The Illustrated Encyclopedia of
BLACK MUSIC

The Illustrated Encyclopedia of

BLACK MUSIC

Consultant: Mike Clifford

Authors: Jon Futrell, Chris Gill, Roger St. Pierre, Clive Richardson,
Chris Trengove, Bob Fisher, Bill Sheehy, Lindsay Wesker

HARMONY BOOKS

Harmony Books/New York

A Salamander Book

Published by Harmony Books
a division of Crown Publishers, Inc.,
One Park Avenue, New York, New York 10016,
and simultaneously in Canada by
General Publishing Company Limited.

HARMONY BOOKS and colophon are
trademarks of Crown Publishers, Inc.
ISBN 0-517-54779-1
ISBN 0-517-54780-5
10 9 8 7 6 5 4 3 2 1
First American Edition

Library of Congress Cataloging in Publication Data

Futrell, Jon.
    The illustrated encyclopedia of Black music

    Includes index.
    1. Afro-American musicians—Bio—bibliography.
I. Gill, Chris. II. Title.
ML106.U3G54   780'.92'4 [B]   82-3090
ISBN 0-517-54779-1 (cloth)   AACR2
ISBN 0-517-54780-5 (paper)

All correspondence concerning the content of this volume should be addressed to Salamander Books Ltd., Salamander House, 27 Old Gloucester Street, London WC1N 3AF, United Kingdom.

This book may not be sold outside the United States of America and Canada.

Credits

Editor: Ray Bonds
Designer: Philip Gorton

Filmset by Modern Text Typesetting Ltd.
Color reproduction by Bantam Litho Ltd., and Rodney Howe Ltd.

Printed in Belgium by Henri Proost et Cie

Contents

THE BREAKFAST BAN DOLPHIN RIDE

Introduction

BLACK MUSIC is the sound the world dances to, a sound of so many facets that it ranges from "pop" to "message". This book is intended as a tribute to the enormous resilience and dedication of all those involved in changing what started as the indigenous music of an oppressed and displaced minority in North America to a music which is now created and performed by musicians from all races and many nations and which reaches out to a worldwide audience.

"The Illustrated Encyclopedia of Black Music" is the fourth in a series published by Harmony Books. Along with its companion volume, "The Harmony Illustrated Encyclopedia of Rock", "The Illustrated Encyclopedia of Jazz" and "The Illustrated Encyclopedia of Country Music", this new book provides the most comprehensive reference source in the field of popular music.

It contains exhaustively researched biographies on all the major artists who through their own success or their influence on the work of others have made black music one of the most vibrant cultural forms of the 20th Century.

We have defined black music as that which has been aimed primarily at a mass black audience; whether it be soul, funk, reggae, jazz-funk or the more popular blues and R&B output, we have defined it as the black equivalent of pop music. Though such music is

6

performed in the main by black artists, and aimed at black ears, countless white musicians, producers, songwriters and recording executives have played a major role in its development which necessitates their inclusion in this volume. By the same token, black music has always reached out beyond the confines of its primary audience and attracted a multi-racial following. It is no exaggeration to state that black music, given its own success and its major influence on the development of rock and pop, is the most dominant music form in the world today. The music itself, and the performers, have tremendous appeal to followers of all races. Multi-racial groups, from the Del-Vikings and their contemporaries through to the likes of Rufus, Heatwave and War fit into any valid definition of black music, while the contributions of white session musicians such as Steve Cropper, Roger Hawkins, Joe South, Larry Carlton, Duane Allman and Steve Gadd have been colossal, and are therefore recorded in this volume. How could race or colour preclude adequate acknowledgement of the tremendous input to the kaleidoscopic world of black music of Jerry Wexler, Leonard Chess, Jerry Ragovoy, Phil Spector, Bert Burns, Leiber and Stoller, and other white producers?

This unique book has been compiled basically within decades, from the 1940s and '50s, unfolding through the personal biographies of its artists the development of black music.

Of course, the careers, of many of the major performers span several decades, but in placing artists' entries within particular decades our decisions have been influenced by considering the era in which they made their major breakthrough. For example, many of the crossover jazz musicians we included have been recording since as far back as the late 1940s, but their entries appear in the 1970s section since that was the time that they changed their music to reach beyond the confines of jazz towards the mass audience who enjoy black music.

Every performer that we and the other authors regard as being of significance will be found either within our elected decade of "first major breakthrough" or by mention within the appendix. Further performers are mentioned in conjunction with their work with a specific individual who has an entry. The index will point readers immediately to names mentioned in any particular entry. As a cross-reference, if an artist who has his own entry is mentioned in someone else's entry, we have indicated it thus (▶), and again the index will help locate him.

Although the entries generally concentrate on actual performers, we have also included a large number of producers and songwriters who have made an important contribution to black music. Similarly there are entries for a number of record companies, mainly major independents which have concentrated very heavily on the propagation of black music and which, in most cases, developed their own unique sound and identity.

In listing recordings we have included albums only, selected on a purely subjective basis as recommended listening. In some instances a performer's most significant work may be recorded on an album which is no longer easily obtainable, in which case the album may have been omitted from the list of recommended recordings, while reference is made to it in the entry. The American label of origin is listed first, the UK label second. Where an album is on the same label in both countries, the record company name is given only once. A dash signifies that the record was not released in the particular territory, although it may be available on import. In the case of the reggae listings, the same formula applies, but with these artists it is the Jamaican/UK record companies that are noted.

MIKE CLIFFORD
ROGER ST. PIERRE
September, 1982

The '40s & '50s

THE ADVENT of the Second World War and the resulting domestic upheaval in the United States were of prime importance in the development of black music. As a consequence of the war there was a major shift in population, particularly among the ever-impoverished blacks who, in search of work, were obliged to move from the Southern states, either West to the shipyards of California or North to industrial centres like Chicago and Detroit. This migrant black population contained not only a significant percentage of talented performers, but also a vast potential audience seeking entertainment of the kind they had grown familiar with 'back home'.

Virtually the entire idiom of Chicago urban blues resulted from musicians like Muddy Waters, Howlin' Wolf, Elmore James and Little Walter moving North from the Gulf States and Delta area. As far as the chronicling of black musical history is concerned, this period saw the beginning of a degree of acceptance by the white audience which gained ground during the '50s, although not without an uphill struggle.

In New York, Harlem had changed from being a suave centre of entertainment for middle-class whites and was becoming a thriving hotbed for black talent. The Apollo Theatre, the massive Savoy Ballroom and the expansive club atmosphere of Small's Paradise all flourished, and big-band jazz was the popular music of the day. The renowned Cotton Club spawned such personalities as Cab Calloway who grew to be one of the most prominent black stars of the late '40s and early '50s. Other major black bands of the period included those led by Lucky Millinder, Lionel Hampton and Erskine Hawkins, who recorded prolifically and attracted massive followings. Emulation by white bands was rife; they would even make use of the black leaders' arrangements in live shows. However, numerous featured sidemen from the black bands went on to gain reputations as first-rate jazz men.

Another development was the emergence of 'rhythm & blues' as a musical idiom. Although it was patronisingly labelled 'race' music at first, *Billboard* (the main US music trade paper) replaced the term with 'Rhythm and Blues' as its chart heading on June 17, 1949, and, following the initial post-war success of pioneering independent labels like Atlantic, Savoy and Specialty, the early '50s brought an enormous increase in new companies concentrating on rhythm and blues.

From coast to coast, record companies were launched in efforts to capitalise on the commercial potential of the massive increase in urban black populations. In New York, Atlantic—formed by Herb Abramson and Ahmet and Nesuhi Ertegun, sons of the Turkish Ambassador—also became a strong jazz label; in Chicago, Len and Phil Chess's label concentrated on recording bluesmen, but also dabbled in jazz; Sid Nathan in Cincinnati, Ohio, kept his options open with his King/Federal combine, King carrying country music along with gospel and R&B, while Federal was primarily R&B. Billy Ward's Dominoes were also in Nathan's fold and had their first big success in the '50s. Meanwhile, across on the West Coast, Art Rupe's Specialty and Eddie Mesner's Aladdin were reaping healthy sales among the black communities of California.

Radio play also had a role in breaking a hit disc, and an interesting aspect of the record company/radio station relationship emerged in the '50s: a company had to be careful not 'to put all its eggs in one basket' as it were, for stations were reluctant to programme several discs on the same label. The answer was to change the origin of the

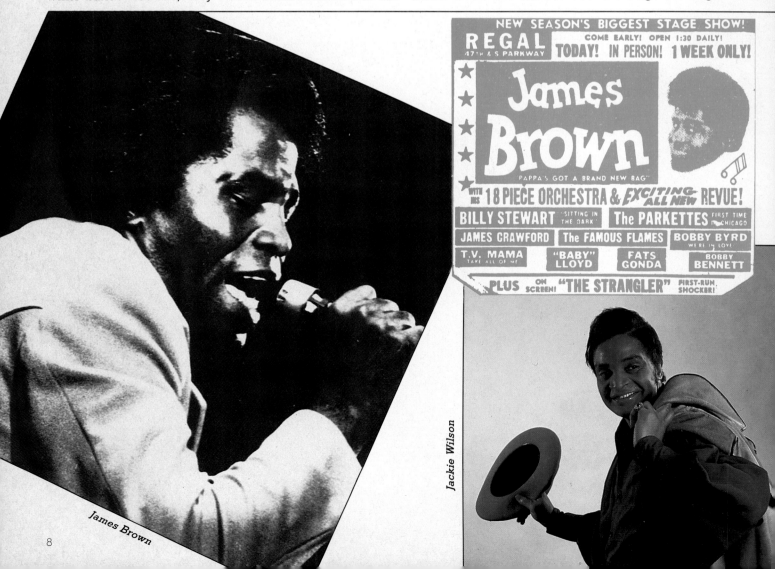

James Brown

Jackie Wilson

8

product. George Goldner, for example, launched Rama in New York and hit paydirt when his fifth release, the Crows' **Gee,** 'crossed over' to go top 20 on the pop charts early in 1954. Had he followed up this success with other potential winners on Rama he might have found airplay limited. He therefore set up subsidiary logos Gee, End and Gone. He could then count on airplay for the Teenagers (on Gee), Imperials (on End) and Dubs (on Gone), ostensibly three separate label entities but in fact all housed under one roof.

Competing for sales from New York was Al Silver with his Herald/Ember combine. Silver's earliest success actually pre-dates Goldner's by a year since Faye Adams scored three consecutive R&B chart-toppers on Herald with **Shake A Hand** (in the fall of 1953), **I'll Be True** (early 1954) and **Hurts Me To My Heart** (October 1954). Sister-label Ember was soon to yield a classic performance with the Five Satins' **(I'll Remember) In The Still Of The Nite.** Silver also cast his net further afield, and a trip South to New Orleans was rewarded with a good catch from sessions by Ernie Kador, Tommy Ridgley and rocking tenor-sax player Les Allen, whose **Walking With Mr Lee** enjoyed good sales without aspiring to the national charts.

The New Orleans connection was not unique to Al Silver, however, and Bobby Robinson also managed to capitalise on the quality of indigenous talent there. Robinson was one of the few blacks to gain a foothold among independent record companies. Based at a record shop in Harlem, he had street-level insight into what was selling, and this may have sharpened his awareness of the commercial potential of material from outside areas. His Robin/Red Robin labels charted R&B with the Rainbows, the Scarlets and the Vocaleers, and the '50s saw him start numerous others, some in partnership with his brother

Danny, including Fire, Fury, Fling, Vest, Holiday, Everlast and Enjoy. While Bobby had an ear for talent, his ventures were financially erratic, and new logos would emerge as previous ones were declared insolvent. Towards the end of the decade he scored handsomely with Wilbert Harrison from Florida, whose **Kansas City** (Fury) topped the pop charts, Lee Dorsey and Bobby Marchan from New Orleans, and Gladys Knight and the Pips, who were from Atlanta, Georgia, but had travelled to New York when **Every Beat Of My Heart** began to sell on Vee-Jay. Robinson swiftly signed the group to Fury and re-recorded the same song!

Mention of Vee-Jay takes us from New York to Chicago, where Vivien Carter and the late Jimmy Bracken had formed the label in 1953, primarily as an outlet for local talent. Their 'open-door' policy resulted in a wide range of black music styles comprising the company's output, with their first couple of discs displaying the total diversity of the down-home blues of Jimmy Reed and the doo-wop harmonies of the Spaniels. Apart from further extensive output in these styles—the roster came to include bluesmen like John Lee Hooker and Eddie Taylor along with vocal groups the Dells, Eldorados and Impressions—Vee-Jay also built a strong catalogue of gospel and jazz and, at the end of the decade, solo soul/R&B singers, to match their competitors across on South Michigan Avenue, Chess, who were also hyperactive in all facets of black music.

The Chess brothers became kingpins in the field of Chicago urban blues, dominating the R&B charts during the early and mid-'50s with material now regarded as classic in its idiom and highly influential in the subsequent development of popular music. Hits came from the dynamic harp of Little Walter **(Juke, Mean Old World)**, the powerful

B.B. King

Chuck Berry

guitar and rumbling vocals of Muddy Waters (**Long Distance Call, Hoochie Coochie Man**), and the throaty roars of Howlin' Wolf (**How Many More Years, Smokestack Lightnin'**). Such was the pulling power of the Chess/Checker combine that when other Chicago blues labels went into demise, any acts with talent or sales potential soon found themselves in the Chess fold, notably Otis Rush and Buddy Guy from Cobra.

As these 'indies' began to gain a firm foothold in the market, some major companies formed R&B offshoots in an attempt to catch sales in the black market without prejudicing their mainstream pop product. RCA, whose Victor logo did score R&B hits with the Du Droppers and Big John Greer, launched Groove to successful effect with Mickey And Sylvia (**Love is Strange**), though the subsequent Vik and 'X' were short-lived, and RCA reverted to their main identity, which had, after all, also had substantial hits with Arthur 'Big Boy' Crudup and Piano Red (aka Dr Feelgood) in 1950/51, Red scoring five top-10 R&B winners, including **Rocking With Red** and **Right String But The Wrong Yo Yo.**

Columbia meanwhile reactivated their OKeh logo, a 'race' label of pre-war heritage, and for some three years from 1951 did well with some fine material by Big Maybelle and Chuck Willis. Maybelle, a large lady with voice to match, was, along with Dinah Washington, a worthy successor to 'classic' blues singers like Bessie Smith and Ma Rainey. A tangential but relevant point of note is that while Maybelle and Dinah both emerged at the turn of the decade, Dinah, signed to Mercury, somehow managed to aspire to speedy recognition in the jazz field, and such 'respectability' led to more than a dozen R&B top-10 hits before Maybelle managed to chart with the

great melancholy **Gabbin' Blues** on OKeh in 1953. Both were fine singers, recorded with worthy jazz/blues orchestrations, but somehow Maybelle was destined to remain in relative obscurity, lauded by just the blues (and later, soul) cognoscenti; sadly, Dinah died in 1963 (of a sleeping pill overdose) and Maybelle in 1972.

To return briefly to OKeh and Chuck Willis, Chuck was destined to be overshadowed by the more egocentric performers of the mid-'50s; he scored on OKeh with gems like **My Story, I Feel So Bad** and **Don't Deceive Me,** then joined Atlantic in 1956, soon to score national hits with **C. C. Rider** and **Betty And Dupree.** He was dubbed 'King Of The Stroll' as that dance craze spread, but did not live to reap the rewards his talent deserved, dying during surgery for a stomach ulcer in 1958 as his tragically-apt hit record climbed the charts—**What Am I Living For/Hang Up My Rock 'n' Roll Shoes.**

Passing mention must also be made at this point, while still discussing the urban North, of Fortune Records, run in Detroit by Devorah Brown with an assortment of blues, doo-wop and R&B, her roster including one Choker Campbell, who went on to gain some repute with a later Detroit label, Motown.

In the Mid-West King/Federal had grown from jumpblues roots in the late '40s to figure strongly in the R&B market of the mid-'50s. The decade began with a bang as the Dominoes went 'pop' with the risqué **Sixty Minute Man,** and Wynonie Harris kept the humour rolling with **Bloodshot Eyes.** The Charms, led by Otis Williams, also crossed-over to pop with **Hearts Of Stone** in 1954, and Little Willie John was to emulate this success with compound interest during the next couple of years, his tuneful, rangy tenor voice equally impressive on ballads and beat,

Muddy Waters

Wayne Bennett

charting with **Fever, Need Your Love So Bad, Leave My Kitten Alone** and a host of others. Instrumentally, Bill Doggett went gold with **Honky Tonk,** following in the footsteps of saxman Earl Bostic's **Flamingo,** but from among Sidney Nathan's expansive roster the most dynamic artist to emerge was James Brown, whose debut **Please, Please, Please** made the R&B top-10 in summer 1956.

Down South were other notable independent labels. Sam Phillips' Sun in Memphis was devoted to earthy blues by Rufus Thomas, Little Milton, Junior Parker and sundry others before Elvis Presley's fusion of blues and country styles opened the floodgates of and for rock 'n' roll; Johnny Vincent's Ace, in Jackson, Mississippi, had its main source of talent down-river in New Orleans—Huey 'Piano' Smith, Earl King and Big Boy Myles, Smith making the national charts with goodtime R&B items like **Rocking Pneumonia** and **Don't You Just Know It** while white R&B singer Frankie Forde over-dubbed his vocals onto Smith's backing track for **Sea Cruise** and sold a million; Ernie Young's Nashboro/Excello in Nashville featured gospel and blues, making extensive use of material recorded by Jay Miller down in Crowley, Louisiana. Artists like Slim Harpo, Whispering Smith and Lightnin' Slim sold locally, but rarely aspired to the national charts—such recognition was limited to breakouts like the Gladiolas' **Little Darlin',** Lillian Offitt's **Miss You So** (Excello) and the Crescendos' **Oh Julie** (Nasco).

Further West in Houston, Texas, Don Robey was building a successful empire, purchasing Duke Records to add to his already buoyant Peacock label, and thus acquiring the eminently successful Johnny Ace, who scored a string of R&B top-10 hits with moody wistful ballads before accidentally killing himself playing Russian roulette on Christmas Eve in 1954, **Pledging My Love** being a posthumous smash hit. Robey's other major star was Bobby 'Blue' Bland, an emotive baritone singer whose powerful delivery exuded oceans of blues and gospel influence, and whose 1957 pop hit **Farther Up The Road** and 1959 R&B smash **I'll Take Care Of You** on Duke prefaced a chart career which continues into the 1980s.

The West Coast spawned fewer R&B independents during the 1950s, maybe because labels like Specialty, Modern/RPM, Aladdin and Imperial not only maintained their initial impact but—with the exception of Aladdin (bought by Imperial)—grew with the passing years, Specialty through Lloyd Price, Guitar Slim and Little Richard, Modern with B.B. King, the Cadets and Etta James, and Imperial with Fats Domino. One new label did emerge, however, when the Hollywood-based Class charted during 1958 with Bobby Day's **Over & Over** and **Rocking Robin,** and then with Eugene Church's **Pretty Girls Everywhere.**

Just as these new independents emerged during the 1950s, so, of course, some from the 1940s grew in status, notably Atlantic, probably due to the musical enthusiasm of management—the Erteguns were avid fans of the music they were marketing, as was Jerry Wexler (who joined the company when Herb Abramson was beckoned by Uncle Sam). The company's roster looks like a who's who of 1950s R&B, with Ruth Brown, LaVern Baker, Ray Charles, Clovers, Coasters, Drifters, Joe Turner, Clyde McPhatter . . . .

The 1950s also gave us names like Sam Cooke, Chuck Berry, Roy Hamilton, the Midnighters, Percy Mayfield, Nappy Brown, some better known than others but all important in the evolution of black music.

Bobby Bland   Ray Charles   Bo Diddley

Johnny Ace

Johnny Ace's career came to a dramatically abrupt end on Christmas Eve 1954 when he shot himself dead while playing Russian roulette backstage at Houston's City Auditorium. At the time he was the biggest artist in black music, acclaimed by the trade magazine *Cashbox* as 'The most programmed R&B artist of 1954'.

Born John Marshall Alexander Jr in Memphis, Tennessee, on June 9, 1929, Ace served in the Navy during World War II then joined Adolph Duncan's band as pianist before a stint with that seminal Memphis group the Beale Streeters, which also included

Bobby Bland(▶) and Earl Forrest. Like Bland, Ace was signed by Don Robey to the Houston-based Duke (▶) label and made his debut in 1952 with **My Song,** which topped the R&B charts and, like much of his subsequent output, was a pensive love ballad sung in a warm baritone.

Billed as a double-header with Willie Mae 'Big Mama' Thornton of **Hound Dog** fame, Ace toured constantly and seemed destined for superstardom, as evidenced by the posthumously released **Pledging My Love,** which became his biggest seller.

Recordings:
Johnny Ace Memorial Album
Duke/Vocalion)

Atlantic Records

Formed in 1947 by the unlikely combination of a Turk and a New York Jew, Atlantic Records has, for more than 30 years, traded on recorded excellence and an almost unique association with various black musical forms. Pursuing an interest in jazz and blues, Ahmet and Nesuhi Ertegun the two sons of the former Turkish Ambassador to the United States, began life in the music business promoting jazz concerts in Washington DC with their friend from the East Coast, Herb Abramson. Ahmet felt that the record industry might afford a man a reasonable living without the necessity of working five days a week.

After a couple of abortive attempts to start a label, Ahmet approached his dentist for a $10,000 loan, realising the need for adequate financing for the project. The dentist, Dr Sabit, duly obliged, and Atlantic Records was launched, with Abramson as president, and Ahmet, the younger of the Erteguns, as vice-president.

The early records featured artists Errol Garner, Joe Morris, Tiny Grimes and Eddie Sanfranski, and Atlantic soon earned placings in *Billboard* magazine's *'Hot In Harlem',* a list of best-selling 'race' discs. **Blue Harlem** by Grimes and **Love Grooving** by Morris (trumpet player with the Lionel Hampton Band) were early Atlantic successes. But the record that gave the label national prominence was **Drinkin' Wine Spo De O Dee** by bluesman Brownie McGhee's brother Stick, which Abramson and Ertegun re-recorded after receiving an order for the single (on a minor label) from one of their Southern distributors.

Stick McGhee's original recording of the song was then bought by Decca Records, and Atlantic found themselves in stiff competition with a major label, although eventually outselling the Decca version. At this time, it was common practice for independent labels to pay a one-off session fee to all performers — usually a negligible amount, and only $10 in the case of McGhee — and there was little contractual aggravation in cutting an identical version. Atlantic, however, began to establish a royalty system, and were rewarded with long-term agreements with their future signings.

Abramson and Ertegun met further opposition from a national company, Capitol, as they negotiated for the signature of powerhouse R&B performer Ruth Brown(▶). Persuaded by her friends and manager Blanche Calloway (sister of Cab), Ruth pacted with Atlantic, recording the popular **So Long** and **It's Raining** in 1949.

Confident about their ability to compete in the music market, Atlantic spread their collective wings, travelling from the East Coast to discover new talent. They recorded Professor Longhair (using his real name, Roy Byrd) and Blind Willie McTell (under the name Barrelhouse Sammy), and even cut a couple of country records after a trip to the South, and then picked up the Clovers, the Cardinals and Joe Turner.

After their 1950 R&B hit with Ruth Brown's **Teardrops From My Eyes,** Atlantic became an acknowledged power in the black music arena, with burgeoning sales and a thriving artist roster, which was soon to include Ray Charles(▶), LaVern Baker(▶) and the group which spearheaded Atlantic's international success, the Coasters(▶).

Although the label had experienced reasonable sales with other vocal groups, most notably the Clovers, whose material had been supplied in part by Ertegun (under the anagram Nugetre), it was the Coasters who opened new horizons, achieving monumental sales, due in no small part to their mentors Jerry Leiber and Mike Stoller(▶). The early '50s saw the arrival of Jerry Wexler to the company and, from 1953, he began to supervise sessions with Ertegun and long-time engineer Tom Dowd, Abramson having received notice from the American Armed Forces to serve two years conscription in Germany as a dentist — ironically, considering the source of Atlantic's original funding.

Wexler was an old-time jazzer, with his roots and ambitions firmly in music, and he began his career as a writer for *Billboard,* the American trade paper, later moving to music publishing (and initially turning down a job with Atlantic in that capacity), before teaming up with Ertegun.

In the two years until Abramson's return in 1955, Atlantic scored with 30 top-10 R&B hits from a total output of approximately 100 sides (including those on subsidiaries Cat and Atco). Wexler's main role in this success was as a promotion man, but he was soon to work in the studio, cutting his teeth with Clyde McPhatter(▶) and the Drifters(▶) on the Jesse Stone song **Money Honey.** Stone, incidentally, had played an important part in Atlantic's field trips to the South, searching out new acts, and also wrote **Cole Slaw,** one of the label's earliest R&B hits, by saxophonist Frank Culley, as well as arranging much of the company's product.

Above: The See See Rider lady LaVern Baker.

Money Honey was a big R&B record, and was followed by five further chart successes for the Drifters, including **Such A Night** and Ertegun's **Watcha Gonna Do.** Unfortunately, McPhatter suffered the same fate as Herb Abramson, being drafted before he could fully capitalise on the Drifter's success, eventually returning to Atlantic for a solo career.

Ray Charles was an investment which quickly paid off, Atlantic picking up his contract for $2,500 after Swingtime, Charles' then current label, found itself in financial difficulties. Ivory Joe Hunter, another notable R&B/blues performer, had a similar recording background to Charles before signing to Atlantic and charting with one of the company's first pop hits, **Since I Met You Baby,** in 1956.

The return of Abramson saw an expansion for the Atco subsidiary with Wynonie Harris, Guitar Slim and Bobby Darin (**Splish Splash**) scoring in '57/'58. The Coasters were also signed to Atco, providing Atlantic with its first million-selling single, **Searchin',** in 1957. Sadly, at a time when the company was performing so well, Abramson decided it was time to go, a situation no doubt aggravated by the position of his by then estranged wife Miriam, who had been with Atlantic since its inception.

Along with Ahmet's brother Nesuhi, who had become director in charge of the jazz catalogue, Ahmet and Wexler raised $300,000 to buy Abramson out. After a series of failed labels, Abramson now runs the A-1 Studio in New York and manages veteran blues performer Louisiana Red (who had a 1971 album release on Atlantic).

Established as a successful crossover label, Atlantic further progressed in the pop and R&B markets with astute signings and an uncanny feel for music that the Erteguns and Wexler loved. Chuck Willis(▶), the resurgence of the Drifters with Ben E. King(▶) as lead singer, and jazz artists like the Modern Jazz Quartet and the Jazz Workshop (featuring Charlie Mingus) provided Atlantic with both hit singles and a solid album catalogue, a development helped in no small way by Nesuhi, an avid jazz fan who saw good business sense in looking for long-term album security.

Ben E. King went on to solo success, and made the US top 10 with Ahmet's **Stand By Me.** Further distribution deals provided Atlantic with some unlikely instrumental successes, including **Stranger On The Shore** by Acker Bilk, **Apache** by Jorgen Ingman and **Alley Cat** by Danish pianist Bent Fabric, which was astonishingly voted R&B Record Of The Year in 1962. The company did lose acts, however, most notably Clyde McPhatter and Ray Charles, both of whom went on to cut a steady stream of hits for other labels.

The advent of the '60s saw the emergence of the soul superstar, and Atlantic had their full quota — Aretha Franklin(▶), Wilson Pickett(▶), Don Covay(▶), Solomon Burke(▶) (later produced by Bert Berns who had also taken on the production mantle for the Drifters, replacing Leiber and Stoller). Atlantic also distributed the Stax product, taking this independent label from Memphis under its aegis and maintaining a consistent cash flow which allowed Stax to expand, and not flounder like many of its counterparts who had to wait months for income from the major companies.

The inter-relationship between Stax and Atlantic was best demonstrated by the recordings of Otis Redding, whose product appeared both on the Stax subsidiary Volt, and on the Atco label. In fact, Tom Dowd engineered the singles that broke Redding nationally, **I've Been Loving You Too Long, Respect** and **Satisfaction.**

Another profitable deal was that set up by Atlantic with Rick Hall's Fame label, which was based at his studio in Muscle Shoals(▶), Alabama. Utilising the outstanding rhythm section at the studio, Wexler cut much of Atlantic's finest work, starting with Wilson Pickett's **634—5789**, with Hall engineering.

Just over a year later, in February 1967, Wexler returned to Muscle Shoals to produce the label's newest signing, Aretha Franklin, recording the majestic **I Never Loved A Man (The Way I Love You)** and **Do Right Woman Do Right Man.** Their association produced countless classic albums and singles, earning Wexler a couple of music industry Best Producer awards, most notably for **Lady Soul**, arguably the finest soul LP of all time. The Fame connection also brought Clarence Carter into the Atlantic fold. Atlantic's own studio in New York, and the Criteria set-up in Miami, have also been conducive to the label's sound.

Other ladies enjoyed success with Atlantic during the early '70s, including Jackie Moore and Betty Wright, and Bonnie, of Delaney & Bonnie, who introduced Atlantic to good old white rock 'n' roll, adding another dimension to the company's output (though she had a solid background in black music having been the only white singer ever to be a member of Ike and Tina Turner's legendary back-up vocal team, the Ikettes).

With rock music taking a stranglehold on album and single sales, Atlantic moved quickly and effectively, establishing themselves in the market with Buffalo Springfield, Crosby, Stills, Nash & Young, Led Zeppelin, Emerson Lake and Palmer and, more recently, Genesis (and Phil Collins), AC/DC, Foreigner and the Rolling Stones, whose Rolling Stones Records label they distributed in the States. Zeppelin also supplied a label, Swan Song, and this provided a series of top 10 albums with Bad Company.

The Muscle Shoals connection provided Atlantic with the Allman Brothers Band. Duane Allman had worked sessions at the studio and impressed Wexler, who set up a deal to handle Capricorn, a label owned by the brothers' manager Phil Walden.

On the pop front, Atlantic scored with Sonny & Cher, the Rascals, the Troggs (whose **Wild Thing** was available on both Atco and Fontana, with the royalties split down the middle), Abba and the Bee Gees.

Meanwhile the soul output had been superbly maintained by Roberta Flack, Donny Hathaway and a host of others.

The expanding Atlantic operation became an attractive stock option to investors and a deal was signed with Warner Brothers in 1967 for an exchange of shares, and the security of big company finance. Warners themselves were bought out in 1972 by the Kinney Corporation, which inaugurated the Warner Brothers/Elektra/Atlantic combine, known universally as WEA.

It has been a worldwide success story. In Britain, Decca provided Atlantic's original outlet via the London American label before giving the company its own logo identity. Polydor then continued the good work, again under Atlantic's own label, before WEA eventually set up its own UK operation.

Rock historian and broadcaster Charlie Gillett has told the entire Atlantic Records story in his masterwork *Making Tracks*, published by W.H. Allen & Co.

Recordings:
This Is Soul (Atlantic)
History Of Rhythm & Blues Vols 1-6 (Atlantic)
Supersoul (Atlantic)
Soul Getogether (Atlantic)
Uptown Saturday Night (Atlantic)

History of Rhythm & Blues. Courtesy Atlantic Records.

LaVern Baker

LaVern Baker recorded for King and Columbia before singing with Atlantic(▶) and finding fame in 1952. She stayed with the Atlantic label until 1965, recording a whole string of hits in the intervening years, ranging from the pop-influenced **Tweedle Dee** to the gospel-slanted **Shake A Hand** and the definitely bluesy **See See Rider**, the later tracks making full use of her ability to wring emotion out of a good lyric.

Born in Chicago on November 11, 1929, her career was long and fruitful and she was one of the first R&B artists to win a large audience among whites. However, although her records pointed the way to the soul era, her star went into decline when soul became popular in the early '60s.

Recordings:
See See Rider (Atlantic)

Hank Ballard

With his 1960 million-seller **The Twist** (covered with even greater success by Chubby Checker(▶)), Hank Ballard launched a new dance craze on the world. However, although his name might have been new to white audiences, particularly those in Europe, he was already well established in the forefront of R&B.

Born in Detroit, Michigan, on November 18, 1936, as John Kendricks, Ballard settled in Atlanta, Georgia, and in 1953 joined Lawson Smith, Norman Thrasher, Billy Davis (later replaced by Arthur Potter) and Henry Booth (replaced on his death by Sonny Woods) as lead singer with a promising group called the Royals. Ballard took the place of Charles Sutton, who had a throat infection (Sutton later rejoined as replacement for Thrasher).

On signing with King (▶), the group's name was changed to the Midnighters (to avoid confusion with the Five Royales(▶), already an established King act). The Four Falcons was the original choice of name until it was discovered that there was a fast-rising Detroit act called the Falcons.

In 1954 they notched three million-sellers (a remarkable achievement for a black act in that era) as Hank Ballard and the Midnighters with **Work With Me, Annie, Sexy Ways** and **Annie Had A Baby** (something of a trilogy in terms of lyrical content!).

Six years later, **The Twist** burst the world wide open for them. Ballard was booked to appear on Dick Clark's important 'American Bandstand' TV show in Philadelphia, but he was hung up on a girl in Atlanta and failed to show for rehearsals. Incensed, Clark arranged with the Philly-based Cameo-Parkway (▶) company for a cover version to be cut by the then unknown Chubby Checker (it was Clark's wife who dreamed up that stage name).

Finger Poppin' Time gave Ballard and his outfit another 1960 hit but their fortunes went into decline and the Midnighters broke up in 1968, Sonny Woods moving into record distribution, Norman Thrasher becoming a producer and Lawson Smith getting involved with black power.

Working the rock 'n' roll revival shows, Ballard formed a new set of Midnighters (Frank Stadford,

Walter Miller, Wesley Hargrove) and recorded for Silver Fox and Chess (▶) (where Ballard was re-united with Ralph Bass, producer of his earlier King/Federal hits).

Ballard then linked up with another former mainstay of the King stable, James Brown (▶), and appeared on the latter's stage shows as well as contributing a sickeningly ingratiating monologue on Brown's 1973 **Get On The Good Foot** album.

Recordings:
The Jumpin' Hank Ballard
  (King/London)
Hank Ballard's Biggest Hits
  (King/—)

Dave Bartholomew

Noted New Orleans trumpeter/ bandleader Dave Bartholomew sold 100,000 copies of **Country Boy** on De Luxe in 1949 then discovered and propelled Fats Domino(▶) to fame, co-writing most of his hits.

As a producer, Bartholomew had hits with Lloyd Price(▶), Shirley and Lee(▶), Smiley Lewis, Guitar Slim, Huey Smith, Frankie Ford and others.

Jesse Belvin

An exceptionally influential balladeer in the Nat 'King' Cole(▶) mould, Jesse Belvin was born on December 15, 1933, in Texarkana, Arkansas. Starting out with Big Jay McNeely's band he recorded as a transient member of a wide variety of doo-wop groups, including the Cliques, the Sheiks and the Sharptones, and had a 1953 R&B hit on Specialty(▶) as one-half of Jesse and Marvin with **Dream Girl.**

Belvin wrote the **Earth Angel** hit for the Penguins and is thought to have written countless other songs credited to others.

He recorded solo for a large number of labels, notably Specialty, Kent/Modern(▶), Class and Jamie, and had huge hits with the smooth **Goodnight My Love** (Modern, 1956), **Funny** and **Guess Who** (both on RCA, 1959).

A talented pianist, Belvin was an important catalyst on the Los Angeles recording scene, helping many acts to get started. He died in a car crash in 1960 at the age of 27.

Recordings:
But Not Forgotten (Kent/—)
The Casual Jesse Belvin
  (Crown/—)

Wayne Bennett

Cited by many top American artists as the finest guitarist in black music, Chicago native Wayne Bennett has, ironically, only ever had one record released in his own right—the unsuccessful 1967 single **Casanova** (Giant).

Best known for his classic guitar fills behind the vocalising of Bobby 'Blue' Bland(▶), Bennett was on the soul star's 1960's classics for Duke before leaving in 1965 to work with Operation Breadbasket. He rejoined Bland in the late '70s.

A member of the house bands at the Apollo, New York; Regal, Chicago; Howard, Washington; and Uptown, Philadelphia, Bennett has worked on-stage with many of the black music greats, including

Aretha Franklin(▶), Lou Rawls(▶), Jimmy Smith(▶), Cannonball Adderley(▶), Gene Ammons and Dexter Gordon.

As a session man he has played on recordings by Ramsey Lewis(▶), Tyrone Davis(▶), the Chi-Lites(▶), Jackie Wilson(▶), Hamilton Bohannon(▶), the Independents(▶), Jerry Butler(▶), Jimmy Reed, Otis Rush, Buddy Guy, Junior Wells, the Mighty Clouds Of Joy, the Soul Stirrers, Fats Domino(▶) and Little Junior Parker.

Recordings:
No album releases.

Chuck Berry

When Bob Dylan lauded Smokey Robinson(▶) as 'America's greatest living poet', he may have flipped a coin to make the final decision, because an equally valid contender in a similar idiom is Chuck Berry, whose lyrical output over the decades may not incorporate Smokey's delicate analogies, but can surely match his thematic originality.

Cars, teenage lifestyle and music are the prime ingredients of Berry's writing output: **Maybellene** has Berry's V8 Ford chasing the Cadillac which is taking his girl away; **No Money Down** has him describing the components and extras of his dream car to the auto salesman; **School Day,**

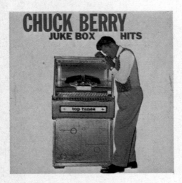

Juke Box Hits. Courtesy Chess Records.

Sweet Little Sixteen, Almost Grown are teenage-life sagas; **Johnny B. Goode** and **Bye Bye Johnny** are beginning and continuation of a storyline tale of country-boy-turned-rock 'n' roll-star. And so the chronicle of Berry's material could continue through his lengthy string of hits, the first wave of which spanned the years 1955 to 1960.

The story began, however, in San Jose, California, where Charles Edward Berry was born on October 18, 1926. The family moved eastwards to St Louis, Missouri, early in the 1930s and there the young Berry gained some musical experience in sacred and secular styles, singing in the local church choir and in the school glee-club, causing some raised eyebrows at the time with his version of the Jay McShann blues **Confessin' The Blues.** He trained as a hairdresser, then worked in an auto-factory while performing with a small combo in the evenings and at weekends.

Early in 1955, Berry put a couple of songs on tape, trekked North to Chicago and combed the clubs and bars to find blues-king Muddy Waters(▶). The venture bore fruit in a Southside club, where Waters suggested that Berry should go see

Leonard Chess; he did—Leonard was duly impressed, and signed Berry to Chess (▶), where he promptly cut **Maybellene,** which scored a No. 1 R&B hit.

A prolific recording career followed, both in terms of output and success, Berry doing frequent sessions with sidemen who were the cream of the Chicago blues scene—pianists Johnny Johnson, Otis Spann, Lafayette Leake; bassist Willie Dixon; drummers Eddie Hardy, Fred Below or Odie Payne—and reaping rich reward with hits like **Brown-Eyed Handsome Man, Roll Over Beethoven, Let It Rock,** and other classics.

Apart from his inventive lyrics,

Berry's distinctive contribution to his discs was his guitar-playing, particularly the instrumental introductions which prefaced most of his hits, incisive flurries of clean-picked notes pouring forth from his Gibson guitar—that to **Sweet Little Sixteen** was stolen note for note by the Beach Boys for their **Fun, Fun, Fun** hit. Solos would be performed at gigs as Berry travelled across stage in a bow-legged squatting position—his trademark duckwalk. Because of his constant hit-status, he was also committed to celluloid in the rock movies *Go Johnny Go* and *Rock Rock Rock,* while a workout of **Sweet Little Sixteen** at the 1958 Newport Jazz Festival created a

Above: Chuck Berry performs his inimitable 'duck walk'.

startling impact in *Jazz On A Summer's Day.*

In 1959 there began a semi-mysterious chain of events which culminated in Berry being convicted on a charge of violating the Mann Act for allegedly transporting a minor across a State line for immoral purposes. Chess maintained his disc output during Berry's incarceration, but sales dwindled after 1960 and it was four years before his regained liberty resulted in fresh material and more hits, helped along by the publicity gained from covers of his classics by the Rolling Stones.

Above: Still rocking it... the ageless Chuck Berry.

As 1964 brought chart action for **Nadine, No Particular Place To Go** and the wry **You Never Can Tell,** Chuck embarked on his first tour of Britain, and though his guitar work paled in comparison with the subtleties of co-star Carl Perkins, Berry was nonetheless still a dynamic performer--in marked contrast to the indifferent performance of his live shows in more recent years.

Back in the USA in 1966 a large cash advance persuaded Berry to sign with Mercury, whereon **Club Nitty Gritty** was original, bluesy and chunky, but most other material was a waste of talent, comprising rehashes of the great

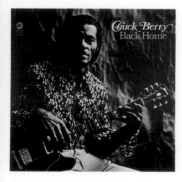

Back Home. Courtesy Chess Records.

Chess sides and some flirtations with the rock market (recording a live LP at Fillmore West with Steve Miller). Dismal sales resulted, and by 1969 Chuck was back with Chess, where **Back Home** was an aptly titled LP.

The early 1970s brought a vogue for recording veteran bluesmen in 'London Sessions': Chess had Chuck Berry cut on a studio set, then a live set in Coventry, the latter yielding a lengthy version of an old risqué blues, **My Ding-a-Ling,** and it was this kitsch allusion to sex which brought Chuck a transatlantic chart-topper in 1972. An intriguing, reassuring **Bio** album came next, but Chess was becoming a spent force, and Berry

began spending more time touring than recording.

He is now a standard, if hackneyed, attraction at cosmopolitan jazz festivals and rock oldies shows, his last recorded venture being a **Rock It** LP for Atlantic(▶) in 1979, the musical quality of which failed to inspire either sales or fans.

Recordings:
Golden Decade Vols. 1, 2, 3 (—/Chess)
Motorvatin' (—/Chess)
Juke Box Hits (Chess)
St Louis to Frisco to Memphis (—/Philips)
Spotlight On . . . (—/Chess)
Bio (Chess)
Rock It (Atlantic)

Bird Groups

As long as there have been vocal groups performing and recording, so long has there been a need for the groups to find a name; a family unit can usually use their own name—different generations will be familiar with the Mills Brothers, Treniers(▶), Tavares(▶) or Jacksons(▶) —but otherwise a combination of brainpower, coincidence and democracy is necessary to arrive at the right word to splash on billposters and record labels.

In the early 1950s the international success achieved by the Ink Spots(▶) served to inspire groups of teenagers throughout the USA who had been harmonising on street-corners, in subway passages or in hallways with the belief that they, too, could make the big time. But what name to choose? Some thought of automobiles (Cadillacs, Edsels), some of musical sounds (Harptones), some of luxurious cloth (Satins, Velours), and many of birds, perhaps comparing the sound of their harmonies to the mellifluous songs of nature.

Trends manifest themselves from time to time and thus we have the Larks, Cardinals, Swallows, Wrens and Blue Jays—named after small tuneful birds—as well as the Crows, Penguins and Pelicans, birds with perhaps less of a reputation for

sweet songs and attractive plumage. However, even these groups had precursors, such as the Orioles and the Ravens who began to gain repute as hit vocal groups during the late 1940s.

The Orioles, led by the delicate tenor voice of the late Sonny Til, started recording in 1948, enjoying good sales with **It's Too Soon To Know** on Jubilee, then topping the R&B charts during 1949 with **Tell Me So** and maintaining regular output until **Crying In The Chapel** hit No. 1 R&B in 1953. They continued to record for some years without further chart action. Ahead of them in popularity were the Ravens, formed by Warren Suttles and Jimmy Ricks in 1947, when they hit with **Ole Man River,** led by the rumbling bass voice of Jimmy Ricks. They continued to record prolifically through the 1950s, though chart recognition was limited to early-'50s R&B hits on National and Mercury.

Going into the 1950s we find the Robins hot on the West Coast for Savoy, RCA and Spark with gritty jump tunes, while in New York there were the Larks, on Apollo, with **Eyesight To The Blind** and **My Reverie** in mellow ballad style, likewise the Cardinals' **Shouldn't I Know** and **Wheel of Fortune** on Atlantic, with the Swallows adding a bluesy approach, the Baltimore group scoring on King with **Will You Be Mine** and the risqué **It Ain't The Meat It's The Motion.**

The Cool Cool Penguins. Courtesy Dootone Records.

By 1954 the 'bird groups' were breaking new ground with crossover pop hits, the Crows being first when **Gee** went top 20 on Rama in April, then the Penguins finished the year going Hot 100 with **Earth Angel** (Dootone). From the West Coast came the Pelicans and the Jayhawks, from the East emerged the Wrens and the Quails. The Carey family began singing in Chicago and the Flamingos were born, struggling through early years on Chance to find fame in 1956

with **I'll Be Home** on Checker, followed at the end of the decade by a string of Hot 100 hits on End, including top 20 for **I Only Have Eyes For You.**

So with the passing of the rock 'n' roll years, the bird groups waned—some, like the Flamingos and Larks, metamorphosed into soul stylings. A new bird name

Rhythm And Blues Hit Vocal Groups (including the Penguins) Courtesy Atlantic Records.

emerged from Detroit in 1959 when the Falcons (who included Wilson Pickett(▶), Sir Mack Rice (later a Stax(▶) performer/writer, Eddie Floyd(▶) and Joe Stubbs) brother of Four Tops(▶) leader Levi), went top 20 with **You're So Fine** on Unart, then hit again in 1962 with the gospel passon of **I Found A Love** (Lupine), but this was an exception, a reminder of a faded era.

Bobby Bland

Bobby 'Blue' Bland must surely be one of the best singers, regardless of musical genre, never to have made an impression on the British charts. The majority of his American hits, which almost invariably crossed-over from the R&B charts to the national Hot 100, were classy, stylish performances sung in a distinctive bluesy baritone voice over precise, brassy orchestrations.

Robert Calvin Bland, born on January 27, 1930, in Rosemark, Tennessee, grew up to the sound of rural blues by Blind Lemon Jefferson, but his world changed when the family moved to Memphis in 1944. The city was a hotbed of blues' activity, with radio shows presented by Sonny Boy Williamson and B.B. King(▶), while Howlin' Wolf was an active and influential local performer.

After a short spell with a gospel group, Bland became valet for B.B.

Below: Bobby Bland (left) in partnership with B.B. King.

King from 1949-50 then spent three years as driver for Rosco Gordon(▶). Bland also sang with the Beale Streeters, a loosely knit aggregation which lasted six years but never recorded. Also in the group were Billy Duncan, Earl Forrest and Johnny Ace(▶) but not, as has often been reported B.B. King nor Rosco Gordon; they were all closely associated. At Gordon's instigation, Bland recorded some sides with arranger Ike Turner which were issued on the West-Coast based Modern label. Bland recalls that company bosses the Bihari brothers were not very impressed and suggested he should "forget singing and buy himself a plough"! While on military service, Bland performed in a talent show in Houston, Texas, where he was spotted by local record executive Don Robey and promptly signed to Duke Records.

The contract with Duke placed Bland under the musical guidance of Joe Scott, trumpeter and arranger with Bill Harvey's Band. Scott was to become the long-time mentor to Bland's extensive and successful career, constructing solid brass arrangements to carry the melodic blues-drenched voice into the charts for almost a decade. Though pacted to Duke in 1954, it was 1957 before Bland first hit the charts, with the gritty lilting **Farther Up The Road.** Then, after a hiatus limited to R&B hits, the onset of the '60s saw a string of hits comparable with the best of today's superstars, with some 30 chart entries over 10 years, including soulful gems like **I Pity The Fool, Turn On Your Lovelight, Call On Me, Ain't Nothing You Can Do, Ain't Doing Too Bad** and **Rocking In The Same Old Boat.** Besides Scott's imaginative arrangements, these recordings featured the superlative guitar work of Wayne Bennett(▶) whose playing style provided the perfect foil for Bland's vocal artistry.

For some eight years Bland had worked on stage using Junior Parker's band (with Pat Hare on guitar) but from 1962 he had led his own large band (usually a 10 to 12 piece outfit) with Bennett prominently featured along with saxplayer Mel Jackson who was still with him into the '80s, Bennett having left in 1965 and returned in late '70s.

Later recordings adapted to contemporary soul stylings, though with no less artistry, then, in 1972, Duke was bought out by ABC Records, who maintained Bland's contract, attempting to broaden his appeal to the rock market but still with no loss of his basic blues' spirit; indeed they even teamed him up for recordings with B.B. King(▶). ABC has in turn been absorbed into MCA, with Bobby 'Blue' Bland remaining on contract.

Produced more recently by Al Bell and Monk Higgins, Bland's LPs like **Sweet Vibrations** and **Try Me I'm Real** have recaptured the essence of the Joe Scott era, and 45s are still keeping him in the charts (Joe Scott had died in 1979).

Recordings:
Introspective Of The Early Years (ABC/-)
Two Steps From The Blues (Duke/Vocalion)
Woke Up Screaming (—/Ace)
Dreamer (ABC)
Get On Down With (ABC)
California Album (ABC)
Try Me I'm Real (MCA/—)
Together 'Live (ABC) with B.B. King

Below: Bobby Bland pictured live at a London concert in 1982.

James Brown

Despite the varied quality of his recorded output in recent years, James Brown remains one of the most successful black artists of all time and arguably the most influential figure in modern black music. During the course of the last quarter century or so, he has broken box-office records throughout the world, released countless million-selling singles and albums, created a whole new set of criteria for exciting live performance, led some of the most exhilarating and well-drilled bands ever, and practically invented funk single-handed. He may not now be quite the force he once was—he is after all pushing 50—but it seems likely that posterity will agree with Arthur Conley when he sang in **Sweet Soul Music:** '. . . he's the King of them all y'all.'

James Brown was born near Augusta, Georgia, on May 3, 1933. Like many other Southern blacks before and since, he endured an early life of extreme poverty (and had brushes with the law), and first came to music via gospel. Brown formed the first Famous Flames during 1954 and they included his long-time associate Bobby Byrd. They quickly won a local reputation as a group to save the most hardened sinner, with Brown already showing the uninhibited vocal style, with its whoops, falsetto cries, screams and gasps, that he was later to make famous. Nevertheless, it was not long before gospel material was pushed into the background in favour of secular songs. One of these—**Please Please Please**—came to the attention of King Records, who immediately signed James Brown and the Famous Flames. King released the song as the group's debut recording, and it became a major R&B chart success.

Although **Please Please Please** was a secularised gospel song, Brown and the Flames followed up its success with a series of numbers which conformed more to the R&B mainstream of the time. These failed to make much of an impact, and it looked as if **Please Please Please** was simply a false start. From 1956 to 1958 the group toured the chitlin' circuit, scratching a living as best they could like dozens of other similar units. But in September 1958 they went to New York to record and this time picked a winsome ballad, **Try Me,** which echoed the gospel undertones of their previous hit. Brown's agonised vocals perfectly complemented the song's yearning quality and the record became the group's second major hit.

Above: James Brown live! A soul-stirring event.

Sex Machine. Courtesy Polydor Records.

This time there was no mistake. Already developing the shrewd business sense that was to become legendary in the music industry, Brown put together a regular six-piece backing band and released 11 hit records between January 1959 and February 1961. An indication of his spreading influence, even at this point, is the fact that of these numbers at least three—**I'll Go Crazy, Think** and **Night Train**—became standard fare for the British horn-based R&B outfits that were beginning to burgeon around this time.

While the hits kept on coming, Brown developed a stage act that matched the wild fervour of his recordings. At the beginning of the '60s his singers and the small band had metamorphosed into an entire Revue, complete with its own support acts, its centrepiece being Brown's own dynamic stage show. Anyone who has not seen James Brown live has missed one of black music's most electrifying sights, and at this time he was probably at his peak as a performer.

He was as exciting to watch as he was to listen to, punctuating his impassioned exhortations with dazzling displays of footwork and deft bodily contortions that made him sometimes appear to be made of rubber. Again, his influence has been inestimable—countless other black acts have followed in his nimble footsteps, as have not a few white rock acts.

This period of consolidation culminated in 1962 with a live recording made at New York's famous Apollo Theatre. The resulting double album, **Live At The Apollo**, is Brown's *chef d'oeuvre*, and a watershed record in several ways. It was one of the very first live recordings; it was one of the most successful albums by a black artist up until that time; and it was a perfect example of what a live album should be. The raw excitement of Brown's voice, the interplay between his staccato vocal patterns and the well-oiled machine that was his incredible band, and the exhilarating rapport between Brown and his ecstatic audience, all provided the elements of a legendary recording. It fuelled the best parties for a decade, and although long deleted it's worth selling your granny to get a copy. **Live At The Apollo** also heralded the start of Brown's acceptance by the American white audience, and indeed the international market. He followed it with **Prisoner of Love,** a single which was a pop hit and started him on the road to superstardom. It may be, however, that Brown's business astuteness provided the real turning-point, because at this time he broke his contract with King and recorded his next hit, **Out Of Sight,** for Mercury subsidiary Smash. It seems that Brown was unhappy with King's promotional efforts and, rightly or wrongly, felt that the company did not realise quite what an exceptional talent they had on their hands. Whatever the truth of the matter, the ploy worked perfectly. **Out Of Sight** was a big hit, King quickly made their peace with Brown and welcomed him back into the fold, and thereafter James Brown enjoyed the company's best efforts. He did, however, continue for a time to release strictly instrumental records for Smash, many of them versions of his vocal hits on King. These featured organ and piano solos which were accredited to Brown himself though it has often been rumoured that they were, in fact, the work of Bobby Byrd. This swift label-jump illustrates one aspect of James Brown's shrewdness, but it has always been accepted in the music industry that no one fools with the Godfather of Soul. Brown's reputation as a hard businessman is something he holds in common with many other major black artists—Chuck Berry and Ike Turner come immediately to mind—and without a doubt years spent playing the chitlin' circuit hone the business mind better than any number of management courses. Brown took this further than most, his investments including ownership of several black radio stations which, no doubt, helped assure continual exposure for his recordings.

The next few years saw a succession of classic hits like **Papa's Got A Brand New Bag, I Got You** and **It's A Man's Man's Man's World,** and when King Records disappeared in 1970 Brown signed with Polydor and continued the run with singles like **Get Up I Feel Like Being A Sex Machine** and **Hey America.** (All these singles were hits in the UK, and it's worth mentioning that by this time James Brown and his various entourages were regular visitors to Britain, enjoying enormous success with crowds who had quite literally never seen anything like it before.)

James Brown started off as a rhythm & blues singer in the '50s, became the No. 1 black artist and a star of international stature in the '60s, and continued to have hits, draw capacity crowds, and influence the course of popular music in the '70s. James Brown's music—the arrangements, the horn patterns, the heavily syncopated beat, the long single chord passages overlaid by repetitive vocal figures—has been enormously influential. Several of his own musicians have made a name for themselves in various incarnations—Maceo and the King's Men, Fred Wesley and both the J.B.s and the Horny Horns, Bootsy Collins—and a whole slew of funk bands owe much to Brown's pioneering work. Sly and the Family Stone(▶), who provided the link between R&B and rock that was to spawn a whole generation of bands like the Blackbyrds(▶), Earth—Wind and Fire(▶) and the Ohio Players(▶), were directly influenced by Brown's music, adding psychedelic overtones and a looser, less slick image to take the music a stage further on.

Below: James Brown. He said it loud, he's black and he's proud, and he led a nation with that chorus.

Also not to be underestimated is James Brown's importance as a political figure. Although, like most self-made businessmen, he can hardly be classed as a radical, Brown has nevertheless made a considerable contribution to the movement towards black unity and awareness in America. Right back in 1968 he recorded what was to become practically the anthem of the movement, **Say It Loud, I'm Black And I'm Proud,** and kept up the stream of black consciousness with numbers like **Get Up, Get Into It, Get Involved.** Just how important he was to black Americans, at least in the mid-60s, may be judged by the fact that a hastily arranged James Brown TV spectacular had the effect of getting people off the streets during one of the fierce inner-city riots of the time. Lyndon Johnson himself commended Brown for his action, and in a way the situation illustrated the ambiguity which Brown has always presented politically. On the one hand he's 'Soul Brother Number One', and important figurehead of black American culture, a unifying influence, a man who constantly preaches black awareness and cohesion. On the other hand he is almost a stereotype of the American Dream, a genuine rags-to-riches hero who is legendary for his autocratic attitude, for running an extremely tight ship as far as his band and entourage are concerned, and for no-nonsense business practices. Certainly, if self-help is the name of the game, James Brown sets a remarkable and flamboyant example.

The last few years have seen the man keeping a lower profile as artists and bands of a newer generation, many the inheritors of his rhythmic innovations, have taken the centre stage. That is not to say he is a spent force by any means—his 1976 album **Body Heat,** for example, became one of his biggest sellers, and in the intervening years he has fought with not inconsiderable success in the jungle of the disco market. In 1981 he hit with **Rap Payback,** the James Brown response to the success of records by 'rappers' like the Sugar Hill Gang and Kurtis Blow, and he continues to tour to critical acclaim if not to sold-out houses. After 20-odd years of success, he is, however, no longer quite the force he once was—even legends are subject to the whims of musical fashion. Again, at this particular point confusion reigns about his recording plans—having left Polydor for TK with **Rap Payback** (and **Soul Syndrome,** its accompanying album), he has split from the troubled TK in turn and Island Records have announced a new deal.

What is certain is that even if he were never to set foot in a recording studio or concert hall again, James Brown has an assured place in the pantheon of modern black music. He has been at the top of the tree for three decades, and has pioneered new directions in the music during the whole of that period. Like many other key figures in popular music, he has recorded his fair share of the banal, the repetitive and the just plain boring. But there again, it has often seemed as if every week brought a new James Brown record.

Because he has recorded so much, the following discography is highly selective, and includes albums which are deleted but worth searching out. **Solid Gold** is a double album offering a pretty fair overview of the man's entire career, and is probably the best bet if you just want one example of James Brown in your collection.

Recordings:
Soul Syndrome (TK/RCA)
Solid Gold (Polydor)
Body Heat (Polydor)
Soul Classics, Vols. 1-3 (Polydor)
Get Up Offa That Thing (Polydor)
Get On The Good Foot (Polydor)
Revolution Of The Mind (Polydor)
Live At The Apollo (King/Polydor)

Live At The Apollo.
Courtesy King Records.

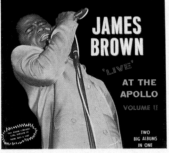

Nappy Brown

Southern-born and church choir schooled, Napoleon 'Nappy' Brown moved North to Newark, New Jersey, and between 1954 and 1961 released more than 25 singles for the then important Savoy label, several of them were giant R&B hits.

Blessed with an incredibly rich baritone voice, he developed an emotive style, based on holding notes in extended vibrato, which later degenerated into a gimmick-laden hiccup delivery.

Several of Brown's records, including **Pitter Patter** (1955) and **Cried Like A Baby,** crossed over onto the pop charts while his slow ballads, notably **The Right Time,** set the pattern for the deep-soul style which was to become so important in the '60s.

Brown suddenly disappeared from the scene for a decade—some thought he was dead, others that he was in prison, while he claimed later he had merely retired to work on a bus—but he then returned to the studio in 1959 to cut what must surely rate as one of the great undiscovered soul classic albums of all time for the obscure New York based (and short lived) Elephant V label.

Thanks For Nothing was cut in a tiny studio which was located beneath an Italian restaurant and which shook every time a subway train passed. It was produced by Herb Rooney (of the Exciters(▶)) and the little-known but enormously talented Thomas Kaye, who wrote the majestic and spine-chilling title cut which was almost Dylanesque in its lyrical impact. With backings from Wilson Pickett's stage band, the Midnight Movers, each of the nine tracks was a masterpiece and Brown's voice, rid of its earlier gimmicks, was magnificent. Since then he has moved into the gospel world, cutting sides for Jewel with the Bell Jubilee Singers.

Recordings:
Thanks For Nothing
(Elephant V/—)
That Man (Route 66/—)

Ruth Brown

'Miss Rhythm' was born on January 30, 1928, in Portsmouth, Virginia, and joined Lucky Millender's band at the age of 16. She was later sacked and left stranded in Washington DC, but Cab Calloway's sister Blanche gave her a gig at her Crystal Cavern and soon after took her up to the Apollo in New York.

Signed to Atlantic Records(▶) in 1949 by Herb Abramson, Ruth Brown was the label's most prolifically recorded artist throughout the '50s, with some 87 releases including the 1950 R&B chart-topper **Teardrops From My Eyes** and such classics as **Mama He Sure Treats Your Daughter Mean, Oh What A Dream** and **Lucky Lips.**

On numerous package shows she topped the bill, even above such pop stars as Pat Boone, but with the advent of the '60s her stylings were sounding old-fashioned though she did cut some admirable jazz-slanted material with the Thad Jones/Mel Lewis Big Band.

Recordings:
The Best Of Ruth Brown (Atlantic)
The Big Band Sound Of Thad Jones And Mel Lewis Featuring Ruth Brown (United Artists)
Black Is Brown And Brown Is Beautiful (Buddah)
The Real Ruth Brown (Cobblestone)

Ray Charles

At different times during his near 40-year musical career, Ray Charles has been hailed as a genius, revered as a phenomenon, and dismissed as a showbiz sell-out. He is possibly the most consistently misunderstood of the great black music stars, and latterly certainly the most consistently underrated, but his contribution to the development of the music has nevertheless been enormous. The most influential vocalist of his era, a powerful and versatile instrumentalist, and an individualistic writer and arranger, Ray Charles more than anyone helped to develop the R&B of the '50s into the soul of the '60s, at the same time opening the door to wide commercial acceptance.

Born Ray Charles Robinson on September 23, 1930, in Albany, Georgia (he later shortened his name to avoid confusion with boxer Sugar Ray Robinson), Charles was permanently blinded at the age of six by what was later diagnosed as glaucoma. Nevertheless, he enjoyed a happy if unluxurious childhood in Greenville, Northern Florida, and showed early signs of musical talent. He was exposed to most of the influences that would later come out in his own music—gospel and blues from the local church and local bars, jazz, swing and country music from the radio.

Sent to the State School for the Blind at St Augustine at the age of seven, Charles remained there until he was 15, concentrating on musical studies. By his early teens he was already doing gigs as a piano player, and when his mother died in 1945 he decided to quit school and become a full-time musician.

These early years found him gaining experience in a variety of places—Jacksonville, Orlando, Tampa, Seattle (he joined R&B star Lowell Fulsom's(▶) band for a time) and Los Angeles. His first permanent group was a trio consisting of himself on piano and vocals, Gosady McGee on guitar and Milt Garred on bass—it was called the McSon Trio, after the Mc in McGee and the Son in Robinson. At this time Charles was greatly influenced by the work of both Nat 'King' Cole(▶) and the then popular blues singer Charles Brown, and recordings made for several small labels reflect those influences. Many of the sides recorded around this period are still available, on a variety of re-issue labels.

However, it was not until Charles signed with the up-and-coming Atlantic Records(▶) that his career really started to take shape. His first sides for the company, recorded in 1952 and 1953, did not differ radically from the material previously released on the smaller labels, but Charles was beginning to find his own identity. **Mess Around,** an up-tempo 12-bar written by Atlantic boss Ahmet Ertegun, pointed the way to the future. Recorded with a group of top New York session men, the cut featured Charles letting loose with a more impassioned blues and gospel-tinged singing style that was a thousand miles away from Nat Cole's jazzy intimacy. In 1954 Charles tasted real success for the first time with **It Should've Been Me,** a wry semi-spoken novelty blues that reached the upper echelons of the R&B chart.

With his career under way Charles began to experiment, allowing more of himself into his music and completely excising the early Cole/Brown influences. He secularised gospel forms, either writing to a 16-bar gospel pattern or adapting existing church-based songs. **I Got A Woman** was the first major success to utilise this formula, and many others followed, including **Hallelujah I Love Her So, Lonely Avenue, I Want To Know, Talkin' 'Bout You, Yes Indeed** and **Tell All The World About You.** At the same time the blues influence was also coming to the fore, and several great 12-bar R&B performances date from this period, including **Blackjack, Get On The Right Track Baby** and **Mary Ann.**

Not the least part of Charles' success in the mid-'50s was his band. Formed in 1954 following the success of **It Should've Been Me,** it was a seven-piece featuring musicians like David 'Fathead' Newman(▶) and Hank Crawford(▶), who could not only play funky blues and gospel but also more than hold their own when it came to Parker and Gillespie-style hard bop. When the group played the Newport Jazz Festival in 1958 it caused a sensation; to this day Charles has never worked with any but the best musicians.

The big breakthrough, however, came in 1959. The way Charles tells it, **What'd I Say** was written almost by accident, composed on the spot to fill out a particularly long live set. True or not, the record synthesised all the elements that Charles had used up until then. To a hypnotic semi-Latin electric piano riff (incidentally, one of the first appearances of electric piano on record), he added a wild call-and-response vocal routine that had him swapping phrases with his female backing group, the Raelets, and the whole record was imbued with a kind of semi-religious intensity. It was blues, gospel, rock 'n' roll and soul put together in one explosive package, and its success was enormous and immediate. Ray Charles was suddenly in the top 10 of the pop charts.

In many ways 1959 was the peak year for Ray Charles. As well as

Above: For nearly forty years, Ray Charles has sat near the top of the pile of R&B performers, and is still a major concert attraction.

album would come out of a collaboration between Charles and a sympathetic contemporary producer. Assuming that his health holds—and at some periods in the past it has given cause for concern—there seems no reason why Ray Charles should not continue to do his personal thing for years to come. He is in the odd position of being a living legend whose most seminal work is well in the past, yet who is still more than capable of turning in majestic performances both in concert and on record.

Ray Charles is one of the most imitated singers in popular music, particularly by white rock singers like Joe Cocker and Eric Burdon, while one of Stevie Wonder's(▶) early albums was full of his songs and titled **Tribute To Uncle Ray.** He is a key figure in the international popularisation of black music, and the creator of some of the most emotionally wrenching and exhilarating music ever made. His place in the history of popular music is assured.

Discography covers only recent albums and reissued early work. Much early Atlantic material is also available on Japanese and European import. Very early material has been bought and sold dozens of times, and may turn up on all sorts of labels.

Recordings:
Love And Peace (Atco/London)
True To Life (Atlantic/London)
Ray Charles Live (Atlantic)
The Great Ray Charles (Atlantic)
The Greatest Ray Charles (Atlantic)
The Genius Of Ray Charles (Atlantic)
The Best Of Ray Charles (Atlantic)
25th Anniversary In Show Business (Atlantic)

Country And Western Meets Rhythm And Blues. Courtesy EMI Records.

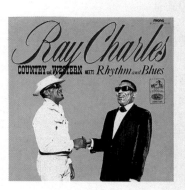

scoring massive pop success with **What'd I Say** he cut a magnificent live album in Atlanta (featuring a long soul-shaking version of **Drown In My Own Tears**), and paved the way for future developments by cutting his first tracks with strings. Nevertheless, he was not to remain with Atlantic much longer. Following an offer which Atlantic were unable or unwilling to match, Charles joined ABC-Paramount at the end of the year.

The conventional wisdom is that, artistically, Charles had given of his best before arriving at ABC. However, his early years with the company resulted in some of his finest recordings, particularly of blues-based material and some of his biggest hits. Particularly notable are **Them That Got, I Wonder, I've Got News For You, I'm Gonna Move To The Outskirts Of Town** and **The Danger Zone. Georgia On My Mind,** from the 1960 album **Genius Hits The Road,** reached the top 30 in Britain and established him internationally. **Hit The Road Jack** kept the charts warm for him until 1962 when he recorded his first album of country songs, **Modern Sounds In Country And Western Music.**

At the time, the idea of a soul and jazz star turning his hand to country music was outlandish. Blacks and hip whites regarded country as strictly for the hicks, while the country audience was not yet used to black artists covering its tunes. But the potentially disastrous idea turned out to be a winner. Charles himself, always a country fan, was a natural for the simple, strong melodies and primal emotions of country. Despite the misgivings of many critics and the loss of some fans, Charles had enormous success with both the album and singles pulled from it, particularly **I Can't Stop Loving You.** This Hank Williams' song was a massive hit on both sides of the Atlantic, and was largely responsible for creating the middle-of-the-road white audience that has stayed with Charles to the present day. Other hits from the same album included **You Don't Know Me** and **Born To Lose.**

In 1962 Ray Charles sold more than $8,000,000 worth of records—not a tremendous amount by today's standards, but then a phenomenal figure. He had become a major international star, in a position to tour with a large band and entourage, and to record when and with whom he pleased. He was in demand for TV shows and prestigious concert dates all over the world, and it would have been surprising had he not relaxed and coasted a little—he had been making a living from music for around 15 years. In fact, after this period, most of his albums followed roughly the same pattern. There would be a couple of blues or R&B songs, a country song or two, perhaps a standard, perhaps an example of more contemporary material. His live appearances also began to assume a more predictable pattern, a far cry from the excitingly innovative Newport and Atlanta appearances of the late '50s. Tuxedoed, Charles presided over a tightly-disciplined band and a chorus that rarely had a chance to stretch out.

But Charles was still capable of delivering the goods. Gems which date from the '60s include a classic 1967 version of McCartney's **Yesterday,** and an equally affecting version of **Eleanor Rigby.** The '70s saw the odd nugget—**Heaven Help Us All** on the album **A Message From The People, Living For The City** on **Renaissance,** the Ray Charles/Cleo Laine version of **Summertime, I Can See Clearly Now** on **True To Life** and a searing version of **We Had It All** on **Love And Peace.**

The '70s did see one change, namely a shift to total independence as far as recording went. From 1968 to 1973 Charles' records were issued on his own Tangerine label, but marketed and distributed by ABC. In 1973 he quit ABC in favour of his own label, renamed Crossover. In 1977 he agreed to an arrangement with his old company Atlantic whereby the company marketed and distributed Crossover.

Now in the '80s it seems unlikely that Ray Charles is going to make any radical changes in the formula which has kept him at or near the top for the last 20 odd years—although it would be interesting to see what kind of

The Coasters

To paraphrase Rudyard Kipling: If you can keep your head while all around you are losing theirs, and maintain a sense of humour, and find a band capable of putting down a solid dance beat, then what you have may well turn out to be the Coasters, that legendary vocal quartet who added a large dose of fun to the classic era of rock 'n' roll.

The group have such an involved history that it would need an entire book to adequately chronicle their three decades of personnel variations and hit discs—in fact, R&B authority Bill Millar wrote one, published in the UK by Star Books in 1975—but suffice it to mention here that the legend began in 1949, rooted in the Robins who scored local R&B hits around their Los Angeles hometown on labels like Savoy and RCA before signing to Spark. At this point songwriters/producers Jerry Leiber and Mike Stoller(▶) came to the fore. Their material was to become a major factor in the success of The Coasters during the 1950s, and their first main launch-pad was Spark Records which they incepted in 1954 as a vehicle for their own production output. The Robins proved an ideal vehicle for the duo's collaborations, and sales' reaction improved to such effect that **Smokey Joe's Cafe** aspired to the R&B top 20 late in 1955.

This hit attracted the attention of Atlantic, who soon did a deal with Leiber/Stoller which included acquisition of the Spark back-catalogue. Unfortunately, the Robins' management didn't approve, which resulted in Leiber and Stoller persuading lead voice Carl Gardner and bassman Bobby Nunn to leave the group, joining forces with Billy Guy and Leon Hughes to form the Coasters, the name being derived from their West-Coast origins.

Down In Mexico was an auspicious debut, an R&B top-10 hit in spring 1956, while follow-up **One Kiss Led To Another** made the pop charts briefly that September, paving the way for a string of smash hits spanning some five

years, albeit with varying personnel. The main change was the departure of Nunn and Hughes, who were replaced by tenor Cornell Gunter and bass Will 'Dub' Jones. Their first session with the group yielded **Yakkety Yak,** the Coasters' first pop chart-topper, in summer 1958.

Hits poured forth combining the magical ingredients: group vocals led by Gardner's earthy good-humoured tenor, contrasted by Jones' rumbling bass, on inventive Leiber/Stoller lyrics punctuated by King Curtis's(▶) raunchy tenor-sax solos and embellished by Mickey Baker's catchy guitar phrases. One amazing guitar solo in **I'm A Hog For You** (though not by Baker) consists of the same single-string note repeated 47 times, so phrased as to fit perfectly! The songs, like **Searchin', Charlie Brown, Poison Ivy** and **Little Egypt,** have come to be considered rock 'n' roll classics, be they tales of romance or sagas of schooldays and teenage life.

By the end of 1961, the hits had dwindled to minor status, and another personnel change saw the departure of Cornell Gunter and arrival of Earl Carroll from the Cadillacs. The standard of material declined, as did the frequency of Atco releases, and it was 1964 before the Coasters next hit with

Vocal class and plenty of laughs equalled the Coasters.

Tain't Nothin' To Me, an amusing tale of failed bar bravado cut live at the Apollo Theatre. Their connections with Leiber/Stoller had been severed just prior to that hit, but the Atco contract ran until 1966, and was fulfilled by some rather dismal material, though the final release was a splended revival of Louis Jordan's jumping **Saturday Night Fish Fry.**

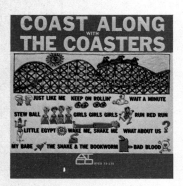

Coast Along. Courtesy Atlantic Records.

The group returned to the Leiber/Stoller fold in 1967 signing with Columbia soul subsidiary Date to be produced by the duo in a more contemporary idiom. Discs like **Soul Pad** and **She Can** resulted, artistically fine in style but commercial failures, and the label was soon discontinued. Next stop was a solitary single on Lloyd Price's(▶) Turntable label in 1969, then in 1971 King Records (▶) bought all the Date material, did a little doctoring in the studio with over-dubs, and managed to score a hit with the group's revival of the Clovers'(▶) hit **Love Potion No. 9,** with the bass voice of Ronnell Bright added.

Since then the Coasters have continued to tour with varying personnel, and even managed another disc outing in 1976 on Wilson Pickett's(▶) Wicked label, the flip-side of the record being philosophically entitled **The World Keeps On Turning.**

Recordings:
20 Great Originals (—/Atlantic)
On Broadway (King/London)

Nat 'King' Cole

From a schooled pianist playing mellow sophisticated 'club blues' in West-Coast bars in the mid-1940s, to a popular entertainer enjoying worldwide renown as a melodic balladeer in the 1960s, that was Nat Cole.

Born Nathaniel Adams Cole on March 17, 1919, in Montgomery, Alabama, he made his first public appearance playing piano in a talent show at the Regal Theatre, aged just four! The 1940s saw him establishing a reputation with accompanists Oscar Moore, guitar, and Wesley Prince, bass, as the Nat Cole Trio, primarily an instrumental unit in mellow jazz style, though Cole would occasionally oblige customer requests and sing.

The trio began recording for the emergent Capitol label in 1943, the start of a lifelong association with that company for Cole, but as the years passed it became apparent that Cole himself was the talent the public wanted, and the trio disbanded in 1948 when **Nature Boy** became a solo hit for him, swathed in plush orchestration.

The suave ballad style became

the norm for Cole as songs like **Mona Lisa** and **Too Young** rose high in the charts, but while his appeal soon waned in the R&B market, it blossomed for the mass popular audience, resulting in a prodigious stream of successes throughout the 1950s and well into the '60s. Major hits came with lilting singalongs like **Rambling Rose** and **Those Lazy Hazy Crazy Days of Summer,** and he entered the movie world singing the theme song **The Ballad of Cat Ballou** in duet with actor Stubby Kaye for the spoof Western in 1964, while perhaps his finest record was the R&B-tinged **Let There Be Love,** which featured a brilliant solo from blind British jazz pianist George Shearing.

Nat had contracted cancer, however, and though a lung was removed in surgery in January 1966, he tragically died on February 14 that year. His daughter Natalie Cole(▶) carried on the family tradition and became a soul star in her own right.

Recordings:
Nat King Cole And Trio And Big Band 1944 (Jazz Anthology)
Best Of Vols 1, 2 & 3 (Capitol)

Sam Cooke

Sam Cooke was shot to death in a Los Angeles motel room on December 10, 1964. The court verdict was 'justifiable homicide'. Cooke had, it appears, entered a lady's room in the middle of the night and been shot when he tried to molest her, though it has since been opined that it was all a tragic accident — he had taken the wrong room key by mistake. Whatever the truth of the matter, the man often credited with being 'the father of soul' music was dead.

This Is Sam Cooke. Courtesy RCA Records.

Cooke left behind a legacy of fine recordings, and a lot of dross too. However, while the material RCA chose for him — often lightweight pop and show tunes which were being used to try to cast him in an 'all-round entertainer' role — was not always of the best, his vocals were never less than superb with their trend-setting phrasing and his style was always unique. His record sales ran to more than 15 million, far short of Fats Domino's 60 million or the 50 million logged by James Brown(▶), but his influence over other artists far exceeded theirs.

Otis Redding(▶), Al Green(▶), Smokey Robinson(▶), Johnny Nash(▶), Arthur Conley(▶), Marvin Gaye(▶) and, perhaps most of all, Rod Stewart — all acknowledged their debt to Cooke and also recorded his material, as did the Animals (a hit with **Bring It On Home To**

Above: The legendary Bo Diddley plays guitars of all shapes and sizes.

Me) and Herman's Hermits (who scored with **Wonderful World**).

One of eight sons of the Rev. Charles S. Cooke (after his death one brother, L.C. Cooke, recorded a tribute album), Sam Cooke was born in Chicago on January 22, 1931, and first performed with two sisters and a brother as the Singing Children. In his teens, he joined the Highway QCs, who eventually became a leading gospel group. R.B. Robinson of the already established Soul Stirrers (who had originally been a Texas group) coached the new act and when the Stirrers' lead singer Robert Harris decided to retire, Cooke was invited to take his place.

From 1950 to '56, Cooke sang lead on a host of gospel hits for the Soul Stirrers, including the majestic **Touch The Hem Of His Garment.** Specialty(▶) label A&R director Bumps Blackwell recognised the potential of Cooke's voice and persuaded him to sing secular music, albeit under the pseudonym of Dale Cook. His distinctive voice could not be disguised, however, and the gospel world was outraged. (After several Dale Cook releases, Cooke quit the Soul Stirrers and was replaced by Johnnie Taylor(▶) who went on to soul stardom at Stax(▶)).

Specialty boss Art Rupe offered to release Cooke and Blackwell from their contracts and leased them the tapes of **You And Me,** an attractive pop-soul number they had cut with a white girl chorus. Blackwell took the tapes to Bob Keene who issued the number on his Keen label and saw it sell some two-and-a-half-million copies (1957). Forgetting previous qualms, and never one to miss a trick, Art Rupe rushed out an earlier recording, **I'll Come Running Back To You,** so that Specialty got its own piece of gold the same year.

Only Sixteen and **Wonderful World** (1959) were further Keen hits for Cooke, both adding a gospel-style vocal to a popular song to produce what was to become known as soul music.

While himself moving on to the major RCA label (in 1960), Cooke also put a lot of energy into setting up his own Sar label to highlight the talents of others. His partner was J.W. Alexander, a former member of the Pilgrim Tavellers

group and by then Cooke's manager. (Alexander still sang from time to time, and a hard-to-find but most enjoyable blues album, **Raw Turnips And Hot Sauce,** produced by Harold Battiste, was issued on Thrush Records in the '60s.)

Sar released R&B hits by the Sims Twins, Johnnie Taylor (**Rome Wasn't Built In A Day**) and the Valentinos (the Womack brothers — Bobby Womack(▶) was later to marry Cooke's widow). Another early business partner of Cooke's was white trumpeter/bandleader Herb Alpert who, with Jerry Moss, went on to set up A&M Records.

Cooke's RCA sides, most masterminded by Hugo and Luigi who years later set up Avco Embassy records and scored with the Stylistics(▶), included everything from the much-emulated **Chain Gang** to the 1962 million-seller **Twistin' The Night Away,** which rode the dance craze, to the brilliant blues-laced **Night Beat** album which included his own **Laughin' And Clownin',** one of the finest new blues' compositions of the '60s, and on to pure show-biz schmaltz **Shake, Good News, Tennessee Waltz, Shake Rattle And Roll, Hey Man** (later re-worked by Arthur Conley(▶) as Sweet Soul Music) and **Cupid** were all classics.

Cooke also helped other artists along. Lou Rawls(▶) featured as second voice on **Bring It On Home To Me,** Billy Preston(▶) toured with Cooke as his organist and is heard on the classic Cooke version of Willie Dixon's **Little Red Rooster** which bears the famous aside from Cooke: 'Play it Billy, ask 'em Ray, Lord have mercy!' (the Ray was not Ray Charles(▶) as has often been stated, but a West Coast sessionman). Cooke also encouraged his great friend Muhammed Ali, then known as Cassius Clay, to venture into the recording studio for MGM, a session which yielded an awful album but a far from bad version of Ben E. King's(▶) **Stand By Me.**

Straddling the worlds of gospel, soul, R&B, blues, pop and MOR and fronting a tight-knit R&B combo, a big band or a mass of strings, Sam Cooke was in every way a musical giant. His material is still widely available through a mass of re-issues and 'Best Of' collections, many on budget labels.

Bo Diddley

A fortunate coincidence of circumstance and environment resulted in the world of rhythm & blues being graced by 'The Originator'—as Bo Diddley calls himself with some justification—but he might easily have become a classical violinist instead of a rock 'n' roll/R&B giant.

Born Ellas McDaniel in McComb, Mississippi, on December 30, 1928, and raised by his mother's cousin, Mrs Gussie McDaniel, young Diddley was taken to Chicago at the age of five, and soon afterwards began studying violin under the classically trained Prof. O.W. Frederick. This tutoring lasted some 12 years, but meanwhile Diddley was also gaining musical inspiration from Baptist church services.

Early R&B influences were in complete contrast—Diddley liked the suave balladry of Nat Cole(▶), the ebullient humour of Louis Jordan and the unorthodox guitar work of John Lee Hooker(▶)—while walking the streets of Chicago brought him into contact with the blues style which had migrated from the Mississippi Delta to become identified as indigenous to the Windy City. Guys like Muddy Waters(▶) and Little Walter gigged in local clubs and bars, and Diddley would hear their playing as it filtered onto the streets.

As a teenager he had been given a guitar by his sister, and he taught himself to play well enough to form his own small group in the early 1950s, setting up on street corners to play earthy blues: Diddley on vocals and guitar with Frank Kirkland (drums), Jerome Green (maraccas) and sometimes Billy Boy Arnold (harp). By this time he was married, and exploring many avenues to remain solvent, including a spell as a boxer, then as a construction worker, before coming to realise that his music could also pay the bills.

Diddley auditioned for Chess(▶) in 1954, cutting I'm A Man and Bo Diddley, the latter a landmark in musical history with its throbbing jungle rhythm, powerful beat, gruff vocal and hypnotic guitar lick. The disc was released on Checker in spring 1955, climbing swiftly to No. 2 in the R&B charts and providing a solid foundation for years of inimitable Diddley material to follow.

With his regular band expanded to include his sultry half-sister 'The Duchess' on rhythm guitar, Diddley maintained a phenomenal

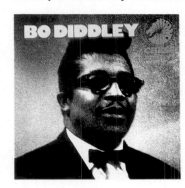

Bo Diddley. Courtesy Chess Records.

output of mainly original material, often lyrically unorthodox with strong humour content after the style of Louis Jordan, yet not obviously derivative. Hits I'm Sorry (with The Moonglows(▶) doo-wopping in support) and Cracking Up were almost mainstream ballads, the latter providing Diddley's first crossover pop hit in summer 1959, but top-20 smash Say Man was more typical, with Diddley and partner trading insults in black jive humour over frantic rhythm support.

In the early 1960s Diddley's repertoire became the staple diet of dozens of British R&B groups in the 'beat boom', songs like Road Runner, Pretty Thing, Mona, Who Do You Love, I Can Tell and You Can't Judge A Book By The Cover gaining good mileage in performance royalties while also charting R&B for Diddley in the USA.

As well as singles, both hits and flops, he also cut a prodigious quantity of LPs, mainly during the 1960s—in fact, any disc collection with less than a half-dozen Diddley albums is hardly representative! The material was still mainly original, and the performances mainly predictable, but Diddley's humour and enthusiasm positively ooze from the grooves. Perhaps more distinctive were a pair of albums cut in 1967 and supervised by Phil and Marshall Chess. One combined Bo, Muddy Waters and Little Walter as Super Blues, and the other had Bo, Muddy and Howlin' Wolf(▶) as The Super Super Blues Band.

Around 1970, social consciousness got to Diddley and producer Bob Gallo cut him in rather heavier musical context for the LP Another Dimension, but the non-Diddley songs left him sounding uncomfortable; the idea was tried again with similarly uninspiring results on Big Bad Bo in 1974. Shortly before that, in 1972 and 1973, Diddley's performance was committed to celluloid in the music movies Let The Good Times Roll and Keep On Rocking.

While he continued to fulfil a heavy schedule of live shows, touring throughout the US and Europe, his disc career was less active, partly because of the demise of Chess, and it was 1976 when he signed with RCA to record a disappointing album 20th Anniversary of Rock 'n' Roll, from which Not Fade Away was a flop 45 (it was Diddley's revival of Buddy Holly's interpretation of the Diddley sound!).

Since then he has continued to tour, latterly as support act to British new wave bands who mirror his energy if not his talent, and a whole new generation of music fans are beginning to appreciate Bo Diddley, Originator!

Fats Domino

Home for Fats Domino is a plush pink mansion on Marais Street in New Orleans, on the fringe of a ramshackle black locale where he grew up more than 50 years ago and from which he emerged to become a star of worldwide reputation by playing the music indigenous to his hometown.

Antoine Domino was born on February 26, 1928 one of nine children in a family with little musical background. He became interested in the piano at an early age when a cousin left an old upright with the family, and was fortunate to be given some guidance in learning to play it by

This Is Fats. Courtesy London Records.

his brother-in-law, guitarist Harrison Verrett.

Young Domino quickly gained proficiency, spending most of his teens playing and singing in local clubs and bars; it was at the age of 17 while playing in Billy Diamond's band that the leader/bassist tagged him 'Fats' and the affectionate nickname stuck to the rotund youngster. Domino was still playing nights in juke-joints and working days in a factory when he came to the notice of prominent New Orleans trumpeter/bandleader Dave Bartholomew(▶) and was invited to join his band.

A long success story began in 1949 when Imperial Records president Lew Chudd signed Domino and the Bartholomew Band to his label, and a December session yielded The Fat Man, a rolling boogie song with limited lyric but infectious atmosphere which hit the R&B charts early in 1950, and garnered sales in excess of a million copies. Domino continued to enjoy success in the R&B market for some five years, his style reflecting the influence of boogie giants like Albert Ammons and Meade Lux Lewis combined with local talent like Paul Gayten, Pleasant Joseph and Leon T. Gross (Archibald), plus a hint of the triplets of Little Willie Littlefield.

He broke into the US national pop charts in late 1955 with the rollicking Ain't That A Shame, and for the next eight years was a regular and prominent name in the top 50, scoring international hits with songs like I'm In Love Again, Blueberry Hill, Blue Monday, Whole Lotta Loving, I'm Ready, Waking To New Orleans and Be My Guest. He had a total of 22 million-selling singles, still something of a record for a black artist. His popularity also resulted in cameo parts in several rock exploitation movies like Shake Rattle & Rock, Disc Jockey Jamboree and The Big Beat, while the superior The Girl Can't Help It featured Domino singing Blue Monday.

The 1960s saw some dilution of his music with the occasional addition of strings, and his material became less convincing in terms of aesthetic content; by the end of 1962 declining sales brought a change of direction, Domino signing to ABC Paramount where his output was tailored to apparent contemporary needs. Red Sails In The Sunset was an immediate top-50 hit, combining piano triplets with swirling strings, but the consistency of his Imperial material was not to be emulated—a dozen releases yielded but one more hit, Heartbreak Hill, and by late 1964 Domino and Paramount had parted.

Early in 1965 he joined Mercury, the brief association yielding a

Below: Fats demonstrating his pounding, up-tempo piano style.

couple of abysmal singles, though the company taped Domino in concert in Las Vegas and managed to produce one of the best live albums in the R&B idiom, **Domino '65.** The contract lapsed and, following two years of recording inactivity, he formed his own label, Broadmoor, cutting two singles before being signed by Reprise in 1968. The recording hiatus had one pleasing result in that Domino was free to travel abroad and in March 1967 he made his British debut at the Saville Theatre, delivering an electrifying performance each night for a week.

Reprise released one album, **Fats Is Back,** produced by Richard Perry, and held one back as being unsatisfactory, while half-a-dozen singles garnered small sales, **Lady Madonna** aspiring to No. 100 in the US charts.

From then on, Fats was content to live quietly at home with his wife Rosemary and their eight children, taking his pick of cabaret dates and occasional overseas tours, until in 1978 he went down the road to Sea-Saint Studios to cut an entertaining LP, **Sleeping On The Job,** licensed by Agram Records in Germany and Sonet elsewhere in Europe. There have been rumours of more new material in vintage New Orleans style, but it has yet to manifest, and Domino is now content to perform and tour when the desire and finance are right!

Recordings:
Be My Guest (—/Sunset)
Fats Domino Story Vols 1-6 (—/United Artists)
Legendary Masters (United Artists)
Fats Is Back (Reprise/Valiant)
Domino 65/Live In Las Vegas (Mercury/Philips Int.)
Sleeping On The Job (—/Sonet)

The Drifters

One of the best-loved black vocal groups of all time, with dozens of hits to their name, the Drifters have carved out a special niche for themselves in the history of popular music. Like Chuck Berry, their forte has been providing the soundtrack to the standard American teen fantasy—cuts like **Save The Last Dance For Me, Under The Boardwalk, Up On The Roof** and **Saturday Night At The Movies** are evocative anthems for anyone who grew up in the early '60s.

During the three decades of their existence, the Drifters have undergone countless personnel changes. Like the Temptations and many other vocal outfits, the group has remained in the public consciousness as a name and a distinctive sound rather than as a specific collection of individuals (after the fashion of a football team!). Over the years, the Drifters have had a variety of lead singers, and more than 30 others have passed through the ranks as back-up vocalists.

The first line-up comprised lead singer Clyde McPhatter(▶), the Thrasher brothers Gerhardt and Andrew, and bass singer Bill Pinkney. All had sung previously with gospel groups, and early Drifters' cuts reflected this influence. The four originally came together in 1953 and started recording for Atlantic. They were an immediate success as far as the R&B charts were concerned, scoring heavily with numbers like **Money Honey, Honey Love** and **Whatcha Gonna Do,** but failed to make any impact

Above: The Drifters, pictured in 1972, with the earstwhile Johnny Moore still at the helm. His is one of the sweetest voices in soul.

on pop listings. The period from 1955 to 1958 is one of some confusion. McPhatter left to join the army and subsequently pursued a solo career, David Baughn briefly taking his place; Johnny Moore joined as lead singer in 1955, but was almost immediately drafted. Continual disagreement with manager George Treadwell (then husband of Sarah Vaughan) led to him sacking the entire group in 1958, and attaching the name 'Drifters' to an entirely different outfit.

This group had often supported the Drifters Mk I on Apollo Theatre bills, and were known as the Five Crowns. They sported a lead singer named Ben E. King(▶) who could easily step into the shoes of the great Clyde MacPhatter, and success for them was almost immediate. Under the aegis of legendary producers Jerry Leiber and Mike Stoller(▶) the new Drifters recorded **There Goes My Baby** in summer 1959. It was, for the time, a revolutionary sound, and its use of a string section, kettle drums and other quasi-classical devices marked it out from the crowd. **There Goes My Baby** outsold all previous Drifters releases by far, reaching No. 2 in the American pop charts in August 1959.

The follow-up, **Dance With Me,** also made the American top 20 and established the group as a hit act in the UK. Suddenly, the Drifters could do no wrong, and hit followed hit. **Save The Last Dance For Me** reached No. 1 in America and No. 2 in the UK in autumn 1960, making the Drifters one of the hottest acts around. Although he sang lead on the record, by the time **Save The Last Dance For Me** was released, Ben E. King had left to pursue a solo career (with considerable success, at least initially). He was replaced by Rudy Lewis, another former gospel

singer, who took the lead on a remarkable string of hits that included **Some Kind Of Wonderful, Please Stay, Sweets For My Sweet** (later covered in the UK by the Searchers), **When My Little Girl Is Smiling, Up On The Roof** and **On Broadway.** Ironically, although he sang lead on as many records as Clyde McPhatter and more than Ben E. King, Rudy Lewis was never destined to enjoy the fruits of success; he died in summer 1964.

In the meantime, Johnny Moore had returned from the army in 1963, rejoined the Drifters, splitting lead duties with Lewis. Now he took over again, remaining as lead vocalist through all vicissitudes until late 1980, returning again briefly in 1981 before forming his own group. The hits continued, with **Under The Boardwalk, Sand In My Shoes, Saturday Night At The Movies, At The Club** and **Come On Over To My Place** taking the group into the mid-'60s.

With Beatlemania changing the face of popular music and Atlantic concentrating on their solo soul stars and their newly acquired heavy rock outfits, the Drifters' record sales began to slow down, though they worked continuously in cabaret on both sides of the Atlantic. At the same time, frenetic personnel changes had brought about a situation whereby several outfits of ex-members were touring under names like the Original Drifters (a group led by Bill Pinkney), further confusing the listening public.

It was also at this time that the Drifters began to gain higher chart placings in the UK than in the US, and it was the group's British popularity that led to what was virtually a second career, starting in 1972. Following a successful re-issue of **At The Club** and **Come On Over To My Place** by Atlantic,

the group contracted to teenybop label Bell, which teamed them with British hit writers like Roger Cook, Roger Greenaway and Tony Macaulay. The result was another raft of hits between 1973 and 1976, most of whose titles reflected a continuing concern with the teenage ethos—**Kissin' In The Back Row Of The Movies, Down On The Beach Tonight, Can I Take You Home Little Girl,** and so on. Many critics have dismissed the Drifters' Bell output as nothing more than re-treads of earlier triumphs, but in fact the British material suited the group quite as well as many of the Brill Building songs that they had earlier recorded. British popularity was further demonstrated by the enormous success of the 1975-released album which collected together 24 hit tracks from both Atlantic and Bell days.

Although the hits dried up again after Bell was absorbed by Arista in 1976, the Drifters have continued to be a popular touring act, working regularly in clubs and cabaret. An indication of their continuing popularity is the fact that **Save The Last Dance For Me** was a small hit in Britain when issued again in 1979, almost 20 years after its first release.

In 1980, Johnny Moore—who has sung lead on nearly 80 per cent of all the Drifters' recordings to date—left for a short-lived solo career with British label Magnet. Moore rejoined the Drifters for a short spell, but decided to leave again when the group's manager Faye Treadwell (second wife and widow of George Treadwell) severed an 11-year association with British promoter Henry Sellers. Under Sellers' management, Moore, who now keeps a home in London, pulled in two other longserving ex-Drifters, Clyde Brown and Joe Blunt, to form a new group called, sardonically, Slightly Adrift. Meanwhile Faye Treadwell brought Ben E. King back into the Drifters to resume the mantle of lead singer. Bill Fredericks, who sang lead on several of the group's Bell records, rejoined at the same time.

Recordings:
24 Original Hits (Atlantic)
Golden Hits (Atlantic)
I'll Take You Where The Music's Playing (Atlantic)
Every Nite's A Saturday Nite (Arista)
Saturday Night At The Club (Atlantic/Pickwick)

Duke/Peacock

Though based in Houston, Texas, the Duke, Peacock and Backbeat labels found their richest vein of talent in Memphis, from which source label boss Don Robey signed up Bobby Bland(▶), Johnny Ace(▶), ex-members of the Beale Streeters, Rosco Gordon(▶), O.V. Wright(▶) and others.

In the '40s, Robey owned the Bronze Peacock, a black nightclub in Houston where ,in 1947, bluesman T.Bone Walker(▶) introduced Clarence 'Gatemouth' Brown to Robey who became the latter's manager and set up the Peacock label as an outlet. Buying the Duke label in 1952 from Memphis DJ James Mattis, Robey signed Johnny Ace, who gave him a run of big hits. His label also issued Willie Mae 'Big Mama' Thornton's original of **Hound Dog.**

Little Junior Parker was signed in 1954, Bobby Bland came to the company a year later and became its mainstay right through to the '70s, when ABC bought Robey out (he died in 1975). Little Richard's(▶) earliest records were on Peacock but it eventually became a purely gospel label (Mighty Clouds Of Joy, Dixie Hummingbirds etc), while Backbeat released discs by O.V. Wright and R&B-influenced white artist Roy Head, whose **Treat Her Right** (1964) was a big hit with blacks.

Using such peerless musicians as Johnny Otis's(▶) band (on the Johnny Ace sides), guitarists Wayne Bennett and Pat Hare, trumpeter/arranger Joe Scott, tenor-sax man Bill Harvey (on Bland, Brown and Parker records) and pianist James Booker (behind a host of artists), Robey ensured high quality to his labels' output. Many of the releases bore songwriting credits to one 'Deadric Malone'. There was no such person; Robey would buy songs outright from down-at-heel young black songwriters for a fistful of dollars and assign credits to the mythical Malone.

Recordings:
The Duke And The Peacock (—/Island)

Billy Eckstine

Back in 1945 there were just 17 certified million-selling records. Two of them were to the credit of Billy Eckstine (born Pittsburgh, July 8, 1913). Subsequently, the mellow-voiced crooner notched another five million-sellers (the last in 1951) and has topped 10 million in total sales.

Discovered by bandleader Earl Hines at Chicago's De Liso Club in 1939, Eckstine became a regular vocalist with Hines for four years, during which time he discovered Sarah Vaughan on an amateur night at the Apollo Theatre, New York. With the couple sharing vocals, the Earl Hines Orchestra became a major attraction, but Eckstine hankered after a bigger share of the limelight and left in 1943, originally with the idea of just working as a singer, but his agent suggested he set up his own big band.

That band was the catalyst for what was to become the be-bop modern-jazz movement: Charlie Parker, Dizzy Gillespie, Miles Davis(▶), Art Blakey, Fats Navarro, Gene Ammons, Dexter Gordon and Lucky Thompson all came from the Eckstine band. By 1947 each of the players had made his own name and the band split up, but by that time Eckstine was a big star, known as 'The Fabulous Mr B', and had already seen **Cottage For Sale** and **Prisoner Of Love** go gold (both on National).

Signing long-term to MGM, he made a speciality of recording highly personalised versions of oldies, earning further gold discs for **Everything I Have Is Yours** (1947), **Blue Moon** (1948), **Caravan** (1949), **My Foolish Heart** (1950) and **I Apologise** (1951).

In 1965, Eckstine was signed to Motown(▶), who made no attempt to submerge him beneath the Detroit Sound (as they did later with Jerry Butler(▶)), but recorded him in a style totally sympathetic with what his public had come to expect—lush strings and smooth orchestrations underlying mellow melodic songs.

A later stint at Stax's(▶) Enterprise label was somewhat more adven-turous. A debut set, **Stormy**, produced and arranged by Isaac Hayes(▶), was in the usual Eckstine mould but, ironically, the next two sets, produced by Eckstine himself, took the veteran straight over into soul music.

Recordings:
Gentle On My Mind (Tamla Motown)
Stormy (Enterprise/—)
Senior Soul (Enterprise/—)
Greatest Hits (Polydor)

The Five Royales

In the realms of those nebulous vocal groups who recorded during the 1950s, it was a distinct advantage to have a competent songwriter in your midst. Such was the fortune of The Five Royales who included the eminently talented Lowman Pauling among their number, and his material carried the group through three phases of chart status.

The Five Royales. Courtesy King Records. (Note group name spelling variation on this reissued album).

The group comprised Lowman and Clarence Pauling, Johnnie Tanner, Johnny Moore and Obediah Carter, and began singing together as a gospel group, the Royal Sons Quintet, in 1948. Switching to the secular style, they topped the R&B charts in 1953 with **Baby Don't Do It** and **Help Me Somebody** on Apollo, signed to King and scored with **Think** in 1957 (also a hit for James Brown(▶)), then with **Dedicated To The One I Love** in 1961 (also a hit for the Shirelles(▶)).

Subsequent discs appeared on ABC, Vee Jay, Home of the Blues, Todd (including a new version of **Baby Don't Do It**) and Smash, with personnel variations bringing in Otto Jefferies.

Recordings:
24 All Hit Tunes (King/—)

Lowell Fulsom

Born in Tulsa, Oklahoma, in 1921, to a black mother and an American Indian father, Lowell Fulsom (alternatively spelt Fulson on some releases) worked the Southern States blues circuits, playing mostly acoustic music before moving to the West Coast, after World War Two service, and adopting an electric guitar style.

Signing to the Los Angeles label Swingtime, he scored big with **Every Day I Have The Blues** (1949) and began touring widely (Ray Charles(▶) was his pianist for a while), recording for Aladdin, Chess(▶) subsidiary Checker and Kent/Modern(▶), who took him into a style which bridged the gap between R&B and soul.

His **Tramp** classic was covered by Otis Redding(▶) and Carla Thomas(▶) on Stax(▶), while Fulsom himself did a great version of **Funky Broadway** (a hit for Wilson Pickett(▶)).

Switching to Jewel, he was cut at Muscle Shoals(▶) in the rock-influenced 'heavy blues' style which Howlin' Wolf(▶) and Muddy Waters(▶) were also dabbling in, though Fulsom did it with somewhat less disastrous results.

His compositions, notably **Reconsider Baby** and **Black Nights** have become standard fodder for black American artists of all musical persuasions.

Recordings:
Lowell Fulsom (Chess Blues Masters/—)
Tramp (Kent/—)
Now! (Kent)
In A Heavy Bag (Jewel/Polydor)
Love Maker (Big Town/—)

Rosco Gordon

Memphis-based singer and pianist Rosco Gordon was born in 1933. By 1948 he was one of the best known singers in his native city. He employed Bobby Bland(▶) as his driver('Because I was the only one in our crowd who owned a car!' recalled Bland in years later).

Gordon liked to play illegal gaming tables, which gave Bland the chance to front the Gordon band from time to time and pave the way for his own singing career. Produced by Ike Turner(▶) for Sam Phillips, Gordon hit with **Booted** (leased to Chess(▶)) and **No More Doggin'**.

Later, switching to Vee Jay, he scored with **Just A Little Bit**, which song became standard fare with British R&B groups in the '60s, while his sax-laden backings and strong vocals made him a big favourite with West Indian record buyers. Gordon eventually moved to New York, recorded for his own small soul label then went into semi-retirement until returning to the stage in 1982 for his first visit to the UK. Note: Gordon's christian name has often been published with and 'e' (ie Roscoe). Rosco is the correct spelling.

Recordings:
Keep On Doggin' (Mr R&B)
The Best Of Vol. 1 (—/Ace)

Roy Hamilton

Unchained Melody, the biggest selling R&B record of 1955, was typical of Roy Hamilton's output. Sung in a baritone which owed its appeal to conventional clarity of tone rather than to the quirky inflections which became known as soul singing, it was a performance of great power.

Born in Leesburg, Georgia, on April 16, 1929, Hamilton had topped the R&B charts in 1954 with **You'll Never Walk Alone**, and his big-ballad style won him enormous popularity through such numbers as **If I Loved You, Ebb Tide** and **You Can Have Her** (a 1961 hit).

Hamilton, who died of a heart attack in 1969, heavily influenced The Righteous Brothers(▶) who had hits with a number of his songs (they cut all those listed above).

Recordings:
You Can Have Her (Epic/—)
Greatest Hits Vols 1 & 2 (Epic/—)
Warm Soul (MGM)

Wilbert Harrison

With his reading of the Leiber/Stoller(▶) composition **Kansas City** (Fury, 1959), Wilbert Harrison (born North Carolina, January 6, 1929) came up with one of the true all-time standards of black American music.

A host of records for a series of obscure labels seemed likely to doom him to the tag 'one-hit wonder', but in 1969 he took his novel one-man-band format (a style forced on him by economics rather than choice) to Sue and enjoyed a big hit with **Let's Work Together**. He was even a success with rock audiences when he toured as support for Creedance Clearwater Revival.

Recordings:
Let's Work Together (Sue/London)
Shoot You Full Of Love (Juggernaut/—)

Screamin' Jay Hawkins

One of the most bizarre characters in black music, Jalacy 'Jay' Hawkins was born in Cleveland, Ohio, in 1929, and raised in an orphanage.

As a youngster he took up boxing and was good enough to win the 1947 Golden Gloves competition and was a professional for a short time.

Working as singer/pianist with Tiny Grimes, Lynn Hope and other R&B names he cut his first record, **Coronet Boogie,** in 1951 and turned to music full-time in 1953. He recorded for a variety of labels, showing a penchant for novelty songs with sardonically humorous lyrics of which the eerie **I Put A Spell On You** (OKeh 1956, and later also a hit for Nina Simone(▶)) proved to be the biggie.

Adopting a voodoo/crypt image (copied later by Screaming Lord Sutch, Arthur Brown and others) Hawkins wore cloaks, was carried on stage in a coffin and held a skull with flashing eyes! He blended theatrics with a mixture of rock 'n' roll, R&B and blues, sung in a resonantly deep, husky-tinged voice.

I Hear Voices (1962), **Feast Of The Mau Mau** (1967), various recordings of **Spell** and the outrageous grunt-laden **Constipation Blues** (1967) have assured him an ardent if small following, particularly in France and the UK.

Recordings:
The Night And Day Of Screamin' Jay Hawkins (—/Planet)
I Put A Spell On You (OKeh/Direction)
What That Is! (Mercury)
Screamin' The Blues (—/Red Lightning)

Below: Screamin' Jay Hawkins lets loose.

veer more towards Tin Pan Alley than the R&B mainstream.

Recordings:
Best Of The Ink Spots (MCA)
Stanley Morgan's Ink Spots
  In London (—/Golden Hour)

Little Willie John

Co-written by Eddie Cooley and Otis Blackwell under the pseudonym John Davenport, **Fever** (later covered successfully by Peggy Lee and now a standard) gave Little Willie John a 1956 million-seller on King (▶) (it was to be just one of 14 huge hits for the label). By the end of the year hit total sales had topped seven million and his biggest hit was yet to come, the impassioned **Talk To Me, Talk To Me** (1957). His burst of successful creativity continued through till 1961, when the hits stopped.

Any chances of a comeback were ended dramatically when he got into a drunken brawl in a Seattle cafe and stabbed to death a railroad employee, Kudall Roundtree. Convicted of manslaughter, he was incarcerated in Washington State Penitentiary where he died of pneumonia on May 26, 1968, aged just 30.

Born in Camden, Arkansas, on November 15, 1937, Little Willie John had recorded for Prize, Savoy and Rama by the time he was 16. He toured with the Paul Williams band as well as making several appearances with Count Basie and Duke Ellington. Signed to King by Sid Nathan in 1955, he scored immediately with a revival of Titus Turner's **All Around The World** (a 1969 hit for Little Milton (▶) under the new title **Grits Ain't Groceries**), followed by the soulfully bluesy **I Need Your Love So Bad** (a subsequent hit for James Brown (▶) and, years later, for Fleetwood Mac). Then came **Fever**.

John's sister Mable John was a member of the Raelets and recorded several classic soul sides for Stax. (▶).

Recordings:
Come On And Join Little Willie John At A Recording Session (King/London)
Free At Last (Gusto)

Kent/Modern Records

Founded in Los Angeles in 1945 by the white Biharri brothers—Jules, Joe, Saul and Lester—Modern Records and its subsidiaries (Kent contained most of the soul music output), made an early reputation in the blues' field through Lightnin' Hopkins, John Lee Hooker, B. B. King (▶) (signed to the company's RPM label by Ike Turner (▶)), Jimmy Witherspoon and a host of others.

Soon broadening its outlook to cover the whole gamut of black music, the company, issued a series of sides by Etta James (▶), Bobby Bland (▶), Little Richard (▶), Z. Z. Hill (▶), Lowell Fulsom (▶), the Cadets, Johnny Moore's Three Blazers and numerous other major black acts.

Recordings:
Rock 'n' Roll Festival (Kent/—)
Teenage Rock 'n' Roll Party
  (—/Ace)

John Lee Hooker

When the British beat boom of the mid-'60s focused attention on American blues and R&B musicians, John Lee Hooker was one of the chief beneficiaries, having a minor UK hit with **Dimples** (1964) and winning a lot of club action with **Boom Boom** and **San Francisco** on which the back-up vocals were provided by the Vandellas(▶) who, like him, were based in Detroit.

Born on August 22, 1917, in Clarksdale, Mississippi, Hooker played with Robert Nighthawk and other blues legends in Memphis before moving to Detroit in 1943. Signed to Modern(▶) in 1948, he notched a million-seller with the compulsive **Boogie Chillun** from his first session.

Since then his output has been enormous. Recording as Texas Slim, Johnny Williams and John Lee Booker, as well as under his own name, he has worked for a profusion of labels, including Chess(▶), King(▶), DeLuxe, Chance, Vee-Jay(▶) (which label enjoyed the benefits of his mid-'60s hits), and, more recently, Liberty, Stax(▶), Probe, ABC and Tomato.

His 1982 UK concerts on the same bill as B.B. King(▶) and Bobby Bland(▶) were a triumph, showing that, even in his 60s, he has lost none of the raw cutting power of his vocal and guitar work.

Recordings:
House Of The Blues (Chess/Pye International)
Best Of John Lee Hooker (Vee-Jay/Joy)
Big Soul (Vee-Jay/Joy)
Free Beer And Chicken (ABC)
That's Where It's At (Stax/-)
The Cream (Tomato/-)

Howlin' Wolf

A massive 270lb of snarling blues aggression, Chester Burnett (born Aberdeen, Mississippi, June 10, 1910) learned his gritty vocal style and stinging guitar work from country blues man Charlie Patton and his harmonica from Sonny Boy Williamson (Rice Miller), before being discovered by Ike Turner(▶) while playing in a Memphis club. Turner recorded him for Modern while Sam Phillips cut him for his own Sun label and for Chess.

Moving to Chicago with a Chess contract in his pocket, Howlin' Wolf churned out a succession of major blues/R&B hits between 1954 and '64 and made a heavy impact on the rock world, his material being covered by such luminaries as the Rolling Stones, Cream, 10 Years After, the Yardbirds, Manfred Mann, Rod Stewart, Doors, Electric Flag and Little Feat. In 1972, the Rolling Stones encouraged him to come to London and Wolf cut an album which utilised the playing of Eric Clapton, Ringo Starr, Stevie Winwood, Bill Wyman, Charlie Watts and Ian Stewart.

An experiment in heavy-rock, **The Howlin' Wolf** album bore the title tag: 'This is Howlin' Wolf's NEW ALBUM. He doesn't like it. He didn't like his electric guitar at first either.' Wolf's devoted fans didn't like the set either, nor did they grow to like it! His experimental sessions with Bo Diddley(▶) and Muddy Waters(▶) were similarly slated but, in retrospect, can be said to contain some worthwhile music.

In 1973, already a sick man as a result of several heart attacks, Howlin' Wolf went through the windshield of his car in a road accident, suffering kidney damage

Above: 65 years old, and still cooking, John Lee Hooker knocked 'em dead on his 1982 tour with Bobby Bland and B.B. King.

which eventually led to his death. He is remembered for such masterpieces as **Spoonful, Little Red Rooster, Back Door Man, Killing Floor** and **Smokestack Lightning** (which was a British pop hit!).

Recordings:
Howlin' Wolf (Chess/—)
Poor Boy (Chess)
Message To The Young (Chess)
The London Howlin' Wolf Sessions (Rolling Stones)
Chester Burnett AKA Howlin' Wolf (Chess)

The Ink Spots

Formed in 1934 by Jerry Daniels, tenor vocals; Charles Fuqua, tenor vocals, guitar, ukelele; Ivory Watson, baritone vocals, guitar; and Orville 'Hoppy' Jones, bass vocals, guitar, the Ink Spots were the grand-daddies of all black vocal groups, rivalled only by the Mills Brothers.

In 1939, Bill Kenny replaced Daniels as lead singer and the Ink Spots scored with the ballad **If I Didn't Care**, setting a style followed by black vocal groups ever since with a harmonised accompaniment providing fills behind a strong lead voice.

It was Jones who gave the group their famed 'talking chorus' gimmick. With his death in 1944 and then those of Watson and Fuqua the line-up changed over the years, but the Ink Spots worked through the '40s, '50s, '60s and into the '70s as a continued inspiration to other black artists even if their music did

B.B. King

Living up to his name, Riley B. 'Blues Boy' King (born in Itta Bena, near Indianola, Mississippi, on September 16, 1925, and raised by foster parents) has strode majestically through the world of the blues.

Though purists have sometimes criticised his fearless steps into other areas—the first bluesman to introduce massed strings, to reach out and grab a mass audience, to acknowledge the importance of country ('It's the white man's version of the blues', he once said)—few would deny that he is THE king. Record sales alone justify that title, surpassing those of any other blues artist, and his artistry and influence over other players back up the claim.

Ironically, for a man regarded by many (and not only blues freaks) as the world's greatest lead guitarist, King confesses that he cannot play rhythm (rating Steve Cropper as the master of that idiom), nor can he sing and play at the same time—which explains why he adopted the call-and-response pattern of plantation work-songs, alternating powerful vocal lines with dazzling guitar licks to create a style which has become an integral part of the blues playing tradition.

King's cousin, the legendary country blues guitarist/singer Bukka White, was a major influence on his style and so was the more sophisticated jazz-angled urban blues playing of T. Bone Walker and the pure jazz of Charlie Christian.

King's first break came when he joined Radio WGRM in Greenwood, Mississippi, and was spotted by Sonny Boy Williamson II (Rice Miller) who was then hosting the 'King Biscuit Boy' radio show, on the far more important station WDIA in Memphis, sponsored by a flour company. King was given a 10-minute slot as a DJ, which helped supplement his earnings as a musician. By the time he left, his show had grown in both time and popularity and was taken over by another WDIA stalwart, Rufus Thomas(▶). (It was WDIA station manager Don Kearn who dubbed King 'The Beale Street Blues Boy', soon shortened to plain 'B.B.')

King's first record release was in 1949 with **Miss Martha King.** Then he was signed to Modern Records'(▶) RPM subsidiary by Ike Turner(▶), who was working as roving talent scout for the label. During an 11-year stint at RPM, King forged his peerless reputation. Recording in Memphis, he cut the atmosphere-laden **Three O'Clock Blues** (1950) with Ike Turner on piano, Willie Mitchell(▶) on trumpet and Hank Crawford(▶) on alto-sax, and saw it stay at No.1 on the R&B charts for 18 weeks.

New B.B. King records appeared on the market almost every other week. As later happened with James Brown(▶), King often had several records on the R&B chart at the same time. All were marked by King's vocal mix of high-falsetto and gospel-influenced tenor, played off against

Below: Revered by musicians and audiences from all walks of life, Riley B. 'Blues Boy' King gives it all.

Above: B.B. King captivates another generation at a recent concert.

his guitar improvisations which featured a torrent of notes, often 'bent' over a vibrato sound. It was a style of playing which influenced dozens of bluesmen (notably Otis Rush and Buddy Guy), as well as such diverse musicians as Eric Clapton and Jimi Hendrix(▶).

Again, a worthwhile comparison can be made with Steve Cropper. Just as King could never play rhythm and Cropper cut only minimal solos, so King's appeal was in the sheer welter and complexity of notes while Cropper's lay as much in the notes he left out as the ones he played—in a way, a contrast of sheer dazzle against restrained taste.

B.B. has since made a name for himself as one of the hardest-working musicians in the world, gigging an average of 300 days a year and spending most of the other 65 in the recording studio. At Modern/RPM, he cut hundreds of sides.

Every Day I Have The Blues, a 1955 million-seller, **Sweet Little Angel, Sweet Sixteen** and **Rock Me Baby** were among King's RPM masterpieces—all of them much covered by other artists. In 1961, King switched to the major ABC label (later appearing on their Bluesway subsidiary) and the hits continued with gems like **Don't Answer The Door** and **Lucille** (a number dedicated to his guitar, which he called by that name), usually recorded in Chicago, produced and co-arranged by Johnny Pate (better known for his work with such smooth soul acts as the Impressions(▶)) often using Quincy Jones(▶) as band-leader and co-arranger.

The classic **Live At The Regal** (1964) album revealed the depth of King's continuing appeal to blacks at a time when, in general, they regarded blues as somewhat passé. Like other bluesmen, however, King realised there was a whole new white audience to be won and he started working with white rock musicians (notably Leon Russell, Joe Walsh and Carole King) for the **Indianola Mississippi Seeds** set in 1970.

Before that, King had his biggest and most innovative hit with the haunting **The Thrill Is Gone** (1969), which featured a stunning string arrangement. King had recorded with strings before but never in such an imaginative way. Also on the **Completely Well** album, which yielded the hit, was the extended **Cryin' Won't Help You Now/You're So Mean,** one of the most vibrant jam sessions ever committed to disc, his young backing musicians (Herbie Lovelle, drums; Paul Harris, electric piano; Hugh McCracken, guitar; and Gerry 'Fingers' Jemmott, bass) getting such a heavy groove going that King is heard to exclaim: 'What are y'all trying to do—kill me?'

Produced by Bill Szymczyk, that and the next few ABC/Bluesway albums were King at his mightiest, but later offerings, reflecting the influence of his astute manager Sidney Seidenberg (who also managed Gladys Knight and the Pips(▶)) perhaps tried to move him too far in the direction of sophistication (aiming to capture the soul market, the rock freaks and MOR listeners as well, rather than the traditional blues market).

Albums were recorded in Los Angeles, in London (at Abbey Road and guesting such unlikely luminaries as Ringo Starr, Steve Marriott and Klaus Voorman!), live at the University of Mississippi and at Cook County Jail, Chicago, with big orchestras and with rock groups and, notably, in partnership with his friend from the Memphis days, Bobby 'Blue' Bland. The quality has ranged from misconceived and uninspiring (though King's personal contribution on each album has been faultless) to unquestionably brilliant. At times challenged by the other two Kings of the blues' world, Albert King(▶) and Freddie King(▶), he was never surpassed by them (by coincidence, his own father's name was Albert).

Over the past 30 years B.B. King has recorded hits in a hotel bedroom, in a converted garage and in the most sophisticated studios in the world, with material ranging from his own superb compositions to country songs and even Broadway standards, and with musicians ranging from the best

Midnight Believer. Courtesy ABC Records.

of black America to British pop stars, but always he has been, truly, a King on all of his countless albums and hundreds of singles, continually updating his music to please an ever-growing audience.

Recordings:
From The Beginning (Kent/—)
The Jungle (Kent/—)
Live At The Regal (ABC Paramount/HMV)
Lucille (ABC Bluesway/Stateside)
Completely Well (ABC Bluesway/Stateside)
Indianola Mississippi Seeds (ABC-Probe)
In London (ABC-Probe)
Together For The First Time . . . Live (with Bobby Bland) (ABC)

Freddie King

The R&B instrumental **Hide Away** and cuts like **I'm Tore Down, Lonesome Whistle Blues** and **San-Ho-Zay** made Freddie King the undisputed king of the blues scene at the turn of the '60s, his records outselling those of B.B. King(▶), Jimmy Reed, John Lee Hooker(▶), Bobby Bland(▶) and all the opposition at that time.

Born in Longview, Texas, on September 30, 1934, King moved to Chicago as a teenager and first recorded for El Bee in 1956, but it was in 1960 that he broke through, signing with King(▶) subsidiary Federal and enjoying three major hits from his very first session for them: **Have You Ever Loved A Woman, See See Baby** and **Hide-Away.** 77 further titles (30 of them instrumentals) were released by King over the next six years before he switched to Atlantic(▶) in 1968 for two albums produced by King Curtis(▶).

Rock star Leon Russell then signed King to his Shelter label and, thanks to producing three superb albums and featuring the bluesman on his tours, Russell turned King into a superstar.

In 1974, British producer Mike Vernon signed King to RSO and recorded the **Burglar** album which featured Eric Clapton and Gonzalez(▶) in support.

One of the blues world's three Kings (B.B. and Albert(▶) being the others), King died a relatively young man on December 27, 1976, following a heart attack at a Dallas gig on Christmas Day.

Larger Than Life. Courtesy RSO Records.

Recordings:
Let's Hide Away And Dance Away With Freddie King (King/—)
His Early Years (—/Polydor)
Texas Cannonball (Shelter/—)
Woman Across The River (Shelter/A&M)
Burglar (RSO)
Freddie King 1934-1976 (RSO)
Best Of Freddie King (Shelter)
Greatest Hits (—/A&M)
Hideaway (—/Gusto)

King Records

Syd Nathan launched his King group of labels in Cincinnati, Ohio, in 1944, as a showcase for country and western artists (a role which was continued down through the years), but soon realised there was also an emergent record market among the black population.

In 1947, Henry Glover was brought in with the particular responsibility of building an R&B catalogue, a task he carried out with great aplomb for more than 25 years, ensuring a flood of releases—some mediocre, some good and more than a few excellent—on such subsidiary labels as Federal, De-Luxe, Starday and Bethlehem.

The R&B jump bands of Bullmoose Jackson, Lucky Millinder, Tiny Bradshaw and Wynonie Harris were native to the Mid-West (Oklahoma being a particularly rich source for such talent), while the company's geographical location was such as to attract artists from both East and West Coasts and from the South as well as from the Mid-West.

The list of artists whose records passed into the King catalogue is vast, among the notables being Champion Jack Dupree (from New Orleans), Johnny 'Guitar' Watson(▶) (from Los Angeles), James Brown(▶) (from way down in Georgia), Little Willie John(▶)(from Arkansas), Hank Ballard(▶) (from Detroit), organist Bill Doggett (from Philadelphia), and Otis Williams and the Charms (from Cincinnati itself). The wide catchment area involved is the main reason why the company never developed the family-type feeling which was to exist at later companies like Motown(▶), Stax(▶), TK(▶), Philadelphia International(▶) and, to a lesser degree, Chess(▶), all of whom tended to draw their talent from artists resident in their base city.

But while many artists did flit into then flit straight out of the King story, others showed more durability, none more so than James Brown whose extraordinary success virtually carried the company through the '60s. Once he left, to join Polydor, the operation collapsed.

King's back catalogue was bought up by Nashville-based Gusto, who are now content to churn out re-packages of old material, which at least ensures that all those classic recordings don't lie buried in the vaults—a recent example in the UK being the re-issue of Nina Simone's(▶) Bethlehem recording **My Baby Just Cares For Me**, which made a serious tilt at the charts in 1982.

Jerry Leiber and Mike Stoller

Jerry Leiber and Mike Stoller were the most important writing/production team in late '50s and early '60s R&B and rock 'n' roll. Responsible in one way or another for dozens of classic cuts by the Coasters(▶), the Drifters(▶) and solo artists like Ben E. King(▶) (as well as working with Presley), Leiber and Stoller added wit, finesse and an unerring commercial sensibility to the early flowerings of mainstream black pop music.

Leiber and Stoller were Jewish kids raised in Baltimore in a racially mixed area, cutting their teeth on the blues, R&B and country music. They began writing together as teenagers—Leiber generally the lyrics and Stoller the music—and started scoring successes in the early '50s with artists on the small independent R&B labels.

Cuts from this period include **Good Good Whiskey** by Amos Milburn, **Hard Times** by Charles Brown and **That's What The Good Book Says** by the Robins.

An important break came in 1956 when Atlantic bought the catalogue of Los Angeles-based Spark Records, for whom the Robins recorded. The Robins became the Coasters, were signed to Atco, and the first of a long line of Leiber and Stoller written and produced hits was released: **Riot In Cell Block No. 9.** The record established the pattern of Coasters/Leiber/Stoller collaborations to come; it was a 'playlet', with a definite scenario and storyline, and an undercurrent of wry, knowing humour. Over the next few years the team released some of the period's most evocative and entertaining records, including **That Is Rock & Roll, Poison Ivy, Along Came Jones, Searchin', Yakety Yak, Little Egypt, Charlie Brown, Down In Mexico** and **Smokey Joe's Cafe.**

During this period, Leiber and Stoller also wrote and produced for other Atlantic acts like Ruth Brown(▶), Joe Turner and LaVern Baker(▶), and were commissioned to revive the flagging fortunes of the Drifters. Although the group had previously had several R&B chart successes, it was the Leiber and Stoller produced **There Goes My Baby** which cracked the pop market for them. The song was not written by the duo, but was in many ways a landmark recording, especially in its marrying of strings and R&B vocals. **There Goes My Baby** took the Drifters to No.2 in the pop charts and initiated a run of Leiber and Stoller produced hits, including classics like **Save The Last Dance For Me, Up On The Roof,** and **On Broadway** (also co-written by Leiber and Stoller). Following Ben E. King's departure from the Drifters, the pair were also responsible for King's classic **Stand By Me.**

Mention must also be made of **Hound Dog,** the song Leiber and Stoller originally wrote for blues singer Willie Mae 'Big Mama' Thornton. Later covered by Elvis Presley, the song went on to become a huge international hit. Nevertheless, many prefer the Thornton version, not least the writers themselves, who first became aware of the Presley cut when they heard it on the radio. However, they consequently met Presley and collaborated with him on a whole run of material including **Jailhouse Rock.**

After a relatively low-profile period in the '60s Leiber and Stoller revived their partnership in the '70s, but devoted most of their energies to rock acts. Their work with the Coasters, the Drifters and their contemporaries remains their most fitting testimony. Leiber and Stoller (along with Phil Spector(▶), one of their protégés), did much to revolutionise the way black music was viewed by the public at large, helping to make R&B and its related strains very much a part of the pop mainstream. To their credit, they achieved this largely without watering it down or over-prettifying it. Examples of their work can be found on Coasters, Drifters and other compilations.

Little Richard

'My Music is the healing music, it makes the blind see, makes the lame walk, it makes the deaf hear and the dumb talk!'—such is Little Richard's claim for his prolific and generally exciting output, and while such physical miracles may not actually manifest, Little Richard, who was the self-proclaimed 'Georgia Peach', has certainly proved himself a dynamic entertainer over the years in the fields of R&B, rock 'n' roll, gospel and soul.

Richard Wayne Penniman was born on December 5, 1935, in Macon, Georgia, into a large family with a heavily religious background, growing up as a Seventh Day Adventist then forsaking the faith to run away from home to perform in a medicine show. As his family background dissolved, Richard was taken care of by a white Macon couple, Ann and Enotris Johnson, both of whom were to feature incidentally in his subsequent musical career— Miss Ann in an intense bluesy song of that name and Enotris as co-writer of smash hit **Long Tall Sally**.

Richard's musical involvement began in earnest in 1951 when he won a talent contest in Atlanta as Little Richard, the prize being a recording contract with RCA. Two sessions yielded eight songs, a varied mixture of melancholy blues-ballads and frantic jump-blues, his intense tenor voice displaying the influences of rich throaty Roy Brown and gospelly blues-wailer Billy Wright. Success was very limited with the four singles, however, and by late 1953 he had signed with Don Robey's Houston-based Peacock(▶) label.

Good Golly Miss Molly. . . Courtesy Specialty Records.

Richard was with Peacock for some three years, recording with the Tempo Toppers' vocal group on some good-humoured jump-blues material with raunchy combo support, but his handful of singles remained restricted to local sales. He also played one-nighters around the South-East and Southern States, and at the instigation of Lloyd Price(▶) in New Orleans sent a demo tape to Art Rupe at Specialty Records(▶) in Hollywood. Rupe liked what he heard, negotiated a release from Peacock with Don Robey, and sent producer Robert Bumps Blackwell to New Orleans to cut some sides on Richard at Cosimo Matassa's renowned J&M Studio.

The results came to write a new chapter in the annals of rock 'n' roll: debut **Tutti Frutti** charted in late 1955, followed over the next two years by such gems as **Long Tall Sally, Rip It Up, Ready Teddy, Lucille, Good Golly Miss Molly** and **The Girl Can't Help It**, the latter also the title-song of arguably the best ever rock 'n' roll movie (Richard appeared in a cameo performance as he did in *Don't Knock The Rock* and *Mr Rock 'n' Roll*).

Though his disc performances were inimitable, powerhouse shouted vocals over frantic thumping piano and torrid sax solos, they did inspire a host of cover-versions, but his raw impact usually won the day.

Then an amazing thing happened—at the height of his popularity, in 1957, while touring in Australia, Richard suddenly relinquished rock 'n' roll. He threw his jewelry off the Sydney Harbour Bridge and turned to religion, enrolling at Oakwood College in Huntsville, Alabama. His recording career became understandably schizoid, with Specialty lifting album tracks to perpetuate pop-chart status, while Richard began cutting gospel songs for a variety of labels, including Coral, End, Goldisc and Mercury, the latter under the direction of Quincy Jones(▶).

The winds of change began to swirl a little by 1962: Richard's vocals can be heard on some Little Star 45s credited to his band the Upsetters, then came a Mercury single **He Got What He Wanted**, a secular song with undertones of gospel. A 1963 deal with Atlantic(▶) yielded gospel sides, but 1964 took Richard back to Specialty with the storming rocker **Bama Lama Bama Loo**. Rupe's label was on the decline by now, however, and a Vee Jay(▶) contract gained Richard's signature, resulting in an uncertain mixture of soul-tinged new material and crass rehashes of the Specialty classics.

The soul connection soon ruled with a nice version of the ballad **Without Love**, followed by a superb outing of impassioned soul-gospel-blues, the Don Covay(▶)-penned **I Don't Know What You've Got But It's Got Me**, his only chart hit on Vee Jay. When the label folded Richard made some interesting raunchy soul sides for Modern(▶) and Kent(▶), moving on again to OKeh in 1966. His debut **Poor Dog** charted briefly; then followed the epic soulful gems **Hurry Sundown**—a scintillating movie theme—and **Don't Deceive Me**, before the man toured England and recorded **Get Down With It**, his most torrid rocker in years.

Above: The self proclaimed 'Georgia Peach'—Little Richard.

Lean times ensued—brash soul dancers on Brunswick, attempts at R&B with a contemporary production on Reprise, a deal which actually yielded three LPs, one produced by Richard in Muscle Shoals(▶), one by H.B. Barnum (▶), and **The Second Coming** reuniting him with Bumps Blackwell.

The Fabulous Little Richard. Courtesy Specialty Records.

(Some of the Reprise sides such as **King Of Rock 'n' Roll** and **Green Power** were enjoyable music but they weren't vintage Little Richard.) Subsequent discs have appeared on Green Mountain, Manticore and Mainstream.

Meanwhile, Richard's live performances have varied in quality and idiom—his image changing from stand-up pianist in baggy zoot-suit to an embarrassing gay poseur in make-up, tight pink jumpsuit and headband emblazoned 'The King'. Latterly he has returned to religion as a touring evangelist, in 1981 decrying the immorality of homosexuality from a pulpit in New Orleans while his sidemen gathered money from the congregation before the performance began—the 'King of Rock 'n' Roll reduced to 'Stealing In the Name of the Lord'.

Recordings:
20 Original Hits (Specialty)
Rip It Up (Vee-Jay/Joy)
Mr. Big (Vee-Jay/Joy)
Is Back (Vee-Jay/Joy)
Cast A Long Shadow (Epic)
The Modern Years (—/Ace)

Frankie Lymon & the Teenagers

Perhaps it's unfortunate that Frankie Lymon & the Teenagers were so young, so long ago, because their hit records are rather more enduring in the public mind than are the group themselves. When Diana Ross hit the charts late in 1981 with her revival of **Why Do Fools Fall In Love**, it was the song that jogged memories rather than the Teenagers, who cut the original hit.

Frankie Lymon was born in Washington Heights, New York, on September 30, 1942, and raised in a musical family along with three brothers and a sister. At school in 1954 he heard a practice session by the Premiers—four schoolmates named Herman Santiago, Joe Negroni, Jimmy Merchant and Sherman Garnes—and was accepted into this group, who were soon asked to audition for Gee Records.

With Lymon's piping, eager young voice upfront, the Teenagers debuted with **Why Do Fools Fall In Love** at the beginning of 1956 and reached the top 10 in American and British charts. Further hits followed in similar shrill jumping style, like **I Want You To Be My Girl** and **I Promise To Remember**, and the group rose to international stardom through movies and tours. During a British visit Lymon was recorded solo on **Goody Goody**, and sowed the seeds of discontent within the group. By late 1957 they had split up.

Frankie continued solo, with Gee being absorbed into the Roulette company, recording some good rock'n'roll sides with his voice broken and matured, but the hits stopped and he sank into a drug problem which eventually led to his death on February 28, 1968. Sherman Garnes died, during surgery, in 1981.

Recordings:
Why Do Fools Fall In Love (—/Pye Int.)
Teenagers (Roulette/—)

Johnny Mathis

Reputed to be the first black American entertainer to reach millionaire status, Johnny Mathis (born San Francisco, September 30, 1935) recorded output down the years from his singing with Columbia in 1956 (when he earned a gold record for **Wonderful, Wonderful**) was a million miles from the mainstream of black music. Then, all of a sudden, the man who had cast himself in the mould of a black Tony Bennett or Frank Sinatra became an authentic soul singer when he travelled down to Sigma studios and discovered the Philly Sound.

Working with Thom Bell(▶), he cut a string of superlative singles to carry him into the '80s, including the soul-tinged MOR Christmas song, **When A Child Is Born**, a re-make of the Stylistics'(▶) **Stone In Love With You**, and his big disco hit **Gone, Gone, Gone**. His duets with Deniece Williams(▶) also

proved fruitful, the duo scoring with **Too Much Too Little Too Late** and **You're All I Need To Get By** in 1978. In 1980 Mathis celebrated 25 years of recording for Columbia.

Recordings:
All Time Greatest Hits (Columbia/CBS)
When A Child Is Born (Columbia/CBS)
99 Miles From LA (Columbia/CBS)
Killing Me Softly (Columbia/CBS)
The Mathis Collection (Columbia/CBS)
That's What Friends Are For (With Deniece Williams) (Columbia/CBS)

Clyde McPhatter

His was the first voice to make the otherwise cloying sentimentality of **White Christmas** acceptable to ears hardened to the sound of urban R&B. The soaring clear tenor tones of Clyde McPhatter singing lead on the Drifters'(▶) 1954 R&B smash was aural magic. McPhatter, born on November 15, 1933, in Durham, North Carolina, the son of a baptist minister, developed his vocal talents singing with the gospel group the Mount Lebanon Singers. He was lured into the secular world at the age of 17 as lead tenor with Billy Ward's Dominoes, to feature in contrasting moods, like the impassioned melancholia of **The Bells** and the jumping blues **Have Mercy Baby.**

Clyde McPhatter Live At The Apollo. Courtesy Mercury Records.

Above: Smooth balladeer Johnny Mathis hit a soul groove in the late '70s.

McPhatter quit the Dominoes in 1953 to form the Drifters, scoring with gems like **Money Honey** and **Such A Night,** but was drafted into the USAF in 1954. Upon discharge in 1956 he signed with Atlantic(▶) as a solo, recording songs like **Treasure Of Love** and the chart-topping **A Lover's Question** before signing a remunerative contract with MGM in 1959.

This was a brief unsuccessful venture, and he soon moved to Mercury with more rewarding results. **Ta Ta** went top 30, and the jumping percussive **Lover Please** top 10 during his five-year spell with the label, which also yielded several pleasing LPs. McPhatter then joined Amy in 1966, Muscle Shoals'(▶) sessions spawning the soulful singles **A Shot Of Rhythm & Blues** and **Lavender Lace,** but sales were low and the deal lapsed.

In 1967 he moved to London, but two Decca sessions the following year failed to produce anything memorable, being vocally shallow and crassly orchestrated. **Denver** was a solitary 1969 release on B&C with little impact, and McPhatter was obliged to return to the USA when his work-permit expired in 1970. Back home, producer Clyde Otis persuaded US Decca to sign him, and a superb **Welcome Home** album resulted under the aegis of 'Ronnie, Norman & Earl', who must be Philadelphian alumni Baker, Harris and Young. A track entitled **Please Give Me One More Chance** was sadly appropriate, but the album didn't sell. Clyde McPhatter died in June 1972, a sad broken figure, a tragic end for a fine voice.

Recordings:
Live At The Apollo (Mercury/—)
Songs Of The Big City (Mercury/—)
Welcome Home (Decca/MCA)

The Moonglows

Among the foremost of the classic doo-wop vocal groups to gain national recognition during the 1950s were the Moonglows, a quartet from Louisville, Kentucky, consisting of Bobby Lester, Alexander Graves, Prentiss Barnes and distinctive bass singer Harvey Fuqua. After making their disc debut on the short-lived Champagne label, they were signed to Chicago-based Chance Records at the instigation of renowned DJ Alan Freed. They scored regional hits with the ballads **Secret Love** and **I Was Wrong,** but when Chance folded too in 1955, they were promptly signed up by Phil Chess(▶) for his family company.

The mellow ballad **Sincerely** proved a hit debut, despite being deprived of major pop status by the McGuire Sisters' cover-version, and **Most Of All** was a big R&B hit before the beaty **See Saw** reached the US national top 30 late in 1956 (it also featured in the movie *Rock Rock Rock*).

The group maintained a dual identity for a while, singing ballads as the Moonglows on Chess, and jump tunes as Bobby Lester and the Moonlighters (Checker), but disc sales were spasmodic until 1958, when the bass lead of Fuqua on **Ten Commandments Of Love** helped the disc to achieve top 30 status.

Soon after this the group split, though Fuqua recruited the Marquees to substitute for the remaining contract period, and they in turn metamorphosed into the Spinners(▶) on Tri-Phi/Motown. Fuqua remained busy, however, reforming a group for a **Return Of The Moonglows** LP on RCA, as well as being one of Motown's most active producers during the '60s and masterminding Sylvester's career in the '70s.

Recordings:
Moonglows (Chess—All Platinum/—)
Return Of The ... (RCA/—)

Johnny Otis

It may be something of a paradox that a white man, the son of Greek immigrant parents, should come to be known as 'The Godfather of Rhythm & Blues', but the facts reveal that Johnny Otis is eminently worthy of such accolade. Born in Vallejo, California, on December 28, 1921, with a family name of Veliotes, Otis gained musical inspiration from the big-band jazz of Count Basie and Duke Ellington, learning to play drums, then moving on to piano and vibes, and gaining experience playing in bands with Harlan Leonard and Count Prince Matthews.

By the mid-1940s Otis had his own band, scoring a hit with **Harlem Nocturne** on Excelsior in 1946, and after a spell on the road settled down in Los Angeles to open the Barrelhouse Club in 1948, in partnership with the late Bardu Ali, which featured the local stars of R&B. Otis proved to have an ear for talent, his first discoveries being the Robins and Little Esther (Phillips)(▶), and by 1950 he and his protégés were scoring numerous hits on Savoy.

The early 1950s saw him form a touring R&B revue while also finding time to produce hits for Johnny Ace(▶) and Little Richard(▶) on Duke/Peacock(▶) Records. His travels took him to Detroit, where he spotted emergent singers Jackie Wilson(▶), Little Willie John(▶) and Hank Ballard(▶), then the Johnny Otis Revue began recording for Capitol as the rock 'n' roll years arrived.

Willie & The Hand Jive was a top 10 smash for Otis in 1958, and **Ma (He's Making Eyes At Me)** became popular for Marie Adams with the Review. Further hits followed on Capitol for a couple of years, before Johnny moved to King with rather uninspiring results, then took a rest from performing.

It was 1969 before the next Otis output manifested, a fine blues-based LP, **Cold Shot**, on Kent(▶), yielding R&B hit 45 **Country Girl**, featuring his son Shuggie on Hendrix(▶)-inspired guitar along with newer talents Delmar Evans and Gene Connors. The Otis Band was also connected with **Snatch & The Poontangs**, a highly risqué LP on Kent! This success prompted Johnny to organise a Revue to play the 1970 Monterey Jazz Festival where he featured veteran R&B giants like Joe Turner, Little Esther and Roy Brown; the Show was committed to disc by Epic, who also signed Otis to contract, **The Watts Breakaway** appearing on an OKeh 45.

In 1974 Otis launched his own Blues Spectrum label, re-recording R&B greats like Charles Brown Joe Turner, Pee Wee Crayton and Joe Liggins with his own combo, but not always with memorable results. Then, after a lull in his

Below: Johnny Otis, and his all-new show band.

28

activities, he returned to disc with a fresh Johnny Otis Show on Alligator in 1982.

Recordings:
Johnny Otis Show (—/Charly)
Formidable (Capitol/Specialty)
Pioneers of Rock Vol. 3 (—/Starline)
Rock 'n' Roll Hit Parade (Dig/Flyright)
Cold Shot (Kent/Sonet)
Live At Monterey (Epic)

The Platters

Perhaps the best-known of the many vocal harmony groups who trod a rags-to-riches path during the rock 'n' roll years of the 1950s are the Platters, who managed to climb from the obscurity of regional R&B charts to worldwide stardom.

Initially a quartet comprising Tony Williams, Alex Hodge, David Lynch and Paul Robi, the group met entrepreneur Buck Ram in Los Angeles in 1953 and were signed to Federal Records, but met little success until Ram made an inspired personnel change, recruiting Zola Taylor as a contrasting female voice, to be known as the Platters' 'dish' while Hodge was replaced by Herb Reed. They continued to record for Federal, picking up local sales, until Ram managed to place them with Mercury as virtual 'make-weights' in a deal involving the Penguins, who had just made the national charts with **Earth Angel**.

That feat was promptly emulated by the Platters, whose first four records on Mercury all reached the national top 5 during the year from the fall of 1955 to late 1956; **Only You, The Magic Touch, The Great Pretender** and **My Prayer** were fine lyrical ballads, the latter two topping the charts, led by Tony Williams' clear soaring tenor. The hits continued to flow throughout the next five years, chart-toppers **Twilight Time** and **Smoke Gets In Your Eyes** aspiring to the realms of pop standards in The Platter's distinctive ballad stylings, albeit wrapped in rather lush orchestrations.

In 1961 Tony Williams quit to pursue a solo career, and auditions yielded Sonny Turner as a replacement, but despite maintaining a similar mode of performance the hits didn't come so readily. The group made a good living on the cabaret circuit, though, and continued a steady output of albums until leaving Mercury in 1965.

The Platters. Courtesy Mercury Records.

A change of musical direction followed more personnel changes —Sandra Dawn replaced Zola, and Nate Nelson took over from Paul Robi—and the group pacted with Musicor in 1966, taking a more

Encore! Courtesy EMI Records.

soulful inclination and switching up-tempo to score with lilting beaters like **I Love You 1000 Times** and **With This Ring,** while albums contained re-workings of their Mercury hits.

Subsequent years have brought innumerable changes of personnel and record labels and a profusion of lawsuits. The 'Buck Ram Platters' are touring minions of their ageing manager, who slaps injunctions on any original member who dares to quote the group name in show billings under any guise, and so the tarnished legend of the Platters wends its way around supperclub circuits!

Recordings:
Best Of ... Vols. 1 & 2 (—/Philips)
20 Classic Hits (—/Philips Int)
Encore Of Golden Hits (Mercury/—)
More Encore Of Golden Hits (Musicor/Stateside)
Going Back To Detroit (Musicor/Stateside)
Sweet Sweet Lovin' (—/Stateside)

Lloyd Price

Although a familiar name among cognisant R&B and soul fans, Lloyd Price is perhaps less well-known generally than the title and hook of one of his biggest pop hits, the favourite airplay oldie **Pesonality**, but his recording career spans three decades and a variety of styles.

Born on March 9, 1933, in New Orleans, Price was from a musical family and learned to play the trumpet before forming his own small band to play local clubs. By 1949 he was broadcasting on radio WBOK, for whom he wrote a station jingle which metamorphosed into a song called **Lawdy Miss Clawdy.**

Early in 1952 Art Rupe, owner of Specialty Records(▶), visited New Orleans in search of someone to match Fats Domino's(▶) success, and was impressed by Price's impassioned delivery of **Clawdy** at an audition. Lloyd was duly signed to Specialty and the song became a smash hit in summer 1952. Some further R&B success followed, but

Price was drafted in 1953 and emerged from service to find Little Richard(▶) established as the label's new star.

A move to Washington brought him into contact with Harold Logan, and their lengthy business relationship started with the launch of KRC Records. Price cut the ponderous bluesy ballad **Just Because**

Above: Lloyd Price is now an astute businessman.

for KRC then sold the track to ABC, whereon it reached the national top 30, launching a pop career which yielded a host of hits, including chart-topper **Stagger Lee** and the brash-but-catchy singalongs **Personality** and **I'm Gonna Get Married.**

Price's gritty vocals and some brassy arrangements, combined with his business acumen, were reaping steady royalties, resulting in the launch of Double L Records in 1963 (Wilson Pickett(▶) made his solo debut for the label), then Turntable in 1969; his musical style meanwhile moved towards heavy soul.

Price also recorded for Monument, Ludix, Jad, GSF, Wand(▶)

(fine soul and a great ballad **Mr & Mrs Untrue**), then joined forces with Don King Productions to launch his LPG label in 1976; he remains active in New York as an aware music businessman.

Recordings:
Original Hits (Specialty)
Best Of ... (—/(ABC) Starline)

The Royals

Not to be confused with the successful Jamaican group of the same name, the Royals hailed from Detroit and comprised Lawson Smith, Norman Thrasher, Billy Davis and Henry Booth with Hank Ballard(▶) brought in as lead singer.

When they pacted with King Records, their name was changed to the Midnighters to avoid confusion with the Five Royales(▶), who were already successful for the label. With a revised line-up, they won massive commercial success as Hank Ballard and the Midnighters, commencing with the million-selling **Work With Me Annie** on King subsidiary Federal in 1954.

Recordings:
No album releases as the Royals.

Shirley and Lee

Shirley Pixley (born 1937) and Leonard Lee (born 1935) were teenagers of just 14 and 15 years old respectively when they cut their first record in their native New Orleans and as Shirley and Lee were dubbed 'The Sweethearts Of The Blues'.

I'm Gone (Atlantic(▶)) made No.2 R&B and was followed in 1956 by the million-selling **Let The Good Times Roll** (Aladdin), which has become a classic R&B standard (also a hit as part of a medley for Bunny Sigler(▶)).

The duo also recorded for Warwick and Imperial, and made a living through the late '60s by appearing on revival shows. Shirley (now Shirley Goodman following marriage) returned with a major disc dancer hit, **Shame, Shame, Shame** on All Platinum subsidiary Vibration in 1974 as Shirley and Company.

Recordings:
Let The Good Times Roll (Aladdin/—)

Specialty

Art Rupe's Los Angeles-based Specialty R&B label made a dramatic impact on emerging rock 'n' roll through a run of major hits by Little Richard(▶), Larry Williams(▶) and Jerry Byrne. It also yielded some classic blues sides by Roy Milton, Percy Mayfield, Guitar Slim and others.

Specialty was launched in 1946 and scored early with Roy Milton's **R.M. Blues**. In 1952, Rupe started looking beyond LA for his material and found a rich source in New Orleans, selling a million copies of Lloyd Price's(▶) **Lawdy Miss Clawdy** that same year. The Crescent City also yielded the brilliant **Things That I Used To Do** by Guitar Slim and, in 1955, Little Richard's **Tutti Frutti,** first of a solid run of international hits for Specialty by that extrovert showman.

Producers Sonny Bono (later of

Sonny and Cher) and Bumps Blackwell, in Los Angeles, and Harold Battiste, in New Orleans, played a major role in the label's success, but when raw rock 'n' roll stopped selling in 1959 and black audiences turned from R&B to the smoother soul sounds of the '60s, Specialty lost its momentum and became merely a rich source of archive material.

Recordings:
This Is How It All Began
Vols. I & II (Specialty)

The Treniers

The Treniers, essentially a family group, are something of a paradox in that their recording career spanned some 20 years and more than a dozen labels, yet failed to yield a single chart hit, pop or R&B, though they featured in four rock 'n' roll movies!

Twins Claude and Cliff Trenier, born in Mobile, Alabama, on July 14, 1919, were the nucleus of the group, which also included brother Buddy and nephew Skip, plus Jimmy Johson (bass), Don Hill (sax), Gene Gilbeaux (piano) and Henry Green (drums). Their recording debut was on Mercury in 1947 with **Buzz Buzz Buzz;** from there they moved on to Coral and London before joining OKeh in 1951, whereon their brand of jumping R&B liberally laced with humour was displayed on more than a dozen singles. Four years later they switched to sister-label Epic.

The group's lively stage act had outstanding visual impact, leading to cameo spots in the movies *Don't Knock The Rock, The Girl Can't Help It, Calypso Rhythm* and *Juke Box Rhythm,* performing their OKeh and Epic material.

More records followed on Groove, RCA and Vik, and the Treniers were in demand for many TV shows, leading to cabaret circuit bookings, which helped to maintain their career for many subsequent years.

Recordings:
Go Go Go (Epic/—)

Vee-Jay

Vee-Jay was a company which foundered as much through its overwhelming success as through anything else. 'Over-trading' is the current term for the ailment. Having signed the Four Seasons and, remarkably, secured the US contract on the Beatles, Vee-Jay found itself presssing up records just as fast as they could possibly be churned out. The trouble was, the had to borrow heavily to keep up with demand, distributors were slow to settle, interest charges and commitments to other artists mounted and eventually bankruptcy ensued.

Vee-Jay started from modest beginnings. Jimmy Brackent and his wife Vivian Carter owned a record shop in Chicago from where they set up their label in 1953 after bluesman Jimmy Reed and doo-wop group the Spaniels begged them to put their talents on record.

The initial efforts were issued on Chance but when that label folded, Vee-Jay was set up in its own right and the 1954 Spaniels' hit **Goodnight Sweetheart Goodnight** provided the funding to bring in Ewart Abner and Vivian's brother Calvin Carter to take charge of A&R and sign new acts.

Launched in 1957 as Falcon, a subsidiary soon re-named Abner concentrated on soul music with the Impressions(▶) and, especially, Dee Clark(▶), while Vee-Jay built an ever-expanding roster which ranged from solid blues (from John Lee Hooker(▶), Reed, Memphis Slim, Rosco Gordon(▶) and others), to gospel (Staple Singers(▶), Swan Silverstones, Highway QC's, Caravans, Five Blind Boys, Maceo Woods), R&B (Birdlegs and Pauline, El Dorados), soul (Dells(▶), Gene Chandler(▶), Jerry Butler(▶)), jazz (Eddie Harris(▶), and pop (Beatles, Four Seasons, Frank Ifield).

Offices were opened in Hollywood, California, and the future looked assured, but Vee-Jay had too many artists, too much product, too many commitments and too slow a cashflow, and in May 1966, it collapsed, though its product is to this day regularly re-issued via various labels on both sides of the Atlantic.

It was ironic that black music built the company but pop music (usually regarded as being far more commercially attractive) effectively killed and buried it!

Dinah Washington

If Sam Cooke was 'The Father Of Soul' then Dinah Washington was assuredly the mother of the idiom. Like Cooke, she had best-sellers in her own right but, more importantly, she had an enormous stylistic influence over the generation which followed her—most notably over the young Aretha Franklin(▶) (Dinah was a family friend who shared a strong gospel background with the Franklins).

Despite the strong church influence, however, Dinah Washington was a fiery woman who once beat her husband up on stage—using his own saxophone to do it! Born Ruth Jones in Tuscaloosa, Alabama, on August 29, 1924, she grew up in Chicago and made an early impact fronting the Lionel Hampton Band.

She first recorded jazz, for Keynote, then, signed to Mercury, she broadened her output to take in pop, blues and even country material—all of it sung from the soul, which at that time was revolutionary for secular music—developing superb phrasing and a way of singing across the beat. Her majestic appearance in the *Jazz On A*

Above: Urban blues/R&B veteran Muddy Waters.

Summer's Day movie won much acclaim and was followed by her biggest hits, **What A Difference A Day Makes** (1959) and a neatly rocking duet with Brook Benton(▶) on **Baby You Got What It Takes** (1960).

Her most soulful records included **This Bitter Earth,** produced by Clyde Otis, and her work with Quincy Jones(▶) whom she knew from Lionel Hampton days.

Her tempestuous life, which bore many parallels to that of Billie Holliday, ended just as tragically— she died of a sleeping-pill overdose on December 14, 1963.

Recordings:
Golden Hits (Mercury)

Muddy Waters

Though his music has stayed within the confines of the Chicago urban blues idiom, Muddy Waters has wielded an enormous influence over musicians black and white alike in almost every field of popular music from rock to soul.

Born McKinley Morganfield, in Rolling Fork, Mississippi, on April 4, 1915, he grew up on a plantation at nearby Clarksdale and was discovered in 1941 by Library Of Congress folk-music researcher Alan Lomax, who recorded him singing primitive rural blues.

Moving to Chicago in 1943, Waters soon became immersed in the vibrant blues scene there, recording for Aristocrat in 1945, hav-

Spotlight On Dinah Washington. Courtesy Philips Records.

ing acquired an electric guitar thanks to an uncle. When Aristocrat became Chess(▶), Waters soon established himself as their leading artist, a role he fulfilled till the label's demise many years later (even when Bo Diddley(▶) and Chuck Berry(▶) were outselling him, he was still recognised as Chess's father figure).

With his half-brother Otis Spann on piano, Little Walter on harmonica, Jimmy Rogers on second guitar, the Muddy Waters' band had a succession of classic hits, including **Rolling Stone, I've Got My Mojo Working, Tiger In Your Tank** and **I'm A Man,** all of which became standard material for any self-respecting British R&B/beat band in the '60s (among the most influenced being the Rolling Stones). What's more, each member of Waters' band became a recording star in his own right, Little Walter actually managing to outsell Waters himself in the mid-'50s.

Hard Again. Courtesy Blue Sky Records.

Between 1950 and 1958, Waters had 12 US R&B hits—but even such sales failed to reflect adequately his stature—and during the '60s and '70s he became a major concert draw with rock as well as blues audiences, latterly recording for white blues/rock star Johnny Winter's Blue Sky label. Waters is probably the most-recorded of all blues artists, save, perhaps, B.B. King. Most of his work is still available via a wide range of re-issues on secondary labels.

Recordings:
At Newport 1960 (Chess/Pye International)
Chess Masters (Chess)
McKinley Morganfield AKA Muddy Waters (Chess)
Hard Again (Blue Sky)
I'm Ready (Blue Sky)

Larry Williams

Larry Williams and his girlfriends, **Short Fat Fannie, Bony Moronie, Dizzy Miss Lizzy** and **Mary Ann,** made quite an impact on the rock 'n' roll scene in the late '50s, rivalling Specialty(▶) labelmate Little Richard(▶) in both style and impact.

While Richard temporarily retreated into gospel, the demise of rock 'n' roll found Williams forming a working partnership with Johnny 'Guitar' Watson(▶) and cutting some superb soul sides for OKeh.

Born in New Orleans on May 10, 1935, Williams moved to San Francisco at 18 and formed his own band, the Lemon Drops, as well as playing piano with Roy Brown and Percy Mayfield. Moving back to New Orleans in 1955, he became

pianist for Lloyd Price(▶) who introduced him to Art Rupe of Specialty. Rupe recorded the youngster on the Price song **Just Because** which went to No.2 in the US chart.

Williams followed this blues-angled ballad with a string of frenetic rockers, earning gold discs in 1958 with **Short Fat Fannie** and **Bony Moronie** (both his own compositions) which, though in the Little Richard vein—pounding piano, honking saxes etc.—were marked by Williams' own vocal gimmicks (including the snatches of whistling which became his hallmark).

Williams teamed with Watson in 1960 and they formed a joint production company. One of their collaborations was a hilarious duet on **Beatle Time,** now a rare collectors' item in the UK since it was only issued in a limited edition of a hundred or so and was sold by mail order by Mike Vernon. At the time Vernon was working for Decca for whom he produced a live album, **The Larry Williams Show,** when Williams toured the UK (with Watson as his guitarist as well as sharing vocals) in 1965. Another LP, **Larry Williams On Stage,** was cut during the same tour, for Island, with Screaming Lord Sutch doing the introductions.

Williams re-worked his old Specialty hits for an OKeh album, **Greatest Hits,** which included a great version of **Slow Down** and also showed he could handle a slow blues as well as a rocker. Then came the **Two For The Price Of One** duet set with Watson for the same label, which ranged from the storming title track to the insistent Williams-penned **Love Is A Funny Thing,** and the gently rocking version of the Cannonball Adderley(▶) hit **Mercy, Mercy, Mercy.**

After a long spell in semi-retirement, Williams returned on Fantasy with **The Resurrection Of Funk** album.

Recordings:
Here's Larry Williams (Speciality)
Greatest Hits (OKeh/—)
Two For The Price Of One (OKeh/—)
The Resurrection Of Funk (Fantasy/—)

Chuck Willis

Harold 'Chuck' Willis died of a stomach ulcer on April 10, 1958, aged just 30. A few months later the prophetically titled **What Am I Living For?** climbed to No. 15 and sold a million copies.

Born in Atlanta, Georgia, on January 31, 1928, the self-proclaimed 'Sheik Of The Blues' (he wore a bejewelled turban) and 'King Of The Stroll' first sang in Red McAllister's band. Discovered and subsequently managed by top local DJ Zenus Sears in 1952, he was signed to OKeh and scored R&B top-10 entries with **My Story, Going To The River, Don't Deceive Me, You're Still My Baby** and **Feel So Bad** between 1952 and '54. Besides charting, these songs became much-recorded R&B standards.

Willis also wrote hits for Ruth Brown (▶), Patti Page, Eydie Gorme, the Five Keyes, Wanda Jackson, the Cadillacs, Don Cornell and others (later, his songs were also recorded by Elvis Presley, the Drifters (▶) and Buddy Holly).

After his initial stint as an R&B maestro, Willis found a second career in 1956 when he switched

to Atlantic (▶) and became a major rock 'n' roll star with such masterpieces as **It's Too Late, C.C. Rider, Betty And Dupree** and **Hang Up My Rock & Roll Shoes.**

The chances are that, had he lived, Chuck Willis could also have undergone the transition into soul music; certainly his voice was distinctive and emotive enough.

Recordings:
I Remember Chuck Willis (Atlantic)

Jackie Wilson

A singer with a hit record career spanning three decades, and possessing one of the finest tenor voices in the popular music idiom, yet now remembered mainly just by the congnoscenti and for a few typical hits . . . such is the lot of Jackie Wilson.

Born in Detroit, Michigan, on June 9, 1934, he had talent in his fists as well as in his voice, having a brief spell as a boxer in the late 1940s and winning the amateur Golden Gloves welterweight title. His singing had its roots in the church, and his performing career began with the Ever Ready Gospel Singers before he took to the secular path in 1951 for a session with Dizzy Gillespie's Dee Gee label.

Later that year Wilson sang in a talent show at the Paradise Theatre, Detroit, where he was heard by Billy Ward, whose group —the Dominoes—were hot with **Sixty Minute Man.** Ward was impressed, took his phone number, then called him some months later when Clyde McPhatter(▶) quit the Dominoes, enlisting Wilson as replacement to sing lead or second tenor. He was with the group for some four years as they maintained a prodigious output on King/Federal, his soaring tenor tones distinctive in his melismatic delivery of ballads like **Rags To Riches.**

When the Dominoes moved to Decca in 1956, Wilson stayed with them for a while before leaving in search of solo recognition. He was spotted singing in a local club by Al

Green—then manager of Johnny Ray and LaVerne Baker(▶)—who signed him up and placed him with Brunswick Records under the supervision of house bandleader Dick Jacobs.

Wilson has remained a Brunswick artist ever since, being the mainstay of their roster for more than a decade. His lengthy succession of hits, in styles which managed to change with the passing times, include the rocking **Reet Petite** (1957) (at which time he was involved with Berry Gordy Jr. who went on to form Motown(▶)), the lilting **Lonely Teardrops** and the classy balladry of **To Be Loved** (1958). He maintained such stylistic variations, combating the brash orchestration through the years until 1963, when an injection of the then contemporary R&B feeling resulted in **Baby Workout.**

In 1966 Wilson's recording location changed from New York to Chicago. With the move came a transfusion of new ideas from producers like Carl Davis and Sonny Sanders, leading to more mainstream soul output of danceable yet ear-catching songs. **Whispers, Higher and Higher** and **I Get The Sweetest Feeling** sold well and confirmed Wilson's status as a hot soul star.

The formula had lost its commercial impact by the early '70s, though, and Wilson began searching for new ideas and material. A brief liaison with Eugene Record and the Chi-Lites(▶) bore limited fruit then tragedy struck on September 29, 1975, when Wilson suffered a heart-attack while singing at the Latin Casino in Camden, New Jersey. He lapsed into a coma, suffered severe brain damage, and has since been confined to Cherry Hill Medical Centre in New Jersey.

Recordings:
My Golden Favorites (Brunswick/Coral)
Spotlight On (Brunswick/—)
My Golden Favorites Vol. 2 (Brunswick/—)
Somethin' Else (Brunswick/—)
Soul Galore (Brunswick/Coral)
Greatest Hits (Brunswick)
Very Best Of (—/Brunswick)
Nobody But You (Brunswick/—)

By Special Request. Courtesy Brunswick Records.

The '60s

BLACK MUSIC entered the '60s in the same state of confusion and lack of direction as did rock 'n' roll, the earthy ethnic approach which had marked the mid-'50s seeming in danger of being overwhelmed by a desire to follow the dictates of Tin Pan Alley in an attempt to please—or, at least, not actively offend—a wider, largely white, pop audience.

Judged on standings in *Billboard* magazine's all-important R&B charts, the biggest record of 1960 with black audiences was **Baby (You Got What It Takes)** by Brook Benton and Dinah Washington—a decidedly MOR-influenced record by two of America's leading cabaret entertainers.

Despite having begun her career as a raw and very influential jump-blues singer in the late '40s, Dinah Washington had, by 1960, become well entrenched in the Ella Fitzgerald syndrome of being a so-called 'quality singer' while Brook Benton, like Billy Eckstine, Johnny Mathis and Sammy Davis Jr, had put himself in a similar bag among male singers.

The success of **Baby (You Got What It Takes)** reflected what was happening generally in black music at the turn of the decade, the penchant for doo-wop, blues and the gutsy black rock 'n' roll style of Little Richard, Larry Williams and Bo Diddley having given way, in the main, to more pop-orientated sounds.

Where the Drifters' 1959 use of strings on **There Goes My Baby** was a novel extension of R&B, with the strings enhancing the overall soulful feel of the record, their use on records by Fats Domino, Lloyd Price, Jackie Wilson, Brook Benton and even by the great blues singer B.B. King was merely blatant sweetening to attract the pop market and transform the artists concerned into 'all-round entertainers', opening the doors to Las Vegas and similar big-paying gigs, which had previously been the almost exclusive preserve of white artists.

It was not until 1964 that the real sound of black music in the '60s—soul music—came to full fruition (ironically, it was the year in which, for some inexplicable reason, *Billboard* chose not to print any R&B charts!). Until that sudden flowering, only a handful of artists could claim to be making a major contribution to what was to be the most significant change in black music yet to occur.

Whereas R&B had been an amalgam of the blues and mainstream pop music influences, and rock 'n' roll had been created from a marriage of blues with hillbilly country music stylings, soul was the far more radical marriage of the fervent feel of gospel music to secular lyrics.

The traditional blues singers had built their careers knowing that they sang 'the Devil's music' and thus had no right to meddle with religious music. But in the late '50s, Ray Charles, who till then had enjoyed only a modest career singing straight blues/R&B, earned himself the title of 'The Genius' by his blatant mixture of the intensity of gospel music with secular lyrics, even going so far as to borrow the actual tunes from gospel music, as when he put new lyrics to **This Little Light Of Mine** and transformed it into **This Little Girl Of Mine.**

In 1959, Ray Charles imbued **What'd I Say?** with all the fervour of a holly-roller prayer meeting and with one record turned black music on its head and the birth of soul was the result. For the next three years, Charles stayed on course with **Hit The Road Jack, Sticks And Stones, Unchain My Heart, Hide Nor Hair** and many others.

Charles' claim to be the father of soul music must be shared with the late Sam Cooke, who produced an even greater shock to gospel sensibilities for, as lead singer of the ultra-successful Soul Stirrers, he, unlike Charles, had been very much a part of the gospel music establishment.

Initially hiding behind the alias of Dale Cook, he barely changed his singing style but, by substituting secular lyrics—often of pure banality but sometimes, as in **A Change Is Gonna Come,** verging on the pure poetic—he committed the heresy of crossing over from the spiritual to the profane. It was a switch which was to be followed by many others in the ensuing years (Johnnie Taylor, his successor as lead singer with the Soul Stirrers, was one who made the change with great commercial success).

There had been a lot of hypocrisy within the world of gospel music, because while its purveyors sang of purity of spirit and deed, the sexual exploits of so very many of them were legend in black America. The birth of soul music was in many ways a release, allowing singers to learn their trade in church but then make their living catering to this world rather than to the next. 'Began vocal career in church, singing gospel' was to become THE cliché of black soul artists' biographies.

The title of Cooke's **A Change Is Gonna Come** was, then, prophetic in more than one way: the song's lyric reflected the awakening of black self-assertion in America —the fight to register the vote, to de-segregate buses and schools and so on—and the title itself heralded the advent of soul, a whole new dimension in black music. No wonder that, despite his dabblings with pure pop and even show-business schmaltz, Sam Cooke was to become revered among black artists. In terms of record sales, his achievements were well behind those of Nat 'King' Cole (total sales 75 million), Fats Domino (60 million), James Brown (50 million), the Supremes (50 million) and Ella Fitzgerald (25 million). Even Chubby Checker could claim to have surpassed his 15 million records sold. But Cooke has been, arguably, the most influential black-music stylist of all time, his inflections and his material being heard in

Jimi Hendrix

The Supremes

the work of Otis Redding, Lou Rawls, Arthur Conley, Al Green and countless others.

James Brown merits a very special place alongside Charles and Cooke in black music's hall of fame. Though his music was heavily rooted in the blues tradition, Brown too showed strong gospel influences and his tremendous sense of rhythm made him not only one of the first truly great soul artists (the self-proclaimed title of 'Soul Brother Number One' not being undeserved) but the unchallenged father of funk.

Surprisingly, the floodgates of soul music did not open overnight. A slow transition lasting three years or so took place as teenage singers steeped in the doo-wop tradition gradually and almost stealthily took elements of gospel singing and transferred them to their popular songs.

Just as the R&B boom of the immediate post-war years and the rock 'n' roll boom of the '50s had been fired by the entrepreneurial visions of a handful of independent record labels, so the new sounds of the '60s were largely propagated by new independent companies and, significantly, some of them were black owned and operated.

Berry Gordy Jr, a black Detroit car worker, began his music career writing hits for Jackie Wilson in 1957, and then used the earnings generated by this success to finance productions of his songs performed by other local artists, like Marv Johnson, whom he signed to United Artists, and William 'Smokey' Robinson and the Miracles, whose efforts he leased to Chess and Gone, two estabished outlets for black music, the former steeped in blues, the latter in doo-wop.

Gordy was not convinced, however, of the ability of such labels to break his artists and, consumed with the belief that he was right on the new direction which black music was taking, he formed his own label, Tamla, operating out of a converted house in his hometown. After a few minor hits, he reached No.1 for the first time in 1961 with the Miracles' **Shop Around**. In 1962, Mary Wells' **You Beat Me To The Punch** and the Contours' **Do You Love Me** were also chart-toppers for his new company.

Gordy's empire (with Motown, Soul, V.I.P., and other logos added to his roster of labels) grew so rapidly that by 1966 he could claim that Tamla Motown, as it had become, was the single most successful black-owned corporation in the United States. The company's slogan 'The Sound Of Young America' and its nickname of 'Hitsville USA' were well merited as by that time the company had notched no fewer than nine No.1 singles on the mass-audience national pop chart with an artist roster that could boast the Temptations, Stevie Wonder, Marvin Gaye, the Supremes, Junior Walker and the Four Tops among its many talents. In that one year, Gordy's company enjoyed 30 weeks atop the *Billboard* R&B charts, which was really some achievement.

Soul music had taken America by storm but by the mid-'60s Gordy's artists had become increasingly pop-orientated and were no longer purveying the raw undiluted soulfulness of gospel singing, all his artists having been carefully groomed to be able to move effortlessly into the lucrative 'all-round entertainer' territory.,

It was left to another notable independent label, Atlantic Records, to provide the market with the real thing. Atlantic's A&R men, headed by Jerry Wexler, who had helped the rise of rock 'n' roll by recording many of the most influential of the '50s blues and R&B artists, could see what their own release of **What'd I Say** was doing.

They signed boy-preacher Solomon Burke from Philadelphia and in 1963 he enjoyed his biggest hit with **If You Need Me,** a cover version of a song by a Detroit-based singer named Wilson Pickett who had been lead vocalist with the Falcons. Never one to miss a trick, Jerry Wexler also signed Wilson Pickett to the company and soon hit pay-dirt with **In The Midnight Hour,** co-penned by Pickett and Booker T and the MGs' guitarist Steve Cropper, and recorded at the Stax studio in Memphis.

As leader of the Falcons, Pickett had enjoyed a top-10 hit in 1962 with perhaps the most uninhibited of all secularised gospel songs, the intense and almost totally demented sounding **I Found A Love.** His gospel scream, combined with the Memphis Sound of Stax (and later using Muscle Shoals musicians too) was pure soul and his Atlantic recordings remain exciting to this day.

Atlantic's connection with Stax had arisen in 1961 when Carla Thomas's pop-soul song **Gee Whiz** had taken the Southern states by storm and was picked up for national distribution by Atlantic. In the '40s and '50s, the South had provided much of the music which had grabbed the attention of black populations which had migrated in force to the Northern cities and out to the West Coast; again, in the '60s, the music of the South, and especially of Memphis and Muscle Shoals, was going national.

While Jim Hall's Fame studios in Muscle Shoals fuelled not only Atlantic but Chess and many, other Northern companies, Stax's product was the exclusive preserve of Atlantic. Besides sending its own artists to the Stax Studios, Atlantic also handled Stax's own artist roster, some of whom, like Sam and Dave, the Mar-Keys and Otis Redding, had records out on the Atlantic or Atco labels as well as on Stax's own labels. Carla Thomas and her father Rufus, Booker T and the MGs, Eddie Floyd, Albert King, Johnnie Taylor and many others kept the Stax studio on East McLemore Avenue busy day and night.

While Wexler sent Pickett down to Memphis, he took another Detroiter, Aretha Franklin, to Muscle Shoals.

Smokey Robinson

Jimmy Cliff

Aretha had been struggling to find direction under her earlier recording deal with Columbia, but Wexler immediately came up with the right format, thanks to the Fame studio team, and turned her overnight into 'Lady Soul'.

Nor did Atlantic content themselves with these two main sources of Southern genius—they also had a deal with Henry Stone's set-up down in Miami, where the Criteria Studio also became a regular calling point for the company's artists as well as pushing local talent Atlantic's way.

In the midst of this soul explosion came the British invasion of the American pop charts. Insatiable demand for black American music, which was widely covered by groups in the UK, brought worldwide focus to bear on black music. Without the unbridled endorsement given by the Beatles, it is doubtful if Berry Gordy's Motown Sound could ever have achieved its international stature, or even its American pop success as quickly as it did. By the same token, the Rolling Stones not only helped generate new white interest in the blues singers of the '50s but, by their endorsements of the Atlantic/Stax sounds, also helped soul to gain international acceptance.

Besides Memphis, Muscle Shoals and Miami, other Southern centres such as New Orleans (where Allen Toussaint and his partner Marshall Sehorn built on what Fats Domino had achieved by encouraging a whole new generation of Crescent City stars), Atlanta, Jackson and even Nashville (where Bobby Bland, Joe Simon and others did much of their recording) all played a part in the evolution of soul. Out West in Los Angeles, a host of independents were doing their bit for the new music, and major companies too were finding it a good source of revenue—Capitol, with Lou Rawls, Bettye Swann and Candi Staton; Imperial/Minit with a host of artists, many recorded in New Orleans.

All over the US, major cities were developing their own particular brand of the soul sound: in Philadelphia, Kenny Gamble and Leon Huff, Jerry Ragavoy and others had their slant; New York was burgeoning with talent, ranging from the sweet pop-soul of the Chiffons and Phil Spector's various acts to the mellow soulfulness of Freddie Scott and Chuck Jackson (besides Atlantic, New York could boast such black music labels as Scepter/Wand, Shout and Sue).

Over in Chicago, Chess Records followed Atlantic's lead in dabbling heavily in Southern soul, using its network of regional distributors to find new talent as well as steering some established doo-wop and R&B performers like the Dells and Etta James in the soul direction. Chess was helped enormously in keeping afloat by the British beat groups' reliance on their Chuck Berry and Bo Diddley catalogues, and the sudden surge of white interest (particularly in Britain and Europe) in their massive blues roster featuring Muddy Waters, Howlin' Wolf, Sonny Boy Williamson, Elmore James, Little Walter, Willie Dixon and a host of others. Many of these artists were able to build a new career by winning over rock audiences and participating in the blues revival, which spawned a whole crop of new white stars on both sides of the Atlantic, including Fleetwood Mac, John Mayall and Johnnie Winter.

Vee-Jay too enjoyed success in soul music to add to its blues impact, though the label (which by the early '60s had in large part shifted to the West Coast) went bust before it could really build on the success of Jerry Butler and others. The Windy City boasted a host of small labels like Mar-V-Lus, One-Der-Ful, Dakar and Daran, as well as being home to some of the other established heavies in black music.

Mercury (owned by the giant Dutch company Philips), Brunswick (allied to MCA/Decca), and OKeh (the black music subsidiary of Columbia) all made Chicago a base for their activities and issued a steady stream of worthwhile soul records. But the real success story of Chicago in the '60s belongs to one man—Curtis Mayfield.

After the departure of original lead singer Jerry Butler for solo fame, Mayfield re-worked his group, the Impressions, dropping their original doo-wop flavoured style for something quite different. He borrowed virtually the entire sound of the famed gospel group the Swan Silvertones, including the whispered falsetto style of their lead singer Claude Jeter, and turned it into something which seemed to be totally original.

The Impressions enjoyed 25 smash hits in the decade before Mayfield went solo in 1970 to help create what would be the sound and direction of another new decade. Besides his success with the Impressions, Mayfield's contribution to the '60s as a writer and producer for local Chicago talent was enormous. Major Lance, Jerry Butler, the Five Stairsteps, Gene Chandler, Walter Jackson, and many others all rode the '60s charts with the help of Mayfield's genius.

The recurring thread of gospel roots can be found in almost every artist in the decade. Most falsetto stars of the time, be they Mayfield with the Impressions, or Eddie Kendricks with the Temptations, owed their style to Claude Jeter; Wilson Pickett and James Brown took their screaming styles from Ira Tucker of the Dixie Hummingbirds; David Ruffin and Marvin Gaye sounded close to Julius Cheeks of the Sensational Nightingales and Aretha Franklin not only sounded like Clara Ward but had, in fact,

Albert King

Wilson Pickett

been encouraged in her teens by that very lady.

The last three years of the decade saw changes just as dramatic as those which had taken place in its early years. The new breed of producer/songwriter at Motown (most notably Norman Whitfield) managed to steer the company away from the dangerous (in aesthetic terms) move towards cabaret stylings and into a new assertiveness. Curtis Mayfield and James Brown too were to be vital contributors to the last major movement of the decade — the emergence of black pride.

Brown's earlier efforts had, in the main, been strictly in a dance craze vein, pairing infectious rhythms with lyrics which simply extolled the virtue of a particular dance or were sexually rather than politically assertive (**Out Of Sight, Papa's Got A Brand New Bag, Sex Machine**). But with **Say It Loud, I'm Black And I'm Proud, I Don't Want Nobody To Give Me Nothing (Open Up The Door And I'll Get It Myself)** and others he set up a clarion-call echoed by Mayfield with his Impressions' songs of hope like **We're A Winner, Choice Of Colours, Mighty Mighty, Spade And Whitey, This Is My Country,** Syl Johnson's **Is It Because I'm Black?** and others.

The increasingly political content of black music reflected a nation in turmoil — skyrocketing crime rates, civil unrest, the death of Dr Martin Luther King, the emergence of the Black Power and even more radical groups like the Panthers, the war in Vietnam, the explosion in drug abuse — all gave new sources of lyrical content to black music which, in the early days, had contented itself largely with affairs of the heart and dance crazes.

While the blues had been largely based on self-pity and the bemoaning of one's lot, this new music took a more positive stance, demanding a new deal rather than merely regretting the lack of one. Black music was speaking out, and loudly at that, on all the political and social issues which were causing America such tremendous traumas in a decade which seemed full of 'long hot summers', injustice, violence and the seeds of social revolution.

It was not a question of wishful thinking, the music was a reflection of what was actually happening: the '60s saw the worlds of sport, film, TV, politics and even big business open up for black America. It was a decade which mixed tragedy with hope for the future, but one which left many older blacks in a state of shock as their way of life, albeit low-ranking but at least predictable, was swept aside in a tide of violence and rapid change.

While the young blacks grabbed at their new-found opportunities and turned their backs on traditional black American culture, their parents often held on to it dearly and rather than follow the new political and socially conscious forms of soul, returned to the blues.

Between them, Bobby Bland and B.B. King enjoyed more than 50 hit singles during the decade, and the blues audience was also buying large quantities of records by Little Milton, Junior Parker, Albert King, Freddie King and even such down-home performers as Jimmy Reed and John Lee Hooker. Moreover, the blues had won an important new audience among white rock fans, especially in Europe where such a cult developed that dozens of young white groups first reached for fame by utilising the blues idiom.

Jamaica, too, was seeing enormous cultural changes. In the early '60s the airwaves and the sound system of the island had been happy to play the music of black America, particularly the jump blues of Rosco Gordon and Wynonie Harris and the New Orleans shuffle beat of Fats Domino, but when the advent of soul put those styles into decline in America, Jamaican audiences didn't take to the new sound. Producers on the island therefore decided to make their own recordings to cater for local tastes, and so ska was born. (Listen to an early Prince Buster or Laurel Aitken record and compare it with the rhythms of late '50s Fats Domino and Smiley Lewis.) Ska led on, by 1967, to the subtler sounds of rock-steady which, in turn, led to reggae.

In the UK, 1968-69 saw the skinhead movement take Jamaican music to its heart and a whole slew of reggae discs made the pop top 20. It was something of a false start, however, as the mass acceptance of reggae as an art form rather than merely a gimmicky style was some way off. It would take the rise of Bob Marley to superstar status in the mid-'70s to persuade white British audiences, and both black and white America, to take reggae albums seriously instead of simply dancing to the occasional single.

By the '70s black music had reached the covers of *Time, Newsweek* and *Life* magazines, and achieved unprecedented international acceptance by the end of the decade when it embarked on a whole new venture. Just as in previous decades, the cross-pollination of black and white music was bringing about a completely different sound. White rock musicians took the blues form, extemporised on it, injected it with psychedelia and created heavy rock, as purveyed by the Cream, Led Zeppelin and Jimi Hendrix (a black musician but playing in a rock idiom).

Inevitably, black musicians borrowed back and the emergence of Sly and the Family Stone in 1968, the new sounds of the Isley Brothers, the ambitious productions of Norman Whitfield and even B.B. King's first tentative recordings with white musicians served to close the '60s and open the door to the brave new world of the '70s which was destined to be a decade every bit as revolutionary.

Edwin Starr

Martha Reeves

Barbara Acklin

Born in Chicago on February 28, 1943, Barbara Acklin joined the famed New Zion Baptist Church Choir at the age of 11. Her first recordings were made with the St Lawrence label in 1964 under her own name, and as Barbara Allen.

While working as a receptionist at Brunswick Records' offices in Chicago she submitted a song called **Whispers** to A&R boss Carl Davis, which resulted in a big hit for Jackie Wilson(▶). Barbara then duetted on her own song, **Show Me The Way To Go**, with Gene Chandler(▶) for a hit before launching her solo career at the company with the massive **Love Makes A Woman** (which was co-penned by Eugene Record of the Chi-Lites(▶)). Other hits include **Just Ain't No Love** and **Am I The Same Girl**, the original vocal version of Young-Holt Unlimited's million-selling **Soulful Strut** instrumental. She also wrote further material with Record.

Recordings:
Love Makes A Woman
(Brunswick/MCA)
Seven Days Of Night
(Brunswick/MCA)
Someone Else's Arms
(Brunswick/MCA)
A Place In The Sun
(Capitol)

Laurel Aitken

Born in Cuba in 1928 Laurel Aitken, arguably the godfather of ska, originally trained as a plasterer. He moved to Jamaica in 1956 and found an entry into music via Vere Johns, who during that period was staging amateur talent shows. His recording of **Little Sheila** in 1960 for Chris Blackwell's Starlight label established him as a star in Jamaica; the disc topped the island's charts for over two months. It was a rumbustious boogie that highlighted Aitken's gritty blues vocal delivery and featured a zany saxophone solo. It was in 1960 that the heavy demand for Jamaican music, still very R&B orientated, caused

Emile Shalett to establish his Bluebeat label in Britain for which he immediately snapped up Aitken. A stack of popular singles were released by Shalett, including **Mary Lee, Bartender, Bouncing Woman** and **Kansas City.**

After departing from Bluebeat Aitken's recordings surfaced on a variety of labels: EMI, Direct Records' Rio outlet, R&B and Ska Beat. His band during this time included Georgie Fame's trumpet player Eddie Thornton and Rudy Jones on saxophone. A brief flirtation with Doctor Bird Records brough forth the delightfully filthy **Fire In My Wire**, a favourite in rock-steady circles in 1968.

Aitken's next stop was with the West Indian brothers Harry, Carl and Jeff Palmer and their Pama label. About this time Aitken fell behind on his weekly £1.50 paternity payments and was arrested after a gig in Birmingham. Without a bean to his name but offered the choice of paying a £200 fine or gaol, he signed up to Pama and paid the fine with his advance royalties.

The Pama period is generally remembered as his most successful, coinciding as it did with the emergence of skinheads in Britain and their devotional interest in rock-steady and ska. He cut such classics as **Pussy Price** which bemoaned the cost of living, the scathing **Landlords And Tenants** and **Jesse James**, still a popular title over a decade after its release.

With the emergence of Two-Tone music in Britain during 1980 and the ska revival movement, Arista Records' I-Spy label gave Aitken another crack at the whip with two new original compositions, **Rudi Got Married** and **Honey Come Back To Me.** He will be remembered as a genuine ska innovator. His **Little Sheila** was released three years before the more infamous Prince Buster(▶) got started.

Recordings:
Scandal In A Brixton Market
(—/Pama)
The High Priest Of Reggae
(—/Pama)
Fire In Your Wire (—/Doctor Bird)

Ska With Laurel (—/Rio)
You Left Me Standing (—/Trojan)

Above: P.P. Arnold's main success has been in session singing.

Arthur Alexander

Arthur Alexander's two best records, **Anna** and **You Better Move On** (both self-penned and from 1962 sessions for Dot), were covered by the Beatles and the Rolling Stones respectively, while he himself did a great cover of Lowell Fulsom's(▶) **Black Nights.**

One of the first stars to emerge from Rick Hall's Muscle Shoals(▶) studio, Alexander (born Sheffield, Alabama, 1942) had a subtle, understated approach which was enhanced by very simple uncontrived arrangements, giving his records a haunting quality (**Go Home Girl**, 1963, was another classic).

After a decade in the doldrums, a fine Tommy Cogbill-produced Warner Bros album (1972) and the minor hit **Everyday I Have To Cry A Little** (1975) reminded the world of one of Southern soul's first heroes.

Recordings:
You Better Move On
(Dot/London)
Arthur Alexander
(Warner Bros/—)

Steve Alaimo

White purveyor of so-called 'blue-eyed soul' on which he showed a strong James Brown(▶) influence, Steve Alaimo became a US teen idol thanks to exposure on Philadelphia-based pop TV shows (notably 'Where The Action Is'). His real impact on black music, however, came when he became Henry Stone's right-hand man at TK records and helped to guide the careers of George and Gwen McCrae(▶), Betty Wright(▶), Clarence Reid, Latimore(▶), Little Beaver(▶), K.C. and the Sunshine Band(▶) and many others.

Recordings:
Where The Action Is (ABC-Paramount/—)

Duane Allman

Duane Allman found fame in the late '60s and early '70s with his brother Gregg as the Allman Brothers Band rock group, but his earlier session work had already put him on the black music map. His powerful slide guitar playing was much in evidence on some of the classic soul recordings of the '60s, including **Hey Jude**, Wilson Pickett(▶), **The Road Of Love**, Clarence Carter(▶), **The Weight**, Aretha Franklin(▶), **Games People Play**, King Curtis(▶), which won Curtis a Grammy award as best instrumental of the year, and Johnny Jenkins' **Down Along The Cove.**

It was Allman who suggested to Wilson Pickett that he record **Hey Jude.** Pickett was reluctant, but was persuaded after hearing Allman's guitar arrangement. It deservedly sold upwards of a million singles in the US as one of the most imaginative cover versions of a Beatles' song. In return, Pickett nicknamed Allman 'Skyman', because 'He's always up, man'. Through his work with Jerry Wexler on the Aretha Franklin sessions, Allman was recommended to Eric Clapton, whose **Layla** album was being produced by Atlantic house-producer Tom Dowd. It was Allman who provided the soaring guitar for the title track.

Born in Nashville in 1946, Allman absorbed the guitar styles of the local blues players after moving to Florida. His first bands were blues and R&B orientated, and it was this music which provided the underlying content for the Allman Brothers.

Tragically, Duane Allman was killed in a motorcycle accident on October 29, 1971. Fittingly, Jerry Wexler provided the eulogy at his funeral.

Recordings:
An Anthology (Capricorn)
An Anthology, Vol.II (Capricorn)

Seven Days of Night: Courtesy MCA.

Roland Alphonso

Coxsone Dodd has often said of tenor saxophonist Roland Alphonso that he is the best musician he has ever worked with. That tribute from the head of reggae's most influential label, Studio One(▶), does credit to a musician whose skill is at the very core of the development of Caribbean music. **Phoenix City**, **El Pussy Cat**, **James Bond** and **Guns Of Navarone** are a sample of the internationally famed recordings Alphonso made all his own while a member of Studio One house band, the Skatalites(▶).

Born in Cuba on January 12, 1931, his mother took him to Jamaica two years later, where after a spell in the country they settled in the island's capital, Kingston. At the age of 10 he enrolled at Stone Hill Industrial School and showed his first signs of an interest in music. He began to play the drums but 18 months later his mother changed all that when she brought him a saxophone. Leaving school when he was 17, Alphonso spent a year playing the island's coastal clubs with the Eric Deans Band. His recording career began in 1960 when with Coxsone Dodd he assembled the now legendary studio band, the Skatalites. This group was the spawning ground for many great reggae talents and during the early to mid-'60s it was almost impossible to escape their loony yet finely groomed swing percolating from the island's juke boxes and radios. Alphonso was in particular demand, his frequently manic saxophone style spattered throughout the Jamaican charts on literally dozens of records. He later developed the sonorous talking saxophone that was distinguished by its quirky jumping style.

His output in the '70s was minimal largely due to a severe heart attack that halted much of his recording activities and opened his eyes to Christianity. However his legend will linger on in the form of at least 12 versions—at the last count—of his immortal **Jah Shakey** rhythm, which he originally cut with Coxsone.

Recordings:
The Birth Of Ska (Treasure Isle/—)
Ska Authentic (Studio One/—)
Best Of The Skatalites
  (Studio One/—)
The Best Of Roland Alphonso
  (Studio One/—)
King Of Sax (Winro Records/—)

Bob Andy

Bob Andy, real name Keith Anderson, first emerged in the late '60s with a string of Jamaican hits, notably **Going Home**, **Unchained**, **Feeling Soul** and **My Time**. With his highly distinctive voice and songwriting ability he quickly achieved superstar status in the Caribbbean, his reputation enhanced by his commendable contribution to the original Paragons(▶) line-up.

International recognition came in 1970 with a version of the classic Simone and Irving song **Young Gifted And Black**—regarded as a cornerstone of early '70s reggae hits—recorded with his close friend and later I-Threes(▶) member, Marcia Griffiths. Andy's genius is best observed in his Studio One compilation **Bob Andy's Songbook**. As with many Jamaican artists Andy was to enter many dif-ferent studios and work with a variety of producers, notably Harry J and the island's only female producer of note, Sonia Pottinger. His time with Ms Pottinger spawned such memorable singles as **Slow Down**, **Ghetto Stays In The Mind**, and what is regarded as the definitive Andy album, **Lots Of Love And I**.

An album, **Slow Down**, released in 1977, was the last heard from the singer, who has seemingly abandoned music in favour of an acting career.

Recordings:
Songbook (Coxsone/—)
Music Inside Of Me (Sound
  Tracs/—)
Lots Of Love And I (High Note/—)

P.P. Arnold

Pat Arnold started her career as a session singer in Los Angeles, where she had been born in 1946. Spotted by Ike Turner(▶), she became a member of the Ikettes backing vocal team, and came to the UK with the Ike and Tina Turner(▶) Revue in 1966, when they appeared as support act to the Rolling Stones.

Deciding to stay in London, P.P. signed to the Immediate label, run by the Stones' then manager Andrew Loog Oldham, and had a UK top 20 hit in 1967 with her emotive reading of Cat Stevens' **First Cut Is The Deepest**, backed by the Nice. P.P. appeared in the musicals *Catch My Soul* and *Jesus Christ Superstar* then returned to session work.

Recordings:
Kafunta (—/Immediate)

Ashford and Simpson

Nick Ashford and Valerie Simpson established their reputation as one of Motown's(▶) most gifted songwriting teams before launching their own career with two beautiful but unsuccessful albums for that company. In 1973 they left Motown for Warner Bros and were rewarded with a string of major hits.

Valerie, who had formed a gospel group known as the Followers, met Nick, who had moved to New York from Detroit, at the White Rock Church in Harlem. They landed staff jobs as songwriters at Scepter/Wand(▶) writing material for, notably, Chuck Jackson(▶) and Maxine Brown(▶).

One day, when they were both feeling down, they wrote **Let's Go Get Stoned** to vent their feelings. Picked up by Ray Charles(▶) it gave him a 1966 smash and made their reputation.

Joining the staff at Motown in Detroit, they wrote **You're All I Need To Get By**, **Ain't No Mountain High Enough** and **Ain't Nothin' Like The Real Thing**, the first two for Marvin Gaye(▶) and the other for Tammi Terrell(▶) (the latter was also a hit for Diana Ross(▶)), then **Reach Out And Touch Somebody's Hand** and **The Boss** for Diana Ross.

The warmly sensual **Gimme Something Real** and **I Wanna Be Selfish** albums launched their Warner Bros golden era which, besides yielding highly listenable albums, gave them transatlantic smashes with **Don't Cost Nothing**, **It Seems To Hang On** and **Flashback**.

Recordings:
Gimme Something Real (Warner
  Bros)
I Wanna Be Selfish (Warner Bros)
A Musical Affair (Warner Bros)

Mickey "Guitar" Baker

Veteran of a thousand New York recording sessions, guitarist Mickey Baker was born McHouston Baker, Louisville, Kentucky, October 15, 1925.

His distinctive guitar licks were almost as much a factor in the success of the Coasters(▶) as was King Curtis's(▶) rollicking sax.

Baker played on Ruth Brown's(▶) **Mama He Treats Your Daughter Mean** masterpiece for Atlantic then went on to record with Little Willie John(▶), Nappy Brown(▶), Screaming Jay Hawkins(▶) and many others, being employed regularly by Atlantic(▶), King(▶), OKeh(▶) and Savoy.

He had a smash of his own in 1956 when he paired with Sylvia Vanderpool as Mickey and Sylvia for the haunting **Love Is Strange** which sold 800,000 copies on Groove and which was then picked up by RCA Victor for their Vik label, total sales finally topping a million.

Sylvia (born New York, March 6, 1936) went on to marry Joe Robinson and set up the All Platinum group of labels.

Baker has recorded instructional albums on guitar playing for various specialist labels and written several text books including the best-selling "Jazz Guitar".

Recordings:
Take A Look Inside (—/Big Bear)
Blues And Jazz Guitar
  (—/Kicking Mule)

Darrell Banks

Darrell Banks died in 1970 at the age of 32, shot in a gun duel with a policeman who had been having an affair with his girlfriend. It was just one of many violent deaths in America. It robbed soul music of one of its best writers and singers.

Born in Buffalo in 1938, Banks won his first contract with Revilot in Detroit and broke R&B charts wide open with **Open The Door To Your Heart** (at the time he was singing part-time with the Daddy B. Combo and working as a cement finisher). In 1967, Atlantic bought the rights to the hit, and nine more tracks from Revilot, to make up the **Darrell Banks Is Here** album.

Three years later, Stax(▶) subsidiary Volt issued **Here To Stay**, which featured versions of Jerry Butler's(▶) **Only The Strong Survive** and Percy Sledge's(▶) **When A Man Loves A Woman**, along with the easy-rocking **No One Blinder (Than A Man Who Can't See)**, one of the finest ever samples of the Memphis Sound.

Recordings:
Darrell Banks Is Here (Atco/—)
Here To Stay (Volt/—)

Below: Singing and writing partners Ashford and Simpson.

Homer Banks

A prolific songwriter on the staff of Stax(▶) (**If Loving You Is Wrong** for Luther Ingram(▶), **Are You Sure** for the Staple Singers(▶)), Banks had his own moment of glory with **60 Minutes Of Your Love**, recorded for Minit some time earlier in Memphis, with Isaac Hayes(▶) on piano (and production by David Porter(▶)).

Born in Memphis on August 2, 1941, Banks was in Soul Consolaters gospel group while at high school and in 1964 made a solo debut with **Lady Of Stone** (Genie), which was picked up by Minit for national distribution. He wrote at Stax with Johnnie Taylor(▶) and others, and now writes with Carl Hampton for, notably, Randy Brown(▶).

Recordings:
No album releases

The Bar-Kays

Al Jackson, drummer with Booker T & the MGs(▶), took an early interest in the Bar-Kays and helped groom them in a similar mould to the MGs—a tight-knit, funky R&B instrumental combo. The work paid off in 1965 when **Soul Finger**, a compulsive dance instrumental with added party noises, became an international success for the then line-up of Jimmy King (guitar), Ronnie Caldwell (organ), James Alexander (bass), Carl Cunningham (drums), Phalon Jones (saxophone) and Ben Cauley (trumpet). The resultant album included the equally potent **Knucklehead** with its scorching harmonica and versions of **You Can't Sit Down** and **Hole In The Wall** that marked them as a band to watch. Otis Redding(▶) thought so too, grooming them to be his regular backing band on live gigs.

It was en route to a Redding gig on December 10, 1967, that tragedy struck. The light-aircraft carrying Redding and the Bar-Kays crashed into the frozen Lake Monono, Wisconsin. Ben Cauley was the only survivor of the crash while James Alexander was fortunate that there had not been sufficient room for him on the plane and he had travelled separately.

Unwilling to let the Bar-Kays' name die, Alexander formed a new line-up of equal potency but different musical direction, gradually moving into the world of black rock.

Below: Stirring up a storm—the Bar-Kays.

The early '70s found the Bar-Kays being used as the Stax Studios second house band. When Gulf & Western bought the company, a massive album release (some 30 in all) meant two weeks of intensive recording operated on a shift system between the Bar-Kays and Booker T & the MGs/the Mar-Keys(▶). The Bar-Kays were on Isaac Hayes'(▶) **Hot Buttered Soul** and he came to rely on them heavily as his studio band.

Joining Alexander in the new line-up were Larry Dobson (vocals), Charles Allen (trumpet), Harvey Henderson (tenor sax), Winston Stewart (keyboards), Lloyd Smith (guitar), Michael Beard (drums) with Frank Thompson (trombone), Mark Bynum (keyboards), Sherman Gray (percussion) added to bring the line-up to 10 by 1979.

Stax sets like **Gotta Groove, Black Rock, Do You See What I See** and **Cold Blooded** and an appearance in the *Wattstax* movie failed to turn them into a major act however and it was not until they switched to Mercury that their star really began to shine.

Their 1979 label move was followed by a 1980 album release, **Injoy**, which saw the band conform to the noises common to contemporary records, far removed from their Stax roots. Produced by Memphis-based Allen Jones, the group had a hit with **Move Your Boogie Body**.

A new career and a new sound embarked on, the Bar-Kays began to release albums of growing funk sophistication, aimed fairly and squarely at a black, club, reaction. From their 1981 album, **As One**, came the R&B hit **Boogie Body Land**. Then again, in 1982, their **Night Cruisin'** release contained the hit single, **Hit And Run**.

Recordings:
Soul Finger (Volt/—)
Gotta Groove (Volt/—)
Black Rock (Volt/—)
Cold Blooded (Volt/Stax)
Money Talks (Volt/Stax)
Injoy (Mercury)
Night Cruisin' (Mercury)

H.B. Barnum

H.B. Barnum has earned more than 90 gold albums and 160 gold singles as a writer, arranger and/or producer with artists such as Count Basie, Cannonball Adderley(▶), Frank Sinatra, Sammy Davis Jnr, Fats Domino(▶), Little Richard(▶), the Drifters(▶), Lou Rawls(▶), Nancy Wilson(▶), Etta James(▶), Johnny Bristol(▶), the Osmonds, Chairmen Of The Board(▶) and a host of Motown artists from the Supremes(▶), to the Temptations(▶), the Jacksons(▶), and the Marvelettes(▶).

Early successes included the Hollywood Argyles' **Alley Oop** and Bee Bumble and the Stingers' **Nut Rocker**. O.C. Smith's(▶) **Hickory Holler's Tramp**, Freda Payne's(▶) **Band Of Gold** and Honey Cone's **Want Ads** were among later chart records.

Proficient on nine different instruments, Barnum is best known for his piano playing and cut some enjoyable albums of his own for RCA Victor in the early '60s, which also revealed his talent as a vocalist.

Recordings:
The Big Voice of Barnum — H.B. That Is! (RCA Victor)
Everybody Loves H.B. — Barnum That Is! (RCA Victor)

Richard Barrett

Philadelphia-born performer/songwriter/producer/manager Richard Barrett started with Angels (on End) then had hits as a member of the Valentines (**Tonight Kathleen** and **Lily Maybelle**, 1957). He produced Frankie Lymon and the Teenagers(▶) **Why Do Fools Fall In Love** and hits for the Chantels, as well as making numerous solo records himself.

As A&R man for George Goldner (owner of Gone/End), Barrett signed the Isley Brothers(▶), the Flamingos and Little Anthony and the Imperials(▶). After joining Swan Records in 1964 he became longtime manager/mentor of the Three Degrees(▶).

Recordings:
No album releases.

Fontella Bass

It was the Svengali-like talents of Ike Turner(▶), discoverer of so many greats in black music, not least his own wife Tina, which gave Fontella Bass (born on July 3, 1940) her first break. Turner lifted Fontella from her role as pianist/organist with the band led by Oliver Sain in her home city of St Louis, Missouri, and put her vocals on record via his Prann label.

After further releases on Bobbin and Sonja (another Turner label), Fontella scored a duet with Bobby McClure on Checker in 1965. **Don't Mess Up A Good Thing** went top five R&B and was quickly followed up by her biggest solo hit, the classic **Rescue Me**, which made No.1 R&B and No.4 pop. Its rather modest chart status in the UK belied its long-lasting impact on soul fans.

Recovery also made some impact but Fontella's sado black-leather image failed to turn her into an established artist and, apart from a 1969 Paris-recorded album with her jazz trumpeter husband Lester Bowie, she languished in obscurity until 1971 when she had a run of modest soul hits produced by Oliver Sain for Jewel/Paula.

Recordings:
The New Look (Checker/Chess)
Free (Jewel/Mojo)

Madeline Bell

American-born singer Madeline Bell arrived in Britain in the '60s in the cast of the black gospel touring package *Black Nativity* and stayed to join the burgeoning music scene. She became an in-demand session singer, then joined other top musicians to form Blue Mink in the late '60s. A classy pop-rock band with an above-average line in songs, Blue Mink enjoyed a run of British hits between 1969 and 1973, including **Melting Pot**—a clever plea for racial tolerance—**Good Morning Freedom, Banner Man** and **Randy**.

Since then Bell has returned to session work and cabaret, often making TV appearances singing MOR-type material. She is now also the queen of jingles in Britain, much in demand for her clear pleasant voice and technical proficiency.

Recordings:
This Is One Girl (—/Pye)

William Bell

William Bell's classic ballad, **You Don't Miss Your Water (Till The Well Runs Dry)**, was the third hit record for Jim Stewart and Estelle Axton's Memphis-based Satellite Records which, after a name-change to Stax(▶), was to become one of the major forces in black music through the '60s and early '70s. Bell, who had started his singing career as a member of the Del Rios, was to be a mainstay of the label throughout that period, scoring with such numbers as **I Forgot To Be Your Lover, A Tribute To A King** (cut following the untimely death of fellow Stax artist Otis Redding(▶)) **Eloise (Hang On In There), Happy**, and, his biggest success, as a duet with Judy Clay, on **Private Number**.

A prolific songwriter, Bell cowrote several major songs with Booker T. Jones (of Booker T and the MGs)(▶), including Albert King's(▶) smash **Born Under A Bad Sign**. When the Stax label foundered, Bell signed to Mercury and cut two albums including one recorded at Allen Toussaint' Sea-Saint studio in New Orleans, but it did not match the class of his prolific output for Stax.

Recordings:
The Soul Of A Bell (Stax)
Tribute To A King (Atco)
Bound To Happen (Stax)
Coming Back For More (Mercury)

Brook Benton

Born Benjamin Franklin Peay on September 19, 1931, in Camden, South Carolina, the son of devout Baptist parents, Brook Benton received his musical grounding with the locally based Camden Jubilee Singers, travelling around the South. Moving to New York at 17, he earned a living pushing a handcart round the city's garment district. He then joined the Bill Landford Spiritual Singers, returning South on a tour with them before switching to the Golden Gate Quartet spiritual group.

Back in New York, Benton formed the Sandmen R&B vocal group while holding down a day job as a truck driver. He entered the recording business cutting demo discs of songs (some 500 in all) for such major artists as Nat 'King' Cole(▶), Roy Hamilton(▶) and Clyde McPhatter(▶) before making some unsuccessful singles for Epic and Vik.

His first minor hits came with **The Wall** and **A Million Miles**

Above: William Bell, former Stax superstar.

From Nowhere, but it was on signing for Mercury and teaming up with their A&R man/producer Clyde Otis and arranger Belford Hendricks that the charts burst wide open for him, leading to a phenomenal run of 21 gold records within just five years, a dozen of them in the first 18 months, beginning with the prophetic **It's Just A Matter Of Time** in 1959.

Benton's rich warm tones had an across-the-board and international appeal with both black and white audiences of all ages. His hits ranged from the novelty **Boll Weevil Song** through to the jaunty **Kiddio,** the mellow ballad **This Bitter Earth** and the haunting **I Was Born To Sing The Blues** and he was one of the first black singers to establish himself as an album artist.

Mercury pulled off a masterstroke when they teamed him with the tempestuous Dinah Washington(▶) for **Rockin' Good Way,** which contains the memorable impromptu aside 'Move over, you're in my spot!' The first take, blunders and all, was released and its refreshing spontaneity helped it sail to gold-record status.

Leaving Mercury, Benton was signed to Reprise (then owned by Frank Sinatra) who cut him on the brilliant **Laura What's He Got (That I Ain't Got),** which included a great version of Bobbie Gentry's country classic **Ode To Billie Joe.**

In 1970 Benton switched to the Atlantic(▶) subsidiary Cotillion and cut his timeless classic version of Tony Joe White's **Rainy Night In Georgia.** He had several albums for the company before moving on to Brut (the perfumery company

folded the label before his album could be released), Stax (the company being in its terminal throws didn't help) and All Platinum, with diminishing success, though his appeal as a concert draw continued unabated.

Recordings:
Hot Millions Of The '50s and '60s (—/Philips)
Lie To Me (Mercury)
This Bitter Earth (Mercury)
Born To Sing The Blues (Mercury)
Laura What's He Got (That I Ain't Got) (Reprise/—)
Brook Benton Today (Atlantic)
The Gospel Truth (Atlantic)
Do Your Own Thing (Atlantic)
Mr Bartender (All Platinum)

Otis Blackwell

Black singer/pianist Otis Blackwell (born 1931) has recorded prolifically—his debut song **Daddy Rollin' Stone** (reissued in UK on 1981 Flyright LP) became a classic via much later revivals by Derek Martin (on Sue) and the Who—but he is best known as a composer, notably for Little Willie John(▶) **(Fever),** Dee Clark(▶) **(Hey Little Girl),** Jimmy Jones(▶)**(Handy Man),** Jerry Lee Lewis **(Great Balls Of Fire)** and a string for Elvis Presley (notably **Don't Be Cruel, All Shook Up** and **Return To Sender).**

Recordings:
Singing The Blues (Joe Davis/Flyright)

Big Maybelle

Big in name, size and voice, Maybelle Smith (born 1926, Jackson, Tennessee) was something of an

institution at New York's Apollo Theatre and other black venues through the '50s and '60s. She recorded prolifically for Epic with backing bands which included bluesmen Brownie McGhee and Mickey Baker(▶) and jazz names like Panama Francis.

In the '60s she was dubbed 'The Mother Of Soul' and cut the superb **Pure Soul** album in that idiom; it also has an excitingly inventive version of the pop hit **96 Tears.** Switching to Scepter, she cut the definitive version of the emotive **Don't Let The Sun Catch You Cryin',** which the same label also recorded with Chuck Jackson(▶).

Sadly, Maybelle died in 1972.

Recordings:
Gabbin' The Blues (Epic/—)
The Pure Soul Of Big Maybelle (Epic/CBS)
The Soul Of Big Maybelle (Scepter)

Bob and Earl

Bob and Earl's infectious dancer **Harlem Shuffle** was one of the records which set the British soul explosion in motion in 1963 but it was not until re-issued in 1969 that it made the UK top 10 (first-time round it had been top 50 in America on Marc Records).

Bob was Bobby Relf (aka Bobby Garrett), Earl was Earl Nelson (aka Earl Cosby, aka Jackie Lee, aka Jay Dee!). To add to the confusion, the original Bob had been Bobby Byrd (aka Bobby Day of **Rockin' Robin** fame)! Nelson had joined Byrd in the latter's well-known group the Hollywood Flames (Nelson sang lead on that group's 1957 hit **Buzz Buzz**) before they recorded as Bob and Earl for Class between 1957 and 1959, when Bobby Relf replaced Byrd to cut sides for Chene, Tempe, Loma and Mirwood.

As a solo, Relf recorded for Flair, Cash, Dot and (as Bobby Garrett) for Mirwood, besides writing Love Unlimited's(▶) debut hit **Walking In The Rain.** Nelson had solo releases with Class and Ebb, as Earl Cosby on Mira and Keyman, and as Jackie Lee on Mirwood, with which label he hit top 10 in

1965 with **The Duck** (the album of the same name containing a glut of songs in the same vein but all of them highly infectious disco belters). In 1973, using the name Jay Dee, Nelson cut a superb album for Warner Bros.

Through all these name and label changes, Bob and Earl stuck close to a lightweight but high-energy fun sound which owed a lot to producer Fred Smith and not a little to Barry White's(▶) arranging talents.

Recordings:
Bob And Earl (Mirwood/Jay Boy)
Bob And Earl Together (Mirwood/Joy)
The Duck (Jackie Lee) (Mirwood/Joy)
Come On In Love (Jay Dee) (Warner Brothers)

Gary US Bonds

Gary US Bonds was born Gary Anderson in Jacksonville, Florida, on June 6, 1939. His first singing experience was with a streetcorner doo-wop harmony outfit called the Turks in his adopted home town of Norfolk, Virginia, and they caught the attention of speculative record producer and record-store owner Frank Guida. Guida was anxious to involve himself in the making, rather than the retailing, of records, and moved swiftly to revitalise a local studio—the Norfolk Recording Studio—which had gone bankrupt. Although his only other experience had been on a couple of budget productions for Atlantic (with the Sheiks and Tommy Facenda), Guida started his own label, Legrand Records.

His first session was **New Orleans,** a song penned by himself and colleague Joe Royster. Guida recruited young Anderson (as second choice) to handle lead vocals, and set to work 'with my eyes closed', he remembers. It was this general inexperience which resulted in a raucous undisciplined master, sounding like the product of a drunken binge recorded in a dustbin. Anderson was horrified, and even more so when Guida sent promotional copies of the

Dance 'Til Quarter to Three... Courtesy Top Rank.

Above: Gary US Bonds, still hot over 20 years later.

single to local radio stations in a sleeve bearing the inscription 'Buy US Bonds'. Believing the record to be a public-service announcement, programme directors were happy to give it air time!

New Orleans took off nationally in October 1960 making the American top 10 and the UK top 20. Inspired—and probably astonished—Guida went to work again, and proved (thankfully) that he hadn't learned a thing.

Quarter To Three was party-time all over again, with the addition of saxophonist Gene Barge augmenting the Church Street Five, Guida's house band. The frenetic pace and direction were, maintains Guida, considered judgements, but Anderson—now known as Bonds—says he and the boys were steaming, 'absolutely bombed', and he thought it was the worst record he had ever heard!

Nevertheless, **Quarter To Three** followed **New Orleans** to the upper reaches of the charts, and Guida kept up the momentum, and the capricious sound, with **School Is Out, Dear Lady Twist, Seven Day Weekend** and **Twist Twist Senora**. Although Bonds eventually ran out of hits, he remained with Legrand until the late '60s, before moving into the lounge club and 'oldies' circuit where he maintained a reasonable standard of living and kept his voice in shape.

It was at a club venue that Bonds was to meet his second saviour, rock star Bruce Springsteen, who was paying homage to the legendary rock 'n roller. Unaware of Springsteen's eminence, Bonds had to be convinced that he was in the company of a superstar, although quickly getting the message when the two duetted on **Quarter To Three**.

Anxious to maintain this collaboration, Springsteen booked time at New York's Power Station studio and began work with co-producer Miami Steve Van Zandt on **Dedication**, with Bonds' group and Springsteen's E Street Band in support. Although hardly a throwback to Bonds' earlier recordings, **Dedication** is nonetheless a hard-driving rasping set which evokes fond memories of Guida's 'dustbin' sound.

Recording note: All the classic Bonds' material is available on a **Greatest Hits** collection, released in 1981.

Recordings:
Greatest Hits (Ensign)
Dedication (EMI)

Booker T & the MGs

Booker T & the MGs (MG stood for Memphis Group) originally came together as the house rhythm section for Stax Records(▶), and provided the backing for a multitude of tracks by Stax stars like Otis Redding(▶), William Bell(▶), Rufus Thomas(▶) and Sam and Dave(▶). Jones' spare, logical keyboard (usually organ) styling, Steve Cropper's mean, lowdown blues guitar, 'Duck'Dunn's steady-as-a-rock bass and Al Jackson's metronomic drumming gelled into a sound that was not only instantly identifiable, but set a whole style for soul backup and instrumental groups in the '60s.

The MGs' sound was effectively displayed on the group's first hit single **Green Onions,** released in 1962 (and in which Lewis Steinberg not Dunn, played bass). Simple to the point of minimalism, the record was nevertheless a masterpiece of understated funk—the hippiest kind of 'club' music, sounding as if it had emerged blinking from some steaming basement. Although the group only toured together sporadically (spending most of their time, usually together, playing on other people's hits at Stax), other hits followed up until the end of the '60s; notable were the incisive

Chinese Checkers in 1963, the strutting **Bootleg** and **Outrage** in 1965, the funky **Hip Hug Her** in 1967 and the semi-calypso styled **Soul Limbo** in 1968. During this period the group also did well with albums, and continued to provide the characteristic clean, disciplined Stax sound for the label's artists, often with the Mar-Keys(▶) horns who also played on the MGs own records (Cropper and Dunn, in fact, had started their careers as members of the Mar-Keys).

1969 saw an interesting departure for the group when they scored the soundtrack for the Jules Dassin film *Uptight,* an effective re-working of *The Informer,* set in Cleveland, Ohio, and concerned with the Black Power movement. The score, in turn haunting and propulsive, played a considerable part in the success of the film and threw up a hit single, **Time Is Tight.** This was one of the group's biggest successes, and its B-side, **Johnny I Love You,** showed the direction that Booker T was going to follow in that it demonstrated his considerable vocal talents.

Despite the fact that what they played was quintessentially black music, a direct descendant of urban R&B of the '50s, the members of the MGs were a heterogeneous quartet. Jones and Jackson were black, while Cropper and Dunn were white; Jones had studied at Indiana University while Cropper had a rural upbringing; the tall, lean Cropper in the early '60s affected a greasy, swept-back hairstyle that made him look more like a bluegrass mandolin player than an ace bluesman, while pipe-smoking 'Duck' Dunn often looked more like a farmer than a musician. Nevertheless, the group they played in was always a model of cohesion; Jones and Cropper in particular worked pefectly together, swapping lead and accompanying roles effortlessly, while Dunn and Jackson sometimes seemed like one musician.

In the late '60s the MGs started to fade out their live appearances, which were anyway never that frequent, and although they continued to record, it seemed that the inspired days were over. They were now releasing more MOR-orientated sides like **Hang 'em High** and **Mrs Robinson** that simply didn't allow them to do what they did best—which was to hit a groove and work it for all it was worth. The MGs continued studio work together up until 1972, when they went their separate ways.

Dunn and Jackson continued playing sessions in Memphis, most notably for Al Green(▶), Cropper concentrated on production while Booker T moved to California, married Rita Coolidge's sister Priscilla, and recorded several albums with her which ranged in quality from mediocre to dire. Although **Johnny I Love You** showed that Jones possessed an attractive and expressive voice, none of the vaguely country-flavoured material he recorded with his wife allowed him to show it off to best advantage. Jones' production projects, however, such as Bill Withers'(▶) brilliant debut album **Just As I Am,** proved more successful.

In 1973 Stax issued an album titled simply **The MGs** but it was far from vintage stuff and neither Jones nor Cropper played on it, being replaced by Carson Whitsett and Bobby Manuel. Jones and Cropper returned in 1976 to cut a

Above: Booker T. Jones, leader of the MGs.

reunion album for Asylum, **Universal Language**—although Willie Hall replaced Al Jackson who had been murdered by an intruder at his home in 1975. Sadly, it lacked the bite and attack that characterised the MGs at their best, and is hardly an essential album. The best memorial for the group remains their work for Stax in the early '60s. Jones was influential in making the organ and electronic keyboard common elements in modern rhythm sections, and Cropper was an influence on many of today's rock and soul players.

Most recently, Cropper and 'Duck' Dunn have surfaced as part of the Blues Brothers Band, put together for the *Blues Brothers* movie that was largely a tribute to the soul music of the '60s. The movie was fine and the band was great.

Recordings:
Green Onions (Atlantic)
Melting Pot (Stax)
Time Is Tight—The Best Of Booker T And The MGs (Atlantic)

British R&B

British R&B is usually thought of in terms of guitar-based groups like the Rolling Stones, Yardbirds and Manfred Mann who started their careers by offering regurgitated Howlin' Wolf(▶), Bo Diddley(▶) and Chuck Berry(▶) material. But, roughly when these groups were coming to the fore—the early 60's—another caucus of bands was offering R&B of a different type. Instead of Wolf and the Chicago bluesmen, their influences were Louis Jordan, Ray Charles(▶), James Brown(▶), early Motown(▶) and early Stax(▶), roughly speaking the artists then popular with black Americans rather than ageing blues heroes.

At the forefront of this movement were former rock 'n' roll pianist Georgie Fame and his band the Blue Flames, Zoot Money and his Big Roll Band, the Night-timers, Chris Farlowe and the Thunderbirds and the Erroll Dixon Band. Unlike the R&B guitar bands, these outfits were popular with blacks—

West Indians and American GIs based in Britain—and featured black artists like vocalists Herbie Goins, Ronnie Jones and Dixon, trumpeters Eddie 'Tan-tan' Thornton and Harold Beckett, guitarist Ernest Ranglin and percussionist Speedy Acquaye. Many of the musicians had a background in jazz, and former jazz clubs provided a nucleus of venues for the music—London's Flamingo Club and Klook's Kleek were two of the most famous.

Several of the bands—Fame and the Blue Flames in particular—were also among the earliest popularisers of reggae, then in its infant stages and known as ska or blue-beat. Most of the bands featured horns and exhibited a high degree of musicianship, and although few made the big time they paved the way for British soul. The legendary Geno Washington(▶) and the Ram Jam Band, Jimmy James(▶) and the Vagabonds and other British-based soul groups all evolved, as did their audiences, out of the earlier scene.

Although Georgie Fame later pursued an idiosyncratic career which encompassed jazz on the one hand and pop/MOR on the other, and Chris Farlowe had several pop hits, most of the artists in this field were hit hard by the psychedelic explosion of the late '60s. Overnight, horns were shed and beads donned, usually to little effect. However, the ground had been laid for a British black music scene that a generation later, at the dawn of the '80s, began to find a strong and individual voice.

Maxine Brown

The self-penned sweet-soul ballads **All In My Mind** and **Funny** rocketed Maxine Brown into the charts in 1961. Both were produced by Tony Bruno, owner of the Nomar label on which they appeared. A glamorous former model, Maxine was born in Kingstree, South Carolina, and began her career with the Royaltones, the Manhattans and other New York-based gospel groups.

After her early success, she switched first to ABC and then to Wand, being paired by the latter label with Chuck Jackson(▶) for some fine duets, including a powerful version of Sam and Dave's(▶) **Hold On, We're Comin'**.

Solo hits included **Ask Me, It's Gonna Be Alright** and **Oh No, Not My Baby**, which was covered successfully by Manfred Mann. Later records appeared on Epic, Commonwealth United and Avco.

Recordings:
Spotlight On Maxine Brown (Wand/—)
Saying Something (with Chuck Jackson) (Wand/—)
Hold On, We're Comin' (with Chuck Jackson) (Wand/—)

Solomon Burke

Dubbed 'King of Rock & Soul' by the Atlantic publicity machine during his golden years in the early 1960s, Solomon Burke is a striking, robust, regal man with vocal strength and quality to match his physique. Born in Philadelphia in 1936 into a religious family, such was his precocious talent that he was a soloist in church by the age of nine (two of his younger brothers were members of the

Showstoppers who scored big in the UK with **Ain't Nothin' But A House-party** (1968)), had his own radio show 'Solomon's Temple' and made personal appearances as 'The Wonder Boy Preacher'.

Burke's disc debut came in 1955 on Apollo Records, his material bridging the idiomatic gulf between sacred and secular with songs like **I'm All Alone,** a melancholy love ballad with religious overtones, the arrangement and delivery bearing comparison with Johnny Ace(▶) and Roy Hamilton(▶).

1959 brought a move to Singular, but the few sides issued were soon picked up for re-issue on Atlantic(▶), to whom Solomon signed in 1960, his eight-year tenure yielding hits of great quality and quantity. The country ballad **Just Out Of Reach** opened his chart account, going top 30 in the fall of 1961, while the gospel-soul intensity of **Cry To Me** provided a stylistic contrast, and subsequent hits continued to vary between mellower soul—**If You Need Me, You're Good For Me, Tonight's The Night**—and more energetic performances like **Everybody Needs Somebody**.

Burke scored regularly on Atlantic until 1968, the socio-soul ballad **I Wish I Knew (How It Would Feel To Be Free)** being his last Atlantic hit before moving to Bell. There he promptly made tracks to Muscle Shoals(▶) to produce himself on a superb LP of Southern R&B, the title-track **Proud Mary** providing a hit single with a great cover of the Creedance

The Best Of Solomon Burke. Courtesy Atlantic Records.

Clearwater Revival's classic.

His next move was to MGM, where **Electronic Magnetism** was an artistic and commercial disaster in progressive style, but **We're Almost Home** took a step in more soulful direction in 1972. Two years later Solomon joined ABC Dunhill; a Martin Luther King tribute LP, **I Have A Dream**, had some success, then he teamed with arranger Gene Page(▶) who had moulded Barry White's(▶) career, and the result was White soundalikes **Midnight & You**(Dunhill) and **You and Your Baby Blues** (Chess)(▶).

In 1979 Burke signed with the emergent independent label Infinity—distributed through MCA—cutting a fine LP, **Sidewalks Fences and Walls**. The soulful title cut was just breaking as a single when Infinity folded—Burke had been pacted via a production deal through Jerry 'Swamp Dogg' Williams Jr's(▶) Atomic Arts Inc, which had also yielded a 1978 Amherst outing **Please Don't You Say Goodbye To Me**—and Burke has remained unattached since.

Recordings:
Best Of . . . (Atlantic/—)
Proud Mary (Bell)

Sidewalks Fences and Walls (Infinity/—)
From The Heart (—/Charly)

Prince Buster

Despite his name of Prince, the unquestionable King of ska(▶) (or blue-beat as it was known in Britain) was Prince Buster, who churned out a succession of classic dance records during the '60s, scoring hit singles throughout the Caribbean and in Europe.

Greatest Hits. Courtesy Fab Records.

Born Buster Campbell in Kingston, Jamaica, on May 24, 1938, he was named by his railroad worker father after Bustamente, the great Jamaican statesman. He attended Central Branch School and St Anns, but unlike many of the Alpha School graduates, showed no great interest in music until his late teens. In fact, his passion was for boxing; he became known as the Prince after one particularly violent confrontation between rival gangs of 'rude boys' in Kingston's famed Orange Street (long the centre of the city's music business, incidentally) and would have become a professional prize fighter had he not eventually drifted into music.

Buster used to meet up nightly with friends in a small 'spasm' band after weight training. From bashing old saucepans and sticks to make a rhythm, he found the pluck to enter a talent contest at Tilly Blackman's famous Glass Bucket Club, winning for three weeks in a row and becoming a member of the resident band there, which also featured singers Derrick Morgan(▶) and Eric Morris.

Encouraged by his father and by the band's drummer, Arkland Park (known locally as Drumbago), Buster began recording in the early '60s, backed by the Drumbago All Stars, the Les Dawson Blues Unit, or the Rico Rod-

riguez(▶) Blues Band, who shared back-up on his 1963 debut album **I Feel The Spirit**. This included such masterpieces as **Run Man Run, Wash All Your Troubles Away** (a ska version of the classic spiritual), the infectious instrumental **Spirit Of Africa, Madness** (the track that made his reputation among the disco crowds in the UK) and the bitingly political **Black Head Chinaman** (his involvement in radical Jamaican politics was to cause him problems with the authorities from time to time).

Issued in the UK on the tiny Blue Beat label (a subsidiary of Melodisc, a company which Emile Challot, it was once said, sarcastically, ran out of the pockets of his enormous overcoat!), Buster's records made his name rank among the mod 'in-crowd' alongside those of James Brown(▶), Otis Redding(▶) and various black American artists. But even before his albums hit the stores in Britain, Buster had a sensational concert at Brixton Town Hall in London. He also toured France and Spain to packed houses.

Buster's records concerned themselves with everything from Jamaican gang violence (**Al Capone**) to that ultimate anthem to male chauvinism, **Ten Commandments,** and the lewd **Big Five**, while his classic **Judge Dread**(▶) inspired the British DJ/reggae performer who took the title as his stage name. One of his biggest sellers **Rough Rider,** which was released in 1967 and sold in excess of 130,000 copies, was recently revamped by the UK pop/ska outfit The Beat.

For much of the '70s Buster concentrated more upon cabaret performances in Jamaica and abroad. He has in addition worked closely with a number of reggae artists, having production credits on hits by John Holt, Dennis Brown(▶), Alton Ellis(▶), the Heptones(▶) and the Ethiopians(▶).

He owns 10 record stores in the Caribbean and spends much of his time supplying records for juke boxes, on which he now has practically a monopoly in Jamaica. He recently attempted a comeback in the wake of the UK 2-Tone ska/rock-steady revival movement but failed.

Recordings:
I Feel The Spirit (—/Blue Beat)
Fabulous Greatest Hits (Fab/Melodisc)
Sister Big Stuff (—/Melodisc)
Jamaica's Greatest (various artists) (—/Melodisc)

Below: Prince Buster, tough, talented king of ska.

Above: Former Impression Jerry Butler, who carved out a satisfactory solo career.

Jerry Butler

Jerry Butler's parents were part of the mass black migration from the South up to urban Chicago which began in earnest in the '30s and by the '40s had become a floodtide.

Butler, born in Sunflower, Mississippi, on December 8, 1939, was just three when his family moved North (his father got a job on the railroad) and his life-story mirrors the aspirations of the many thousands who made the same trek. From poor beginnings, Butler became not only a major—and very wealthy—entertainment star but also built a highly successful business as the major distributor of imported beers in 'The Windy City'.

He started singing at 15 in church choirs, which led to membership of the Northern Jubilee Gospel Singers who sang for the Travelling Soul Spiritualistic Church, where he met up with the younger Curtis Mayfield(▶). For a while they travelled separate paths, Mayfield singing with the Alpatones (also spelt Alfatones) while Butler was in a doo-wop group, the Quails.

The two were to link up as members of the Impressions(▶), auditioning for the Vee-Jay label, who recorded them on **For Your Precious Love** and to Butler's trepidation, and the others' annoyance, billed it as by 'The Impressions With Jerry Butler'.

The record was an instant hit, selling 150,000 copies in the first two weeks. Vee-Jay immediately groomed Butler as a solo star while the Impressions went into, thankfully temporary, doldrums. While trying to hold the group together, Mayfield continued working with Butler, writing songs and playing guitar for him.

Specialising in smooth ballads at that time, Butler had a run of Vee-Jay hits: **He Will Break Your Heart** (1960, a Mayfield song), **Find Yourself Another Girl, I'm Telling You,** the vocal hit version of Johnny Mercer and Henry Mancini's **Moon River** and **Make It Easy On Yourself.**

Butler also recorded duets with Betty Everett(▶), and, more recently, Thelma Houston, scoring in 1964 with **Let It Be Me,** as well as writing material for Jackie Wilson(▶), Otis Redding(▶), Count Basie and others, and visiting the UK to appear on TV's 'Ready, Steady, Go' in 1965.

When Vee-Jay collapsed, Butler was snapped up by Mercury who, after scoring with **Mr. Dream Maker** and a couple of modest albums in his usual mode, had the foresight to link him with the then obscure Kenny Gamble and Leon Huff(▶) over in Philadelphia.

It was a magic teaming, resulting in the million-selling **Only The Strong Survive** (arranged by the then novice Thom Bell(▶) and later the subject of an outstanding cover version by Elvis Presley) and two classic albums, **The Ice Man Cometh** and **Ice On Ice,** making play on his 'Iceman' nickname given him by noted Philadelphia DJ George Wood, and earned both for his cool vocal delivery and for his ice-cool beers!

Gamble and Huff opened Butler's horizons, moving him into a more contemporary style with up-tempo and mid-pace items to balance the ballads. The three of them co-penned **Hey Western Union Man** (re-titled **Send A Telegram** for the British market) on **The Ice Man Cometh** album, and it was one of 1968's finest and most imaginative soul records. A flop initially in the UK, it was re-promoted and charted in 1970 when he flew in to London to collect his Blues And Soul magazine award as 'Number One Vocalist'.

Deciding to concentrate on their own Philadelphia International(▶) label Gamble and Huff stopped producing Butler in 1970 and, though he had a big 1970 duet album **One Plus One** with Gene Chandler and a 1971 million-selling duet with Brenda Lee Eager (leader of Peaches, his backing vocalists) on **Ain't Understanding Mellow,** his career flagged until he was signed by Berry Gordy Jr to Motown(▶) in 1975.

It took a year for the first album under the deal to emerge and Motown avoided the mistake they made with Chuck Jackson(▶). Though the company's distinctive sound was certainly utilised, it was not allowed to submerge Butler's distinctive voice, and a run of pleasing albums and singles have ensued.

Butler's extra-curricular activities have continued. With brother Billy Butler (best known for his OKeh collectors' classic **Right Track**) he ran the Stax(▶)-distributed Fountain and Memphis labels and the Chicago South-Side-based Butler Music Workshop which cultivates young writers, producers, arrangers, musicians and singers, among the luminaries of which have been Chuck Jackson and Marvin Yancey of Independents(▶) fame, Natalie Cole(▶) and Terry Callier.

Recordings:
For Your Precious Love (with the Impressions) (Vee-Jay/—)
Make It Easy On Yourself (Vee-Jay/Joy)
Delicious Together (with Betty Everett) (Vee-Jay/Joy)
Mr Dream Merchant (Mercury)
The Soul Goes On (Mercury)
The Ice Man Cometh (Mercury)
Ice On Ice (Mercury)
It All Comes Out In My Song (Motown)
Love's On The Menu (Motown)
Two To One (with Thelma Houston) (Motown)

Donald Byrd

Trumpet and fluegelhorn virtuoso Donald Byrd (born Detroit, December 1932), established himself as a premier musician in New York, while working with Art Blakey and Max Roach.

He began leading his own groups in the '60s, while pursuing his musical studies, which resulted in a Masters Degree in Music Education from the Manhattan School of Music. Later, he attained a Ph.D in teaching from Columbia University.

His recording career took hold in the early '70s with a series of methodical and percussive jazz/soul albums, the pattern of which was set by **Ethiopian Knights** (1972) and **Black Byrd** (1975). The latter gave his then-record company Blue Note the biggest selling album in their 35 year history.

Byrd's teaching career continued at Howard University Washington DC, where, as Chairman of the Black Music Dept. he taught youngsters who subsequently worked in his band, and whom he later produced as the Blackbyrds(▶).

Recordings:
Stepping Into Tomorrow (Blue Note)
Ethiopian Knights (Blue Note)
Black Byrd (Blue Note)
Love Byrd (Elektra)

And 125th St NYC. Courtesy Elektra Records.

Cameo-Parkway

Philadelphia-based songwriters Bernie Lowe and Kal Mann set up the Cameo label as a vehicle for a song called **Butterfly** which they had written for white rock 'n' roller Charlie Gracie. It was a smash hit and, aided by a glut of talent in Philly and plenty of exposure via the locally based but nationally networked *American Bandstand* TV show, hosted by Dick Clark, they were able to churn out a seemingly endless procession of teen-orientated hits. As a result they have often been cited as the guilty persons who spelled the end of raw rock 'n' roll and the advent of banal pop, which dominated the charts until the advent of the Beatles and the beat boom.

But amidst all the pap from Timmie Rogers, Bobby Rydell and the rest, were plenty of gems aimed at the R&B/soul market. Chubby Checker's **The Twist** and his follow-ups were the biggest sellers, but records from the Orlons (**Wah-Watusi, South Street** and the hilarious **Them Terrible Boots**), the Dovells, with Len '1-2-3' Barry as lead singer (**Bristol Stomp, Bristol Twisting Annie**), Dee-Dee Sharp (**Mashed Potato Time**) and Bunny Sigler(▶) (**Let The Good Times Roll & Feel So Good**) kept Cameo and its Parkway subsidiary in the limelight. Most of the recordings were made in the company's studios, located in an old theatre, under such producers as John Madara, Kenny Gamble and Leon Huff.

Lowe and Mann had sold out in 1963 and in 1968 the company folded, its catalogue being picked up by its one-time accountant Allen Klein, who was later to be controversially involved both with the Beatles and the Rolling Stones.

With the demise of Cameo-Parkway, the Jamie/Guyden group of labels (of which there were dozens) became the prime outlet for black vent of Gamble and Huff's Philadelphia International(▶).

Recordings:
The American Dream: The Cameo-Parkway Story 1957-1962 (—/London)

James Carr

Like Sam Cooke(▶) and Johnnie Taylor(▶), James Carr emerged from the ranks of the Soul Stirrers gospel group to become a great solo soul singer. Born in Memphis on June 13, 1942, he grew up in Shreveport, Louisiana, but it was on returning to Memphis and signing with Goldwax(▶) boss Clinton Claunch and coming under the management of Phil Walden (who also looked after Otis Redding(▶) and Duane Allman(▶)) that he made his mark.

Black country singer/songwriter O.B. McClinton(▶) wrote much of Carr's material, including the classic breakthrough, **You've Got My Mind Messed Up,** a haunting soul ballad. A brilliant version of the Chips Moman/Dan Penn soul standard **Dark End Of The Street** and the lilting **You're Pouring Water (On A Drowning Man)** confirmed Carr's mastery of the R&B ballad idiom, and they were all helped by sympathetic playing from some of the best Memphis session men outside Stax(▶) and Hi(▶) (Carr usually recorded at Sam Phillips' legendary Sun studio, source of the early Elvis hits).

Recordings:
You Got My Mind Messed Up (Goldwax/Stateside)
A Man Needs A Woman (Goldwax/Bell)

Clarence Carter

Blind singer-guitarist Carter was originally one half of Clarence and Calvin, who recorded for Duke. In 1965 they joined Rick Hall's Muscle Shoals(▶) studio to record for Atco. Calvin was injured and retired, but Clarence stayed on to record a string of soul hits like **Thread The Needle, Looking For A Fox** and **Slip Away** for Atlantic.

Carter's speciality was a sly, sexy lyric sensibility coupled with an attacking delivery, so it was ironic that his biggest hit by far, **Patches,** was a sentimental epic that slipped perilously close to MOR territory. Released in 1970, it made the top 10 on both sides of the Atlantic.

Carter eventually quit Muscle Shoals to sign with ABC/Dunhill and record a series of self-produced albums. His more recent recordings don't measure up to the standard of the Muscle Shoals tracks, all of which are unfortunately now deleted. Carter was formerly married to soul singer Candi Statton(▶).

Recordings:
This Is Clarence Carter (Atlantic)
The Dynamic Clarence Carter (Atlantic)
Testifyin' (Atlantic)
Sixty Minutes With Clarence Carter (Fame/—)
Patches (Atlantic)
I Got Caught (ABC)

Alvin Cash

Born in St Louis, Missouri, on September 15, 1939, Alvin Cash moved to Chicago and, as Alvin Cash and the Crawlers, had an initial hit with **Twine Time** on the much-collected One-Der-Ful R&B label's Mar-V-Lus subsidiary.

The Crawlers—Cash's four brothers—were a song and dance team (they did some shows as dancers with Frank Sinatra) while his backing band became known as the Registers.

Cash carved a niche for himself in the mid-'60s with his simple but effective dance records, such as **Alvin's Got A Boogaloo, The Philly Freeze** and **Funky Washing Machine.** A friend of Muhammed Ali since 1960, Cash was encouraged by the boxer to record **Ali Shuffle** in the '70s with the respected musician/producer Willie Henderson.

Recordings:
The Philly Freeze (Mar-V-Lus/President)

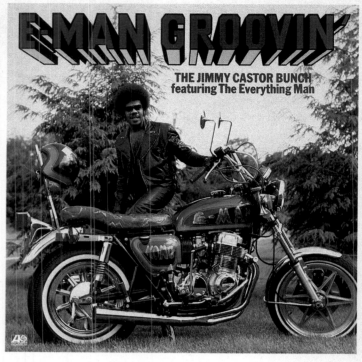

E-Man Groovin'. Courtesy Atlantic Records.

Jimmy Castor

Born in New York on June 22, 1943, Castor has had an amazingly diverse career, which has tended to overshadow his importance in any one style. Normally considered a gimmicky purveyor of dance-orientated novelties, Castor in fact began in 1957 as a tenor voice in several youthful doo-wop groups, including Frankie Lymon's (▶) brother Lewis' group the Teenchords. By 1960 Castor had moved from singing to playing saxophone and was featured in that capacity on the Dave 'Baby' Cortez' hit **Rinky Dink.** He continued as sideman and session player in New York until the short-lived Latin craze of 1966 gave him a nationwide smash hit with **Hey Leroy, Your Mama's Callin'.**

Unable to follow the hit, Castor drifted back to session work until the formation of the Jimmy Castor Bunch in 1972. Originally recorded for CBS, their debut album **It's Just Begun** actually appeared on RCA where the track **Troglodyte,** a ridiculous piece of electronic funk, took off all by itself to become one of the year's biggest hits. Once again, another hit was not forthcoming but in 1974 Castor signed with Atlantic and managed to come through with a run of consistent hits, including **Bertha Butt Boogie, E-Man Boogie, King Kong** and the aptly titled album **The Everything Man.**

He toured the UK in 1975 with the successful Atlantic Super Soul package featuring Sister Sledge(▶), Ben E. King(▶) and the Detroit Spinners(▶), but was unable to ride the disco boom of the late '70s. He reappeared in 1982 on the Salsoul label with a new smash hit, **E-Man Boogie 82.**

Recordings:
It's Just Begun (RCA)
The Everything Man (Atlantic)
E-Man Boogie 82 (Salsoul/—)

Below: Jimmy Castor—king of the Bunch.

Below: Donald Byrd, trumpeter with and producer of the Blackbyrds.

The Chambers Brothers

Thanks to a black hippie image and ultra-high-volume rock-influenced music, the Chambers Brothers won themselves a mass white audience and an acceptance in rock circles matched by few black artists.

Brothers Lester (harmonica/cowbell/vocals; born April 13, 1940), Willie (guitar; born March 2, 1938), George (bass; born September 26, 1931) and Joe (guitar; born August 22, 1942) were raised in Lee County, Mississippi, and pooled their savings to travel down to Houston, Texas, to cut early sides for Peacock(▶). But it was on moving to Los Angeles that they began to make an impact with—at that time—a mixture of folksy blues with the emphasis on lightly amplified guitars and harmonica.

An appearance at the 1965 Newport Folk Festival won plaudits, and early records for Vault in LA included the superb **People Get Ready** album, highlighting a great version of the Curtis Mayfield(▶) song, as well as the Womacks'(▶) **It's All Over Now**, Lowell Fulsom's(▶) **Reconsider Baby** and the compulsive original **Tooka Tooka**.

The Chambers Brothers added a new drummer to their line-up when they discovered Briton Brian Keenan playing at the Ondine Club in New York. Moving into a brash highly-amplified rock influenced style, the fivesome landed a major contract with Columbia and became a feature of major rock concerts following their 1968 hit **Time Has Come Today**. Vault re-issued an exuberant version of **Shout** to chart the same year and the Brothers also scored with a powerful version of Otis Redding's(▶) **I Can't Turn You Loose** from their acclaimed **A New Time,**

A New Day album. 1971's **New Generation** album yielded the hit single **Funky**, but the group faded when Keenan left soon after.

Recordings:
People Get Ready (Vault/Vocalion)
Shout (Vault/Liberty)
The Time Has Come (Columbia/CBS)
A New Time, A New Day (Columbia/CBS)
New Generation (Columbia/CBS)

Gene Chandler

Born in Chicago on July 6, 1937, Gene Chandler rocketed to fame in 1962 with the ponderous novelty song **Duke Of Earl** (Vee-Jay), whose style harked back to the early '50s doo-wop era and hardly seemed to auger for a creatively productive future. Teaming up with Curtis Mayfield's(▶) writing and production skills put Chandler into a more orthodox uptown-soul vein and a steady stream of hits ensued, including **Rainbow** (Vee-Jay 1962), his signature tune to this day, **Just Be True** and **Nothing Can Stop Me** (both on Constellation) and **Groovy Situation** (Mercury). He also cut successful duets with Barbara Acklin(▶) (**From Teacher To The Preacher** on Brunswick) and Jerry Butler(▶) (**Ten And Two** on Mercury) and teamed up again with Curtis Mayfield in 1972 when he signed to the latter's new Curtom label!.

The mid-'70s was a lean time for Chandler but his fortunes were revived when long-time stalwart Chicago-producer Carl Davis signed him to Chi-Sound in 1978 and another string of hits began, including **Get Down** (1978), **When You're Number One** (1979), and **Does She Have A Friend** and **Rainbow '80** in 1980.

Chandler's forté is soft, mellow,

Above: Chubby Checker, who twisted to stardom.

soulful ballads but he has also come up with consistently attractive dance material.

Recordings:
Duke Of Earl (Vee-Jay/—)
The Girl Don't Care (Coral)
The Gene Chandler Stituation (Mercury)
Here's To Love (Chi Sound/20th Century)
There Was A Time (MCA)

Chubby Checker

Though it was Hank Ballard who came up with **The Twist** (and had a huge US hit in the process) it was Ernest Evans, better known as Chubby Checker, who set the hips of the world atwirling when his version sold three million copies in 1960.

Born on October 3, 1941, Checker worked in a local chicken market whose owner, Henry Colt, was so impressed with his singing that he took the youngster to Kal Mann, who signed him on a long-term contract to Cameo Parkway(▶) and wrote his first record, **The Class**. The wife of American DJ Dick Clark was at that debut session and remarked that Checker looked like a young Fats Domino—and came up with the name Chubby Checker to fit.

An immediate hit, **The Class** was on the US chart for 19 weeks and was re-promoted a year later, spending another 19 weeks on the chart, through into 1962. 1961 produced three more million-sellers, **Pony Time** (co-written by Don Covay(▶)), **Let's Twist Again** (which re-worked the successful Twist format) and **The Fly**. In 1962 both **Slow Twistin'** and **Limbo Rock/Popeye** achieved gold disc

status and he recorded **Down To Earth**, an enjoyable album of duets with long-serving Philly soulstress Dee Dee Sharp.

Despite successful European tours and worldwide sales of more than 15 million, Checker's star soon went into eclipse as the public tired of dance-craze songs and his bland lightweight voice.

Recordings:
For Twisters Only (Parkway/—)
18 Golden Hits (Cameo Parkway/—)
Checkered (Chalmac/London)

Chess Records

Jewish immigrants from Poland, Leonard and Phil Chess settled in Chicago in 1928 and by the '40s ran a chain of bars on the city's Southside. Given the largely black population locally, they settled on a black music policy when opening their Macomba night-spot and featured artists like Billy Eckstine(▶) and jazz saxophonist Gene Ammons.

In 1947 they opened a recording studio and set up the Aristocrat label to service the demand among their clientele for records by acts who appeared in the club. A new musical dimension was added when Sunnyland Slim, a blues pianist, got them to give him a recording session. Slim brought with him a young Mississippi-born singer/guitarist who went under the pseudonym of Muddy Waters(▶). With time left over at the end of the session, some sides were cut showcasing Waters, and one of these, **I Can't Be Satisfied**, sold in the thousands.

The brothers immediately realised that, besides Chicago's indigenous black population, who liked the sophisticated sounds of jazz, the city was teeming with immigrants freshly arrived from the plantations of the South and that their tastes were firmly for the blues, especially if the music was amplified and urbanised, thus providing a link between their roots in the country and their new faster lifestyle in the city.

With Leonard Chess producing, Waters quickly became a major star while his band spawned such talents as Little Walter, Otis Spann and Jimmie Rogers, who all became stars in their own right for the company. The name was changed from Aristocrat to Chess in 1950 (a link with the past: the first Chess release was by Gene Ammons).

Chicago's top bluesmen flocked to the fold: Howlin' Wolf(▶), Elmore James, Sonny Boy Williamson (Rice Miller), Eddie Boyd and later Buddy Guy all had successful careers with the company. The Chess-owned Ter-Mar studio became a magnet

Bo-Diddley & Company.
Courtesy Chess Records.

Above: Buddy Guy, one of many Chess Records' successes.

and soon developed its own house band, led by bass-player, song-writer, arranger and producer Willie Dixon (author of such classics as **Little Red Rooster**). In later years, even the Rolling Stones made the pilgrimage to Ter-Mar at 2120 South Michigan Avenue, where they cut part of their second album.

Eager to find even more talent, Leonard Chess started making field trips, selling records from the back of his car and making contacts with Southern entrepreneurs like Sam Phillips in Memphis from whom he leased Jackie Brenston's 1951 hit **Rocket 88**, and Stan Lewis down in Shreveport Louisiana. The Checker subsidiary appeared in 1953; Argo (mainly jazz and gospel, though Etta James(▶) was also signed to it) and Cadet followed soon after.

John Lee Hooker (from Detroit) and Lowell Fulsom(▶) (from the West Coast) joined the blues roster, while the company also got into rock 'n' roll with Chuck Berry(▶) and Bo Diddley(▶), and into doo-wop with Harvey and the Moon-glows(▶), the Monotones and others.

By the mid-'50s, the Chess/Checker roster covered the whole gamut of black American music (and even had a couple of white acts). Soul groups like the Dells(▶) and the Radiants, solo R&B singers like Jimmy McCracklin(▶), soul sisters like Etta James(▶), KoKo Taylor, Sugar Pie DeSanto(▶) and Fontella Bass(▶), and soul brothers like Maurice and Mac(▶) and Clarence 'Frogman' Henry(▶) all found their outlet with the Chess Corporation and, besides the Chicago sessions, artists were recorded in many other locations (Etta James, for instance, was sent down to the Fame Studios in Muscle Shoals(▶) to revive her career).

Surpassed among black-orientated companies only by Motown(▶) and Atlantic(▶) in sales power, Chess had established itself as an immensely influential corporation, covering a wider range of music than Motown and, arguably, getting closer to the roots than the more commercially orientated Atlantic.

In 1969 it all ended though. Leonard Chess died on October 16 and, losing the heart to carry on alone, Phil Chess decided to concentrate on the radio station they had owned for years (and which had played such a major part in breaking their records), while Leonard's son Marshall left to work for the Rolling Stones.

The company was sold to the massive GRT tape company, who ran it in tandem with their GRT, Janus and Westbound labels for a few years and had a few more hits (notably Chuck Berry's **My Ding-A-Ling**) before selling the labels and all the archive material to the New Jersey-based All Platinum company who released all the artists and contented themselves with releasing album re-packages of old material.

This is Chess. Courtesy Chess Records.

Recordings:
Pop Origins (Chess/—)
Sing A Song Of Soul (Checker/-)
Chess Golden Decade Vols 1-8 (—/Chess)
Chess/Janus Mobile Discotheque (—/Chess)
Good Ole Rock 'n' Roll Vols 1, 2, 3 (Vee Jay/Joy)
Doo Wop Doo Wop (—/DJM)
Best of Chess Doo Wop (—/Chess)
Golden Age of R&B (Chess/—)

The Chi-Lites

The Chi-Lites have been among the most consistent hit makers of the last 20 years of soul harmony vocal groups. Although they have undergone one or two line-up changes, including the temporary departure of writer Eugene Record, the cool falsetto of lead singer Marshall Thompson has been their ever-present trademark. Their combination of falsetto lead and clean even-toned harmonies is now recognised as having influenced many vocal groups. It was a style that the Temptations(▶) adopted for a while and it had an even greater impact on the Stylistics(▶), who, with Russell Thompkins Jr playing Marshall Thompson's role, scored a succession of massive hits in the mid-to-late '70s.

The group first appeared as the Chanteurs on the renowned Vee Jay label, before beginning to

Above: The Chi-Lites who have harmonised for 20 years.

record as the Chi-Lites (a name derived from their hometown Chicago) on a variety of small and colourfully named local labels. They have served their longest tenure with the Brunswick label, for whom the driving protest song **Give More Power To The People** was their first international chart success. There then followed an almost unbroken succession of hits throughout the early-to-mid-'70s beginning with the doleful semi-spoken **Have You Seen Her, Oh Girl**—with its memorably plaintive harmonica intro, the chillingly atmospheric **Coldest Days Of My Life, Lonely Man, A Letter To Myself, Stoned Out Of My Mind**, and then a buoyant twist in style (broken only by the tongue-in-cheek pathos of **Homely Girl**) which included **I Found Sunshine** and **Too Good To Be Forgotten**. Indeed, between the explanatory titles **Coldest Days Of My Life** and **I Found Sunshine** The Chi-Lites had unearthed and mastered a whole range of styles and emotions.

Eugene Record left the group, saying that they had gone as far as they could. He was replaced in the vocal line-up by Vandy 'Smokey' Hampton, while another long-serving member, Creadel 'Red' Jones, was replaced first by the deep-voiced David 'Doc' Roberson and then by Charles 'Chuck' Rogers.

Meanwhile, Record capitalised on the happy coincidence of his name and career by releasing the album **The Eugene Record** on WEA. Although he later rejoined his old colleagues, Record may have been right when he said the group had gone as far as they could; the disco boom of the '70s clove the world of traditional soul in two, and the Chi-Lites were just one group of former great importance who were left with a lot of ground to make up.

They have changed labels several times recently, unable to create the kind of tight-knit liaison they had with Brunswick in their halcyon days. Among the group's less successful recent recordings are reworkings of some of their greatest hits, which might have been better left alone. Come 1982, the group were touring with their original line-up but still searching for a road back to the top.

Recordings:
Give More Power To The People (Brunswick)
Greatest Hits (Brunswick)
Greatest Hits Vol. II (Brunswick)
Heavenly Body (20th Century)
The Fantastic Chi-Lites (Brunswick)

The Chiffons

The early '60s yielded a host of tales derived from the 'formularised' aspect of American pop music—i.e. strike a hit formula then bleed it to death—and the Chiffons provided an adequate example of the system. This quartet of young black office-girls, led by Judy Craig (born 1946), with Barbara Lee (1947), Patricia Bennett (1947) and Sylvia Peterson (1946) in support, began singing demo records for Brooklyn-based Bright Tunes Productions, and after flopping with their first disc outing on Big Deal, signed with the Laurie label. Fame came quickly thereafter as the 'doo lang doo lang' intro of **He's So Fine** spent a month atop the US pop charts in spring 1963. It was a brash, shrill teenage love-song, followed in similar vein by **One Fine Day** and **A Love So Fine**.

Their stylised delivery, lacking the gritty impact of contemporaries like the Crystals(▶) or the gospel roots of Motown's emergent Supremes(▶) and Vandellas(▶), nevertheless managed to survive almost three years, and the lilting **Sweet Talkin' Guy** gained top 10 status in 1966. The Chiffons' personnel also recorded on Laurie subsidiary Rust as the Four Pennies with limited success. Their career as the Chiffons lingered on with decreasing sales as they became resident on the 'rock oldies' circuit.

He's So Fine has come to be judged in the US law courts as the inspiring source of George Harrison's hit **My Sweet Lord,** and the Chiffons have recorded their version of the latter on Laurie.

Recordings:
Sweet Talkin' Guy (Laurie/London)
Greatest Hits—Pick Hits Of The Radio Good Guys (—/Philips)

The Cimarons

Formed in 1967 by friends who met weekly at a north London Methodist youth club, this octet can rightfully claim to be the first major British-based reggae band. Until the early '70s the Cimarons survived by backing, in the studio and on the road, Jamaican rock-steady singers visiting the UK. This tutored the group in reiterating contemporary hit songs and led to them being invited to tour Africa at the height of the Biafran war. Upon returning they cut their first single, **Mammy Blue,** for Downbeat Records.

They toured on their own as a fully fledged band and recorded two albums in quick succession: **In Time** incorporating reggae versions of popular soul songs, and **On The Rock,** made in Jamaica. Signed to the international Polydor label at the end of the '70s they cut the uneven **Maka** album and a fine live album, recorded at London's Roundhouse, that included their epic **Ethiopian Rhapsody.**

So adaptable are the Cimarons that they can be heard on an album by Australian pop singer/songwriter Gary Shearston, and their latest album is an intriguing collaboration with Paul McCartney, **Reggaebility,** that sets to reggae some Beatles songs, and others owned by McCartney's publishing company.

Current membership, recently brought up to full strength with ex-Matumbi(▶) drummer Jah Bunny, consists of Sonny Binns keyboards, Franklyn Dunn bass, Locksley Gichie guitars and Winston Reid vocals.

Recordings:
Live (—/Polydor)
Reggaebility (—/Pickwick)

Above: Dee Clark, co-author of '60s soul classic You Can't Sit Down.

Dee Clark

One of the most tuneful of the '60s black vocalists, Dee Clark was soulful enough for black audiences and pop enough for white. He had his great day in 1961 when **Raindrops** made No. 2 in the US charts after a string of top-30 records on Vee-Jay and its subsidiaries, which had started in 1958 with **Nobody But You.**

Born Delecta Clark in Blythville, Arkansas, on July 11, 1938, Clark grew up in Chicago and recorded gospel with the Hambone Kids for OKeh in 1952 before joining R&B group the Goldentones who became the Kool Gents and were contracted to Vee-Jay, which soon recognised Clark's solo talents.

Clark co-penned **You Can't Sit Down** for Phil Upchurch(▶) while on tour with the guitarist and, after his golden Vee-Jay period, cut sides for such labels as Constellation, Columbia, Wand and Liberty before having another, albeit brief, taste of glory in 1975 with a one-off disco hit.

Recordings:
You're Looking Good (Vee-Jay/Joy)
Keep It Up (—/Charly)

Jimmy Cliff

Born James Chambers, in St Catherine, Jamaica, in 1948, and raised by his father, Cliff moved to Kingston in 1962 after dropping out of college in search of music stardom. His first record was **Daisy Got Me Crazy** with Count Boysie at Federal Studios. It did nothing. Nor did his second release, **I'm Sorry,** for Jamaican sound system operator Sir Cavaliers.

His career began to take off when he teamed up with Chinese-Jamaican producer Leslie Kong. Still only 14 years old, Cliff wrote **Hurricane Hattie,** inspired by a hurricane that had swept across South America that year. It was a local hit.

In 1964 the Jamaican parliament, particularly Edward Seaga—then leader of the opposition—was eager to promote reggae music abroad. A tour of America was sponsored with Byron Lee and the Dragonaires(▶) backing a number of singers including Cliff. Unfortunately the tour flopped, partly due to the Dragonaires' inability to produce authentic yard-style rhythms. Cliff, however, met Island Records' boss Chris Blackwell, who the fol-

Below: The Cimarons, Britain's first major reggae band.

The Harder They Come. Courtesy Island Records.

lowing year convinced the singer he should work in England. Cliff complied, but it wasn't until the late '60s that he began to make an impact on the charts. He had been working with English rock musicians, Mott The Hoople's Ian Hunter and Mick Ralphs and UK domiciled American vocalists Doris Troy(▶), Madeline Bell(▶) and P.P. Arnold(▶).

His first two singles failed and his album **Hard Road To Travel** revealed a desire to break away from reggae into a more general area of pop. He covered Procul

Above: Jimmy Cliff, a vastly underrated talent.

Harum's **Whiter Shade Of Pale**, **Let's Dance**, previously recorded by the first white group signed to Motown, the Hit Pack, and the Spencer Davis Group's **Can't Get Enough**. It consolidated a strong club following without selling in vast quantities.

In 1968 Cliff went to Brazil representing Jamaica in an International Song Festival. He sang **Waterfall** which was previously released as a single in Britain, but had failed to take off. It went clear in Brazil and he stayed on to play more live shows and write new material. Out of this period came **Wonderful World Beautiful People**, an international hit in 1969. At last he was a star and the next year he consolidated his top-10 status with a version of Cat Stevens' **Wild World**.

Cliff's reputation gained greater impetus through his material for

other artists: **Let Your Yeah be Yeah** for the Pioneers(▶) and **You Can Get It If You Really Want It** for Desmond Dekker(▶).

His desire to be an international pop star took him to Muscle Shoals(▶) to cut an entirely non-reggae album, **Another Cycle**. It was his first major error of judgement, from which he has never really recovered. Without being strong enough for American soul audiences the album additionally disaffected him from his roots-reggae fans.

That LP was recorded during the filming of his starring role in Perry Henzell's film *The Harder They Come*. The film was a box office smash in Jamaica. Cliff became the island's first superstar, with critical acclaim awarded to the film and to Cliff for his performance as the central character.

Sadly the film and the soundtrack album, featuring the title song written by Cliff, failed to ignite an international reaction. Defeated, the singer severed his ties with Island, against the advice of Blackwell, and accepted a hefty advance from EMI (Warner Brothers in the US). The first fruit was **Unlimited**, an uneven crop of reggae and soul songs that further exposed the absence of roots. He was increasingly envious of Bob Marley's(▶) success, but, unlike him, he refused to stay in one category. Neither would he record in one studio, preferring to cut half an album in Jamaica and the other half in the US.

Cliff has continued to make albums that fuel his devotional cult following and testify to his immense songwriting and vocal abilities, but his attempt to cover too many ethnic styles has disorientated the wider public and led to his fall from grace. It is widely believed, however, that one day he will find the right ingredients and claim his place among the elite.

Recordings:
Hard Road To Travel
(A&M/Trojan)
The Harder They Come
(Mango/Island)
The Best Of Jimmy Cliff (Island)
Give Thanx (Warner Brothers)

Mitty Collier

Mitty Collier's sole Chess(▶) album was titled **Shades Of A Genius**. It was a sadly prophetic title, for though it contained the lady's remake of the James Cleveland-penned gospel standard **I Had A Talk With My God Last Night** which, as **I Had A Talk With My Man Last Night**, stands as one of the greatest deep-soul performances of all time, it was her first and final LP.

Other tracks, notably her version of the much-covered Ray Charles(▶) hit **Drown In My Own Tears** (a Henry Glover composition), were similarly majestic, but Mitty, a native of Birmingham, Alabama, and 23 at the time of the recordings, slipped straight back into obscurity.

Recordings:
Shades Of A Genius (Chess/—)

Dave and Ansell Collins

Dave Barker, a session vocalist and Ansell Collins, a keyboards player, were working for producer Lee Perry(▶) in Kingston, Jamaica, in the late '60s, and joined forces in 1971 for the ska single **Double Barrel**. Released on the Techniques label, it topped the Jamaican and UK pop charts in March of that year. It was the first record ace reggae drummer Sly Dunbar(▶) ever played on.

The similarly styled **Monkey Spanner** enjoyed the same international success. After cutting an album Collins and Barker parted company, Collins becoming a top-class session player and Barker, resident in the UK, singing with a number of undistinguished soul groups. They attempted a comeback in 1981 without success.

Recordings:
Double Barrel (Techniques/Trojan)

Arthur Conley

Dubbed 'The Crown Prince Of Soul', Arthur Conley (born April 1, 1946) cut a brief run of promising records during the mid-60s but failed to ascend to the throne. The late Otis Redding(▶) heard a Conley demo of **I'm A Lonely Stranger**, took the youngster under his wing and released the record on his own Jotis label.

Redding then took Conley to

Muscle Shoals(▶), where some tracks were cut under the guidance of Rick Hall at Fame, but it was the Redding-produced **Sweet Soul Music**, an anthem of praise to the greats of soul music (who all got a mention in the lyric), which crashed him into the US top-10. The song was based on Sam Cooke's(▶) earlier hit **Yeah Man** and Cooke's influence could be detected in Conley's vocal stylings, but the musical backdrop was pure Stax(▶)/Atlantic(▶) Sound.

A re-make of **Shake Rattle And Roll**, the witty **People Sure Act Funny** and the admirable dancer **Funky Street** were all classics of the genre but failed to lift Conley out of the second division.

Recordings:
Sweet Soul Music (Atlantic)
More Sweet Soul (Atco)
Soul Directions (Atlantic)

The Contours

The Contours were one of the early acts signed by Tamla Motown(▶) boss Berry Gordy. Following a tip from Jackie Wilson(▶) (cousin to one of the group members), Gordy signed them to his namesake label and wrote **Do You Love Me** for them. The resulting record, with its spoken introduction, wild vocals and socking backbeat, became a big hit and an instant classic. (In Britain cover versions by beat groups Brian Poole and the Tremeloes and the Dave Clark Five became hits despite their obvious inferiority to the original.)

However, the Contours were beset by personnel changes and seemed unable to capitalise on their promising beginning. They put out several other interesting records (notably **First I Look At The Purse**) but ended up playing second fiddle to Motown's big vocal group acts like the Four Tops(▶). The group eventually folded in 1968, and lead singer Dennis Edwards was picked by Norman Whitfield to replace the departed David Ruffin in the Temptations(▶).

Although they notched up a posthumous hit in 1970 with **Just A Little Misunderstanding**, The Contours' real claim to lasting fame lies with **Do You Love Me**. Both these tracks and other Contours work can be found on various Motown compilation albums.

Below: Arthur Conley praised that **Sweet Soul Music** *in the mid-60s.*

Dave 'Baby' Cortez

Moving from Detroit to New York, Dave 'Baby' Cortez (born Dave Clowney) wrote hits for LaVern Baker(▶) and Clyde McPhatter(▶), recorded as a member of the Pearls for Atco and Onyx, and played piano on many sessions before switching to organ and going to No. 1 on the pop chart with the lightweight R&B instrumental **The Happy Organ** on Clock. The follow-up, **Whistling Organ,** was a smaller hit, but in 1962 he bounced back with the catchy **Rinky Dink** for Chess.

Besides his own prodigious output for various labels, Cortez played on the early Gladys Knight and the Pips(▶) hits for Bobby Robinson's Fire/Fury set-up.

Recordings:
The Golden Hits Of (Clock/ London)
Rinky Dink (Chess/—)
Soul Vibration (All Platinum)

Don Covay

A key member of Atlantic Records' famed 'Soul Clan' in the '60s, Don Covay was born the son of a Baptist preacher in Orangeburg, South Carolina, in March 1938, and soon began singing in the family's Cherry-Keys gospel group. Growing up in Washington DC, Covay joined the seminal local group the Rainbows (in which Billy Stewart(▶), Marvin Gaye(▶) and other luminaries also served) in the late '50s.

When Little Richard(▶) came into town, Covay won himself a solo slot on the rock 'n' roll star's stage show. Richard recorded Covay under the name Pretty Boy and **Bip Bop Bip** was released on Atlantic, but before starting his long regular stint with that label, Covay recorded for a host of other labels including Sue(▶), Columbia, RCA, Big Top, Cameo(▶) and Landa, having modest success with **Pony Time** (1962) and **Popeye Waddle** (1962).

In 1964, Don Covay and the Goodtimers were signed to the tiny Rosemart label, which was distributed by Atlantic. When **Mercy Mercy** gained chart status, Atlantic took over the contract and followed through with a run of great records, including **Sookie Sookie** and **See Saw,** which were hot favourites in British discotheques as well as among black Americans. They were recorded—as were many Atlantic hits of the time—at the Stax Studios in Memphis, with Booker T and the MGs(▶) providing the rhythm section and the Mar-Keys(▶) the horns.

Co-written by Covay and the MGs' guitarist Steve Cropper, **Sookie Sookie** and **See Saw** were punchy, hard-biting slabs of up-

See Saw Courtesy Atlantic Records.

Don Covay, a key member of the Atlantic Records 'soul clan'.

tempo Southern soul in the vein of **Chain Of Fools,** which Covay wrote for Aretha Franklin(▶) (who also scored with **See Saw**).

Always blues-influenced, Covay ventured into that idiom in the early '70s with his **The House Of Blue Lights** album and then moved first to Janus then to Mercury (doubling as a producer and A&R man as well as an artist). He cut a novel reggae-flavoured version of Chuck Berry's(▶) **Memphis** in 1973, following through with the belting **It's Better To Have (And Don't Need).** In 1976, Covay cut the **Travelin' In Heavy Traffic** album for Philadelphia International but it lacked the potency of his earlier work.

Covay's strength has always been in his songwriting and his studio work. Distinctive on record, his voice lacks the raw power of many of his contemporaries and on-stage he needs all the amplification aid he can get, which perhaps explains why he has spent most of his time in the recording studio.

Recordings:
Mercy (Atlantic/—)
See Saw (Atlantic)
House Of Blue Lights (Mercury)
Super Dude 1 (Mercury)
Hot Blood (Mercury)

The Crusaders

Rivalling the Four Tops for longevity, the band that was eventually to become world-famous as the Crusaders first came together in Texas in the early '50s. Felder, Sample and Hooper, along with the fourth founder-member, trombonist Wayne Henderson, formed an all-purpose band, the Swingsters, which undertook gigs around Houston and on the Texas small-time circuit. Playing material that varied from B.B. King to Dizzy Gillespie by way of Stan Kenton, the band—which was also the nucleus of a floating coterie of other musicians—laid down the beginnings of the eclectic style which was to develop into the Crusaders' unique blend of jazz-funk.

Seeking wider horizons, in the early '60s the quartet split for California. Now known as the Jazz Crusaders, they landed a contract with Pacific and recorded a number of sides over the next few years. As was to become their habit, they used top musicians to fill the bass chair and add extra instrumental voices. However, despite laying down some excellent funky jazz during this period, they were somewhat ahead of their time—they were too jazzy for a wide audience, and jazz critics found them too basic. Fellow-musicians and music industry cognoscenti were broader-minded, and the four became stalwarts of the West Coast session scene.

In 1970 the band dropped the 'Jazz' from their name and became simply the Crusaders, embarking on a style that has since become a byword for finely-honed, disciplined yet inventive instrumental

Below: The Crusaders have had a near-30-year run.

music. Success began to build, helped by the endorsement of many top rock and soul artists. The Average White Band(▶), for example, recorded **Put It Where You Want It** from **Crusaders I** and show a debt in the sound of both their horn arrangements and their rhythm section. By the same token, most modern session reed players tend to derive in about equal proportions from Wilton Felder and King Curtis(▶).

The early '70s saw the band consolidating their reputation with superb albums like **Second Crusade, Unsung Heroes** and **Scratch,** as well as recording with artists as diverse as Joan Baez and Van Morrison. In 1975 Wayne Henderson left to pursue a solo career (his first solo album **Big Daddy's Place** was released in 1977), and the band has carried on with a basic nucleus of three members ever since. As always, however, supple-

Rhapsody And Blues. Courtesy MCA.

mentary instrumental duties are fulfilled by only the very best musicians. Robert 'Pops' Popwell held the bass chair for a number of years, brilliant white guitarist Larry Carlton was regularly featured during the late '70s, and others who have recorded with the band over the years include musicians of the calibre of bass player Chuck Rainey, guitarist David T. Walker, and Billy Preston on keyboards.

By the mid-'70s the Crusaders

Above: An inspiration to all reed players, Crusader Wilton Felder. The band members are respected session musicians and have enhanced many West Coast recordings. Their style has evolved into a successful blend of jazz-funk.

had also become an in-demand live act. In 1975 the Rolling Stones asked the band to support them on a UK tour, and they became the only instrumental group to tour with the Stones, before or since. In 1976 they toured the UK alone to enormous acclaim, and now perform to SRO audiences in the US and throughout the world.

Images was the first Crusaders album to go gold, although previous albums had dominated the jazz charts and made good showings in the pop charts. 1978 saw the first solo album by a member of the Crusaders, **Rainbow Seeker** by Joe Sample. Felder's **We All Have A Star** followed, and Sample's second solo outing, **Carmel,** was followed by Stix Hooper's debut, **The World Within.** These solo efforts were generally well received both by the critics and the public.

In 1979 the Crusaders entered a new phase when they recorded the title track of the album **Street Life** with vocalist Randy Crawford(▶). Released as a single it was a huge hit, setting Randy Crawford on the road to superstardom and establishing the Crusaders as a force for the '80s. The 1980 album **Rhapsody and Blues** featured the hit **Soul Shadows,** a beautiful and evocative song sung by Bill Withers, while the 1981 album **Standing Tall** brought British vocalist Joe Cocker back into the limelight. His soul ballad, **I'm So Glad I'm Standing Here Today,** stands as one of his best performances.

There is no reason why the Crusaders should not continue to prosper through the '80s and beyond. They are mature musicians at the height of their powers, men who have paid their dues and come to terms with the business. Without a doubt their sinuous, supple yet hard-centred music will continue to make friends and influence people.

Recordings:
Old Shoes And New Socks (Chisa/ Rare Earth)
Crusaders I (Chisa/Island)
Chain Reaction (ABC)
Southern Comfort (ABC)
Street Life (MCA)
Standing Tall (MCA)

The Crystals

Towards the end of 1961, a quintet of Brooklyn schoolgirls began singing for spare-time cash and landed a recording contract with Philles, a new label being launched by producer Phil Spector(▶). Dee Dee Kennibrew, Dolores 'La La' Brooks, Mary Thomas, Barbara Alston and Pat Wright were the first Crystals, Barbara singing lead on the debut **There's No Other** and follow-up **Uptown.** During 1962 Mary Thomas quit to get married, leaving a quartet whose name leapt to the top of the charts with **He's A Rebel.** The phrasing of that last sentence is important—while **Rebel** carried a label-credit to the Crystals, the singer was actually Darlene Love, with studio singers in support.

Early 1963 brought **Da Doo Ron Ron,** an amazing driving, dominating, powerhouse disc with percussion and brass epitomising Spector's legendary 'wall of sound' production, topped by rasping soulful vocals, and it became a transatlantic smash hit, followed by the marginally more restrained **Then He Kissed Me.** In October 1963, just prior to a British tour, Pat Wright was replaced by Frances Collins, and the quartet continued to sing out the Philles contract.

Spector dropped the Crystals in 1964, and their career ended with a couple of Motown-inspired discs on United Artists in 1965-6.

Recordings:
He's A Rebel (Philles/London)
Greatest Hits (—/Phil Spector Int)

King Curtis

Fort Worth-born King Curtis—real name Curtis Ousley—started out

King Curtis at Fillmore West. Courtesy Atlantic Records.

Above: Immaculate but not impactive, the Delfonics.

as a session tenor-sax player in the '50s, basing himself in New York, and was featured on records by artists as diverse as the Coasters(▶) and Buddy Holly. His gritty, chicken-scratching solo on the Coasters' **Yakety-Yak** was both a highlight of the record and a typical example of his style at that time. As well as adding magic to recordings by other people and going on the road as leader of a back-up orchestra, Curtis soon started recording under his own name, cutting a number of jazz sides for Prestige with sidemen like Brother Jack McDuff and Eric Gale(▶) before moving into the mainstream of R&B and coming up with several tracks which have stood the test of time, notably the Curtis versions of soul standards, **Night Train** and **Honky Tonk,** and the self-composed **Soul Serenade** and **Soul Twist.** (The latter rode the twist craze to hit status in 1962.)

Later Prestige recordings encompassed further modern jazz sessions with luminaries like Nat Adderley, Wynton Kelly and Paul Chambers, and a superb blues album (**Trouble In Mind** on Status) on which he sang and played guitar, as well as saxophone. While by no means disgraced as a jazzer it was obvious that his real talent lay in the field of R&B and soul. By the late '60s he was ensconced at Atlantic(▶), the natural home for a man of his particular talents, providing back-up for Atlantic stars like Aretha Franklin(▶) and cutting albums under his own name. Favoured sidemen were musicians like guitarist Cornell Dupree(▶), bassists Jerry Jemmott and Chuck Rainey, keyboard man Richard Tee and legendary drummer Bernard Purdie as well as his stage band regulars who included Paul Griffin on piano, and Melvin Castle on cornet.

Perhaps Curtis' best memorial is the amazing 1971 live album **King Curtis At Fillmore West.** Recorded at the same time as Aretha Franklin's **Live At Fillmore West,** it shows the tenor man at the height of his powers, demonstra-

ting to the full his syncopated, almost percussive approach to saxophone playing. Fiery and propulsive on belters like **Memphis Soul Stew** and **Changes,** airy and melodic on **Soul Serenade,** King Curtis shows how he got his name. The band, of course, was the best soul band around at the time, featuring Cornell Dupree, Truman Thomas on electric piano, Jerry Jemmott, Bernard Purdie, Pancho Morales on congas, Billy Preston(▶) on organ, plus the Memphis Horns. The album was simply a triumph. On August 31, 1971, King Curtis was stabbed to death outside an apartment building he owned on 86th Street, New York. He was just 37 years old. But his spirit lives on in the work of dozens of horn players, notably Grover Washington Jr.(▶), David Sanborn and Tom Scott(▶).

Recordings:
Soul Serenade (—/Specialty)
King Curtis At Fillmore West (Atlantic)
Live At Smalls Paradise (Atco/—)
The Best Of King Curtis (Atlantic)
Instant Groove (Atco)

Tyrone Davis

Owner of one of the most emotive voices in soul music, Chicago-based Tyrone Davis (born Greenville, Mississippi, 1938) cut **Can I Change My Mind** for Ray Charles' Tangerine label without success. Later he recorded the song again, for Carl Davis's Dakar label, and this time earned a gold disc, thanks to a far less frenetic approach which brought out all the power of the haunting lyrics.

Davis issued the track as a B-side and it took some months to surface but by December 1968 it had gone US top 10. **Turn Back The Hands Of Time** (1970), **You Keep Me Holding On** (1971) and **I Had It All The Time** (1973) were all equally pungent performances, and throughout the '70s Davis showed an ability to turn out consistently good albums.

Recordings:
Can I Change My Mind (Dakar/—)
Turn Back The Hands Of Time (Atlantic)
Love And Touch (Columbia/—)
Greatest Hits (Dakar/Brunswick)
Let's Be Closer Together (Columbia/CBS)

Sam Dees

At 6 feet 4 inches and over 200 pounds, Sam Dees is one of the biggest songwriters in every sense. He is also one of the finest at creating the romantic soul ballad. Born in Birmingham, Alabama, he moved to Rochester, New York, as a child. Returning to the Southern states in the mid-'60s, his songs began to be recorded by Clarence Carter(▶) and Z.Z. Hill(▶).

As an Atlantic Records(▶) recording artist, he has had intermittent success, scoring with a mid-'70s single **The Show Must Go On.** Many of the best soul albums of today have a Sam Dees composition on them. Dees' songs have been recorded by Tyrone Davis(▶), Z.Z. Hill, the Persuaders, Loleatta Holloway(▶), Frederick Knight(▶), Booker T. Jones(▶) and Sylvia Robinson.

Recordings:
The Show Must Go On (Atlantic)

Desmond Dekker

Dekker's contribution to rocksteady and the development of reggae with his producer/guardian Leslie Kong is incalculable. Their recordings between 1967 and 1971 (when Kong died, aged 38 after a history of cardiac trouble) were the first Jamaican sounds to attract a mass white audience, particularly in the UK where Dekker was adopted by the essentially working-class skinhead movement. Many white people were first introduced to reggae through his records and, later, those of Bob Marley(▶).

Born in Trenchtown, Kingston, Jamaica, in 1943, and orphaned at an early age, he began his working life as a welder, but by the mid-'60s he was a singer with the Aces band, a studio ensemble employed by producers Lloyd Daley 'The Matador' and Duke Reid. The group enjoyed some individual success with their **Generosity** single and later evolved into the Righteous Flames.

Desmond Dekker and the Aces burst onto the UK pop charts in 1967 with the single **007 (Shanty Town),** released on Pyramid. Two years later they reached No. 1 in the UK, the first reggae act to achieve that honour, with **The Israelites.** The single charted twice again on re-release. **It Mek, Pickney Gal, You Can Get It If You Really Want It** and **Sing A Little Song** (which was released in 1975 on Cactus) all charted. **The Israelites,** incidentally, was the first reggae record to make any impact in America, where it charted.

After Kong's death Dekker's career went into decline. The loss of his mentor and adopted father was such a blow he is believed to have wanted to throw himself into Kong's grave.

Abortive projects followed and in 1980, with skinheads and ska back in vogue in the UK he signed to Stiff Records for whom he promptly cut an encouraging

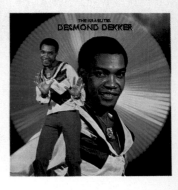

The Israelites. Courtesy Pyramid Records.

album versioning his previous hits. In 1981 he made the **Compass Point** collection with British blue-eyed soul singer Robert Palmer producing. Neither succeeded in re-activating his chart career. He will be remembered, however, as reggae's first superstar.

Recordings;
This Is Desmond Dekker (—/Trojan)
Black And Dekker (—/Stiff)
Desmond Dekker Sweet Sixteen Hits (—/Trojan)

The Delfonics

Purveyors of diaphanous sophisto-soul, the Delfonics—William and Wilbert Hart and Major Harris vocals—were early protegés of Philadelphia-producer Thom Bell (▶), who wrote and produced their big hit **La-La Means I Love You** in 1968. An album of the same name followed, as did further successful singles like **Ready Or Not Here I Come.**

Although their material was immaculately sung and produced, the group as an entity lacked punch, and they found their territory largely captured by the Thom Bell-produced Stylistics(▶) in the early '70s. Nevertheless, the compilation album **The Delfonics Super Hits** is worth looking out for.

Recordings:
The Delfonics Super Hits (Philly Groove/Bell)

The Dells

One of the longest serving acts in black music, the Dells began in 1953 as the El Rays while still at high school in Harvey, Illinois. The then line-up of Marvin Junior, John Funches, Chuck Barksdale, Lucius McGill and Mickey McGill recorded without success for Checker, and Lucius McGill left before they changed their name to the Dells and signed with the Chicago-based

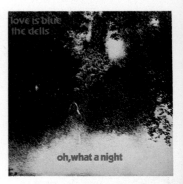

Love Is Blue. Courtesy Chess Records.

Vee Jay label. Funches left four years later, as the result of a car accident, to be replaced by Johnny Carter, who had been with the Flamingos.

Signing to Chess's Argo subsidiary in 1962, The Dells had a minor hit with (Bossa Nova) Bird before rejoining Vee Jay in 1964. Two years later Vee Jay, who had boasted both the Beatles and the Four Seasons on their roster as well as a host of soul acts, collapsed through poor administration rather than lack of sales success, and the Dells returned to Chess with whom they enjoyed a run of hits, which has continued through the '60s, '70s and into the '80s.

Beautifully arranged and faultlessly performed songs like **Stay In My Corner** (1968), a 1969 re-recording of their 1956 R&B hit **Oh What A Night,** and the almost symphonic medley **Love Is Blue/I Can Sing A Rainbow** and a run of

Above: The Dells learned the secret of longevity — 30 year's worth!

consistently entertaining albums have made the vocal team perennial favourites of black America. An adventurous 1974 outing, **The Dells Vs The Dramatics,** saw them teamed up with the Dramatics(▶) by Chess in response to Motown's pairings of acts like the Supremes(▶) and the Four Tops(▶).

They even managed to sail through and emerge untainted from the disco explosion of the '70s, and their rich and instantly recognisable harmonies, plus mellow lead vocals from Junior and Carter, have ensured them pop acceptance while in no way undermining their ethnic roots.

Recordings:
Love Is Blue/I Can Sing A Rainbow (Chess)
Greatest Hits (Chess)
The Dells (Cadet/Chess)
The Mighty Mighty Dells (Cadet/Chess)
Face To Face (ABC/—)
I Touched A Dream (20th Century Fox)
Whatever Turns You On (20th Century Fox)

Sugar Pie De Santo

Small in stature, big in voice, Sugar Pie De Santo (born Peylia Balington, in Brooklyn, of Filippino extraction), was raised in San Francisco. She was discovered by Johnny Otis in the mid-50s and recorded for Federal, Aladdin, Check and Veltone before touring with the James Brown(▶) Revue in 1960.

Showing a heavy blues influence, she recorded for Checker and her classic **Soulful Dress** (1964) led to her inclusion on one of the Folk Festival Of The Blues packages which toured Britain and Europe. She also recorded a great duet with Etta James(▶), cut in Muscle Shoals(▶).

Above: Lights burned brightly, if briefly, for the Delfonics.

Recordings:
Sugar Pie De Santo (Checker)

Detroit Emeralds

At the pop end of the soul spectrum, the Detroit Emeralds had a brief, but certainly bright, blaze of glory in the early '70s with some unquestionably attractive recordings, of which **Do Me Right, With This Ring,** their first million-seller **You Want It You Got It** and **Feel The Need In Me** stand out.

Guitarist, arranger and songwriter Abe Tillmon, his brother Ivory Tillmon and James Mitchell Jnr made their first records for the Ric-Tic label, which was bought out by Motown(▶) in 1968. Switching to Westbound, they had a spell of success, but it ended abruptly when Ivory Tillmon and Mitchell left in 1974. Reforming in the late '70s the group failed to regain their earlier prominence.

Recordings:
Do Me Right (Westbound/Janus)
You Want It You Got It (Westbound/Janus)
Abe James And Ivory (Westbound)
I'm In Love With You (Westbound)
Feel The Need (Westbound)
Let's Get Together (Westbound/Atlantic)

Jessy Dixon

In recent years black gospel music has undergone some transition as performers more influenced by contemporary sounds have emerged to compete with the older, traditional aspects of the genre. Jessy Dixon is a guy who has crossed the bridge from involvement with classic quartets and choirs to become a leading light

among the 'born again' element.

Born in San Antonio, Texas, Jessy spent most of his life in Chicago and derived inspiration from great quartets like the Ward Singers and Dixie Hummingbirds. His first professional involvement was playing piano for the Ward Singers. He joined James Cleveland's Gospel Chimes, which prompted him to form his own group, and the Jessy Dixon Singers were booked onto the Newport Jazz Festival in 1971, where he was spotted by Paul Simon and signed to perform a solo spot in Simon's touring show.

Dixon and his group were soon signed to Light Records, where their output veers towards the soul-contemporary idiom.

It's All Right Now, recorded for Light subsidiary Word, was released in 1979, and is a good example of Dixon's reverent work.

Recordings:
It's All Right Now (Word)
Live Rhymin' (Columbia/CBS) (Paul Simon featuring the Jessy Dixon Singers)

Ernie K. Doe

Born Ernie Kador in New Orleans in 1937, ninth of 11 children of a Baptist preacher, Ernie K. Doe topped the US charts in 1961 with the attractive novelty song **Mother In Law** (Minit), which featured Benny Spellman(▶) contributing the deep-voiced vocal responses to Doe's plaintive story-line.

It was a one-off hit but, summing up as it did the whole 'Crescent City Sound' of the '60s, it built Doe a reputation which assured steady work for years after. In the early '70s Allen Toussaint(▶) produced the **Ernie K. Doe** album for Janus.

Recordings:
Mother In Law (Minit/—)
Ernie K. Doe (Janus)

Above: Tough-guy Dorsey has his share of soul talent.

Lee Dorsey

Lee Dorsey was born in 1926, and before taking up a musical career made a living as a professional boxer. In fact, it was boxing that brought him to New Orleans, where he met up with producers Allen Toussaint(▶) and Marshall Sehorn in 1961. They matched Dorsey's distinctive, almost fragile voice with a nonsense lyric and a piano-and-horns-based arrangement, and watched the result—**Ya Ya**—go on to sell a million (**Ya Ya** was covered by Joey Dee in the US and by Petula Clark, of all people, in Europe). The follow-up, **Do-Re-Mi,** was released the same year to gain equal popularity, and become something of an R&B standard— Georgie Fame was only one of many artists who covered it.

The combination of Dorsey, Toussaint and Sehorn was obviously a winner, producing a unique sound that was strangely compelling. Nevertheless, the team's next few releases made only minor impact, and a lull followed the collapse of Fire Records, the company to whom they had leased the tracks. But by 1965 Dorsey had joined the Amy/Mala/Bell complex, and the hits began to flow again. **Ride Your Pony,** also destined to become an R&B standard, hit the American charts, and international success came the year after with **Get Out Of My Life Woman.** Remembered as much for Toussaint's delicate but bluesy piano work as for Dorsey's haunting vocal, the record set the standard for a string of major hits like **Confusion,** the brilliant **Working In The Coalmine,** and the wry **Holy Cow.** Live appearances during this period showed that Dorsey could back his recorded success with a capable stage act, and he was particularly appreciated in Britain where soul fans regarded him as something of a giant.

Although the hits dried up, Dorsey recorded many more fine sides in the '60s with Toussaint and Sehorn, including gems like **The Greatest Love, Neighbour's Daughter** and **A Mellow Good Time,** not to mention some excel-lent duets with deep-soul singer and stablemate Betty Harris. He was still making records sporadically in the mid-'70s although by that time Allen Toussaint himself had come to the fore as a solo artist.

Lee Dorsey has achieved enough to occupy a permanent niche in the history of black music, having cut a good many tracks that combine charm, orginality and real soul. Look out for greatest hits compilations.

Recordings:
The Best Of Lee Dorsey (Fire/Island)
The Best Of Lee Dorsey (—/EMI Regal Starline)
The New Lee Dorsey (Amy/Stateside)
Yes We Can (Polydor)

Lamont Dozier

Detroit born and bred, Dozier is most famous as one third of the most successful songwriting partnership in black music history, Holland/Dozier/Holland(▶). After splitting with Motown(▶), the three established their own short-lived Invictus label in 1967, whereupon Dozier tentatively began his solo recording career, in the company of fellow Invictus signatories Freda Payne(▶) and Chairmen of the Board(▶).

With the demise of Invictus, Dozier pursued his singing ambi-

Out Here On My Own—Courtesy ABC Records.

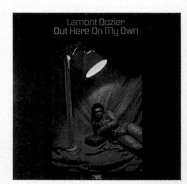

tions with ABC, Warner Brothers and Columbia, making a respectable mark with singles **Fish Ain't Bitin'** and **Let Me Start Tonite,** and the ballad-laden Columbia album, **Working On You.**

Recordings:
Bittersweet (Warner Brothers)
Working On You (Columbia/CBS)

Doris Duke

Despite a relative lack of commercial success, Doris Duke is regarded by aficionados as one of the finest exponents of the deep soul idiom. Born Doris Curry in the small town of Sandersville, Georgia, she spent her early career with such gospel outfits as the Raspberry Singers, the Evangelistic Gospel Singers, the Davis Sisters and the Caravans before switching to secular music as a backing vocalist in New York in 1963 (she can be heard on recordings by such diverse artists as Aretha Franklin(▶), Dusty Springfield, Jackie Wilson(▶) and Frank Sinatra).

Using her first husband's surname, she recorded in her own right for Hy-Monty in 1967 as Doris Willingham (she was being managed by Donald Height, himself a soul singer of some repute in U.K. 'Northern Soul' circles). Doris toured Europe in 1968 as back-up singer with Nina Simone and adopted the stage name Doris Duke on her return Stateside, linking up with legendary producer Jerry Williams Jr (aka Swamp Dogg: 'The world's most successful failure' in his own words). The result was the classic **I'm A Loser** album and single for Wally Roker's short-lived Canyon label. Culled from the album, **To The Other Woman (I'm The Other Woman)**—a masterpiece in the soul rap genre—made US R&B top 10 in early 1970 and the album went top 20.

On the demise of Canyon, Williams signed Doris Duke to Mankind Records and produced a second highly-rated album **A Legend In Her Own Time.** A subsequent LP recorded in London for Contempo, using British producers, arrangers and musicians, was far less successful and since 1975 her career has languished in obscurity.

Yes We Can. Courtesy Polydor Records.

Recordings:
I'm A Loser (Canyon/Charley)
A Legend In Her Own Time (Mankind/Mojo)
B.C. (Columbia/CBS)
Flight Time (Sandra)

Jackie Edwards

Born Wilfred Edwards in St Elizabeth, Jamaica, on August 22, 1939, young Jackie began singing at the tender age of 12. He grew up a neighbour of Alton Ellis(▶) on Maxfield Avenue, Kingston, and made his debut public performance on the Vere Johns Talent Show. His initial bias was towards sentimental balladeering and he was greatly influenced by Nat King Cole(▶).

At 20 he cut **Your Eyes Are Dreaming** which went straight to No. 1 in Jamaica. Among his first recordings were **Tell Me Darling** (eight weeks at No. 1) and **Heaven Just Knows.** With the great ska boom not having yet gained momentum, it was what Jamaican mass audiences wanted and he soon became the island's top artist.

Outside reggae, he is now probably best known as a songwriter, though, had he been a black American, he would certainly have made a major mark in soul circles with his superlative 1966 Island soul album **In Demand,** which was produced by white Jamaican Chris Blackwell and contained two classic but neglected self-penned cuts, **I Feel So Bad** and **L.O.V.E.**

Edwards had made the move to Britain in 1962, being brought over by Blackwell when he set up Island Records, though initially signing his protégé to Decca for a gospel EP. (Blackwell is, incidentally, a member of the family of Crosse and Blackwell of baked-bean fame!) Edwards subsequently cut gospel and reggae but, mostly, soul for Island on a total of seven albums. His greatest commercial triumph came in 1966 when Britain's Spencer Davis Group took his **Keep On Running** to No. 1 on the pop charts, also scoring with his **Somebody Help Me,** while he penned the **Come On Home** hit for Wayne Fontana.

His association with Island terminated with the sublime rocksteady soul of his **Put Your Tears Away** album in 1969; he then switched to CBS Direction and, in 1970, released the **Let It Be Me** set. He has maintained a low public

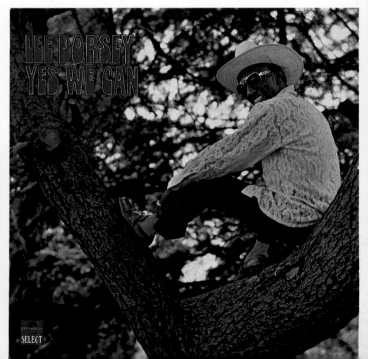

profile since that time. A consistent album maker, and infrequent public performer, it was his work with the Dynamics and afterwards with producer Bunny Lee that reaped the greatest rewards.

Recordings:
The Most Of (—/Island)
Put Your Tears Away (—/Island)
Sincerely (—/Trojan)
Let's Fall In Love (—/Third World)

Donnie Elbert

Donnie Elbert began singing professionally in 1954 and started recording for De Luxe in 1957 when he scored his first US hit with the ballad **What Can I Do?** (a song he later re-recorded in Jamaica as **The Wedding**). Following an album for De Luxe, he switched to Chicago's Vee Jay label and came

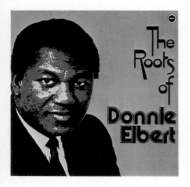

*The Roots Of Donnie Elbert.
Courtesy Ember Records.*

up with the quarter-million seller **Will You Ever Be Mine?** before being drafted into the US Army.

Returning to the recording scene in 1961, Elbert recorded for Parkway in Philadelphia and Checker in Chicago, as well as Jalynne and Cub in New York, and turned down an offer from Harvey Fuqua at Motown before starting his own Gateway/Upstate label in 1964. He quickly came up with a hat-trick of hits with **Run Little Girl, A Little Piece Of Leather** and **You Can Push It Or Pull It.** The irresistibly catchy **Little Piece Of Leather** (on Island's Sue Label in UK) was a big disco hit and established Elbert's name with British soul fans.

Elbert visited Britain on a promotional visit, married an English girl and settled in the UK for six years, recording for several labels (including an album of Otis Redding(▶) cover versions for Polydor) and showing a considerable reggae influence in his work. In 1970 he returned to the USA with tapes of two songs he had recorded in Britain. **Can't Get Over Losing You** was leased to Rare Bullet and gave him a national hit, while his reworking of the old Supremes(▶) hit **Where Did Our Love Go?** (recorded in his characteristic high-pitched falsetto style) was leased by All Platinum and went top 20 on both sides of the Atlantic. Switching labels yet again, to Avco, Elbert, re-recorded another old Motown standard, the Four Tops(▶) **I Can't Help Myself,** and logged another international hit—making 1972 the pinnacle year of a career which has since slipped back into obscurity.

Recordings:
The Roots Of Donnie Elbert (—/Ember)
Stop In The Name Of Love (—/DJM)

The Elgins

One of Tamla Motown's second division groups in the mid-'60s, the Elgins recorded as the Emeralds (for States) and as the Downbeats (for Backbeat) before signing with Motown's VIP subsidiary.

Saundra Edwards sang lead on a trio of 1966 American hits—**Put Yourself In My Place, Darling Baby** and **Heaven Must Have Sent You** (the last-named did not make the UK charts until 1971 by which time Saundra had been replaced in the group by Yvonne Allan, formerly of the Donays).

Other members of the Elgins were Johnny Dawson, Cleotha Miller, Robert Fleming and Norman McClean.

Recordings:
Darling Baby (VIP/Tamla Motown)

Alton Ellis

Born in Trenchtown, Kingston, Jamaica, in July 1944, Ellis grew up in a healthy musical environment: his father played guitar and organ in a Methodist church and his mother sang in a choir. He had intended to become a professional dancer but with his primary influences, singing duo Higgs(▶) & Wilson, distilling an irresistible flavour into American soul standards, he changed boats midstream and formed R&B duo Alton & Eddy, with Eddy Perkins.

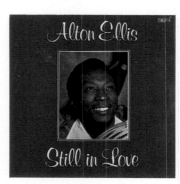

*Still In Love.
Courtesy Trojan Records.*

Their first signing was to Coxsone Dodd's Studio One(▶) for the singles **Murial** (1962) and **My Heaven.** With Perkins in search of a solo career, Ellis hung around Studio One to make two albums: **Rock & Soul** (incorporating hit singles **Let Him Try, I'm Just A Guy** and **Mad Mad**) and **Mr Rock Steady** (including his most popular rock-steady statement, **Get Ready To Do The Rock Steady**).

By 1966 Alton and his backing band the Flames had pacted to Duke Reid's Treasure Isle. Releases were **Dance Crasher** and **Cry Tough.** It was his rendering of **Willow Tree** that convinced Dodd he wanted the singer back in his fold. Dodd sent him to America for three months in 1967, following the death of his mother. There he cut R&B sides with an Afro/American band.

On returning home he discovered that his **Remember That Sunday** album was among the best sellers. In this definitive Ellis collection he attacked the legal disputes he was having with Dodd and Reid whilst baring his soul over the breakdown of his marriage and his mother's death.

1969 saw him off to Canada to

*Above: Lorraine Ellison,
a one-hit wonder.*

work with Keith Hudson(▶) on the **Big Bad Boy** set. He has since remarked that Hudson was, in his view, the only producer to treat him fairly financially. Before leaving Jamaica he deposited two albums with producer Lloyd Daley 'The Matador', **Blackman's Pride** and **Going Back To Africa,** issued in 1971 and 1972 respectively.

Since 1972 he has been resident in London, where his activities included discovering lovers' rock star Janet Kay(▶), writing the blueprint of Althea & Donna's **Uptown Top Ranking** and recording material with the Grove Muzik and Third World companies.

Recordings:
Remember That Sunday (JA)
Sunday Coming (Studio One/Bamboo)
Girl I've Got A Date (Treasure Isle/—)
Still In Love (—/Trojan)
Love To Share (—/Third World)

Shirley Ellis

Lincoln Chase, writer of **Such A Night** for the Drifters(▶) and of **Jim Dandy** for LaVern Baker(▶) and a recording star in his own right with a wide variety of labels, began tutoring Shirley Ellis (born New York, 1941) in 1958 when she left the Metronomes.

In the mid-60s he wrote her a trio of nursery-rhyme-inspired novelty soul songs: **The Nitty Gritty** (later a hit for Gladys Knight & The Pips(▶)), **The Name Game** and **The Clapping Song,** all issued on Congress and all top-20 hits, **The Clapping Song** earning a gold record.

However, her career fizzled out as quickly as it had flared and, apart

from a small hit on Columbia in 1967 with **Soul Time,** she made no further impact.

Recordings:
The Name Game (Congress/—)
Soul Time (Columbia/CBS)

Lorraine Ellison

When Frank Sinatra cancelled a recording date at New York's A&R Studios at the last minute, the time and the assembled orchestra were utilised by producer Jerry Ragavoy to come up with one of the all-time classics of soul music—Lorraine Ellison's highly emotive **Stay With Me Baby.** It was a record which proved to be maybe just too much over the top to achieve major chart success but which in subsequent years was destined to become one of the most sought-after collectors' items in black music.

Born in Philadelphia, where she started her career as a gospel singer (leading the Ellison Singers

Stay With Me. Courtesy Warner Bros Records.

on the Sharp label), Lorraine recorded for Warner Brothers from 1966 through to 1969 but proved to be a one-hit wonder. She had more success as a songwriter, in partner-

ship with Sam Bell (songs for Garnet Mimms(▶), Linda Jones, and Howard Tate(▶)).

Recordings:
Stay With Me (Warner Bros)

The Essex

The five members of the Essex got together while serving in the US Marines. Walter Vickers and Rodney Taylor teamed up in Okinawa then were posted to Camp Lejeune, North Carolina, where Billie Hill and Rudolph Johnson joined them. Feeling the need for a female voice to round out their attractive vocal harmonies, they added Anita Humes, whom they had heard singing in an NCO club.

On a short leave, they did the rounds of record companies, signed to Roulette and had an immediate million-seller with **Easier Said Than Done** (1963), following through quickly with **A Walkin' Miracle,** another instantly appealing slab of pop-soul, showcasing Anita Humes' lead vocals.

Recordings:
Easier Said Than Done (Roulette/—)
A Walkin' Miracle (Roulette/—)

Betty Everett

Born in Greenwood, Mississippi, in November 1939, Betty Everett started her career in the gospel field before moving to Chicago and, after a single on One-Der-Ful (**Your Love Is Important To Me**), notched her first hit with **You're No Good.** She swiftly followed up with **It's In His Kiss (The Shoop Shoop Song)** which, despite competition from other versions (notably that cut by Ramona King), hit No.6 in the US pop charts in March 1964 (on Vee Jay). Later that year she teamed up with Jerry Butler(▶) for **Let It Be Me** (also on Vee Jay),

which made No.5, and spawned the artistically highly rated **Delicious Together** album.

Despite a flow of often pop-slanted soul recordings over the years for ABC Paramount, MCA, and, in recent years, Fantasy (including an album co-produced by Johnny 'Guitar' Watson(▶) and Lou Rawls'(▶) one-time producer Dave Axlerod), Betty has failed to recapture her early success, though her vocal talents remain undiminished.

Recordings:
Delicious Together (with Jerry Butler) (Vee Jay/Joy)
It's In His Kiss (Vee Jay/Fontana)
Happy endings (Fantasy)
Love Rhymes (Fantasy/—)

The Exciters

Produced by Leiber and Stoller(▶) with arrangements by Teacho Wilshire, the Exciters' sound was pure New York, borrowing not a few tricks from Leiber and Stoller's work with the Drifters. The group, consisting of Herb Rooney, his wife Brenda Reid, Carol Johnson and Lilian Walker, all hailed from the Jamaica suburb of New York.

Strong songs furnished by Bert Berns, Burt Bacharach and Van McCoy (▶) and a contract with United Artists saw them break through in 1962 with **Tell Him** (which went top 10) and establish themselves with follow-ups like **Get Him** and **Doo Wah Diddy** (the cover of which was a big hit for Manfred Mann).

I Want You To Be My Baby (Roulette 1965) and their version of **A Little Bit Of Soap** (earlier a hit for Garnet Mimms(▶) and the Enchanters) issued by Bang in 1966, gave the Exciters further successes. Ronnie Pace and Skip McPhee replaced Johnson and Walker, and Rooney found new success for the group in the UK during the late '70s with the advent

of the Northern Soul cult, which made a fetish of old '60s uptown soul sides.

Recordings:
The Exciters (Roulette/—)

Fifth Dimension

An immensely successful and highly sophisticated black vocal act, the Fifth Dimension managed to cross their appeal over from soul to MOR audiences thanks to some superb songs from the then unknown Jimmy Webb and Bones Howes' imaginative arrangements and production.

The original line-up consisted of girl members Florence LaRue Gordon (born 1943) and Marilyn McCoo (born 1934), both natives of Los Angeles, and male members Billy Davis Jr (born 1939), Lamont McLemore (born 1939) and Ron Townson (born 1933), who all hailed from Louisiana. Working first as the Versatiles then as the Vocals, they were touring with Ray Charles(▶) when discovered by manager Marc Gordon who signed them to rock star Johnny Rivers' Soul City label (and also married Florence).

The soulful **Go Where You Wanna Go** was their first hit; their first million-seller came in 1967

The Magic Garden. Courtesy Liberty Records.

Above: The Four Tops made a sensational return to the charts in 1981.

with **Up, Up And Away** from the magnificent **The Magic Garden** album. (When McCoo and Davis got married later, the ceremony was performed in a hot-air balloon —a touch of the Hollywood showbiz style which was to prove their undoing when it came to their credibility as a soul music act.)

Stoned Soul Picnic went gold in 1968, the classy **The Age Of Aquarius** LP went gold the next year, but the increasing slickness of their act polished off the gritty edge of soulfulness which had been their earlier forté and their recordings soon became listless wallpaper music. McCoo and Davis went on to record as a duo, scoring with **You Don't Have To Be A Star** in 1977.

Recordings:
Up, Up And Away (Soul City/Liberty)
Stoned Soul Picnic (Soul City/Liberty)
The Magic Garden (Soul City/Liberty)
The Age Of Aquarius (Soul City/Liberty)

Below: The Fifth Dimension: pop at the top.

Four Tops

Almost unbelievably, the Four Tops have been together with the same line-up for nearly 30 years. Detroit-born Levi Stubbs started to make his mark in amateur talent shows around the Motor City in the early '50s, and recruited Renaldo Benson, Abdul 'Duke' Fakir and Lawrence Payton to form the Four Aims in 1954. Success hardly came overnight however. The next 10 years saw the group signed to Chess(▶), Singular, Riverside and Columbia without making any significant impact, and it was not until 1964 when they signed to Motown(▶) that they hit the jackpot.

At this time Motown was riding the crest of a wave, capitalising on the success of acts like Stevie Wonder(▶), the Miracles(▶), Martha and the Vandellas(▶), Mary Wells(▶), and, latterly, the Supremes(▶). In fact the Supremes were Motown's first real stars, the prime interpreters of the Holland/Dozier/Holland(▶) sound, and the group who carried the Motown sound through to the white pop market in a big way. The Supremes' success pointed to the possibilities for a male counterpart, the masculine version of the Detroit Sound. So Berry Gordy signed the Four Aims, renamed them the Four Tops, assigned writing and production duties to Holland/Dozier/Holland, and watched them become one of Motown's biggest and most consistent acts. Success was almost immediate. Their first record for the company, **Baby I Need Your Loving,** was a hit, and in 1965 **I Can't Help Myself** became a US No.1, an international hit and a million-seller. The similarly styled follow-up, **It's The Same Old Song,** repeated their chart success and established the Tops as a headlining act.

Right from the beginning, the Four Tops' hallmark was the smouldering, powerful voice of lead singer Stubbs. It was Stubbs' voice which set the group apart, while the other elements of the Tops' collective personality made them in many ways the archetypal '60s black vocal group. Levi laid down an authoritative lead; the three others provided muscular harmony back-up that set it off perfectly. On stage, Stubbs dominated vocally while most of the choreography was undertaken by Fakir, Payton and Benson. The formula—a piquant mixture of the familiar and the outstanding- worked again with the yearning **Loving You Is Sweeter Than Ever,** a hit in summer 1966.

But nothing the group had so far done had prepared the public for what was to come next. No.1 on both sides of the Atlantic, a multi-million seller, one of Motown's classic records and one of the best singles of all time in any category, **Reach Out I'll Be There** combined a great Holland/Dozier/Holland song with inspired production and a spine-tingling, dramatic, all-stops-out vocal by Levi Stubbs. The record seemed to come out of a clear sky, demonstrating the growing confidence and resources of Motown as an innovator as well as a commercial record company. It attracted considerable attention and admiration from music business insiders as well as massive sales. Phil Spector(▶) characterised the record as 'black Dylan', and whether or not you consider his comment relevant, there's no doubt that **Reach Out** presaged Motown's move towards more rock-styled 'contemporary' material in the late '60s. The lyrics may have been fairly standard—a man reassures his lover that he will be there to help no matter what—but the style, the sound as a whole, took Motown into new territories.

It was a hard act to follow, a *tour de force* that couldn't be repeated. Nevertheless, Holland/Dozier/Holland acquitted themselves well with the Tops' next two releases—**Standing In The Shadows Of Love** in late '66 and **Bernadette** in early '67. While neither record had quite the magic of **Reach Out,** they both utilised Stubbs' pleading voice well, and helped consolidate what had now become a recognisable Tops/Motown sound.

In 1967, however, the Tops lost their writers and producers when Eddie and Brian Holland and Lamont Dozier defected from Motown to form Invictus Records. The group continued to have hits on both sides of the Atlantic, including more classics like **Don't Walk Away Renee, If I Were A Carpenter, Do What You Gotta Do, It's All In The Game, Still Water (Love),** and **Simple Game,** but by 1969 they were beginning to feel overlooked among the plethora of talent that the label was now handling. Norman Whitfield, who had taken over from Holland/Dozier/Holland as Motown's musical mentor, wanted to concentrate on the Temptations(▶) and, anyway, was taking the Motown sound in a harder, funkier, rockier direction. Notwithstanding the pioneering breakthrough of **Reach Out,** the Tops were essentially a conventional lead-and-back-up vocal group. They split from Motown, but despite rumours and counter-rumours have always maintained that their departure was essentially amicable.

The Tops may have left Motown in search of new ideas and directions, but they didn't really find them at ABC/Dunhill, the company to which they signed in 1972. **Keeper Of The Castle** was a top 10 hit in late '72, and **Sweet Understanding Love** charted a year later, but neither song represented any radical development for the group. If anything, the songs were average compared to the gems which highlighted their Motown career. However, the signing at least kept the Tops recording, and the next few years saw a steady trickle of albums and singles of varying quality and success.

During this relatively fallow period the Four Tops were still undertaking a full schedule of live work, touring regularly throughout the US and Europe. The British public in particular has always had a soft spot for the Tops, and the group has never had any difficulty filling large halls. As a live act, the Tops tend to be something of an anomaly, falling somewhere between the tight, highly-disciplined choreography of groups like the Temptations and Gladys Knight and the Pips(▶), and the looser, more casual approach of contemporary pop and rock acts. There's little radical about their live repertoire, but there again they have a massive backlog of hits to call upon. There are still few finer spectacles in black music than Levi Stubbs in full flight with his three cohorts grooving behind him.

Ordinarily, the story might have ended there, with the Tops heading towards comfortable semi-retirement in cabaret and on the nostalgia circuit, but at the beginning of 1982 things started happening all over again for them. Having signed to Casablanca in 1981, the group released an album, **Tonight,** which immediately yielded two big hits, **When She**

Above: The Top's majestic lead singer Levi Stubbs, still groovin', some 30 years' on.

Was My Girl and **Don't Walk Away.** Both songs are in the relaxed, pop-soul genre that the group handle so well, and although they don't approach the majesty of the classic Motown sides, they have brought the talents of the Four Tops to a whole new generation of record buyers.

Ultimately, the Four Tops are important not for being great innovators but for doing what they do so well, so consistently and over such a long period. A conventional black vocal group with an exceptional lead singer, they've made the most of their chances and produced a great deal of glorious music that will be remembered when more pretentious efforts are long forgotten.

The discography is selective, confined to compilations of their classic Motown work and their recent successful album.

Recordings:
Anthology (Motown)
Four Tops: Greatest Hits (Motown)
Tonight (Casablanca)

Right: The Four Tops pictured during the early '60s, at about the time they signed for Motown.

Tonight. Courtesy Casablanca Records.

Eddie Floyd

Eddie Floyd was never one of Stax's major stars, but nevertheless he wrote and recorded one of the '60s most-remembered soul anthems, **Knock On Wood**. Along with Sam & Dave's(▶) **Hold On I'm Coming** it became part of the repertoire of virtually every amateur band aspiring to play soul music, eventually achieving cliché status. **Knock On Wood** was a hit on both sides of the Atlantic in 1967, and Floyd was able to follow it up with two more minor hits in the same year, **Raise Your Hand** and **Things Get Better**. Despite releasing a good many sides over the course of the next few years, including several with Mavis Staples(▶), he never regained major hit status. Unlike many soul stars he was not able to rely on live work to keep his career buoyant, being a somewhat ungainly stage performer.

He recorded some mediocre disco-orientated material for Malaco in the mid-'70s and is still recording but it's best to look out for the Stax greatest hits collection listed below.

Recordings:
Rare Stamps (Stax)

Foundations

Writer/producer Tony Macauley got his run of big hits off to a good start in 1967 when he came up with the million-selling **Baby Now That I've Found You** for the multi-racial British pop/soul band Foundations.

Build Me Up Buttercup gave the eight-piece aggregation a second million-seller the following year but, when lead singer Clem Curtis was replaced by Joey Young soon after, their career foundered. They broke up in 1970, though a group containing some of the original members emerged to re-

Below: Better looking half of Inez & Charlie Foxx team!

work the name for several years.

Recordings:
Greatest Hits (—/Golden Hour)

Inez & Charlie Foxx

From Greensboro, North Carolina, come brother-and-sister duo Inez and Charlie Foxx, he a keen basketball player and she a skilled dressmaker before the call of music came to the fore. Inez, born September 9, 1942, began singing gospel with the Gospel Tide Chorus before taking the solo plunge in New York around 1959, while Charlie, born October 23, 1939, developed talents as a songwriter and record producer.

In 1962 the duo were signed by Juggy Murray's Sue label, and early 1963 saw the release of their debut **Mockingbird** on the Symbol subsidiary, an appealingly rhythmic, if basic, adaptation of a nursery rhyme, with Inez' soaring soulful voice supported by Charlie's baritone responses. The disc was a top 10 smash, and follow-ups like **Ask Me** and **Hurt By Love** sold well, but the company soon folded and the Foxx team moved to Musicor Records, bowing in with **No Stranger To Love**.

The company launched an R&B outlet, Dynamo, whereon the soulful **I Stand Accused** and insistent **Count The Days** scored. Their dynamic stage act pivoted on a wailing delivery of **Accused**, culminating in Charlie walking offstage cradling his sister in his outstretched arms, still delivering her impassioned lyrical plea.

While Charlie continued as a producer, Inez signed solo with Stax in 1969, and was last heard on a fine album for Stax subsidiary Volt, **Inez Foxx At Memphis**.

Recordings:
Mockingbird (Sue/UA)
Greatest Hits (Musicor/Pye Int)
At Memphis (Inez Foxx solo)
  Volt/—)

Below: Aretha Franklin, truly the 'Queen Of Soul'. Her power and phrasing have influenced two decades of black music.

Aretha Franklin

Aretha Franklin's explosive vocal delivery and ability to freeze a single word or phrase into an emotional outcry for love or liberation, has made this lady the leader of the pack for more than 20 years. Born on March 25, 1942, in Memphis, Tennessee, Aretha remembers hearing music from her earliest days. 'We were always singing', she recollects.

Aretha's father was an accomplished preacher, whose sermons have been recorded on over 70 albums released on the Chess label. As Pastor of the New Bethel Church in Detroit, he led the church choir. When he first noticed his daughter's extraordinary voice, he promoted the diminutive Aretha to soloist, and she soon became something of a local celebrity, despite the glut of gospel talent in the area.

Acknowledging her ambition to sing and play the piano professionally, and with a solid musical family tradition behind her—legendary gospel singer Clara Ward was her aunt—Aretha went out on the road with her father, and began recording for the Detroit label JVP.

The JVP sessions were very productive, with Aretha's prodigious ability flourishing in these new surroundings. Family friend Sam Cooke(▶) encouraged Aretha to turn to the world of secular music, and she recorded a

Lady Soul. Courtesy Atlantic Records.

Aretha. Courtesy Arista Records.

series of demos under the guidance of jazz pianist Teddy Wilson's bassist Major Holly. Holly's endeavours in New York brought Aretha into contact with Columbia Records A&R supremo John Hammond, who duly signed her to the label in 1960. 'She was the best natural singer I'd heard since Billie Holiday', comments Hammond.

Aretha, her Columbia debut, was released in 1961, with Hammond producing, but the uneasy mixture of R&B, jazz and standards was something of a disappointment, despite reasonable sales. On reflection, the move to a different environment and the choice of unfamiliar material may have subdued the natural exuberance in Aretha's approach. After all, she had shown nothing but fire in her gospel work. Her second Hammond-produced album was **The Electrifying Aretha Franklin,** with Aretha again struggling in uncharted waters, although she did see chart action with **I Surrender Dear** and **Rock-A-Bye Your Baby With A Dixie Melody,** the choice of which sums up this whole uneasy musical episode.

Aretha's career was now being guided by Ted White, whom she had married in Detroit, and he became a major influence in her music during their time together. White's vision of Aretha as a jazz/pop singer à la Nancy Wilson(▶) added to the confusion in these formative days of her career. With production taken over by Bob Mersey in 1962, Aretha cut three albums under his supervision, the best of which, **The Tender, Moving, Swinging, Aretha Franklin,** enjoyed some success.

Laughing (1962) and **Unforgettable — Tribute To Dinah Washington** (1964) were the other Mersey-produced collections, although Aretha also worked with Bobby Scott, Bob Johnston and Clyde Otis. Otis, in fact, came closest to capturing the real Aretha Franklin during her time with Columbia — he had been hired because of his work with Brook Benton(▶), although he took a retrograde step with the jazzy **Yeah** set (1965).

Aretha's last release with Columbia was the **Soul Sister** album in 1965, and White signed her to Atlantic Records(▶) the following year. With veteran Atlantic producer Jerry Wexler anxious to work with the young lady he described as 'the best black singer around', they began recording together early in 1967 at Muscle Shoals(▶), Alabama, and cut **I Never Loved A Man (The Way I Love You),** and **Do Right Woman — Do Right Man.**

Wexler had immediately captured the essence of Aretha Franklin, the soul singer, as her unbridled power was let loose on a series of mainstream R&B songs. Ronnie Shannon's **I Never Loved A Man . . .** was certified gold shortly after release, and the resulting album (finished in New York) followed its seven-inch namesake in the gold department.

By the summer of '67, Aretha had become the biggest female star on

Above: Aretha swings through her classic singles during a 1968 tour of Europe. She left audiences emotionally exhausted.

the pop and R&B charts with three more million-sellers, **Respect, Baby I Love You** and **Chain Of Fools.** She won the NATRA poll as Singer Of The Year, and collected a host of trade paper honours as Female Singer Of The Year for both singles and albums. Her second Atlantic LP, **Aretha Arrives,** was also a million-seller.

With a recording pattern established, Wexler employed a mixture of contemporary writers for Aretha's albums, although her own songs (in collaboration with Ted White) were used to good effect. The culmination of this formula was the **Lady Soul** album, arguably the all-time soul classic recording.

Lady Soul included Otis Redding's(▶) **Respect,** Ray Charles'(▶) **Come Back Baby,** Don Covay's(▶) **Chain Of Fools, Ain't No Way** by sister Carolyn Franklin(▶) and Ted White and **Since You've Been Gone (Sweet Sweet Baby),** her and White's own contribution. With the pulsating NY Atlantic Studios' rhythm section supplying the foundation, Aretha added her percussive piano and scorching vocals to as fine a set of soul works as you will hear. The appearance of Eric Clapton on **Good To Me As I Am To You** provided this master guitarist with one of his finest moments. **Respect** earned Aretha her first two Grammy awards, as R&B Singer Of The Year and for Best R&B Recording.

Aretha's first major tour of Europe was in 1968, which did much to push **Think** (a Franklin/White composition) into various European top 10s; she had scored little success there with singles before then, although **Respect** had made the UK top 20 in the summer of '67. A live album, **Aretha In Paris,** recorded during this jaunt, was her fourth Atlantic release, preceding the excellent **Aretha Now,** which contained **Prayer** and **Think.**

This period, however, was beset with personal problems for Aretha, not least the break up of her marriage to White, and she stumbled through 1969 with just one major hit **See-Saw** (by Don Covay and Steve Cropper), and a neglected, but underrated album, **Soul '69,** which may have suffered through the inclusion of **Elusive Butterfly** and **Gentle On My Mind.**

After 15 months of reflection, Aretha returned to recording at the Criteria Studios in Miami, with **Call Me** restoring her to the singles' chart in 1970. The resulting album from these Florida tracks, and subsequent New York sessions, was **This Girl's In Love With You,** an LP which has been the cause of much critical disagreement over the years. Many felt that Aretha had lost her earlier aggression, which Wexler put down to personal problems. 'She was just coming out of her divorce with Ted White. It was a miserable time for her', he said.

However, she had still performed superbly on a majority of the cuts, particularly the semi-autobiographical **Son Of A Preacher Man,** and the two Lennon/McCartney classics, **Let It Be** and **Eleanor Rigby,** both recorded to 'widen' Aretha's appeal. Although Wexler felt that **The Weight** was a mistake, which lyrically it may have been, it nonetheless featured some superb guitar work by Duane Allman(▶).

During 1970, Aretha toured Europe again, and began work on the **Spirit In The Dark** album (titled **Don't Play That Song** in the UK). With her personal life on the up-and-up (she was soon to give birth to a son, Kecalf), and a reversion to out and out R&B material, Aretha let loose once more. Says Wexler: 'We went back to southern players, the Dixie Flyers, a Memphis band we had in Miami at the time, and then there was the Muscle Shoals rhythm section. I feel that this album relates directly to **Lady Soul.'**

Below: Yet another change of image for Aretha, who Jerry Wexler called 'the best black singer around'.

Both the title track and **Don't Play That Song** were best-selling singles, with Wexler successfully continuing his collaboration with co-producer Tom Dowd and arranger Arif Mardin. At the end of 1970, Wexler committed the cardinal sin of involving Aretha in more rock-orientated material, and cut Elton John's **Border Song.** 'I fell into the same trap twice', Wexler observed later, 'Once was with **The Weight,** and you're not supposed to repeat your mistakes—but I did. What was wrong with the song was that black audiences didn't know what the hell the lyric was all about.'

Amends were soon made, however, as the follow-up, **You're All I Need To Get By** (by Ashford/Simpson(▶)), quickly charted, and then came four consecutive US gold singles, **Bridge Over Troubled Water, Spanish Harlem, Rock Steady** and **Day Dreaming,** although only **Spanish Harlem** scored in the UK. Aretha's albums kept up the pace as well, with **Live At Fillmore West, Young Gifted And Black** and **Amazing Grace** all earning American gold discs.

The **Fillmore** set, Aretha's second concert recording, was the cause of some initial trepidation from Wexler, who was unsure what the reaction to an R&B artist would be in San Francisco's premier rock venue. His fears were unfounded though, as Aretha quickly conquered the audience, turning in a particularly memorable performance, and a classic duet with Ray Charles. Wexler remembered the occasion: 'I'm particularly pleased, always was, with the sound we got on that album. The rhythm on that recording is so clear. One reason that this thing was so great was because she was using King Curtis(▶) and his musicians as her road band.'

Young Gifted And Black was cut in Miami and New York and featured some of Aretha's previous singles, without being particularly notable. **Amazing Grace,** however, was another kettle of fish, returning Aretha to the gospel arena of the New Temple Missionary Baptist Church of Los Angeles, in partnership with the Reverend James Cleveland and his Southern California Community Choir.

On home territory once again, Aretha showed herself to be a musical evangelist of the highest order, as she utilised her commercial know-how on a series of seminal spirituals. In the album's sleeve notes, John Hammond predicted that 'this album will go down in history as both Aretha's finest hour, and the final breakthrough of black gospel music to mass appreciation'.

A change of producer (Quincy Jones(▶)) did not prove fortunate for the 1973 set **Hey Now Hey (The Other Side Of The Sky),** although her sister Carolyn's song (co-penned with Sonny Saunder) **Angel** hit the US top 20. The year was best remembered for Aretha's concert performances at major American venues like the LA Forum, Houston Astrodome and Boston Gardens, and gold single No. 14 **Until You Come Back To Me** by Stevie Wonder(▶), Clarence Paul and Morris Broadnax).

A return to Wexler/Dowd/Mardin produced **Let Me In Your Life** (1974), with Aretha more involved in the studio work, as she had been for **Hey Now Hey,** and **I'm In Love** followed **Until You Come Back To Me** into the US top 20. But after her second album release in 1974, **With Everything I Feel In Me,** Aretha's career seemed to flounder. She remained busy with TV appearances and live dates, and even picked up an honorary Doctor of Law degree from the Bethune-Cookman College in Dayton, Ohio, but the recording magic was fast disappearing.

Aretha's final major '70s LP was **You** (1975), which utilised the writing talents of Chuck Jackson (the erstwhile partner of Marvin Yancey, not the singer who recorded for Wand, Motown and All Platinum), Ronnie Shannon, sister Carolyn, Frederick Knight(▶) and Van McCoy(▶). Her work from the Curtis Mayfield(▶)-produced movie score **Sparkle** to her final Atlantic album **La Diva** is best forgotten, despite the recruitment of Van McCoy (**La Diva,** 1979), Lamond Dozier(▶) (**Sweet Passion,** 1977) and Mayfield again (**Almighty Fire,** 1979) as producers.

Life away from recording also proved turbulent as Aretha battled against continual weight problems, hospitalisation, and the near-fatal shooting of her father during a robbery at his home. It was evident that a change was coming and a move to a new record company inevitable.

In 1980, Aretha signed with Arista Records, and renewed her relationship with Arif Mardin, who part-produced **Aretha** (with Chuck Jackson) as her debut for the label. The clever mix of contemporary and classic material returned Aretha to the charts, first with the Doobie Brothers' **What A Fool Believes** and then the Otis Redding standard **Can't Turn You Loose.**

Her 1981 album, **Love All The Hurt Away,** also produced by Mardin, contained a rip-roaring version of the Sam and Dave soul masterpiece **Hold On I'm Coming** (for which she received a Grammy award), and a duet with George Benson(▶) on the title track. The use of the session musicians who make up the band Toto (former backing outfit for Boz Scaggs) seemed to move Aretha to a performance not heard since the mid-70s. Jerry Wexler is in no doubt as to her standing in the music business: 'Aretha is as good now as she's ever been', he says, 'She's probably even better. To my mind, Aretha is the greatest gospel singer alive. As a soul artist, no one can touch her.'

Recording note: Aretha's early work with Columbia was re-packaged as **The Great Aretha Franklin – The First Twelve Sides** in 1973, while **I Never Loved A Man The Way I Love You** and **Aretha Arrives** are now available as a double album set: **2 Originals Of Aretha Franklin.** Sadly, **Lady Soul** and much of her earlier work is now out of print. The JVP recordings are available in the States on the Checker label.

Recordings:
Songs Of Faith (Checker/—)
The Great Aretha Franklin (Columbia/Embassy)
All Time Greatest Hits (Columbia/—)
I Never Loved A Man The Way I Loved You (Atlantic/—)
2 Originals Of Aretha Franklin (—/Atlantic)
Lady Soul (Atlantic)
Aretha Now (Atlantic)
Aretha In Paris (Atlantic)
Soul '69 (Atlantic)
This Girl's In Love With You (Atlantic)
Spirit In The Dark (Atlantic)

Above: Marvin Gaye, one third of Motown's superstar triumverate with Smokey Robinson and Stevie Wonder, was a former session musician with a multi-instrument talent.

Live At Fillmore West (Atlantic)
Young Gifted And Black (Atlantic)
Amazing Grace (Atlantic)
Hey Now Hey (Atlantic)
Let Me In Your Life (Atlantic)
You (Atlantic)
Aretha (Arista)
Love All The Hurt Away (Arista)
Collections:
Aretha's Gold (Atlantic)
Aretha's Greatest Hits (Atlantic)
Best Of Aretha Franklin (Atlantic)
Ten Years Of Gold (Atlantic)

Carolyn Franklin

Youngest of three famous singing daughters of the Rev. C.L. Franklin (Aretha(▶) and Erma(▶) are the others), Carolyn Franklin was born in Memphis, Tennessee, in 1944. She grew up against a background of Baptist church gospel singing and went on the road for five years as one of sister Aretha's back-up singers, before launching her own recording career with RCA. Besides writing several songs for Aretha, including the hit **Baby Baby Baby,** she wrote sister Erma's hit **Don't Wait Too Long** as well as many of Erma's vocal arrangements.

Recordings:
This Is Carolyn (RCA)

Erma Franklin

Though totally overshadowed by the popular success of elder sister Aretha(▶), Erma Franklin at times got very close to her in terms of artistry, especially on the spine-tingling Bert Berns/Jerry Ragavoy classic **Piece Of My Heart.**

Along with Aretha, and their younger sister Carolyn(▶), Erma grew up in a musical background, singing in their father's choir before branching out into secular music.

Erma's best work, including a great version of Jimmy Reed's **Big Boss Man** and **Don't Catch The Dog's Bone** (written and also recorded by Carolyn), was cut for the New York-based Shout label. She has also recorded for Epic and MCA.

Recordings:
Soul Sister (MCA)

Bobby Freeman

Starting out with the Romancers on Dootone at the age of 14, singer/pianist Bobby Freeman (born San Francisco, June 13, 1940) wrote **Do You Wanna Dance** in 1958 and took it to US No.5 on Josie. He also hit with **Betty Lou Got A New Pair Of Shoes, Shame On You Miss Johnson** also on Josie and **Shimmy Shimmy** on King. The frenetic Sly Stone(▶) produced **C'Mon And Swim** in 1964, which was a hit on Autumn.

A talented dancer, Freeman had a classy stage act with his firebrand mix of rock 'n' roll, R&B and soul. One of his finest recordings, though, was the clever rocking soul ballad **Heartbreaker.**

Recordings:
Get In The Swim With . . .
(Josie/—)
The Lovable Style Of (King/—)

Marvin Gaye

Marvin Pentz Gaye Jr, the son of a minister, was born in Washington DC on April 2, 1938. His professional career, both as a singer and—less famously now—as an instrumentalist, is as old as the pioneering Motown record label with which his name is indelibly associated. Indeed, his very first album, **The Soulful Moods of Marvin Gaye,** was Motown's(▶) second album release.

Over the years, Gaye evolved, in the company of label-mates Smokey Robinson(▶) and Stevie Wonder(▶), to form a triumvirate who were among the half-dozen most successful black solo artists in contemporary music.

With the encouragement of his father, Gaye had begun vocalising in church at a very early age. By the time he was five, he was singing in a Kentucky church convention. Three years later he was singing spiritual duets with his brother Frankie, and started to take an interest in learning instruments, beginning on the most readily available, his father's church organ, from which he graduated to piano, guitar and, eventually, his pet love, drums.

By the time he was old enough to hang around on street corners, Gaye was singing tenor in kerbside doo-wop groups, and that was how he encountered his first professional outfit, the Rainbows. The group was Washington's premier vocal outfit of the day and boasted Don Covay(▶) and Billy Stewart(▶) among its line-up. Gaye would regularly fill in for absent group members.

At the end of his school career, Gaye yielded to his father's concern over his future and joined the Air Force. He loathed it, however ,and in 1957 was given an honourable discharge. Returning to Washington, Gaye formed his own group, the Marquees, with a friend, Reese Taylor, and two singers, remaindered from the now disbanded Rainbows. Under the auspices of Bo Diddley(▶), the Marquees recorded **Wyatt Earp** on the OKeh label.

Meanwhile the Moonglows(▶), one of the most popular vocal groups of the day, had split up and their leader, Harvey Fuqua, came to Washington looking for the components of a new Moonglows group. He heard the Marquees singing **The Ten Commandments of Love** and was impressed enough to recruit them, en bloc, to become the new Moonglows.

The new Moonglows retained the former group's recording contract with the legendary Chicago label, Chess(▶), for whom they recorded **12 Months of the Year** and **Unemployment** during 1959. Neither was successful. The Moonglows struggled on, but without Marvin, who moved to Detroit with Fuqua, seeking work.

Fuqua signed to Anna records, owned by Motown president Berry Gordy's sister, Gwen. The two were married, while younger sister Anna, after whom the label had been named, began to be seen around with Gaye. They too were married, in 1961, and when Gwen decided to join label forces with her brother Berry, Gaye found himself with a Motown recording contract.

Above: The young Marvin Gaye, who became a Motown veteran.

Early Years. Courtesy Tamla Motown Records.

In his first official capacity at Motown, Gaye was a session drummer and back-up vocalist, although, as two Motown veterans, Smokey Robinson(▶) and Martha Reeves(▶) (who was an A&R secretary at the time) recall, he was already a multi-instrumentalist and would play just about anything on any session he was offered. In fact, he became drummer for Robinson's group the Miracles(▶) and played on their live performances for two years. He also sang back-ups for the Marvelettes(▶), and in one way or the other was associated with most of the early Tamla Motown singles.

In 1961, Gaye made his first tentative bid for solo stardom with **Let Your Conscience Be Your Guide,** and his first album **The Soulful Moods Of Marvin Gaye,** hit the streets. Two further singles, **Sandman** in January 1962, and **Soldier's Plea,** released a year after his solo debut in May 1962, failed to make any impact. Gaye was unhappy about their failure and so, in mid-1962, Gordy took a greater personal interest in Gaye's recordings. He matched him with producer Mickey Stevenson(▶) and the formula was an instant success: **Stubborn Kind of Fellow** (co-written by Gaye, Stevenson and George Gordy, and featuring his former admirer, Martha Reeves with the Vandellas(▶) on backing vocals) became a massive R&B hit and crossed-over into the Billboard national top 40.

With that breakthrough, the pattern for Gaye's continued success through the rest of the '60s was well and truly established. He stayed under the production aegis of Stevenson for follow-ups **Hitch Hike** and **Pride And Joy,** and was in turn produced by Berry Gordy himself and Holland/Dozier/Holland(▶).

Gaye continued to score solo hits with **Can I Get A Witness** and **You're A Wonderful One** until, in May 1964, he released a brace of singles with Mary Wells(▶), the first of four female vocalists with whom he has been successfully teamed over the years.

By now Gaye had released four solo albums, but his pairing with Mary Wells—at that time just about the biggest artist at Motown—heralded the beginning of a parallel career as a duo, and aside from the two singles, they recorded a successful album **Together.**

Two solo singles later, Gaye found himself back in the studio with another Motown lady, Kim Weston(▶), with whom he recorded the moderately successful **What Good Am I Without You,** in 1964. The full fruits of that partnership came three years later with the barnstorming album and single **It Takes Two.** Meanwhile, Gaye released a string of solo hit singles, including his first two R&B chart No. 1s, **I'll Be Doggone** and **Ain't That Peculiar,** in 1965.

Vastly encouraged by the success of the Gaye/Weston album and single, Motown instituted what was to become Gaye's most memorable pairing, with the late Tammi Terrell(▶). A three-year relationship of perfect professional empathy and great personal friendship was launched with the duet **Ain't No Mountain High Enough,** in mid-1967. Virtually forsaking his solo career, Gaye recorded a blaze of chart hits with Terrell, including **Your Precious Love, Ain't Nothing Like The Real Thing** and **You're All I Need To Get By.**

Even after Gaye's solo international breakthrough with **I Heard It Through The Grapevine,** in 1968, and **Too Busy Thinking About My Baby,** the two continued recording together, scoring with **What You Gave Me** and **The Onion Song.** The partnership was tragically sundered with Tammi's sudden death in 1970, at the age of 24, and the stricken Gaye immured himself, away out of the public view. He was rarely seen in the studio and made no stage appearances at all.

However, in early 1971, he launched phase two of his remarkable career, with the release of the superlative **What's Going On** album. It was an entire conceptual breakthrough and at once elevated him from the rank of masterful pop singer, to master producer/composer and stinging social commentator. Even taken out of the darkly brooding context of the album, this material marked the emergence of Gaye as a creative force to fuel other major black artists, attracting cover versions from Diana Ross(▶) (**Save The Children**), Aretha Franklin(▶) (**Wholly Holy**), Gil Scott-Heron(▶) (**Inner City Blues**), Quincy Jones(▶) and the late Roland Kirk(▶) (**What's Going On**).

Gaye's next major project was to compose a dramatic score for the film *Trouble Man,* one of an avalanche of 'blaxploitation' movies which followed in the wake of *Shaft.* The soundtrack was released in February 1973.

Later that year, Gaye turned his attention away from the perpetually troubled urban ghettos, but maintained the whole-album concept with the release of the sensual **Let's Get It On,** the sleeve inscribed with T.S. Eliot's nugget: 'Birth, copulation and death, that's all the facts, when you get down to brass tacks'. But, as one English review pointed out, Gaye seemed to have dispensed with the birth and death, the better to concentrate on copulation!

The album was a phenomenal success. Within weeks of its release, while sales were still gathering momentum, the album **Diana and Marvin** was released, Ms Ross becoming the fourth and latest of Gaye's female singing partners.

Below: Now exiled in Belgium, Gaye's plans are uncertain.

Above: Gaye's live appearances, although sporadic, have always been well received.

Above: Dobie Gray captured the imagination of a generation with his '60s recording of The In Crowd.

In 1974, at Oakland Coliseum, California, Gaye fronted a 34-piece orchestra, back-up singers and rhythm section for his first stage appearance in six years. The results were issued on **Marvin Gaye Live**, under three sub-headings: 'The Beginning', including **Inner City Blues** and **Trouble Man**, 'Fossil Medley', comprising several of Marvin's early pop hits, and 'Now', comprising **Let's Get It On** and **What's Going On.**

Gaye's next studio album, in 1976, plied the sensuous image of **Let's Get It On,** although not quite so successfully, and again there was another comparatively lengthy interval, filled with live and compilation recordings, before Gaye released another studio set, in 1979. Perhaps the reason for the delay was partly explained on the record itself: **Here My Dear** was an extraordinarily heartfelt collation of Gaye's thoughts, feelings and observations concerning the break-up of his second marriage. There was even a story that the royalties from the album were earmarked for Gaye's alimony payments. He had possibly over-estimated the capacity of his established audience for the kind of morbid voyeurism needed to fully appreciate the album's contents, but Gaye's music, as ever, was coming directly from the soul.

Gaye subjected his fans to another nervous wait, before holding out cause for hope with the announcement, in late 1980, of another studio album, to be titled **In Our Lifetime.** The nail-biting was over in early 1981, and Gaye was back in his self-assured role with a subtly crafted and sensuously strutting collection.

Behind the scenes, however, Gaye was having both personal and business problems. His wife's affair with Teddy Pendergrass—who had been, he thought, one of his best friends—had left a deep scar. Troubles with the Internal Revenue Service over the tax dues led to the seizure of his recording studio and he fled to Hawaii, setting up home in a converted bread delivery van!

A UK tour produced nightmares for the promoters. By now an unpredictable, almost unmanageable artist, Gaye swung from highs—giving some impressive performances—to lows. He blew TV dates and turned up hours too late for a scheduled show in front of HRH Princess Margaret.

Motown's Berry Gordy bailed Gaye out of some of his troubles but eventually despaired. Gaye moved home to Belgium and then terminated his long association with Motown. He has since been recording on the Continent and his fans await the results with a mixture of eager anticipation and trepidation.

Recordings:
What's Going On (Motown)
Let's Get It On (Motown)
Trouble Man (Motown)
Anthology (Motown)
Live (Motown)
Best Of Marvin Gaye (Motown)
Here My Dear (Motown)
In Our Lifetime (Motown)

Goldwax Records

Though never as internationally successful as Stax—its major rival in Memphis—the Goldwax label, founded in 1965 by Quinton Claunch and Rudolph 'Doc' Russell, released many memorable recordings (mostly recorded in nearby Muscle Shoals, Alabama). James Carr(▶) came close to rivalling Otis Redding(▶) when he cut the soulful **You're Pouring Water On A Drowning Man,** while Spencer Wiggins and Mighty Sam made a succession of classy records for the label.

Recordings:
Cellar Full Of Soul Vols 1 & 2 (—/Bell)

Dobie Gray

Despite his long-standing success in the US, Dobie Gray has so far been unable to crack it in Britain, being blighted with a run of 'turntable hits', which have won him considerable critical acclaim but scant commercial reward. Few artists have, in artistic terms, so cleverly blended black and country music as Gray, but he first came to attention through straight R&B, hitting the US Hot 100 in 1963 with **Look At Me** (Cor Dak), then following through two years later with **The In Crowd** (Charger), a big favourite among UK mod audiences at the time and later an in-demand 'Northern Soul' item among collectors.

Born in 1943 in Brookshire, Texas, Gray had moved to Los Angeles to make his records, but it was on reaching Nashville eight years later that he really found his musical niche, thanks to the Mentor Williams' composition **Drift Away.** The Gray-Williams' combination was a winner and they gave MCA a string of superb records which leaned towards the swamp-rock idiom whenever the tempo went up, and rated as country/soul masterpieces on the ballad side. Gray's trio of MCA albums, **Drift Away, Loving Arms** and **Hey Dixie** and his Troy Seals-produced Capricorn album **New Ray Of Sunshine** gave him three great years.

In 1979 he bounced back again with the disco favourite **You Can Do It** (Infinity) but, again, sales failed to match the exposure and the heavily financed label, which had determined to make Gray a superstar, failed to live up to expectations and quickly folded.

Recordings:
Drift Away (MCA)
Loving Arms (MCA)

R. B. Greaves

A halfbreed black/American Indian, Ronald Bertram Aloysius 'R.B.' Greaves was the son of an Air Force captain and born on a US air base near Georgetown, British Guyana, on November 28, 1944. Raised on a Seminole reservation in California, he began songwriting at the age of 12.

In 1963 he travelled to England to sing in clubs as Sonny Childe (recording for Polydor with his group the TNTs) and trade on being a nephew of Sam Cooke(▶). Six years later he took a song titled

Take A Letter Maria to Atlantic(▶) president Ahmet Ertegun and the resultant record sold four million copies. He followed this up by hit versions of **Always Something There To Remind Me, Fire And Rain** and **Whiter Shade Of Pale.**

In 1973 he recorded for Ember but his career was already fading.

Recordings:
To Be Cont'd (as Sonny Childe) (—/Polydor)
R. B. Greaves (Atco)

Willie 'Little Beaver' Hale

Willie Hale has enjoyed parallel careers—as a prolific Miami-based session guitarist, and as a singer recording in his own right for TK's(▶) Cat label.

Born in Forrest City, Arkansas, August 15, 1945, he was heavily influenced by blues' musicians passing through his hometown and, at 13, he started playing guitar, working with saxophonist Arthur Pryor in Clifton Walker's band, the Savoys. It was Pryor, in fact, who dubbed Hale 'Little Beaver', on account of his two big front teeth, which were prominent as a child.

In 1962, Hale moved to Mississippi and joined the road band of Birdlegs and Pauline who had just scored with the soul classic **Spring.**

By 1964 his base had switched to Miami where he played local gigs and record sessions (including backing Big Maybelle(▶) on several songs).

Under the title Frank Williams and the Rocketeers, featuring Little Beaver, his own first releases were on Phil-L.A. Of Soul, a tiny label which released some real gems by a range of artists in its short lifespell.

When the band broke up, Hale was taken to Cat by producer Willie Clarke and played the guitar parts on Betty Wright's(▶) **Clean Up Woman** smash before scoring in his own right with the blues ballad **Joey**, title cut from his first album (1972). The 11-min 26-sec long blues laced soul ballad **Katie Pearl** was lifted from the same album and also charted.

The 1974 hit **Party Down** took Hale into a straight disco-soul groove and subsequent albums and singles have found him offering an enjoyable blend of music which has ranged from almost downhome blues and soul dancers, right through to lushly orchestrated instrumentals.

A classy singer and inventive guitarist (his playing shows strong jazz influences), Hale has written material for Latimore(▶), Timmy Thomas(▶) and Gwen McCrae(▶) and played on sessions for those artists and others, including Aretha Franklin(▶), Clarence Reid and rock stars Pacific Gas and Electric Co and Al Kooper.

Recordings:
Joey (Cat/President)
Party Down (Cat/President)
Black Rhapsody (Cat/—)
When Was The Last Time (Cat/—)

Betty Harris

Betty Harris's reputation far outshines her commercial success, but to many addicts of the deep-soul idiom she remains one of the greatest singers ever to have graced

the soul charts. It was the Jubilee label which first unearthed her talents, in 1963, with a superb version of Solomon Burke's(▶) **Cry To Me**, produced by Bert Berns.

Based in New Orleans, she soon beat a track to Allen Toussaint(▶) and Marshall Sehorn's Sansu Enterprises, and under their tutelage cut some beautiful ballads, as well as a version of Lee Dorsey's(▶) up-tempo **Ride Your Pony.** Her memorable duets with Dorsey, who was also a Sansu artist, included **Love Lots Of Lovin'** and **Take Good Care Of Our Love.**

From Sansu she moved to SSS International with less success, though **There's A Break In The Road** rates as one of her best records.

Recordings:
Soul Perfection (—/Action)

Eddie Harris

Abrasive tenor player Harris (born in Chicago in 1936) has recorded more than 40 albums, his best work being available on the Atlantic label. He first came to attention with his version of **Exodus** in 1960, for the Liberty company, before pioneering electronic reed effects on his 1967 set, **The Tender Storm.**

Further electrical adventures resulted in his masterwork to date, **The Electrifying Eddie Harris** (1968), although his collaboration with pianist Les McCann on two LPs, **Swiss Movement** and **Second Movement** (recorded at the Montreux Jazz Festival), has considerable merit. His later albums have seen him singing (moderately well), but more for the sake of experimentation than for effect.

Recordings:
The Explosive Eddie Harris (Sunset/—)

Below: Rasping tenor player Eddie Harris is a 40-album veteran.

Oh Happy Day! courtesy Buddah Records.

The Exciting Eddie Harris (Kent/-)
Steps Up (Steeplechase/—)
The Tender Storm (Atlantic)
The Electrifying Eddie Harris (Atlantic)
Swiss Movement (Atco)
Second Movement (Atco)
I Need Some Money (Atlantic)
Best Of (Atco)

Major Harris

Richmond, Virginia-born Major Harris joined the hit-making smooth-soul group the Delfonics(▶) in 1971 and quit two years later to

sign with Atlantic(▶), first as solo then leading his own Boogie Blues Band (Dennis Dozier, lead guitar; Alfred Pollard, keyboard; George Harris, sax; Sylvester Bryant, trumpet; Eric Bodner, violin; Tyrone Hall, trombone; Michael 'Sugar Bear' Foreman, bass; Allison Hobbs, Phyllis Newman, Karen Dempsey, backing vocals) which, despite its name, was in the sophisticated soul bag.

Signed to Philadelphia's WMOT productions, Harris had moderately successful albums issued via Atlantic.

Recordings:
My Way (Atlantic)
Jealousy (Atlantic)
Major Harris And The Boogie Blues Band (Atlantic)

Edwin Hawkins Singers

Early in 1969 an Oakland, California, radio DJ started giving heavy play to a track lifted from an album recorded privately by the North California State Youth Choir and sold at concerts to raise funds. Soon other DJs across the US were picking up on the cut, the Pavilion label signed the choir under a new banner, the Edwin Hawkins Singers, and Buddah stepped in with a national distribution deal.

Titled **Oh Happy Day!**, the record not only stormed the American charts, reaching No. 4, but became the first gospel record to make a major mark in the UK, where it went to No. 2.

Born in Oakland in August 1943, choir director Edwin Hawkins subsequently released several further albums with his choir, but with rapidly diminishing success. Dorothy Morrison, whose wailing lead vocals (matching Aretha Franklin(▶) in intensity) had dominated the hit above the mass choir sound, went on to a mildly successful career as a solo soul singer.

Recordings:
Oh Happy Day! (Buddah)
He's A Friend Of Mine (Buddah)
Children (Get Together) (Buddah)

Jimi Hendrix

Born Johnny Allen Hendrix in Seattle, Washington, on November 27, 1942, his name was changed by his father in 1946 to James Marshall Hendrix. At the age of 16 he spent time in the 101st Airborne Division, meeting Billy Cox (later to play bass in his Band Of Gypsies).

On discharge, Hendrix entered the music business, playing guitar in pick-up bands on various tours, supporting artists including B.B. King(▶), Ike and Tina Turner(▶), Solomon Burke(▶), Jackie Wilson(▶), Tommy Tucker(▶), Sam Cooke(▶), Little Richard(▶) and Wilson Pickett(▶). Settling in New York, he worked with the Isley Brothers(▶) and King Curtis(▶) on the club circuit.

The then girlfriend of Rolling Stones' Keith Richard persuaded Animals' bass player Chas Chandler to check out 'an amazing guitarist playing in Curtis Knight's band'. Recognising Hendrix's latent genius, Chandler sold his own guitars to buy equipment and eventually brought Hendrix to Britain.

Chandler recalls sharing a flat with Hendrix: 'He would lock himself in the toilet for seven or eight hours at a stretch practising new licks. If he wasn't playing guitar himself, he wanted to be out all the time checking other acts. We saw some pretty dire guitarists but he told me he could always learn something new, even from the worst of players.'

Once in London, Hendrix' showmanship and flashy playing (using such Johnny 'Guitar' Watson(▶)/T. Bone Walker gimmicks as playing with his teeth and with the guitar behind or above his head) made him the sensation of the club circuits, drawing such luminaries as Pete Townsend, Eric Clapton and the Beatles to his gigs and landing him a Polydor recording contract.

In 1967, a successful European tour, hit singles with **Hey Joe** and **Purple Haze** and the **Are You Experienced?** album turned Hendrix into a superstar, aided by his black hippy-freak image. 54 dates in 47 days, gold awards for the **Axis Bold As Love** and **Electric Ladyland** albums and cult status made 1968 his zenith year.

Amid personal and business wrangles, drug problems and trouble with the authorities, the Jimi Hendrix Experience (Noel Redding, bass, Mitch Mitchell, drums) broke up in early '69. The all-black Band Of Gypsies (Billy Cox, bass, Buddy Miles(▶), drums) followed soon after but was short-lived, Hendrix walking out on an audience of 19,000 people in the middle of the second number at a gig in Madison Square Garden, New York, in January 1970.

Later that year, he played an undistinguished set at the Isle of Wight Festival. It was to be his final major concert.

On September 18, he was found dead in his London flat, having suffocated on his own vomit. Drink and drug abuse had deprived rock 'n' roll of a genius.

Recordings:
Are You Experienced? (Polydor)
Axis Bold As Love (Polydor)
Electric Ladyland (Polydor)
Band Of Gypsies (Polydor)

Right: Genius Jimi Hendrix.

Clarence 'Frogman' Henry

The novelty song **Ain't Got No Home**, replete with bull-frog impressions, hurtled Clarence Henry to international stardom in 1957, then, four years later, he enjoyed an even bigger success with the gently rocking Bobby Charles' composition **But I Do**, produced by Allen Toussaint(▶) and Paul Gayten.

Henry (born Algiers, New Orleans, March 19, 1937) had a few minor hits afterwards but soon settled back into a less spectacular though comfortable niche, singing his attractive, if dated, brand of R&B in the clubs and bars of his native city, recording an album in 1979, **New Recordings**.

Recordings:
Alive And Well (—/Pye)
New Recordings (CFH)
Clarence 'Frogman' Henry (Roulette/—)

Hi Records

Founded by the late Joe Cuoghi, Memphis-based Hi Records was eventually run by its mainstay artist, trumpeter Willie Mitchell(▶). Hi established its name via R&B/country instrumentals by white artists Ace Cannon and Bill Black (Elvis's erstwhile bassist). On Black's death, Mitchell's band started recording as the Bill Black Combo (with increasingly black-sounding output) as well as the Willie Mitchell Combo.

In later years the advent of Al Green(▶), Otis Clay, Syl Johnson(▶) Ann Peebles(▶) and her husband Don Bryant took Hi into vocal music, with Mitchell producing and his band providing the backings. The Hi label is now part of Cream Records.

Recordings:
River Town Blues (Hi/London)

Z.Z. Hill

Arzel Hill—Z.Z to his fans—was

Hendrix's Electric Ladyland. Courtesy Polydor.

born in 1940 in Naples, Texas, singing locally before being taken out to Los Angeles by his brother Matt to record **You Were Wrong** (dubbed 'a classic' by the trade paper *Record World*). Signed to Kent Records, Hill cut a string of

Z.Z. Courtesy United Artists Records.

superb blues-tinged R&B/soul records through the '60s, including **You Don't Know Me, If I Could Do It All Over** and **Have Mercy Someone**, before forming his own

Above: R&B's great Z.Z. Hill.

Hill label and logging his biggest hit in 1972 with **Don't Make Me Pay For His Mistakes**, leading to a UA contract.

Hill rates along with Bobby Bland(▶), O.V. Wright(▶), Little Johnny Taylor(▶) and Little Milton(▶)

in the forefront of contemporary R&B vocalists.

Recordings:
A Whole Lot Of Soul (Kent/Action)
The Best Thing That's Happened To Me (United Artists/—)

Justin Hinds And The Dominoes

Justin's first big hit was for Duke Reid in 1964, with the classic **Carry Go Bring Come**. It set a pattern from which Hinds rarely deviated, his expressive country/gospel tenor getting sympathetic support from the two Dominoes, backed by the Treasure Isle house band led by Tommy McCook. Hinds stayed with Reid until 1972 and the combination produced some of the best-ever Jamaican music—both ska(▶) and rock-steady.

In the ska style, **King Samuel, Botheration, Jump Out Of Frying Pan, The Ark, Peace and Love** and **Rub Up Push Up** are all well worth hearing. Rock-steady brought forth further gems, from the transitional **Higher The Monkey Climb, No Good Rudie, Once A Man, Drink Milk**, a new version of **Carry Go Bring Come**, an anguished version of the Rip Chords' **Here I Stand**, right up to the sublime **Save A Bread**. Lyrically Hinds is masterful, utilising the rich Jamaican tradition of proverb and parable to reflect the wide range of issues thrown up by a society in transition from rural to urban life.

From 1972 onwards, Justin was largely inactive, as was his mentor Reid. After Reid's death in 1975, Justin cut two albums for Jack Ruby which were released on Island Records and Mango respectively. A couple of singles, including a buoyant **Dip And Fall Back** and the third re-cut of **Carry Go Bring Come**, were also issued though without much success.

Since 1978, Hinds has recorded for Sonia Pottinger, who had taken over Reid's company after his death and was issuing old and new material on her High Note label. Sides like **What A Weeping, Rig-Ma-Roe Game** and **Wipe Your Weeping Eyes** showed Hinds'

beautiful voice to be still intact.

Largely ignored by the many overseas fans who discovered Jamaican music in the '70s, Hinds has always enjoyed a special following in Jamaica itself. The late Bob Marley(▶) was a long-time fan, as are many others who favour sincerity and originality over trendiness and gimmickry.

Recordings:
Jezebel (—/Island)
Greatest Hits (Treasure Isle/—)

Holland/Dozier/Holland

Eddie Holland (born Detroit, October 30, 1939) left college to work for Berry Gordy's music publishing company, singing demos and co-writing songs before being launched by Gordy as an artist through a contract with United Artists.

When Gordy decided to set up his own Motown(▶) group of labels, Eddie Holland was one of his first signings and enjoyed a US top-30 hit in 1967 with the beat ballad **Jamie**. His style was very much in the mould of Jackie Wilson(▶), a star with whom Gordy had already enjoyed success and whose demos had been sung by Holland.

Early on, Eddie Holland had introduced his brother Brian (born Detroit, 1941) to Gordy, who trained the youngster in the crafts of writing and production. It was Brian who co-produced the Marvelettes'(▶) smash **Please Mr Postman** with Robert Bateman. When Bateman left the company, Gordy paired up Brian Holland with Lamont Dozier (born Detroit, June 16, 1941), who had been involved with the company from the beginning.

Dozier had made his recording debut at age 15 on Fox Records with the Romeos in 1956, leaving the city and the music business soon after to work in New York. In 1958, he returned to Detroit and was introduced to Gordy by childhood friend Ty Hunter who was recording for Anna, a label run by Gordy's sister Gwen.

Recording under the name Lamont Anthony, Dozier had releases on Anna and Melody before

THE JIMI HENDRIX EXPERIENCE ELECTRIC LADYLAND

being teamed with Brian Holland. With Eddie Holland's own recording career on the wane, the duo became a trio and the writer/production credits 'Holland/Dozier/Holland' became the key to gold for Motown with an astonishingly prolific and consistent run of hits for the Supremes(▶), the Temptations(▶), Marvin Gaye(▶), Martha and the Vandellas(▶), the Isley Brothers(▶) and many other acts signed to the label.

Amid a welter of law suits and much acrimony, Holland/Dozier/Holland left the Motown Corporation in 1968 and set up their own Invictus and Hot Wax labels, which immediately continued the hit pattern through such acts as Chairmen Of The Board(▶) (**Give Me Just A Little More Time**, etc), Freda Payne(▶) (**Band Of Gold**), 100 Proof Aged In Soul (**Somebody's Been Sleeping In My Bed**), white soul band Flaming Ember (**Westbound No. Nine**), Laura Lee(▶) (**Woman's Love Rights**) and Honey Cone (**Want Ads**, the company's first US chart-topper in 1971).

Eddie Holland. Courtesy Motown Records.

Working as a duo, Brian Holland and Lamont Dozier notched hits of their own in 1972-3, but by the end of that year the succession of legal wrangles led to the departure of Dozier to sign a solo contract with ABC (he was introduced to the label by old friends the Four Tops(▶) who had moved there from Motown) and Invictus/Hot Wax came to a rapid end.

Dozier's ensuing run of solo albums have met with enormous critical acclaim if not staggering commercial success.

Recordings:
Eddie Holland: Eddie Holland (Motown)
Lamont Dozier: see under own entry

Brenda Holloway

The impassioned slow ballad **Every Little Bit Hurts** (1964) was one of Motown's(▶) biggest selling records in the early days. More important, it was the first hit for the company to be produced outside Detroit, having been recorded by Brenda Holloway (born Atascadero, California) on the West Coast.

Brenda also scored with **When I'm Gone** and her own composition **You've Made Me So Very Happy**, which was later a big hit for Blood, Sweat and Tears. In the '70s she appeared as a session singer on Joe Cocker records.

Recordings:
Every Little Bit Hurts (Tamla/—)
The Artistry Of Brenda Holloway (—/Tamla Motown)

John Holt

Quitting the Paragons(▶) towards the end of the '60s, having enjoyed phenomenal chart action with Treasure Isle singles **On The Beach, Happy Go Lucky Girl** and **Wear You To The Ball,** Holt continued to work with Paragons' mentor Duke Reid but only on an occasional basis, preferring instead to use a number of different producers to suit the varied nature of his material.

On this basis he prospered with singles **Let's Build Our Dreams,** with Reid, **Close To Me,** with Prince Buster(▶), and **Love I Can Feel,** with Clement Coxsone Dodd. With the issue of his brace of Tony Ashfield-produced albums, **The Further You Look** (1973) and **One Thousand Volts Of Holt** (1974), and his stirring cover version of Kris Kristofferson's **Help Me Make It Through The Night** (1975), he established himself as a consummate reggae star appealing to all ages.

A Love I Can Feel. Courtesy Trojan Records.

The quality and quantity of hits kept flowing with the release of Holt's Channel One recorded album and single, **Up Park Camp,** issued the summer of 1975, the title track a re-run of the Heptones'(▶) **Get In The Groove** rhythm, that stayed in the Jamaican charts for 20 weeks.

Since then he has had more than a dozen albums issued in the UK and in Jamaica. He is continually touring America and Europe, and with such titles as **You're All I Got, Wasted Days And Nights** and his most recent success, **Ghetto Queen,** has dominated the reggae singles' charts.

Recordings:
Roots Of Holt (—/Trojan)
Up Park Camp (Channel One/—)
Everybody's Talkin' (—/Trojan)
Dusty Roads (—/Trojan)

Jimmy Hughes

A discovery of Muscle Shoals'(▶) prime mover Rick Hall, Jimmy Hughes (born Florence, Alabama) started as a gospel singer but soon made a forté of singing about sin. His second record **Steal Away** (leased to Vee-Jay, 1963) about adultery was a big hit, and with Hall switching him to Atlantic(▶) Hughes scored again in 1967 with the compulsive **Neighbour, Neighbour,** in which his role was changed to that of victim.

Eventually joining Stax(▶) he had a class album out on the Volt subsidiary in the early '70s. Always strongly blues influenced, Hughes rates with Syl Johnson(▶) and O.V.

Wright(▶) among the unsung greats of Southern soul.

Recording:
Steal Away (Vee-Jay/—)
Why Not tonight? (Atlantic)
Something Special (Volt)

Tommy Hunt

Born the son of vaudeville entertainers in a carnival tent in Pittsburgh, Tommy Hunt eventually settled in Chicago where he joined a group known as the Echoes, which also included Johnnie Taylor(▶). He then moved on to join the famed Flamingos, appearing on their big hit **I Only Have Eyes For You** and four albums, before leaving four years later and, after a struggle as a solo, landing a contract with Luther Dixon of Wand(▶) Records and moving to New York.

Hunt sang back-up on discs by Dionne Warwick(▶), Dee Dee Warwick(▶), the Shirelles(▶), Theola Kilgore and other, mainly Wand, artists as well as scoring in his own right with **Human** and **I Am A Witness,** but he was overshadowed at Wand by Chuck Jackson(▶) and looked for a new deal. Dixon too had moved on and signed Hunt to Dynamo.

In 1968, Hunt toured the US bases in Germany and two years later decided to settle in Europe. He set up home in Wales, becoming a solid draw on the cabaret circuit, though failing to score with any of his numerous recordings. Memories of Wand days made him a hero on Britain's Northern Soul cult circuit and kept him busy throughout the '70s.

Recordings:
Human (Wand/—)
Live At The Wigan Casino (—/Spark)
A Sign Of The Times (—/Spark)

The Impressions

Sam Gooden and Fred Cash started out in Chatanooga, Tennessee, in a group called the Roosters, with Richard and Arthur Brooks.

Gooden moved to Chicago in 1956, Cash followed early in 1958 and they teamed with Jerry Butler(▶) and a then 14-or-so-year-old Curtis Mayfield(▶) to form a new group, which they called the Impressions. **For Your Precious Love** was a massive 1958 hit but the label credit read 'Jerry Butler And The Impressions' and Butler used the resultant publicity to launch himself into a solo career.

With the Brooks brothers brought North to join the group for a while, the Impressions, with Gooden and Richard Brooks taking lead, recorded without real success for Abner, Bandera and Swirl. Their career seemed to be in the doldrums and Mayfield concentrated on writing and playing guitar for Butler's solo hits with Vee-Jay until, in 1961, the Impressions, now down to a trio with the departure of the Brooks brothers, recorded a debut single in New York for ABC Paramount, **Gypsy Woman,** which gave them a hit (covered in the pop market by Brian Hyland). Two years later, the classic Impressions' era got underway with their biggest hit **It's All Right.**

With Mayfield's relaxed, at times almost whispered, high-pitched lead, some great songs from his pen and inventive Johnny Pate's orchestral arrangements, **You Must Believe Me, I'm So Proud,** the gospel-inspired soul anthem **Amen, Keep On Pushing, People Get Ready** and others, the Impressions challenged the Temptations(▶) as soul music's top male group.

The battle with the Motown(▶) act led to a certain Detroit influence creeping into the Impressions' sound in the late '60s, but after two final ABC hits with **We're A Winner** and **We're Rolling On** they switched to Mayfield's newly formed Curtom label in 1968. Here they found a whole new direction with the black-consciousness songs **This Is My Country, Choice Of Colours** and **Mighty Mighty Spade and Whitey.**

In 1970, Mayfield left the group

Below: The Impressions putting across their soul message.

Above: The consummate reggae star John Holt is continuously on the road with his act.

The Isley Brothers

One of the most successful of all black American acts are the Isley Brothers, whose career spans 25 years and includes countless hit records and label affiliations with several of the major record corporations in the US. Their pop and international success has been inconsistent, but within the parameters of the black American market they are acknowledged superstars. The original three Isleys, the brothers Rudolph, Ronald and O'Kelly, began as gospel vocalists performing with their pianist mother, Sallye Bernice Isley, around their hometown of Cincinnati. This was the period when soul music was just emerging in a synthesis of raucous gospel fervour and the harmonies of doo-wop. Inspired by the example of artists like Ray Charles(▶), Clyde McPhatter(▶) and Jackie Wilson(▶), the three brothers, with their mother's blessing, left Cincinnati to gamble on a secular career in New York.

By 1957 they had secured several performing jobs in important black theatres like the Howard in Washington and Harlem's Apollo. Their first record **An Angel Cried** was released on the tiny Teenage label, but success was still a few years away. In 1958 they signed with the New York-based Gone Records, owned by George Goldner, an engaging entrepreneur who had made a fortune in the Latin-American market before discovering Frankie Lymon(▶); Little Anthony(▶) and a whole slew of teenaged doo-wop groups.

At Gone they released four singles, ranging from doo-wop to straight ahead rock 'n' roll, all to no avail. Despite garnering much acclaim as a live act, record sales still eluded them and in 1959 they signed with RCA. Their initial release again made no impact until RCA A&R heads Hugo and Luigi persuaded the brothers to record their improvised live finale to their interpretation of Jackie Wilson's hit **Lonely Teardrops**. The result,

Below: Ernie Isley, guitarist for his brother's band, added a new dimension to their success with his work on the album 3+3 That Lady.

to concentrate on his new label and a solo career, calling in Leroy Hutson as his replacement (Hutson had been working with Donny Hathaway(▶) and Mayfield in the Mayfield Singers studio outfit). Hutson in turn went solo, in 1972, so Gooden and Cash recruited Reggie Torrian and Ralph Johnson and cut the *Three The Hard Way* movie soundtrack. They scored a hit in 1974 with **Finally Got Myself Together,** written and produced by veteran Ed Townsend, and enjoyed a 1975 British hit with **First Impressions.**

Recordings:
For Your Precious Love (Vee-Jay/—)
It's All Right (ABC Paramount/—)
Keep On Pushing
  (ABC Paramount/—)
Big 16 Vols 1 & 2 (—/Stateside)
We're A Winner (ABC Paramount/ Stateside)
This Is My Country (Curtom/ Buddah)
Check Out Your Mind (Curtom/ Buddah)
Times Have Changed (Curtom/ Buddah)
Finally Got Myself Together (Curtom/Buddah)
First Impressions (Curtom/RSO)
Loving Power (Curtom/RSO)
Impressions 16 Greatest Hits (ABC/—)

Big Dee Irwin

Born Defosca Ervin in New York on August 4, 1939, Big Dee Irwin was lead singer with the Pastels on their **Been So Long** ballad hit on Argo in 1957. His duet with Little Eva(▶) on **Swing On A Star** (1963) went top 10 in Britain.

A successful songwriter and producer of Ripple, he has recorded as a solo for at least 10 labels, his best effort being as Dee Ervin with the stunning Muscle Shoals(▶)— recorded **One Part Two Part** (Signpost), which builds into a tumultuous and hilarious finale.

Recordings:
Dee Ervin Sings D. Ervin (Signpost)

entitled **Shout Parts 1 & 2,** climbed the pop charts to No. 47 and eventually sold a million as well as becoming a standard rock number revived by countless artists during the '60s beat boom.

Although they recorded another rock classic while at RCA, **Respectable,** no more hits were forthcoming and they moved to Atlantic Records(▶) where, despite being handled by Leiber and Stoller(▶), the dry spell continued. Quickly moving again (in 1961) to the New York-based Wand label, they began to fare better.

At Wand they were produced by Bert Berns, a Leiber/Stoller apprentice who had gained a reputation for combining Latin rhythms with R&B. The Isley's second session for Berns produced yet another rock classic, **Twist & Shout.** Released in early 1962, the record rode the crest of Chubby Checker's(▶) twist craze wave into the US top 20. It was another year before the rest of the world heard the song from the voice of John Lennon and the Beatles. When released in the UK in July 1963, the Isley Brothers' version reached No. 42.

After enabling the Isleys to tour America and consolidate further their reputation as a killer live act, their influential hit did not enhance their recording career. After supplying the beat groups of the world with yet another rock standard for Wand in **Nobody But Me** they again moved labels. At United Artists Records they recorded several songs without success, including **Who's That Lady** which in 10 years' time would be re-recorded for worldwide consumption.

After the debacle of United Artists (one album—no hits) and the euphoria of having the Beatles drop their name at every possible opportunity, the Isley Brothers, tired of corporate manipulation, formed their own label, T-Neck Records, an almost unheard-of practice for a group (particularly a black one) even to consider in 1964. After one release, distributed by Atlantic, which did not sell, they signed again to the Atlantic label where they recorded the beautiful ballad **The Last Girl** without success. They languished there until late 1965 in blissful ignorance that within two years their young lead guitarist, one James Hendrix(▶), would change the face of rock music forever and achieve major international fame before they did.

During 1965 the Isleys guested on several Motown Review package shows and were offered a contract by Berry Gordy. Gordy handed them over to his hit machine Holland-Dozier-Holland(▶), and in April 1966 they hit the American top 20 with the classic **This Old Heart Of Mine.** They released two excellent albums on Motown, **This Old Heart Of Mine** and **Soul On The Rocks,** and had their first run of consistent hits in their career, **I Guess I'll Always Love You, Got To Have You Back** and **Take Me In Your Arms,** although it was in England that the real chart consistency came.

This Old Heart Of Mine was a minor UK hit in April 1966 reaching No. 45, and in September **I Guess I'll Always Love You** also scraped into the top 50 at No. 47. Two years later, in 1968, fired by a minor soul boom emanating from the Midlands and North of England (the first signs of the Northern Soul syndrome) UK Tamla Motown re-issued **This Old Heart Of Mine** and watched it soar to No. 3 in the chart. At this time many two or more year-old Motown records were hitting the UK chart. **I Guess I'll Always Love You** was the follow-up, reaching No. 11 in January 1969. In April, UK Tamla began picking up their own singles from Isley albums and scored again with **Behind A Painted Smile,** a No. 5 hit.

In between that hit and the next Motown revival, **Put Yourself In My Place** (No. 13 in August 1969), came **It's Your Thing** a No. 30 hit in June '69 on the new Major Minor label. The record had been leased from T-Neck records of America because during Tamla Motown's UK euphoric

Below: The Isley Brothers now comprise five brothers and a cousin.

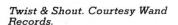

Twist & Shout. Courtesy Wand Records.

Forever Gold. Courtesy T-Neck Records.

period things had fallen apart for the Isleys at Motown USA.

By the middle of 1968, Holland-Dozier-Holland had become entangled in complex law suits with Berry Gordy, which led to their departure for pastures new in the shape of their own label-complex Hot Wax-Invictus (distributed by the successful Buddah Record Company). The Isley Brothers, feeling lost in the Motown factory (their Motown releases, though superb records, could have been by almost any group from the company's roster) followed their producers' example and revived their T-Neck operation, also signing a distribution agreement with Buddah.

In addition to this new, more secure artistic freedom, the Isleys also made a conscious radical change of style. In the heady days of 1969 the self-contained group was what was happening. From the hippie dream of San Francisco's Jefferson Airplane and Grateful Dead to the drug-influenced black rock of Sly & the Family Stone(▶) through the new sparse rhythmic funk of James Brown's(▶) experiments with the repetitious riff of bass, drum and horns, music had changed. So did the Isley Brothers.

They recruited their younger brothers Ernie, on lead guitar, and Marvin, on bass, plus cousin Chris Jasper on keyboards and became a self-contained Isley Brothers—all funk—no horns, no strings. **It's Your Thing,** a song in the James Brown mould of **Cold Sweat** etc., blasted them to No. 1 on the American chart and heralded a new phase of non-stop innovative smash hits like **I Turned You On (Now I Can't Turn You Off), Black Berries, Was It Good To You, Bless Your Heart, Keep On Doin', Work To Do, Warpath, Layaway, Pop That Thing** and **Get Into Something.**

With their new radical image, which was overtly black power in stance, The Isley Brothers became one of the top black acts of the day and in typically militant fashion they released an album entitled **Givin' It Back** (1971), which contained their biggest hit since **It's Your Thing,** a storming version of Stephen Stills' **Love The One You're With.** It almost topped the soul chart and reached the pop top 20.

Frustrated by their inability to break through to pop, although selling consistently in the black market, they included cover versions of rock classics like Dylan's **Lay Lady Lay** and Eric Burden's **Spill The Wine** in the album. The concept was based on the rock market's historical plundering of black hits to the detriment of black performers and the Isley's 'gave it back' in no uncertain fashion. Flushed with this success they recorded another even more successful album, **Brother Brother Brother,** which reached No. 29 on the pop album chart and included more covers, like Carole King's **It's Too Late.** The combination of pumping half-a-million dollars into a stiff movie entitled *It's Your Thing*—a live concert at New York's Yankee Stadium featuring themselves, Ike & Tina Turner and the Five Stairsteps—plus a couple of less than massive singles prompted the Isleys to look around for a more comfortable cushion to fall back on than Buddah.

They found their salvation in CBS Records, who, by 1973, after success in black music through distributing Stax(▶) and Philadelphia International(▶), welcomed the Brothers with open arms. The first album **3+3 That Lady** brought Ernie, Marvin and Chris way out front. Produced by the Brothers, but engineered by Malcolm Cecil and Robert Margouleff, the two synthesiser programmers who were to become so influential in Stevie Wonder's(▶) emergence as a major force in the 70's, the LP was a blistering *tour-de-force* of funk, including originals like the re-worked title track (an international hit of massive proportions) and mainstream rock songs. The rock songs were Seals and .Crofts' **Summer Breeze** (also an international hit) and James Taylor's **Don't Let Me Be Lonely Tonight.**

From the release of **3+3** through to the '80s, the Isley Brothers achieved a much-sought-after goal—consistency. With the Hendrix-styled guitar of Ernie plus Chris Jasper's distinctive synthesiser work laying the background, Ronald, Rudolph and O'Kelly's vocals minted gold like Fort Knox. The albums—**Live It Up** (1974), **Fight The Power** (1975), **The Heat Is On** (1976), **Go For Your Guns** (1977), **Showdown** (1978), **Winner Takes All** (1978), **Go All The Way** (1980), **Grand Slam** (1981) and **Inside You** (1981/82)—and the singles—**That Lady, Summer Breeze, Highways Of My Life, Live It Up, Midnight Sky, Fight The Power, For The Love Of You, Who Loves You Better, Harvest For The World, The Pride, Take Me To The Next Phase, (It's A) Disco Night, Don't Say Goodnight It's Time For Love**—all gained Gold and Platinum awards.

During this period and for no particular reason the Isley Brothers had a habit of sub-titling virtually all their titles Parts 1 and 2, probably out of sheer nostalgia for the days of **Shout.** Not until 1981 did the group hit any kind of snag. In eight years they had sold over 12 million albums without dramatically changing their style since the release of **That Lady,** or touring outside of America. Despite this enormous volume of sales, they still did not feel that they had reached their full potential. As Ernie Isley said in 1980, before associating themselves with CBS their biggest album seller had reached 220,000 but since **3+3** they had not sold less than a million units of any LP. **Grand Slam** in 1981 changed that by not spawning a smash single and taking longer than others to reach that seemingly automatic gold status. In addition to this frustration they also felt that they were still not as consistent in the pop market as they should be. One CBS executive told *Rolling Stone* magazine: 'When you're Platinum in the Soul market who cares about pop crossover?' The Isleys did and as they entered the '80s it looked as though their 25th Anniversary would come with more achievements to attain.

Inside You was the first Isley Brothers' T-Neck album to use additional musicians and strings and pointed new areas for exploration.

Recordings:
The Isley Brothers (—/RCA)
The Isley Brothers Super Hits (—/Tamla Motown)
Timeless (T-Neck/Epic)
Forever Gold (T-Neck/Epic)
Go All The Way (T-Neck/Epic)
Grand Slam (T-Neck/Epic)
Inside You (T-Neck/Epic)

J.J. Jackson

285-lb (20 stone) J.J. Jackson cut his musical teeth arranging for jazz organist Brother Jack McDuff and bluesman Jimmy Witherspoon, and writing pop-soul hits for Mary Wells(▶), Inez Foxx(▶) and the Shangri-Las. Born in the Bronx, New York, J.J. had an R&B No. 1 in the US with **But It's Alright** (1967), which was recorded in Britain. It was the first British-recorded title to achieve this US chart distinction.

He returned to the UK to settle in 1969, signing to MCA and putting together The Greatest Little Soul Band In The Land (later known as Dilemma), a 10-piece backing outfit featuring the cream of the UK jazz scene, including Terry Smith (guitar), Dick Morrisey(▶) (tenor) and reggae trombone man Rico Rodriguez(▶) in its fluctuating line-up.

Recordings:
But It's Alright (—/Strike)
The Greatest Little Soul Band In The Land (MCA)
... And Proud Of It (Perception/—)

Chuck Jackson

Chuck Jackson is the man Tom Jones credits as having the biggest influence over his vocal style. Their voices are indeed very similar, imbued with a rich, dark timbre, but whereas Jones' attempts at soulfulness were contrived, Jackson's came naturally.

Born in the South Carolina town of Winston Salem on July 22, 1937, and not to be confused with the other Chuck Jackson (who came to fame as a songwriter/producer with Marvin Yancey) Jackson moved North to Pittsburgh and joined the famed Del-Vikings vocal group just after their classic **Whispering Bells** hit in 1957. He recorded as a solo for Clock and Beltone before being signed up by Scepter-Wand(▶) house-producer Luther Dixon, who spotted him on a Jackie Wilson(▶) tour bill. Dixon and label boss Florence Greenberg soon realised that they had a potential black superstar on their hands and aimed to capture the kind of success that Dionne Warwick(▶) was giving them on the distaff side of things.

Jackson cut some superb uptempo material, including an ambitious if inconsistent album of Elvis Presley songs, **Dedicated To The King**, and two albums full of cover versions of then current soul hits, **Tribute To Rhythm And Blues** (Vols 1 & 2). As well as his potent vocals, these featured his superb brass-laden nine-piece stage band led by his musical director

and sax player Bobby Scott and with keyboard overdubs by both Jackson and Valerie Simpson. But it was his powerful balladry on numbers like **I Don't Want To Cry** (his first Wand release), **I Wake Up Crying** and **Any Day Now** which brought him most success, particularly since the writing talents of Wand's house team of Burt Bacharach and Hal David were put at his disposal.

Dedicated To The King.
Courtesy Wand

A series of duets with Maxine Brown(▶) (including two whole albums) also won acclaim. Wand recordings were family affairs. Maxine Brown, Dionne Warwick and the Shirelles(▶) contributed back-ups, and Jackson and Tommy Hunt(▶) even recorded versions of the same songs, using the same backing tracks!

After 10 albums for Wand, Jackson left the company when his contract came up in 1967 because Florence Greenberg had refused to cover the cost of getting his band out to a promotional appearance on TV. 'Neither of us would climb down on the issue and though we were both in tears when we made the final goodbye our pride wouldn't let us compromise', recalled Jackson.

Jackson went to Motown: 'Smokey Robinson(▶) called me and suggested I signed to them. I'd always said that was the company I'd go to if ever I left Wand.' He took Yvonne Fair with him: 'The move was beneficial to her—they ended up giving her a couple of big hits—but it was a disaster for me. Motown's thing was to mould an artist into their own sound, but all that meant was I ended up sounding like any other Motown artist rather than like Chuck Jackson.'

The resultant records could, indeed, have been by almost anyone. Jackson didn't stay with Motown for long but, sadly, subsequent forays with Dakar, ABC, All Platinum and other labels have also failed to lift Jackson out of the ruck. A man who was once one of the most distinctive stylists in black music has

languished through producers trying to bring him in line with whatever happens to be the current in-vogue sound.

Recordings:
I Don't Want To Cry (Wand/—)
Any Day Now (Wand/DJM)
Dedicated To The King (Wand/—)
Tribute To Rhythm And Blues Wand/-)
Hold On, We're Coming (with Maxine Brown (Wand/—)
Chuck Jackson Arrives (Tamla Motown)
Through All times (ABC Probe)

Walter Jackson

Long-serving member of the Chicago soul music fraternity, Walter Jackson was born in Pensacola, Florida, in 1939, later moving to Detroit and singing with local bands from the age of 13.

A victim of polio in his late teens, Jackson appears on stage on crutches, but any lack of the dance steps which seemed arbitrary for '60s soul acts was made up for by his rich emotive voice, which, despite an at times irritating hint of lisp, worked well on a string of recordings for OKeh. **It's All Over, Speak Her Name** and **Uphill Climb From The Bottom** are fine examples.

After a lean time in the '70s, Jackson was again actively recording with the dawn of the '80s.

Recordings:
It's All Over (OKeh/—)
Speak Her Name (OKeh/—)
Feeling Good (Chi-Sound/United Artists)

The Jacksons

Starting out as precocious teen talents competing for the same weenybopper/teenybopper audience as the Osmonds and David Cassidy, the Jacksons have matured into one of the most consistently entertaining soul groups around, both in terms of records and live performances.

It was Diana Ross(▶) who brought

Jacksons Live. Courtesy Epic Records.

their talents to Motown(▶) and played an important role in their dramatic breakthrough to instant stardom in 1969 when the label projected Michael Jackson(▶) as a 'child genius', just as they had Stevie Wonder(▶) some years earlier.

The Jacksons' father, Joe Jackson, had been guitarist with the Falcons soul vocal group, and their mother Kathy played clarinet and dabbled at singing blues and country and western. All their children were born in the steel town of Gary, Indiana. Maureen, the first-born, was followed by Jackie (born May 4, 1951), the eldest of what was to be the million-selling quintet, and Tito (born October 15, 1953).

Maureen learned piano and violin from an early age, but Tito was the one with the most intense interest in music, picking up his father's guitar when the old man was out and teaching himself to play. Realising Jackie and Tito's interest, Joe Jackson began giving them proper guitar lessons while his wife taught them the rudiments of vocal harmony.

Jermaine Jackson(▶) was born on December 11, 1954, and as soon as he was old enough to learn to play and sing he was drafted into the emerging family act which was becoming very popular at local social functions and private bookings. A second daughter, LaToya, was born in 1955 and occasionally contributed background vocals at shows

Below: Exceptionally commercial, the Jacksons perform well on record and stage.

as she grew older.

The completion of what was originally to be known as the Jackson 5 came with the births of Marlon on March 12, 1957, and Michael on August 29, 1958. The penultimate Jackson child, Randy, was born on October 29, 1962, and though he played bongos with the group from a very young age, he did not become an official member until Jermaine left the group in 1976. The ninth Jackson child, Janet, was born in 1966.

Although the girls are all musical, none of them has ever been a full member of the Jacksons, but the bonds between them all have remained incredibly close and most of the family still live together.

In 1967, with Michael only nine years old but already acting as a focal point, the Jackson 5—Jackie, Tito, Jermaine, Marlon and Michael —turned professional. Two years later they did a campaign benefit for Richard Hatcher, the mayor of their hometown of Gary.

Diana Ross was among the guests at the show and she instantly recognised the Jacksons' innate talent and was convinced that Motown boss Berry Gordy Jr would

20 Golden Greats. Courtesy Motown Records.

share her enthusiasm. The group was, indeed, signed by Gordy, scoring immediately with their debut Motown single **I Want You Back** (some earlier recordings had appeared without impact on a tiny local label).

Their debut album was titled, appropriately enough, **Diana Ross Presents The Jackson 5**, and the superstar continued to keep a close interest in their career. When she starred in her first 90-minute TV spectacular *Diana*, in 1971, she included the Jackson 5 among the guest artists on both the show and the subsequent soundtrack album.

The early hits of the Jackson 5 were written and produced by 'The Corporation', communal pseudonym for the rich array of songwriters, musicians and producers on the Motown staff. The hits were highly commercial, appealing across the board, with sub-teenage Michael sounding like a show-business veteran. Although both Jackie and Tito could play guitar well and Jermaine was proficient on bass—as evidenced by their live shows—on record it was sufficient that they sang.

Garnering many sales from the predominantly female 'teenybop' audience, the early '70s recordings of the Jackson 5 were pure gold, such smashes as **I Want You Back, ABC, The Love You Save, I'll Be There, Mama's Pearl, Never Can Say Goodbye, Lookin' Through The Windows** giving them a ratio of almost a hit every three months. Carefully groomed in the Motown tradition, their stage shows featured dazzling choreography, and a superbly engineered publicity campaign—including their friendly rivalry with the white teenybop group the Osmonds—kept them constantly in the headlines.

At 13, Michael began a parallel solo career with the 1972 hit single **Got To Be There,** which was

followed by three further charters in a particularly fertile year. His solo career then languished somewhat until it suddenly blossomed again with the sensational success of his 1979 album **Off The Wall** and the string of singles lifted from it.

Tito was the first Jackson to wed, marrying Delores Martes in 1972. A year later, Jermaine married the boss's daughter, Hazel Gordy. Both Tito and Jermaine had solo album releases but without the kind of success Michael had won.

Although the Jackson 5 released consistently big-selling albums it was really their superb singles which captivated their predominantly young audience, hits like **Doctor My Eyes, Hallelujah Day, Skywriter** and **Dancing Machine** keeping up the pace.

In March 1976, the group caused a sensation by not renewing their Motown contract, choosing instead to sign a multi-million deal with Epic. Jermaine, however, stayed loyal to his father-in-law's company and quit the group, being replaced by Randy, and concentrated on a solo career, which was not all plain sailing as he had to wait till 1980 before being rewarded with his first worldwide hit singles.

Changing their name from the Jackson 5 to, simply, the Jacksons, the family group had no such problems, recording a first album for Epic which instantly went gold. Hit singles abounded, **Enjoy Yourself, Dreamer** and **Show Me The Way To Go** each boasting sales figures in the millions. Their second Epic album, in 1977, gave them a title track hit with **Goin' Places**, as well as **Even Though You're Gone.**

But their success was yet to see its highest point. Their 1978 album release contained two of the very biggest records of that year. It was produced by the group themselves, and they wrote most of the songs,

Above: The Jacksons combine perfect timing with harmony.

though calling on the services of the finest West Coast session musicians to provide the backing tracks. **Blame It On The Boogie** and **Shake Your Body (Down To The Ground)** were perfect fodder for the then burgeoning disco craze.

In 1978, Michael was given the chance to fulfil a lifetime ambition to act in a feature film when he appeared in *The Wiz*, a black version of *The Wizard Of Oz*, starring Diana Ross as Dorothy with Michael as the Scarecrow. Though the movie was not unanimously applauded, Michael won much praise for his role.

In 1979, sister LaToya made her bid for stardom, signing a solo contract with Polydor. Her debut album yielded the hit single **If You Feel The Funk.**

In between cutting the third and fourth Jacksons' albums for Epic, Michael released his multi-million-selling **Off The Wall** set which made it seem as though his solo efforts might eclipse the group, but the family came through with their own aptly titled **Triumph** set (1980), from which came the hit singles **Lovely One, Heartbreak Hotel** and **Can You Feel It.**

Extensive touring preceded the release of a double live set late in 1981 and meanwhile the ninth Jackson child, Janet, had become an in-demand television actress.

Recordings:
Diana Ross Presents . . . (Motown)
ABC (Motown)
Looking Through The Windows (Motown)
Skywriter (Motown)
Dancing Machine (Motown)
The Jacksons (Epic)
Destiny (Epic)
Triumph (Epic)

Above: Etta James, whose career has spanned many years and musical idioms.

Etta James

One of THE great voices on the distaff side of soul, Etta James has had a career spanning three decades, her bluesy raw-edged tones proving effective in a range of records which have covered the rock 'n' roll, blues, R&B, gospel and disco idioms.

Born in Los Angeles in 1938, Etta had training in gospel before joining the Peaches rock'n' roll group. In 1955 she was auditioned by R&B bandleader Johnny Otis(▶), who was talent scouting for Modern Records(▶) in LA. The resultant single, **Dance With Me Henry**, was an instant R&B smash.

Lean times followed for Etta, but she was helped by Harvey Fuqua of the Moonglows(▶) who, finding her stranded flat broke in Chicago, persuaded Leonard Chess to pay off her hotel bills in exchange for a session which yielded the heartfelt **All I Could Do Was Cry** (1959) for Chess subsidiary Argo. This hit was quickly followed by a successful Etta and Harvey duo, **If I Can't Have You**, and 18 further solo hits, spread over the next four years.

Arrangers Maxwell Davis and Riley Hampton made a major contribution to such Etta masterpieces as **At Last, Pushover, Stop The Wedding**, while Jackie Wilson(▶) also helped her career along. At Chess(▶) she recorded some superb duets with Sugar Pie De Santo(▶), notably **In The Basement**.

With Etta's sales flagging again, Chess had the brilliant idea of sending her to Muscle Shoals(▶) in 1967 to record at Rick Hall's Fame set-up which included Barry Beckett, Roger Hawkins, David Hood, Jimmy Ray Johnson, Gene 'Bowlegs' Miller, James Mitchell (brother of Willie Mitchell(▶)) and Rufus Thomas's(▶) son Mavell.

The definitive version of **I'd Rather Go Blind**, the dance stormer **Tell Mama** and a powerful reading of Otis Redding's(▶) **Security** were among the Muscle Shoals' cuts. It was the peak of Etta's creativity, although later albums for other labels have yielded many fine moments.

Recordings:
The Soul Of Etta James (Ember)
Top Ten (Argo/—)
Queen Of Soul (Argo/—)
At Last (Argo/Chess)
Peaches (Greatest Hits Double) (Chess)
Sings Funk (Cadet/—)
Deep In The Night (Warner Bros)
Changes (MCA/—)

Jimmy James

Unlike other West Indian bands, Jimmy James and the Vagabonds eschewed reggae and instead exerted a dramatic influence on white British audiences by converting them into soul freaks. With regular appearances at Jeffrey Kruger's Flamingo Club in London's Soho and other mod hangouts around the country the brash, brassy Vagabonds laid down a potent if unsubtle backcloth for James and the ebullient Count Prince Miller, who shared vocals.

Using equipment borrowed from the Who, the group travelled some thousands of miles on one-nighters, spreading **The New Religion**. But while the album of that title (1966) did well, the fans soon realised there was nothing like the real thing and the group's record sales paled besides the increasing flood of classy black product from Stateside, though James did tickle the charts years later with the James Brown-flavoured **You Don't Stand A Chance If You Can't Dance** (1975). Sadly, James was unable to sign for Atlantic(▶)/Stax(▶) in the late '60s as the label's planned replacement for Otis Redding(▶), due to contractual difficulties.

Recordings:
The New Religion (—/Piccadilly)
Life At The Marquee Club (—/Pye)
Open Up Your Soul (—/Pye)

Jewel/Paula/Ronn

The Shreveport, Louisiana-based white entrepreneur Stan Watson has worked in black music—as a retailer (through Stan's Record Shack), distributor, producer and talent scout—since the '40s.

In 1960 he set up his own Jewel/Paula/Ronn group of labels, and though his biggest commercial success came with the trite pop ditty **Judy In Disguise** by John Fred and the Playboys, he has issued a welter of superb blues, R&B (notably by Lowell Fulsom(▶) and soul material. Some of the finest (if too often unacclaimed) Southern black talents have appeared on his labels, including Bobby Patterson, Bobby Powell, Clay Hammond ,Roscoe Robinson and Clarence Carter(▶) (who went on to bigger things with Fame/Atlantic(▶)).

Recordings:
Stan's Soul Shop (—/Charly)

Marv Johnson

Signed to United Artists but produced by Berry Gordy Jr, Marv Johnson paved the way for the latter's 'Motown Sound' with a run of nine consecutive hits from 1959 to 1961, which included **Come To Me, You Got What It Takes** and **More Than Mountains.**

Born in Detroit on October 15, 1938, Johnson had a second stab at chart success when he signed to the Motown Corporation(▶) and scored with **I Miss You Baby** and the perennial favourite **I'll Pick A Rose For My Rose.**

Recordings:
Marvellous Marv Johnson (United Artists)
I'll Pick A Rose For My Rose (Tamla Motown)

Syl Johnson

Mississippi-born Syl Johnson moved to Chicago in 1952 and started his musical career at 14 as guitarist with bluesman Eddie Boyd. While studying at Chicago's Boston School of Music, he gigged with Muddy Waters(▶), Magic Sam, Howlin' Wolf(▶) and Junior Wells, joining Wells' band full-time in 1958 and staying till 1962, as well as recording with Jimmy Reed and Elmore James.

His interests were moving from blues to R&B/soul and he recorded for King in the early '60s, then had his first hits with the self-penned **C'Mon Sock It To Me** and the brilliant **Is It Because I'm Black** on Twi-night.

Willie Mitchell(▶) heard Johnson perform at the Burning Spear club in Chicago and signed him to Hi(▶) which resulted in an R&B No. 1 with **I'm Still Here** (1970). **We Did It** and **Back For A Taste Of Your Love** sustained interest and sales, and he has continued to record superb blues-tinged albums.

Recordings:
Is It Because I'm Black (Twinight/—)
Back For A Taste Of Your Love (Hi/—)

Diamond In The Rough (Hi/—)
Total Explosion (Hi/London)

Johnny Johnson & The Bandwagon

There have been a significant number of occasions when an American act has enjoyed only limited success in its homeland, but has been readily accepted by British fans. One such group was Bandwagon, whose first claim to fame was the US Epic hit **Baby Make Your Own Sweet Music** in mid-1968. **Breaking Down The Walls Of Heartache,** a British hit later in the year, was busy and effervescent, if not a zenith of artistry, with lead singer Johnny Johnson aspiring to full label-credit. The group followed up with **You** and **Let's Hang On** on UK CBS' R&B outlet Direction.

1970 brought a change of label to Bell, and even greater success with UK top 10 hits **Sweet Inspiration** and **Pony Express** but the public soon tired of such brash stereotype, and the group faded.

Recordings:
Johnny Johnson & The Bandwagon (Columbia/Direction)
Soul Survivor (Bell)

Gloria Jones

Gloria Jones' **Tainted Love** was a highly prized collectors' item on the British Northern Soul scene for nearly a decade before it finally secured a UK release on Inferno following the enormous chart success of a cover version by the 'new romantic' group Soft Cell in 1982.

Gloria met with personal tragedy in 1977 when the car she was driving crashed and the rock star Marc Bolan, by whom she had a son, was killed. The tragedy left a deep mark on Gloria but she fought back to make a new life and to continue her promising career as a songwriter and producer. Earlier she had been working at Motown(▶), where she had co-written and co-produced **I Ain't Going Nowhere**

The New Religion. Courtesy Piccadilly Records.

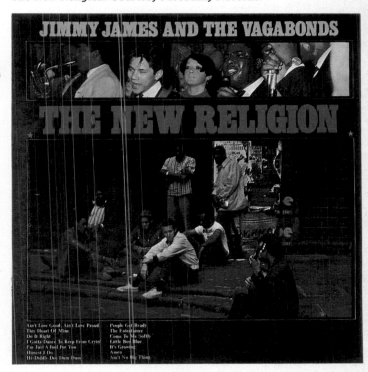

on Junior Walker's(▶) **Peace And Understanding** album, working with Pam Sawyer, an English housewife from Romford who used to send songs off by post to Motown and had several hits even before moving to the States.

After Bolan's death, Gloria and her brother Richard 'The Big Dipper' Jones worked closely with British soul/disco band Gonzales, and her greatest success to date came with their worldwide smash **Haven't Stopped Dancing Yet** for the Sidewalk label.

Recordings:
Vixen (EMI)
Windstorm (Sidewalk)

Jimmy Jones

When the distinctive falsetto chorus of **Handy Man** nestled in the transatlantic top 10 in March 1960, it was the culmination of a whole lot of dues-paying by Jimmy Jones. Born on June 2, 1937, in Birmingham, Alabama, and educated there before moving to New York as a teenager, Jimmy served in the US forces as a cook, but fostered his singing ambitions in his spare time.

His disc career began in 1955 with the vocal group the Sparks of Rhythm, whose output on Apollo Records included a seminal version of **Handy Man,** and continued with the Pretenders (on Rama, Central and Bobby Robinson's Holiday and Whirlin' Disc labels) and the Savoys (on Savoy). Subsequent solo sides on Savoy, Arrow and Epic were commercial flops, and Jones was a rather sad figure when Otis Blackwell heard his demo of an updated **Handy Man.**

Good Timin'. Courtesy MGM.

A contract with MGM resulted, and the record appeared on their Cub R&B subsidiary with chart-shattering impact, emulated by **Good Timin',** another happy beater with falsetto hook. Unfortunately, the vocal gimmick which brought such storming success also proved to have a Midas-type overkill effect, Jones being obliged to punctuate his every song with shrill falsetto, and though he managed a trio of lesser hits on Cub, the bubble had burst within a year. Attempts were made to revive his fortunes on Vee Jay and Roulette, but the formula, and perhaps the talent, had worn too thin, and Jimmy faded into obscurity.

Recordings:
Good Timin' (MGM)

Pat Kelly

Born in Kingston, Jamaica, in 1949, Kelly attended a local technical college before spending a year in America in 1966 studying electronics at Springfield College, Massachusetts. Upon returning home, a close friend, Winston Riley, invited him to replace Slim Smith in a reggae harmony trio, the Techniques. He obliged and with Riley and Bruce Ruffin on harmonies he sang lead.

Their version of Curtis Mayfield's(▶) **You Don't Care** (1967), for Duke Reid's Treasure Isle label, occupied the No.1 position in Jamaica for six weeks. An album of the same name followed. Until 1969, when he quit the group, Kelly also worked at Randy's Studio as an engineer.

Joining producer Bunny Lee's stable of stars as a solo singer he wrote his first major hit. **How Long Will It Take** took off instantly in Jamaica and Britain; in addition to confirming him as reggae's own Sam Cooke(▶), the single was a landmark in the history of the Jamaican recording industry for its employment of strings. Riding this crest of success he went to Britain where Pama Records released an album titled after the single.

The Beatles were then touting for new acts to sign to their Apple organisation and were keen to enlist Kelly. Despite a five-figure enticement, he was stymied by contractual commitments and returned home disillusioned with the music business. Again it was Riley who persuaded him to end a three-year silence and return to the recording studio. The resultant **Lonely Man** album was a fine reggae/soul achievement and the subsequent singles, **Love Oh Love** and **Sing About Love,** were nuggets.

In vogue once more, Kelly teamed up with Lee again and recorded another Mayfield song, **One Man Stand,** that featured the then undiscovered talent of Al Campbell(▶) on harmonies. He went from strength to strength, working with producers Jo Jo Hookim, Duke Reid and Ossie Hibbert on a reggae version of Procul Harum's **Whiter Shade of Pale** and his biggest hit of 1980, **It's A New Day.**

London-based sound-system operator and producer Fat Man signed him in 1980 and issued the perfectly balanced **Sunshine** album, Kelly's songwriting still melodic and romantic and his voice as brittle as ever.

Recordings:
Pat Kelly Sings (—/Pama)
Talk About Love (Sunshot/Terminal)
One Man Stand (—/Third World)

Paul Kelly

Born on June 19, 1940, Paul Kelly worked in his native Miami with the Spades and the Valadeers before landing a solo contract with TK(▶) in 1960 and then being persuaded by producer Clarence Reid to head the Del-Mires. Soon soloing again, he came up with **Chills And Fever** for the local Lloyd label. Buddy Killen—the man behind Joe Tex(▶)—picked the master up for his Nashville-based Dial label. Subsequently Kelly, via Killen, had a run of less successful records on Phillips.

In 1968 he joined his family in New York and concentrated on writing, but when Sam and Dave(▶) were too busy to see him he decided to keep **Stealing In The Name Of The Lord** for himself, contacted Killen again and recorded the number in Muscle Shoals(▶), securing a release on Happy Tiger.

The song (covered superbly by David Clayton-Thomas of Blood, Sweat and Tears) was a masterly exposé of rip-off preachers. Kelly's singing was great and the record went top-five R&B, resulting in Warner Bros picking up the subsequent album from Happy Tiger and recording a further two sets, which highlighted Kelly's perceptive songwriting.

Recordings:
Stealing In The Name Of The Lord (Happy Tiger-Warner Bros./—)
Don't Burn Me (Warner Bros)
Hooked, Hogtied And Collared (Warner Bros)

Albert King

Starting his career in 1948 as a guitarist, Albert King (born Indianola, Mississippi, April 25, 1923) toured as a singer with the Harmony Kings Quartet gospel group before moving to Chicago where he played drums for Jimmy Reed, Jackie Wilson(▶), Brook Benton(▶) and others, cutting his first record as a blues singer/guitarist for Parrot with **Bad Luck Blues** in 1953.

It was six years before King cut his next record in his own right, having moved to St Louis where Ike Turner(▶) recorded him for the locally based Bobbin label on tracks which were later leased to King(▶) for issue in album form.

On signing to the Memphis-based Stax organisation in 1966 King's career really began to take off. Working with the Stax house band (an aggregation of Booker T and the MGs(▶) and the Mar-Keys(▶), King laid down some of the most vibrantly innovative blues sounds ever committed to disc, especially on the mournful **Born Under A Bad Sign** (co-penned by Booker T. Jones(▶) and William Bell(▶)) and the strident **Crosscut Saw.**

The combination of King's mumbled vocals and the stinging guitar lines of his left-handed, strung-upside-down, rocket-shaped guitar (dubbed 'Lucy'), won over white rock audiences as well as a mass black following.

As one of the three Kings of blues music (B.B. King(▶) and Freddie King(▶) being the others) he cashed in on the publicity value of their common surname. B.B. had been born just outside Albert's hometown of Indianola and his father happened to be named Albert so many journalists jumped to the conclusion that the two blues stars must be close relatives, and neither did much to correct this false assumption.

A 6-foot 4-inch, 250lb giant of a man, Albert King plays giant blues which have managed to cut across the usual musical barriers to win wide acclaim.

Recordings:
The Big Blues (King/—)
Travelin' To California (King/Polydor)
Born Under A Bad Sign (Stax)
Live Wire—Blues Power (Stax)
King Does The King's Thing (Stax)
Albert (Utopia/—)
New Orleans Hat (Tomato/—)

Below: Ben E. King, now back in the Drifters' fold.

Ben E. King

In 1958, the late George Treadwell sacked his popular black vocal group the Drifters(▶) on the spot following a show in New York. An unknown young group working as the Crowns were on the same bill and the astute Treadwell—who had copyright on the Drifters' name—recognised their talent and snapped them up to launch as the new Drifters' line-up. In 1959 their debut Atlantic single, **There Goes My Baby**, was a smash hit and introduced fans to the lead-vocal talents of one Benjamin Earl King (born Henderson, North Carolina, in 1938) who had started his singing career in his father's New Jersey restaurant.

Don't Play That Song! Courtesy Atlantic Records.

King sang on such Drifters' classics as **Save The Last Dance For Me** before Atlantic(▶) decided to project him as a solo star, scoring quickly with the two classics, **Spanish Harlem** and **Stand By Me** (a song later covered by Cassius Clay among others). **Don't Play That Song, Tell Daddy,**

Seven Letters, It's All Over and finally **What Is Soul?** (which in both lyrical content and performance gave the most apposite answer to that question) provided King and Atlantic with a string of hits.

Leaving the company in 1969, King failed to find success through subsequent deals with Maxwell/Crewe and Mandala and returned to Atlantic in 1975 to enter the US top 10 with the atmospheric, gently rocking **Supernatural** and in 1977 cut a not wholly successful LP with the Average White Band(▶).

In 1982 the wheel turned full circle when he was asked to rejoin the Drifters as lead singer for a UK tour following the departure from the group's ranks of long-serving Johnny Moore.

Recordings:
Spanish Harlem (Atlantic)
Seven Letters (Atlantic)
Don't Play That Song (Atlantic)
Greatest Hits (Atlantic)
Rough Edges (Crewe)
Supernatural Thing (Atlantic)
Benny And Us (with Average White Band) (Atlantic)
Street Tough (Atlantic)

Frederick Knight

Alabama-born (August 15, 1944) Frederick Knight spent years trudging the streets visiting record companies before becoming the proverbial 'overnight success'. Joe Tex's manager Buddy Killen got Knight a $1,000 advance from Mercury for his debut disc **Throw The Switch**, but they never released it; Capitol issued **Have A Little Mercy** but it flopped and after a frustrating stint in New York, Knight returned South to work as an engineer in the Sound of Birmingham Studio.

Knight's wife Posie and Jerry Weaver co-wrote **I've Been Lonely For So Long** with someone else in mind, but producer Elijah Walker got Knight to cut it and the record was a 1972 international smash, a superb example of gently-rocking Southern soul at its best and somewhat unique in having no drums on it, the rhythm being provided by tambourine and a stool hit with slats of wood.

None of Knight's subsequent records has lived up to this early promise however.

Recordings:
I've Been Lonely For So Long (Stax)
Let The Sunshine In (Juana/—)

Gladys Knight and the Pips

A true child prodigy, winning the televised Ted Mack Amateur Hour at the tender age of eight, Gladys Knight has gone on to become one of soul music's true veterans (her career spanning three decades) while still managing to look young and vivacious.

The story doesn't just belong to her, however, for while the undoubted strength of the act is her bitter-sweet, gospel-wailing-to-smoothly-seductive lead voice, the songwriting and backing vocals of the Pips have also played a vital role.

Gladys was born in Atlanta, Georgia, on May 28, 1944, and sang in the Morris Brown gospel choir before travelling to New York and taking $2,000 for her rendition of Nat 'King' Cole's(▶) **Too Young** on that Ted Mack Show.

Back home she joined the Wings Over Jordan Choir. A family celebration for her older brother Merald

Above: Gladys Knight and her faithful Pips.

'Bubba' Knight (born September 2, 1942) led to the formation of the Pips when the pair sang together with cousins William (born June 2, 1941) and Elenor Guest, taking the name from a third cousin, James 'Pip' Woods, who became their first manager. Elenor was soon replaced by yet another cousin, Edward Patten (born August 2, 1939), and after six years' apprenticeship and unsuccessful recordings for Brunswick, the Pips cut a version of Johnny Otis's(▶) **Every Beat Of My Heart** for local label Huntom.

The record sold slowly at first and the group moved on to a deal with Bobby and Danny Robinson in New York. After a couple of unspectacular releases on Enjoy and Everlast they were switched to the brothers' Fury banner and re-recorded **Every Beat Of My Heart** (with novelty R&B hit-maker Dave 'Baby' Cortez on organ). Meanwhile, Huntom had leased their original version to Vee-Jay(▶) and the group found itself in the unusual position of having two recordings of the same song fighting it out for chart honours.

The Vee-Jay cut won, hitting top 10 in 1961 while the Fury disc went as high as the 40s. Fury hit back, though, with a re-make of Jesse Belvin's(▶) **Guess Who?** and the emotive **Letter Full Of Tears**, both of which charted before the year's end.

In 1963, Larry Maxwell signed them for the new Maxx label he had started with their then manager Marguerite Mays, and the team of writer Van McCoy(▶) and arranger Fred Norman gave them another run of R&B hits, kicking off with **Giving Up** which also made the pop charts.

On the demise of Maxx, the group went back to Atlanta and concentrated on touring and singing on other acts' sessions. Guesting on a 1966 Motown(▶) package tour, they were offered a deal which was to turn them from being merely a respected soul act into international superstars.

One of the first 'name' acts signed by Motown, who till then had largely groomed their own stars from scratch, Gladys Knight and the Pips started off with their new label in a steady fashion. Their first release, **Just A Walk In My Shoes** (issued on the Soul subsidiary), was brilliant but didn't happen, the next, **Take Me In Your Arms And Love Me**, tickled the charts, the third, **Everybody Needs Love**, finally took them back into top-40 territory.

20 Golden Greats. Courtesy Tamla Motown Records.

With the introduction of Norman Whitfield(▶) as producer, the group's product was stunning, both artistically and commercially. Though recorded after the Marvin Gaye(▶) version (which became a No. 1), the Pip's reading of **I Heard It Through The Grapevine** was taken at an altogether more frenetic pace and was one of 1967's most exciting hits. The tortured **It Should Have Been Me** (1968), the revival of Shirley Ellis's(▶) **The Nitty Gritty** (1969) and the potent **Friendship Train** the same year were all classics. They then proceeded to cut superlative ballads like **If I Were Your Woman** (1970), the classic version of Kris Kristofferson's **Help Me Make It Through The Night**, and **Neither One Of Us** (both in 1972).

Coming under the management of the astute Sidney Seidenberg, the group took advantage of a lucrative offer from Buddah when their Motown deal expired in 1973 and, with Gladys now being reckoned by many to have usurped Aretha Franklin(▶) as the Queen of Soul, continued the run of haunting smash-hit ballads with the Jim Weatherly songs **Where Peaceful Waters Flow, Midnight Train To Georgia** (both 1973), **The Best Thing That Ever Happened To Me** (1974), as well as the barnstorming **I've Got To Use My Imagination** (1973) (which was back in the mould of their uptempo Motown hits) and **The Way We Were** (1975), recorded 'live' without Gladys' knowledge!

A Curtis Mayfield-written and produced soundtrack album for the movie *Claudine* and a starring role in the *Pipe Dreams* film (with a soundtrack album produced by Bubba Knight) kept Gladys Knight and the Pips in the public eye.

Buddah also, however, moved the group more towards an MOR audience, even issuing a pretty appalling album of Christmas-theme songs. At the same time there were certain problems within the act. The Pips split and recorded a rather ordinary LP.

Soul fans heaved something of a sigh of relief when Gladys not only rejected plans to turn her into a cabaret-style performer (after all, she'd been able to work the cabaret circuits for years without selling out her artistry), but also kissed and made up with the Pips and signed a new deal with Columbia, bringing in talented ex-Motowners Nick Ashford and Valerie Simpson(▶) to write and produce for the debut Columbia set **About Love**, issued in 1980—some 27 years on from the group's formation.

Recordings:
Gladys Knight And The Pips (—/DJM)
Feelin' Bluesy (Soul/Tamla Motown)
Cloud Nine (Soul/Tamla Motown)
If I Were Your Woman (Soul/Tamla Motown)
A Little Knight Music (Soul/Tamla Motown)
Anthology (Soul/Tamla Motown)
Imagination (Buddah)
2nd Anniversary (Buddah)
I Feel A Song (Buddah)
About Love (Columbia/CBS)

Major Lance

The success Major Lance achieved on a string of hits for the Chicago-based OKeh label through the mid-60s was due as much to the combination of Curtis Mayfield's(▶) superb songs, Johnny Pate's classy brass-infused arrangements and Carl Davis's production as to Lance's vocal talents. It was truly the overall feel of recordings like **The Monkey Time, Hey Little Girl, Um, Um, Um, Um, Um, Um** and **The Matador** which made them such distinctive top 20 chartbusters, keeping Lance consistently in the limelight between 1963 and 1967.

Recording later for Daker, Curtis Mayfield's Curtom label, and the Stax subsidiary Volt (tracks leased from Carl Davis), Lance visited Britain in 1972 as a cult figure and recorded a live album for Contempo at the legendary 'Northern Soul' venue, The Torch, in Stoke-on-Trent.

Recordings:
The Rhythm Of Major Lance (OKeh/Columbia)
Greatest Hits Recorded Live At The Torch (—/Contempo)

Arthur Lee

One of the few blacks to be involved in the late '60s psychedelic explosion, Memphis-born Lee was the lead singer and composer for the influential rock band Love. An unpredictable and sometimes perverse character, Lee was nevertheless the progenitor of several brilliant albums, notably **Da Capo** and **Forever Changes**.

There were various incarnations of Love between 1965 and 1971, all of them under Lee's control, but the group's later work was disappointing. After Love broke up, Lee attempted a solo career, but the spark seemed to have gone. Difficulties caused by his own personality helped him back to obscurity.

Recordings:
Da Capo (Elektra)
Forever Changes (Elektra)

Byron Lee and the Dragonaires

This 14-piece combo of forever changing personnel was assembled during 1953, in Jamaica, by Byron Lee (real name Ken Lazarus) and his manager Ronnie Nasralla, initially to provide backing for singers touring the Caribbean. Harry Belafonte used them more than once.

A Jamaican ska(▶)/swing big-band was so unique that they soon found themselves in permanent demand. By the end of the '50s they had toured extensively throughout the Caribbean and South America, and in 1963 undertook their first headlining tour of major North American cities, currying particular favour in Canada.

By 1966 they were practically a Jamaican national institution. Lee Holdings Ltd was formed to take care of their expanding business empire and they became a major tourist attraction in Kingston and Miami. A measure of the country's esteem for Lee was displayed in 1967 when he was invited to play to an estimated crowd of 35,000 on Jamaica's National Day at Expo '67. The following year the band performed in front of the Queen of England at the Commonwealth Games, in Kingston.

In 1968 the band teamed up with leading calypso exponent the Mighty Sparrow, and until 1974 forged an invigorating bond between reggae and calypso, cutting many sides of celebratory fusion for a number of different producers. Unfortunately, the band had been dogged by inadequate European distribution deals that have stymied the sales of many of their best albums.

Since the mid-'70s Lee has retired from performing and concentrated on producing Sparrow.

Recordings:
Sparrow Meets The Dragon (Spa Lee Records/Trojan)
Reggae Round The World (Dynamics/Dragon)
The Midas Touch (Dynamics/Dragon).

Reggae Fever. Courtesy Select Records.

Laura Lee

Blessed with a grittily expressive voice, Laura Lee was doing with equal potency what won fame and fortune for Millie Jackson(▶)—and doing it a year or so earlier. Based in Chicago, she had some early hits on Chess(▶), but it was on moving to Hot Wax that she made her biggest impact.

Produced by Ronald Dunbar, with great arrangements by McKinley Jackson and Tony Camillo, her later Hot Wax hits like **Crumbs Of The Table** and **Women's Love Rights** were classics of the woman-as-mankiller genre. But perhaps, back in 1972, the world wasn't quite ready for her strident form of feminism, and she failed to consolidate her career, which is a lasting pity as she was a truly exciting pioneer.

Recordings:
Women's Love Rights (Hot Wax)
Two Sides Of Laura Lee (Hot Wax)

Ketty Lester

Ketty Lester might be the archetypal one-hit wonder, but what a giant that one hit was! With its ponderous tinkling piano accompaniment and her emotion-drenched reading of a poetic lyric, **Love Letters** turned a 1945 movie theme song into a 1962 soul classic.

Born in Hope, Arkansas, Ketty moved to San Francisco and sang in local clubs before joining a theatrical troupe and touring Europe. Spells with Cab Calloway's band and the Ziegfeld Follies were followed by an Era recording contract and **Love Letters**.

Recordings:
Love Letters (Era/—)

Ramsey Lewis

Chicago-born pianist Lewis was only 15 when he first began to attract attention with a jazz group called the Clefs, who played in and around his home town. The group signed to Chess Records' jazz label Argo in 1956, and became the

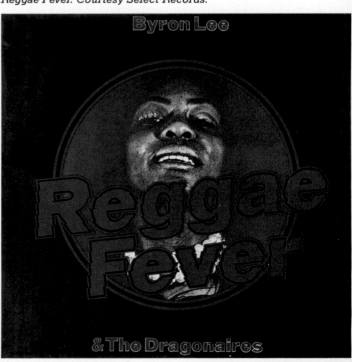

Ramsey Lewis Trio. The next nine years saw the Trio, featuring Eldee Young on bass and Red Holt on drums, record 18 albums and establish a solid reputation in clubs and jazz venues around the US. It wasn't until 1965 that an old Dobie Gray hit, **The In Crowd,** provided the vehicle that carried the Ramsey Lewis Trio to international stardom.

The In Crowd featured Lewis's Junior Mance/Les McCann-influenced soul-jazz styling coupled to a shuffle-rock beat. Its good-time funky feeling propelled it into the US top five. Both the single and the album achieved gold status, as did the similarly styled follow-up singles **Hang On Sloopy** and **Wade In The Water.**

The In Crowd. Courtesy Chess Records.

Young and Holt left the group to form Young-Holt Unlimited(▶) and were replaced by Cleveland Eaton —later to hit with **Bama Boogie**— and Maurice White, who formed Earth, Wind and Fire(▶). Subsequent years saw a succession of jazz/funk/MOR albums of varying degrees of artistic success, and occasional hit singles like **Sun Goddess** and **Spring High.** Nevertheless, many remain convinced that the spare funk of **The In-Crowd** provided the high spot of Lewis's career.

Recordings:
The In Crowd (Argo/Chess)
The Best Of Ramsey Lewis (CBS)

Little Anthony & the Imperials

From the hallways of Brooklyn to the dancefloors of Wigan and Blackpool in Britain's 'Northern Soul' cult, the fame, fortune and talent of Little Anthony & the Imperials were carried by an array of chart hits spanning some 20 years and in styles ranging from street-corner doo-wop to cabaret musicals. Anthony Gourdine began singing with the Duponts in Brooklyn back in 1955, then formed the Chesters with Clarence Collins, Tracy Lord, Ernest Wright and Nat Rogers. An audition with End Records in 1958 brought a disc contract and a name change to the Imperials, whose debut **Tears On My Pillow,** a plaintive teen ballad, soared into the US top 10.

More hits followed on End with Little Anthony up front, but internal conflict within the young group caused a split in 1960. After a four-year hiatus Anthony reformed the group with Collins, Wright and Sammy Strain, signing to DCP Records in 1964 to chart with some fine dramatic soul ballads driven by plush arrangements on songs like **I'm On The Outside**

Above: Ramsey Lewis—had success with jazz-based funk.

Looking In, Going Out Of My Head and **Hurt So Bad.**

Early in 1966 they moved to Veep, launched as an R&B outlet by United Artists, and continued their chart success, moving up to the main UA label in 1969. A further change of fortunes took the group to Janus, then, in 1974 to Avco. They adapted their style to suit contemporary musical needs, but generally retained Anthony's distinctive lead delivery. A brief postscript occurred in 1977 when a group of Imperials led by original member Clarence Collins hit the British charts with **Who's Gonna Love Me** on Power Exchange.

Recordings:
Hits of . . . (Roulette/—)
I'm On The Outside (DCP/UA)
Going Out Of My Head (DCP/UA)
Out Of Sight Out Of Mind (UA/—)

Little Eva

Just like something out of a Hollywood script, the story goes that the husband and wife songwriting team of Jerry Goffin and Carole King heard their babysitter singing one day, got her a recording deal with Dimension, wrote her a song called **The Loco-motion** and saw her take it straight to the top of the charts. The young lady's name was Eva Narcissus Boyd (born Bellhaven, North Carolina, June 29, 1945), the name that went on the record labels was Little Eva.

Subsequent releases were not as highly successful, but numbers like **The Turkey Trot** and **He Is The Boy** remain highly listenable samples of early '60s pop-soul artistry.

Recordings:
The Loco-motion (Direction/
(London)

Little Milton

Milton Campbell, born in Inverness, Mississippi, on September 17, 1934, has been recording for almost 30 years, and started from humble beginnings on Sun Records in Memphis in 1953. Despite possessing a strong blues-drenched voice, and picking deft, biting guitar, he has tended to record material often highly derivative. T-Bone Walker and B.B. King inspired Milton as a teenager, and their guitar styles are reflected in his first discs on Sun and Meteor, but indifferent sales prompted him to move to St Louis-based Bobbin Records under the auspices of

bandleader Oliver Sain. There his repertoire expanded, and output included material with big bands and small combos, though still retaining broad hints of Walker and King.

In the early 1960s Milton's contract was taken over by Chess/ Checker in Chicago, and soon his records began to appear in the national charts, perhaps partly due to a change of style—Chess seemed intent in shaping their artist into a mirror-image of Bobby Bland(▶). The formula bore fruit when Milton covered Bland's **Blind Man** in 1965 and actually outsold the original. Hits like **Who's Cheating Who** and **Grits Ain't Groceries** followed, brassy blues numbers

Below: Little Milton, Mississippi's own powerhouse R&B performer.

73

with roaring vocals and intense delivery, and for some five years the sucess was maintained.

1971 brought a move to Stax and an attempt to blend Milton's blues' heritage into the contemporary soul idiom. It worked beautifully, yielding hits like **Behind Closed Doors** and **Let Me Back In,** while an appearance in the *Wattstax* movie saw him give a stinging rendition of **Walking The Backstreets And Crying.**

The demise of Stax left Milton temporarily stranded until he formed his own Camil Productions, recording some crisp soul-blues back in Chicago, which he placed with Miami-based TK Records. **Friend Of Mine** was a small hit on their Glades outlet, and two albums combined good elements of blues with commercially viable soul. With the expiry of the TK deal, Milton's more recent discs have appeared on the Golden Ear label in Chicago.

Recordings:
Raise A Little Sand (Bobbin/Red Lightnin')
Grits Ain't Groceries (Chess)
Chess Blues Masters (Chess/—)
Waiting For . . . (Stax/—)
Me For You (Glades/—)
Friend Of Mine (Glades/—)

Little Sonny

Born Aaron Willis, in Greensboro, Alabama, October 6, 1952, Little Sonny took his name from the late blues great Sonny Boy Williamson (Rice Miller). Updating a hard biting style of harmonica playing and a bluesy voice into a mixture of R&B and contemporary funk, after obscure singles for a minor labels, he had three much-acclaimed albums for Stax (▶) subsidiary Enterprise, who signed him in 1969.

Sonny honed his craft in the clubs and juke-joints of Detroit where he doubled as a photographer and harmonica player, sitting in with John Lee Hooker, Eddie Burns, Baby Boy Warren and others. His classic instrumental rendition of **Wade In The Water,** from his second album, was one of the finest R&B records of the '70s.

Recordings:
New King Of The Blues Harmonica (Enterprise/Stax)
Black And Blue (Enterprise/—)
Hard Going Up (Enterprise/—)

Shorty Long

Had he lived, Frederick 'Shorty' Long may well have become one of Motown's(▶) biggest stars. An excellent writer, vocalist and producer, he was responsible for several classic cuts during his all too brief career.

The Prime Of Shorty Long. Courtesy Tamla Motown.

Alabama-born Long signed with Motown in 1964, and released **Devil With A Blue Dress** in April of that year. Over the next few years he issued a number of singles which became dance-floor classics, including **Function At The Junction,** and in 1968 hit with the wry **Here Comes The Judge.** These and other excellent cuts made up Long's first album, **Here Comes The Judge,** which combined some great singing, an undercurrent of hip humour and an altogether tougher approach than some of the other artists recording for Motown at the time.

Long's second album, **The Prime Of Shorty Long,** provided more solid evidence of the range of the man's talents with its individualistic versions of material as varied as Fats Domino's(▶) **I'm Walkin'** and **Blue Monday,** and Procul Harum's **Whiter Shade Of Pale,** as well as several more, distinctive self-penned compositions.

Unfortunately Long never had the chance to realise his undoubted potential, as he was killed in a boating accident in 1969, aged only 29. Both his albums are worth looking for in cut-out bins and secondhand racks.

Recordings:
Here Comes The Judge (Motown)
The Prime Of Shorty Long (Motown)

Tommy McCook

A member of that seminal Jamaican studio band the Skatalites(▶), tenor saxophonist Tommy McCook played on countless sessions for Prince Buster(▶) and others and went on to found his own highly-rated instrumental combo, the Supersonics, who scored in 1968 with the catchy **Second Fiddle** for Duke Reid and Treasure Isle Records. They also backed Phyllis Dylon on her 1967 classic **Perfidia** and have subsequently enjoyed a string of fine albums.

Recordings:
Tommy McCook (Treasure Isle/Attack)
Instrumental (Justice)

Taj Mahal

At a time when every young black American was turning his back on the blues and its at times self-pitying lyrics, and getting into the more stridently self-assured soul music of the late '60s to early '70s, Taj Mahal (born New York, May 17, 1942) went against the tide and dug back to the roots.

When blues once again became acceptable, with whites if not blacks, Mahal did another about-face, dabbling in reggae and delving even further back to unearth the African roots of black music. That he managed to sell lots of records and put lots of backsides on seats despite his unorthodox musical policies, says much for his consummate artistry.

Mahal had studied American folk music at university, becoming an acknowledged expert in the subject, and while in Los Angeles he formed a band called the Rising Sons. The band soon broke up but Mahal persevered, getting a deal with Columbia and putting together a superbly tight group which, in his own words, comprised: 'A son of a Texas sharecropper, a Hungarian Jew, a wild-

Above: Going against the grain, young contemporary bluesman Taj Mahal keeping a tradition alive.

eyed Irishman and a crazy swamp spade'.

Jessie Ed Davis on lead guitar, Ry Cooder guesting on rhythm guitar and mandolin, Taj on slide guitar, a great rhythm section and good material made his debut album, **Taj Mahal,** an underground monster on both sides of the Atlantic (**The Celebrated Walkin' Blues** remains, arguably, his best ever record).

The Natch'll Blues, Giant Step/ De Ole Folks At Home and **The Real Thing** spawned more of the same ilk while **Recycling The Blues** had African touches (and some vocal work by the Pointer Sisters(▶)) and **Music Keeps Me Together** brought in a West Indian element.

A steady flow of albums found the 6 foot 4 inch tall Mahal expanding his horizons, introducing traditional African instruments yet managing to be innovative whilst always looking back over his musical heritage. Ironically, since his career has been dedicated to exposing the true richness of black music, his audiences have been predominantly white. He now manages himself, maintaining a frugal approach to his expanding business enterprises.

Recordings:
Taj Mahal (Columbia/Direction)
The Natch'll Blues (Columbia/ Direction)
Giant Step/De Ole Folks At Home (Columbia/CBS)
Happy To Be Just Like I am (Columbia/CBS)
Mo Roots (Columbia/CBS)
Music Fah Ya (Warner Bros)
Anthology Vo. I (Columbia/—)
Going Home (Columbia/CBS)

The Majors

The first-tenor/falsetto lead vocals of Baltimore-born Ricky Cordo made the Jerry Ragovoy (▶)-produced and Philadelphia-based Majors one of the most attractive groups to work the uptown pop/soul style in the early '60s.

Cordo and native Philadelphians Ronald Gathers, Eugene Glass, Frank Troutt and distaff member Idella Morris signed to Imperial and scored in 1962 with **A Wonderful Dream.** This was swiftly followed by **A Little Bit Now, She's A Troublemaker,** the latter co-written by Van McCoy(▶), **What In The World** and a clever cover version of **Twist And Shout.**

Recordings:
Meet The Majors (Imperial/ London)

Mad Lads

Formed in Memphis in 1963 the group (John Gary Williams, lead tenor; Julius Green, tenor; William Brown, baritone; Robert Phillips, bass) were first known as the Emeralds. Stax(▶) changed their name to match their extrovert personalities and released **Sidewalk Surf** in 1964. Their second release, **You Don't Have To Shop Around,** stayed on the US chart for nine months.

On enlisting for army service in 1966, Williams and Brown were temporarily replaced by Quincy Billups and Sam Nelson. On the return of the two original members, Billups joined the much-touted Ollie and the Nightingales (also on Stax) and Nelson became a producer.

At Stax Williams doubled as songwriter, Brown headed the company's editing department and Phillips ran Stax's Satellite record store. Green worked as a fashion designer.

The Mad Lads recorded through till the demise of Stax, their final **Mad, Mad, Mad, Mad, Mad Lads** album being produced by the late Al Jackson of Booker T & the MGs(▶).

Recordings:
The Mad Lads In Action (Volt/—)
The Mad, Mad, Mad, Mad Lads (Volt/—)
A New Beginning (Volt/—)

Above: Martha & the Vandellas kept us 'Dancing In The Street' during the '60s.

The Mar-Keys

Originally an all-white instrumental band, the Mar-Keys were formed as the Royal Spades in high-school days in Memphis. The group's ever evolving line-up started out as Packy, brother of country star Hoyt, Axton (tenor sax), Don Nix (baritone sax), Wayne Jackson (trumpet), Steve Cropper (guitar), Donald 'Duck' Dunn (bass), Jerry Lee Smith (organ) and Terry Johnson (drums).

Axton was the son of Estelle Axton who, with her brother, the country banjo-picker Jim Stewart, ran the Satellite record store. Since the shop happened to be in a predominantly black area of Memphis, the two concentrated on R&B music and when they formed their own Satellite label (soon to be re-named Stax) they released records in that idiom.

Written and arranged by Chips Moman (one of many white Memphis musicians to make a name in black music), the Mar-Keys' debut single **Last Night** sold a million copies. Stewart, who despite his involvement never really had an ear for black music, didn't want to release the disc so, unbeknown to him, the group sent the master tape off to Satellite's distributors, Atlantic(▶), who flipped over it; the record charted before Stewart realised what was happening!

Repeating the same sax-dominated format, the Mark-Keys cut a succession of fine records, including **Morning After, Pop-eye Stroll, Grab This Thing** and **Philly Dog**. Steve Cropper switched from the Mark-Keys to Booker T & the MGs(▶) in time for that outfit's 1962 smash **Green Onions**. Duck Dunn followed suit, replacing Lewis Steinberg, original bassist in the MGs (it was Steinberg who played on **Green Onions**).

In effect, though, the two groups were as one. The Mar-Keys provided the horn sound on MGs' records, the MGs were the rhythm section on the Mark-Keys' discs and the bands appeared on stage as a unit, as well as working together as the house band at Stax on hits by Otis Redding(▶), Sam and Dave(▶), Eddie Floyd(▶), Don Covay(▶), Wilson Pickett(▶) and the host of other stars who passed through the label's East McLemore Avenue studios.

Eventually, the Mark-Keys were reduced to the twosome of Wayne Jackson and Andrew Love who also began recording, with the addition of Floyd Newman (baritone sax), as the Memphis Horns.

In 1965 Packy Axton scored with a new band called the Packers and a record titled **Hole In The Wall**, which was straight out of The Mar-Keys' trick bag.

Similarly, Stax groomed Otis Redding's teenaged backing band the Bar-Kays to follow in the Booker T & the MGs/Mar-Keys mould, not only in sound but as a second house band at the studio. The air-crash which killed Otis Redding also killed most of the Bar-Kays and, on re-forming, the new Bar-Kays went off in a new heavier direction. As for the Mark-Keys the name simply passed into history though the various musicians who had been in the group continued to make major contributions to music.

Recordings:
Last Night (Atlantic/—)
Do The Pop-Eye (Atlantic/—)
The Great Memphis Sound (Stax/—)
Damifiknow (Stax)

Marcels

Although their sound was patterned on other American vocal R&B groups of the '50s and '60s, the Marcels were unusual in that they featured two white singers, Richard Knauss and Gene Bricker. Knauss was the leader of the group, which started after manager Jules Kruspir had held auditions to mould a singing unit to capitalise on the musical approach of the day.

The Marcels' first release was the Rodgers/Hart classic **Blue Moon**, which was a No.1 hit both in America and Britain (1961). Minor successes, including another standard **Summertime**, followed, but the group never sustained their initial impact. Apart from Knauss and Bricker, the Marcels consisted of Ronald Mundy, Fred Johnson and guitarist Cornelius Harp.

Recordings:
Blue Moon (Colpix/—)

Martha & the Vandellas

Dancing In The Street is frequently cited as epitomising the 'Motown Sound', and this million-seller for Martha & the Vandellas from the fall of 1964 certainly contained the ingredients vital to that exciting formula, with crashing percussion, surging rhythm, biting brass and gospel-intense vocals.

Martha Reeves (born July 18, 1941), Rosalind Ashford and Annette Sterling were all natives of Detroit, working as secretaries at Motown Records when the opportunity arose for them to fill in as background singers on Marvin Gaye's **Stubborn Kind Of Fellow**. Their performance was sufficiently impressive for them to be given a

Below: Vandellas have come and gone—but there's only one Martha.

Above: Curtis Mayfield's delicate high tenor led the Impressions to a series of classic soul sides. during the early '60s.

contract — as the Vandellas — on Gordy Records. **Come And Get These Memories,** a husky, bittersweet beat-ballad, which brought them top 30 status in spring 1963, was soon surpassed by the frantic, gospelesque **Heat Wave** and similar **Quicksand** and **Live Wire,** making full use of the duo-syllabic title hook. **Dancing In The Street** maintained their success, as did **Nowhere To Run**—in these last four hits Betty Kelly had replaced Annette and this revised trio scored more than a dozen hits during the next five years.

Martha was accorded feature label-credit on the 1967 disc **Honey Chile** and on all subsequent releases. In 1968, her sister Lois joined the group in place of Betty Kelly. By 1970 the chart-ratings had dwindled, though the Vandellas continued to record and tour, now with ex-Velvelette Sandra Tilley in place of Rosalind. In 1974, however, Martha left to pursue a solo career, first with MCA, then with Arista, and in 1978 with Fantasy, but artistic merit did not convert to commercial acceptance, and she has now joined the circuit of 'oldies' shows with anonymous Vandellas.

Recordings:
Greatest Hits (—/Tamla Motown)
Martha Reeves (Fantasy)
Rest Of My Life (Arista)

The Marvelettes

Though soon eclipsed by the Supremes(▶), the Marvelettes were the first of Motown's(▶) girl groups to strike it rich when they went to No. 1 in 1961 with their debut **Please Mr Postman** (a number subsequently covered by the Beatles which earned a gold disc.

Teaming up at Inkster High School, Detroit, lead singer Gladys Horton and her partners Katherine Anderson, Juanita Cowart and Georgeanna Tillman (all born in The Motor City in 1944) won a talent contest and were introduced to Motown boss Berry Gordy Jr by their school teacher.

Playboy, Beechwood 4-5789, Too Many Fish In The Sea and the gently rocking **Don't Mess With Bill** kept them in the charts through to 1966 but, though she had a superb blues-tinged voice of gospel intensity, Gladys Horton lacked the persona of a Diana Ross(▶), and the group had no strong identity.

Juanita and Georgeanna quit and Anne Bogan replaced Gladys Horton as lead singer of the resultant trio in 1968, getting a minor hit next year with **That's How Heartaches Are Made,** but failing to capture the classic Marvelettes' sound.

The group then disbanded, though various outfits of varying degrees of authenticity have continued to tour using the name, thus reflecting the faceless image of a group who had huge hits with great records but never became stars in the true sense.

Recordings:
The Marvellous Marvelettes (Tamla/Tamla Motown)
Sophisticated Soul (Tamla/Tamla Motown)
In Full Bloom (Tamla/Tamla Motown)
The Best Of The Marvelettes (Tamla/Tamla Motown)

Hugh Masekela

Hugh Masekela was born in the coal-mining community of Witbank, South Africa, and was soon listening to the local percussion bands. But it was the Kirk Douglas movie *Young Man With A Horn* that inspired him to become a musician. After joining an African touring band, Masekela came to

The Boy's Doin' It. Courtesy Casblanca Records.

the attention of prominent white musicians, who arranged for his departure from South Africa. With the help of Johnny Dankworth, Masekela enrolled at the Royal Academy of Music in England, and later received a scholarship from the Manhattan School of Music in New York.

His formal training complete, Masekela entered the world of recording, and was soon successful. He scored on MCA with **Grazin' In The Grass,** which sold four million copies worldwide. He subsequently collaborated with the African band Ojah, and has enjoyed individual acclaim with a variety of albums for various labels, notably **Melody Maker** and **Colonial Man.**

Recordings:
The Boy's Doing It (Casablanca)
Colonial Man (Casablanca)
Melody Maker (Casablanca)

Maurice And Mac

Boyhood friends Maurice McAlister and McLaurin Green formed the Radiants in 1962, signing with Chess(▶) and charting, notably with **Voice Your Choice,** but this ended when Green was called up for army service the following year.

Three years later, the Maurice and Mac duo was formed, scoring on Checker with the Sam and Dave(▶)-flavoured **You Left The Water Running.**

Recordings:
No albums recorded

Curtis Mayfield

The frayed, high tenor of Curtis Mayfield was the antithesis of the accepted gutsy vocal sound of the late '50s and early '60s, but Mayfield led the Impressions through a stream of self-penned soul classics in that era. Born in Chicago on June 3, 1942, Mayfield soon absorbed the rich musical pickings of the local blues, gospel and soul musicians, and was leading his own group, the Alphatones, before he was a teenager.

When the Mayfield family moved to Chicago's north side in 1956, the young Curtis renewed his friendship with Jerry Butler(▶), a former member of Curtis's grandmother's church choir. Butler was eager to involve himself in another group, and joined up with three former Tennesseeans, Arthur and Richard Brooks, and Sam Gooden. He persuaded Mayfield to leave the Alphatones to complete this new aggregate.

The quintet retained the name the Roosters, which Gooden and the Brooks had used in the midsouth (another member, Fred Cash, had stayed behind when the others moved north), and they began working locally. Although the group attracted a good following, they felt that a change of name would better indicate their urban surroundings —there aren't too many live chickens in the city—and they became the Impressions.

Their first hit was **For Your Precious Love,** in 1958, with a label credit of 'Jerry Butler and the Impressions', an unintentional mistake by the record company, which led to the premature departure of Butler, and the not unnatural annoyance of the rest of the unit. 'It created hard feelings among fellows who were all striving equally to make it', says Mayfield.

Accepting Butler's innocence in the episode, Mayfield turned to playing guitar in his band and writing for him, and this period resulted in Butler's first national solo hit, **He Will Break Your Heart.** Devoid of their two leading lights, the Impressions temporarily assumed a secondary role in the Mayfield story, although they remained active, with Fred Cash rejoining the original members.

After two years with Butler, Mayfield, now domiciled in New York, renewed his association with the Impressions as lead singer, cutting **Gypsy Woman** in 1961, which immediately re-established the group. He utilised his unique vocal style on a series of stirring Impressions' singles, including **I'm So Proud, Keep On Pushin', People Get Ready, We're A Winner, This Is My Country, Choice Of Colours, Mighty, Mighty, Spade And Whitey** and the soul anthem to end all soul anthems—**Amen.**

Astonishingly, the Impressions made little commercial impact in the UK, although Mayfield became a temporary demigod among the teenage Mod movement of the time, and his material was played by every aspiring '60s soul band.

Unlike most of the Impressions' contemporaries, the group retained a strong gospel flavour in their product, and although the lyrical content was secular in the strictest sense of the word, Mayfield left no doubt as to the intention of his music. 'They were church songs', he recalls, 'The difference was, I left the word God out'.

In 1970 Mayfield extracted himself from full-time duties with the Impressions, although he continued to produce them for his Curtom label, which he had started in 1968.

His first solo album, **Curtis,** quickly achieved gold status, with the single **Move On Up** giving him his first taste of the British charts. His promotional visit for the record gave UK audiences a chance to see him on stage and he quickly secured a favourable reputation, although many thought 10 years too late.

The early '70s remained Mayfield territory as he scored with **Curtis Live, Roots** and the formidable **Superfly** soundtrack. This latter filmwork was almost unique among movie scores as it stood up as an album in its own right. Two singles, **Freddie's Dead** and **Superfly** went gold, the album platinum.

Mayfield had at last achieved superstardom—rather than just acknowledged excellence — and found himself in the forefront of the new black music momentum which was pushing other more patronised musical forms into the second division. Along with Isaac Hayes((▶), the re-emerging Stevie Wonder(▶) and Marvin Gaye(▶), Mayfield was extending the accepted black sound boundaries to unexplored territory.

He enjoyed further gold albums during this momentum, **Back To The World** and **Sweet Exorcist,** and scored two more film soundtracks, **Claudine** (with Gladys Knight & The Pips(▶)) and **Let's Do It Again** (Staple Singers(▶)). Although warmly received by critics, Mayfield's 1975 set **There's No Place Like America Today** was musically disappointing, despite some pertinent, acerbic lyrics.

His lightweight-funk rhythm section was in danger of being steamrollered by the emerging powerhouse soul units, and he returned to the comparative calm of films for the Cosby/Poitier vehicle *A Piece Of The Action,* for *Short Eyes,* which featured Mayfield in an acting role, and for *Sparkle,* with Aretha Franklin(▶), a surprising non-event, considering

There's No Place Like America Today. Courtesy Curtom Records.

the talent of the collaborators. He also produced Gladys Knight & The Pips and the Staple Singers.

Despite the hesitancy of Mayfield's recent career, prospects are always bright for the genuine giants of music, although it may be difficult for him to recapture the **Amen** days.

Recording note: See the Impressions for selected recordings with that group.

Recordings:
Curtis (Curtom/Buddah)
Curtis Live (Curtom/Buddah)
Roots (Curtom/Buddah)
Superfly (RSO)
Back To The World (Curtom/Buddah)
Sweet Exorcist (Curtom/Buddah)
Move On Up—The Best of Curtis Mayfield (—/Buddah)
Curtis In Chicago (Curtom/Buddah)

O.B. McClinton

Successful white 'blue-eyed soul' acts have been legion—the Righteous Brothers(▶), Roy Head, the Box Tops among them. Black country stars are a much rarer breed—though Charlie Pride did do it with a vengeance, becoming second only to Johnnie Cash in the C&W sales race.

O.B. McClinton, from Senatobia, Mississippi, not only sang country, he sang it in a rich mellow but definitely white redneck accent. Not that he turned his back on black music, however (the lyric of **Country Music That's My Thing** explains his philosophy with its story of why he doesn't sing like James Brown(▶)) for he was a prolific songwriter, his songs, interpreted by such stars as James Carr(▶), Clarence Carter(▶) and Otis Redding(▶), regularly appearing in the R&B chart.

His own records, released on Stax(▶) subsidiary Enterprise, included superb versions of William Bell's(▶) **You Don't Miss Your Water (Till The Well Runs Dry)** and the Temptations'(▶) **I Wish It Would Rain,** sung in country style.

Recordings:
O.B. McClinton Country (Enterprise/—)

Jimmy McCracklin

Rooted in the blues, McCracklin, who is still very active, has taken his career through R&B, rock 'n' roll, soul and back to the blues.

Born in St Louis in 1931, he started as a boxer, winning the US light-heavyweight title before a car accident put paid to that career. He recorded hard-rocking blues for several Los Angeles labels in the late '40s to early '50s, then signed to Chess(▶) and scored with the rock 'n' roll classic **The Walk.** By 1961 he was moving towards soul and scored with the haunting **Just Got To Know,** an R&B No. 2 in 1961, and subsequent superb albums for Imperial/Minit.

Stax took him back to the blues in the early '70s for the great **Yesterday Is Gone** album, produced by Willie Mitchell(▶) and

Below: The multi-talented Curtis Mayfield, who has staying power too.

Blues For Mister Jimmy. Courtesy Sue Records.

Booker T & the MGs(▶) drummer Al Jackson Jr.

Recordings:
Jimmy McCracklin Sings (Chess/—)
I Just Got To Know (Imperial/—)
The Best Of Jimmy McCracklin (Minit/—)
A Piece Of Jimmy McCracklin (—/Minit)
Yesterday Is Gone (Stax/—)

Eugene McDaniels

There was a time during the early 1960s when the name Gene McDaniels was rarely absent from the American Hot 100 through his convincing delivery of lyrical material written by such talents as Bacharach/David, Goffin/King and Pomus/Shuman, but the passing of years have brought a change of roles with McDaniels emerging as a writer of songs of social conscience.

McDaniels was born in Kansas City and his singing had gospel roots at Omaha University and at the Conservatory of Music prior to his emergence with commercial impact on Liberty in 1960. Backed by the brash but controlled orchestration produced by Snuff Garrett, McDaniels made the US top 10 early in 1961 with **A Hundred Pounds of Clay,** a love-song with a quasi-religious basis which incurred the displeasure of several broadcasting authorities at the time. By the end of 1961 he was back in the top 10 with the wry **Tower Of Strength,** which also made the British charts. Songs like **Chip Chip, Point of No Return** and **Spanish Lace** took his appealing tenor voice into the best-selling lists throughout 1962, while a movie appearance in *It's Trad, Dad* yielded the moody **Another Tear Falls.**

The 1970s brought a metamorphosis in the Eugene McDaniels identity, and he moved into a heavier musical direction with fresh sociological awareness, and an Atlantic contract yielded albums like **Outlaw** and **Headless Horseman Of The Apocalypse,** covering a different lyrical spectrum from the earlier era.

Recordings:
Tower of Strength (Liberty)
Outlaw (Atlantic)
Headless Horseman Of The Apocalypse (Atlantic)

Jimmy McGriff

Prolifically recorded jazz/R&B organist James Harrell McGriff was born in Philadelphia on April 3, 1936, and raised in a classical music environment. Starting out playing drums, bass, sax and vibes, he developed an interest in the Hammond organ after hearing townsman Jimmy Smith(▶) and others. When Richard 'Groove' Holmes played at McGriff's sister's wedding, the youngster asked to try out on Holmes' Hammond and was hooked (In later years the pair recorded an album of organ duets for Groove Merchant).

Signed to Juggy Murray's New York-based Sue(▶) label, McGriff hit top-20 Stateside in 1962 with his instrumental reading of Ray Charles's(▶) **I've Got A Woman** and won a following with UK mods thanks to **MG Blues** and other freewheeling Sue singles which were jazzier than Booker T and the MGs(▶) but pop enough to score with the dancers.

In the following years, McGriff recorded nearly 40 albums for an assortment of labels, including Solid State, Groove Merchant, Blue Note and Jam. Of late he has also been experimenting with synthesisers.

Below: Super New Orleans session band the Meters, prime movers on a series of soul classics.

Recordings:
I've Got A Woman (Sue)
Gospel Time (Sue)
Blues For Mister Jimmy (Sue/—)
A Bag Full Of Soul (Solid State)
Electric Funk (Blue Note/—)
Let's Stay Together (Groove Merchant/People)
City Lights (Jam/—)

The Melodians

Tony Brevette, born in Clarendon, Jamaica, and Robert Cogle and Brent Dowe, both from Kingston's Greenwich Town area, assembled as the Melodians in 1965. More than a decade and a half later the group is considered to have been a cornerstone of reggae's vocal-harmony sound despite its comparatively low volume of output. **Little Nut Tree, Sweeter The Sugar** and **Loving Feeling** formed their singles apprenticeship with Coxsone at Studio One(▶). Between 1966 and 1969 they seldom visited a recording studio, except for a couple of sessions with Duke Reid, preferring instead to appear live on-stage at the island's night spots. The decision to concentrate on public performances was fuelled by poor financial rewards from recording.

Their first and biggest hit outside Jamaica came in 1969 when, with producer Leslie Kong, they cut **The Rivers Of Babylon,** the haunting anthem of Rastafari that was to be popularised again in the late '70s by the Anglo/German pop group Boney M(▶). The Melodians' version is reputed to have sold in excess of 75,000 copies in the UK alone. The Melodians and Kong could do no wrong. Two more big hits came in Jamaica, **Sweet Sensation** and **It's My Delight,** besides the first-rate album containing both of them, **Rivers Of Babylon.**

Just at the point where their future seemed assured, the Melodians quit Leslie Kong and began working with Duke Reid. The unit was forever peering back over its shoulder, and survived by cutting new versions of old songs. The group was uninspired and the public became disillusioned with them. In 1974, shortly before Duke Reid's death, they broke up: Brevette—the group's central figure—left for America; Dowe flourished briefly as a solo performer, hitting with **Build Me Up,** but Cogle went into a period of inactivity.

To all intents and purposes the group no longer exists; Brevette, Dowe and Cogle are making a living doing backing vocals and have agreed not to re-form unless contracted to a major record company and a producer who can deliver the goods that Kong did.

However, in 1976, the Melodians did reassemble, in Miami, with producer Harry 'J' Johnson for the **Sweet Sensation** album, re-recording all their formative hits, with the Soul Syndicate providing the rhythm tracks. Snapped up in America and throughout the Caribbean, the album fingers the Melodians' dilemma and that which affects a number of similar vocals units: how to maintain a production and songwriting momentum without continually having to hark back. But even if **Rivers Of Babylon** and **Sweet Sensation** are all we are to hear of the Melodians, it was a worthwhile group.

Recordings:
Rivers Of Babylon (Beverlys)
Sweet Sensation (Harry J)
The Melodians (Island)

The Meters

Like Booker T and the MGs(▶), the Meters have always existed partly as a recording and gigging unit, partly as a studio band backing others. Although never as successful as the MGs, over the course of the years the Meters have stacked up several hits, at the same time establishing themselves as the definitive purveyors of New Orleans funk.

The Meters started in New Orleans, backing Fats Domino(▶) and gigging around the area. They were known as the Hawkettes and then as the Neville Sound, before falling in with ace producer Allen Toussaint(▶). He used them to back Lee Dorsey(▶), and the result was a string of hits for Dorsey in the mid-60s. **Ride Your Pony, Work Work Work, Get Out Of My Life Woman** and **Working In The Coal Mine** were among the classic hits that benefited from the Meters' unique blend of syncopated funk. The line-up at this time comprised Art Neville, keyboards; Leo Nocentelli, guitar; Joseph 'Zig' Modeliste, drums; and George Porter, bass.

Toussaint also used the band to back other star vocalists like Betty Harris(▶), Art Neville's hit-making brother Aaron Neville(▶) and Irma Thomas(▶). In 1969, the Meters first recorded under their own name, with Toussaint and partner Marshall Sehorn producing. The result was several hit singles, including **Sophisticated Cissy** and **Cissy Strut**, and three albums which were all released on Josie, a subsidiary of Jubilee Records. The music was exceptional, a potent blend of clipped quirky rhythms, stripped-down funk and off-beat accents. In many ways, the music the Meters were making at this time paved the way for '70s street-funk.

The Meters moved labels to Reprise in the early '70s, although Allen Toussaint remained their producer. The move heralded a more wide-ranging approach, with extra percussion and horns often added, while material veered more towards rock. **Cabbage Alley,** released in 1972, is a good and varied album, while **Rejuvenation,** released in 1974, combined the band's original New Orleans influences with Sly Stone(▶)-style funk. It's a remarkably successful blend, and the album is possibly their most rewarding recording.

Later albums from the Meters never quite recaptured the inspiration of **Rejuvenation,** and from the mid-'70s onward the band became increasingly involved with rock groups. They suported Dr John and the Rolling Stones on tour, and were the driving force behind a number of rock acts in the studio, from Robert Palmer to Paul McCartney. Nevertheless, their albums—particularly **Cissy Strut,** which is a selection of early Josie tracks, and **Rejuvenation**—show just what can be achieved within instrumental funk limitations.

Recordings:
Cissy Strut (Island)
Cabbage Alley (Reprise)
Rejuvenation (Reprise)
Fire On The Bayou (Reprise)
New Directions(Warner Bros)

Buddy Miles

Miles' powerful drumming was

Above: Besides having solo success Buddy Miles has played with the best.

first heard in the charts on Jaynetts' early '60s classic **Sally Go Round The Roses.** Born in Omaha, Nebraska, he worked from age 13 in bands, backing the Inkspots(▶) Bryan Hyland, Conway Twitty and the Dick Clark Revue.

Joining Wilson Pickett's(▶) band in 1965 he spent a year with the soul giant before teaming up with rock musician Mike Bloomfield to form Electric Flag under the aegis of legendary manager Albert Grossman (the man behind Bob Dylan).

An anarchic mixture of rock, blues and soul influences, Flag produced great music but soon fell apart leaving Miles to form the Buddy Miles Express, a brass-laden aggregation which took the

rock/R&B mix a stage further and was like Blood, Sweat and Tears with funk.

After a run of fine albums, Miles joined Jimi Hendrix(▶) and Billy Cox in the ill-fated Band Of Gypsies, featuring on the album of that name as well as on Hendrix's **Electric Ladyland, The Jimi Hendrix Experience** and **Cry Of Love** albums.

In 1970, Miles put together the Buddy Miles Band and came up with the brilliant **Them Changes** album which spent nearly 18 months on the US charts, the title cut being reissued no fewer than three times to meet public demand. Several further quality albums (including **Collaborations** with Carlos Santana) emerged before the rotund drummer/vocalist faded from prominence.

Besides his own prolific output, Miles was drummer on Aretha Franklin's(▶) **Respect,** Wilson Pickett's(▶) **In The Midnight Hour** and Eddie Floyd's(▶) **Knock On Wood** as well as recording and/or gigging with Gladys Knight and the Pips(▶), Billy Stewart(▶), Ben E. King(▶), Joe Tex(▶), Percy Sledge(▶), James Brown(▶) and many more.

Recordings:
Expressway To Your Skull (Mercury)
Electric Church (Mercury)
We Got To Live Together (Mercury)
Them Changes (Mercury)
A Message To The People (Mercury)
Boogie Bear (Columbia/—)
All The Face (Columbia/CBS)

The Melodians. Courtesy Island Records.

THE ORIGINAL REGGAE SOUND

THE MELODIANS

Sweet Sensation
Rock It With Me
Rivers Of Babylon
It's My Delight

Above: The latterday Miracles perform on American TV's Soul Train Show.

Millie

Millie Small's one big hit, **My Boy Lollipop** (1964), did more than any other record to awaken white audiences to the appeal of Jamaican music (ska, or bluebeat, as it was known at the time).

Leased to Fontana Records by Chirs Blackwell, it provided urgently needed funds to keep his own Island label in business. Island subsequently developed from a pure reggae outlet into a major rock and black music label. **My Boy Lollipop** made No. 2 in the UK chart, thanks to its irresistible bouncy beat and Millie's high-pitched little-girl vocal but although she saw top 40 action with the follow-up **Sweet William**, subsequent records sank without trace.

Recordings:
The Best Of Millie Small
(—/Trojan)

Garnett Mimms

Garnett Mimms recorded some of the most hauntingly soulful ballads of the '60s, records which benefitted not only from his emotive but in no way histrionic vocals but also from the songwriting/arranging/production genius of Jerry Ragovoy(▶).

Born Garnett Mimms in Ashland, Virginia, on November 26, 1935, Garnett Mimms grew up in Philadelphia where his first group was known as Garnett Mimms and the Deltones. Returning from army service he formed a new group called the Gaynors, whose line-up also included Howard Tate(▶). Records for Mercury, Cameo Parkway(▶) and Red Top won only local

success and the outfit folded in 1961.

Undaunted, Mimms and fellow-Gaynor Samuel Bell brought in Charles Boyer and girl singer Zola Pearson to form the Enchanters. Signed to United Artists, they quickly scored with the million-seller **Cry Baby** in 1963. It was to all intents a Mimms' solo performance of an evocative Bert Russell/Norman Meade soul ballad.

By 1964, Mimms had dropped the Enchanters and consistently charted with such marvellous material as **As Long As I Have You, A Little Bit Of Soap, I'll Take Good Care Of You** and **It Was Easier To Hurt Her.** He toured the UK and cut a live album with a Scottish band, Senate, but the '70s saw his kind of uptown soul music in eclipse and an attempt to get into the new disco mode, via an album on Arista (produced by Brass Construction's(▶) Randy Muller) in the mid '70s, failed dismally as it had none of the charm of his earlier output.

Recordings:
Cry Baby And 11 Other Hits
(United Artists)
I'll Take Good Care Of You
(United Artists/—)
As Long As I Have You (United Artists/—)
Live (United Artists)
What It Is (Arista)

The Miracles

When Smokey Robinson(▶) left The Miracles to concentrate on a solo career in 1971, the group had some dificulty in finding a convincing direction. Robinson continued to produce their records at first, but it was not long before the Miracles were handed over to a variety of Motown(▶) 'house' producers, including Marvin Gaye(▶), Willie Hutch(▶) and Freddie Perren.

The group (which kept the

original line-up, less Robinson and his wife Claudette, of Bobby Rogers, second tenor; Ronnie White, baritone; Warren 'Pete' Moore, bass; plus new lead voice William Griffin) put out some half-dozen albums in the '70s of varying artistic and commercial success, although they did have a big hit in 1976 with the single **Love Machine,** taken from the album of the same name. Eventually, wanting more independence to write and produce their own material, the group left Motown for Columbia. Like many other ex-Motowners, they had not had spectacular success since leaving the label.

Recordings:
Do It Baby (Motown)
Love Machine (Motown)
Love Crazy (Columbia/CBS)

Willie Mitchell

Though trumpet is his preferred instrument, Memphis veteran Willie Mitchell is also an adept keyboard man, songwriter, arranger and producer.

The Willie Mitchell Combo has been every bit as synonymous with the 'Memphis Sound' in soul

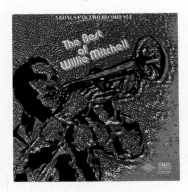

The Best Of Willie Mitchell. Courtesy Hi Records.

music as was the rival Booker T and the MGs(▶) line-up. Indeed, the late Al Jackson Jr served as drummer with Willie Mitchell before becoming a founder member of the MGs.

Jackson's replacement in Mitchell's group was Howard 'Tiny' Grimes, the other mainstays in later years being Mitchell's younger brother James on saxophone, and the Hodges brothers, Mabon 'Teenie' Hodges, Charles 'Dufunny' Hodges and Leroy 'Flick' Hodges, on guitar, organ and bass. Together they have long been the resident band at Hi Records(▶), a company which Mitchell was eventually to head after the death of its founder Joe Cuoghi.

Born in Ashland, Mississippi, in 1928, Mitchell gained his early experience in bands led by Tuff Green and Al Jackson's father (also known as Al). In 1954, Mitchell formed his own combo; they became house band with the House Of The Blues label before joining Hi in 1961 and scoring with such hits as **20-75, Everything Is Gonna Be Alright, That Driving Beat Ram-Bunk-Shus, Bad Eye, Mercy, Soul Serenade** and **Prayer Meeting,** as well as a whole run of albums featuring instrumental versions of then current R&B/soul favourites.

Following the death of Bill Black (who also recorded for Hi), Mitchell and his band took over the mantle of Bill Black's Combo and recorded under that name as well as their own. They were also the house band behind major hits for Al Green(▶), Ann Peebles(▶), Syl Johnson, Otis Clay, Don Bryant and others.

Recordings:
That Driving Beat (Hi/—)
Hold It (Hi/—)
The Hit Sound Of Willie Mitchell
(Hi/London)
Soul Serenade (-/London)
Best Of (Hi/—)

Jackie Mittoo

Born in 1948 into a middle-class family in Kingston, Jamaica, Mittoo was taught to play the piano by his grandmother, a teacher at the Alpha Music School. He'd played his first public engagements by the age of 10 and three years later had passed through two local bands, the Rivals and the Sheiks.

The popularity of the Sheiks led him to the Studio One(▶) stable of Clement Coxsone Dodd, where with Lee Perry(▶) he was employed as a talent scout and producer (often uncredited), in addition to assembling the legendary studio band, the Skatalites(▶) with whom he played piano and organ. They sculptured mid-'60s rock-steady, scoring internationally with singles **Phoenix City** and **Guns Of Navarone** that he co-wrote.

Mittoo joined the Soul Vendors and in 1967 toured Britain, where he recorded his first album, the instrumental set **Jackie Mittoo In London**, released on the Coxsone label. His first single was **Ram Jam**, dedicated to a popular Jamaican club.

A consummate musician with his own label, Vendor, he has worked with countless producers (including Bunny Lee, Duke Reid, Prince Buster(▶)) and artists Bob Andy(▶) Delroy Wilson(▶), the Heptones(▶), Marcia Griffiths(▶), Sugar Minott(▶)). His album tracks often show a strong leaning towards soul and jazz, not every cut being in a reggae idiom. The classy **Now** (Bamboo) set, for instance, is very much in the mode of The Meters(▶). He has also written scores for Broadway shows and presently commutes between his home in Canada and New York, London and Kingston.

Recordings:
Wishbone (Boot/London)
Now (Studio One/Bamboo)
Keyboard King (—/Third World)
Macka Fat (United Artists/Studio One)

Below: Motown's 'magnificent seven': the Supremes and the Four Tops.

Jackie Moore

Born in Jacksonville, Florida, Jackie Moore had a minor hit on Scepter with **Dear John** and was then taken by important Philadelphia DJ Jimmy Bishop to Atlantic Records(▶), who teamed her with producer Dave Crawford. Their co-penned **Precious Precious** earned the lady a gold disc, and she also scored with **Sometimes It Has To Rain In Your Life, Darling Baby** and **Time.**

Recordings:
Sweet Charlie Babe (Atlantic)

Motown

While the Motown Recording Corporation was for some time synonymous with the musical output of Detroit, there was a time some 20 years ago when two other independent disc companies in that city were contesting for a major hold on the R&B market—Devora Brown's Fortune Records, with a background of blues and doo-wop, and Robert West's LuPine Records, with a distillation of gospel and black popular balladry. Then an emergent Motor-city magnate burst through to eclipse both rivals. He was the catalyst who blended the essence of R&B, gospel and pop to secure a major hold on first the local market, and subsequently on the national and international scene. Berry Gordy Jr spent the mid-50s working part-time on the Ford Motor Company production line, but balanced this with a more creative and remunerative vocation, writing songs and producing record sessions. By early 1960 he had accumulated a track-record of some 180 top 100 hits, often in collaboration with Tyran Carlo (a.k.a. Roquel Davis) or Janie Bradford, including million-sellers by Jackie Wilson(▶) (**Reet Petite, Lonely Teardrops**) and Marv Johnson(▶) (**You Got What It Takes**).

Thus Gordy was hardly an assembly-line pauper when he launched the Motown label in June 1960 with the Satintones' **My Beloved/Sugar Daddy.** This doo-wop quintet consisted of James Ellis, Sammy Mack, Vernon Williams, Robert Bateman and Sonny Sanders, and their follow-up, **Motor City,** launched sister-label Tamla a month later. As yet, however, there was no definite 'Motown Sound'—early discs by artists like Mable John, Gino Parks and Eddie Holland(▶) were in the popular beat idiom of their day, Holland sounding like a stand-in for Jackie Wilson, while Hattie Littles adapted a gospel-drenched delivery to the secular market.

It was a combination of pop and gospel roots that began to gel into the classic Motown format during 1960/61, as Gordy brought erstwhile Fortune stalwart Choker Campbell and his band to the Hitsville USA HQ on West Grand Boulevard. Thus began an era of instantly recognisable 'Motown Sound', driven by the crashing rimshot snare beats of Benny Benjamin, the solid bass foundation of James Jamerson, those reedy horn

It Takes Two. Courtesy Motown Records.

riffs and crisp tambourine, with slower material endowed with gospelly piano or organ (usually played by Earl Van Dyke(▶).

Then came a succession of distinctive (and oft-covered) chart hits including Barrett Strong's **Money,** a first million-seller with the Miracles'(▶) **Shop Around,** emulated by the chart-topping **Please Mr Postman** by the Marvelettes(▶), and the Corporation's inception of

a third logo, Gordy, early in 1962 soon to score with the Contours' **Do You Love Me.**

Meanwhile several small independent Detroit labels with Gordy family connections were experiencing financial difficulties, having scored hits but received no payment from distributors. By the end of 1962 Harvey, Miracle, Tri-Phi, Melody and Anna had been absorbed into the Motown Corporation, and with them the contracts of Lamont Anthony (Dozier)(▶) Jimmy and David Ruffin(▶), Johnny Bristol(▶), Jr Walker(▶), the Temptations(▶) and Spinners(▶), sewing the seeds for chart success for years to come. The Temptations went to Gordy, and their No.1 smash **My Girl** set the idiomatic style of lilting balladry, contrasting with the striking exuberance of label-mates Martha & the Vandellas(▶), whose **Dancing In The Street** remains an incomparable blend of R&B/gospel/pop.

Similar elements were to the fore when two new stars emerged during 1963. The strident gospelly intensity of Marvin Gaye's **Pride & Joy** and **Can I Get A Witness,** and the spontaneous power of Little Stevie Wonder's(▶) **Fingertips** were big scorers. The same urgency was evident in the output of the Contours and Four Tops(▶), and even oozed from the lilting groove of Mary Wells' **My Guy,** pushed by that typical splashing percussion and firm but underlying bass. By this time, in the summer of 1964, the Supremes(▶) were ready to assume the mantle of the Corporation's prime hitmakers, topping the charts with **Where Did Our Love Go** and **Baby Love,** then with 10 further discs up to 1969; the Four Tops were also rarely out of the top 50.

Motown's two headlining male groups, the Four Tops and the Temptations, maintained their progress in distinctive and divergent styles, the former largely with punchy beat-ballads from the strident delivery of Levi Stubbs, and the latter with usually more delicate harmonies behind the alternating lead baritone of David Ruffin or high tenor of Eddie Kendricks(▶), though this image was rent asun-

der by the rock-tinged influence of writer/producer Norman Whitfield(▶) in 1969. No, we haven't forgotten the Miracles, but the presence of Claudette Rogers—who later left to have children—precludes their being classified as *male*. They were led by arguably the most recognisable voice in Motown music (if not in soul)—Smokey Robinson(▶). They too enjoyed a prodigious output and high hit quotient, from the poignancy of **Ooh Baby Baby** to the stomping vitality of **Going To A Go Go**, leaning on Smokey's lyrical genius.

The mid-60s saw the inception of further logos, VIP and Soul, with rosters bulging with vocal groups set for subsequent recognition. The Monitors, Elgins and Velvelettes displayed more vintage approach and were soon eclipsed, but the Spinners, Orginals and Gladys Knight & the Pips(▶) were able to grow along with varying contemporary demands.

1967 proved a landmark year when Smokey Robinson and Diana Ross(▶) were accorded feature label-credits on their groups' releases, while Marvin Gaye changed his approach to good effect in duet with Kim Weston and then with the tragic figure of Tammi Terrell(▶) (of whose death only Elaine Jesmer has alluded to with pseudonymous actuality!). There was, strangely, a lack of significant female solo successes—Brenda Holloway, Kim Weston, Liz Lands, Carolyn Crawford, Tammi, Mable John, Yvonne Fair(▶), Barbara McNair all had limited releases/hits, but somehow failed to hold Corporation interest.

The Motown Sound was sustained to the end of the decade, remaining distinctive and definitive, even to the extent that acts joining the roster became moulded to fit the image—Gladys Knight & the Pips, the Isley Bros(▶) and Chuck Jackson(▶) being prime examples of performers whose prior and subsequent output was at odds with the Detroit blend. But the established acts were still winning through with 'the sound,' Marvin Gaye scoring with his version of Gladys Knight's earlier hit **Grapevine** (ironically his rendition

had been recorded first), the Temptations carrying Whitfied's biting arrangements to chart summits, and Diana Ross and the Supremes firing a parting united shot with **Someday We'll Be Together.** But the turn of the decade brought fresh moves and new names, including the emergence of the Jackson Five(▶) with four consecutive R&B chart toppers.

With the dawn of the 1970s came several changes at Motown. The Corporation's roster had suffered two fatalities with the deaths of Shorty Long (drowned in a boating accident) and Tammi Terrell, but this was balanced by the output of the phenomenally successful Jackson Five, discovered by Diana Ross, and signed from the local Detroit-based Steeltown label. A notable split within the ranks occurred when Diana Ross left the Supremes in January 1970 to pursue a solo career, but both she and the group stayed with Motown.

A divergence of style came with the inception of two new logos: Rare Earth being a tentative step into white rock, and Chisa forming an outlet for jazz-based products. Finding Motown established as the most successful black record corporation, Berry Gordy Jr felt it was time to explore alternative media, primarily the movie world, prompting a move for his administrative headquarters from West Grand Boulevard, Detroit, way out west to Hollywood, California. The prime intent was to groom Diana Ross for celluloid stardom, on which basis Motown set about producing a biographical film of the life and tragic death of the legendary jazz-blues singer Billie Holiday, with Diana starring over the supporting Billie Dee Williams. The movie won a degree of critical acclaim and Oscar nominations, though maybe it was the Holiday aspect rather than Ross's talent which 'made' the film, since her subsequent fashion-model role as *Mahogany* is (and largely has been!) perhaps best forgotten.

Below: A superstar among Motown's glittering galaxy, the many-faceted Diana Ross.

Motown Gold. Courtesy Motown Records.

Meanwhile, the geographical relocation had spawned yet another logo, aptly named MoWest, with a delightful Pacific sunset design and a roster including Gloria Jones(▶), Sisters Love, G.C. Cameron(▶) and Tom Clay, a DJ who took the second release into the top 10, the narrative **What The World Needs Now—Abraham, Martin & John,** a bizarre but striking collage of radio-station tapes relating to political assassinations, cushioned with tasteful musical background.

There was a concurrent resurgence for Marvin Gaye's career as he changed his musical direction to the melancholy introversion of **What's Going On, Mercy Mercy Me** and **Inner City Blues,** successive R&B chart-toppers, and this was indicative of the Corporation's musical development. No longer were its discs readily indentifiable stomping gospel-soul rhythms, they were blending into the pattern of contemporary elaborated orchestrations powered by the ever-increasing dominance of throbbing bass-lines.

With the changing times came a changing roster; departures included the Four Tops, Gladys Knight & the Pips, the Spinners, and the Miracles (minus Smokey Robinson, who remains a consistently successful Tamla solo act to this date), to varying success in different pastures, while Stevie Wonder rose to massive crossover popularity by virtue of his creative writing ability and rock-tinged performance. Eddie Kendricks(▶) emerged from the Temptations as a top-line solo act, the Commodores(▶) developed as masterful exponents of ballads and funk, and Diana Ross stuck more to her proven vocal talent, laying a foundation for the entire disco genre with her 1976 smash hit **Love Hangover,** actually a cover version lifted with amazing speed from the Fifth Dimension's original demo pressings. Thus began a whole new ball-game, with the Motown Recording Corporation maintaining its position as market innovator/leader, and the story continues with Motown riding out the disco era while maintaining a degree of artistic integrity and commercial zeal.

The 1980s have brought yet more changes to the roster and the honour-roll of hits, as newer groups like Switch (male) and High Inergy (female) score small hits with regular releases, while Rick James(▶) has emerged as a major figure, his 'punk-funk' image adding a different dimension to the Motown sound, even if rather at aesthetic odds with its more soulful roots. The Temptations have re-joined the company, as have, separately, their erstwhile lead singers Eddie

Kendricks and David Ruffin, but former top Motown names Diana Ross and Marvin Gaye now appear on different labels, RCA and Columbia respectively.

The Motown Sound, Volume 1. Courtesy Motown Records.

A pleasantly surprising and welcome addition is Bettye LaVette, a native of Michigan with a long soulful pedigree, whose debut single **Right In The Middle** gained impressive chart status early in 1982, while Stevie Wonder topped the soul charts with **That Girl,** and Smokey Robinson celebrated his silver anniversary on disc with another hit **Tell Me Tomorrow.** So the Motown story continues, still scoring hits with talent old and new . . .

Recordings:
The First Decade
  (Motown/—)
Motown Memories Vols 1, 2, 3
  (—/Tamla Motown)
Motown Chartbusters Vols 1-10
  (—/Tamla Motown)

Idris Muhammad

Born Leo Morris in New Orleans in 1939, drummer and percussionist Muhammad is one of the most experienced and accomplished musicians around today. He has had two distinct careers—first as a highly rated session drummer, secondly as a leader in his own right. In the first incarnation he was the driving force behind a raft of late '50s and early '60s hits, including Larry Williams'(▶) **Bony Moronie,** Joe Jones' **You Talk Too Much,** The Impressions'(▶) **Keep On Pushing** and **People Get Ready** and the Dixie Cups' **Chapel Of Love.**

In 1974 he signed to Creed Taylor's(▶) Kudu label, and was featured on albums by artists like Bob James(▶) and Grover Washington(▶), as well as releasing records as a leader. He had considerable success before moving to Prestige in 1978. He is now a regular in the disco and R&B charts with music that is a highly listenable mixture of jazz, funk and soul.

Recordings:
Boogie To The Top (CTI)
Fox Huntin' (Fantasy)
Make It Count (Fantasy)
Turn This Mutha Out (Kudu)

Muscle Shoals

Within the spectrum of rhythm and blues music, there have developed a number of quite distinctive area 'sounds' serving to identify the location of a particular recording and/or the origin of the performer. The blues field has its 'Chicago' style, along with sounds indigenous

Above: Philly International stalwarts, the soulful O'Jays.

to the Mississippi Delta or to Texas, while the more contemporary soul idiom boasts 'Memphis' and 'Philadelphia' sounds, and R&B music from New Orleans carries its own identity.

The Southern states seem to create such identities fairly readily, perhaps because of their less cosmopolitan lifestyle, and down in Alabama during the 1960s the small town of Florence began to gain a reputation with the 'Muscle Shoals' sound — Muscle Shoals was the airport serving this town, where writer/musician Rick Hall had opened a recording studio.

Surrounded by a nucleus of white musicians with their souls deeply immersed in Southern R&B, Hall began to produce records which created both local and national interest. Session-credits would boast names like Spooner Oldham, Barry Becket (organ), Jimmy Johnson (guitar), David Hood (bass), Roger Hawkins (drums), who combined to generate a very 'churchy' sound, particularly on slower songs.

Besides leasing his self-financed productions to a variety of labels, Hall produced material on artists sent to the studio by such companies as Chess(▶) and Atlantic(▶).

In 1964 Hall launched his own Fame label, scoring with Jimmy Hughes' **Steal Away**, and that year Joe Tex cut his **Hold What You've Got** hit at the Fame studio, prompting Atlantic Records' interest in the set-up. Hall signed his Fame label to Atlantic distribution, and Atlantic began to use his talents and facilities to record artists like Wilson Pickett,(▶) Aretha Franklin(▶) and Arthur Conley(▶). Their success prompted interest from Chess, who sent Etta James, Irma Thomas and Bobby Moore to Alabama with similar results, while blind star Clarence Carter(▶) and his then wife Candi Statton(▶) also recorded at Fame.

Since then such diverse talents as Otis Rush and Ronnie Hawkins

have used the studio, and the sessioneers have recorded their own LPs under a collective Muscle Shoals identity, while the most notable recent output was an album by Eddie Hinton recorded in November 1977; interestingly, 1981 saw the granting of a liquor licence for the area, which had previously been 'dry'!

Aaron Neville

A member of the Hawketts in the early '60s, Aaron Neville (born New Orleans, 1941) recorded as solo for Minit and had minor success with **Over You** before scoring a No. 2 US hit with his black awareness anthem **Tell It Like It Is** (on Parlo) in 1967. Under the direction of Allen Toussaint(▶) and Marshall Sehorn at Sansu Productions Neville also recorded for Instant, Safari and Bell. His brother Art is a member of the Meters(▶).

Recordings:
Like It 'Tis (Mint/Liberty)

O'Jays

Maybe angling for extra air-play, the O'Jays took their name from popular Cleveland, Ohio, radio DJ Eddie O'Jay; in the two decades which have elapsed since then, their fame has far eclipsed that of their mentor.

The roots of the group lay in a doo-wop outfit formed at Canton McKinley High School. Eddie Levert, Walter Williams, William Powell, Bobby Massey and .Bill Isles recorded together in 1958 as the Mascots before changing their name and recording the dance-craze number **Do The Wiggle** for King(▶) in nearby Cincinnati. It flopped.

H. B. Barnum(▶) took them to Los Angeles-based Imperial where they cut **Lonely Drifter** (1963) and had a minor hit. They followed up with a version of Benny Spellman's(▶) **Lipstick Traces** which did a bit

better, making national action. Numerous follow-ups on both Imperial and the associated Minit label failed to happen as did sides they cut in New York with George Kerr producing; subsequently Isles left.

Singing to Kenny Gamble and Leon Huff's Philly-based Neptune label, they did better with **One Night Affair** and **Looky, Looky** (1970), but it was a false start since the label promptly folded, leaving the group to go off producing themselves without success until Gamble and Huff got their act together again by launching Philadelphia International(▶).

Now down to a trio, Bobby Massey having left to work in record production, the O'Jays took off with a vengeance almost before the ink on the Philadelphia International contract was dry. The combination of their smooth soulful vocalising (Levert usually singing lead, Williams alternating between baritone and tenor, Powell between tenor and baritone), great songs and production from Gamble and Huff and the impressive musicianship of the Sigma Sound Studios band (later to evolve as the nucleus of MFSB(▶)) was pure magic and, from 1972 on, hits like **Back Stabbers, Love Train, For The Love Of Money** made their version of the Philly Sound a chart fixture worldwide.

In late 1975, illness forced William Powell into retirement. His replacement in the trio was Sammy Strain who had spent 12 years as a member of Little Anthony and the Imperials(▶).

Subsequently a run of powerful singles, including the superb **Used To Be My Girl,** and **Girl, Don't Let It Get You Down,** and ever enjoyable albums have kept the O'Jays' flag flying high.

Recordings:
Full Of Soul (Liberty-Sunset)
The O'Jays (Bell/—)
The O'Jays In Philadelphia (Epic)
Ship Ahoy (Philadelphia International)

Family Reunion (Philadelphia International)
Survival (Philadelphia International)
So Full Of Love (Philadelphia International)
The Year 2000 (Philadelphia International)

The Originals

Walter Gaines, C.P. Spencer, Henry Dixon and Freddie Gorman started out at Motown(▶) in 1965 singing back-ups for other artists, for example Stevie Wonder's(▶) **Yester You, Yester Me, Yester Day,** before Marvin Gaye(▶) wrote **Baby I'm For You** for them and they notched their first gold record. A succession of classy singles established them as among the best of Motown's 'second division' vocal groups.

Gaines was born in Augusta, Georgia, and came to Detroit to work as a postman. The other three are native Detroiters.

Recordings:
Green Grow The Lilacs (Tamla Motown)
Down To Love Town (Motown)
Another Time Another Place (Fantasy)

The Orlons

Mainstay of Philadelphia's Cameo label, The Orlons won major exposure on the city's American Bandstand TV show, resulting in a series of hits, including three million-sellers.

Formed at high school, the group broke up after five years but were put back together again with a line-up of Shirley Brickley (born December 9, 1944), Rosetta Hightower (born June 23, 1944), Marlena Davis (born October 4, 1944) and Steve Caldwell (born November 22, 1942). Signing to Cameo, they hit No. 2 in the US chart in 1962 with the million-selling dance number **The Wah-Watusi,** following through quickly with the catchy novelty song **Don't Hang Up,** which also went gold.

A year later their third gold disc came with **South Street** (penned, like the other two, by Cameo bosses Dave Appell and Kal Mann). At Cameo, they also sang back-up for Dee Dee Sharp and Bobby Rydell.

Steve Caldwell and Marlena Davis left in 1964 and Audrey Birchley came in, but the demise of Cameo spelt finis to The Orlons' chart career and later records on ABC and Calla made little impact. The group finally split up when Rosetta Hightower left for a solo career in Britain, where she married arranger Ian Green and recorded for CBS.

Recordings:
Best Of The Orlons (London)

The Paragons

Formed in Kingston, Jamaica, in the early '60s, the Paragons evolved from another vocal group, the Binders, and initially comprised Garth 'Tyrone' Evans, Bob Andy(▶), Junior Menz and Leroy Stamp, trading on revamped American R&B hits, and in particular the soulful harmonies of the Drifters(▶). John Holt(▶), who was quickly to take on the mantle of chief protagonist, joined in 1964 to replace Stamp. Menz quit to become lead singer with the now legendary Techniques, and Howard Barrett, a former member of the Kingston College Choir, was drafted in.

The line-up complete, the group embarked upon extensive live engagements, backed by the now defunct Vikings, playing many of Kingston's major venues and, with Byron Lee(▶), hotels on the island's salubrious north coast. Pacted to Coxsone Dodd's Studio One(▶) in 1964, they committed their American-influenced soul to vinyl with singles **Love At Last, Lover's Dream** and **Good Luck And Goodbye**. A dispute over their musical direction resulted in Andy's acrimonious departure the next year.

Below: Esther Phillips found success with the country classic **Release Me.**

Fruitless searching for a replacement slapped a temporary halt on their recording career. It was an idea of Holt's that set them running again with a completely fresh approach. A new rock-steady beat was the key and the first release during this phase was **Happy Go Lucky Girl**. It was tighter and crisper than anything they'd done before and made them realise that they worked just as efficiently as a trio.

In 1966 they began their celebrated relationship with producer Duke Reid at his Treasure Isle Studio and the hits kept coming: **On The Beach, Wear You To The Ball, In My Neighbourhood, Riding High** and **So Much Pain**, in all, 16 rock-steady classics, all going to No. 1 in Jamaica.

Despite being the most prolific and successful rock-steady group in the Caribbean, with an eager audience in Britain, the group disbanded over a stipendiary disagreement. Evans and Barrett moved to New York to live with their families and Holt set off on what was to be a rewarding solo career.

When American rock group Blondie scored an international hit with their version of **The Tide Is High**, producer Lister Hewan-Lowe assembled the three for a one-off album of re-makes of previous hits, issued in 1981 by Island Records.

Recordings:
Rosalin Sweat (—/Attack)
The Paragons Return ((—/Third World)
Sly & Robbie Meet The Paragons (Mango/Island)

Robert Parker

Sax soloist on numerous R&B records going back as far as Professor Longhair's 1949 cuts for Atlantic and including sessions with Irma Thomas(▶), Ernie K. Doe(▶) and Joe Tex(▶), Robert Parker (born in New Orleans on October 14, 1930) made a run of poorly selling singles for a variety of labels. He finally scored the big 'un

with the infectious dance item **Barefootin'** on Nola in 1966, which hit No. 4 in the US national charts.

The resultant album was full of other equally attractive cuts, which represented New Orleans' R&B at its best, but none of his follow-ups scored big, nor did subsequent records for Silver Fox and other outlets.

Recordings:
Barefootin' (Nola/—)

Lee Perry

Born in St Mary's, Jamaica, in 1939, Perry has been a major force in the development of reggae music during the past two decades. First and foremost as a producer and secondly as a performer, his contribution to the music is incalculable. He shaped a sound that was totally unique and helped launch the careers of several artists, playing a significant role in Bob Marley's(▶) musical development.

Perry (aka Pipecock Jackson, Scratch, the Gong and the Upsetter) started his career in music selling records from Clement Coxsone Dodd's(▶) car. Dodd operated the legendary Downbeat sound system(▶), later training Perry, or Little as he was then known due to his four-foot-eleven-inch stature, to be joint controller and DJ with another man whom destiny had designs upon, Jackie Mittoo(▶). When Dodd moved into the recording business at his Studio One(▶), Perry and Mittoo were employed as talent scouts and apprentice producers/arrangers. Perry acquired the name Scratch when he cut his first record in response to an island dance craze, the **Chicken Scratch**.

Above: Lee Perry, a major contributor in the development of reggae.

Recording under the name King Perry, his first local hits, such as **Doctor Dick** and **Rub And Squeeze** were often quite lewd affairs set to a rock-steady beat. He eventually fell out with Dodd in 1968, probably because of a legal dispute, and committed his feelings to vinyl for Joe Gibbs(▶) on a record called **The Upsetter**, and on another reputed to be about Dodd, **People Funny Boy**.

The ball was now rolling, and working for his own Upsetter label Perry scored with **Tighten Up** by the Untouchables. In the spring of 1969 he achieved a top-20 position on the British pop charts with **Return Of Django**, attributed to the Upsetters, the studio band comprising Aston 'Familyman' Barrett, bass, and his brother Carlton (currently with the Wailers(▶)), drums, and Ronnie Williams, guitar.

Perry's royalties were ploughed into the now legendary Black Ark studio that he built for himself in the back of his home in Washington Gardens, Kingston. Still only a four-track studio, it was here that he perfected the distinctive double-time cymbal sound, a feature of his 1976 international hit **Police And Thieves** with Junior Murvin(▶), the equally famous **Sufferers Time** with the Heptones(▶), and his own indictment of colonialism, **White Belly Rat**.

The studio became a spawning ground for many Jamaican artists, including Susan Cadogan, Max Romeo(▶) and Augustos Pablo(▶). It was there that he recorded his debut album **The Upsetter** that set the tone for even more diverse albums such as **Blackboard Jungle** and **Scratch The Super Ape**. Assisting him in his work was his wife Pauline, who has since left him.

His relationship with Bob Marley, Peter Tosh(▶) and Bunny 'Wailer' Livingstone(▶) (collectively the original Wailers(▶)) was to have a profound effect upon all their lives. Teaming up with them at Studio One, he assisted in the writing and production of reggae classics **Slave Driver, Duppy Conquerer, Small Axe, African Herbsman, Sun Is Shining** and **Kaya**. He collaborated on the definitive early Wailers' album, **Soul Rebel**, and was a strong influence on their commercial breakthrough set, **Catch A Fire**. It is a measure of Marley's regard for the man that he departed from Dodd soon after Perry, and named his record company Tuff Gong as a tribute to Perry who, at the time, called himself the Gong.

In 1978 Perry went to live in Holland where he was introduced to the psychedelic hallucinogenic drug LSD. He worked with a variety of musicians and producers, including many involved with the burgeoning punk-rock scene. Absorbing the reggae and punk working-class kinship he left for Britain, where at Island Records' London studios he cut **Punky Reggae Party** with Marley.

By the turn of the decade, rumours circulating the industry implied that he had lost his mind and was waging a crusade against Rastafarians. A genuine eccentric, he had in fact feigned madness in what became a successful move to liberate himself from the countless freeloaders who surrounded him. He erected an impenetrable fence around his studio, cemented a fish-tank beneath his drumkit and barred anyone with dreadlocks from the premises.

Perry has been comparatively quiet of late, but there is every reason to expect a plethora of new material soon. He is the most successful record producer in the history of reggae and a sample of his idiosyncratic gift can be heard on the 1979 Island Record's compilation, **Scratch On The Wire**.

Recordings:
The Upsetter (—/Trojan)
Cloak And Dagger (Black Ark/ Rhino)
The Upsetter Presents (Lion Of Juddah/—)
The Upsetter Collection (—/Trojan)

Persuasions

Something of an anachronism, the talented Persuasions made a successful '70s career out of the then outdated acappella style of singing, cutting a stream of great albums for a variety of labels and packing concert halls. They knew their craft so well that it often took several listens to one of their records before it dawned that there were no musical instruments, all the sounds being made by human voice (though they did include some instrumental backings on one of their later albums).

Lead baritone Jerry Lawson (born Fort Lauderdale, Florida, January 23, 1944), baritone Herbert 'Tubo' Rhoad (born Bamberg, South Carolina, October 1, 1944), bass Jimmy 'Bro' Hayes (born Hopewell, Virginia, November 12, 1943), and tenors Joseph 'Jesse' Russell (born Henderson, North

Above: 'Look, no bands!' Acappella group the Persuasions found success via Frank Zappa's Straight label.

Carolina, September 25, 1939) and Jayotis Washington (born Detroit, May 12, 1941) came together in the Bedford-Stuyvesant district of Brooklyn in the mid-'60s as members of an amateur group called the Parisians, before deciding to make a career of acappella. They launched the Persuasions in 1968, issuing an accompanied record on Minit a year later.

Rock freak Frank Zappa released their debut **Acappella** album on his Straight label and his bizarre image and nose for publicity helped focus attention on the group. The album met with wide critical acclaim, building an underground following which led to furthur albums via Island, Capitol, MCA and A&M (in 1974, and on which Willie C. Daniels replaced Washington while, on the **More Than Before** set, side two featured a rhythm section).

In 1977, their eighth album, **Chirpin'**, was released on Elektra and was firmly back in the acappella idiom.

Recordings:
Acappella (Straight/—)
Street Corner Symphony (Island)
Spread The World (Capitol/—)
Chirpin' (Elektra)

Esther Phillips

Esther May Jones was born in Galveston, Texas, on December 23, 1935, and grew up in Los Angeles where she was discovered by Johnny Otis(▶) when she won a talent contest at his famed Barrelhouse Club in 1949.

Backed by Otis' R&B jump band, she recorded a host of singles under the name Little Esther for Savoy, Modern and Federal, notching an R&B No. 1 in 1950 with **Double Crossing Blues**. Joining King Records in 1951, and still backed by Otis's band, she recorded prolifically up until 1954, when she retired from the scene for six years.

Returning to the studios in 1960 she surged back to the top two years later with her definitive, emotion-laden version of the old Ray Price song **Release Me**, which established a formula which has since become extremely successful—the marriage of a country and western ballad song with a soul-style vocal treatment. The idea came from Nashville mainstay Lelan Rogers who had signed her to Lenox.

The record went top 10 (and was later successfully covered by Englebert Humperdinck) and re-established Esther Phillips, as she was now known, as a leading singer (she took the name Phillips from an oil-company billboard!).

On the demise of Lenox, Esther Phillips signed with Atlantic and between 1963 and 1970 recorded a string of superb if in the main, only moderately comercially successful records which ran the gamut of pop, soul, jazz and blues styles. Most memorable was her reading of the Lennon/McCartney song **And I Love Him**, which did give her a sizeable hit. She also cut an album for Roulette in 1969 during a temporary split with Atlantic.

Creed Taylor(▶) signed her to his Kudu label in 1971 and she had the benefit of the backing services of New York's foremost jazz session musicians for a series of outstanding albums. The guitar work of Cornell Dupree(▶) and Eric Gale(▶), Gordon Edwards' bass lines, Richard Tee's keyboards and Bernard 'Pretty' Purdie's(▶) rock-solid drumming helped her wring every last drop of emotion out of Allen Toussaint's(▶) moving **From A Whisper To A Scream** and Gil Scott-Heron's(▶) **Home Is Where The Hatred Is** in truly spine-chilling performances which came right from the soul and reflected her own drug-abuse problems.

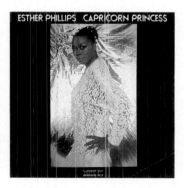

Capricorn Princess. Courtesy Kudu.

Till My Back Ain't Got No Bone, Mr Magic and an update of Little Willie John's **Fever** were other truly classic cuts from the Kudu sessions. Since moving to Mercury, however, she has failed to repeat their brilliance.

Esther Phillips is one of the most truly distinctive singers in black

music—though the much underrated white singer Timi Yuro sounded amazingly similar when she tackled soul/R&B material—and her style, rich in gospel influences and almost screaming with passion, marks her as an artist of stature far greater than her chart success would imply.

Recordings:
Reflections Of Country & Western Greats (Lenox/Ember)
Esther Phillips Sings (Atlantic)
Confessin' The Blues (Atlantic
From A Whisper To A Scream (Kudu)
Capricorn Princess (Kudu)
You've Come A Long Way Baby (Mercury/—)

Wilson Pickett

Behind only James Brown and Otis Redding in the superleague of '60s male soul stars, Wilson Pickett personified the macho, superstud ethos of soul. Known as 'The Wicked Pickett', he cut a slew of electrifying hits between the mid and the late '60s and toured regularly with a full soul revue centred on his hip-grinding overtly sexy stage act.

Born in Alabama in 1942, Pickett first came to the fore as lead singer for the Detroit-based vocal group the Falcons. On **I Found A Love**, released in 1961 on Lupine Records, Pickett was already showing the full-blooded impassioned but controlled vocal style that was to become his trademark. When the Falcons split Pickett signed with Lloyd Price's(▶) Double L label, which gave him his first two solo hits, **If You Need Me** and **It's Too Late**. Strangely perhaps, as Pickett later made a speciality of medium and up-tempo dance numbers, these first two hits were gospel-tinged ballads.

In 1964 Pickett signed with Atlantic(▶), a move which was the beginning of the making of a soul superstar. After a short experimental period in New York he moved down to Memphis to record with the Booker T. Jones(▶)/Steve Cropper axis of musicians, a liaison which produced his first major hit, **In the Midnight Hour**, (which he co-wrote with Cropper). It was one of the seminal cuts of the '60s soul era, a thunderously percussive epic with a memorable brass riff, sly and sexy lyrics and a masterful performance from Pickett that established him once and for all as the cocksure king of stud soul. The number almost immediately became a staple of every amateur soul band from Akron, Ohio, to Shepherds Bush, London, quickly achieving cliché status. Nevertheless, the record had stood the test of time to the extent that its raw excitement and surging power make it as exhilarating today as it was in 1965, and it has been the ruin of the few who have attempted to cover it on record.

Other classic hits followed— **Don't Fight It, 634-5789**—and in 1966 Pickett shifted his recording base to Rick Hall's Fame Studios in Muscle Shoals(▶), Alabama. Backed by the legendary Muscle Shoals rhythm section and horns, Pickett notched up a further slew of winner tracks. Autumn 1966 saw his version of Chris Kenner's **Land Of A Thousand Dances** steaming up the charts and lacerating dance floors on both sides of the Atlantic, while later that year **Mustang Sally** did the same. In Autumn 1967

Above: As wicked as ever, Wilson Pickett breaks loose.

are looking good for Wilson Pickett once again. His powers are little diminished (witness the 1979 single **You Are The One**, comparable with his best) and the beginning of a soul revival in the US is exposing him to a new, younger audience. Whatever the future brings, the body of work he recorded for Atlantic in the '60s assures him of an honoured place in the soul pantheon.

Recordings:
The Best Of Wilson Pickett
(Atlantic)
Wilson Pickett's Greatest Hits
(Atlantic)
The Right Track (EMI)
Pickett In The Pocket (RCA)
Live In Japan (RCA)

The Pioneers

The original Pioneers, formed in 1962, consisted of the Crooks Brothers, Sidney and Derrick, with Glen Adams. In 1968, Sidney teamed up with Jackie Robinson to cut a series of massive hits for Joe Gibbs, starting with the Jamaican No. 1 **Gimme Little Loving**.

They followed this with another number-one, **Long Shot**, about a famous racehorse. Further successes for Gibbs included. **Dem A Laugh, No Dope Me Pony, Catch The Beat** and **Mama Look Deh**, which the Maytals(▶) used as the basis for their classic **Monkey Man**. They then teamed up with Desmond Dekker's(▶) brother George and started recording for Leslie Kong, hitting with **Nana** which they released as the Slickers.

They followed this with another episode in the racehorse saga; Long Shot and a horse named Combat had died in a race at Kingston's Caymanas Park track so the Pioneers cut their classic **Long Shot Kick The Bucket**. Other successes for Kong included the Jamaican chart-topper, **Easy Come Easy Go**, the frenetic **Samfie Man** and **Mother Rittie**. After their tenure with Kong's Beverleys outfit they moved to England, where **Long Shot Kick The Bucket** had got into the top-10. In 1970 the Pioneers toured Egypt and Lebanon, return-

Below: Billy Preston & Syreeta scored with the haunting **With You I'm Born Again** *in 1979.*

Funky Broadway hit big but signalled the end of Pickett's halcyon period.

The late '60s were difficult times for many of the soul stars who had come to the fore in the earlier part of the decade. Flower power and acid rock had made soul increasingly unfashionable, and Pickett's aggressive stance and uptown street-smart image were greatly at odds with the then current brown-rice-and-bells ethos. Strangely, however, his most commercially successful single was a cover of the post-psychedelic Beatles anthem **Hey Jude**.

Fame Studios' then house guitarist Duane Allman(▶) was the prime mover behind Pickett's version, and the future rock hero contributed some stinging guitar licks to the track. But it is very much Pickett's record—his voice ranges from controlled pleading on the verse to virtual dementia as the

song fades out over the repeated brass figures and Allman's licks. It was Pickett's finest record since **Midnight Hour**, but unfortunately it was also more or less his swan-song as far as the big time was concerned.

Having switched to RCA, Pickett kept recording throughout the '70s with varied success—he seemed unable to establish a viable new direction or to find distinctive material. Nevertheless, he kept on working live, and never relinquished the ferocity and intensity that characterised his live work in the '60s. Anyone who has seen the Wicket Pickett in concert will know that it is not an experience easily forgotten — screaming, posing, thrusting, leaping atop a speaker stack the better to preach at his audience, Wilson Pickett is in many ways the absolute paradigm of the soul singer.

At the time of writing the signs

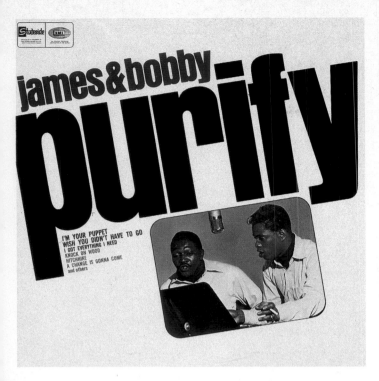

James & Bobby Purify. Courtesy Stateside Records.

ing in 1971 to record in a much more lightweight 'pop' style, achieving a smash with **Let Your Yeah Be Yeah** and enjoying smaller success with **A Hundred Pounds Of Clay** and **A Little Bit of Soap**.

Since 1973, George Dekker has pursued a singing/composing career. Jackie has been a solo singer, whilst Sidney Crooks has concentrated on production work, though the Pioneers have made infrequent records and UK stage appearances.

They were always big favourites of the skinhead teen cult in the UK, with their best records being those they cut between 1968 and 1970

Recordings:
Long Shot (—/Trojan)
Battle Of The Giants (—/Trojan)

David Porter

Songwriting partner of Isaac Hayes(▶) during the golden era of Stax Records and 'The Memphis Sound' in the '60s, David Porter (born in Memphis on November 21, 1941) was originally an insurance salesman, which is how he met Hayes. The pair were soon writing together and turned out such hits as **B-A-B-Y** for Carla Thomas(▶) **Hold On I'm Coming** for Sam and Dave(▶), **I Got To Love Somebody's Baby** for Johnnie Taylor(▶), **Your Good Thing Is About To End** for Lou Rawls(▶) and **The Sweeter He Is** for Soul Children(▶),

When Hayes started to concentrate on his own recording career, Porter took the same course, though with less success. His several albums for Stax did, however, include a few gems, notably a workmanlike version of **One Part, Two Parts**, the Dee Irvin song. His **Victim Of The Joke?** soul-opera concept album smacked of pretension, however, and he soon reverted to writing for other people.

Recordings:
Gritty, Groovy & Gettin' It (Enterprise/—)
Into A Real Thing (Enterprise/—)
Victim Of The Joke? — An Opera (Enterprise/—)
Sweat And Love (Enterprise/—)

Billy Preston

Though still a relatively young man, Billy Preston can boast a career which has spanned three generations of musicians. He is a star both in his own right and as a key session-man in the success of others, from Sam Cooke(▶) to the Beatles.

Born in Houston, Texas, on September 9, 1946, he was raised in Los Angeles and soon developed a talent for keyboard playing, backing gospel great Mahalia Jackson and appearing in a cameo role in the movie *St Louis Blues* by the age of 10. In the early '60s he toured as organ player with both Little Richard and Sam Cooke, first meeting the Beatles on a Little Richard package tour of the UK in 1962.

After early moderately successful recordings for Derby and Vee-Jay (notably the classic instrumental **Billy's Bag**), Preston won a better contract with Capitol, made regular appearances on the 'Shindig' networked US television show, and toured with Ray Charles, who pushed him into the limelight as his protégé.

A visit to the UK with Charles for a much-applauded TV special, saw Preston signing to the Beatles' Apple label as an artist (cutting **That's The Way God Planned It)** and playing on their **Get Back** and **Let It Be** smash hits, as well as with John Lennon's Plastic Ono Band, notably on the 1969 UNICEF 'Peace For Christmas' London Lyceum concert. The band's line-up at that time included Lennon, Yoko Ono, Eric Clapton, Keith Moon, Delaney and Bonnie and Klaus Voorman as well as Preston.

With a major A&M contract, **I Wrote A Simple Song, Outta Space** and **Will It Go Round In Circles** were all early '70s hits for Preston. He also played on many of Sly and the Family Stone's(▶) hits and was a special guest on the Rolling Stones' massive 1975 American tour.

Being managed by Diana Ross's then husband brought him into contact with Motown, which company he joined in

1979, scoring with his own records as well as on duets with Syreeta(▶), in particular the chart-topping **With You I'm Born Again**.

From his roots as a key session-man, Preston has developed into one of black music's most successful vocalists/instrumentalists.

Recordings:
Greazee Soul (Derby/Soul City)
The Most Exciting Organ Ever! (Vee Jay/Island)
That's The Way God Planned It (Apple)
I Wrote A Simple Song (A&M)
The Kids And Me (A&M)
Everybody Likes Some Kind Of Music (A&M)
Late At Night (Motown)
The Way I Am (Motown)

Bernard 'Pretty' Purdie

Veteran of 1,000 recording sessions, Bernard 'Pretty' Purdie is not the world's most modest man, having made a name for himself by erecting a huge banner behind his drumkit proclaiming: 'Pretty Purdie—World's Greatest Drummer'. 'I want to be the prettiest drummer that ever lived—and go on from there!'—he said in 1967.

James Brown(▶), Aretha Franklin(▶), Nina Simone(▶), Brook Benton(▶), Peaches and Herb(▶) are some of the artists who have used his services on stage and/or in the studio. His own 1967 single, **Funky Donkey,** made an impression in UK discos.

Recordings:
Soul Drums (Columbia/Direction)
Soul Is (Flying Dutchman/Philips)
Shaft (Prestige)

James and Bobby Purify

Cousins James Purify (born in Pensacola, Florida, on May 12, 1944) and Robert Lee Dickey (born in Tallahassee, Florida, on September 2, 1939) teamed in 1965 when Mighty Sam quit as lead vocalist with a group in which James played guitar. Working together as a vocal duo, James and Bobby were signed by producer Papa Don Schroeder,

who took them to Muscle Shoals(▶) to cut **I'm Your Puppet,** a 1966 smash with its melodious and simple balladry.

When the duo's popularity declined in the late '60s, Robert Dickey retired, leaving James Purify to continue as a solo until Don Schroeder introduced him to Ben Moore, who became the 'new' Bobby Purify, re-recording **I'm Your Puppet** and eventually signing to Casablanca around 1975.

This second pairing has since split and in 1981 Ben Moore released a superb LP, **Sanctified** (DJM), which revived the familiar pop-disco sound of James and Bobby but failed to achieve any great sales success.

Recordings:
The Pure Sound Of The Purifys (Bell)
James And Bobby Purify (Mercury)

Jerry Ragovoy

An influential white producer of black music in the '60s and early '70s, Philadelphia-born Ragovoy first tasted success when he wrote **This Silver Ring** for George Grant and the Castells in 1954. In 1959 he and his business partner Bill Fox produced the hit group the Majors(▶), and during the '60s he wrote for and produced a number of major and minor black artists, including Garnett Mimms(▶), Erma Franklin(▶) (**Piece Of My Heart**), Freddie Scott, Bobby Freeman(▶), Irma Thomas(▶) (**Time Is On My Side**), Baby Washington and Lou Courtney (for his own short-lived Rags label). One of the high spots of his '60s career was Howard Tate's(▶) superb 1967 debut album, which he produced and largely wrote. (One of the songs on the Tate album, **Look At Granny Run Run,** cropped up on a recent Ry Cooder album.)

What he may be remembered best for, however, is Lorraine Ellison's(▶) amazing **Stay With Me**, which he co-wrote and produced. This emotion-drenched slice of secular gospel is rated by many as the greatest soul record of all and is certainly one of the most powerful. It would have assured Ragovoy's reputation had he produced nothing else.

Below: James & Bobby Purify were our puppets in 1966.

Ernest Ranglin

A regular on Jamaican recording sessions throughout the '60s, Ernest Ranglin was born in Manchester, Jamaica, in 1933, and in his twenties became recognised as the foremost guitarist in the Caribbean, playing resort clubs and hotels as well as recording.

Following the lead of trumpeter Dizzy Reece and alto-saxophonist Joe Harriott, he moved to Britain for a spell and like them made an immediate impact on the London jazz scene, being voted by readers of *Melody Maker* as both 'Number One Guitarist' and 'New Star Of 1964', cutting two acclaimed small combo jazz albums and, with the GBs, a studio pick-up group, a superb R&B extended-play 7-inch featuring the catchy **So-Ho** and **Swing A Ling Pts 1 & 2**.

Ranglin played on many of the classic ska(▶), rock-steady and reggae tracks to come out Jamaica, often working at Studio One(▶) with the Skatalites'(▶) studio band.

Recordings:
Wranglin' (—/Island)
Reflections (—/Island)

Below: The distinctive Lou Rawls.

Lou Rawls

Though, in purely sales terms, his 1970s recordings for Philadelphia International(▶) took him to new peaks, there is no denying that Lou Rawls reached his creative zenith in the '60s.

Given the superb songs and faultless orchestrations, those Philly records would have been hits for any of the artists on the company's roster, submerging as they did Rawls' distinctive style beneath the overall 'Philly Sound'.

But during his long stay with Capitol Records in the previous decade, the man's recordings had been unmistakably Lou Rawls— he had his very own sound.

The combination of Rawls' distinctive voice, H.B. Barnum's(▶) arrangements and Dave Axelrod's production work was majestic.

Though Rawls owed quite a debt to Sam Cooke(▶) (which he repaid by travelling to the Fame Studios in Muscle Shoals(▶) and recording an album of Cooke's songs under the title **Bring It On Home To Me**), Rawls was essentially his own man.

Like Cooke, Rawls had served as a member of the Pilgrim Travellers gospel group and he had, in fact, sung second lead on Cooke's original million-selling version of **Bring It On Home To Me**.

Born in Chicago, on December 1, 1937, Rawls had left the Pilgrim Travellers following a car accident in 1958 and, after a stint in the 82nd Airborne Regiment and working the 'chittlin circuit', he settled in Los Angeles, singing blues and jazz.

For his 1962 debut album, **Stormy Monday**, Capitol teamed Rawls with Les McCann Ltd, a highly rated jazz trio comprising Les McCann, piano; Leroy Vinnegar, bass, and Ron Jefferson, drums. They then matched Rawls with the jazz big bands of Onzy Matthews (for **Black And Blue** and **Tobacco Road** and Benny Carter (for **Nobody But Lou**, on which Dave Axelrod came in as his regular producer) and leased an album of gospel sides he had cut earlier with the Pilgrim Travellers.

The definitive Lou Rawls' album came with his sixth release, **Live!**, recorded at a gig in an intimate night-club setting and introducing the spoken monologue which was to become a Rawls' trade-mark and set the pattern for all the 'rap' records which proliferated in the '70s.

Backed by the small combo of James Bond, bass; Earl Palmer, drums; Tommy Strode, piano, and Herb Ellis, guitar, Rawls made it one of the most atmospheric—and soulful—live albums ever, as he strode through a set mostly comprising blues standards, of which his versions of T. Bone Walker's **Stormy Monday** and John D. Loudermilk's **Tobacco Road** (studio cuts of which he'd featured on previous LPs) were true masterpieces. The album sold half-a-million copies.

With succeeding albums—and they came in rapid succession— Capitol moved their star further and further into the soul mainstream, bringing Barnum in as regular arranger from 1966 to 68.

Soulin' was a certified gold album in 1966 and Rawls had become one of the highest-earning black performers, commanding a then enormous $5,000 a night for his shows, his great triumph coming with a 1967 concert at New York's hallowed Carnegie Hall.

His stand-out singles included THE version of country writer Mac Davis's **You're Good For Me** (1968), **Love Is A Hurtin' Thing** and **Your Good Thing (Is About To End)** which was a sadly prophetic title for Capitol as they lost his services to MGM soon after.

With the new deal, the near seven-year-old Rawls/Axlrod partnership broke up and the MGM output somehow lacked the magic of the earlier records.

Rawls' career then went into something of a limbo situation until his move to Philadelphia International in the late '70s zapped him back into the big time with records like **You'll Never Find Another Love Like Mine** (1976) and **Let Me Be Good To You** (1979), though this output lacked the creative distinction of his Capitol classics.

Recordings:
Live! (Capitol/—)
Soulin' (Capitol)
Carryin' On (Capitol)
Feelin' Good (Capitol)
The Way It Was, The Way It Is (Capitol/—)
Natural Man (MGM)
Silk And Soul (MGM)
Let Me Be Good To You (Philadelphia International)

Red Bird Records

Songwriters/producers Jerry Leiber and Mike Stoller(▶), who made their reputation in the '50s through their work with the Coasters(▶), the Drifters(▶), Elvis Presley and others, formed Red Bird Records in New York in 1964, though the running of the company was eventually taken over by George Goldner (previously involved in such legendary R&B labels as Gone, End, Gee, Rama and Roulette).

Young songwriters from the famed Brill Building 'Hit Factory' on Broadway (where the label was based), such as Phil Spector(▶), Jerry Goffin, Carole King, Ellie Greenwich, and especially George 'Shadow' Morton, gave Red Bird and its subsidiary Blue Cat a string of hits. The Ad-Libs' **Boy From New York City**, the Dixie Cups' **Chapel Of Love**, Alvin Robinson's **Down Home Girl** and the Jelly Beans' **I Wanna Love Him So Bad** and even the white girlie trio the Shangri-Las had a black-pop sound.

Recordings:
Red Bird Goldies (Red Bird)
The Red Bird Era (—/Charly)

Otis Redding

Although many soul stars ran into difficulties in the late '60s in the wake of the psychedelic/heavy rock movement, none was more thoroughly dumped on than Otis Redding. Castigated by the nouveau-hip devotees of so-called 'head' music as a mouther of clichés, a gargling word-swallower concerned with non-cerebral subjects like dancing and gettin' down, Redding suddenly became terribly dated around 1969. What's more, as he had died in 1967 there was nothing he could do to ingratiate himself as popular taste changed. The place in front of the stage suddenly became a place to sit down on rather than dance on, and Redding—and too many other black stars—became yesterday's news.

However, a faithful core of devotees has kept his name alive and his records in print over the past 15 years, and while Moby Grape fans are now somewhat thin on the ground, Otis Redding still has a solid reputation. The truth is that he was one of the soul greats, a marvellous singer (particularly of ballads), a superdynamic live performer and a considerable writer. As it stands, he is among the elect of black music stars, and may well have developed into a superstar like Wonder(▶) or Gaye(▶) had he lived.

Born in Dawson, Georgia, 1941, Redding was brought up in nearby Macon. He first sang in the local church choir and at school, and was soon singing at gigs around his home town. Through a high-school friend, Phil Walden (later to become boss of Capricorn Records), Redding was introduced to local heroes Johnny Jenkins and the Pine-toppers, and in 1959 he went on the road with them as a general

Otis Blue. Courtesy Volt Records.

assistant and occasional singer. In the next couple of years Redding cut several records on small labels with little success, but his real chance came in 1962. Johnny Jenkins was recording in the Stax(▶) studios in Memphis, and the session finished early enough for Redding to cut a couple of his own compositions, **These Arms Of Mine** and **Hey Hey Baby**. Stax boss Jim Stewart was impressed enough to sign Redding on the spot, and **These Arms Of Mine** was issued as a single in November 1962. A heartfelt ballad which showed Redding's impassioned style to be practically fully-fledged even then, **These Arms** made an impression on the US charts and paved the way for Redding's second release, **Pain In My Heart**.

Pain In My Heart was also the title of Redding's first album, a collection that combined covers of R&B hits with self-composed

numbers like **Security** and **That's What My Heart Needs**. Now established as a major new star, Redding had considerable success with most of his material over the next four years. Singles included **That's How Strong My Love Is**, the all-time soul ballad classic **I've Been Loving You Too Long**, **Respect** (later covered by Aretha Franklin(▶)), the frenetic **I Can't Turn You Loose**, the Stones' **Satisfaction** and **Fa Fa Fa Fa Fa (Sad Song)**.

The albums released during this period were of equally high quality and the passage of time only enhances their appeal. **The Great Otis Redding Sings Soul Ballads** showcases some superb material like Jackie Wilson's(▶) **A Woman, A Lover, A Friend** and Jerry Butler's(▶) **For Your Precious Love**. **Otis Blue** is regarded by many as the definitive Otis Redding album; as well as the gorgeous ballads **I've Been Loving You Too Long** and **My Girl**, there are definitive soul renditions of Solomon Burke's(▶) **Down In My Valley** and Sam Cooke's(▶) **Shake**, not to mention a version of B.B. King's(▶) **Rock Me Baby** which features a classic blues guitar solo by Steve Cropper. In fact, there is not a dud track on the album. Both **The Soul Album** and **Dictonary Of Soul** have their share of stand-out tracks, and all in all it is true to say that the highest standards were maintained throughout Redding's album output.

During this period Redding was probably more appreciated in

Europe, particularly in Britain, than on his home ground. He toured regularly between 1964 and 1967, heading the 1965 Stax-Volt tour of Europe, and making other trips to the UK with his own band. As a live act he was in many ways the classic soul performer, dancing, running on the spot, ripping off superfluous items of clothing as the act progressed, never giving less than

Above: Otis Redding's dynamic live performances will remain in the memory of all who saw him.

total energy and commitment to his performance.

Two events happened in 1967, however, which finally brought him the widest recognition. The first was the Monterey Pop Festival. As the only soul artist among rock

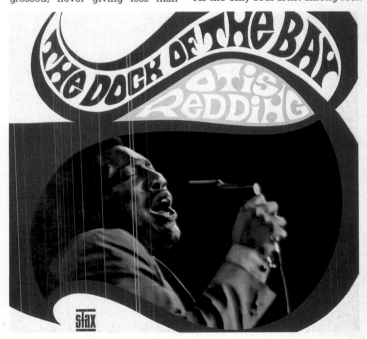

Sittin' On The Dock Of The Bay. Courtesy Stax Records.

acts like Jimi Hendrix(▶) and the Who, Redding scored a surprising success. Fortunately, his performance was captured for posterity in the movie *Monterey Pop*. The second was his death on December 10, as a result of an air crash. Redding's private plane crashed into a lake near Madison, Wisconsin-tour members of the Bar-Kays(▶) were also killed.

Whether **Dock Of The Bay** would have been such a major hit had he not been killed is debatable, but the fact is that it was Otis Redding's biggest single. Released in early 1968, it reached No.1 in the US and No.2 in the UK. More pop styled than most of his other recordings, with dubbed-on seagull sounds, **Dock** is perhaps an indication of the direction Redding might have taken had he lived.

Now, when much of the music of the '60s is being re-appraised, Otis Redding's position as one of that decade's heroes is secure. Via his recordings, he lives—although Atlantic's cut-out policy means that he is not as well represented as he might be. The discography includes both currently available material and albums worth searching out in cut-out bins and specialist shops.

Recordings:
Otis Blue (Volt/Atlantic)
Dictionary Of Soul (Volt/Atlantic)
The Dock Of The Bay
(Volt/Atlantic)
Love Man (Atco/Atlantic)
Tell The Truth (Atco/Atlantic)
History Of Otis Redding
(Atco/Atlantic)
Otis Redding Live In Europe
(Atco/Atlantic)
The Best Of Otis Redding
(Atco/Atlantic)
The Immortal Otis Redding
(Atco/Atlantic)

The Righteous Brothers

There has never been any shortage of white acts attempting specifically black musical forms, although their success has been varied both artistically and commercially. Among the battalions of plagiarists and borrowers in soul music, however, one act stands alone, both uniquely competent and uniquely inspired —the Righteous Brothers. They represent a musical phenomenon, first in a field of one.

Baritone Bill Medley was born in Los Angeles in 1940, high tenor Bobby Hatfield in Wisconsin in the same year. Coming together as the Righteous Brothers in 1963, they had a hit the same year with the R&B styled **Little Latin Lupe Lu.** The cut was released on Moonglow Records (along with an album), and was also a hit for another far less convincing blue-eyed soul act, Mitch Ryder and the Detriot Wheels. However, it wasn't until 1964, when they joined forces with production genius Phil Spector(▶), that the Righteous Brothers came to international prominence.

Spector was already hot, with big hits by the Crystals(▶), the Ronettes(▶) and others under his belt. Having signed the Brothers, Spector worked with them in the studio for a solid three weeks on one song, **You've Lost That Lovin' Feelin'** (written by Spector, Barry Mann and Cynthia Weill). The result of all the toil was quite simply a masterpiece, certainly one of the greatest singles in the history of pop, rated by many as *the*

greatest. Fittingly, it sprang to the No. 1 spot in both the US and the UK singles charts in January 1965.

Spector's 'wall of sound' was a perfect foil for the deep, rich, Ray Charles(▶)-influenced voice of Bill Medley and the higher, gospel-tinged range of Bobby Hatfield. The Spector-produced **Unchained Melody** and **Ebb Tide** were also sizeable hits, and the Brothers stayed with Spector's Philles label for four albums, although much of the material on these was self-produced.

The Righteous Brothers Greatest Hits. Courtesy Verve Records.

Moving to Verve in 1966, the Brothers continued to make both hit singles and excellent albums. **You're My Soul And Inspiration,** another Mann/Weill composition, approached the quality of **Lovin' Feelin'**, and the Brothers' version of **Island In The Sun** was an object lesson in making something out of hackneyed material. The albums were generally worth a listen, and included some worthwhile versions of standard soul songs like **In The Midnight Hour** and **A Change Is Gonna Come.**

The Righteous Brothers eventually split up in 1968 after a massive farewell concert at a Los Angeles football stadium, Bill Medley going on to pursue a not particularly successful solo career, Bobby Hatfield attempting to keep the Righteous Brothers act together with a new partner, Billy Walker. Medley and Hatfield got together again in 1974, had a freak US hit with a death disc called **Rock 'n' Roll Heaven,** and put out a couple of reunion albums before splitting again. Their best testimony remains their early work, in particular, of course, **Lovin' Feelin'.** The Spector-produced tracks can be found on various Spector compilations.

Recordings:
You've Lost That Lovin' Feelin'
(Verve)
Soul And Inspiration (Verve)
Greatest Hits (Verve)

Smokey Robinson

A great singer who is also a great songwriter is a rare creature. Sam Cooke(▶) comes to mind, as does Ray Charles(▶) at his peak, but the greatest of the writer/performers must be William 'Smokey' Robinson. One of the all-time giants of black music, Smokey Robinson would have been well remembered for his songs for the Miracles(▶) and other Motown(▶) artists even had he never sung a note; the fact that he is also the possessor of one of the most distinctive and expressive voices in popular music makes him a genuine phenomenon.

Smokey Robinson was born in February 1940 in Detroit. He formed the Miracles as a high school vocal group in 1955, and met up with Berry Gordy in 1957 while Gordy was still working as an independent producer. Gordy was impressed with the group and cut several sides with them in Detroit, including **Got A Job,** released through End Records, and **Bad Girl,** released through Chess. The records were moderately successful, and Gordy was encouraged by Robinson to set up Tammie—later Tamla—Records, with the Miracles as the first signing. The group at this time consisted of Robinson, Claudette Rogers, Bobby Rogers, Ronnie White and Pete Moore.

1960 saw the first major success for both Tamla and the Miracles. **Shop Around,** a wry song written by Gordy and Robinson, reached No. 2 in the charts and went gold. The group was on its way—the next few years saw a slew of superb hit singles like **What's So Good About Goodbye?, You Really Got A Hold On Me, Mickey's Monkey** and **Ooh Baby Baby.** At the same time Robinson started writing for and producing other artists, such as Mary Wells(▶). The first signing to a new label, Motown, Wells had a raft of hits under Robinson's aegis, including **Two Lovers** in 1962 and **What's So Easy For Two** in 1963. Her biggest hit, the classic **My Guy,** was also a Robinson composition and production; released in 1964, it was one of Motown's first international hits.

Being With You. Courtesy Motown Records.

In 1963 Robinson married Claudette Rogers, who left the Miracles but continued to sing on their records. Moving into the mid-'60s, Robinson entered his classic period as both a writer and performer. From this time until the early '70s Robinson was responsible for literally dozens of classic records—not just hit singles, but some of the lasting triumphs of pop music. With the Miracles there was **Going To A Go-Go, (Come Round Here) I'm The One You Need, I Second That Emotion,** the immortal **Tracks Of My Tears** and **Tears Of A Clown, I Don't Blame You At All** and others. Since 1963 Robinson had been collaborating with the Temptations(▶), and was responsible for many of their most memorable numbers, including **Get Ready,** the glorious **My Girl** and other superb love songs like **The Way You Do The Things You Do, It's Growing** and **Since I Lost My Baby.** Amazingly, Robinson also found time to work with other Motown artists—he wrote and produced the successful **Ain't That Peculiar** and **I'll Be Doggone** for Marvin Gaye(▶) for example.

During this period Smokey Robinson grew into one of the most original and influential forces in music. His songs were covered dozens of times, and seemed to have a particular impact in the UK where **Shop Around** was covered by Georgie Fame and **You've Really Got A Hold On Me** by the Beatles. (The Miracles went to Britain as part of the 1965 Motown Revue and were hailed as 'the Beatles' favourite artists'). Part of Robinson's appeal as a songwriter lies in the fact that he was one of the first post-rock 'n' roll writers to turn in lyrics of any consequence. While few of his songs were revolutionary in their subject matter, being generally concerned with love, requited or otherwise, he had a particular facility for imagery, the finely turned phrase, that was in marked contrast to the hackneyed lyric writing that was the norm at that time. (The lyrics of so-called 'progressive' rock, then beginning to make itself felt, were often no more than collections of new and different clichés.) This facility went hand in hand with an uncanny ability to produce gorgeous melodies that were also instantly memorable. In many cases the results were virtually perfect songs; it is difficult to fault, say, **Tracks Of My Tears** or **My Girl** from any viewpoint. What's more, like only an elect few songwriters such as Cole Porter, Robinson wrote sophisticated songs that were never pretentious. It is doubtful whether Smokey Robinson ever sat down to write a word intending it to be art, yet he contributed greatly to the extension of the art of the pop song and was described by no less an authority than Bob Dylan as being 'America's greatest living folk poet'.

Possessor of one of soul's great high tenor voices, Robinson was and is a uniquely expressive singer whose handling of a ballad is always impeccable. Especially when singing his own material, he has considerable emotional range and demonstrates that a gentle tender approach to soul singing can be as effective as a more strident heart-on-sleeve delivery. As a producer, Robinson was of course instrumental in establishing the early Motown style, which would become 'The Motown sound'. What could be more evocative of the early '60s than the sound of Mary Wells' **My Guy** or the Temptations' **My Girl**—Robinson productions both.

It was, however, Eddie and Brian Holland and Lamont Dozier(▶) who established 'The Motown sound' as an international success, with the Supremes(▶) and the Four Tops(▶). Possibly Smokey Robinson was too much of an individualist to be able to make as great a contribution now that Motown was becoming more of a 'hit machine'. Great as many of Holland/Dozier/Holland's compositions and productions were, they generally had neither Robinson's subtlety nor his originality. After a series of farewell concerts Robinson left the Miracles in 1971 to concentrate on his role as vice-president of Motown Records with special responsibility for new talent.

Right: One of black music's most influential personalities, Smokey Robinson has helped the burgeoning Motown empire flourish over a period of 20 years with his unique musical and business talents.

Above: Former Temptation David Ruffin.

Initially Robinson continued to produce the Miracles, and despite claims that he didn't want to make solo records his first solo effort was not long in arriving. Over the course of the next 10 years Robinson's recorded output was rarely less than interesting, as one would expect, but seldom hit the heights of his golden years in the '60s. The albums tended in general to be more experimental than his previous work—**Deep In My Soul**, released in 1977, for example, was his first album consisting entirely of other people's compositions— and often more reflective and philosophical. **Pure Smokey** contains a song called **Virgin Man** whose subject matter is about as far away as it is possible to get from the more macho concerns of the average soul song, detailing as it does the problems and insecurity of male sexual inexperience.

Most of Robinson's solo albums repay listening and have been moderately successful. At the end of the '70s it looked as if Smokey Robinson was going to continue to bring out albums regularly, keep up his position at Motown and generally coast into middle age. It was not to be however. In late 1981 the title track of Robinson's album **Being With You**, an airy, romantic medium-paced ballad perfectly suited to his sensual voice, became a huge international hit and brought his talents to the attention of a new young audience. There seems no reason why Smokey Robinson should not become as big a star in the '80s as he was in the '60s. Whatever the future may hold, it is difficult to overstate his achievements: writer, singer, producer—Smokey Robinson is among the greats in each category.

Discography is restricted to recent solo albums and compilations of Smokey Robinson and the Miracles.

Recordings:
Where There's Smoke (Motown)
Being With You (Motown)
Anthology (Motown)
Greatest Hits From The Beginning (Motown)
Greatest Hits Vol. 2 (Motown)

The Ronettes

The Ronettes—Veronica 'Ronnie' Bennett (born August 10, 1943), Estelle Bennett (July 22, 1944) and Nedra Talley (January 27, 1946)— were two sisters and a cousin who worked the New York club circuit in the early '60s. They were spotted in 1963, while working at the Pepermint Lounge, by ace producer Phil Spector(▶) who signed them to his phenomenally successful Philles label. Having developed his legendary 'Wall of Sound' production techniques with his previous signings, the Crystals(▶), Spector applied them fully blown to recordings with the Ronettes, with the result that the Ronettes' first release—the Spector/Ellie Greenwich/Jeff Barry song **Be My Baby**—became a million-selling international hit.

The Ronettes were an accomplished group with a strong lead singer in the person of Ronnie Bennett and their talent, coupled with Spector's unique expertise, made them chart regulars for a couple of years. Classic hits included **Baby I Love You, The Best Part Of Breaking Up, Do I Love You,** and **Walking In The Rain**.

With their tight dresses, heavy eye make-up and bouffant hairstyles, the Ronettes had one of the early '60s most potent visual images—the kind of bad girls dreamed about. Spector married and later broke up with Ronnie Bennett, who surfaced in the mid-'70s as Ronnie Spector(▶).

Recordings:
The Ronettes (Philles/Colpix)
The Ronettes Sing Their Greatest Hits (Phil Spector)

Roy C

Shotgun Wedding, a US hit in 1965, a UK hit in 1966 and again in 1972-3, cost just $300 dollars to record and used four white New York teenagers to back Roy C on one of black music's classic novelty numbers.

Born Roy Charles Hammond in New York City in 1943, Roy C sang lead with the Genies on records for Shad, Hollywood, Warwick and Forum before going solo, recording for Black Hawk (who issued **Wedding**) and Shout. After setting up his own Alaga label he recorded a string of singles concentrating on the sordid side of love (**I Caught You In The Act, I Found A Man In My Bed**), which were issued in album form by Mercury with **Sex And Soul** (1973).

Roy C also produced Mark IV's million-selling **Honey I Still Love You** (1974) for Mercury.

Recordings:
Sex And Soul (Mercury)
More Sex And Soul (Mercury/—)

Ruby And The Romantics

Originally formed as the Supremes (but not to be confused with the giant Motown(▶) act of that name), the Romantics changed their name in 1962 when Ruby Walsh joined as lead singer.

The Ohio-based vocal group (Ronald Mosley, Edward Roberts, Geroge Lee, Leroy Fann) topped the pop and R&B charts in 1963 with the pop-flavoured **Our Day Will Come** (Kapp). Succeeding hits on Kapp (including the original of Eddie Holman's(▶) **Hey There Lonely Girl**, titled **Hey There Lonely Boy**) were all in the same lightweight pop/soul vein, as were less successful records for ABC Paramount.

Recordings:
Greatest Hits (Kapp/—)

David Ruffin

David Ruffin's low tenor was the focal point, and perfect contrast, to the otherwise smooth sound of The Temptations(▶). The balance between Ruffin and co-lead vocalist Eddie Kendricks(▶) provided the group with a goldmine of material, of which they took full advantage. Ruffin contributed his talent to classic Temptations' hits, **My Girl, It's Growing, I Know I'm Losing You, Ain't Too Proud To Beg** and **Beauty Is Only Skin Deep**.

Ruffin left The Temptations to go solo in 1968, but achieved little immediate success. This native of Meridian, Mississippi, and brother of Jimmy Ruffin(▶), has yet to see his full potential realised, although he made inroads with **Walk Away From Love** in 1975/76. This Van McCoy(▶) produced single, from the album **Who Am I**, was followed by the promising **Everything's Coming Up Love**. But it seems that David Ruffin will be one step away from sustained success until he rediscovers that raw edge that made him the backbone of The Temptations.

Recordings:
Who Am I (Motown)
Everything's Coming Up Love (Motown)

Jimmy Ruffin

Jimmy Ruffin could have been joint lead singer of the Temptations(▶) but he turned the job down and it went instead to his brother David(▶), while Jimmy became one of Motown's(▶) major solo acts, with such classics as **What Becomes Of The Brokenhearted, I've Passed This Way Before, Farewell Is A Lonely Sound** and **Forever My Love** carrying him through the '60s.

Born in Collinsville, Mississippi,

Below: Jimmy Ruffin, former Motown star.

on May 7, 1939, Ruffin moved to Detroit in 1960 and was immediately pacted to Motown, but in the early days just as a session singer— 'They hired us to do the handclaps and the foot-stomps on things like the Supremes'(▶) **Where Did Our Love Go**' he recalls—while working at a variety of day jobs.

In 1962, he found steady work on the assembly line at Ford Motor Company and stayed there till 1965, though he had his first single, **Don't Feel Sorry For Me**, on the Miracle subsidiary in 1961, and a second, **Since I've Lost You**, on Soul in 1964. Ruffin took time off from work to appear on Motown package tours and when tenor Eldridge Bryant left the Temptations he was offered the job but passed.

Writer James Dean intended to give **What Becomes Of The Brokenhearted** to the Spinners(▶), but Ruffin persuaded the company to let him record it and it was Motown's second biggest '60s hit in the UK, selling half-a-million copies (and being re-issued three times).

Able to concentrate on becoming a full-time performer, Ruffin established himself with entertaining singles and albums, and cut an album of duets, **I Am My Brother's Keeper** (1971), with brother David before leaving Motown a year later, after nearly 12 years with the company. He recorded first for Atlantic in Philadelphia, and then for RSO, scoring in 1980 with **Hold On To My Love**.

Recordings:
The Jimmy Ruffin Way (Soul/ Tamla Motown)
Ruff 'N' Ready (Soul/Tamla Motown)
Greatest Hits (Soul/Tamla Motown)
Jimmy Ruffin (Atlantic/Polydor)
20 Golden Classics (Motown)

Sam And Dave

Sam Moore (born Miami, Florida, October 12, 1935) sang gospel with the Melionaires then worked as a solo in local clubs, meeting Dave Prater (born Ocilla, Georgia, May 9, 1937) in the process. One night in 1958 at the King Of Hearts Club, Moore called Prater up on stage and the pair went down so well that they decided on formal partnership and got a contract with Morris Levy's New York-based Roulette label, recording under producer Henry Glover but without major impact.

Switching to Atlantic(▶) in 1965, they were taken to the Stax(▶) studios in Memphis by Jerry Wexler to record with the famed Stax house-band (an amalgam of Booker T and the MGs(▶) and the Mar-Keys(▶)), with Isaac Hayes(▶) and David Porter(▶) assigned to write and produce.

The resultant records (some issued on Stax, others on Atlantic) were among the most vibrant examples of the Stax sound, displaying a gospel-style intensity but being highly commercial at the same time. On both ballads and up-tempo items, the pair established themselves as soul music's top duo, the sheer quantity and quality of their product putting such other fine acts as Sam and Bill, Pic and Bill and Maurice and Mac(▶) in the shade (though the white 'blue-eyed soul' pair, the Righteous Brothers(▶), matched their success).

You Don't Know Like I Know, I Take What I Want, Hold On I'm Coming (which made a massive impact in the UK), **I Thank You, You Got Me Hummin'** and the 1967 million-selling US No. 2 **Soul Man**, on the up-tempo side, and **When Something Is Wrong With My Baby**, among the ballads, were true classics.

When Stax was sold to Gulf & Western in 1968, rights to the old master-tapes and the duo's current contract reverted to Atlantic, but subsequent Miami recordings flopped. Reportedly on bad terms with each other, Sam and Dave went their separate ways, Sam Moore staying with Atlantic, Dave Prater signing with Alston. Teaming up again in 1971, they recorded for United Artists and in the mid- '70s signed with British label Contempo, but they could not recapture the great days at Stax and eventually split again.

Recordings:
Sam And Dave (Roulette/Major Minor)
Hold On I'm Coming (Stax/—)
I Thank you (Stax)
Soul Men (Stax)
Double Trouble (Atlantic)
Best Of Sam And Dave (Atlantic)

The Shirelles

The Shirelles' claim to fame was a string of 25 pop hits spread over almost 10 years, including two chart-toppers and two songs which have become virtually immortal oldies; now they are generally consigned to the ranks of forgotten greats, and earn paltry dollars playing oldies' revival shows.

Shirley Alston, Doris Kenner, Beverly Lee and Addie Harris formed the Shirelles in 1958, recording briefly for Tiara before their manager Florence Greenberg signed them to Decca. **I Met Him On Sunday** was a top 50 hit, then in 1959 Ms Greenberg launched Scepter Records with the group as mainstay of her roster (which later included a subsidiary label, Wand, and major black artists Dionne Warwick(▶), Chuck Jackson(▶), Tommy Hunt and Maxine .Brown(▶). Hit followed hit, songs like **Will You Love Me Tomorrow, Dedicated To The One I Love, Baby It's You, Soldier Boy** and **Everybody Loves A Lover** soared high in the charts; teenage laments with fine lyrics carried the label through to 1967.

Later material on RCA had little merit or success, and the group were last seen in a major context in the movie *Let The Good Times Roll*.

Recordings:
Golden Hour Of Greatest Hits (—/Pye Golden Hour)
Remember When Vols 1 & 2 (Wand)
Happy And In Love (RCA)

Shout Records

With offices located in the legendary Brill Building on New York's Broadway, Shout Records was the soul arm of the Bang/Shout group of labels founded by white producer/songwriter Bert Berns (he also worked under the names Bert Russell and Russell Byrd). The Brill Building housed dozens of small music-publishing and record companies as well as a rabbit-warren of cubbyhole offices, which were used by New York's top songwriters, including Goffin and King, Ellie Greenwich, Neil Diamond and Leiber and Stoller(▶), earning it the name 'The Hit Factory'.

Born in 1929, Berns started out as a record salesman and session pianist then, in 1960, began writing with Phil Medley and soon came up with the Isley Brothers'(▶) classic **Twist And Shout** (originally recorded by the Topnotes). Berns went on to write for a host of soul artists, including Don Covay(▶), Marv Johnson(▶), The Exciters(▶), Garnett Mimms(▶) and Solomon Burke(▶). His noteworthy hits (most penned in collaboration with a variety of other Brill Building talents) included the Vibrations' **My Girl Sloopy** and the Drifters'(▶) **Under The Boardwalk.**

On Shout (licensed to London in the UK) Berns released classics by Roy C(▶), Erma Franklin(▶), Freddy Scott and others which captured the spirit of the mid-'60s New York soul scene.

Berns died on December 31, 1967, of a heart attack, his publishing and record companies being continued by his widow but soon fading from prominence.

Bunny Sigler

A long-time mainstay of the Philadelphia soul scene, Walter 'Bunny' Sigler was born in the 'City Of Brotherly Love' on March 27, 1941. Singing in local clubs from his teens, he was 23 before he cut his first record for the tiny local label Craig Records. But it was in 1965, when he got together with Leon Huff at Philly's then burgeoning Cameo-Parkway(▶) Records, that Sigler's career took off, thanks to the classic medley **Let The Good Times Roll & Feel So Good** (a format suggested by white producer John Madara who has worked with most of the major black acts in Philadelphia). A hit in its day, the record has ever since remained a collectors' classic because of its energy and irresistible rolling beat. **Lovey Dovey/You're So Fine** was a less successful follow-up in the same vein.

When Cameo-Parkway folded, Sigler moved to the new Neptune label founded by Leon Huff and his partner Kenny Gamble which, in turn, led him onto their highly successful Philadelphia International(▶) roster. Besides recording for the company, Sigler became increasingly active as a writer and producer for other artists working in his home city. He wrote four songs for Joe Simon's(▶) **Drowning In The Sea Of Love** album, which Gamble and Huff produced, contributed three songs on the O'Jays'(▶) **Back Stabbers** set and wrote for Billy Paul(▶), Wilson Pickett(▶) and also the Chambers Brothers.(▶).

Of his own singles, the lively re-make of the Bobby Lewis oldie **Tossin' And Turnin'** stands out. His prolific album output has included much fine material, though it is usually more notable for the quality of the songs than for his vocal performances, which tend to be somewhat bland and undistinctive.

Recordings:
Let The Good Times Roll & Feel So Good (Cameo Parkway/—)
I've Always Wanted To Sing (Gold Mind/Salsoul)
Let Me Party With You (Gold Mind/Salsoul)
My Music (Philadelphia International)

Below: Philadelphian soul veteran Bunny Sigler, who cut the classic Let The Good Times Roll.

Above: Nina Simone, a major '60s vocal influence.

Nina Simone

A somewhat enigmatic figure, Nina Simone has nevertheless been one of the most respected and influential figures in post-war black music. One of the few artists to tread the path between jazz, pop and soul successfully, Simone has also made important contributions to the black consciousness movement via songs like **Old Jim Crow, Mississippi Goddam** and **Young, Gifted And Black.**

Born Eunice Waymon in North Carolina in 1933, Simone taught herself the piano and organ by the age of seven and sang in the local church choir. Her obvious musical talent led to her being given an academic music training, first at high school in Asheville, North Carolina, and then at the famous Juilliard School Of Music. After her family moved to Philadelphia, Simone began working in nightclubs on the East Coast. One such engagement in Atlantic City led to a recording contract with Bethlehem, and she had a massive hit in 1959 with a version of **I Loves You Porgy.**

In the '60s her style broadened from its original jazz base, although her innate taste dictated that she still sought out the best material, whether pure love songs or uncompromising 'protest' songs. A period with Phillips from 1964 to 1967 yielded a version of the Screaming Jay Hawkins(▶) number **I Put A Spell On You** which was an international hit.

In 1967 Simone switched record labels again, to RCA, and entered her most productive and commercially successful period. She had two more single hits, with **Ain't Got No—I Got Life** from *Hair* and the Bee Gees' **To Love Somebody,** and was responsible for a series of albums of consistently high quality. Particularly worth seeking out are **Nina Simone Plays The Blues, Silk And Soul** and **Here Comes The Sun**—all are well produced, thought-provoking, yet at the same time easy to listen to.

In the '70s, Nina Simone began to devote more and more time to political work, and since 1974 has made only sporadic concert appearances. The late '70s saw her apparently beset by both personal and financial problems, neither of which stopped her from recording a superb album, **Baltimore,** for CTI(▶) in 1978. As always, the album contains good songs sung with a sense of emotional commitment, the whole beautifully arranged and produced. Sadly, Nina Simone has recorded nothing since its release.

Recordings:
Baltimore (CTI)
Here Comes The Sun (RCA)
It Is Finished (RCA/—)
The Best Of Nina Simone (RCA/—)
Pure Gold (—/RCA)
The Best Of Nina Simone (Phillips/—)

Below: Golden-voiced Percy Sledge lived up to his recording company's acclaim.

Ska

Ska is the grandfather of modern reggae music and like any creative force its roots are easily traced. The first new music to emerge in the Caribbean this century, it contains elements of mento, a Jamaican calypso of the 19th century, and its predecessor, the more folksie jonkanoo. More recently, it is linked with the American swing ('40s) and R&B ('50s) movements (particularly the music of New Orleans with a strong Fats Domino(▶) influence apparent).

After the Second World War the R&B bug swept across North America (with its rock 'n' roll spinoff) and began to penetrate Jamaica. Many islanders went to find work in the States where they absorbed the new music that was great to dance to. Others heard it at home, broadcast by radio stations in Texas and Florida, and others watched with interest the handful of R&B acts that toured the Caribbean.

It was to meet the demand for Yankee music that the Jamaican sound system emerged. Two of the first operators, Tom The Great Sebastian and Duke Reid The Trojan, sprang up in the early '50s. Another operator, Clement Coxsone Dodd and his Downbeat, with DJ Winston Count Matchouki, started the ball rolling for talking or toasting over rhythms, taking his cue from American disc jockeys

These and others imported recording equipment and as early as 1956 started to manufacture their interpretations of R&B with artists such as Owen Gray, Jackie Edwards(▶), Lascelles Perkins and Roy Panton. Singers, duos and bands prospered.

By 1962 the music was beginning to change. The drummer still held down a firm beat but by then joined by the guitars and keyboards, while the bass player strove for the off-beat that was already being heard on Fats Domino records. This was the start of the lolloping rhythm—more rhythm and less solo improvisation was the idea.

Innovative records like Prince Buster's(▶) **Madness,** the Folks Brothers' **Oh Carolina,** Eric Morris's nursery rhyme adaptation **Humpty Dumpty** and Derrick and Patsy's **Housewife Choice** won an avid 'in-crowd' following among London's mod youth movement, from 1962 on, and as almost all the best ska of the early days appeared in Britain on Melodisc's Blue Beat label, the name 'blue beat' became widely used as an alternative to ska. This was fully developed in the mid-'60s by bands like Tommy McCook(▶) and The Skatalites(▶), Roland and The Soul Brothers and the Don Drummond All Stars.

In 1967 ska was being phased out by the softer more soulful rock-steady rhythm. The legacy is a wealth of exciting material that put Jamaica on the world map with tunes of the calibre of **Phoenix City, Alcatraz** and **Guns Of Navarone.** In 1968/'69 the rhythm changed again, moving into the more gutsy reggae style (originally spelt reggay). This time it was London's 'skinheads' who adopted the Jamaican sound as their clarion call, and the end of the '60s saw a spate of reggae records going top 20 in the UK national pop charts, including Desmond Dekker's(▶) **Israelites** and **It Mek,** the Pioneer's (▶) **Long Shot Kick De Bucket** and Symarip's **Skinhead Moon Stomp.**

The terms ska (or blue beat), rock-steady and reggae are more correctly applied to particular dance styles. It was the contrasting tempos of the three dances which governed the differing form taken by the music.

Selected recordings (all various artists):
Ska '67 (—/Island)
Intensified! (original Ska 1962-'66) (—/Island)
Gems From Treasure Isle (—/Trojan)

The Skatalites

Formed in 1963, the Skatalites were the *crème de la crème* of Jamaica's musical talent at the time. The instrumentalists included Don Drummond(▶) playing trombone, Tommy McCook(▶) and Roland Alphonso(▶) on tenor saxes, Johnny 'Dizzy' Moore on trumpet, Lester Sterling on alto sax, Jackie Mittoo(▶) on piano, Jah Jerry on guitar, Lloyd Brevett on upright bass, and Lloyd Nibbs on drums, although the personnel fluctuated from time to time. The band name was a McCook pun on the Russian space satellite of 1963. They recorded a huge number of records, primarily for Clement Dodd, though they also worked for Duke Reid, Prince Buster(▶) and Philip Yap's Top Deck Records.

The Skatalites lasted for two years; in late 1965, a combination of financial, personal and organisational problems caused them to break up. Clement Dodd persuaded Jackie Mittoo and Roland Alphonso to leave the band and form the Soul Brothers as the Studio One(▶) house band. McCook worked mainly for Duke Reid at the Treasure Isle studios, while the wayward Don Drummond, suffering from a periodic mental problem, finally took his own life on May 6, 1969, in the Bellevue Hospital in Kingston.

The Skatalites' music was a powerful synthesis of American R&B combined with swinging, jazzy 'take-off' solos, forming in the process something uniquely Jamaican—the first music to come out of the post-war colonial independence movement of the West Indies. The music stimulated new dances, the ska, the shuffle and the split. The Skatalites backed every singer of note in the island's studios and cut hundreds of instrumentals under various names. At the same time they laid the foundation for today's Jamaican music.

They attempted a reunion album in 1975, though the results, released on Soundtracs, were not ska(▶) but instrumental reggae of a very high order.

Recordings:
Ska Authentic (Studio One)
Best Of The Skatalites (Studio One/—)

Percy Sledge

Record companies are hardly noted for under-selling their artists, and when Atlantic(▶) released an album by Percy Sledge entitled **The Golden Voice Of Soul** there may have been some potential buyers who questioned the singer's ability to justify the apparent hyperbole. Such fears were allayed, however, at the first sounds of Sledge's rich, warm, sonorous if husky high tenor voice. A repertoire consisting mainly of emotive soul balladry, delivered with more than a hint of gospel intensity, serves to confirm that the 'golden voice' is not simply a product of electronic manipulation in the studio.

Sledge was born in Leighton, Alabama, in 1941, and began his working life as a male nurse while gaining singing experience in various gospel choirs. His recording career had a somewhat audacious start—he walked into a record shop in Sheffield, Alabama, owned by local DJ and disc-producer Quin Ivy, and sang an audition, whereupon Ivy and his partner Marlin Greene promptly arranged a contract with Atlantic.

The haunting balladry of **When A Man Loves A Woman** provided a million-selling debut in summer 1966 and **Warm And Tender Love,** Sledge's version of a New York hit by Joe Haywood, soon followed it into the top 20. For three years the chart status was maintained with melodic consistency through songs like **It Tears Me Up,** the elegaic **Out Of Left Field,** a soulful revival of Presley's **Love Me Tender,** the swaying **Take Time To Know Her** and the tender **Sudden Stop.**

By 1970 the formula had worn thin, however, despite its continued aesthetic qualities, and Sledge faded quietly from the Atlantic roster with a minor R&B hit, **Sunshine,** in summer 1973. But he returned to the charts with healthy vengeance on the Capricorn label in the fall of 1974 with **I'll Be Your Everything,** which had a distinct similarity to his sonorous Atlantic ballads—in fact it was recorded at the same Muscle Shoals studio.

Recordings:
Best Of (—/Atlantic)
The Golden Voice Of Soul (—/Pickwick)
I'll Be Your Everything (Capricorn/—)

Sly & The Family Stone

Sly Stone, who came to be regarded as 'godfather' of psychedelic funk in the early 1970s, in fact had his roots in more orthodox black music heritage with a high school doo-wop vocal group. He began life as Sylvester Stewart in Dallas, Texas, on March 15, 1944, and four years later made his disc debut as a child prodigy with **On My Battlefield For My Lord.** It was high school before his next recording activity, as lead voice with the Viscanes on **Yellow Moon;** he also pooled his talents in other facets of the business, producing records for the Autumn label, and doing DJ work on San Francisco radio.

The Autumn connection started

early in 1964, Sly writing and producing material for Bobby Freeman(▶), who was then moving into the soul era from his late '50s rock'n'roll hits (viz. his original **Do You Wanna Dance**). Freeman had a fine voice, tuneful and powerful, but his first Autumn hit was the beaty banality of **C'mon And Swim,** and Stewart repeated the formula on **S-w-i-m** and **The Duck,** though his inventive musical brain yielded some intriguing B-sides for Freeman—**Friends** and **Cross My Heart** are far from routine, with time-signatures akin to jazzman Dave Brubeck's experiments.

As Freeman faded, Stewart turned his attention to the pop harmony group, the Beau Brummels, who managed a handful of hits during 1965, and the Autumn catalogue also boasts a solo single, **Buttermilk,** by simply 'Sly'. By now his career was entering a new phase, and as psychedelia gripped San Francisco in 1966 Stewart began performing regularly with his band the Stoners, soon to be spotted by Columbia A&R man Dave Kapralik, who signed the group and launched them into the rock world as Sly & the Family Stone with the album **A Whole New Thing.** Thus our man became Sly Stone, being credited as such as producer on **Dance To The Music,** the epic single unleashed on the world as 1968 drew its first breath.

This powerhouse slice of pulsating funk soared into the top 10 of both pop and soul charts, to be surpassed by a subsequent release, **Everyday People,** which went right to the top. **Stand** was another hit 45 and also title track of an LP whence came **I Want To Take You Higher,** a small hit upon release, but soon to be immortalised at the

Woodstock concert as Sly and the massed throng chanted 'Higher' into the warm night air.

The solid funk style was temporarily eclipsed when the lilting brassy **Hot Fun In The Summertime** scored late in 1969, but was back on vogue for the quaintly titled **Thank You Falettinme Be Mice Elf Again,** a chart-topper emulated by the strangely wistful, rambling **Family Affair** in 1971.

Sly was falling into disfavour, however, as he failed to show for several gigs, then spent an eternity delivering an LP, **There's A Riot Going On,** to mixed reaction. Further albums, **Fresh** and **Smalltalk,** appeared without euphoria, and his image became increasingly tarnished, musically and personally. After a period of some readjustment he re-emerged in 1982 in partnership with George Clinton.

Recordings:
Dance To The Music (Epic/Direction)
Stand (Epic)
Greatest Hits (Epic)

Greatest Hits. Courtesy Epic Records.

Above: Sly Stone, the man behind the group behind the Woodstock anthem I Want To Take You Higher.

Jimmy Smith

One of the most extensively recorded artists in any area of black music, organist Jimmy Smith has more than 80 album releases to his credit. Born in Norristown, Pennsylvania, on December 8, 1925, Smith was taught piano by his father and gigged in jazz and R&B groups around Western Pennsylvania between 1941 and 1951, when he settled in Philadelphia and attended music school.

In 1953 Smith heard Wild Bill Davis's use of the Hammond organ and decided to switch instruments, working with the quartet led by Don Gardner (who later had soul hits with Dee Dee Ford) on the R&B circuit. After setting up his own trio (Thornel Schwartz on guitar, Donald Bailey on drums) he landed a Blue Note record deal, which led to a steady flow of albums and an ever-increasing reputation on both sides of the Atlantic with such brilliant sets as **Home Cookin',** **Back At The Chicken Shack** and **Midnight Special.**

Line-ups changed from album to album, Bailey featuring on most but Schwartz being replaced by Quentin Warren who, in turn, gave way on some albums to such guests as Kenny Burrell and Eddie McFadden.

Later Blue Note sets often saw the addition of sax players like Lou Donaldson, Hank Mobley and Stanley Turrentine(▶). On switching to Verve and recording under Creed Taylor's aegis in 1962, a full-blown

Above: The Soul Children, sweetness and sophistication.

big band became a hallmark of Smith's albums—his collaboration with the Oliver Nelson Orchestra on Elmer Bernstein's **Walk On The Wild Side** became so innovatively exciting with his spectacular use of the Hammond keyboard with wild scat phrases underlined by the screaming power of the big band that it catapulted the record right into the pop charts.

Then, organ players were a bit beyond the pale where jazz aficionados were concerned, and Smith alienated purists even more when he started recording versions of old Muddy Waters'(▶) blues hits like **Hoochie Coochie Man** complete with his own gruff vocals. But the idea won him further hits and his star remained bright until the late '60s when the advent of the synthesiser made the organ sound old hat.

Though he experimented with the new keyboard instruments, Smith still recorded mostly on the Hammond organ and saw his fortunes revive when the instrument started coming back into favour in the early '80s.

Recordings:
Back At The Chicken Shack (Blue Note/—)
Midnight Special (Blue Note/—)
The Unpredictable... (Verve)
Any Number Can Win (Verve)
Got My Mojo Working (Verve)
Respect (Verve)
Best Of (Verve)
Get On It (Mercury)

O.C. Smith

Ocie Lee Smith first made his name singing a sophisticated mix of jazz and standards in New York and the holiday resort area of the Catskill Mountains. He made several records before joining Count Basie's band as replacement for vocalist Joe Williams.

Two years later, Smith (born in Mansfield, Louisiana, on June 21, 1936) left Basie to gig again on the US club circuit and in the Far East before settling in Los Angeles where he landed a contract with Columbia Records, cutting **The Dynamic O.C. Smith**, a live album featuring Oscar Peterson's sidemen Herb Ellis, guitar; Ray Brown, bass; and jazz drummer Jimmy Smith on a selection of standards.

In 1965 Smith switched musical track, recording a country-flavoured song, **Son Of Hickory Holler's Tramp**, in a soul vein for his biggest hit (a success on both sides of the Atlantic).

La La Peace Song (1972) was another classy soul song, but for the most part Smith cut sentimental ballads, having some success with his versions of **Little Green Apples** and **Honey** (both in 1968).

Recordings:
The Dynamic O.C. Smith (Columbia/CBS)
Hickory Holler Revisited (Columbia/CBS)
Help Me Make It Through The Night (Columbia/CBS)
La La Peace Song (Columbia/CBS)

Soul Children

Ace songwriters Isaac Hayes(▶) and David Porter(▶) put together the Soul Children specifically as an outlet for their material. Anita Louis (already an established session-singer at Stax(▶)), Shelbra Bennett and John Colbert all came from Memphis, while Norman West was a native of Monroe, Louisiana, and had worked on recordings for Hi(▶) and Smash.

Formed in 1968, the group had regular releases on Stax, establishing themselves with the **Genesis** album (1972). The dramatic single from this, **I Want To Be Loved**, included a long rap and featured rasping male vocals to offset the sweetness of the two girls. **Don't Take My Kindness For Weakness** and the '74 chart-topper **I'll Be The Other Woman** (a response to Doris Duke's(▶) **To The Other Woman**) reflected their concentration on adult lyrics which made **Friction** one of the finest albums to come out of Memphis.

With Duck Dunn and Al Jackson (of Booker T & the MGs(▶)) in their rhythm section, Bobby Manuel on guitar, the Memphis Horns(▶) and the best of the Muscle Shoals(▶) team, plus the Memphis Symphony Orchestra string section, the Soul Children always benefited from the most sophisticated of musical backdrops.

Recordings:
Soul Children (Stax)
Best Of Two Worlds (Stax)
Genesis (Stax)
Friction (Stax)
Open Door Policy (Stax)

Phil Spector

By the age of 24, Phillip Harvey Spector had become a millionaire, produced 15 or so hit records for his own record label, sold more than 20 million records and became more famous than the artists he produced. A genuine original and one of rock and pop's seminal figures, he pioneered the art of the mega-production and made the Phil Spector 'Wall Of Sound' his instantly recognisable trademark. Although primarily a pop producer, he did most of his best work with either black or black-influenced artists, and can take a good deal of credit for breaking black acts with young white audiences and making them an integral part of the 'teen scene'.

Below: Ronnie Spector, whose anguished vibrato personified the Spector sound.

Above: The Spinners (Detroit Spinners in the UK) with their most productive line-up featuring Phillipe Wynne, far right.

Born in New York in 1940, Spector moved with his family to Los Angeles in 1953. He started playing guitar and piano while in high school, and began hanging out with ace R&B writers/producers Leiber and Stoller(▶) who were working in LA studios. In 1958 he formed the Teddy Bears and recorded **To Know Him Is To Love Him,** a somewhat soppy teen anthem. Soppy or not, it was an instant and massive success, making No.1 in the US and No.2 in Britain. Phil Spector, the 'First Tycoon of Teen', was on his way.

The Teddy Bears didn't hit again, but Spector continued producing, first on the West Coast and then in New York with Leiber and Stoller. Hits from this period include Curtis Lee's **Pretty Little Angel Eyes** and **Under The Moon Of Love,** and Ben E. King's(▶) **Spanish Harlem.** The next move was back to the West Coast, where he formed his own Philles label.

Philles' first signing was the black girl group, the Crystals(▶). Their **There's No Other** made the US top 20, but it was their second and third releases, **Uptown** and **He's A Rebel,** that really established Philles. Both records featured elements of what was later to become the 'Spector Sound', and **He's A Rebel** was a US million-seller. A golden age of classic pop singles followed. The Crystals continued to hit with titles like **Da Doo Ron Ron** and **Then He Kissed Me,** and 1963 signings included the Ronettes(▶), who followed their lead with smashes like **Be My Baby, Baby I Love You** and **(The Best Part Of) Breaking Up.** Spector later married Ronettes' lead singer Veronica 'Ronnie' Bennett (Ronnie Spector(▶)).

Spector's *chef d'oeuvre,* though, was what many regard as the greatest pop record of all time, **You've Lost That Lovin' Feelin'** by the Righteous Brothers(▶) where

Spector married the unique black gospel/soul sound of white duo Bill Medley and Bobby Hatfield to a majestic backdrop of sound. Released in November 1965, **You've Lost That Lovin' Feelin'** hit the No.1 spot on both sides of the Atlantic in January 1966. This was probably the zenith of Spector's career. **River Deep, Mountain High,** recorded in 1966 with Tina Turner(▶), was comparable in quality to **Lovin' Feelin'** and is now regarded as a classic, but at the time failed to register in America, despite being a smash hit in the UK. Radio stations simply refused to play it, white stations because it was a black act, black stations because they said it was a white sound. It seems now that Spector was as much as anything the victim of professional jealousy; he had achieved too much too quickly. With Checkmates Unlimited's version of **Proud Mary** the eccentric Spector went right over the top. Said to be the most expensive ever production of a single, **Proud Mary** featured more than 300 musicians for a true 'Wall Of Sound'—and that after two earlier, similarly sized, orchestras had been abandoned and paid off! In the late '60s Spector lived as a recluse and seemed to lose interest in the record business, remaining virtually inactive until the early '70s.

During the '70s Spector worked with John Lennon and the Beatles and other pop acts like Cher, Dion, Harry Nilsson and Kim Fowley, but never quite regained the heights he hit in the '60s. He is nevertheless one of the most important producers of all time, whose pioneering techniques remain a major influence.

Recordings:
Phil Spector's Greatest Hits (Spector/—)
Echoes of the Sixties (—/Phil Spector International)

Ronnie Spector

Formerly lead singer of the Ronettes(▶) and wife of producer Phil Spector(▶), Ronnie Spector (born Veronica Bennett on August 10, 1943) returned to the music scene in the mid-'70s under the aegis of the white rock/R&B outfit Southside Johnny and the Ashbury Jukes. She sang with the band both at live appearances and on record, and cut a single of her own, **Say Goodbye To Hollywood,** with members of the band. In 1981 was signed to Red Shadow Records and released further singles, but has yet to make an impact comparable to the one she achieved when with the Ronettes.

Recordings:
Siren (—/Red Shadow)

Benny Spellman

The evocative **Lipstick Traces** backed with **Fortune Teller,** an attractive song with a Coasters'(▶) style story-line, gave Benny Spellman (born Pensacola, Florida, 1938) a double-header hit on Minit in 1962.

Based in New Orleans, Spellman worked as a session singer for Allen Toussaint(▶), contributing the deep responses to Ernie K. Doe's(▶) lead on the earlier novelty hit **Mother In Law.**

After records for Watch, Alon, Sansu and Atlantic(▶), Spellman dropped out of the music scene to work as a beer salesman, though he still performs at various revival gigs and in local clubs. His material is available on various New Orleans compilations such as **We Sing The Blues** (Imperial/Liberty).

The Spinners

Formed in the mid-'50s, the Spinners (known initially in the UK as the Motown Spinners, and subsequently as the Detroit Spinners—to save confusion with the well-established folk group the Spinners) have been one of the most consistent and long-serving vocal groups in black music.

Four of the original members, Henry Fambrough (baritone), Billy Henderson (tenor), Pervis Jackson (bass) and Bobby Smith (tenor), have provided the solid base of the group while other members at various times have been George Dixon, G.C. Cameron(▶) Crathman Spencer and Phillipe Wynne(▶) who joined in 1971. After adding his distinctive clipped style of lead vocals to many of the group's best records on Atlantic(▶), Wynne too went his own way, eventually being replaced in 1977 by John Edwards, who had been working with the band off and on since 1973, filling in for other members when they fell ill.

Happiness Is Being With . . . Courtesy Atlantic Records.

Starting in Ferndale High School, Detroit, as the Domingos, the quintet won early exposure via a local radio-show spot and their debut record, **That's What Girls Are Made For,** was released by ex-Harvey and the Moonglows'(▶) leader Harvey Fuqua on his Tri-Phi label in 1961 and charted. Tri-Phi was absorbed by Tamla Motown(▶) who switched the group to their labels, first Motown, then VP, and **I'll Always Love You, Truly Yours, Message From A Black Man** and **It's A Shame** established The Spinners' reputation internationally.

The Spinners joined the mass exodus from Motown following the company's move to the West Coast, and signed with Atlantic who had the great idea of teaming them with arranger/writer/producer Thom Bell(▶). From 1972 on, Bell gave them a succession of hits with beautiful soul ballads and mid-tempo items, including **I'll Be Around, Could It Be I'm Falling In Love** and **Then Came You,** on which they were teamed with Dionne Warwick(▶).

The Best of The Detroit Spinners. Courtesy Motown.

When Phillipe Wynne left and Thom Bell moved on to new pastures the group lost much of their vibrancy, but they still turn out consistently enjoyable records which rarely fail to sell in big numbers—their 1980 US/UK reworking of the old Four Seasons number **Working My Way Back To You Babe** was their 12th gold record since joining Atlantic.

Recordings:
Second Time Around
(Tamla Motown)
The Detroit Spinners (Atlantic)
Mighty Love (Atlantic)
Dancin' And Lovin' (Atlantic)
Love Trippin' (Atlantic)
Pick Of The Litter (Atlantic)
Smash Hits (Atlantic)
20 Golden Classics (Motown)

Staple Singers

America's best-known gospel group of the late '50s to early '60s was the Staple Singers, who made a confident stride into the world of secular music when they signed with Stax(▶). Produced initially by Steve Cropper then by Al Bell, they unleashed a succession of super soul records of which the most notable were **Heavy Makes You Happy, Respect Yourself, I'll Take You There, If You're Ready (Come Go With Me), You've Got To Earn It, City In The Sky** and **Be What You Are**; though the lyrics were no longer religious they almost always held some kind of moral.

Mavis Staples' marvellous lead vocals, the thoroughly competent

Above: Pop's still leading the majestic Staple Singers.

back-ups of her sisters Cleotha and Yvonne, and father Pop Staples' own distinctive baritone, were all part of the magic, so too was the big round sound of Pop's guitar playing (which can be heard to particularly good effect on **Jammed Together,** an album of instrumentals which he cut at Stax with Albert King(▶) and Steve Cropper. Until 1970, brother Pervis had been part of the group, but he left to handle their business affairs, at which time Yvonne became a permanent replacement.

The story of this remarkable family group began on December 28, 1915, when Roebuck 'Pop' Staples was born in Winoma, Missouri. He played blues guitar in his teens but then turned to the church, and in 1931 joined the Golden Trumpets, a group which toured churches in his home state. He married Oceola and in 1934 Cleotha was born, followed a year later by Pervis. The family moved North to Chicago where they stayed with Pop's brother, the Rev Chester Staples, Pop singing with the Trumpet Jubilees at evenings and weekends and working at a variety of jobs during the day.

Yvonne was born in 1939 and Mavis in 1940 and, as the children grew older, the Staple Singers evolved, cutting their first record for United in 1954, then moving on to Vee Jay(▶) in 1955, staying with the company for six years during which time they recorded a steady flow of gospel songs, the second of which, **Uncloudy Day,** was a major gospel smash.

Hold On To Your Dream. Courtesy 20th Century Records.

In 1961 Pervis was replaced by Yvonne, at first a temporary arrangement while he was away on army service. That year they moved labels to Riverside, cutting more than 400 sides in just two years, before being contracted to the major Epic label in 1964 and, in 1967, entering the national Hot 100 with their classic Larry Williams(▶)-produced **Why (Am I Treated So Bad)** (later covered in two quite different but equally superb versions by the Sweet Inspirations(▶) and Cannonball Adderley(▶)).

Williams also produced **For What It's Worth,** an inspired song by Stephen Stills and still regarded as a Staples' masterpiece. Buried in the Billy Sherrill-produced **Pray On** album was one secular song—a chilling lead vocal performance by Pervis Staples of the Bob Dylan song **John Brown,** a recording which surely stands as the most powerful indictment of the folly of war ever committed to record.

In 1968 the move to Stax turned the Staple Singers into an act of worldwide mass appeal, as evidenced by their much lauded appearance on the epic 'Soul To Soul' concert in Ghana and, after the demise of Stax, their Curtis Mayfield(▶)-written and produced soundtrack album for the Sidney Poitier/Bill Cosby movie *Let's Do It Again.*

The Staple Singers moved from Stax to Fantasy to Warner Bros, and most recently to 20th Century for the 1981 **Hold On To Your Dream** album, but success of the magnitude they found at Stax has eluded them.

Besides her singing with the family group, Mavis Staples has enjoyed a parallel solo career which yielded fine albums for Stax's Volt subsidiary and a solo soundtrack for a second Poitier/Cosby film *A Piece Of The Action.*

Recordings:
The Best Of (Vee Jay/Joy)
Pray On (Epic/—)
For What It's Worth (Epic/—)
Soul Folk In Action (Stax)
Be What You Are (Stax/—)
Bealtitude: Respect Yourself
(Stax)
Best Of (Stax)
Unlock Your Mind (Warner Bros.)
Hold On To Your Dream (20th Century)

Edwin Starr

Although never one of Motown's(▶) big guns, Edwin Starr (Born Charles Hatcher, in Nashville, on January 21, 1942) had several major hits in the late '60s and early '70s, and was the possessor of an impressive Wilson Pickett(▶)-style voice. Early

hits included **Stop Her On Sight** and **Headline News** (both on Ric-Tic) in 1966, and **25 Miles** in 1969 (on moving to Motown when they bought his previous label). In 1970 Motown's increasing concern with 'street credibility' was reflected in Starr's anti-war song **War** (also one of the few protest songs ever to be a disco favourite) and its follow-up **Stop The War Now.**

After splitting from Motown in 1972, Starr eventually signed with 20th Century, and has since recorded consistently with moderate success. **H.A.P.P.Y. Radio,** a single from the album of the same name, gave him a hit in 1979. A dynamic live performer, Starr has always been able to fill venues, and has been particularly popular in Britain.

Recordings:
Hits Of Edwin Starr (Motown)
Clean (20th Century)
H.A.P.P.Y. Radio (20th Century)

Stax

Always boasting a strong musical fraternity—it was the hometown of W.C. Handy, the so-called 'Father Of The Blues', while Beale Street had long been a noted centre for jazz music—Memphis started to become an important recording centre in the early '50s when Sam Phillips set up his Phillips recording studio and Sun record label, cutting blues, R&B, rockabilly, and discovering Elvis Presley.

Hi Records consolidated Memphis' importance, but it was the 1959 founding of Satellite, soon to become Stax, which really turned 'The Memphis Sound' into a major force on both the American and international music scenes.

Jim Stewart and his sister Estelle Axton ran a record shop called Satellite. It was natural then that they should launch a label and that, given Stewart's background as a country music banjo player, initial releases should be in the C&W idiom. The store, however, was located in a predominantly black-populated district and force of customer demand soon steered musical policy towards R&B.

Local black radio DJ Rufus Thomas(▶) and his daughter Carla(▶) gave Satellite an early hit with **Let Me Be Good To You** and in 1960 Stewart recorded Carla Thomas

Below: The late Otis Redding, one-time chauffeur who became Stax's greatest star.

solo on **Gee Whiz,** which sold a million, distributed by Atlantic(▶).

In 1961, the label name was changed to Stax (the 'St' from Stewart, the 'Ax' from Axton) and set the scene for a decade of enormously influential and commercially successful music-making. Purchasing the disused Capitol Cinema on East McLemore Avenue, Stewart laid it out as a studio and office complex.

Until the late '60s, Stax was to be distributed by and closely connected with Atlantic, and at various times Stax-signed artists appeared on Atlantic and Atco as well as on Stax and its own subsidiaries, notably Volt and Enterprise, while many of Atlantic's own black artists, like Wilson Pickett(▶) and Don Covay(▶), were sent down to Stax to record.

But, whatever the design on the label (originally the Stax label was light blue, later yellow), the Stax sound was unique, and instantly recognisable. Clean, spare, usually only lightly produced (though towards the '70s, large-scale and complex orchestral arrangements were increasingly utilised), it was based on a relaxed but precise rhythm section backed up by punchy horn patterns.

The resident session band was Booker T & the MGs(▶), plus the Mar-Keys(▶) horn section (later on, the Memphis Horns) and, if strings were required, the luminaries of the Memphis Symphony Orchestra. The Bar-Kays(▶) eventually served as a second studio outfit.

Stax's greatest star was Otis Redding(▶), discovered when he visited the studio as chauffeur/odd-job man with Johnny Jenkins and the Pinetoppers and used up some time left over at the end of one of their sessions to cut his 1963 ballad hit **These Arms Of Mine.**

The company also had enormous success with Sam and Dave(▶), Rufus Thomas, Carla Thomas, Eddie Floyd(▶), William Bell(▶), Johnnie Taylor(▶), and Booker T & the MGs, the Mar-Keys, the Bar-Kays, in their guise as recording and gigging bands. In addition, Stax recorded a large 'second division' of artists who were responsible for some great records, including many million-sellers, even if they might have lacked staying power (in some cases) or the ability to reach the heights of the charts (in others).

The Soul Children(▶), the Emotions(▶), Judy Clay, Margie Joseph(▶), the Dramatics(▶), Little Milton(▶) blues master Albert King(▶), Mel and Tim(▶), Frederick Knight, Shirley Brown(▶), the Mad Lads, Ollie and the Nightingales and the remarkable Rance Allen(▶) all had moments of great creativity at Stax. Issac Hayes(▶) and David Porter(▶), originally with the company to write and produce for Sam and Dave and other acts, eventually launched solo careers of their own, Hayes becoming a giant of black music while still with Stax.

Possibly the label's greatest contribution to black music lay in showing that soul music could sell in vast quantities to a crossover (and international) audience, but still remain true to its ethnic roots. The Stax sound was certainly popular but amounted to more than mere easy-to-assimilate pop, rarely compromising itself with either the rock or showbiz formula which Motown(▶), for example, sometimes flirted with.

At the end of the '60s, Stax was bought as a going concern by the

Paramount entertainment arm of the vast Gulf + Western industrial conglomerate. To mark the event, a massive two-week recording binge was undertaken with Booker T and the MGs/the Mar-Keys working one 12-hour shift and the Bar-Kays the other as the company's stars were shuttled through the studios.

In 1972, dissatisfied with the way things were going, Jim Stewart,

Below: The late Al Jackson, then Stax's resident session drummer and founder member of the MGs.

who had been kept on to head things, bought the company back but soon ran into financial difficulties, though the massive seven-hour Wattstax concert which pulled thousands into an L.A. football stadium in 1973 had augured a healthy future. Diversifying into a wide range of musical areas, including rock (with Cargo, Molloch and others), gospel (Rev. Maceo Woods, etc.), blues (Freddy Robinson, Jimmy McCracklin(▶)), black consciousness (Louis Paul, the Sons Of Truth, John DeKasandra), MOR (Billy Eckstine(▶)), jazz (Chico Hamilton) and even country (O.B. McClinton(▶) didn't help; nor too did being ripped off by pirates and bootleggers (hundreds of thousands of counterfeit Isaac Hayes' albums flooded the market).

Another major factor in Stax's problems was Stewart himself. Without the presence of black A & R man Al Bell, it is arguable whether Stax would have ever happened at all. Stewart was notorious among his artists for having little idea of what constituted a hit record—the Mar-Keys, for example, had to send the master tape of their million-selling **Last Night** to Atlantic surreptitiously as Stewart didn't want it released, believing it had no chance. One major Stax artist once confided: 'You always know when Jim is at a session, you can hear him clapping his hands and stomping his feet— out of time with the music!'.

Whatever the causes, the com-

Above: Edwin Starr, a powerful vocalist who has had sporadic success since the '60s.

pany was put into liquidation by its bankers in 1975. At the bankruptcy hearings, the judge made the classic remark: 'Running a record company strikes me as being like playing Russian roulette—with five bullets in the chamber!'.

The company's artists (those left by the time the final crunch came) went their various ways, the McLemore Avenue studio which had once vibrated to so much great music became a ghost-ridden empty shell, and the master-tapes were purchased by Fantasy who, thankfully, have in the ensuing years repackaged them in various forms (and kept the familiar yellow Stax label alive for the purpose).

In later years there was a sad leavening of dross (though still plenty of first-rate material as well), but the prodigious Stax output remains a unique body of work. Most of the music sounds as fresh and exciting today as when it was first recorded, and it is perhaps significant that few of the artists originally with Stax have managed to score significant success with other labels in the ensuing years.

Recordings:
Memphis Soul (Stax/—)
Fillet Of Soul (Stax)
Wattstax (Stax)
Stax 15 Original Big Hits Vols 1 & 2 (Stax)

Mickey Stevenson

Married to Motown(▶) star Kim Weston(▶), Mickey Stevenson was a seminal producer/songwriter for the company, being head of A&R from 1959-67, producing sides for Marvin Gaye(▶), Stevie Wonder(▶), Mary Wells(▶), Martha and the Vandellas(▶), the Four Tops(▶), The Supremes(▶), the Temptations(▶) and the Marvelettes(▶), as well as his wife.

His compositions include Martha and the Vandellas' **Dancing In The Streets**, Marvin Gaye's **Pride And Joy** and **Hitch Hike**, Stevie Wonder's **Nothing's Too Good For My Baby** and Kim Weston's **Love All The Way**. He also recorded in his own right with modest success.

Recordings:
Here I Am (Ember)

Billy Stewart

While the ghettos of New York City have spawned a plethora of black musicians, the more suburban climes of Washington DC are not without their talented offspring. Such was Billy 'Fat Boy' Stewart, born on March 24, 1937. His early musical background was in the Stewart Gospel Singers before high school brought him into contact with the doo-wop vocal group the Rainbows, whose sometime members also included Marvin Gaye(▶) and Don Covay(▶).

Billy's solo disc career began with the keyboard instrumental **Billy's Blues** on Chess in 1956, while he was pianist in Bo Diddley's(▶) band, then came **Billy's Heartaches** on OKeh in 1957. But it was his vocal talents that bore most fruit when **Reap What You Sow** scored in summer 1962, the first of several fine ballads to chart in the distinctive Stewart style incorporating 'word doubling' and a little scat singing.

The hit era spanned some seven years, yielding hits like **I Do Love You, Sitting In The Park** and a unique treatment of **Summertime**, laden with vocal gimmicks, yet beautifully performed and bridged with a masterful sax solo. That was in summer 1966, his career zenith; thereafter the hits waned somewhat, though Billy toured constantly, and even reached England briefly yet memorably. Then, in

Below: Keyboard player and vocalist Billy Stewart.

the early hours of Saturday January 17, 1970, Billy Stewart and three members of his band were tragically killed when their car plunged off a bridge into the River Neuse in North Carolina.

Recordings:
Golden Decade (—/Chess)
Unbelievable (Chess)
Cross My Heart (Chess/—)

Barrett Strong

Barrett Strong has gone down in history as the man who cut the original of **Money**, the Berry Gordy Jr/Janie Bradford song which was the 1960 smash hit on the back of which Gordy launched his Tamla Motown(▶) empire (it was issued on Gwen Gordy's Anna label). Later it was a renowned Beatles' album cut and a UK hit for Bern Elliott.

Born in Mississippi, on February 5, 1941, Barrett moved to Detroit before meeting Gordy. After spells with Atlantic(▶) and Tollie he went back to Motown in the early '70s to co-write and co-produce with Norman Whitfield for the Temptations(▶) and Undisputed Truth(▶) as well as cutting an album of his own.

Recordings:
Stronghold (Capitol)

Studio One

Countless blue beat, ska and reggae artists have spent some time at Studio One, in Brentford Road, Kingston, Jamaica, the now legendary base of producer Clement Coxsone Dodd, the erstwhile operator of the equally legendary Downbeat sound-system.

Although many artists alleged unfair treatment by Dodd, there is no denying the success rate of the label (particularly when Jackie Mittoo(▶) and Lee Perry(▶) were employed there), as references in this book will bear witness.

Sue Records

The Sue label was founded in New York by black producer/performer Juggy Murray and scored its biggest successes with Ike and Tina

Above: Florence, Mary and Diana—the Supremes, the most influential female vocal group of the '60s.

Turner(▶), Inez and Charlie Foxx(▶) (whose images were cultivated in the same mould) and organist Jimmy McGriff(▶). The then infant Island Records leased several tracks from Sue for release in the UK and registered the Sue name and a distinctive red and yellow label design.

Under the guidance of the late Guy Stevens (later a seminal figure in the development of London's undergound psychedelic rock scene), the UK Sue label issued material not just from US Sue but from a host of American outlets. Many of the records were obscure but almost all were classics.

Stevens' legendary auctions of rare soul imports as a club DJ and most of all his work through Sue (with records by Ike and Tina, Wilbert Harrison(▶), Bob and Earl(▶), Larry Williams(▶)—including a UK-produced album, O.V. Wright(▶), Willie Mabon, June Bateman, Chris Kenner, Big Al Downing, Bobby Lee Trammell, Louisiana Red, Roscoe Shelton, the Olympics, Harold Burrage, Baby Washington, James Brown(▶) and many others) made him a major figure in the rapid development of the burgeoning British soul scene.

Much material from US Sue was later issued in the UK by Decca (on London American) and United Artists.

Recordings:
The Sue Story (Vols 1, 2 & 3) (—/Sue)
The Sue Story (—/London)

The Supremes

Above: Combining beauty with composure, The Supremes in the late '70s.

Originally formed in Detroit's Brewster projects in 1959, the embryonic Supremes, then known as the Primettes, consisted of Mary Wilson, Florence Ballard, Diane (Diana) Ross(▶) and Betty Anderson. The four girls were, like many teenagers of the late '50s, heavily influenced by the popular doo-wopping trend and in particular by the hugely successful Frankie Lymon and the Teenagers(▶) group.

Their name came from a local amateur male group—the Primes (who were in fact the forerunners to the Temptations(▶))—and the girls would follow the group to various engagements in typical random fashion. After Betty Horton left they enlisted Barbara Martin and came to the attention of the Detroit-based Lupine label. Lupine were hot with the Falcons (who consisted of Wilson Pickett(▶), Eddie Floyd(▶), Mack Rice and Joe Stubbs, brother of Levi of the Four Tops(▶), but were unable to sell many Primettes records. The recording contract did enable the girls to make more live appearances however.

By 1960, Detroit was showing the signs of an emerging black music scene. Local song writer Berry Gordy had used his royalties from Jackie Wilson hits to finance recordings by his discoveries Smokey Robinson(▶) and the Miracles(▶). The records were moderate hits enabling Gordy, with help from Robinson, to set up Tamla Motown(▶) records and begin a search for talent; they soon found the Primes and shortly afterwards the Primettes, who had become a trio again with the departure of Barbara Martin. Diana Ross lived close to Smokey Robinson and after the girls left Lupine she pestered him for an audition with Gordy. Gordy was interested and, although insisting they remain in school, used them regularly as back-up vocalists for other acts like Marvin Gaye(▶) and Mary Wells(▶).

In 1962, after renaming them the Supremes, Motown cut them as a group and released their first album **Meet The Supremes**, produced and mostly written by Smokey Robinson. Their first taste of success came in the early months of 1963 when **Let Me Go The Right Way** entered the R&B charts at No.26 for a week and peaked at 90 on the pop charts in a six-week run. Previously they had hit the pop charts at 95 with **Your Heart Belongs To Me** in August 1962. A year later **A Breathtaking Guy** hit 75 on the pop charts, and in late 1963 the girls were assigned new producers in Holland-Dozier-Holland(▶) and international fame was just a hit away. In January 1964 **When The Love Starts Shining Through His Eyes** climbed to No.22 on the pop charts. During the summer of that year they took to the road in an all-star package-show somewhere down the bottom of the bill. While the group were touring, Motown released **Where Did Our Love Go** and by the end of the tour the Supremes were topping the bill and the record was topping the charts—all over the world.

From 1964 to 1967, under the guidance of Holland-Dozier-Holland, they emerged as the most successful female singing group in record history. Hits like **Baby Love, Come See About Me, Stop! In The Name Of Love, You Keep Me Hanging On, I Hear A Symphony, Back In My Arms Again, You Can't Hurry Love** came at breathtaking speed, one after another. Spurred by the Beatles' constant endorsement of Motown's material around the world, the Supremes were the toast of almost every nation.

To meet the public's insatiable demand for material they recorded several banal albums such as **A Little Bit Of Liverpool, Sing Country And Western, We Remember Sam Cooke, Merry Christmas** and **Sing**

Rodgers And Hart, although, between the dross, Holland-Dozier-Holland continued to provide them with brilliantly conceived epics of three-minute pop neatly contrived to appeal to all creeds and colours. In 1966, as recognition for her part in their success, the group became Diana Ross and the Supremes. This was the first stage in Berry Gordy's long-term plan to turn Ross into a solo star. It prompted Florence Ballard to leave the group at its height for a short-lived tragic solo career and rapid personal decline towards her death in 1976. Her replacement was Cindy Birdsong, a member of Patti LaBelle(▶) and the Bluebelles.

After the departure of Holland-Dozier-Holland, the Supremes were given to other producers with great success. **Love Child** and **I'm Living In Shame** kept up the consistency until late 1969 when Diana Ross finally took the plunge into a solo career. Prior to her departure they had hit a low point in sales, with singles like **The Composer** and **No Matter What Sign You Are** barely achieving top 30 status. The last Diana Ross and the Supremes single, aptly and deliberately called **Someday We'll Be Together** (December 1969), was their first No.1 since **Love Child** in November 1968. All together the group had 12 No.1 singles between November 1964 and December 1969, as well as a further eight top-10 records.

Diana's replacement was Jean Terrell and it was expected that the group would be unable to overcome her loss. But in April 1970, they were back in the top 10 with **Up The Ladder To The Roof**, followed by other top-20 hits through to 1972, including **Stoned Love, Nathan Jones** and **Floy Joy.** A coupling with the Four Tops kept the hits coming but the changing face of black music, with its new political awareness, was no place for three nice harmonising girls and, with the departure of Cindy Birdsong and then Jean Terrell, Mary Wilson was left to struggle alone with several line-up changes.

The last really consistent Supremes was the line-up of 1976, which featured Mary, Scherrie Payne (from Glasshouse and a sister of Freda(▶)) and Susaye Green (from Wonderlove). Their two albums, reuniting the group with Holland-Dozier-Holland in 1976, **Mary, Scherrie And Susaye** and **High Energy**, the latter featuring the hit single (No.40, July 1976) **I'm Gonna Let My Heart Do The Walking,** were a tremendous return to form.

Unfortunately, with insufficient promotion, the records failed to register strongly enough and in 1977, after several highly successful English cabaret tours, the girls went their separate ways, Scherrie and Susaye as a very short-lived duo and Mary as a solo. In 1978 Mary toured the UK with the two new Supremes, Karen Ragland and Karen Jackson, but the dream was over and the Supremes were no more. A sad postscript came in 1980 when Mary Wilson sued Motown over the use of the name and had to tour England as 'Mary Wilson of the Supremes'. The name will never die!

Recordings:
Supremes Sing Motown (Tamla Motown)
Supremes A Go Go (Tamla Motown)
Anthology (Tamla Motown)
Join The Temptations (Tamla Motown)
20 Golden Greats (Tamla Motown)
Early Days 1961-1964 (Tamla Motown)
Floy Joy (Tamla Motown)
High Energy (Tamla Motown)

Swamp Dogg

Jerry Williams Jr, alias Swamp Dogg, once wrote: 'Where else but in America could a person own a Rolls-Royce, a Cadillac Eldorado Mark IV, a Mercedes limousine, an estate in Long Island, an apartment in Hollywood and still be considered a failure?'

Certainly, while Williams has long been a well-respected name among soul buffs, he remains an unknown to the wider public, despite a whole host of highly inventive recordings under both his names, and productions on a number of artistically superior if commercially modest soul artists, including Doris Duke(▶) and Irma Thomas(▶).

Born in Portsmouth, Virginia, in July 1942, he recorded singles as Jerry, Little Jerry Williams and plain Jerry Williams for Roulette, Ember, V-Tone, Loma, Calla, Cotillion and other labels, before coming up with his bizarre Swamp Dogg alter-ego and recording highly innovative albums for Canyon, Elektra, Cream, TK(▶) and Island, notable for their imaginative lyrics and wry vocal approach.

Recordings:
Total Destruction To Your Mind (Canyon/Contempo)
Rat On (Elektra/—)
Gag A Maggot (TK/President)
Have You Heard This Story? (Island)
Cuffed Collared And Tagged (Cream/—)

Bettye Swann

One of the unsung heroines of soul music, Bettye Swann (born Betty Jean Champion at Shreveport, Louisiana, on October 24, 1944,

the seventh of 14 children) was the Queen of the deep-soul ballad, making some of the most hauntingly soulful sides on record. She moved to Los Angeles in her teens and joined the Fawns before debuting on Money with the self-penned **Don't Wait Too Long.** In 1965 she hit the US top 10 on the same label with another of her own songs, **Make Me Yours.**

When Money folded in 1968 she switched to Capitol and was teamed with producer Wayne Shuler (whose father ran the seminal rockabilly/R&B label Goldband in Louisiana). Shuler coupled the songstress with classic country songs and such Nashville-style ingredients as steel guitars and strings, and the first big hit came with a version of country star Hank Cochran's **Don't Touch Me.** The album of the same title was a true gem, featuring material by Don Gibson, John D. Loudermilk and even the Bee Gees, along with a version of Otis Redding's(▶) **These Arms Of Mine,** but despite the varied ingredients, the mix came out as pure Southern soul.

A second set, **Don't You Ever Get Tired (Of Hurting Me)?,** had another Cochran song as its title cut, and everything from the choice of material, to the arrangement, the playing and Bettye's performances, spelt spine-tingling magic. Great versions of **Today I Started Loving You Again** and **Stand By Your Man** helped make it a classic album.

Rick Hall, at Fame Studios in Muscle Shoals(▶), then took over production and **Victim Of A Broken Heart** was a hit, as was a new version of **Today I Started Loving You Again.**

Below: Jerry Williams, still something of a cult figure.

Above: Little Johnny Taylor who for some reason was often confused with Johnnie Taylor.

Recordings:
Make Me Yours (Abet-Money/—)
The Soul View Now (Capitol/—)
Don't You Ever Get Tired (Of Hurting Me)? (Capitol/—)

The Tams

The Tams are an example of that paradox of musical taste which sometimes gives American acts belated success in Britain when they are perhaps passé in their homeland. It was almost bizarre to see this quintet of rotund black guys nearing middle-age getting rapturous applause from a young London audience in the early 1970s, a decade after their initial US hits. Charles and Joseph Pope, Robert Lee Smith, Floyd Ashton and Horace Kay, all from Atlanta, Georgia, spent their formative musical years singing in hometown clubs before charting with the plaintive **Untie Me** on Arlen in 1962.

A management deal with Bill Lowery and a personnel change with Albert Cottle replacing Ashton, brought a move to ABC Records, whereon the Tams attained chart consistency with hits like **What Kind Of Fool (Do You Think I Am), You Lied To Your Daddy, Hey Girl Don't Bother Me** and **Be Young Be Foolish Be Happy,** all easy-tempo items with ear-catching hoarse lead vocals and throaty gospel-tinged harmonies.

Through Lowery's productions, the group later had discs on 1-2-3 Records and Capitol, then in 1971 found themselves top of the British charts with the re-issued **Hey Girl,** but further success has eluded them.

Recordings:
A Little More Soul (ABC/Stateside)
Be Young Be Foolish Be Happy (—/Stateside)

Howard Tate

A superb singer who never received the recognition he deserved, Tate's main claim to fame is a marvellous album released in 1967 on Verve, **Get It While You Can**. Produced by ace soul producer Jerry Ragovoy(▶), the album was a potent mixture of uptown blues and mellow soul that showcased Tate's classic vocals to perfection. One single pulled from the album **Ain't Nobody Home** became an R&B hit.

A later Warners album did not reach the same standard as the Verve set, and **Get It While You Can** is definitely the one to look for in cut-out bins and specialist shops.

Recordings:
Get It While You Can (Verve)

Little Johnny Taylor

Born in Memphis, Tennessee, in 1940, Johnny Young started singing gospel with Mighty Clouds Of Joy and as he was the youngest member was dubbed 'Little Johnny'. He moved to Los Angeles to solo as a bluesman and became Little Johnny Taylor with a Galaxy contract, cutting the classic **Part Time Love** blues ballad in 1963.

With the like-named Johnnie Taylor(▶) coming to prominence on Stax(▶) at the same time, there was some confusion between the two, especially when Johnnie cut a version of **Part Time Love** (the tale goes that his mother turned up for a show only to realise she'd bought a ticket for the wrong act!).

Moving to Ronn, who often paired him with Ted Taylor, Johnny Taylor scored with **Everybody Knows About My Good Thing**, **Open House At My House** and other personal-situation numbers, usually about two-timing women.

Recordings:
Little Johnny Taylor (Galaxy/Vocalion)
Everybody Knows About My Good Thing (Ronn/Mojo)
Open House At My House (Ronn/Contempo)
The Super Taylors (with Ted Taylor) (Ronn/Contempo)

Johnnie Taylor

One of the most powerful singers in black music, Johnnie Taylor has during the course of his long career known success in the blues, R&B soul and disco fields. Born in Arkansas on May 5, 1938, Taylor started out in gospel with the Soul Stirrers (who had earlier included Sam Cooke(▶) in their line-up), recording for several small labels before signing with Stax(▶) in 1965.

Most of his early cuts for the company were blues-styled and only moderately successful, until in 1968 he registered a major smash with **Who's Making Love**. This '60s classic, with its wry lyrics and irresistible dance beat, was followed by a series of singles which cast Taylor in the role of the hip philosopher of soul. Tracks like **Jody's Got Your Girl And Gone**, **Steal Away**, the million-selling **I Believe In You** and **I've Been Born Again** sustained Taylor's success into the '70s.

In 1975 Taylor split from Stax to join Columbia, a move which led to massive commercial success. His first album for the company, **Eargasm**, was a collection of highly produced soul ballads that made No.5 in the US charts and went gold. An even greater success was a single pulled from the album, **Disco Lady**, a catchy novelty song full of sexual double talk. It made No.1 on the US charts in 1976, went platinum, and provided Taylor with an international hit.

Taylor has never quite repeated that success, but has recorded consistently, mainly in a 'sexy disco'

Johnnie Taylor. Powerful blues-styled vocalist who found success in the disco market.

mould. His best material is indubitably on Stax, the two **Chronicle** albums covering his most worthwhile cuts.

Recordings:
The Johnnie Taylor Chronicle (1968-1972) (Stax)
The Johnnie Taylor Chronicle (1972-1974) (Stax)
Eargasm (Columbia/CBS)
Rated Extraordinaire (Columbia/CBS)
Ever Ready (Columbia/CBS)

Ted Taylor

Ted Taylor's high-pitched and at times almost maniacally emotional voice might not be to everyone's taste, but there is no denying it made his version of **Ramblin' Rose** (OKeh) one of the most exciting soul records of the early '60s.

A native of Okmulgee, Oklahoma, Taylor moved to California and was in the Cadets at the time of their **Stranded In The Jungle** classic; he also recorded with the group's alter ego, the Jacks.

Combining a strong Roy Brown influence with gospel fervour, he recorded solo for Ebb in 1958 with the rock 'n' roll number **Keep Walking On**, before stints at Peacock and OKeh, his biggest hit for the latter label being the blues-tinged **Stay Away From Me** (1965), though it was **Ramblin' Rose** which made his reputation.

Spells at Top Rank, Atco(▶) and other labels eventually led him to Louisiana-based Ronn Records, a subsidiary of Jewel-Paula(▶), for which company he recorded prolifically, making a speciality of storyline ballads and hitting in 1968 with the Muscle Shoals(▶) recorded **Strangest Feeling**. He also recorded duets with Little Johnny Taylor(▶), notably the **Super Taylors** album, co-produced by Jewel Akens of **Birds And The Bees** fame.

Recordings:
Ted Taylor 1976 (Ronn/Contempo)
You Can Dig It! (Ronn/—)

Below: Bettye Swann: personification of Southern Soul.

Super Taylor. Courtesy Stax Records.

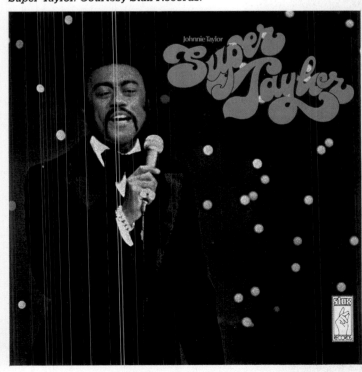

The Temptations

Utilising the dual talents of David Ruffin(▶) and Eddie Kendricks(▶), the Temptations carved out a slice of soul history for themselves with a seemingly uninterrupted stream of hit singles and albums from 1964 on. Then, when the two left to pursue solo careers, the Temptations continued on the chart trail with new lead voice Dennis Edwards (formerly of the Contours(▶)).

The raucous tenor of Ruffin was the perfect foil for the effortless, fluent high tenor of Kendricks and, with astute choice of songs from the Motown(▶) hierarchy, the group never looked back from the day **The Way You Do The Things You Do** entered the American top 20 in March 1964.

The Temptations were formed in 1961, a combination of Otis Williams and the Distants (Williams, Melvin Franklin and Eldridge Bryant), and two survivors from the Primes, Kendricks and Paul Williams. Although this line-up began recording a year later, it wasn't until Ruffin replaced Bryant in 1963 that the unit received more than passing acknowledgement from the Motown staff.

In these early days all Berry Gordy and his burgeoning empire did was 'write it, then record it'. There was no magic formula—just a mountain of talent looking for guidance. And the Temptations were happy to cut anything they were given, particularly when the young singer and writer from the Miracles, Smokey Robinson(▶), came by with some surplus material.

Possibly feeling some vocal empathy with Kendricks, Robinson produced his own **The Way You Do The Things You Do** for the group at the end of '63, providing

Kendricks with a cute pop poem and a distinctive vocal arrangement of which the singer took full advantage.

Although **I'll Be In Trouble** and **Why You Wanna Make Me Blue** were less successful, the Temptations were at the top of the American charts with another Robinson-produced song, **My Girl**, at the beginning of 1965, with the

Wish It Would Rain. Courtesy Motown Records.

spotlight now on Ruffin.

Ruffin's gospel background (he had been with the Dixie Nightingales and the Soulsters in the late '50s) was obvious from his hard driving and emotional reading of this Robinson classic; he performed as well on the follow-up **It's Growing**. 1965 was a vintage year for The Temptations, with **Since I Lost My Baby** and **My Baby** also making the US top 10. Ironically, from this prodigious output only **My Girl** and **It's Growing** made any chart impact in the UK, both barely making the top 50, and then for just one week apiece.

With the introduction of Norman Whitfield(▶) as writer/producer in 1966, the Temptations took on a

rougher edge to their sound, and Ruffin found himself out front as the acknowledged lead vocalist. He was featured on the group's singles **Ain't Too Proud To Beg, Beauty Is Only Skin Deep, (I Know) I'm Losing You** (all 1966), **All I Need Is You, You're My Everything** and **(Loneliness Made Me Realize) It's You That I Need** (all 1967). **Beauty** and **Losing You**

Above: The Temptations showing their handiwork at a London concert. They've covered the field, from pop (The Way You Do The Things You Do) to social commentary (Cloud Nine).

were both UK top 20 chart entries.

It was becoming obvious that Ruffin would want to strike out on his own, and he did so in 1968, but

Above: The Temptations, circa 1964. Tempus fugit ...

not before contributing to **I Wish It Would Rain** and **I Could Never Love Another.** His replacement was Dennis Edwards, former lead tenor of the Contours, and a singer who with his powerful gruff-edged voice slotted in nicely as Whitfield tried to change the Temptations' image to a group identity rather than lead singer plus four, coming up with arrangements which, rather than relying on a lead backed by restrained harmonies, bounced the contrasting voices—from Williams' high tenor through Edwards' lead to Franklin's sonorous bass—off each other. Motown was also moving into the Woodstock era, aware that social commentary was commercially viable, with the Norman Whitfield/Barrett Strong(▶) song **Cloud Nine,** a drug/ghetto opus, setting the pace at the end of 1968, and earning a Grammy Award.

Whitfield and Strong continued their urban themes with **Runaway Child, Running Wild, Don't Let The Joneses Get You Down, I Can't Get Next to You,** their 'age of Aquarius' masterpiece **Psychedelic Shack,** and **Ball Of Confusion.**

At the beginning of 1972, the Temptations earned their first platinum single, for **Just My Imagination,** a return to a wistful slow ballad format, although this honour was soured slightly by the departures of Kendricks (for a solo career) and Williams (because of serious illness). Their respective replacements were Damon Harris (formerly with the Vandals) and Richard Street (from the Monitors, another Motown group).

The Harris/Street/Edwards/ Franklin/Williams' aggregation scored in 1971/72 with **Superstar, Take A Look Around, Papa Was A Rolling Stone** and **Masterpiece.** The albums **Masterpiece** (noted for its extended work-outs of material like Bill Withers(▶) **Ain't No Sunshine**) and **All Directions** went gold, and **Papa** picked up two Grammys. In 1974, the Temptations' **Anthology** triple-album was released, showcasing 37 of the group's record and stage hits, and sealing a decade of chart action. Sadly, it also proved to be a neat parcel of what would remain their best work as they have never since been able to reach such heights of creativity.

Despite the solid **A Song For You** album in 1975, which picked up another gold disc, the departure that year of Harris (replaced by Glenn Leonard) and of Dennis Edwards in 1977 knocked much of the aggressiveness out of the group's approach. Louis Price took Edwards' place as lead vocalist as the unit moved from Motown to Atlantic, recording two fair sets, **Hear To Tempt You** and **Bare Back,** although both were a far cry from the heady days when they had worked with Robinson and Whitfield.

In 1980, after much legal toing and froing, The Temptations returned to Motown, with Dennis Edwards rejoining the group, for his second spell, on the album **Power.** The group have since cut **The Temptations,** released at the end of 1981.

Recordings:
Anthology (Motown)
Cloud Nine (Motown)
Masterpiece (Motown)
Sing Smokey (Motown)
20 Golden Greats (Motown)
Power (Motown)
The Temptations (Motown)

Tammi Terrell

When complications arising from a brain tumour operation took the life of Tammi Terrell on March 16, 1970, the world of soul music was deprived of one of its brightest and prettiest children. Born Tammi Montgomery in Philadelphia in 1946, she pursued an active academic life at high school, graduating to the University of Pennsylvania to study medicine and major in psychology, but gaining musical experience through a number of talent shows. It was this medium that brought her to the attention of Luther Dixon, who soon signed Tammi to Scepter/ Wand Records, whereon she made her debut in 1961.

A brief spell with the James Brown(▶) Revue yielded a disc on his Try Me label, and she also recorded for Checker before joining Motown(▶) in 1965 under her married name of Tammi Terrell. **I Can't Believe You Love Me** was a small debut hit early in 1966, followed by **Come On And See Me.** Then the Corporation paired her in duet with Marvin Gaye(▶), and this successful partnership spent the next three years virtually resident in the upper reaches of the transatlantic charts.

Ain't No Mountain High Enough and **Your Precious Love** —two beaty love-songs with memorable lyrics and ear-catching hooks —set the pace late in 1967. Tammi's sweet soulful tones proved a perfect contrast to Marvin's rich gospel-tinged vitality. Subsequent hits like **Ain't Nothing Like The Real Thing** and **You're All I Need To Get By** have since transcended national barriers and are now regarded as classic pop hits.

Tammi began to suffer violent head pains while pursuing a busy touring schedule, and diagnosis revealed a malignant tumor. Operations were performed, and she seemed to recover; deemed fit enough to sing agin, she and Marvin resumed their touring, only for Tammi to collapse in his arms on-stage one night. Further surgery failed to save her life, and **The Onion Song** was destined to become a posthumous hit in spring 1970.

Recordings:
The Early Show (—/Wand-Marble Arch)
Irresistible (Motown)
The Onion Song (with Marvin Gaye) (—/Sounds Superb)
Greatest Hits (Motown)

Joe Tex

From being a second-rate Little Richard(▶)/James Brown(▶) imitator, Joe Tex developed into one of the most distinctive—and successful— artists in soul music and a prime member of Atlantic Records'(▶) 'Soul Clan'.

Born in Baytown, Texas, on August 8, 1933, Tex won a local talent contest in his teens, the first prize being a trip to New York to appear at the Apollo Theatre (Johnny Nash(▶) was another contestant). Tex went down well enough at the Apollo to be booked to stay on for a further four weeks.

Recording for King(▶) from 1955-7, for Ace from 1958-60 and for Anna in 1960, Tex tried out on a wide range of material (reissued in album form via King and Checker)

Above: Joe Tex, who had bumped for 25 years, died in Navasota, Texas, in August 1982.

as he struggled to find a musical identity, but gradually he evolved his own secular form of philosophical sermonising. He was also busy writing songs for others, including Jerry Butler(▶), Ernie K. Doe(▶) and James Brown (who charted in 1961 with Tex's **Baby You're Right**). Tex also cut a single, **Wicked Woman** (Jalynne), backed by Brown's band.

It was meeting up with Nashville-based country musician/music-publisher Buddy Killen that cracked it wide open for Tex, and Killen set up the Dial label specifically as an outlet for the black singer's talent. A promising album was leased to London Records' subsidiary Parrot, then a long-term deal was signed between Dial and Atlantic in 1965, when the testifying **Hold What You've Got** turned Tex into a hot property and set the pattern for a string of hits in his new role as a homespun country-preacher.

A Woman Can Change A Man, I Want To Do (Everything For You), a brilliant version of Bobby Bare's **Detroit City, The Love You Save (May Be Your Own), Don't Let Your Left Hand Know (What Your Right Hand Is Doing)** were all in the classic Tex lilting ballad mould, but as early as **C.C. Rider,** on his 1965 **The New Boss** album, Tex proved he could also handle a real belter with aplomb. Soon he was leavening the ballads with some great dance records, with super-witty lyrics as their trademark, as on **You're Right, Ray Charles, S.Y.S.L.J.F.M. (The Letter Song), Skinny Legs And All** (recorded live), all of which revealed him to be not only a class performer but one of soul music's most inventive songwriters.

In 1970, Tex and his band visited Britain as part of the 'Soul Together' package tour with Sam and Dave(▶)

and Arthur Conley(▶). On returning to the States, Tex took up church work as a real preacher, but returned to the charts in 1972 with **I Gotcha.**

Tex's long partnership with Buddy Killen continued (Dial now being handled by Mercury). The early and mid-'70s proved relatively lean but he saw chart action again in 1977 with **Ain't Gonna Bump No More (With No Big Fat Woman),** from the **Bumps And Bruises** set.

1978 produced two Tex albums; **Rub Down,** leased by Dial to Epic, included the delightfully titled **You Might Be Digging The Garden (But Somebody's Picking Your Plums),** while **He Who Is Without Funk (Cast The First Stone)** featured the dance-floor hit **Loose Caboose** and **Who Gave Birth To The Funk,** which was co-penned by the talented but underrated black country singer O.B. McClinton(▶) (whose own output on the Stax(▶) subsidiary Enterprise is well worth checking).

These two sets were adequate proof that Tex's ability to come up with catchy songs and imaginative lyrics was undiminished, but he died of a heart attack in August 1982.

Recordings:
Another Man's Woman (Power/—)
Hold On It's Joe Tex (Checker/—)
The Best Of Joe Tex (King/—)
The Best Of Joe Tex (Parrot/—)
Hold What You Got (Atlantic/—)
The New Boss (Atlantic/—)
The Love You Save (Atlantic/—)
Live And Lively (Atlantic)
Buying A Book (Atlantic)
I Gotcha (Dial/Mercury)
Joe Tex Spills The Beans (Dial/—)
Bumps And Bruises (Epic)
Rub Down (Epic)
He Who Is Without Funk (Cast The First Stone) (Dial/—)

Above: Rufus' talented daughter Carla Thomas.

Carla Thomas

Daughter of Rufus Thomas(▶), Carla duetted with her father on 'Cause I Love You (1959) which was to be the first minor hit for Satellite Records (shortly to be renamed Stax(▶)). The company's first million-seller came in 1960 when she soloed on the twee teen ballad Gee Whiz (Look At His Eyes), which was issued nationally on Atlantic(▶).

After a couple more releases Carla was switched back to Stax's own label and had several hits, including one with the Isaac Hayes(▶) song B-A-B-Y in 1966 and a duet with Otis Redding(▶) which revived the Lowell Fulsom(▶) blues' hit Tramp (and led to a joint Thomas/Redding album).

Later she was paired with Johnnie Taylor(▶) and with William Bell(▶), as well as continuing with her solo recordings.

Recordings:
Comfort Me (Stax/—)
Carla Thomas (Stax/—)
King And Queen (with Otis Redding) (Stax)
The Queen Alone (Stax)
Love Means (Stax/-)

Above: Rufus Thomas hit big while Walking The Dog!

Irma Thomas

Working as 'the singing waitress' at the Pimlico Club, New Orleans, Irma Thomas (born in Pontachoula Louisiana, in 1941) was discovered by local bandleader Tommy Ridgley who took her to the Ronn label for the 1958 R&B hit Don't Mess With My Man. Switching to Minit and produced by Allen Toussaint(▶) she had local success with I Done Got Over It, It's Raining, Ruler Of My Heart and the original of Pain In My Heart (which was later a hit for Otis Redding(▶)).

When Minit was brought into the Liberty family of labels, Irma was moved to their Imperial logo and achieved national success with Take A Look, Wish Someone Would Care and other fine deep-soul numbers, including Time Is On My Side, covered later by the Rolling Stones.

She switched to Chess(▶) in 1967 and had an R&B hit with Good To Me, but subsequent records for Canyon, Roker and Fungus (all produced by Jerry 'Swamp Dogg' Williams(▶)) were commercial flops, although they pioneered the domestic-situation songs and rap treatment later exploited with dramatic success by Millie Jackson(▶).

Irma has toured throughout the US and Europe, but is now content to work local New Orleans night spots. She is one of the unsung greats of the soul idiom.

Recordings:
Take A Look (Imperial/Minit)
Wish Someone Would Care (Imperial)
In Between Tears (—/Charly)
Hip Shakin' Mama (—/Charly)

Rufus Thomas

Truly the doyen of soul music, Rufus Thomas (born Collierville, Tennessee, March 28, 1917) began his career in 1935 as a comic with the Rabbits Foot Minstrels. In the '40s he started deejaying on Radio WDIA, Memphis, the first black-owned radio station in the US (he kept his show right through till the mid-'70s). He also ran talent shows which gave early breaks to B.B. King(▶), Bobby Bland(▶), Little Junior Parker and Isaac Hayes(▶).

Starting out in the jump-blues idiom he made one record in 1941, recorded for Star Talent in 1949 and in 1951 under Sam Phillips (the man who discovered Elvis) for Chess(▶), notching an R&B hit in 1953 for Phillips' own Sun label with the raucous Bearcat.

Teamed with his daughter Carla(▶) he gave Stax (Satellite as it was then) their first hit with 'Cause I Love You (Carla went on to solo hits while Rufus' son Marvel became a prominent session musician). In 1963 he had a big solo hit with the novelty dance songs Walking The Dog and The Dog, and in the early '70s firmly established himself as the Memphis Sound's song-and-dance man with such successes as Can Your Monkey Do The Dog, Do The Funky Chicken, Do The Funky Penguin and (Do The) Push And Pull.

Recordings:
Walking The Dog (Stax/London)
Do The Funky Chicken (Stax)
Did You Hear Me (Stax)
Crown Prince Of Dance (Stax)
If There Were No Music (Avi/Pye)

Toots & the Maytals

The raucous voice of Toots (real name Frederick) Hibbert has been an intrinsic part of Jamaican music on its path from ska and rock-steady through to the development of reggae. If it wasn't for the presence of Bob Marley and the Wailers(▶), Toots & the Maytals would arguably have been the supreme reggae group.

The group is continually recording and touring, and despite the often poor record sales, concerts never fail to sell out well in advance. Like James Brown(▶), Toots has rhythm flowing through his veins and it's his use of his musical adrenalin that people flock to see.

Toots began singing in a local church in his birthplace, Maypen, Jamaica. In 1962, he moved down from the hills and formed the Maytals (called the Vikings for their first four years) with backing vocalists Raleigh Gordon and Jerry Matthias, immediately recording at the Brentford Road headquarters of Clement Coxsone Dodd(▶). The group's debut single for Studio One(▶), Hallelujah, was an instant hit on the island. It was followed in the charts by Six And Seven Books Of Moses and Never Grow Old, which consolidated the group's popularity and their energetic 'straight-from-church' mode of singing.

Their stay with Dodd was short-lived, however, the group soon teaming up with leading sound-system operator Prince Buster(▶). Buster would spin Domino, Pain In My Belly, Little Flea and Dog War on his sytem and they'd soon be hits. In fact Dog War is regarded as a classic of the ska genre and is still reckoned to be able to pack any dance floor.

In 1966, the group switched again, this time to Byron Lee's BMN stable which provided them with the co-operation of Lee's fabulous Dragonaires on harmonies. That year they won the Jamaican Festival Song Competition with Bam Bam and changed their name to the Maytals. The Maytals dominated the Jamaican charts with Fever, It's You, Never You Change and the slow bluesy Daddy. That same year The Sensational Maytals album was released; it is now a highly-prized collectors' item.

Their runaway success was brought to an abrupt halt when Toots ran foul of the island's ganga (marijuana) laws and served two years in prison. When he was released, the group went to Chinese/Jamaican producer Leslie Kong and the influential Beverly's label, and it was Toots' penal experiences that gave rise to the group's biggest commercial success. 54-46 That's My Number was a hit in Jamaica and Britain, and the Maytals further reinstated themselves on the reggae scene by winning another Jamaican National Song Festival.

The Best Of Toots And The Maytals. Courtesy Trojan.

Other Kong hits were Just Tell Me, Reborn, Bim Today and Do The Reggay—the first record to have the word 'reggae', albeit spelt differently, in its title. By the time of Kong's death, in 1971, the group had recorded many of their greatest achievements: Pressure Drop, Sweet And Dandy, Monkey Man and Water Melon, songs that were to become the staple diet of young British musicians during the late '70s '2-Tone' movement.

The group returned to Byron Lee and started work on their first album for the Dynamic label, the much-acclaimed Funky Kingston. The album displayed a shift away from ska, and included a scorching version of the Kingsmen's '60s hit Louie Louie (which had started life earlier still as a minor R&B success for Richard Berry), as well as the more retrospective Redemption Song and It Was Written Down.

In 1976, Toots took his group on American and European tours and by the time they reached London the title track from their Reggae Got Soul album was in the pop charts. That album includes such

Reggae Got Soul. Courtesy Island Records.

notables as Steve Winwood, Eddie Quansah, Dudu Pukwana, Rico(▶) and Tommy McCook(▶).

The group made history in September 1980 when they played London's Hammersmith Palais. A live album of that show was mixed and pressed and put into the shops within 24 hours, which is just the speed Toots Hibbert likes to operate at: double quick and always twice as soulful. Although his Maytals have visibly aged and on a recent tour two girl singers were substituted for Gordon and Matthias, Toots is alive and kicking with years of exhilarating music ahead of him.

Recordings:
The Sensational Maytals
  (BMN/—)
Funky Kingston (—/Dragon)
Reggae Got Soul (—/Island)
Toots Live (—/Island)

Oscar Toney Jr

Produced by white mainstays of the Memphis R&B scene Chips Moman and Papa Don Schroeder, the rich-voiced Oscar Toney Jr won fans on both sides of the Atlantic for his relaxed brand of deep soul with classic versions of such soul standards as **Dark End Of The Street, Do Right Woman—Do Right Man** and **For Your Precious Love**.

Toney's all-white backing band of Reggie Young (guitar); Bobby Emmons (keyboards), Tommy Cogbill (bass) and Gene Chrisman (drums) set the lead for many other young white musicians who provided much of the class in studio bands, backing black artists in such Southern centres as Memphis, Nashville, Muscle Shoals(▶), Atlanta and Miami.

Recordings:
For Your Precious Love
  (Bell/Stateside)

Allen Toussaint

Among the more enigmatic figures in contemporary black music is the multi-talented Allen Toussaint, a Capricorn born on January 14, 1938, in New Orleans. Toussaint's abilities as songwriter/producer, pianist extraordinaire and sometime performer have proved catalytic in maintaining the quality of R&B records emanating from the Crescent City for almost three decades. He is a shy, reserved person in public, and conducts a rather private image off-stage, but he has been a dynamic force in the recording studio, furthering the cause and success of considerable local talent.

Growing up in a city rich with piano players, Toussaint imbibed the styles of veterans like Kid Stormy Weather and Leon T. Gross (Archibald), Paul Gayten and Professor Longhair, and the then upcoming Fats Domino(▶) and Huey Smith, to form his own fluid, dextrous style. He became touring pianist with hit duo Shirley & Lee(▶), in which role he was spotted in 1955 by Dave Bartholomew(▶), long-time collaborator with Fats Domino, and hired as a studio session player to work with major acts like Smiley Lewis and Lloyd Price(▶).

Right: Toots Hibbert who, with his Maytals have reached the plateau of reggae groups.

His recording debut as a 'name artist' was relatively inauspicious when in 1958 an album of piano instrumentals by 'Al Tousan' was placed with RCA, who also took publishing rights to his tunes like **Java** (destined to become an MOR standard). Individual fame eluded him, though, and he concentrated more on his studio work with other artists, a move which proved vital to New Orleans during the years of musical transition from raunchy R&B to the relative sophistication emergent in the soul idiom.

Working for Joe Banashak's Minit /Instant label combine, and writing both in his own name and as Naomi Neville (his mother's maiden name), Toussaint was responsible in the early '60s for hits by Aaron Neville(▶), Benny Spellman(▶) Ernie K-Doe(▶) and Irma Thomas(▶), with styles ranging from the brash gimmickry of K-Doe's **Mother In Law** to the wry subtelety of Spellman's **Over You** and the intense balladry of Irma's **Ruler Of My Heart**. The Toussaint touch was further evident in the output of Lee Dorsey(▶) (**Ride Your Pony** etc.), the Meters(▶), Betty Harris(▶), Barbara George and a host of others, while

he also dabbled again as a solo artist on Seville and Alon.

By 1965, Toussaint had come into frequent contact with Marshall Sehorn, a rotund genial white gent from Carolina, but a persuasive businessman with a background of record promotion and production. The two teamed up to launch Sansu Enterprises, soon opening Sea-Saint Recording Studio, which has become the leading studio in Louisiana, recording local and national talent. While recognising his own limitations as a solo performer—he feels happier channelling his ideas through others—Toussaint has been persuaded to cut some further albums, **Toussaint** in 1971 for Tiffany/Scepter, **Life, Love And Faith** in 1972 for Reprise, and **Southern Nights** for that label in 1975, while his hit productions continued with Labelle's(▶) **Lady Marmalade**. He remains an active writer, producer and performer in New Orleans today.

Recordings:
Life, Love And Faith (Warner)
Motion (Warner)
Southern Nights (Reprise)

Doris Troy

A prolific session singer and heroine of the Beatles—who signed her to their Apple label for a short time—Doris Troy was born Doris Payne in New York in 1937, daughter of a Baptist preacher. Starting off in gospel music she worked with a jazz trio known as the Halos before gaining success as a songwriter, penning the Dee Clark(▶) hit **How About That**.

She was working as an usherette at Harlem's Apollo Theatre when James Brown(▶) took an interest in her career, which eventually led to a contract with Atlantic(▶) and her massive 1963 hit **Just One Look**, with its attractive staccato vocal and shuffling beat.

Further less successful records for Atlantic and spells with Capitol and Calla led her in 1969 to settle in the UK where, besides session work, she recorded for People and Mojo as well as Atlantic.

Recordings:
Just One Look (Atlantic)
Doris Troy (Apple)
Stretchin' Out (—/People)

Ike & Tina Turner

For many years hardly a month passed without news of a new album, single or tour by Ike and Tina Turner and their Revue, and so prolific is their combined recorded output on a bewildering variety of labels that it would take an entire encyclopedia to chronicle the full extent of their careers! Ike was born in Clarksdale, Mississippi, on November 5, 1931, and began his musical career as a DJ at radio WROX. His ear for talent became apparent very quickly, and he was soon to form the Kings Of Rhythm, a band of local musicians who, fronted by singer/saxman Jackie Brenston, charted with **Rocket 88** (often cited as the first true rock'n' roll record) on Chess(▶) in 1951. Ike became talent scout for Modern Records, recording people like Bobby Bland(▶), Howlin' Wolf(▶) and B.B. King(▶), then moved to St Louis to further his own performing career with the Kings Of Rhythm, now a revue featuring various singers.

This revue attracted the attention of a young lady called Annie Mae Bullock; 'Little Annie' came to sing with the band, impressed Ike, and became Tina when they recorded **A Fool In Love** in 1960, which became a top 30 hit on Sue(▶). There followed several hits on that label over the next two years, the raunchy impassioned **It's Gonna Work Out Fine** (Tina in vocal duet with Mickey Baker) reaching the top 20 in the fall of 1961.

Sue encountered financial problems, however, and this, combined with Ike's continual hunt for better deals in placing his productions, led to the Turners spending some six years from 1963 on label-hopping in search of hits and security: from Sue to Sonja, Innis and Kent(▶) where the crunching call-and-response gospel style of **I Can't Believe What You Say** scored in 1964, to Loma, Warner, Kent/Modern, Sue (again), Tangerine, Cenco then Philles, where Phil Spector(▶) produced them on the epic **River Deep Mountain High** in 1966. Then came Pompeii, Blue Thumb (for a great blues album **Outta Season**) and Minit, where the seductive **Come Together** scored in 1970.

Minit was bought by Liberty, who took over the Turners' contract and struck paydirt with the dynamic **Proud Mary** in 1971; Liberty were in turn absorbed by United Artists, whereon Ike and Tina maintained a prodigious output of albums—a dozen!—up to 1974, getting chart action with singles like **Sexy Ida, Sweet Rhode Island Red** and the belting **Nutbush City Limits**.

The Very Best Of . . . Courtesy United Artists Records.

The Turners developed a dazzling stage show, centred on the sexuality of scantily clad Tina and the Ikettes backing-group (who scored in their own right with the

Above: Now divorced, The Turners turned out many soul classics in the 60s/70s which should have afforded Tina some clothes!

bouncy **Peaches 'n' Cream**), while Tina's throaty vocals adapted well to a repertoire of storming beat or sultry blues. The partnership faltered with their divorce in the mid-70s, Tina being lured into a solo career with limited success, while Ike concentrated on production at his Bolic Sound Studio at home in Los Angeles.

Recordings:
I'm Tore Up (Ike Turner (Modern/ Red Lightnin')
Kings Of Rhythm Vo. 1 (Ike Turner) (—/Ace)
Peaches (Modern/Mojo)
So Fine (Pompeii/London)
River Deep Mountain High (Philles/A&M)
Outta Season (Blue Thumb)
Come Together (Liberty)
Live At Carnegie Hall (UA)
Airwaves (UA)
Very Best Of (UA)
The Edge (Fantasy/—)
Turns The Country ON (UA/—)
Rough (Tina Turner) (UA)

Stanley Turrentine

Turrentine (b. Pittsburgh 1934) is an excellent tenor saxophonist who is a classic example of a modern genre—the veteran jazzman turned crossover/easy-listening artist. He worked the jazz and R&B circuits in the '50s with everyone from Lowell Fulson to Tadd Dameron. The '60s saw him working and recording with his then wife, organist Shirley Scott, but it was not until the '70s when he signed with CTI(▶) that his star really began to rise.

A series of typical CTI albums followed — well-produced, often with strings or chorus—until Turrentine signed with Fantasy in 1974. Since then he has ploughed much the same furrow (pacting with Elektra in 1979), gaining increasing attention from fans of classy crossover music.

Recordings:
Sugar (CTI)
Inflation (Elektra)
Tender Togetherness (Elektra)
Use The Stairs (Fantasy)
Stanley Turrentine (Blue Note)
New Time Shuffle (Liberty)

The Tymes

Back in 1959, George Hilliard and Donald Banks, from Virginia, met local Philadelphians George Williams, Albert Berry and Norman Burnett and began singing together as the Tymes, entertaining in the city's clubs and bars for a couple of years until they were spotted and signed to the flourishing Parkway(▶) label, which was riding the heights of the twist era in 1962.

The group debuted early in 1963 with **So Much In Love,** a shuffling harmony love-ballad in complete contrast to Parkway's other output, and soared to the top of the US pop charts that summer, closely following with the similarly styled **Wonderful Wonderful.** This success was maintained to a lesser extent during 1964, but the formula soon wore thin, and the group moved on to MGM, then briefly to Winchester (which they owned with Leon Huff) before pacting with Columbia in 1968.

Trustmaker. Courtesy RCA Records.

People was a top 40 hit in swirling orchestral style, but the appeal was not sustained, and it was some time later, in 1974, before the Tymes returned to better fortunes, now on RCA but without Hilliard, scoring transatlantic hits with lilting beaters **You Little Trustmaker** and **Ms Grace,** Charles Nixon handling some lead vocals. They subsequently expanded to include two female members, with **Diggin' Their Roots,** a later LP on RCA.

Recordings:
Cameo Parkway Sessions
  (—/London)
People (Columbia/Direction)
Trustmaker (RCA)
Diggin' Their Roots (RCA)

Phil Upchurch

Co-written while on tour by Dee Clark(▶), Kal Mann and Cornell Muldrow, the boisterous instrumental **You Can't Sit Down Pt 2** (Boyd) with its honking sax, chunky guitar and solid organ lines gave the Phil Upchurch Combo an out-of-the-blue 1961 million-seller.

A well-respected Chicago-based session guitarist, Upchurch began getting session calls in 1958 at the age of 19, playing on records and stage dates with the Spaniels, Jerry Butler(▶) and Porter Kilbert, before becoming a regular fixture at the Chess(▶) studios. At Chess he worked with ace bluesmen(▶) Muddy Waters(▶), Howlin' Wolf(▶) and Otis Rush as well as the company's soul acts like the Dells(▶) and the session orchestra the Soulful

Below: Veteran tenor player Stanley Turrentine has moved successfully from R&B and jazz to crossover jazz/funk.

U-Roy. Courtesy Trojan Records.

Strings (his guitar is heard at its most potent on their 1967 hit **Burning Spear**).

Upchurch has since played with Quincy Jones(▶), George Benson(▶) and many others, as well as recording a string of his own albums for a variety of labels.

Recordings:
You Can't Sit Down
  (Boyd/—)
Darkness, Darkness
  (Blue Thumb)
Phil Upchurch (TK)

The Upsetters

The 1969 chart hit **Return of Django,** which reached No. 5 in the UK, was the general public's only glimpse of a prolific Jamaican studio band whose raison d'etre was to interpret the ideas of the producer Lee Perry(▶) into marketable reggae wax.

Perry, who had numerous singles under his own name from 1963 onwards, underwent a period of particularly intense creativity from 1969-1974, composing, producing and master-minding a slew of releases instrumentals, notably **Django, Dry Acid, Clint Eastwood, French Connection** and **Dollar In The Teeth.**

Others, however, were way ahead of their time: tracks like **Sypriano** and **Bulky Skank** were early examples of D.J. talkover reggae, while numbers like **Tackio** and **Tipper Special** pioneered the amputatory techniques of dub.

The line up of musicians was fluid, but stalwarts included organist Glen Brown, baseman Jackie Jackson, percussionist Scully Simms and pianist Keith Sterling. Lee Perry's sound effects, zany percussion noises and manic semi-spoken vocals were also an essential ingredient of a crisp, bouncy and infectious sound.

Recordings:
Scratch On The Wire (—Ireland)
The Upsetter Collection
  (—Trojan)
The Best Of Lee Perry And The Upsetters (—Pama)

U-Roy

Born Ewart Beckford, in 1943, and raised in the Jones Town area of Kingston, Jamaica, U-Roy was to become the greatest and best-loved of all reggae DJs. Using shrieks, shouts and screams he employed his extraordinary voice to extend the DJ's role to where vocals and instruments became inseparable.

He served his apprenticeship with two local sound-systems(▶), Dicky's Dynamic and Tit For Tat, and quickly established himself as the most sought-after toaster on the island. His recording career began almost by accident. He improvised over two dub tracks cut at King Tubby's studio, which was still being built. Tubby was impressed and took him to Duke Reid's Treasure Isle Studio.

It's his work with Reid that U-Roy will be best remembered for. Using contemporary hits of The

Version Galore. Courtesy Trojan Records.

Paragons(▶), featuring lead singer John Holt(▶), he shouted phrases as if in responce to the lines contained within the songs. Thus it appeared as though song and toasts were recorded at the same time. A string of classic hits followed during his prolific period between 1969 and '72: **Happy Go Lucky Girl, You'll Never Get Away, Version Galore, On The Beach,** in addition to **Wear You To The Ball, Wake The Town** and **Rule The Nation,** were simultaneously in the Jamaican top 10.

By 1974, in the face of stiff opposition from rival DJs Big Youth(▶), I-Roy(▶) and Dennis Al Capone(▶), his career began to flag, and when Jamaican radio stations began to restrict airtime given to 'talkover' DJs he felt the squeeze more than many.

Bunny Lee reactivated U-Roy's career in 1975, using him to voice-over records by Johnny Clarke(▶) and Jackie Edwards(▶). **Jump For Joy** and **Heavy Duty Festival** proved that the DJ had lost none of his stamina. He regained further lost ground with **Joyful Locks** and **Gorgon Wise**.

The following year he toured Britain and secured a recording contract with Virgin Record's expanding reggae roster on its Front Line subsidiary. Perhaps the best-remembered moment of his visit was a show with the Revolutionaires at London's Lyceum, captured on an EP entitled **Live At The Strand**.

Conquering Africa, in particular Nigeria, with the album **Rasta Ambassador** for Virgin, he has since slipped into semi-obscurity.

Recordings:
Version Galore (Vols 1 & 2)
  (—/Trojan)
Dread In A Babylon (—/Virgin)

Earl Van Dyke

Variously credited as the Earl Van Dyke Six, Earl Van Dyke and the Soul Brothers and Earl Van Dyke and the Motown Brass, outfits led by organist Van Dyke undertook instrumental duties for Motown(▶) in the late '60s and early '70s. As well as accompanying Motown acts on the road, the various aggregations were responsible for a number of cuts, mainly instrumental versions of Motown classics like **Too Many Fish In The Sea, I Can't Help Myself** and **Runaway Child Running Wild**. Some are still available on compilations of early Motown material.

Recordings:
That Motown Sound (Soul/Tamla Motown)
The Earl Of Funk (Soul/—)

The Wailers

Bob Marley(▶), Peter Tosh(▶) and Bunny Wailer(▶) expanded their vocal group into a complete self-contained band when they left producer Lee Perry(▶), taking with them his highly respected studio rhythm section of Aston 'Familyman' Barrett, bass, and his brother Carlton 'Carly' Barrett, drums.

By the time of Marley's last album, **Uprising** (1980), the band additionally featured Junior Marvin(▶), lead guitar; Al Anderson, rhythm and lead guitar; Tyrone Downie and Earl 'Wire' Lindo, keyboards, and Alvin 'Seeko' Patterson, percussion.

Several members have been featured instrumentalists on outside projects before and after Marley's death (including albums and live shows by Tosh and Wailer), although as a group they only issued two singles under the collective name. Both instrumentals, the first was **Eastern Memphis** (1976), on the band's Cobra label, and the second **Work** (1977), issued on Tuff Gong. Neither was released outside Jamaica.

Recordings:

See under Bob Marley, Peter Tosh and Bunny Wailer entries.

Wailing Souls

Wailing Souls were formed in Kingston, Jamaica, in 1965 when Winston 'Pipe' Matthews, George 'Buddy' Haye and Lloyd 'Bread' McDonald as the Renegades recorded for the Federal and Matador labels. In 1968 Haye dropped out to attend art school, and Oswald Downie and Norman Davies were recruited. With their name changed to Wailing Souls, the group went to work with Clement Coxsone Dodd(▶) at Studio One(▶). This was the beginning of what many consider to be the greatest of all reggae vocal groups. Their 17-year career has been less than prolific, yet every track is distinguished by deft songwriting and mesmerising harmonies led by the fractured neo-gospel lead of Matthews.

This early line-up went to Bob Marley's(▶) Tuff Gong studio in Hope Road, Kingston, between 1971 and '72. Confusion between Marley's Wailers(▶) and the Wailing Souls, given the remarkable similarity between their harmonies, caused the latter to change their name to Pipe and the Pipers.

Dropping Downie and Davies in 1974, the group re-emerged as Atarra with Haye back in the line-up in addition to Joe Higgs, the man who virtually single-handedly had given Marley's Wailers their sound. He wove the same spell for

Wailing. Courtesy Jah Guidance Records.

the quartet as they switched their name back to Wailing Souls. Higgs left after a brace of singles, the remaining members drafting Rudolph 'Garth' Dennis from a temporarily inactive Black Uhuru(▶). This membership has remained intact ever since.

The group has from that time worked almost exclusively out of the famed Channel One studio. An early hit, **War**, was picked up by the UK independent label Greensleeves, who have been issuing the group's most recent work. Two singles were put out on the group's own Massive label. **Bredda Gravalicious** and **Feel The Spirit** both cropped up on their second album, **Wild Suspense**, released in the UK by Island Records. It was regarded by those who claim to know as the definitive harmony group album, and included a sterling re-vamp of **Row Fisherman**, previously cut for Dodd and incorporating musical muscle from such notables as drummer Sly Dunbar(▶), bassist Robbie Shakespeare(▶) and keyboards player Ansell Collins(▶). But it nonetheless bombed out.

Pacting with producer Henry 'Junjo' Lawes, who records the Roots Radics for Greensleeves,

Above: Ace tenor saxophonist Junior Walker.

Wailing Souls stormed the reggae charts in 1980 with **Kingdom Rise, Kingdom Fall, Who No Waan Come,** and **Sweet Sugar Plum** and **Old Broom** for Dunbar and Shakespeare's Taxi outlet.

Recordings:
Wailing (Jah Guidance/—)
Fire House Rock
  (—/Greensleeves)

Road Runner. Courtesy Tamla Motown Records.

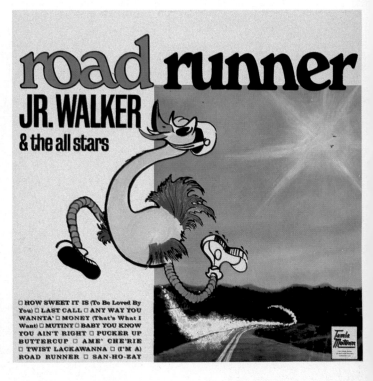

Above: American Geno Washington led one of the finest British soul groups in the '60s, the Ram Jam Band.

Junior Walker

Always neck and neck with King Curtis(▶) in the ace tenor-sax stakes, Junior Walker was nevertheless something of an anomaly in Motown's(▶) mid-'60s stable. Primarily an instrumentalist, he was one of a kind among the groups and solo singers and his music was distinctly different from the rest of Motown's output. Walker played tough, gritty, down-home music not far removed from the honking '50s R&B of players like Sil Austin and Red Prysock, whereas in the mid-'60s Motown was normally dealing with uptown soul with the Supremes(▶), the Four Tops(▶) and the Temptations(▶).

Certainly Walker's early output included some of the hottest music Motown ever released—cuts like **Shotgun, Road Runner, Shake And Finger Pop** and **Shoot Your Shot** had a raw, wild vitality that is still exhilarating. The formula was simple—Walker's gruff functional vocals alternated with his rasping tenor, the whole being driven along by his cornily-named but capable band the All-Stars.

In the late '60s and early '70s Walker began to tone down his style somewhat, concentrating on more melodic material and smoothing the rough edges of both his vocals and saxophone playing. The result was major international hits like **What Does It Take (To Win Your Love), Walk In The Night** and **Take Me Girl I'm Ready.** However, he had not forgotten how to produce the funkiest of dance sounds, as can be seen from album cuts of the period like **Soul Clappin'** and **Gimme That Beat.**

The next few years found him out of the limelight as smoother disco sounds held sway, but he still continued to tour regularly both in the US and in Europe. Walker is the archetypal tenor man, face contorted with effort, neck veins bulging, and because his recorded sound is relatively lightly produced he is usually able to reproduce it successfully on stage.

Motown put some muscle behind Walker again in the mid-'70s, recording party albums like **Whopper Bopper Show Stopper** and **Hot Shot** to capitalise on the burgeoning disco market. However, the spark that fired his prime cuts seemed now to be only flickering.

Recordings:
Anthology (Motown)
Greatest Hits (Motown)
Smooth Soul (Motown)
Whopper Bopper Show Stopper (Motown)

Dee Dee Warwick

Dee Dee worked with her older sister Dionne Warwick(▶) on many a New York session (and as member of the Drinkard Singers gospel group) before Dionne's elevation to stardom. Dee Dee had her own solo career, however, turning out some fine records in a less MOR style than her sister, notably for Mercury.

Recordings:
I Wanna Be With You/I'm Gonna Make You Love Me (Mecury)

Dionne Warwick

Working alongside sister Dee Dee(▶) and aunt Cissy Houston(▶), Dionne Warwick was one of the most active backing singers on the New York scene during the early '60s, both on records and for stage shows at the Apollo Theatre in Harlem. Born in East Orange, New Jersey, on December 12, 1941, she grew up in a family soaked in gospel-music tradition and sang with the family gospel group the Drinkard Singers. She studied music from the age of six, eventually landing a scholarship at Hartt College of Music.

Burt Bacharach and Hal David,

then house producers/songwriters for the Scepter/Wand(▶) group of labels, recognised Dionne's unique vocal style when she worked with them on the Drifters'(▶) hit **Mexican Divorce** and signed her up. They scored immediately with **Don't Make Me Over,** and followed through with the 1963 million-seller **Anyone Who Had A Heart.** Another gold disc came a year later with the Bacharach/David song **Walk On By.**

Although she suffered from cover versions by white British rivals, notably Cilla Black, who hit big with her version of **Anyone Who**

Then Came You. Courtesy Atlantic Records.

Had A Heart in 1964, and also covered **Alfie,** and Sandie Shaw, Dionne Warwick won a big transatlantic following. At home she was almost a fixture in the charts

Above: Dionne Warwick; the combination of writers Burt Bacharach and Hal David earned her a string of gold discs in the '60s.

through to 1969, by which time she had strayed somewhat from her original role as a commercial soul singer into the realm of show tunes and schmaltz (**I'll Never Be In Love Again,** in 1969, being her last big Scepter hit).

Switching to Warner Bros in 1971 (and for a time adding an e to her surname, Warwick becoming Warwicke) she recorded Brian Holland and Lamont Dozier(▶) material and worked with Jerry Ragovoy(▶) and then Thom Bell(▶) as her producers. But it was not till she switched to Atlantic(▶) and was paired by them with the Spinners(▶) for **Then Came You,** a gold No. 1, that her flagging career was revived.

Moving to Arista and produced by Barry Manilow, she had a million-selling album in 1979 with **Dionne,** which included hit singles **I'll Never Love This Way Again** and **Deja Vu.** Further Arista albums have kept up the pressure.

Recordings:
Greatest Hits Vols I, II, III, IV (—/Hallmark)
Sings Her Very Best (Springboard/—)
One Hit After Another (Springboard/—)
Dionne (Arista)
No Night So Long (Arista)

Geno Washington

As a 17-year-old GI stationed in Britain, Geno Washington would get up on stage and sing at Jeff Kruger's Flamingo Club, in Wardour Street, London, with Zoot Money's Big Roll Band or whoever was on stage on the particular night.

Eventually, Washington, who didn't sing professionally in his native USA till the late '70s, took over the Ram Jam Band from Errol Dixon, who had himself replaced Ram Jam Holder. He became a massive cult figure on the UK soul

Shake A Tail Feather Baby. Courtesy Piccadilly.

club circuit in the mid-'60s — where his faithful legions of followers made the chant 'Geno, Geno, Geno' an institution — under the astute management of Rick and John Gunnell, who had been managers of the Flamingo and also

looked after Zoot Money, Georgie Fame, John Mayall and other luminaries of British R&B/soul.

With re-runs of American soul hits, Washington's first album spent 42 weeks on the UK charts, the second 30, but he failed to consolidate with hit singles. A comeback on DJM in the late '70s again found him filling clubs but failing to score on singles' charts.

Recordings:
Hand Clappin', Foot Stompin, Funky—Butt . . . Live! (Piccadilly)
Hipsters, Flipsters (Piccadilly)
Shake A Tail Feather (Piccadilly)

Johnny 'Guitar' Watson

Although much influenced by such great Texan bluesmen as T-Bone Walker, Lowell Fulsom(▶) and Clarence 'Gatemouth' Brown, Johnny 'Guitar' Watson nevertheless managed to develop his own highly distinctive clipped style of guitar playing.

Born in Houston, Texas, on February 3, 1935, Watson moved to Los Angeles at age 13 and served his musical apprenticeship in the bands of Big Jay McNeely and Chuck Higgins. Bandleader Johnny Otis(▶) discovered him via a radio talent show and got him a deal with King Records'(▶) Federal subsidiary in 1952, where he cut the futuristic **Space Guitar** instrumental and the original of his classic **Gangster Of Love**.

Switching to RPM he had a big

Above: Mary Wells came under the auspice of Smokey Robinson, who provided her with hits like The One Who Really Loves You *and* My Guy.

hit in 1955 with **Those Lonely, Lonely Nights** and then started touring with Sam Cooke(▶), Jackie Wilson(▶), Ruth Brown(▶) and others, and developed an exciting stage act, which was to teach more than a few tricks to Jimi Hendrix(▶) (he took T-Bone Walker's stunt of playing the guitar with his teeth a stage further by doing it while performing a handstand!).

A steady stream of records for a variety of labels (including Keen — Sam Cooke's original label) gave

him R&B hits like the atmospheric **Three Hours Past Midnight** and the original of **Looking Back** (Escort), which was later popularised with rock audiences by John Mayall. He also cut MOR ballads and piano instrumentals for Cadet. Teaming up with Larry 'Bony Moronie' Williams(▶) he formed a joint production company (V.I.P.—'Very Important Platters') and the pair toured together, visiting the UK where they recorded two live albums, mainly of Williams' rock 'n' roll material, while back Stateside Watson produced Little Richard(▶) for Epic.

Spending the years 1966 to '69 with OKeh, the pair released a superb LP, **Two For The Price Of One,** which took them firmly into a contemporary soul groove. Watson then moved to Bell and on again to Lizard. The release of a live album cut with Taj Mahal(▶) was thwarted by the label folding.

By now producing for Cannonball Adderley(▶) (who scored with a jazz-funk version of his **Mercy, Mercy, Mercy**), Betty Everett(▶) and Nancy Wilson(▶), he also recorded with Frank Zappa and George Duke(▶). In 1975 he scored a monster hit with **I Don't Want To Be A Lone Ranger** from the brilliant **I Don't Want To Be Alone, Stranger,** an album full of his natural sardonic wit and inventive playing.

1976 brought a worldwide contract with the British-based DJM label which spawned a slurry of critically acclaimed and commercially successful, if sometimes rather monotonous, albums of blues-slanted funk. He also scored with the singles **I Need It** and **A Real Mother For Ya.** Then, in 1981, came yet another label change, this time to A&M.

Watson's biting guitar licks and his instantly recognisable talk-sing style of vocalising make him one of the most distinctive as well as one of the most colourful characters in black music.

Below: Johnny 'Guitar' Watson, complete with star spangled trousers, has made the blues/funk guitar market all his own.

Recordings:
I Cried For You (Cadet/—)
Two For The Price Of One (with Larry Williams) OKeh/—)
I Don't Want To Be Alone, Stranger (Fantasy)
Ain't That A Bitch (DJM)
A Real Mother (DJM)
Family Clone (DJM)
That's What Time It Is (A&M)

Watts 103rd Street Rhythm Band

Grits And Cornbread (Mo Soul) gave the Los Angeles-based instrumental funkers the Soul Runners a 1967 R&B hit. Changing their name to Watts 103rd Street Rhythm Band, they scored again almost immediately with the atmosphere-laden Booker T & The MGs(▶) flavoured **Spreadin' Honey** (Keymen).

Adding vocalist Charles Wright (producer of Caesar and the Romans' **Those Oldies But Goodies**) they got a deal with the major Warner Bros label, were produced by LA ace Fred Smith, and, in 1969, went pop top 20 with the compulsively funky **Do Your Thing**, following through with **Love Land** (1970) and **Express Yourself** (1971), before Wright left to pursue a solo career.

The band provided back-up for a couple of tongue-in-cheek street-funk albums by black comedian Bill Cosby, notably **Hurray For The Salvation Army Band**. Group members James Gadson (drums), Bernard Blackman, Raymond Jackson (trombone) and Melvin Dunlap (bass) worked in Bill Withers'(▶) band on-stage and on records and Gadson and Dunlap went on to establish reputations as two of the foremost black session musicians on the West Coast.

Recordings:
Hot Heat And Sweet Groove
(Warner Bros/—)
Together (Warner Bros/—)
Express Yourself (Warner Bros/—)
In The Jungle Babe (Warner Bros)

Mary Wells

Motown's(▶) major female star until the arrival of Diana Ross(▶) and The Supremes(▶), Mary Wells cut a slew of hits for the company in the early '60s before fading back into semi-obscurity. Born in Detroit in 1943, she came to the attention of Motown boss Berry Gordy at one of the auditions he used to hold for local youngsters in the early days of the company. Gordy placed Wells' career under the control of Smokey Robinson(▶), who provided her with hits like **The One Who Really Loves You, You Beat Me To The Punch** and **Two Lovers** in 1962, and **What's So Easy For Two, Laughing Boy** and **Your Old Standby** in 1963.

However, Mary's biggest hit was the immortal **My Guy**, a huge smash that spearheaded Motown's international success. Again written and produced by Smokey Robinson, **My Guy**'s loping beat, infectious melody and affectionate sentiments made it one of the early '60s most memorable records. Nevertheless, Wells left Motown in 1964, probably sensing that Diana Ross was destined to become the queen bee.

Unfortunately, she never hit the heights again, other labels being unable to capture the appeal of her Motown cuts, although **My Guy** became a top 20 hit again in Britain when it was re-released in 1972. The late '70s found her semi-retired and living in San Francisco, occasionally performing her old hits for appreciative audiences in local music bars.

Recordings:
Mary Wells' Greatest Hits
(Motown)

Norman Whitfield

One of the most inventive songwriters/arrangers and producers in black music, Norman Whitfield is a native New Yorker, born in 1943.

He joined the Motown(▶) staff soon after the company's inception and enjoyed his first top-10 credit as writer of Marvin Gaye's(▶) 1963 hit **Pride And Joy**. Further successes came with songs for the Marvelettes(▶) (notably **He Was Really Saying Something** and **Too Many Fish In The Sea** in partnership with Eddie Holland(▶) and, in the former case, the group's regular writer Mickey Stevenson(▶)) Kim Weston(▶) (Stevenson's wife) and the Velvelettes (**Needle In A Haystack**) all of which artists he also produced.

It was with **I Heard It Through The Grapevine** that Whitfield first collaborated with Barrett Strong(▶). Gladys Knight and the Pips(▶) had the first hit with the song (in 1967), but when Marvin Gaye's less frenzied but more hypnotic version was released the following year it became an even bigger seller, topping the charts on both sides of the Atlantic (ironically, it had actually been recorded before the Gladys Knight version and put in cold store). Smokey Robinson and the Miracles(▶) also recorded a memorable version of the song (hidden in an album) and all three readings, although each was unique in its approach, held hints of the new direction which Whitfield and Strong would be giving to Motown's music.

Strong had given the label one of its earliest hits with his original of **Money** (a song covered by the Beatles among others) and his work was also full of rock influences.

The Whitfield/Strong partnership created the so-called 'psychedelic soul' idiom, using the Temptations (▶) as the medium for a whole new sound which yielded a succession of smash hits, including the raucous **Cloud Nine, I Can't Get Next To You, Runaway Child Running Wild, Psychedelic Shack** and the hauntingly beautiful ballad **Just My Imagination** (a 1971 chart-topper).

Following the lead of rock music, Whitfield and Strong took soul into the realms of extended cuts

Above: Former big band vocalist Nancy Wilson.

with symphonic pretensions—**Papa Was A Rolling Stone**, for example, stretched to more than 12 minutes, while the acclaimed **Solid Rock** (1971) album featured extended versions of Bill Withers'(▶) **Ain't No Sunshine** and the Whitfield/Strong song **Stop The War Now**.

Splitting with the Temptations, Whitfield used Undisputed Truth (▶) as the vehicle for further records in a similar mode then, after leaving Motown to establish his own WEA backed Whitfield label, discovered and masterminded Rose Royce(▶).

Mary Wilson

An original member of The Supremes(▶), Mary Wilson was born in Mississippi, on March 6, 1944, and grew up in Detroit. After Diana Ross(▶) left the Supremes (1969) and the short run of hits with her replacement Jean Terrell singing lead came to an end, Mary soldiered on until she was the only original Supreme left.

She still tours, singing all the old hits, but now billed as 'Mary Wilson of the Supremes' since Motown(▶) own the group name.

Recordings:
Mary Wilson (Motown)

Nancy Wilson

Nancy Wilson, a classy jazz singer with more than a hint of sophistication, was born on February 20, 1940, in Chillicothe, Ohio. She became established as a vocalist during her teenage years, and in 1959 cut an album for Capitol with Billy May's Orchestra. By this time she was already playing live shows for supper-club audiences and gaining some exposure on local TV.

In the early '60s, Nancy was working in Columbus, near her hometown, doing local TV spots, when the Cannonball Adderley(▶) group came to play in town. She went to see the group perform, and was asked to sing a couple of numbers, impressing Adderley to the extent that he suggested that they might cut an LP together for Capitol.

The album was duly recorded in 1963, soon after which **Tell Me The Truth** gave Nancy her first single, and within a year she was in the top 20 with the delightful, lilting wistful love song **(You Don't Know) How Glad I Am**. She maintained a consistent output of albums for Capitol since then, accruing an impressive list of hit singles. She went top 30 with **Face It Girl It's Over** in 1968, and reached the R&B top 10 in 1974 with **You're Right As Rain**.

While she may not set the charts alight any more, Nancy Wilson keeps an international reputation and remains a major concert and cabaret attraction.

Recordings:
How Glad I Am (Capitol)
I've Never Been To Me (Capitol)
Music On My Mind (Capitol)
The Very Best Of . . . (Capitol)

For **Stevie Wonder** entry see next page

O.V. Wright

One of the most soulful of all black singers, Overton Vertis Wright cut a surfeit of spine-tingling deep-soul records over a period of some 20 years without scoring a major breakthrough.

Born in Memphis, Tennessee, on October 9, 1939, Wright joined the Sunset Travellers gospel group while in his teens, going on to work with the Spirit Of Memphis Quartet and the Highway QCs. In 1964 he cut **That's How Strong My Love Is** for Goldwax(▶) in Memphis, but over at neighbouring Stax(▶) the already established Otis Redding(▶) rushed out a cover version which took the chart honours.

O.V. Wright. Courtesy Backbeat Records.

Wright had featured on Sunset Travellers' sides for Houston-based Duke-Peacock Records(▶) and in 1965 label boss Don Robey signed him to a long-term contract with the companion Backbeat label. Wright's second Duke single, **You're Gonna Make Me Cry**, a plaintive ballad, was a big hit and became a soul standard. **8 Men 4 Women**, about 'the jury of love', made similar impact.

After a run of fine recordings for Backbeat, Wright began working under the aegis of Memphis mainstay Willie Mitchell(▶) with equally pleasing results, and continued to record artistically superb if commercially limited sides through the '70s. He died prematurely in 1980.

Recordings:
If It's Only For Tonight
(Backbeat/—)
8 Men 4 Women (Backbeat/Island)
Nucleus Of Soul (Backbeat/—)

Above: Stevie Wonder, who began life as Steveland Morris, was a virtuoso harmonica player before his teens.

Stevie Wonder

Born Steveland Morris in Saginaw, Michigan, May 13, 1950, Stevie Wonder is perhaps the most prodigiously creative figure in contemporary music.

His family moved the ninety miles from Saginaw to Detroit when Stevie was still a child, by which time he had already begun to show an interest in music. By the age of eight, having amassed a range of instruments, donated by relatives and neighbours, Wonder was already proficient on drums, bongoes, piano and harmonica.

Blind since birth, Wonder is a sufferer/benificiary of that one sensory deprivation which has so ironically aided the development of many a musical talent. Through a neighbourhood friend, he was introduced to Ronald White of the Miracles(▶), who were signed to a small, local R&B company, Tamla Motown, who described themselves as 'Hitsville USA'. Wonder's ebullient talent so impressed White, producer Brian Holland and eventually label boss Berry Gordy, that he was signed to his first recording contract at the age of nine.

At first Gordy was simply holding him in reserve; grooming him and setting up the special contractual arrangements required to satisfy American child labour laws. These included a trust into which Wonder's earnings were paid until he attained the age of 21.

Motown was still a small, struggling company and Gordy was obviously taking more of a chance with Wonder than he had with any other artist. Although his abundant, blossoming talent was there to see and hear, Gordy could not be sure that he hadn't signed a novelty act; a little blind kid with a sweet voice who would be good for very little mileage. In fact Wonder's first release **Mother Thank You** (originally titled **You Made a Vow**) was designed to exploit exactly that aspect of his potential.

But the accent was still on grooming and the fact that the record didn't sell bothered neither Wonder nor the company. He was 12 and simply delighted to have cut a record. A similar fate befell the next release, **I Call It Pretty Music**, although it did fare marginally better.

Contract On Love followed and although it too enjoyed only moderate sales, Wonder was beginning to make his reputation through live appearances on the Hitsville touring shows, a readily identifiable inspiration to the teenage audiences. Indeed his unbridled, adolescent energy, combined with such a precocious and unselfconscious musical talent made him a much hotter live artist than had hitherto been reflected by his record sales. It was after he had virtually brought the house down, in front of what was legendarily the toughest audience in the country, at the Apollo Theatre in New York's Harlem, that Gordy made a decisively smart move; he allowed Wonder to record live. The result was **Fingertips**, a brash and exuberant R&B shouter, which made full use of the current call and response influence of gospel music. Wonder's irrepressible energy was communicated to the audience and then handed back to him, as though unveiling the secret of perpetual four/four motion, and all to the tune of Stevie's impelling, joyful harmonica playing.

Fingertips spent 15 weeks at number one in the charts, and while it was still there, the live album **Twelve-Year-Old Genius** was released, containing this first hit. It too went to number one. Wonder was now 13 (the album having been thus titled because it has been recorded some weeks before—something about which the proud 13-year-old felt distinctly ambiguous) and had achieved a record industry 'first', with an album and single simultaneously at number one on their respective charts.

It was then that Steveland Morris became Little Stevie Wonder, an amalgam of just two of the affectionate nicknames by which he was known in the company: Little Stevie and The Boy Wonder.

But, despite Gordy's obvious faith in the Motown prodigy, he was unable to find material apposite to Stevie's special talent, which would consolidate that early success. As the Motown sound began to take a grip of the charts through a string of hits from the Miracles and the Supremes(▶) the formula began to emerge. But Wonder remained outside the mainstream of Motown formula material, repeatedly plying the harmonica novelty with which he had made both his own and the company's name; **Workout, Stevie, Workout** reached only the middle thirties in the chart of October 1963, **Hey Harmonica Man** managed 29 in June 1964, while **Castles In The Sand** never got higher than 52 in February 1964.

Wonder's catalogue of woes continued even through the company's first attempt to bring him into line with the conventional pop/church four-beats-to-the-bar style with which his label mates had by now made Motown a household word. **High-Heel Sneakers** sported the most mature lyric that Wonder had had to contend with, but its highest chart position of 59 forced Motown to conclude that it was perhaps a little too ethnic for the label's new-found white pop audience. The sentiment was modified and the rhythm uprated for his following release, **Uptight (Everything's All Right)**, in January 1966. The song soared to a tenacious 14-week stay at number three in the chart. Devoid of the harmonica gambit, it established Wonder not only as a vocalist—being his first major hit since the largely instrumental **Fingertips**—but also as a songwriter. S. Judkins was credited along with Sylvia Moy and Henry Crosby. Confusion about his various surnames are explained only obliquely by Stevie; whereas Morris was on his birth certificate, Judkins was the name of his real father and Hardaway, the name of his stepfather. But it was as Steveland Judkins that he had signed the songwriting contract.

In fact Wonder had been writing since he was 12 and the commercial success of **Uptight** simply gave him the foothold he needed. From that moment, he was involved in the writing of almost every song he recorded. Having been left behind for so long while the Motown machine forced on, he felt he owed no particular fealty to the formula which others at Motown so assiduously adhered to during the company's peak years. His songs contained a great deal more Stevie Wonder than they did Motown. As an artist of growing importance in a company whose bedrock was its formula, he happily drew his inspiration and influences from a shockingly disparate range of sources, including Ray Charles(▶) (inevitably), the Rolling Stones (with whom he toured in 1964 and whose song **Satisfaction** he cites as a reference for his contribution to **Uptight**), Neil Sedaka and Stan Getz.

The success of **Uptight** enabled Wonder to ally his rogue talent to Motown's account books and thereby to justify his stubborn independence. While not exactly at loggerheads with them, he was open to compromise rather than capitulation when it came to music policy. Two such compromises were **Nothing's Too Good For My Baby** and **With A Child's Heart**, released in rapid succession in early 1966 in an effort to retain the momentum created by **Uptight**. Neither did exceptionally well, given Wonder's new-found status as an international artist, reaching number four and number eight respectively.

Then, with what was to become typical unaccountability, he recorded Bob Dylan's **Blowin' In The Wind**, a wistful folk song which had already seen chart action at the hands of Peter, Paul & Mary. It reached number nine, as did **a Place In The Sun**, five months later.

Wonder's career was temporarily becalmed with subsequent releases **Travelin' Man** and **Hey Love**. Then in June 1967, **I Was Made To Love Her**, two-and-a-half minutes of pure attack, rocketed him back into the limelight, holding the number two slot in the singles chart for 15 weeks.

His musical horizons continued to expand; over the next two years, he penned **Shoo-Be-Doo-Be-Doo-Da-Day**, **For Once In My Life** and **My Cherie Amour** (originally put out as the B-side to **I Don't Know Why**, an unusually inferior Wonder song which only reached number 39 on the singles chart).

In late 1969, Wonder scored his first British number one with **Yester-Me, Yester-You, Yesterday**, but it was a retrospective release (having been recorded a year or two earlier, during the same session as **My Cherie Amour**) and, he considered, a retrogressive move on the part of the corporation. While taking stock of shifting musical trends (West Coast

Signed, Sealed And Delivered. Courtesy Motown Records.

The Jazz Soul of Stevie Wonder. Courtesy Stateside.

psychedelia was becoming all-prevalent), Motown were releasing quite a few old numbers. This was anathema to a tireless experimentalist like Wonder who was not above publicly castigating the label's conservatism. Conversely, Wonder appeared to be involving himself in ever-more off-beat projects, including the release of an instrumental album under the name Eivets Rednow . . . Stevie Wonder spelled backwards.

Fellow artists were beginning to benefit directly from Wonder's sure-footed studio technique as he developed his production skills on Martha and the Vandellas(▶), Rita Wright (sister to Syreeta, Wonder's soon-to-be wife) and white 'underground' act Rare Earth. Indeed, Stevie began to place a much greater emphasis on backroom activities and as long ago as 1969, publicly considered retirement from live performing and recording,

Fortunately, he didn't pursue that ambition, but was obviously gravitating towards production control, at least of his own material (yet another challenge to the restrictive modus operandi of the corporation). His big chance came when, after the chart success of the single **Signed, Sealed And Delivered** in June 1970, Wonder produced, in its entirety, the album of the same name. It won an award for best soul album of 1970 and, though pleased by this success, Stevie Wonder, the complete musician, was extremely dubious about the quasi-racial categorisation.

It was around this time that Berry Gordy responded to the growing influence of West Coast music by starting up an operation in Los Angeles. It was the beginning of a move that would only be complete when the entire Motown organisation had been transplanted to the West Coast, and Wonder took advantage of the ensuing disruption to distance himself yet further from what Motown were still pleased to call their 'family'.

He had also met, fallen in love with, and became engaged to Syreeta Wright(▶), a former Motown secretary with musical aspirations of her own. Wonder credited her with some lyrical contributions to his late 1970 album **Where I'm Coming From,** a thoughtfully titled protestation of his independence from Motown. In fact, in the light of subsequent, wholly unrestricted work, **Where I'm Coming From** can be seen as much more of a protest than a significant musical development. But for Motown, it was also a portent. Wonder was soon to attain the age of 21, he would gain control of all the money which had been kept in trust for him—making him an instant millionaire—and his contract would be up for renewal.

As might have been predicted, Wonder struck for freedom. He assembled a talented, committed and loyal team, moved to New York and set up his own production company, Taurus Productions, and his own publishing company, Black Bull Music, Inc. He was now answerable to nobody but himself, and was now solely responsible for the conceptualisation, structure, direction, production and writing of his own music and he lost no time in making almost perversely radical changes. But Wonder still needed an international distribution network for his records, something he could not set up independently overnight. Motown came instantly back into the picture and he was obliged, yet again through negotiation, to try and minimise the strictures of a corporation contract.

So far as the sound was concerned, the most radical change of all came through his immersion in new keyboard and computerised instrument technology. The first album of the new Wonder era was **Music Of My Mind,** utilising a battery of high-tech machinery—ARP synthesizer, Moog, clarinet—most of which he either programmed or played himself. It was in every respect a one-man album, the one which he might well have dreamed of making during his last few years in the Motown camp. It was subtle, explorative (to put it mildly) and utterly personal. But it was also the tentative first flight of a new liberated musical spirit; at times a little too ponderous and intense for some of the partying, good-time fans of the old Motown days. But moreover it was progressive, and so were the live shows which supported it. Wonder was playing to discerning, mature audiences of all musical tastes. The 'soul' tag was becoming less relevant—on its own at least—and his resentment of labelling in general, more apparent.

In January 1973, **Talking Book** expanded on the innovative ideas introduced on **Music Of My Mind.** But it was an album of much greater depth and structural range, yielding a varied clutch of Wonder standards: **You Are The Sunshine Of My Life, You've Got It Bad Girl, Superstition** and **Blame It On The Sun.** It also became his first platinum album.

Seven months later came **Innervisions,** a more introspective, linear progression from **Talking Book,** the mood epitomised by the darkly powerful **Living For The City.** The song conveyed an anxious intensity which a group of journalists were invited to share while being driven blindfold around New York, before being taken to the studio to preview the album. In contrast, although emotionally just as provocative, was the baleful lament to lost love, **All In Love Is Fair.** One other significant inclusion was **Higher Ground,** a song which dealt with the idea of a second chance at life for, while on a tour to promote the album, Wonder was involved in a serious road accident, his recovery from which constituted exactly that: a second chance.

With business associate Ira Tucker keeping a round-the-clock vigil at his bedside, he spent four days in a coma, and was in a semi-coma for a further week. The distraught Tucker elicited the first signs of a return to consciousness while singing the lyrics to **Higher Ground** directly into his friend's ear. Although by no means fully fit, Wonder made a reassuring public appearance, just two months later, as a surprise guest at an Elton John concert in Madison Square Garden.

Three months after that, he made music business history with a virtual one-man sweep of the Grammy awards, taking five out of the six for which he had been nominated, including the prestigious Best Album award for **Innervisions.**

Shaken by the accident into an even greater, spiritual introspection, Wonder released the brooding and elusively titled **Fulfillingness' First Finale** in mid-1974. Its obscure meandering mysticism and self-absorption rendered it even less accessible than the previous album, but advance sales alone ensured that by September 1974, it was America's best-selling album, and at the Grammy Awards of March 1975, Wonder repeated his performance of the previous year, scooping a total of five awards.

By the spring of 1975, his contract was yet again up for renewal. Encouraged by rumours of Wonder's eternal discontentment at Motown, two other large labels, Epic and Arista, had the temerity to join in the bidding. In the event, Motown outbid them both, retaining their number one superstar with a contract which allowed him unprecedented freedom. Financially too it was a landmark, guaranteeing him an income of 13 million dollars and a 20 per cent-plus royalty share over the next seven years. As a previous reference work has pointed out, not only was it the highest amount ever negotiated in a recording contract, it was very nearly equal to the total of the previous two highest although cynics believe this was a publicity hype. Of the new liberties it allowed him, he would now be able to designate which of his tracks were released as singles (a constant bone of contention as regards some of his more personal songs), and could now take credit for outside production work on other labels. Motown had also been planning to release a Stevie Wonder anthology album, something of which he disapproved and which he was now empowered to quash. This meant the destruction of 200,000 copies which Motown had already pressed.

With the previous album, Wonder had already begun to acquire a reputation for tardiness. Now with his newly negotiated libertarian contract and under no pressure to work to a company schedule, he gave free rein to his dilatory perfectionism. 1975 went by and though he had announced his intention to issue a double album, **Thank You For Letting Me Into Your Home,** in the autumn, it failed to appear. At the Grammy ceremony in March of the next year, Paul Simon collected the Best Album award and made a point of wryly thanking Steve for not having released an album in 1975.

In fact the delay was understandable, for although those who waited expectantly didn't realise it, this was to be Wonder's most ambitious project to date, a rangy double album which appeared to spark off in every direction and catalogue his every mood and emotion. It was infinitely more uplifting than **Fulfillingness.** He had been through a creative torrent and just selecting and trimming from the massive amount of material had been enough to delay substantially the album's release. When it did arrive, at the beginning of October 1976, it had been re-titled **Songs In The Key Of Life** and had busted out of its two-album format to the extent that another four songs had been included on a separate, 7-inch, 33rpm disc. Within a week it had climbed to number one in the chart, the fastest ever rise for a double album.

Songs In The Key Of Life was Wonder's *tour de force;* expansive, varied and multi-thematic, and in contrast to the two or three albums which preceded it, multi-textural. There were a couple of ill-fitting sentiments and incidences of rather heavy-handed preaching. As one critic contended, his flighty poeticism needed to undergo some kind of intellectual screening process. Since it doesn't, you have to take him, warts and all. Wonder was by then operating as a one-man music company and deferred to nobody. Even over the minutest technical details he was the supreme authority, and the sentiments of his songs were not the result of a think-tank committee. The range of material was massive; and from the untamed exuberance of Wonder's jazzy tribute to Ellington, **Sir Duke,** to the percussive, Latinesque **Another Star,** it was at once a seething, but disciplined collection. It was acclaimed as the album of the seventies and, at the Grammy Awards ceremony of the following March, many recalled Paul Simon's jesting of the previous year in a new light as Wonder walked off with top honours for Best Album, Best Male Pop Performer, Best Male Rhythm & Blues Performer and Best Producer, bringing his Grammy total to 14 over a span of just three albums.

Below: Working in isolation, Stevie alone knows how much has been recorded. The world waits for further releases.

Right: Though respected throughout a wide range of musicians, Stevie Wonder is not without his critics, who comment on 'heavy-handed preaching', and point to the relatively unsuccessful and elusive Journey Through The Secret Life Of Plants.

It's hard for anyone without Wonder's disability to imagine how acutely attuned he may be to aural stimulation, and to what extent he is able to visualise inwardly on the basis of what he hears, feels or simply just *senses,* in a way in which most of us, distracted by irrefutable visual images, would be incapable. He certainly doesn't appear to feel disqualified from deriving some kind of sensual stimulation from even the most obviously visual sources. He 'watches' television—sometimes for hours on end—and his penchant for a night out at the movies is well known. He has some kind of compensatory system—or perhaps more than one—which allows accessibility to the kind of stimuli for which most of us would rely almost totally on our visual sense. To accept this, without necessarily understanding it, puts Wonder's next project into a more acceptable context: it was a movie soundtrack.

The film *Secret Life Of Plants* was the screen representation of a book by an American biologist and deals with the plants' ability to feel sense. Perhaps his own secret life, feeling and sensing beyond the normal capacity, made him especially empathetic. Perhaps his own metaphysical flights of fantasy were best suited to interpreting such an oblique and elusive concept. Perhaps the film-makers simply wanted the most imaginatively soulful writer in the world to score their film.

 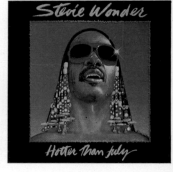

Innervisions. Courtesy Motown Records.

Hotter Than July. Courtesy Motown Records.

It was fully three years before the double album **Journey Through The Secret Life Of Plants** landed on the turntable. It adhered to its single-minded floral concept admirably, but in doing so it robbed us of the myriad subtle ambiguities of Wonder working to his own, rather than somebody else's, discipline. It wasn't a Stevie Wonder album in the sense that a follow-up to his life's masterpiece should have been. Moreover, unable to impress as a separate entity, it was the souvenir to a film that most people never got to see (it wasn't even released in Britain). Melodic, well-structured songs like **Black Orchid** and **Send One Your Love** were interlarded with rambling, wafty orchestral passages no doubt neatly tailored to the film's requirements, but lacking the essential spontaneity of Wonder's free-form work. Critically, it was received with tepid bemusement although it sold moderately well. It takes more than one slip from grace to depose a living legend.

The response to his audience's disquiet was perhaps the most becoming gesture of a consummate musical genius: he lopped literally years off his habitually lengthy gestation period and came up with the barnstorming **Hotter Than July** in late October 1980. It was a climactic event for British audiences who had had a preview of some of the tracks during Stevie's jubilant September tour (he has always felt comfortable in front of UK audiences).

The album contained a selection of love songs, both delicately mysterious and raucously passionate, a statement of pure indignation in **I Ain't Gonna Stand For It**—Wonder cheerfully writing himself a vocal part, in a range which he doesn't even possess—and two heartfelt homages; one to the late reggae superstar Bob Marley (**Master Blaster**) and one to assassinated civil rights campaigner Martin Luther King (**Happy Birthday**). The inner sleeve of the album features a photograph of King on one side, along with Stevie's own testimonial, and a plea for support in his efforts to have King's birthday, July 15, declared a national American holiday. To that end, the song constitutes just one part of this continuing, vigorous campaign.

Hotter Than July yielded no fewer than four consecutive hit singles and again his reserve about the full commercial exploitation of more personal songs was put to the test with the release of the tearfully plaintive ballad **Lately.** Not for the first time did Wonder bend to the persuasive business sense of Berry Gordy.

Once asked how he coped with the pressures of being a world leader in musical terms, he responded unselfconsciously and with tongue in cheek, 'That doesn't bother me. I knew what the job entailed before I took it.'

Recordings:
Signed, Sealed, Delivered (Motown)
Where I'm Coming From (Motown)
Music Of My Mind (Motown)
Talking Book (Motown)
Innervisions (Motown)
Fulfillingness' First Finale (Motown)
Songs In The Key of Life (Motown)
Journey Through The Secret Life Of Plants (Motown)
Hotter Than July (Motown)

The '70s

WHILE THE '70s certainly brought enormous stylistic changes, perhaps even more important to the development of black music was the fact that the decade was the first in which black people started to make really big money out of their fellow blacks. Traditionally, the business side of black music had always been the province of white, usually Jewish, entrepreneurs, but following the lead Berry Gordy Jr had set in the '60s, increasing numbers of black businessmen found their way into personal management, the ownership of booking agencies and recording studios and, most importantly, the ownership of record companies and publishing houses.

Freedoms which had been fought for and won in previous years, largely thanks to the activities of the National Association For The Advancement Of Coloured People (NAACP), had led to a steady rise in living standards. While many blacks still found themselves at the very bottom of the social ladder, others had become part of a new and assertive black middle-class which possessed real purchasing power.

It wasn't just to avoid accusations of racism that consumer-product orientated companies and their advertising agencies started using black actors in TV commercials and newspaper ads—they were after the black consumer's spending power.

Movie makers were not slow to realise that they too could grab a share of the green power which was going hand-in-hand with emergent black power. Dollar bills aplenty could be coaxed over the box-office counter by the right 'blaxploitation' epic and, following the success of *Shaft*, a host more followed.

Music—with an emphasis on hard funk—was an integral part of their success, setting the mood of the streets. Isaac Hayes did the soundtrack for *Shaft*, Curtis Mayfield did *Superfly* and several others, Bobby Womack's music was heard in *Across 110th Street*, and many other major stars of black music (James Brown, Millie Jackson, Mavis Staples, Gladys Knight and Diana Ross included) found work in the film studios of Hollywood and New York where previously Quincy Jones was the only black to be heavily involved in working on movie soundtracks.

Despite the controversy it created, the American TV series *Roots* by William Haley was an enormous success worldwide, and served to kindle a wide intrest in the black heritage. Many musicians re-discovered their African and Caribbean cultural roots and individuals adopted African and Muslim names, following the early lead of Muhammed Ali (Cassius Clay), who was anxious to nullify his slave connection. Indigenous African instruments such as the kalimba started to be featured on black-music records (in just the same way as white musicians like the Beatles had in the '60s discovered Indian

music and utilised the sitar and the tabla).

The tremendous upsurge in the black arts saw the emergence of black comedians, like Richard Pryor and Franklin Ajaye who appeared in the hilarious *Car Wash* movie for which Norman Whitfield and Rose Royce contributed a superb musical score. Black actors too were making their mark—on TV, in the movies and on the Broadway stage. In the US, *The Wiz* introduced us to the black musical, while from South Africa the spectacular staging of *Ipi Tombi* with its native costumes and music dazzled audiences from London to Zurich to New York and became one of theatreland's longest running shows.

Reggae found its way onto the screen and the theatre stage too. Horace Ove's 1969 documentary *Reggae* had been exceptionally well received (especially considering the extremely low budget of just £9,000 with which it had been made), while Jimmy Cliff's *The Harder They Come* and the later *Babylon* (featuring Dennis Bovell and his music along with a storyline which pointedly highlighted the realities of UK black ghetto life) won awards and wide audiences.

Reggae, in fact, came of age in the '70s. Despite a period of near dominance of the pop charts beginning in the late '60s, the music had until then been regarded by white audiences as mere dance fodder, but the emergence of Bob Marley to superstardom focused attention on the political and sociological importance of its lyrical content. In maturing, reggae also split into a variety of distinctive styles ranging from the compulsive rhythms of the 'toasters' to the gently romantic tones of 'lovers rock'.

American black music had entered the '70s hesitantly. The simple, direct dance music which had brought Stax, Atlantic and Motown such succes in the previous decade was on the wane (though the emergence of Philadelphia International assured the soul music idiom of a continued, if rather more sophisticated, existence), being replaced by a diversity of new styles which, like white rock-music, generally suffered from over-production and pretentiousness.

The development of multi-track recording allowed imaginations to run riot, sometimes (as in the case of much of Norman Whitfield's production work) with exciting results but too often with an emasculation of the music. This trend was made even worse by the so-called disco explosion which started innocuously enough with the astounding multi-million sales of George McCrae's **Rock Your Baby** and Carl Douglas's **Kung Fu Fighting.** These at least were in the earlier tradition set by Wilson Pickett's **In The Midnight Hour** and like records, but the slide downwards continued with an increasingly effete and whitened sound aimed more and more at the liberated gay audience which was dominating the disco scene.

Sylvester, Village People, Keith Barrow, Chic and others

Donna Summer

Peter Tosh

made some good records it is true, but where was the ballsiness of the earlier R&B and soul scenes? By the mid-'70s (the middle of the disco boom) black music really had reached its nadir.

Shalamar's trite medley of Motown oldies **Uptown Festival,** which started a massive trend for segue records, gave no hint of the superb music they were to make later; Motown, Stax and Atlantic could no longer boast of being specific styles; the Supremes, the Three Degrees and others had purged their music of any notable content of soulfulness in order to reach out to middle-class, middle American, middle-of-the-road audiences. Although the arrival of the disco-inspired extended 12-inch single gave artists a hitherto unknown degree of artistic freedom, few exploited properly the opportunity the 12-inch gave for creatively developing a tune, contenting themselves in too many cases with astoundingly boring repetition which served to keep the dancers out on the floor but hardly made for inspired home listening.

Moreover, there was even a danger of a white takeover of black music. True, *Saturday Night Fever* (the movie which turned disco from being a somewhat hip underground movement into pure pre-packaged consumerism) had featured Tavares and Trammps, but its soundtrack was dominated by the derivative soul-influenced music of the Bee Gees who, in the search for a mass audience, castrated black music. Nevertheless, they filled dance floors with a brand new audience.

There had to be a reaction to all this and it came eventually from a rather surprising source.

Tiring of the banalities of so-called 'disco-music' (which, in any case, had never caught on with hard-core dance enthusiasts in the UK), British DJs, who had tried to keep up the excitement of their performances, turned from what had become the barren wastes of soul to jazz.

Ironically enough, in a bid to keep some bread on the table, American jazz musicians had been injecting dance rhythms into their previously largely self-indulgent and introspective modern-jazz stylings.

The meeting point became known as 'jazz-funk' and, following the lead of Donald Byrd and of Blackbyrds, a group he had masterminded, such jazz names as Herbie Hancock, John Handy, Hank Crawford, Freddie Hubbard, the emergent Japanese star Sado Watanabe, the Crusaders and others spearheaded this new movement, quickly realising that they would need to add vocals to provide a leavening to their instrumental sounds. Herbie Hancock found his personal answer in the vocoder, an electronic device which enabled him to create artificial vocal sounds to great effect on his massive hit **I Thought It Was You.**

In Britain, the jazz-funk movement was taken up by home-grown acts like Shakatak, and local disco-soul bands like Imagination, Light Of The World and Linx began to make an international impact.

Synthesisers played a major part in jazz-funk and were picked up on by soul acts as well being utilised notably well by Stevie Wonder (who by the middle of the decade had become THE superstar of black music) and mass string arrangements virtually vanished overnight (the victims of increasingly high session fees for musicians).

As the '70s drew to a close, however, there were signs that black music was digging back to earlier more earthy roots; an R&B flavour was coming out in many records; and the Hammond electric organ was making something of a comeback after a decade in the doldrums (it was used to great effect on Carrie Lucas's 1979 hit **Dance With Me**).

The '70s was a bewildering decade of cross-currents which followed the assertiveness of the black athletes' protest at the 1968 Mexico City Olympics and the increasingly militant lyrics of reggae to, on the other hand, a meeting of the ways with white rock music and the mainstream of pop.

Where, in the '60s, the soul music buyer could safely order records unheard, knowing that very few bad ones were being released, the '70s yielded a profusion of musical garbage on the black-music scene which made even its most devoted fans begin to despair.

Yet, amidst all the pap, the boring monotony of so many funk records, the blandness of most disco, the schmaltz of black show-biz, the pretentiousness of much of the supposed new-wave black superstars, lurked some true gems and some very solid new talents, which at least enabled the followers of black music to look forward with expectancy to the new decade of the '80s.

What's more, the '70s was the decade when black music became an institution. Music, judged on a record by record basis, counted more than did image. It didn't matter that the act was old, in the doldrums and, according to the critics, strictly passé. If it came up with the right record it could happen all over again and in this way many big stars of earlier years were able to chart again.

The '70s failed to produce many truly great soul stylists, apart from Michael Jackson, Teddy Pendergrass, Millie Jackson and Randy Crawford, whereas the '60s had spawned a profusion (Sam Cooke, Otis Redding, Wilson Pickett, Lou Rawls, Smokey Robinson, Curtis Mayfield, Aretha Franklin, Nina Simone, Marvin Gaye, Stevie Wonder and Diana Ross)—but it did produce an ever-increasing diversity of musical styles under the general banner of black music.

It is doubtful whether in years to come we will look back on the '70s with the same air of nostalgia which surrounds the golden '60s, but not everything about the decade was transient and much was achieved, if only in terms of laying the ground for a solid future.

George Benson

Issac Hayes

QUINCY JONES I HEARD THAT!!

Diana Ross

The Abyssinians

Perhaps more than any other reggae group the Abyssinians built and developed their style and technique upon the morality of Rastafari—truth and rights. Founder member of the trio was Bernard Collins (aka Jah Satta), with backing vocals provided by the Manning brothers, Linford and Donald. A third brother is Carlton, the featured vocalist with rock-steady rooted ensemble Carlton & The Shoes, whose records **You And Me, Love Me Forever, This Feeling** and **Happy Land** were the musical seeds with which the Abyssinians were originally sown. So intrinsic were the two groups that when Carlton & the Shoes' **Sweet Feelings** single was issued in Britain the label on the disc proclaimed it to be by the Abyssinians.

The group emerged from obscurity in 1969 with the self-produced chant song, **Satta Massa Gana.** Cut at Studio One(▶) it featured the bass playing of Heptone(▶) Leroy Sibbles and former Gaylad B.B. Seaton on guitar. The disc is an unequivocal reggae classic that even a decade after its initial release has lost none of its impact and stands as one of the most devotional Rastafarian songs ever recorded.

The Abyssinians followed their impressive debut with a stack of truly exquisite records. At Studio One these were **Declaration Of Rights, Let My Days Be Long** and **Poor Jason White,** titles which were later to appear on the group's own Clinch label, formed after an acrimonious departure from Coxsone Dodd's Studio One stable.

In 1972 the group began working with producer Lloyd Daley, also known as the Original Matador. The most significant release from this period was a return to the theme of **Satta Massa Gana** on **Yim Mas Gan,** the lyrics chanted in the African language of Amharic. In 1975 they were approached by producer Geoffrey Chung with a view to recording an album. From those early sessions with Chung came the classic single, **Tenayistil-in Wandimae,** which marked their breakthrough into the British reggae charts. The group was established and the remaining fruits of those sessions were gobbled up when they appeared 18 months later on the remarkable **Forward To Zion** album.

By the time the group came to record its **Arise** album it was split into songwriting and vocal factions. The Abyssinians eventually disbanded professionally although recent rumours of a regrouping and fresh recording activities have rekindled fervour and interest.

Recordings:
Forward To Zion (Sound Tracs/Klik)
Arise (Front Line)

Cannonball Adderley

Alto saxophonist Adderley (1928-1975) was a Charlie Parker stylist who came to prominence in the late '50s as part of Miles Davis' legendary band. Other members were John Coltrane, Philly Joe Jones, Red Garland and Paul Chambers. A muscular player who combined a strong blues' feel with bop phrasing, Adderley lost some jazz

Somethin' Else. Courtesy Blue Note Records.

purist fans when he began to get involved with the embryonic soul-jazz movement in the early '60s. Numbers like **Work Song, Jive Samba** and **Sack O' Woe** were rooted in the R&B tradition and brought Adderley a whole new audience.

Adderley had a knack for finding funky piano players like Bobby Timmons, long-time cohort of Joe Zawinul (an Austrian by birth) who later started Weather Report(▶)) and George Duke(▶), and it was Zawinul who brought Adderley his greatest success in the late '60s with **Mercy, Mercy Mercy** and **Country Preacher,** both crossover hits.

Recordings:
Mercy, Mercy, Mercy (Capitol)
Country Preacher (Capitol)
Coast To Coast (Milestone)

Rance Allen

Soul music has often been described as 'Gospel music with secular lyrics'. The Detroit-based Rance Allen Band reversed the process, taking the Temptations'(▶) **Just My Imagination** and re-working it as **Just My Salvation,** and transforming Archie Bell and the Drells'(▶) disco smash **(There's Gonna Be A) Showdown** into an impassioned religious song.

Even when not singing of God, the group, which comprises brothers Rance, Tom, Steve and Esau Allen, and later their cousins Judy, Linda and Annie Mendez, relied on message songs like **See What You Done,** a mother's lament when her son returns from Vietnam a junkie.

Signed to Stax's Gospel Truth subsidiary, the group had considerable chart success hinged on Rance's spine-tingling falsetto lead vocals.

Recordings:
The Rance Allen Group (Gospel Truth/—)
Brothers (Gospel Truth/—)
Sanctified (—/Stax)

Althea and Donna

Two middle-class black schoolgirls from Kingston, Jamaica, Althea and Donna were teamed up by producer Joe Gibbs with an old backing track to cut the whimsical JA-dialect **Uptown Top Ranking.** After building an underground following among white and black kids alike, it burst into the UK chart in January 1978 and raced straight to No.1. Since then, zilch.

Recordings:
Uptown Top Ranking (—/Frontline)

Joan Armatrading

Born in St Kitts, West Indies, on December 9, 1950, Joan Armatrading was one of five children. The family emigrated to Birmingham, England, in 1958, where Joan was raised on a musical diet of Gracie Fields (**Little Donkey** was the first record she ever bought), Jim Reeves and Nat King Cole(▶).

Performing in a local production of the rock musical *Hair,* she met and formed a partnership with another expatriate West Indian, lyricist Pam Nestor. The two moved to London in 1971, where they signed a recording and management deal with the Cube label. Cube, however, could see commercial potential solely in Joan and, when the Gus Dudgeon-produced album **Whatever's For Us** was released, the label took it upon itself to credit it to Joan alone. Resulting tensions served only to sour the partnership and make Joan unhappy. She spent the next two musically unproductive years extricating herself from the Cube contract.

When she finally debuted for a new label, A&M in 1975, the album **Back To The Night** showed her to be her own potent lyricist. Produced by ex-Ram Jam Band and Vinegar Joe guitarist Pete Gage, the album met with no great commercial success. This led A&M to switch to veteran producer Glyn Johns for **Joan Armatrading.** This time the power, passion and mood of Joan's songs gelled with the warmth and confidence of Johns' production. Johns was obviously impressed, not only with Joan's songwriting talent, but also with her able guitar-playing, which he actively encouraged her to develop. He said later that it was the best album he had ever been associated with—and that from a veteran who has worked with the Eagles and the Rolling Stones.

The critics and public went some way towards endorsing Johns' opinion. **Joan Armatrading** became one of the top-selling British albums of 1976 and yielded the hit single **Love And Affection.** A&M complemented the natural momentum by mounting a huge publicity campaign and 'Armatrading' became a most unlikely household name.

Her association with Johns continued through two subsequent studio albums, **Show Some Emotion** and **To The Limit,** and the live set **Steppin' Out.** Then, in a move more lightheartedly adventurous than critical to her music, she went to New York to record the album **Me, Myself, I,** for no other reason it seems than that she had met and liked the album's producer Richard Gottehrer. She admitted to not having heard any of his productions. A subsequent LP **Walk Under Ladders** scored a minor hit with the title track.

Joan is a singer/songwriter of rare individuality. But her trenchant style and rugged stage persona disguise an underlying diffidence and slight discomfort at being under the spotlight. She considers herself first and foremost a songwriter and might happily have remained so had it not been for her early involvement with Cube.

Below: UK reggae pioneers Aswad, from London's Ladbroke Grove.

Recordings:
Whatever's For Us (—/Cube)
Back To The Night (A&M)
Joan Armatrading (A&M)
Show Some Emotion (A&M)
To The Limit (A&M)
Steppin' Out (A&M)
Me, Myself, I (A&M)
Walk Under Ladders (A&M)

Aswad

Pioneers of UK reggae, Aswad was formed in 1976 by Angus Gaye and Brinsley Forde (who remain the nucleus of the band) with bass guitarist George Oban. Inspired by the music and success of Bob Marley and the Wailers(▶), the group, with additional members Donald Griffiths on lead guitar and Courtney Hemmings on keyboards, took their demo tapes to Island Records and in that same year released their first single **Back To Africa.**

With support and encouragement from Island's Leslie Palmer, the group was quick to consolidate a position with both roots and rock audiences through frequent appearances on the nation's pub and college circuit. A favourable reaction to **Back To Africa** gave rise to a further single in that year, **Three Babylon,** still a popular song at their live shows, and an album, **Aswad.**

Based in London's Ladbroke Grove and Harlesden—where they would rehearse in a room at the back of Venture Records—they were familiar with the social injustices and police harassment that distinguish urban ghetto life. They believed in emancipation through Rastafari and ultimately repatriation to Africa.

However there was conflict within the group as to how they would musically interpret their lyrics and this led to a year of inactivity while their music was reassessed, and the band was subjected to a number of changes of membership. Courtney Hemmings quit and an additional bass guitarist, Tony 'Gad' Robinson, who had always been on the periphery of the group, joined.

Re-assembled and pacted to Grove Music, with a distribution link with Island, Aswad emerged in 1978 with the captivating **Hulet** album. Reckoned to be a blueprint for UK reggae, it nevertheless exposed existing musical friction within the group. Gaye and Forde were moving away from the broader-based reggae of Marley into an area of rhythmically tougher Jamaican roots reggae while Oban used the album as a platform for an interest in American jazz/rock fusion.

Such divergent tastes led to Oban leaving soon after the release of **Hulet,** followed by Donald Griffiths. Using a shifting line-up to augment the Gaye, Forde and Robinson nucleus, under the guidance of their manager/producer Mikey Campbell, the group aligned itself to a number of charities including Rock Against Racism.

With reggae music making an impact upon the 'live' circuit and garnering attention from the media, it was inevitable that the film industry would eventually pick it up. Originally planned for television, Franco Rosso's *Babylon* went on general release towards the end of 1980 with Brinsley Forde in the central role.

A film about reggae music and starring Forde was fuel for Aswad and the turbulent reggae industry in the UK. A soundtrack album was issued, assembled by Dennis Bovell(▶). Among a number of notable inclusions it featured two of Aswad's most outstanding singles to date, **Rainbow Culture** and **Warrior Charge,** which were justifiably enormous hits on the reggae market in 1980—Rastafari in the context of rich melodies and insurmountable rhythms that really did charge. In the 18 months since **Hulet,** Aswad had matured into a musical force to be reckoned with. Joined on stage and on record by trombonist Vin Gordon they took to the road again. Gaye's drumming had never been brighter and crisper, nor Forde's lead vocals so anguished and fraught.

1981 saw Grove/Island issue a commendable remix of the group's finest moments on a **Showcase** package, released when the news broke that Aswad had parted company with Island and had just signed a global deal with CBS. After five years of learning and reshaping, Aswad are ready to take on the world.

Recordings:
Aswad (—/Island)
Hulet (—/Grove-Island)
Showcase (—/Grove-Island)
New Chapter (Columbia/CBS)
New Chapter In Dub (—/Grove Music)
Not Satisifed (Columbia/CBS)

Atlantic Starr

Atlantic Starr's nucleus comprises three brothers—Wayne I., Jonathan and David E.Lewis—who broke up into three local bands, Newban, Exact Change and Unchained Youth. These eventually came together as Atlantic Starr, an eight-man-one-woman-band. Having lived in the same neighbourhood on the East Coast, they moved across to California together and chose to live in the same housing complex.

Brilliance. Courtesy A & M Records.

In 1976, the group became a professional outfit, when they were invited to go to the French Alps to play at a black ski festival. The industry was first introduced to them when they placed at the Spinners'(▶) 20th Reunion. Together with songwriter, producer and arranger Bobby Eli, one of the men behind the sound of Philadelphia, they released their first album **Atlantic Starr** in 1978, then their second **Straight To The Point** in 1979. Both albums contained disco but not pop hits; songs such as **Stand Up, Gimme Your Luvin'** and **Let's Rock 'n' Roll.**

They signed with A&M in 1977, and their original choice of producer was James Anthony Carmichael, the Commodores'(▶) producer, but due to prior commitments he was unable to produce them until 1980. Their third album, **Radiant,** contained the American pop hit **When Love Calls.** For this album, saxophonist Damon M. Rentie was replaced by Koran Daniels.

Current line-up is: Clifford Archer, bass; Sharon Bryant, vocals, percussion; Porter Carroll, Jr., drums, vocals; David Lewis, guitar, vocals; Koran Daniels, saxophone; Jonathan Lewis, trombone, percussion; Wayne Lewis, keyboards, vocals; Joseph Phillips, congas, flute, percussion; William Sudderth III, trumpet.

Recordings:
Atlantic Starr (A&M)
Straight To The Point (A&M)
Radiant (A&M)

Patti Austin

Patti is the West Coast-raised daughter of a professional jazz musician and was inculcated in the show-business tradition at the age of four when her father took her to a concert by jazz singer Dinah Washington. Patti ended up on stage, singing Sammy Cahn's **Teach Me Tonight.** She was adopted as band leader/producer Quincy Jones'(▶) goddaughter, again through her father, and although she always expressed an interest in being taken under Jones' wing as a performer, he declined, for fear of spoiling her at too early an age.

Nevertheless, Patti pursued her

Above: Showing very little emotion, the highly individual talent of Joan Armatrading.

interest in a musical career with a small-time record contract which resulted in a few singles. Her first album didn't appear until she signed to the CTI label(▶)—owned by the successful East Coast commercial-jazz producer Creed Taylor—having already established herself as an in-demand backing vocalist and session singer for advertising jingles in New York (an alternate and highly lucrative sideline, which she has always maintained, despite her steady progression as a recording artist).

After several albums of varying artistic merit, some produced by Taylor and some not, Patti's personal relationship with Taylor deteriorated (an unfortunate but recurring problem within the CTI stable). At the end of her CTI contract, and almost as a tribute to Taylor's essential wiliness, she described him thus: 'He looks like Jimmy Carter and thinks like Richard Nixon.'

Now working more closely with Quincy Jones, Patti began to expand her portfolio as a session singer with contributions to Jones' own recordings and Jones-produced albums for other artists. She made the superb duet with George Benson(▶) on **Give Me The Night,** with the song **Moody's Mood For Love,** an extemporised vocal version of what was originally a sax solo by the tenor player James Moody for his rendition of **I'm In The Mood For Love** (and previously recorded by British R&B(▶) artist Georgie Fame.

The culmination of her life-long ambition to be produced by Jones in her own right could not have happened more aptly, for it was Patti's Jones-produced album from 1981, **Every Home Should Have**

One, which launched Jones' own label, Qwest, he having been working out his own contract on A&M Records.

Recordings:
End Of The Rainbow (CTI)
Say You Love Me (CTI)
Havana Candy (CTI)
Body Language (CTI)
Every Home Should Have One (Qwest)

Average White Band

The six-piece jazz/soul outfit, Average White Band, was formed in Scotland in 1972, consisting: Alan Gorrie, bass; Mike Rosen, trumpet; Onnie McIntyre, guitar; Roger Ball, keyboards, saxes; Malcolm Duncan, tenor sax; Robbie MacIntosh, drums. Shortly afterwards Rosen was replaced by guitarist Hamish Stuart. The members already knew each other as they had toured the Scottish club circuit with various bands. Their musical styles, tastes and personalities blended easily, with Alan Gorrie and Hamish Stuart constituting the songwriting and vocal partnership central to the group's identity.

They first signed to MCA and debuted with the very creditable **Show Your Hand,** critically acclaimed but publicly ignored. There followed a switch to Atlantic, at the personal behest of co-founder and producer Jerry Wexler(▶). There, a string of albums under the production of Arif Mardin began with the eponymous **Average White Band,** spawning the million-selling single **Pick Up The Pieces** and propelling the band towards inter-

national stardom.

Although they were the first British band to capture the essence of US funk/soul, Average White Band ironically became more successful in the States than in their homeland. By February 1975, the album and single were at the top of the respective US charts. But tragedy struck almost on the eve of their first major success, when drummer Robbie MacIntosh died of heroin poisoning at a party in Los Angeles. MacIntosh was replaced—originally as a temporary measure—by Brighton-born black drummer Steve Ferrone (ex-Brian Auger Oblivion Express, ex-Bloodstone(▶).

Quizzed on the band's name, Stuart and Gorrie had often evinced some embarrassment at saddling the band with a joke name. The absurdity of it was now highlighted when Ferrone was persuaded to enlist as a full-time band-member.

The band took advantage of America's favourable tax laws, and their own mounting popularity, to domicile themselves on the West Coast. They cut another Mardin-produced album **Cut The Cake,** Gorrie and Stuart's songwriting partnership becoming ever keener. However, their 1976 album **Soul Searching** hinted at the beginning of a creative slide. Their next LP, the live double **Person To Person,** excellent though it was by most live standards, didn't redeem them. In search of a new gambit, they recorded with ex-Drifters(▶) vocalist Ben E. King(▶) for the album **Benny And Us.** King then accompanied them on a European tour in support of the album.

Their last album with Arif Mardin was the sophisticated but low-

Above: The Average White Band perform with Ben E. King in London during their mid-70s European tour.

key **Warmer Communications.** Switching to RCA, they produced themselves on the ambiguously received **Feel No Fret** (1979) and had a couple of moderate hits with their own Latinish composition, **Atlantic Avenue,** and an off-beat, staccato rendition of the Bacharach/David classic **Walk On By.** A radical change of direction for the album **Shine** took them to the disco charts with the frenetic dancer **Let's Go Round Again.**

Recordings:
Show Your Hand (MCA)
Average White Band (Atlantic)
Cut The Cake (Atlantic)
Soul Searching (Atlantic)
Warmer Communications (Atlantic)
Person To Person (Atlantic)
Feel No Fret (RCA)
Shine (RCA)

Roy Ayers

Born in California on September 10, 1940, vibist Roy Ayers carved a solid niche in the jazz/funk disco market from the late '70s with hits like **Running Away, Freaky Deaky, Heat Of The Beat** (with Wayne Henderson) and **Get On Up, Get On Down.** Although a highly respected jazz vibist in the early '60s, Ayers had tasted commercial success as an integral part of flautist Herbie Mann's bands and had featured on three of Mann's hit Atlantic albums.

Prior to joining Mann, Ayers had been a self-confessed musical snob, never venturing out of his strictly jazz sphere. Mann opened the vibist's ears to R&B and soul, which led to the formation of Ubiquity, the group with which he signed to Polydor Records in 1970. Heavily criticised by jazz aficionados, Ayers nevertheless reaped great artistic and financial rewards with Polydor.

1978's **Running Away** is an undisputed disco classic which established Ayers in the European market, but he seemed to be unable to consolidate his success in the changing black music market of the early '80s and moved unsuccessfully into vocalising. But the 1981 release of **Africa Centre Of The World** was a return to a much more mainstream jazz feel on several cuts, besides being full of obvious Nigerian influences.

Never an artist of overt influence Ayers will undoubtedly continue to be a high-quality interpreter of current black music trends with a jazz feel. He still produces his group Ubiquity for Elektra Records.

Recordings:
Everybody Loves The Sunshine (Polydor)
Let's Do It (Polydor)
Lifeline (Polydor)
You Send Me (Polydor)
Africa Centre Of The World (Polydor)

Azymuth

Brazilian group Azymuth burst on to the scene in 1979 with a track called **Jazz Carnival** from their **Light As A Feather** release of that year, a percussively-damaging jazz-funk instrumental that filled floors all round the world.

The group was formed in 1971 by Jose Roberto Bertrami, keyboards; Alex Malheiros, bass; and Ivan Conte (Mamao), drums. Playing music which is heavily influenced by Latin styles, the group is based in Rio de Janeiro. Stanley Clarke's **Light As A Feather**, was the title track of their first American album, which they have since followed with two more energetic sets.

Recordings:
Light As A Feather (Milestone)
Outobro (Milestone)
Telecommunication (Milestone)

J. J. Barnes

A great hero of Britain's Northern Soul cult in the '70s, J.J. Barnes started his career in his home town of Detroit with the Don Davis-produced **Free At Last** (Golden Hit), billed as James Barnes and the Agents.

Barnes worked with various Detroit labels, before joining the legendary Ric-Tic label, a subsidiary of Golden World, and making some noises in the UK with a version of the Beatles' **Day Tripper**. He cut enough tracks for an album but when Motown(▶) bought Golden World in 1966 (to eliminate fast-rising competition) they were put on ice and not released till years later (and then only in the UK).

Don Davis then signed Barnes to his Groovesville label (material was later issued in album form by Volt in the US). These and his 1968/69 recordings for Revilot became UK collectors' items, fetching up to £20 each in the early '70s.

Barnes has written material for Edwin Starr(▶), the Fantastic Four, Steve Mancha, the Dram-

atics(▶) and others.

Recordings:
Rare Stamps (Volt/—)
The Groovesville Masters (—/Contempo)
Ric-Tic Relics (—/Tamla Motown)
Born Again (—/Perception)

Gary Bartz

Baltimore-born Bartz began playing alto saxophone, aged 11, at his father's jazz club, the North End Lounge. When Max Roach came to town, Bartz sat in, and Roach told him to look him up next time he was in New York. Bartz joined the Roach/Abbey Lincoln group in the early '60s.

In 1965, he moved to Art Blakey's group, eventually embarking on a solo career in 1967, though he also played on stage and on record with Roach and McCoy Tyner.

At the beginning of the '70s, Bartz teamed with the Miles Davis(▶) group, whilst continuing to record solo albums, including **Home, Harlem Bush Music-Taifa, Harlem Bush Music-Uhuru, Juju Street Songs, I've Known Rivers & Other Bodies** and **Singerella: A Ghetto Fairy Tale**.

Bartz dislikes being categorised as a 'jazz musician'. He once said: 'Music is my religion ... to call someone's religion "jazz" is an insult ... people let you down, music won't'. Born and raised in a racially tense part of America, he has always reflected black consciousness and African culture.

On signing to Capitol Records in 1977 his music became more commercial and better distributed. His tenth album, **Music Is My Sanctuary**, was his first for the label.

In 1980, Bartz signed to Arista Records, debuting with **Music**. Just previous to that, he had been musical co-ordinator and arranger, and actor, in a successful off-Broadway show, *Bebop: The Hip Musical*. From his Arista album came a hit single, **Magic**, which featured old jazz-to-funk friends James Mtume and Reggie Lucas, prominent '70s soul songwriters.

Recordings:
Music Is My Sanctuary (Capitol)
Love Affair (Capitol)
Music (Arista)

Archie Bell and the Drells

Originally formed during high school days in Houston, Texas, the Drells were put back together again when Archie Bell finished army service in Germany. Bell and his younger brother Lee, together with Willie Parnell and James Wise worked the chittlin' circuit of Southern States' black clubs before the monotonous yet highly danceable **Tighten Up** (Atlantic) shot them to prominence in 1972.

The song had been cut in their hometown and originally released on Ovied, a label formed for the purpose by their manager. When it became a regional hit, Atlantic picked it up for national distribution and signed the band, following through with **Here I Go Again**, produced in Philadelphia by Kenny Gamble and Leon Huff for the **Showdown** album.

Further sessions in Muscle Shoals(▶) (produced by Phillip Mitchell) and New York brought more success before the band

switched from Atlantic to Gamble and Huff's new Philadelphia International(▶) label and moved their recording base to Philly.

Recordings:
Tighten Up (Atlantic)
Here I Go again (Atlantic)
Dance Your Troubles Away (Philadelphia International)
Where Will You Go When The Party's Over (Philadelphia International)

Thom Bell

Classically trained Thom Bell entered the soul music field with the quirky 1968 Showstoppers' hit **Ain't Nothin' But A House-Party**, which

Above: Roy Ayers, **Running Away** *with success*

he arranged. As he later confessed, the whole thing was a shambles but somehow it worked, having an irresistible good-time atmosphere and, though only a local Philadelphia hit in the US, it was a UK smash (also charting on re-release a couple of years later).

Bell learned the idiom quickly, and with his imaginative orchestral scores and a string of great songs, co-written with Linda Creed, he produced some of the very finest samples of the sophisticated Philadelphia vocal group soul sound, working with The Delfonics(▶), the Stylistics(▶), the Detroit Spinners(▶) and many other acts.

Dance Your Troubles Away. Courtesy Philadelphia International.

Above: George Benson, master guitar player and smooth vocalist, moved from the jazz mainstream to the international soul market.

George Benson

Benson exemplifies 'crossover', a self-explanatory word originally used to describe the process by which mostly jazz-based music is infused with enough commercial appeal to find favour in the pop market, and now often taken to mean the music itself. In fact, after years as a jazz and R&B guitarist in various combos Benson's solo success, when it did come, was phenomenal.

A native of Pittsburgh, Pennsylvania, Benson began playing guitar at the age of eight. By the time he began working professionally, he was an accomplished vocalist as well, combining the two functions in a number of early Pittsburgh R&B groups; he also performed as a vocalist on recordings for Columbia and A&M Records.

Moving to New York in 1963, Benson worked on Blue Note jazz sessions, notably with Brother Jack McDuff, and on his own solo debut on Columbia. He was obliged to hide his vocal talent under a bushel during a long tenure with Creed Taylor's(▶) CTI label as a house guitarist. In this capacity, he worked on albums by Freddie Hubbard(▶), Ron Carter, Hubert Laws(▶), Herbie Hancock(▶), Esther Phillips(▶) and Miles Davis(▶), and also turned out a number of solo sets, including **White Rabbit**, for which he earned a Grammy nomination.

Although his virtuosity as a guitarist is regarded by many to have been the mainstay of his musical ability, privately Benson was paying as much heed to the development of his rangey fluid voice and, more importantly, combining this with his eloquent guitar style to produce the unique, syncopated scat-singing/guitar which has become one of his best known trademarks.

Benson stayed with CTI until the early '70s, when he switched to Warner Brothers, who fatefully matched him with their house producer, Tommy LiPuma.

It was under LiPuma's deft production that Benson moulded the pattern for his astonishing success. The result was the album **Breezin'**, a long-searched-for hybrid of commercial jazz which went on to outsell every previous jazz album. It eventually notched up double-platinum sales and simultaneously conquered the jazz, R&B and pop charts. Benson had become what his record company described as 'an across-the-board people's hero'.

Breezin' yielded two major hit singles: the title track—ironically, an instrumental—and the seductive Leon Russell ballad, **This Masquerade**, through which the whole record-buying world was given a chance to savour Benson's vocal abilities. With sales still mounting and Benson's audience still multiplying, Warner Brothers rammed the point home by releasing his follow-up album **In Flight**, again utilising LiPuma's perfectly empathetic production technique; it quickly became Benson's second platinum-selling LP.

Meanwhile, Benson had contributed to the soundtrack of the Muhammad Ali bio-pic, *The Greatest,* and had a huge hit with the largely vocal theme tune, **The Greatest Love Of All.**

In Flight was composed of six long tunes, and yielded no obvious hit single, but as Benson's remarks at the time suggested, the success of **This Masquerade** was not going to tempt him toward the self-imposed musical strictures of the three-minute hit-song formula: 'I'm basically an album artist', he stated confidently.

Benson's recording success not only reactivated back-catalogue material on CTI, A&M and Columbia, but also opened the door for him as a live attraction, and he was able to pack auditoria wherever he played. His own outgoing virtuosity, plus a band which included, among others, keyboard-players Ronnie Foster and Jorge Dalto, enabled him to create a scintillating stage show in which he could recreate the excellence of his recorded work.

This aspect of Benson's overall appeal was showcased on his next LiPuma-produced set, the live double **Weekend In L.A.** After creating enormous impact as a live entertainer in New York during 1977, Benson had ended the year in Los Angeles with a superb performance, in front of a suitably enthusiastic crowd, at Hollywood's best-known music venue, The Roxy. **Weekend In LA**, containing Benson's highly individualistic reworking of the Drifters'(▶) **On Broadway** (which had undoubtedly been an emotional highlight of his New York shows), was released in January 1978 and created great additional momentum for Benson's tour of Japan, Europe and Australia. The same year, he also played for President Carter, in a concert organised at The White House, and further assured his international celebrity status by endorsing two of the Ibanez company's handmade guitars, model number GB-20 and GB-10 (Benson used the smaller GB-10). Both **Weekend In LA** and the following double studio album **Livin' Inside Your Love** (bearing the single **Love Ballad**) went platinum.

Benson's popularity may have found its own level (a platinum album can't be said to signify a diminution in popularity), but his fifth Warner album, produced as a co-project by Quincy Jones(▶) for Jones's new label, Qwest, signalled a very definite and even greater upsurge in his fortunes.

Jones, a multi-talented musician, and a prime force on the American jazz and contemporary music scene for more than two decades, had long harboured an ambition to work with Benson. The two had discussed it even before Benson's initial success in 1973 with **Breezin'**. The formation of Jones's own label seemed to provide an opportunity, and so he and Benson, having renewed their discussions, approached Warner Brothers, to whom Benson was still contracted, about the possibility of involving both labels. That agreed, Jones selected material for the album and had it approved by Benson.

The resultant **Give Me The Night** may have led Benson to recant slightly on his earlier assertion that he was primarily an album artist. With all the panache and craft previously exhibited in his collaboration with Michael Jackson(▶) on the album **Off The Wall**, Jones, along with his now firmly established partner, British songwriter Rod Temperton, gave Benson a collection of chart-topping singles. Jones had given free rein to the verve and variety of Benson's vocal style, from the immediate impact of such dance tunes as the title track and **Love X Love**, to the rangey, jazz-blues duet with Patti Austin(▶), another Qwest artist, on **Moody's Mood**. Temperton, one-time keyboard player with Heatwave(▶) and the author of all their hits, contributed five songs.

Jones's approach was to highlight Benson's vocal capacity so that, as he said, 'Instead of the world's greatest guitarist, who can also sing', we hear, 'a great singer, who is also the world's greatest guitar player'.

Recordings:
Breezin' (Warner Brothers)
In Flight (Warner Brothers)
Weekend In LA (Warner Brothers)
Livin' Inside Your Love (Warner Brothers)
Give Me The Night (Warner Brothers/Qwest)

Biddu

Born into a middle-class Indian family, Biddu came to Britain and eked a living in a doughnut factory until getting his first break as a songwriter and producer with Beacon Records in 1969. Early to appreciate the commercial potential of a rather bland but unquestionably highly danceable whitewashed brand of black music (i.e. disco), he not only scored through his production work with soul-influenced British artists like Tina Charles and the Real Thing(▶) but won a niche for himself via the Biddu Orchestra, a sort of James Last/Ray Conniff of the disco world.

His busy and lush arrangements full of all the in-vogue syn-drum, hi-hat and plunking bass gimmicks of the era won him major chart success on both sides of the Atlantic during the mid to late '70s, but by the '80s his music was passé and he had slipped into the movie world.

Recordings:
Futuristic Journey (CBS)

Barry Biggs

Biggs, born St Andrews, Jamaica, December 1953, initially made a living from singing backing vocals in the mid-'60s for producers Clement Coxsone Dodd at Studio One(▶) and Duke Reid at Treasure Isle. By the end of the decade he had sung backing vocals for Byron Lee and the Dragonaires(▶) and spent six months with the Crystalites, contributing to Derrick Harriot's(▶) best-seller **Eighteen With A Bullet**.

Signing to the Dynamic label, he enjoyed unparalleled commercial success with singles **Work All Day** and **Sideshow** (1976) and **You're My Life** and **Three Ring Circus** (1977), that all did well on the UK, and Jamaican pop charts. He subsequently abandoned a solo career and returned to Byron Lee.

Between 1977 and '79 he cut two albums with producer Bunny 'Striker' Lee, neither of which has been released. He returned to chart form with **Wide Awake In A Dream** in 1980 and two years later with **A Promise Is A Comfort To A Fool**, both topping the reggae charts.

Recordings:
The Dynamic Mr Biggs (—/Creole)

Mr Biggs (—/Trojan)

Big Youth

Undoubtably the most-loved and the most successful of all the great reggae DJs to emerge in the '70s, Big Youth was raised in poverty, sharing the same deprivation as the youths who listened to his music, and it was this lifestyle that was reflected in his chant-like proclamations. Born Manley Augustus Buchanan in Kingston, Jamaica, in February 1955, he acquired the nickname Big Youth prior to joining the legendary Lord Tippertone Hi Fi sound system as resident toaster in 1971. Previously he had trained as a mechanic.

His first record was released in 1972 by Gregory Isaacs' and Errol Dunkley's African Museum label. Entitled **Movie Man** it was a version of Dunkley's popular **Movie Star** and although not charting was all the encouragement this team needed to release a succession of sides: **The Best Big Youth, Tell It Black** and **Phil Pratt Thing**.

Big Youth's breakthrough came in the summer of '72 when his **S-90 Skank**, produced by Keith Hudson(▶), rocketed to the top of the Jamaican charts. The record is dedicated to a model of Japanese motorbike and promptly sparked off a dance craze on the island. The following year Big Youth recorded his debut album, **Screaming Target**, issued only in the UK, on the Trojan label, and produced by Augustus 'Gussie' Clarke. It included such fine rhythms as Leroy Smart's **Pride And Ambition** and Lloyd Parks' **One One Coca Fill Basket** and is rightly regarded as one of the best DJ/toaster talkover albums ever released and certainly one that Big Youth was hard pressed to match.

By now an established artist, he formed two labels to issue all his self-produced recordings — Negusa Negast and Augustus Buchanan. There followed one of his most prolific and creative periods with such splendid tracks as **Dread In A Babylon, African Daughter** and **Natty International Dread**. The labels ground to a temporary halt due to stipendiary problems, only to be reactivated in 1976 after his first album with producer Prince Tony. **House Of Dreadlock**, became one of the biggest selling reggae albums in the UK that year.

The period from 1975 to 1978 is regarded as his most influential. Inspiring other DJs, Trinity and Prince Jazbo in particular, he dominated the reggae charts in Jamaica, the USA and Britain with **Notty No Jester, Yabby Youth, Mosiah Garvey** and a version of Ray Charles' **Hit The Road Jack**. In 1977 Big Youth toured Europe with Dennis Brown(▶), receiving ecstatic notices everywhere he performed.

Recordings:
Screaming Target (—/Trojan)
Dreadlocks Dread (Klik/Front Line)

The Blackbyrds

The individual members of The Blackbyrds were formed into a group while engaged in jazz studies at Howard University, Washington DC, by Donald Byrd(▶). Trumpet player Byrd was already a well-established working jazz musician and he knew that practice was as valuable as theory in a musical education. Thus The Blackbyrds' first major success, with the single **Walking In Rhythm** from their second album **Flying Start**, came while they were all still at college. Byrd also produced the Blackbyrds, thus vicariously, perhaps, producing the kind of soul and pop-influenced jazz, or crossover music, which at that time wasn't possible for him as his own mode.

The Blackbyrds continued to chart regularly over the course of five Byrd-produced albums (three went gold); **Walking In Rhythm** was followed by another chart hit, **Happy Music**. This recording success and their jazz breeding created a demand for the group as a live act. They were meritoriously described as a 'musicians' band, and they toured extensively in the US and Britain. They had grown entirely

Below: The Donald Byrd-produced Blackbyrds earned three gold albums in the '70s.

independent of their founder and namesake by their sixth LP, **Better Days,** which was produced by keyboard wizard and former member of Frank Zappa's Mothers of Invention, George Duke(▶).

Although the Blackbyrds had become used to providing their own material, the group's overall sound had always been shaped by Byrd. They now welcomed the opportunity to shed the lengthy instrumental solos which had frequently betrayed their unfashionable jazz roots, and tightened their sound and aligned their more commercial aspirations to Duke's pop experience. They also expanded their line-up to include a new vocalist and percussionist.

As an experiment in practical music study, the Blackbyrds were a great success for their university, although only one member, keyboard player Kevin Toney, eventually earned his degree. Several of his colleagues, faced with the problem of apportioning their time between their studies and the increasingly successful group, opted to abandon their studies.

Nevertheless, Toney insists, the group's pioneering activities have left their mark on Howard University, where students still earn credits for taking time off to perform as part of their education, while the school's own jazz ensemble has recorded several albums.

Recordings:
The Blackbyrds (Fantasy)
Flying Start (Fantasy)
City Life (Fantasy)
Unfinished Business (Fantasy)
Action (Fantasy)
Better Days (Fantasy)

Black Slate

These British roots-rockers worked on the north London reggae circuit during the mid-70s, and eventually hit in 1977 with their anti-mugging single **Sticks Man.** Originally assembled to back visiting Jamaican reggae artists recording or appearing live in the UK, they quickly built up their own following and by the end of 1975 were performing shows in their own right. A large portion of their appeal can be attributed to their enigmatic lead singer Keith Drummond and the mellifluous bass work of Elroy Bailey, which can be heard on literally thousands of UK reggae releases—mostly in the lovers rock(▶) style.

Lay Your Head On My Shoulder, Live Up To Love and the instrumental **Piano Twist** were all popular live numbers that provided the basis for their first nationwide UK tour in 1978. A year later they introduced their music to the European market, thanks to the success of **Sticks Man,** which had been included on a compilation. Back in Britain Black Slate launched their own TCD label and entered the charts with **Mind Your Motion.**

1980 was their best year to date. A TCD cut, **Amigo,** was picked up by the pop label Ensign Records. A happy-go-lucky singalong praising Rastafari, it climbed to No.7 on the national charts. Further sales were notched up when Ensign remixed and re-released their only album, **Black Slate.**

The summer of 1981 witnessed the release of their appropriately titled second set, **Sirens In The City,** and a headlining international tour taking in Australia and America.

City Life. Courtesy Fantasy Records.

Recordings:
Black Slate (—/Ensign)
Sirens In The City (—/Ensign)

Black Uhuru

Surfacing simply as Uhuru (the Swahili word for freedom) in 1975 on the Jamaica-based Dynamic label with a reworking of an old R&B tune, **Folk Song,** the group comprised founder Derrick 'Duckie' Simpson, Don McCarlos and Garth Dennis. However, Dennis was being sought by another vocal group, Wailing Souls(▶), and McCarlos made no secret of his solo singing ambition, which he was later to achieve.

Back at square one, Simpson recruited ghetto youth Michael Rose, who had previously recorded with producer Niney The Observer when he first cut **Guess Who's Coming To Dinner,** his own composition inspired by the film of the same name which starred Sidney Poitier. The song was later to become one of Black Uhuru's most popular.

Rose took lead vocal duties and, to accompany Simpson on backing version of Bob Marley's(▶) **Natural Mystic** and **I Love King Selassie,**

Sinsemilla. Courtesy Island Records.

harmonies, Errol Nelson was borrowed from the Jays. The trio entered King Tubby's Studio with Prince Jammy (aka Jammys) in 1977 to begin work on their first album, **Love Crisis.** The album included a

a song about Rastafari. The group's commitment to Rastafari was to dominate their material from that time.

Shortly after **Love Crisis** appeared in Britain, Nelson was recalled by the Jays, and New Yorker Puma Jones was brought in to replace him. Born and raised in Harlem and trained as a social worker, Jones had rejected the system of black integration within the American social fabric and had arrived in Jamaica on a journey to trace her cultural roots—ultimately back to Africa. As a dancer she had worked with cult reggae figure Ras Michael and his Sons of Negus, and through them was introduced to Simpson and Rose.

Black Uhuru immediately embarked upon a five-track **Showcase** package with all original material. They agreed that in order to be 'forward' in their collective black consciousness they couldn't record other people's songs. **Showcase**

contained **Abortion, Guess Who's Coming To Dinner** and **General Penitentiary** and was a landmark vocally, lyrically and rhythmically, utilising the exemplary drum and bass partnership of Sly Dunbar(▶) and Robbie Shakespeare(▶). Virgin Records in England added further tracks and issued the album in Europe.

Signed to Chris Blackwell's Island label in 1980, the group issued its most critically acclaimed set thus far, **Sinsemilla.** Rose's songs had become sprawling landscapes of mankind's inhumanity and Jones, who had previously been slighted for not contributing to the overall sound, emerged a useful asset.

Although the most commercially viable, their later album **Red** didn't quite maintain the impetus set by its epic predecessor. But word of the group was spreading across Europe and in 1981 they performed their first major British and American dates to packed houses and excited reviews. Clearly the threesome have much to offer.

Recordings:
Love Crisis (Prince Jammys)
Showcase (D-Roy)
Black Uhuru (Virgin)
Sinsemilla (Island)
Red (Island)
Chill Out (Mango/Island)
Tear It Up—Live (Mango/Island)

Bloodstone

Charles McCormick, Willis Draffen, Charles Love, Henry Williams, Roger Durham and Melvin Webb worked in Kansas City as the Sinceres, moving out to the West Coast in the late '60s to record under that name before returning home, picking up instruments, developing a rock-influenced style in the Sly Stone(▶) mode and adopting a new name—Bloodstone (minus Webb).

Touring Britain in 1972 as an unknown support act to Al Green(▶) they created a sensation and were signed by the British label Decca. Their second album for the com-

Below: Michael Rose of Black Uhuru, from the UK tour, 1981.

pany, produced by Mike Vernon, a British R&B aficionado who had scored modest success with other black American acts, yielded the massive American hit **Natural High**. A superb sweet-soul ballad, it captured the spirit of black America despite having been recorded in the unlikely location of Chipping Norton, a country market town in Oxfordshire, England.

After Webb's departure and Durham's death (in 1973); more albums were cut which contained further fine material but each was less successful than is precursor and, despite a stint at Motown(▶), the group fell into obscurity.

Recordings:
Natural High (London/Decca)
Riddle Of The Sphinx
(London/Decca)
Unreal (London/Decca)

Blue Magic

Part of Philadelphia's WMOT set-up (which has rivalled Philadelphia International(▶) in output), but leased to Atlantic, Blue Magic have recorded a string of consistently classy albums which have few peers when it comes to the sophisticated end of the soul vocal-group spectrum.

Brothers Vernon and Wendell Sawyer and their partners Richard Pratt, Keith Beaton and Ted Mills have recorded such classics as **Three Ring Circus, Magic Of The Blue** and **Sideshow**. All these recordings have also benefited from the talents of producer Bobby Eli, arrangers Norman Harris and Vince Montana, and the regular team of ace musicians at Sigma Sound studios in Philly.

Recordings:
Blue Magic (Atlantic)
Magic of the Blue (Atlantic)
Thirteen Blue Magic Lane
(Atlantic)

Hamilton Bohannon

Bohannon is a well-respected artist in music circles, but his insistence on maintaining control over all aspects of his work may be largely responsible for his fluctuating fortunes. His personal style and sartorial elegance, including the ever present button-hole flower, are redolent of his gentlemanly Southern origins; he is a native of Georgia.

Graduating from Atlanta's Clark College with a BA in musical education, Bohannon began teaching, only to discover that the classroom was not for him. As a drummer, he joined a local Georgia band, where he met and was inspired by a young guitarist named Jimi Hendrix(▶).

Bohannon also encountered Stevie Wonder(▶) during those early years on the road, and spent the years from 1965 to 1967 touring America and Europe as Stevie's drummer. Observers at Motown(▶) were impressed and the label appointed Bohannon as its top bandleader and he found himself responsible for the live music arrangements for all the Detroit label's top acts. Under the banner 'Bohannon and the Motown Sound' he headed a 27-piece band on tour with Marvin Gaye(▶), Diana Ross and the Supremes(▶), the Four Tops(▶), the Temptations(▶), Smokey Robinson(▶), Gladys Knight & the

Pips(▶), the Miracles(▶), the Spinners(▶), and Martha Reeves and the Vandellas(▶).

When Motown moved from Detroit to the West Coast, Bohannon elected not to follow. He formed his own group and had his first international hit via the percussive dominance and irrepressible beat of **South African Man** (1975). That success formed the pattern

South African Man. Courtesy Brunswick Records.

for the unambiguous hard-partying of several subsequent hits, from albums such as **South African Man, Insides Out** to the very direct **Dance Your Ass Off**.

There followed a comparative lull—ironically through the disco boom, which was fuelled by a much flimsier European sound—before Bohannon attempted to crash back with the hopefully titled **Phase II**, on the Mercury label. His next Mercury album, **Summertime**

Below: Marcia Barrett of Boney M, phenomenal late '70s, Europe-based pop-disco group.

Groove, received a slightly warmer reception, with **Let's Start The Dance** becoming a favourite club track. But Bohannon has not been able to recreate the impact of his mid-'70s material, and appears to have been slightly overtaken by the proliferation of similarly angled dance-music of the post-disco era.

Recordings:
South African Man (Brunswick)
Insides Out (Brunswick — later reissued on London)
Dance Your Ass Off (Brunswick)
Bohannon's Best (Brunswick)
Phase II (Mercury)
Summertime Groove (Mercury)

Boney M

Responsibility for the astonishing success of Boney M rests firmly with one man—Frank Farian, a successful German producer and composer. But had Farian not also been a failed would-be artist, Boney M would never have existed. The impact they made when they did arrive counterpoised much of the drear earnestness of late '70s rock and pop and put the fun value of the manufactured group firmly back at the top of the charts.

Boney M, or rather the four people who came to be known as such, didn't actually perform on the first single put out under that name. **Baby Do The Bump**, released in Europe in 1975, was sheer wish-fulfilment on the part of Farian, a long-time soul and R&B fan, who put the record together using his own heavily disguised vocals, backed by a chorus of female session singers.

Although the record didn't score in Farian's native Germany, he

found himself with a hit in Holland. Thus the need to back it up with TV appearances required him to create a real Boney M as soon as possible.

The group was formed from four expatriate West Indians, each of whom had been striving, with limited success, to make it on the German pop scene. Marcia Barrett, from Jamaica, moved to London with her family while she was still of school age; she then worked in London as a secretary, before moving to Germany to begin a singing career. Maizie Williams, from Montserrat, also arrived in Germany via London, where, after finishing school, she had been at various times a model, singer, and beauty queen.

Bobby Farrell moved to Holland from his native Aruba (Antilles) when he was just 15. He joined a soul group and subsequently became active on the German pop circuit. Liz Mitchell, the most experienced of the four when Boney M was formed, had been in the Hamburg production of *Hair*, and had subsequently sung in two German pop groups.

Boney M was not put together quite overnight. Farian, mindful of the future potential of anyone recording under what was now a chart name had taken his time in selecting the components of Boney M. It wasn't until 1977 that **Daddy Cool** became the internationally best-selling follow-up to **Baby Do The Bump**.

In fact, 1977 was a banner year for Boney M, yielding no fewer than four hit singles: **Daddy Cool, Sunny, Ma Baker** and **Belfast**. With the three girls hand-picked for their attractiveness and the manic court-jester gyrations of

Farrell, Farian combined his unerring, commercial screening process and electronic studio-craft, to produce unchallenging pop-disco of the broadest family appeal.

The group's greatest single success came in the summer of 1978, when their singalong rendition of the Melodians' reggae spiritual, **Rivers Of Babylon**, quickly shot to No. 1 in the UK charts (incidentally becoming its British record company's fastest-selling single ever) and scored massively throughout Europe and the US. With cool nerve, the single was then flipped and re-released on the UK market, so that the original B-side, **Brown Girl In The Ring**, made the same record a hit all over again, still with **Rivers Of Babylon** on the other side! It was a gambit probably unequalled in the annals of commercial pop cynicism, and one essential pointer to the enduring tolerance of their pop audience is that it bore them no hard feelings whatsoever.

Applying their even-keeled formula, Boney M have reworked material from such disparate sources as the Yardbirds (**Still I'm Sad**), Roger Miller (**King Of The Road**) and Neil Young (**Heart Of Gold**), while among the equally diverse subjects to pass under their junior microscope have been American gangsters of the 'Thirties (**Ma Baker**), the political situation in Northern Ireland (**Belfast**) and even the 19th century Russian warlock, **Rasputin**.

Since 1979, when they had hits with **El Lute** and **Gotta Go Home**, from the **Oceans Of Fantasy** album, they have undergone something of a cooling-off period. However, they released a greatest hits package, and a low-key studio album, **Boonoonoonoos**, at the end of 1981.

Recordings
Nightflight To Venus (Atlantic/Hansa-Atlantic)
Oceans Of Fantasy (Atlantic/Hansa-Atlantic)
The Magic Of Boney M (Atlantic/Hansa-Atlantic)
Boonoonoonoos (Atlantic/Hansa-Atlantic)

Ken Boothe

Emerging in Kingston, Jamaica, towards the end of the '60s Boothe is a protégé of Clement Coxsone Dodd's Studio One(▶) stable. His tender youthful phrasing is captured on the seminal **Mister Rock Steady** album.

Boothe received UK airplay with his rock-steady interpretation of Sandie Shaw's winning Eurovision Song Contest entry, **Puppet On A String**. By the mid-'70s he was a household name in Jamaica and the UK with a number of classic Lloyd Charmers-produced sides, notably a rendition of David Gates' **Everything I Own**, which topped the UK pop charts in November 1974, and the following year's **Crying Over You** that stayed just outside the top 10.

Both singles are included on his definitive retrospective album **Who Gets Your Love?**, issued some years later, that focuses on his strength as a sweet-ballad crooner with producers Phil Pratt, Bunny Lee and Lloyd Charmers.

By the end of the decade he was producing his own material with sporadic commercial success, although enlisting Bunny Lee for the

I'm Just A Man album, cut at King Tubby's and mixed by the supreme reggae/soul singer Pat Kelly(▶). He scored with the single **You're No Good** in 1979.

Recordings:
Black Gold And Green (—/Trojan)
Everything I Own (—/Trojan)

Bootsy's Rubber Band

see P. Funk

Dennis Bovell

Born in Barbados in 1953 into a family of Seventh Day Adventists, but brought up in South London, Dennis Bovell is the eccentric guitarist with leading UK reggae band Matumbi(▶), and is central to its popular reggae sound. He is also pursuing a quirky solo career, and his experience of the '60s pop boom and a love of Jamaican dub music combine to produce bizarre unstylized music that defies categorisation.

Bovell's love of dub led to him running his own sound system called Jah Sufferer, which he operated every Friday night in a North London club. A confrontation with the police on one of these gigs led to his six-month imprisonment on remand before being cleared of a charge at an appeal court.

For many years Bovell has been a central figure in UK reggae, and at one point he was featured playing on no less than 18 singles in the British reggae top 20. His talents as a producer are recognised by those in and out of reggae. He was called upon to produce the Pop Group and later the tribalistic white reggae of the Slits. His own solo ventures have extended to **I Wah Dub** which, as the title suggests, explores his passion for bass and drum-based instrumental music, and the varied pot-pourri of his double album **Brain Damage**.

Bovell also contributed to, and compiled the **Babylon** soundtrack album, as well as producing Linton Kwesi Johnson(▶) and I-Roy(▶).

Below: Seminal rock steady stylist Ken Boothe.

Brass Construction. Courtesy United Artists Records.

Recordings:
I Wah Dub (—/EMI)
Brain Damage (—/Fontana)

Brass Construction

Originally formed as Dynamic Soul by British Guyana-born Randy Muller in the early '70s, Brass Construction came to prominence in 1976 with the self-titled United Artists' debut album which remarkably broke in the United Kingdom before America. One of the very first, if not the only, debut disco-orientated records to reach top-10 UK album status, it spawned two smash hits and highly influential singles in **Movin'** and **Changin'**. For the previous four years Muller had concentrated on string arrangements on productions by his manager Jeff Lane, and the Muller Brass Construction sound was shaped and refined down through a string of uniquely original international hits by B.T. Express(▶) and Spider's Webb.

Muller and Lane and Brass Construction were without doubt one of the most important catalysts in the whole '70s disco movement and Brass Construction gave rise to many imitators, not the least of which was the equally successful Mass Production(▶). Brass Construction's subsequent albums, creatively entitled **II, III, IV, V,** etc., never really consolidated the promise of **Brass Construction**, although **II** did include one exciting single hit in **Ha Cha Cha**. The band toured the UK successfully in 1977 with the Detroit Spinners(▶), and Muller continued producing B.T. Express and even revitalised the career of '60s soulster Garnett Mimms(▶) with the Arista release **What It Is**, basically a case of Mimms replacing Muller on a standard sounding Brass Construction track.

In 1979, while completing **Brass Construction V**, Muller formed Alligator Bit Him productions and commenced work with a new group, Skyy(▶). Muller signed the band to New York-based Salsoul Records and enjoyed moderate success with them until his third production **Skyyline** smashed through to US pop and international success in late '81/'82. The first single from the album **Call Me** topped the US soul chart and broke the pop top 30.

Now well-entrenched as a hit producer, Muller continued to attempt to bring Brass Construction back to prominence, but the 1982 12-inch release, **Can You See The Light,** showed little of the undeniably influential and original style and class of 1976's **Movin'**. Despite this, Brass Construction will remain in the history books as a group that pioneered a complete change of direction for black music in the '70s. No one has yet come along with anything quite as unique as their arrangement of reed, brass and strings.

Recordings:
Brass Construction (United Artists)
Brass Construction II (United Artists)
Movin'/Changin' (—/United Artists 12" Single UK Only)

Can You See The Light
(EMI-America 12″ Single)

The Brecker Brothers

There can be no more in-demand session horn players than New York-based Randy (b.1945) and Michael Brecker (b.1949) not just in the black music field, for their playing and arrangements can be found in the credits of pop, rock, jazz and soul albums. As a recording entity in their own right, the Brecker Brothers are an informal outfit, now signed to Arista Records, who produce albums that are a fusion of every music they come into contact with. From their 1978 set, **Heavy Metal Be-Bop,** came their biggest hit to date, **East River,** the album title being a perfect description of its sound.

Recordings:
The Brecker Brothers (Arista)
Heavy Metal Be-Bop (Arista)
Detente (Arista)
Straphangin' (Arista)

Brides of Funkenstein

see P. Funk

Dee Dee Bridgewater

Dee Dee Bridgewater was born in Memphis, Tennessee, and raised in Flint, Michigan. She began singing professionally when she was 16, performing in nightclubs around Michigan. Later, while attending the State University, she joined the Illinois Jazz Band that toured Russia.

In June 1970, Dee Dee passed an audition to become lead vocalist with the Thad Jones-Mel Lewis Big Band. During her four years with them, she appeared on their **Suite For Pops** album. This led to session work with Norman Connors(▶), Stanley Clarke(▶), Roland Kirk, Pharoah Sanders, Roy Ayers(▶) and Dizzy Gillespie.

She landed the part of Glinda, the Good Witch, in the 1974 Broadway production of *The Wiz,* winning a Tony Award for Best Supporting Actress.

In 1976, she made an album for Atlantic Records(▶) but it was never released. Two years later she signed to Elektra-Asylum Records and made **Just Family,** produced by Stanley Clark. George Duke(▶) produced her second album, **Bad For Me,** released in April 1979. Moving away from her jazzy leanings, she cut a soul album, **Dee Dee Bridgewater,** produced by Thom Bell(▶), in October 1980.

Recordings:
Just Family (Elektra-Asylum)
Bad For Me (Elektra-Asylum)
Dee Dee Bridgewater
(Elektra-Asylum)

Johnny Bristol

A native of Morganton, North Carolina, Johnny Bristol was stationed near Detroit while serving with the US Air Force. Teaming up with Jackie Beaver they began working local clubs as a duo and came to the attention of Gwen Gordy, sister of

Motown(▶) founder Berry Gordy and wife of Harvey Fuqua (then leader of the legendary Moonglows(▶), later a successful producer with Motown and latterly manager/musical mentor of Sylvester(▶)).

Signed to the Fuqua's Tri Phi label, Johnny and Jackie cut a dozen records, the first being **Do You See My Love For You Growing** (later a hit for Junior Walker(▶)) and the second **Someday We'll Be Together** (which was re-recorded by Diana Ross and the Supremes(▶) some years later, selling two-and-a-half million copies).

When Tri Phi was swallowed up by the burgeoning Motown empire, Beaver left for Georgia and a subsequent solo career with various labels. Bristol, however, stayed in Detroit and became Fuqua's assistant in Motown's Artist Development Department. The pair teamed up as songwriters and producers and over the next six years rivalled that other great Motown partnership of Holland-Dozier-Holland(▶) in terms of success.

Bristol gave Junior Walker a long run of hits as well as being responsible for such other successes as Edwin Starr's(▶) **Twenty Five Miles,** David Ruffin's(▶) **My Whole World Ended,** Marvin Gaye(▶) and Tammi Terrell's(▶) **Ain't No Mountain High Enough** (also a smash for Diana Ross) and **Yester-Me, Yester-You, Yester-Day** for Stevie Wonder(▶).

By the time Bristol's contract with Motown came up for renewal in 1973, the company had moved from Detroit to the West Coast, and there had been a lot of internal upheaval, with many of the top artists leaving for new pastures. Bristol followed suit, signing a new deal as a house producer for CBS, producing O. C. Smith's(▶) **The La La Song,** Boz Scaggs' (▶) **Slow Dancer** album and working with Buddy Miles(▶), as well as taking time out to produce Jerry Butler's(▶) **Power Of Love** album for Mercury.

After CBS turned down his idea of recording an album with himself as featured vocalist, Bristol persuaded them to let him negotiate an outside deal with MGM, which resulted in the smash hit **Hang On In There Baby** (released 1974) and a much-lauded album, Bristol writing all the material. H.B. Barnum(▶), another former Motown veteran, contributed some richly textured arrangements and the album took soul music to a new peak of sophistication, without in any way sounding contrived. A follow-up album (for Polydor in 1976) showed similar craftsmanship.

Returning to producing, Bristol had further success with Tavares(▶), Tom Jones, Johnny Mathis(▶) and others before, in 1981, issuing another brilliant but less commercially successful album **Free To Be Me** for Hansa.

Recordings:
Hang On In There Baby (MGM)
Bristol' Creme (Polydor)
Free To Be Me
(Hansa/Ariola/Hansa)

Below Johnny Bristol has done a good job of hanging on in as a singer songwriter producer.

Dennis Brown

Dennis Emmanuel Brown rates as one of the best-loved reggae singers to emerge in the last decade. He has always set himself the highest songwriting and vocal standards and has been rewarded by a trail of hit singles. Born in Kingston, Jamaica, in February 1956, he enjoyed the comforts of a middle-class background. His father was a television script-writer and actor and his brother was a popular figure because of his role as 'Man Man' in the radio series 'Life In Hopeful Village'.

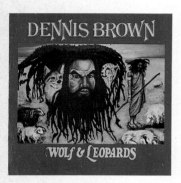

Wolf & Leopards. Courtesy EMI Records.

Brother Basil introduced Brown to his first professional group, the Falcons. He and Noel Brown (no relation) with Scotty and Cynthia Richards built up a reputation on the island's cabaret circuit, busting into the big time via the Smashville '68 concert held in the National Arena with King Curtis(▶), Miriam Makeba and Byron Lee & the Dragonaires(▶) on the same bill.

Lee subsequently introduced Brown to producer Derrick Harriot, with whom he recorded **Lips Of Wine** issued some years later as **Obsession**. Meanwhile, the Falcons' manager Ms Ivy took Brown to meet Clement Coxsone Dodd at Studio One(▶) where he cut his first release, a version of the Impressions'(▶) **No Man Is An Island**, which became the title of a best-selling album in 1972.

Winding up his full-time education in 1974 and still only 17 years old, Brown teamed up with the innovative young producer Winston 'Niney The Observer' Hollness, a relationship that was to have a profound effect on the sound of mid-70s reggae. The firm timbre of his voice, rare in one so young, sent Brown's singles soaring to success: **Westbound Train, Cassandara, Ride On Ride On** (a duet with Big Youth(▶)) and **No More Will I Roam** were among the most popular. That year he toured the UK supporting Toots and the Maytals(▶).

Brown's biggest commercial breakthrough came in 1979 when **Money In My Pocket** and **Ain't That Loving You** took his records out of the reggae charts and installed him firmly in the pop spectrum. Lazer Records, a label licensed to the mighty WEA corporation, attempted to capitalise with the **Money In My Pocket, Live At Montreaux, Joseph's Coat Of Many Colours** and **Spellbound** albums, but failed because of inconsistent material and inadequate promotion.

Brown has been comparitively quiet of late, concentrating on the expanding American market where A&M Records has released the substandard **Foul Play**.

Recordings:
No Man Is An Island (Studio One/—)
Wolves And Leopards (DEB/EMI)
Visions Of Dennis Brown (—/Lightning)
Best Of Dennis Brown (Joe Gibbs/—)

Peter Brown

White Chicago-based Peter Brown built his own home studio, played almost everything himself and sent the tapes to Miami-based R&B label TK(▶). The result was an R&B No. 1 with **Do Ya Wanna Get Funky With Me** (1977), the first-ever 12-inch single to go gold.

Subsequent recordings have established Brown firmly in the mainstream of contemporary black music, despite his ethnic origins.

Recordings:
Do Ya Wanna Get Funky With Me (TK)
Stargazer (TK)

Randy Brown

Brown is a Memphis singer who inherited the songwriting skills of Homer Banks(▶) and Carl Hampton when they finally emerged from the ruins of the collapse of the Stax(▶) label. Banks and Hampton had been important writers and producers at Stax, responsible for Johnnie Taylor's(▶) **Who's Makin' Love,** Luther Ingram's(▶) **If Loving You Is Wrong,** and The Staple Singers'(▶) **If You're Ready (Come Go With Me).**

Brown's debut album, **Welcome To My Room,** established a strong future identity for him, and featured the warm seductive Memphis inheritance of Otis Redding(▶) and Al Green(▶).

Recordings:
Welcome To My Room (Parachute)
Intimately (Parachute)
Midnight Desire (Casablanca)

Shirley Brown

Shirley Brown's 1974 Stax hit **Woman To Woman** created a whole genre of 'dialogue' records with one lady telling another lady to leave her man alone (or to keep him, and welcome!). Born in West Memphis, Arkansas, on January 6, 1947, Shirley moved North to East St Louis with her family, gaining early experience singing (from the age of 14) in church and local clubs before a long stint as opening act for blues singer Albert King(▶). King took her back South to sign with Stax(▶) at the age of 23, and record under the guidance of the late Al Jackson Jr, (drummer with Booker T and the MGs(▶)), and later with David Porter(▶).

Woman To Woman was actually penned for, but turned down by, Inez Foxx(▶). It shot to No. 1 in the US R&B charts and was a pop hit. Since the demise of Stax, Shirley Brown has recorded with modest success for Arista.

Recordings:
Woman To Woman (Stax)
For The Real Feeling (Stax)
Shirley Brown (Arista)

Peabo Bryson

Southern soul balladeer Peabo Bryson enjoys unparalleled success in America and in the environs of his native Southern Carolina but is yet to achieve more than a small cult following outside the US. He first appeared on the soul scene in America's deep south in the late '60s, employed as a songwriter for a band called Moses Dillard and the Textile Display. A regular church attender, he had written songs almost as a hobby. Writing for a group provided the ideal platform for his love ballads and paeans of spiritual rejoicing.

Bryson's association with Dillard led to a contract with Bang Records as a producer and songwriter in 1970. Bang was operated by Ilene Berns, the widow of Bert Berns, an influential soul writer, producer and occasional performer. She ran two labels, Bang being pop-orientated and Shout(▶) the R&B division. In 1975 she launched Bullett and with it Peabo Bryson's first single, **Underground Music,** an up-tempo funk record, unrepresentative of his later work. It was at this time that Bryson met producer Johnny Pate with whom he has worked ever since. Their first album, **Peabo,** also came in 1975.

Bullet ground to a halt and it was up to Capitol Record's Larkin Arnold to pact the Bryson/Pate partnership to his expanding R&B roster. Bryson's first release with this deal was **Reaching For The Sky,** a truly classic album that drove home the singer's enormous vocal range and flair for melody. **Crosswinds,** in 1979, traced a similar pattern of steamy sensual ballads. Since then Bryson's records have been consistently inconsistent. **We're The Best Of Friends,** recorded with another Capitol singer Natalie Cole(▶), lacked cohesion because they recorded their tracks separately. **Paradise** found

Below: B.T. Express keep on churning out the funk.

him back on course again, as did **Turn Back The Hands Of Time,** a collection of remixed Bullett recordings issued in 1981.

Eager to shift Bryson's records outside Amercia, Capitol teamed him with Roberta Flack(▶) for the live album **Live And More.** But Flack, without her former partner Donny Hathaway(▶), sounded lost, and Bryson uncomfortable duetting on Flack/Hathaway songs.

Bryson records continue to sell well in America, although not with soul fans who tend to find his music too elaborately produced, nor in Europe where his music isn't funky enough for radio and club exposure. He remains an underrated talent.

Recordings:
Peabo (Bullett)
Reaching For The Sky (Capitol)
Crosswinds (Capitol)
We're The Best Of Friends (with Natalie Cole) (Capitol)
Paradise (Capitol)
Turn Back The Hands Of Time (Capitol)
Live And More (with Roberta Flack) (Atlantic)

B.T.Express

Originating in Brooklyn, New York, in 1972, the group arrived at their present name via several changes of identity, the last being Brooklyn Transit Express, which was fashionably shortened in 1973 to B.T. Express.

They made their first impact with the trenchant metronomic disco single—the title track from their first album—**Do It Till You're Satisified.** Both single and album went gold in the US on Scepter's Roadshow label. Still with Roadshow, the sound-effect laden **Express** became something of a theme tune, and also the band's third gold record.

Do It 'Til You're Satisifed.
Courtesy EMI Records.

Their second LP, **Non-Stop,** came close to repeating the chart action of their first album, and yielded two hit singles, **Give It What You Got,** and **Peace Pipe.** The band's producer, Jeff Lane, who had more or less discovered them, was retained when they signed to Columbia and released the album **Energy To Burn.** This was followed by **Function At The Junction** and **Shout It Out.**

Meanwhile, the band's original line-up of eight, was gradually modified; first when the only female member, Barbara Joyce Lomas, elected to pursue a solo career. Later, Michael Jones and Leslie Ming both left, while the recruitment of guitarist Wesley Hall brought the group's strength back up to six. It was in this form that B.T. Express began a new decade

Above: Burning Spear, A symbol of the West Indian search for freedom—and a new pair of trousers!

with the proclamatory 1980, an album which further suffused their fading hard-disco image with a variety of styles and moods. They followed this with **Old Gold, Future Gold,** which included remixes of previous hits.

Recordings:
Do It Til You're Satisifed (Roadshow/EMI)
Non-Stop (Roadshow/EMI)
Energy To Burn (Columbia/EMI)
Function At The Junction (Columbia)
Shout It Out (Columbia)
1980 (Columbia/Pye)
Old Gold, Future Gold (Columbia/Excaliber)

Burning Spear

Without doubt, Burning Spear is the embodiment of Jamaican roots music. Through a wealth of magnificent recordings he has come to symbolise the spiritual majesty of a displaced race of peoples searching for freedom and ultimately for repatriation to Africa, a destiny prophesied by his cultural source of inspiration—black civil-rights leader Marcus Garvey. The words of Garvey have featured prominently on all of Burning Spear's recordings since his punitive days with Studio One(▶) over a decade ago. He is one of the most potent forces in reggae; having began as a cult figure he is now a driving omnipresence.

Born Winston Rodney in St Ann's Bay on the north coast of Jamaica— also the birthplace of Bob Marley(▶) and Garvey—he took the name of the late Kenyan statesman Jomo Kenyatta when he started recording for Clement Coxsone Dodd in 1969. The single **Door Peeper,** which sank without trace because it ignored the then popular reggae mould of carefree dance music, was typical of his subsequent recordings, an almost chant-like Rastafarian prayer.

Although Burning Spear is essentially a solo singer, two others were co-opted as backing singers and songwriters during the early days at

Studio One: Rupert Willington and Delroy Hines. For the next five years Spear continued to record for Dodd with little commercial success. **Joe Frazier** made the Jamaican top five in 1972, **Foggy Road, Swell Headed, Ethiopians Live It Out, New Civilisation, This Population** and **Creation Rebel**, all classics of the genre, were largely ignored at the time of their release.

A stipendiary dispute dissolved the Spear/Dodd team, and by the end of 1974 Spear was back on the North Coast where he was approached by sound system operator Jack Ruby(▶). Ruby wanted exclusive discs to play on his system and Spear responded with **Marcus Garvey**. It set the island alight and Jamaica became gripped with Burning Spear mania. Fired by the record's success, Ruby released the equally splendid **Slavery Days** and the **Marcus Garvey** album. Issued by Island Records in the UK, the album was acclaimed an unequivocal success and a major landmark in reggae.

Marcus Garvey. Courtesy Island Records.

Burning Spear Live. Courtesy Island Records.

Although by now recognised as a major musical force, Burning Spear was having little effect upon contemporary Jamaican music, except as a champion of Marcus Garvey's teachings. At the end of 1975 he experimented with self-production and released **Travelling** as a single on his own label. In addition, he produced sides for Phillip Fullwood and a group from St Ann's called Burning Junior. A second album, **Man In The Hills**, showed him in a less militant mood.

The termination of the relationship with Jack Ruby coincided with the departure of Willington and Hines. Lyrically at something of an impasse, Spear used the following months at Harry J's Studio to record the underrated **Dry And Heavy** album, for the most part re-workings of unsung classics from his Studio One days.

Accompanied only by his trumpet player Bobby Ellis, Burning Spear paid his first visit to the UK in October 1976. With Ellis and the nucleus of indigenous London reggae rockers Aswad(▶), Spear had just one day in which to rehearse for two consecutive nights at the capital's Rainbow Theatre. Despite this ramshackle organisation, the shows were triumphs for Spear and reggae, creating a stir similar to Bob Marley's Lyceum show a year earlier. An impressed and grateful Spear invited Aswad to join him in Jamaica to record the **Marcus' Children** album. It marked a return to the defiance of earlier recordings, including the kaleidoscopic track **Civilised Reggàe**, and eventually surfaced in England, retitled **Social Living**, on Island's One Stop subsidiary.

Much of 1979 was spent working at his Garvey Lawn recreation centre in his home town, and laying new tracks at Bob Marley's Tuff Gong Studio in Kingston's Hope Road. Switching to EMI the fruits of this time are found on **Hail H.I.M.**, which he co-produced with the Wailers'(▶) bass guitarist Aston 'Familyman' Barrett. The primal, resolute, questioning vocals splashed across a patchwork of metaphysical rhythms, are the hallmarks of Burning Spear.

Recordings:
Studio One Presents Burning Spear (Studio One/—)
Rocking Time (Studio One/—)
Marcus Garvey (Fox/Island)
Dry And Heavy (Mango/Island)
Social Living (Burning Spear/Island)
Hail H.I.M. (Burning Spear/Island)

CTI

During the '70s, CTI and its sister label Kudu virtually cornered the market in that hybrid music best described as jazz/funk/easy-listening. They have come up with the occasional classic and established an individual and easily recognisable 'sound', at the same time using the talents of the very best jazz musicians in a tasteful and often creative way. The formula is simple—jazz soloist over light funk beat with orchestral backing—and, with variations, has sold a great many records and given good musicians deserved financial reward.

CTI is the creation of Creed Taylor (born Lynchburg, 1929) who was previously a staff producer for jazz label Verve. Having had success with artists like Kenny Burrell, Wes Montgomery and particularly Jimmy Smith(▶), Taylor branched out in the early '70s with CTI (Creed Taylor International). Using Rudy Van Gelder's New Jersey studios and always with himself as producer, he quickly established the label as a commercial force. Artists who record or have recorded for CTI/Kudu include Airto, Joe Beck, George Benson(▶), Joe Farrell(▶), Jim Hall, Bob James(▶), Esther Phillips(▶) (her version of **What A Difference A Day Makes** was an international hit in 1975), Grover Washington(▶), Idris Muhammad(▶), Stanley Turrentine(▶) and Hank Crawford(▶).

CTI artists often play on each other's albums, and studio musicians are in any event of the very highest calibre. Although he has been criticised for commercialising jazz, Taylor has helped to revive interest in the music as well as providing a viable outlet for some of its most distinguished practitioners.

Cameo

As labelmates of George Clinton, it was unlikely that Cameo wouldn't be a little influenced by him—Clinton's major project, Parliament(▶), were also on Chocolate City Records—and when New Yorker Larry Blackmon put together the first Cameo album, in 1977, there were tinges of Clinton: uncut funk with R&B vocals, though sometimes with sanitorium-style mumblings substituted for singing.

As the Players, Blackmon's first incarnation of a group had released a single, **Find My Way**, in 1975. This song appeared on the first album, and was then re-cut for the feature film *Thank God It's Friday*, appearing again on a later LP.

Cameo's first two albums included the hit singles **Rigor Mortis, It's Serious** and **It's Over**. Maintaining Clinton's sense of humour, Blackmon began to move Cameo's sound away into territory of their own. They became an organised version of a Clinton project, and undertook enormous touring schedules to refine their sound and cement their identity. During five years of Cameo albums, the band have stayed on the road almost constantly, and as a 12-piece they were totally self-contained and absolutely tireless.

1978 saw their third album **Ugly Ego**, which contained the singles **Insane** and **Give Love A Chance**. Their fourth, **Secret Omen**, was released in 1979. Blackmon-produced, these were essential club-material albums — raucous dance-inducing stormers, and silky and soulful smoochers. From that fourth album came hit singles **I Just Want To Be** and **Sparkle**. The 1980 releases **Cameosis** and **Feel Me** included singles which were pillars of the R&B charts: **We're Goin' Out Tonight, On The One, Shake Your Pants, Keep It Hot.**

In 1981, still with tongue-in-cheek, Blackmon and pals featured themselves in English medieval costumes for their seventh venture, **Knights Of The Sound Table**, which produced the hit **Freeky Dancin'**. By now, the sound was miles away from the meandering shambles of Clinton's outfits. It had become horny, funky, rich and very tight.

The line-up presently stands at: Blackmon, numerous instruments; Anthony Lockett, guitar/vocals; Gregory Johnson, keyboards; Thomas Campbell, keyboards; Stephen Moore, vocals; Tomi Jenkins, vocals; Charles Singleton, vocals; Aaron Mills, bass; Jeryl Bright, horns; Arnett Leftenant, horns; Nathan Leftenant, horns; Vince Wilburn, drums.

Recordings:
Cardiac Arrest (Chocolate City/Casablanca)
We All Know Who We Are (Chocolate City/Casablanca)
Ugly Ego (Chocolate City/Casablanca)
Secret Omen (Chocolate City/Casablanca)
Cameosis (Chocolate City/Casablanca)
Feel Me (Chocolate City/Casablanca)
Knights Of The Sound Table (Chocolate City/Casablanca)

Cameron

Rafael Cameron was born in Guyana, and came to America when he was 22. On the streets of New York, he recognised Randy Muller of Brass Construction(▶), went up and talked to him, and the two became friends, playing together in an occasional steel drum ensemble called the Panharmonics.

Muller, who was also writing and producing for Skyy(▶), used that band for Cameron's eponymous first album (1980). From the second album, **Cameron's In Love**, released in 1981, came the single **Funtown USA**.

Recordings:
Cameron (Salsoul)
Cameron's In Love (Salsoul)

Below: Esther Phillips scored for CTI in 1975 with **What A Difference A Day Makes.**

G.C. Cameron

G.C. Cameron ('The G.C. doesn't stand for anything, it's just my name') is an ex-lead vocalist with the Spinners(▶) (called the Detroit Spinners in the UK, to avoid confusion with a popular Liverpool folk group). G.C. joined the group in 1968, on his return from the Far East where, as a soldier in the marine corps, he had begun his singing career in the nightclubs of Okinawa.

He was sent home wounded to Detroit in 1967, whereupon his friend Dennis Edwards, then a member of the now defunct Motown(▶) group the Contours(▶), suggested he audition for the Spinners. Within 12 days, with Cameron at the head, the Spinners were opening the show for Marvin Gaye(▶) at Harlem's Apollo Theatre.

During Cameron's three-year tenure with the Spinners, their biggest hit was the Stevie Wonder(▶)-penned **It's A Shame.** When the group left Motown, Cameron remained on a solo contract and had varying success, on both Motown and its subsidiary Mowest with **Act Like A Shotgun, No Matter Where, Let Me Down Easy** and **It's Hard To Say Goodbye To Yesterday** from the soundtrack of the film *Cooley High.*

G.C. duetted with Stevie Wonder's ex-wife Syreeta(▶) on a track from her album **Stevie Wonder Presents Syreeta.** Three years later, they recorded an entire album, **Rich Love, Poor Love,** produced, directed, written and arranged by Motown house producer Michael L. Smith.

Recordings:
Love Songs And Other Tragedies (Motown/−)
G.C. Cameron (Motown)
You're What's Missing In My Life (Motown)
Rich Love, Poor Love (with Syreeta) (Motown)

Al Campbell

Born in Kingston, Jamaica, on August 31, 1954, Campbell sang as a boy in church and was still in his early teens when a close friend, Junior Mennes of the Techniques, introduced him to influential rocksteady / reggae producer Duke Reid. Reid was impressed by the range and timbre of his voice and his precocious songwriting ability, but nevertheless insisted Campbell complete his education. He complied, but quickly assembled the Three Lads vocal trio with Freddie McGregor(▶) and Earnest Wilson.

Campbell is another graduate of the Clement Coxsone Dodd harmony school for whom he sang backing vocals on many Jamaican hits during the late '60s and early '70s. His biggest commercial achievement, and a cornerstone of lovers rock(▶) and roots reggae, was with producer Phil Pratt in 1975 when he wrote and recorded **Gee Baby,** the number that won him a devotional audience in the UK and finally established him in Jamaica.

Leaving Pratt in 1978 after two albums that deftly showcased his rich soulful voice, he has since cut top-quality sides with a variety of producers, in addition to producing others. An almost permanent resident of the UK he is a consistent feature of the reggae charts, reaffirming his popularity in 1980 with the single **Late Night Blues.**

Above: Chic, built around the talents of Bernard Edwards and Nile Rodgers.

Recordings:
Gee Baby (−/Sunshot)
Loving Moods (−/Ital)
Ain't That Loving You (−/Greensleeves)

Larry Carlton

Fluid guitarist Larry Eugene Carlton (born Torrance, California 1948) began his professional career with a group at Disneyland after a musical education completed at the California State University.

In 1969, Carlton became musical director and principal composer of an American NBC children's TV show, and also appeared as the character 'Johnny Guitar'.

His move to the lucrative world of sessions and jingles (after a stint with the 5th Dimension(▶)) resulted in a reputation which secured him a role with the Crusaders(▶) in 1973. His recorded output with this erstwhile jazz unit is best demonstrated by his guitar solo contributions on the **Crusaders 1** and **Southern Comfort** sets.

Carlton's solo recording career, begun in 1968 with an album for Uni, was established with **Singing/Playing** (1974), where he was accompanied by his Crusader soul mates. Further albums have included **Larry Carlton** (1978), **Live In Japan** (1979) and, most recently, **Sleepwalk** (1982). He also contributed the guitar work on the 'Hill Street Blues' TV show theme.

Carlton's seemingly effortless virtuosity has not been well balanced by his so-so vocals, although eight bars from his Gibson ES 335 or Valley Arts Stratocaster are alone worth the price of any album.

Recordings:
Singing/Playing (MCA)
Larry Carlton (Warner Bros)
Live In Japan (Warner Bros)
Sleepwalk (Warner Bros)

Chairmen Of The Board

General Norman Johnson had a much-loved hit as lead singer of the Showmen in the early '60s with that New Orleans' anthem to rock 'n' roll, **It Will Stand.** When Holland/Dozier/Holland(▶) left Motown(▶) in 1969 to establish their own Invictus/Hot Wax group of labels, they teamed Johnson up with Eddie Custis (who was to leave after their second album), Danny Woods and Canadian-born Harrison Kennedy as the new company's flagship act under the appropriate name Chairmen Of The Board.

Though they all had turns at lead, it was General Johnson's quirky hiccup-laden style and his superb songs which became increasingly showcased, selling a million-plus copies of **Give Me Just A Little More Time.** Johnson also scored with **You've Got Me Dangling On A String, Pay To The Piper, Everything's Tuesday, Working On A Building Of Love, Elmo James,** the frenetically exciting **Finders Keepers** and the original of **Patches,** a memorable Johnson ballad later covered with great success by Clarence Carter(▶).

Kennedy, Woods and Johnson all went on to cut solo albums of varying quality and Johnson wrote and produced (with Greg Perry) for other Invictus/Hot Wax acts, notably Honey Cone. Harrison having left, Johnson and Woods toured the UK in 1976 with six musicians as Chairmen Of The Board but they were merely trading on past glories and broke the act up immediately after, Johnson having signed to Arista as a solo.

Although short-lived (the group only recorded as a unit for three years), Chairmen Of The Board nevertheless produced a whole crop of brilliant records.

Recordings:
Give Me Just A Little More Time (Invictus)
In Session (Invictus)
Bitter Sweet (Invictus)
Skin I'm In (Invictus)

Chic's Greatest Hits. Courtesy Atlantic Records.

Chic

Sailing in on the coat-tails of mid-

'70s disco, Chic have developed into the most consistently adventurous and satisfying ensemble of that genre. They can claim to be the biggest selling act signed to Atlantic Records(▶)—the label that previously boasted such heavyweights as Otis Redding(▶) and Aretha Franklin(▶).

The meteoric success of the group is due to two marketing ploys: first the sound, a linear jazz chord progression that has proved great to dance to, and, second, the stylish mode-Francais album and publicity concepts. This reached its apex on the international hit single **Good Times** that lyrically paraded a microcosm of their tongue-in-cheek hedonism.

At the nucleus of what is now the Chic Organisation are Bernard Edwards (bass guitar) and Nile Rodgers (lead guitar), who are the songwriting, performing, production and marketing heart of the band. Edwards was born in Greenville, North Carolina, and has lived in New York since he was 10. He studied tenor saxophone in junior high schol, opting for the electric bass upon enrolling in the Performing Arts High School. Rodgers was born on the Triborough Bridge en route to Queens General Hospital and was raised in Greenwich Village, New York, and Hollywood. He played hard rock with New World Rising at Max's Kansas City during his folk era, prior to studying classical music and jazz. He was a regular with the famous Apollo Theatre house band.

The pair met in 1972 in the Big Apple Band, backing New York City who scored on both sides of the Atlantic with **I'm Doing Fine Now**. They toured the US and Europe and cut their own demos. It was in February 1977 that they began work on the rough rhythm of **Everybody Dance**, which was engineered by a DJ friend of theirs, Rob Drake. Adopting the moniker Chic in June of that year, they had some success with **Dance, Dance, Dance**, which was beginning to interest major record labels. Two weeks after backing the vocal group Luther at Radio City, Chic was signed to Atlantic Records.

In the interim period several new faces had entered the line-up as touring and recording members. New York-born drummer Tony

Thompson had spent a year with Labelle(▶) before joining up with Edwards and Rodgers in June '76. Their lead singer, Alfa Anderson, stepped into the limelight after the original lead vocalist, Norma Jean Wright, quit to pursue a solo career.

Born in Augusta, Georgia, Alfa sang on the soundtrack of the film *The Wiz* and has toured the US, Europe and West Africa with Luther and Raw Sugar. The second regular vocalist is Luci Martin, a native New Yorker, who travelled with the touring companies of *Hair* and *Jesus Christ Superstar* before meeting Edwards and Rodgers through her friend Norma Wright.

By the release of their third album, **Risque**, in 1979, Edwards and Rodgers were ready to tackle external production projects. They worked on Sheila B. Devotion's first hit single, **Spacer**, and then embarked on an album to rekindle the flagging career of their fellow Atlantic Records signing, Sister Sledge(▶). The pair wrote, produced and played on all the tracks. The resulting **We Are Family** sounded remarkably like a Chic album and spawned three best-selling singles, including the title track.

By now the duo couldn't put a foot wrong and were drafted in to work with Diana Ross(▶). By all accounts they were turbulent recording sessions and Motown finally took the tapes away and remixed them. The **Diana** set is nevertheless a Chic-produced classic that reinstated the superstar in the pop charts.

More recent projects have turned sour. An album with Johnny Mathis(▶) has been shelved for not being typical of his style, and Debbie Harry's solo album **Koo Koo**, which they produced, bombed out—possibly due to the conflicting musical styles within it.

A second Sister Sledge album and their own **Real People** showed that their records would not automatically chart. The music was as strong as ever but the public wasn't interested. The same fate befell last year's classic **Take It Off** album, for which they rejected strings and brought in a dominant horn section.

Selected recordings:
Risque (Atlantic)

Below: Bassist Stanley Clarke.

Les Plus Grandes Success Du Chic (Atlantic)
Real People (Atlantic)
Take It Off (Atlantic)

Johnny Clarke

Born in Trenchtown, Kingston, Jamaica, in July 1955, Johnny Clarke cut his first disc at 17 with **God Made The Sea And Sun**. It flopped but a year later he gained some recognition with **Everyday Wondering** and **Julie Don't You Know** with producer Rupie Edwards. Clark's breakthrough, like those of many other struggling young reggae singers, came when he met producer Bunny Lee(▶) and a fountain of hits followed: **Enter Into His Gates With Praise, Rock With Me Baby, If You Should Lose Me, None Shall Escape The Judgement, Move Out Of Babylon** and **Joshua's Word**.

Johnny Clarke quickly became the single most important act in the Bunny Lee stable, which in addition sheltered and groomed Cornel Campbell Horace Andy, Derrick Morgan(▶) and Linval Thompson(▶). Clarke was further exalted by being twice voted artist of the year by the readers of Jamaica's *Swing* music magazine.

In 1976, signed to the expanding Virgin Records reggae roster, he defined the mood of mid-70s reggae with the popular **Rockers Time Now** album, issued in July of that year, the title track being a revamp of Hopeton Lewis' rock-steady classic **Take It Easy**. This album and others of that period were called 'flying cymbals' records due to a new drumming technique developed by Sly Dunbar(▶).

Clarke and Lee soldiered on with Virgin in Europe, pumping out many cover versions of popular songs. Marley's(▶) **No Woman No Cry** and **One Love**, Shirley Bassey's **Never, Never, Never** and the Claredonian's **Win Your Love**, prompted Clarke's nickname Mr Do Over Man. His second and final album for Virgin (February 1977) was appropriately titled **Authorised Version**.

Since then Clarke has settled down to cut many satisfying records with Lee, in 1978 re-establishing firm ties with the UK through London's Third World Records, operated by the ubiquitous Count Shelley. It was Shelley who issued the album **King In The Arena** (1978), the title cut being a major reggae hit that proffered many cover versions.

A capable singer, although more popular than influential, Clarke has been a consistent feature of Jamaican music for several years. He recently (1981) topped the UK reggae charts with **Can't Get Enough**.

Recordings:
Put It On (Vulcan)
Rockers Time Now (Virgin)
Johnny Clarke Disco Dub (Attack)
King In The Arena (Third World)
Don't Stay Out Too Late (Paradise)
Showcase (Third World)
Originally Mr Clarke (Clocktower)

Stanley Clarke

Although Stanley Clarke began in jazz, he has been to funk and back, influencing a generation, and taking bass guitar out of the rhythm section and into the spotlight. Along with Jaco Pastorius and Louis Johnson, Clarke treats his

strings in a way that bass guitarists never used to; pulling them, banging them, and moving his hands up the fretboard so quickly he is able to play lead fills.

Born on June 30, 1951, Clarke began with violin and cello, moving on to classical double-bass at age 13. At the Philadelphia Musical Academy he studied classical music but, naturally, was also exposed to the music his peers were listening to; namely, rock, jazz and soul.

In 1970, he went to New York, and although he was due to start college, jumped at the chance to audition for Horace Silver's group. He got the job, staying with Silver until he joined Joe Henderson's band, where he met Chick Corea (▶). Soon after, Clarke and Corea formed Return To Forever, which also included Lenny White on drums, and numerous guitarists, (particularly Al Di Meola.)

Return To Forever made seven supercharged albums during their existence. While with the band, Clarke also played a series of live and recording dates with Pharoah Saunders, Stan Getz, Carlos Santana, Dexter Gordon, Art Blakey and Aretha Franklin(▶)—a wide variety of music, but Clarke could play it all.

During his RTF days Clarke had begun his solo career, frequently using his RTF colleagues. In 1974, his debut, **Stanley Clarke**, appeared on Nemperor, distributed by Atlantic(▶). A year later, his second album, **Journey To Love**, contained something so funky, it had to become an R&B hit single: **Silly Putty** was a jerky instrumental that featured Clarke's bass playing almost a central melody.

On his solo albums, the versatile Clarke experiments with jazz and funk, most noticeably the 1979 live/studio set **I Wanna Play For You**, which included saxophonists Stan Getz and Tom Scott(▶), percussionist Airto Moreira, and guitarist Jeff Beck. Turning his hand to production, Clarke again chose diverse projects: the rock guitar of Roy Buchanan, the jazz/soul fusion singing of Dee Dee Bridgewater(▶).

Rocks, Pebbles and Sand. Courtesy Epic Records.

In 1981, Clarke teamed up with George Duke, and the Clarke/Duke Project toured the world, released an album, and scored a pop hit single with **Sweet Baby**. Soon after, Clarke became part of a Lenny White(▶) project, an album entitled **Echoes Of An Era** that saw current-day jazz heroes revisiting old jazz standards.

Recordings:
Stanley Clarke (Nemperor)
Journey To Love (Nemperor)
Schooldays (Nemperor)
Modern Man (Nemperor/Epic)

I Wanna Play For You (Nemperor/Epic)
Rocks, Pebbles And Sand (Epic)

Merry Clayton

Merry Clayton captured the adulation of rock audiences with her performance as the Acid Queen in the stage version of Pete Townsend's rock opera *Tommy*. Her subsequent solo recordings have shown a consistent tendency to grab at white as well as black markets, perhaps to the detriment of their commercial potential as they have failed to totally please either faction.

But if heavy sales of her own records have largely eluded her, Merry has the consolation of having made a valuable contribution as session singer on the hits of a huge and diverse range of other artists, including Elvis Presley, the Rolling Stones, Ray Charles(▶), the Supremes(▶) and almost every major act which has recorded on the West Coast.

Merry was born in Los Angeles and moved to the West Coast in 1952. In 1962 she recorded a duet, **You're The Reason I'm Living**, with Bobby Darin and enjoyed a hit. Then she joined Ray Charles' backing girl vocalists, the Raelets and married his musical director, the jazz saxophonist Curtis Army.

She left the Raelets to form Sisters Love, who were eventually to record for Motown(▶), but quickly settled for a solo career, interspersed with prolific session work. Her backing vocal on **Gimme Shelter** on the Stones' **Let It Bleed** album was so well received that she cut the song as title track for her debut Ode album.

Recordings:
Gimme Shelter (Ode/A&M)
Merry Clayton (Ode/A&M)

George Clinton

See P. Funk

Billy Cobham

Born in 1944 in Panama, drummer Billy Cobham played with various New York R&B and jazz outfits before joining Miles Davis(▶) in 1968. Leaving Davis after three albums, he had a spell with the jazz-rock aggregation Dreams before joining guitar virtuoso John McLaughlin's Mahavishnu Orchestra. During his spell with Mahavishnu he attracted much attention for his powerfully propulsive style, and was in demand as a session man for artists like James Brown(▶), Herbie Mann and Larry Coryell.

Cobham released his first solo album, **Spectrum**, in 1974. It featured rock guitarist Tommy Bolin and was both critically acclaimed and commercially successful. Cobham then formed a band around horn players the Brecker brothers(▶), and the outfit's three albums, **Crosswinds**, **Total Eclipse** and **Shabazz**, contained excellent material played with fire and imagination.

However, his next band, an all-star aggregation featuring keyboard man George Duke(▶), was not as successful. By now Cobham was aiming at a jazz-funk/disco audience and, despite moments of inspiration, his band often seemed to fall between several musical stools.

The Cobham/Duke band was short-lived, and the release of **Magic** in 1977 saw a return to form which has been maintained on later releases. Cobham continues to be highly regarded both as a drummer/percussionist and as a composer/arranger, and in recent years has been passing on his expertise at Billy Cobham Drum Clinics all over the world.

Recordings:
Spectrum (Atlantic)
Crosswinds (Atlantic)
Total Eclipse (Atlantic)
Shabazz (Atlantic)
Funky Thide Of Sings (Atlantic)
Life And Times (Atlantic)
Live On Tour In Europe (Atlantic)
Magic (Columbia/CBS)

Natalie Cole

Born in 1950 in Los Angeles, the daughter of the great jazz trio leader and, later, popular singer, Nat 'King' Cole(▶), Natalie was unavoidably influenced throughout her childhood by the musical styles of her father and his many musical friends and acquaintances.

She made her first stage appearance at the age of 11, singing **It's A Bore** in a production of *I'm With You* (a black version of *Gigi*) at The Greek Theatre, Los Angeles, in a cast which included her father and Barbara McNair.

Her musical ambitions became even wider after meeting Taj Mahal(▶) at the University of Massachusetts in Amherst. It was he who pointed out the alternatives to the conventional, tailored soul packaging, and she was impressed by his ability to assimilate various black folk styles. Natalie loved Amherst and stayed on for an extra year as a waitress in a club called The Pub. While there she joined a band (which she ended up fronting), who performed around local clubs at weekends. She made her first professional appearance on July 4, 1971.

Natalie credits her father, whom she always preferred to watch from among the audience rather than from behind the stage, as an 'unintentional influence'. In fact, Natalie's musical influences were much more widespread, taking in early Motown(▶), Marvin Gaye(▶), the Supremes(▶), and the Temptations(▶), and the contemporary rock of people like Leon Russell, Janis Joplin and the Allman Brothers. Natalie also kept a keen eye on those she deemed to be her contemporaries: Sly Stone(▶), Donny Hathaway(▶) and the Pointer Sisters(▶). As her club engagements increased, she developed a suitably eclectic repertoire which included **Honky Tonk Women**, **Killing Me Softly**, **You Are The Sunshine Of My Life**, **Que Sera Sera** (à la Sly Stone), and **Mona Lisa** (the only song of her father's that she ever performed).

Her most fateful encounter came when, after a lengthy club tour as a solo artist which began at the Copa Cabana, in 1973, she met Chuck Jackson and Marvin Yancy, while appearing at Mr Kelly's in Chicago, in October 1974. Jackson and Yancy took her to Curtis Mayfield's (▶) Curtom Studios, where they wrote and produced an entire album for her. The result, **Inseparable**, was offered to Capitol, Nat 'King' Cole's old label, and a deal was struck.

Natalie made the most auspicious start possible, the album going straight to the top of the R&B charts and spending more than a year on the pop chart. It also yielded two big hit singles, **This Will Be** and the title track. At the 1976 Grammy Awards, she scooped the New Artist of the Year award and the Best R&B Female Vocal Performance for **This Will Be**. That same year, Natalie and Marvin Yancy were secretly married, further cementing the partnership of Cole, Jackson and Yancy, and Capitol.

Soon Natalie began contributing material to her albums, and for an overnight star who has managed to sustain success over seven albums and a string of hit singles, her repertoire has been amazingly varied: 'I consider myself a singer', she says, 'but not any particular kind of singer. I like to sing everything from Joni Mitchell to Count Basie.'

For Natalie, one of the most gratifying personal aspects of her career to date is that the Cole dynasty continues through Capitol: 'Daddy would have been pleased . . . I think my being on Capitol would have knocked him out.'

Recordings:
Inseparable (Capitol)
Natalie (Capitol)
Unpredictable (Capitol)
Thankful (Capitol)
Natalie . . . Live (Capitol)
I Love You So (Capitol)
Happy Love (Capitol)

Bootsy Collins

See P. Funk

Above: Natalie Cole, talented in her own right—more than a chip off the old block.

135

The Commodores

Since they first began to rumble with the 1974 single and album **Machine Gun**, the Commodores have vied with Earth, Wind & Fire(▶) for the mantle of the world's number-one soul-dance band. It's an unofficial tussle in which they may lately have come off second best, but the Commodores are still a phenomenal force, thanks mainly to the lyrical and melodic power of songwriter Lionel Richie.

The group were formed at college in their common hometown of Tuskegee, Alabama, a heritage of which they are zealously proud. All six members still live in the town, which has a population of only 11,000, and they frequently communicate with each other over CB radio. To round off this picture of internationally famous millionaire pop stars living in small-town domestic bliss, most of the group are married to girlfriends from local school days.

Four of the current line-up met at school, at the Tuskegee Institute: guitarist Thomas McClary, pianist, saxophonist and singer Lionel Richie, and trumpeter William King (recruited from the school's marching band) formed a trio known as the Mystics. When another school band, the Jays, broke up, keyboard player Milan Williams joined the trio, and the four elected to change their name, selecting the word 'commodore' at random from a dictionary.

Along with two short-lived members the four began playing regularly in nearby Montgomery. As their local reputation grew, Tuskegee Institute, increasingly proud of its musical progeny, sent the Commodores to play at a benefit concert at New York's Town Hall.

Here they were spotted by Benjamin Ashburn, a native of Harlem, and a shrewd marketing man with a public relations background. Ashburn made no direct approach to the group at the time, but the following year, aware of his interest, they contacted him, because they were in need of management and career guidance. And guide their career Ashburn did. He auditioned them at Small's Paradise club in Harlem, signed them to a management deal, and without benefit of a recording contract, set about formulating a seven-year plan for projecting the Commodores into international fame. He has become such an integral part of the group's promotion and identity that he is often referred to as 'the seventh Commodore'.

That summer, the two latest recruits left the group (one was drafted) and Richie, King, McClary and Williams were joined by the other two current Commodore members, vocalist and drummer Walter Orange, and bass player Ronald LaPraed.

Suzanne DePasse, vice president at Motown(▶), saw the Commodores at Small's Paradise and from then on their signing with the label was just a matter of time. Meanwhile, DePasse offered them the opportunity to open for Motown superstars the Jackson 5(▶) on a worldwide tour. As a result, The Commodores subsequently headlined in Japan and the Philippines.

In 1972, they signed their recording contract with Motown. Three singles presaged their first album, by which time the group had already established a niche in the specialist soul market. But it was with their fourth single, a simple but frenetic synthesiser instrumental called **Machine Gun**, that their fortunes changed with a vengeance. It was a hit on both sides of the Atlantic, and went gold in the countries in which the group had toured—Japan and the Philippines—vindicating the heavy-touring aspect of Ashburn's masterplan.

With **Machine Gun** creating its own momentum, the group spent the next two years touring with the Rolling Stones and Stevie Wonder(▶). Subsequent single releases —**Superman, I Feel Sanctified** and **Slippery When Wet**—and the two 1975 albums **Caught In The Act** and **Movin' On**, broadened the band's range of music and dominated the soul charts. Hidden among the wave-after-wave of pure attack in the band's dance tracks was the mellifluous charm of Lionel Richie's nascent songwriting skill. Earlier speculative ballad releases like **Sweet Love** and **Just To Be Close To You** had failed to crossover internationally but ballads were soon to be their forté.

After virtually stealing the show while on support to the O'Jays(▶) on a massive 42-city American tour, the Commodores became a headline act. The controlled diversity and maturity of their 1976 album, **Hot On The Tracks** (their first platinum album), primed an international audience for the release, in 1977, of **Commodores** (retitled **Zoom** in the UK) and its star track **Easy**, a drifting, stunningly melodious ballad which not only brought recognition for Richie's songwriting, but also for his warm commanding vocal style. In that same year, the Commodores received some welcome additional publicity, co-starring with the then

Above: The superb Commodores.

reigning disco queen, Donna Summer(▶), in the film *Thank God It's Friday*, and contributing to the soundtrack with their up-tempo stomper **Too Hot To Trot**.

After an obligatory live album in 1977, the LP **Natural High**, in 1978, provided ultimate proof of Richie's worth as a sentient balladeer. The majestic **Three Times A Lady** went double platinum in the US, while in the UK it became Motown's biggest ever single. Richie apparently began writing the song during a group soundcheck, at which his father was present: 'He told me that in 35 years of marriage, he'd never told my mother how much she meant to him. I decided I wasn't going to wait 35 years to tell my wife, Brenda.'

The song garnered several international awards from music publications and institutions and highlighted the latent affinity between soul and country music, with Richie winning the ASCAP Nashville Country Songwriter Award. Richie has since written massive hits for country superstar Kenny Rogers.

Richie's ballads became as much a mainstay of the group's appeal as the up-tempo dance material, and The Commodores have maintained the balance through the subsequent albums, **Midnight Magic** and **Heroes**. **Still** was an attempt to repeat the success of **Three Times A Lady**, and Richie has even tried his hand at lavishly produced pure gospel with **Jesus Is Love**. Outside The Commodores, he duetted with Diana Ross(▶) to score a huge hit with his self-penned theme tune to the movie *Endless Love*.

Recordings:
Machine Gun (Motown)
Caught In The Act (Motown)
Movin' On (Motown)
Hot On The Tracks (Motown)
Commodores/Zoom (Motown)
Live! (Motown)
Natural High (Motown)
Greatest Hits (Motown)
Midnight Magic (Motown)
Heroes (Motown)

Con Funk Shun

In 1968, high-school friends Mike Cooper and Louis McCall formed a band called Project Soul. For three years, the band gigged around their home state of California. In 1972, they moved to Memphis and changed their name to Con Funk Shun. Over the next few years, they backed many famous Stax Records(▶) artists and when the company allowed them studio time of their own they cut two singles for the Memphis label Fretone Records, owned by one-time Stax president, Estelle Axton.

In 1976, they signed to Mercury Records, and their debut arrived in the same year. From their second album, **Secrets**, released in 1977, came the No. 1 American soul single **Ffun**.

In terms of stage shows, their brand of horny funk was comparable to the Ohio Players(▶), the Commodores and Kool and the Gang(▶), but they were never able to crossover with their singles.

Their third album, **Loveshine**, was released in 1978, and again there was a No.1 soul hit, **Shake And Dance With Me**. This pattern continued through the '70s and into the '80s with soul hits like **Chase Me, Let Me Put Love On Your Mind, Da Lady** and **Lady's Wild**. Throughout the decade or so of their existence, their line-up has been surprisingly stable: Michael Cooper, lead vocals, guitar, sitar; Karl Fuller, trumpet, flugelhorn, trombone; Paul Harrell, soprano and tenor saxophones, flute; Cedric Martin, bass guitar; Louis McCall, drums; Felton Pilate II, lead vocals, trombone, keyboards, guitar; and Danny Thomas, keyboards.

Recordings:
Secrets (Mercury)
Loveshine (Mercury)
Candy (Mercury)
Spirit Of Love (Mercury)
Touch (Mercury)

The Congos

Formed in Kingston, Jamaica, in February 1976, the Congos consist of lead vocalist Cedric Myton (ex-Bell Star, the Tartans and Royal Rasses(▶); 'Ashanti' Roy Johnson, tenor vocals, occasional actor and now solo performer, and Watty Burnett, baritone vocals, who had previously cut musical teeth with Jimmy Cliff(▶) and Bob Marley(▶).

They cut the album **Congo** at Harry J's Studio in Kingston, but came to international attention when the UK based Go-Feet label issued the quintessential 1979 Lee Perry(▶) produced **Heart Of The Congos** set.

Recordings:
Heart Of The Congos (—/Go Feet)

Norman Connors

Born in Philadelphia on March 1, 1948, Connors came to prominence as a much-sought-after jazz drummer in the mid-to-late '60s. After stints with avant-garde doyens

Take It To The Limit. Courtesy Pye Records.

Archie Shepp and the late John Coltrane, Connors joined the Pharoah Sanders group, appearing on four albums. By the early '70s he had organised his own group, and in 1972 signed to Buddah records. He became highly influenced by the then current vogue for soft ethereal balladeering that was dominating the soul charts (Stylistics(▶), Chi-Lites(▶), Delfonics(▶), etc.,). He began experimenting with a combination of voices and almost cocktail-lounge jazz with his third Buddah album **Slewfoot**, but reaped the full reward with the 1976 release **You Are My Starship**, which included several hit singles, among them the title track and **Betcha By Golly Wow**.

In 1978 he signed to Arista where his influence began to wane after the **This Is Your Life** album. His last album, **Take It To The Limit**, was released in 1980 since when he has concentrated on production. Among the vocalists who came to prominence via Connors' leadership are Dee Dee Bridgewater(▶) Michael Henderson, Jean Carn and Phyllis Hyman(▶).

Recordings:
Slewfoot (Buddah/—)
You Are My Starship
 (Buddah/Pye)
The Best Of Norman Connors
 (Arista/Buddah)
This Is Your Life (Arista/Buddah)

The Controllers

This Miami-based four-piece vocal group, whose reputation and respect within musical circles has so far exceeded their commercial success, was formed in 1965 in their hometown of Fairfield, Alabama.

They waited nine years for their first single success, an anguished ballad, **Somebody's Gotta Win, Somebody's Gotta Lose**, delivered in timbrous deep-soul style by lead singer Reginald McArthur. They were produced on TK subsidiary Juana by Frederick Knight(▶).

Recordings:
In Control (Juana/—)
Fill Your Life With Love
 (Juana/—)

Below: Norman Connors, settled for 'cocktail-lounge-jazz'.

Above: Keyboard wizard Chick Corea played a leading role on Miles Davis' Bitches Brew *classic before launching Return to Forever.*

Chick Corea

Brought up in Massachusetts, keyboards player Chick Corea (born 1941) moved to New York in 1960 and spent the next decade building an impressive reputation as a jazz session man. In 1969, he joined Miles Davis(▶), playing an important part on many of his most influential albums, including **In A Silent Way** and **Bitches Brew**.

The beginning of Corea's band, Return To Forever, was actually a 1972 solo album of that name featuring bassist Stanley Clarke(▶), drummer Lenny White(▶) and other star musicians. An electric expedition into territory that covered Latin, jazz and rock, **Return To Forever** set the tone for a series of albums that continued through the '70s. Their quality varies from undeniably brilliant to occasionally tedious, but as examples of what can be done within the jazz-rock genre they are always worthy of attention.

Guitarist Al DiMeola joined Return To Forever in 1974, and he, White and Clarke have since established considerable reputations as solo performers.

Corea, a frequent recipient of jazz poll awards, has moved confidently between mainstream jazz and jazz-rock since the demise of RTF. Amongst his most recent work is a superb album dedicated to Duke Ellington and John Coltrane, **Three Quartets**.

Recordings:
Return To Forever (ECM)
Hymn Of The Seventh Galaxy
 (Polydor)
No Mystery (Polydor)
Romantic Warrior
 (Columbia/CBS)
Musicmagic (Columbia/CBS)
Live (Columbia/CBS)

Solo:
Light As A Feather (Polydor)
Where Have I Known You Before
 (Polydor)
Three Quartets (Warner Bros.)

Hank Crawford

After first coming to prominence as musical director and saxophone soloist in Ray Charles'(▶) big band (switching from baritone to alto), Benny Ross 'Hank' Crawford (born Memphis, Tennessee, December 21, 1934) formed his own seven-piece band in 1963. He soon became a prolific recording artist in his own right, being an early exponent of the jazz-funk idiom, notably on sax though he has also recorded on piano.

Crawford's mood-laced style has always had a strong R&B/blues flavour, and a steady stream of albums, on first Atlantic(▶) (10 or so sets) and then Creed Taylor's Kudu(▶) label, established a firm reputation.

Recordings:
Mr Blues (Atlantic/—)
After Hours (Atlantic/—)
Help Me Make It Through The Night (Kudu)
We Got A Good Thing Going (Kudu)
Don't You Worry 'Bout A Thing (Kudu)
Cajun Sunrise (Kudu)

Randy Crawford

Born in Macon, Georgia, in 1952, Randy Crawford was brought up in Cincinnati, Ohio, although her vocal style retains the 'deep soul' essence of her birth State. She began, in common with countless other soul vocalists, to perform and perfect her art at school and in church. By the age of 15 she was performing regularly at a Cincinnati nightclub.

On holiday from school, between her junior and senior years, she was engaged to play for two weeks at a club in St Tropez, France. This engagement was extended to three months and resulted in Randy being offered management and recording contracts on the spot. Resisting the allure of instant stardom on the French Riviera, Randy returned to the States and resumed her school career. However, even before graduating, she was playing six nights a week at Cincinnati's Buccaneer club. It was there that she was spotted by an East Coast talent scout and signed up to perform in New York where she later met and sang with George Benson(▶).

In 1972, she signed a management contract with John Levy, who also managed the alto saxophonist Cannonball Adderley(▶). Randy was guest vocalist on Adderley's last album, **Big Man.** In 1973, Levy took her to the music capital, Los Angeles, where two years later she made her first important move, away from the club circuit and into the international arena.

The occasion was a concert by a group of jazz all-stars (including Joe Sample of the Crusaders(▶)), under the ad hoc title World Jazz Association, given in front of a capacity five-and-a-half thousand audience at the city's Shrine Auditorium. The show was mainly in honour of the recently deceased Adderley, and Randy did a set which included a recreation of her role as 'Carolina' on the **Big Man** album. The show was recorded and some of Randy's set was used as the basis for her first album, including a flawless and emotive rendition of Bernard Igher's modern jazz standard **Everything Must Change**, conducted by Quincy Jones(▶).

With the release of the **Everything Must Change** album on Warner Brothers, and capitalising on the momentum created by her rapturous reception at the Shrine, Randy formed her own five-piece band and undertook her first

lections of her, Randy was chosen.

The song, **Street Life**, from the album of the same name, was one of the Crusaders' most potent, evocative and, above all, commercial releases and, with Randy's searing heroic vocal, it gave the band their biggest ever international success for both the single and album. The vocal on the single **Street Life** was uncredited, but the interest generated by Randy's performance was sufficient to popularise her name. Furthermore, her association with the Crusaders continued. She accompanied them on two European tours, opening the show with her own set, then returning to join the band for the climatic **Street Life.**

Between the two tours, the Crusaders produced Randy's next album **Now We May Begin**, from which the Joe Sample ballad, **One Day I'll Fly Away**, became Randy's first major solo hit. It earned her the Most Outstanding Performance award at the influential Tokyo Music Festival of 1980, with the Best Song award going to Sample.

This symbolic relationship came to an end when Randy turned to veteran producer Tommy LiPuma to take the helm on her next album, **Secret Combination.** (It was LiPuma's deft commercial jazz production which brought Randy's old colleague George Benson to international prominence with the albums **Breezin** and **In Flight**). Randy immediately consolidated her reputation with the pensive Tom Snow/Nan O'Byrne composition **You Might Need Somebody** .

Recordings:
Miss Randy Crawford (Warner Bros)
Raw Silk (Warner Bros)
Now We May Begin (Warner Bros)
Secret Combination (Warner Bros)
Windsong (Warner Bros)

Andrae Crouch

Born in Los Angeles into a family steeped in religion, Andrae Crouch was perhaps destined to evolve into a leading light in contemporary gospel music. He and his twin sister Sandra had a devoutly Christian upbringing, and their entwined musical career first blossomed with a group emerging from the choir of the Church of God In Christ. The COGIC, who included Billy Preston(▶), Edna Wright (later Honeycone(▶)), Gloria Jones, Sandra 'Blinky' Williams (later with Motown(▶)) and Frankie Spring, as well as the Crouch twins, gained some popularity around LA, and cut an album for Vee Jay(▶).

Andrae then pursued his education further, though continuing to sing, and soon teamed with Perry Morgan to form the nucleus of a new group named the Disciples. This aggregation diverged from traditional gospel styles to build an image which carried them to a new audience, and Andrae Crouch & the Disciples, contracted to Light Records, began to sell records and gain appeal by using more secular funky rhythms in support of their sacred message. Crouch became the first gospel artist signed to Warner Bros' fledgling gospel wing in 1981.

Recordings:
This Is Another Day (Word/DJM)
Live In London (Word/DJM)

Crown Heights Affair

Four 14-year-olds from Bedford-Stuyvesant, New York City, appearing together as Neu Day Express, happened to meet producers/writers/arrangers Freida Nerangis and Britt Britton. The

result was a contract with De-Lite Records, a change of name to Crown Heights Affair, and the formation of an eight-piece commercial funk group.

William Anderson, guitar; Muki Wilson, bass; Raymond Rock, drums and lead vocals; Bert Reid, tenor sax; Raymond Reid, trombone; Howard Young, keyboards; James Baynard, trumpet; and Phil Thomas, lead vocals, produced four hit singles—**Dreaming A Dream, Every Beat Of My Heart, Foxy Foxy,** and **Dancin'**—with their first two albums. With De-Lite having signed a distribution deal with Phonogram, the 1978 release of their third album, **Dream World**, gave them an international pop hit, **Galaxy Of Love.**

For their next album Skip Boardley replaced Howard Young and they had a further hit with **Dance Lady Dance** (1979). Hoping a change of producer might yield even sweeter fruits, Bert DeCoteaux stepped in for their fifth album **Sure Shot** and **You Gave Me Love** scored in 1980.

Unlike De-Lite stablemates Kool And The Gang(▶), CHA output has of late been unspectacular, members choosing to move into production of other acts.

Recordings:
Foxy Foxy (De-Lite/Polydor)
Dot It Your Way (De-Lite/Polydor)
Dream World (De-Lite/Mercury)
Dance Lady Dance (De-Lite/Mercury)

Culture

Culture (Joseph Hill, lead vocals, and Albert 'Ralph' Walker and Kenneth Paley, harmonies) leapt into the reggae vocal group arena occupied by the Mighty Dia-

Below: Randy Crawford, a genuine '70s and '80s superstar.

Secret Combination. Courtesy Warner Bros Records.

national tour of the States. Retaining the same small jazz combo formula, Randy released two further albums: **Miss Randy Crawford** in 1977, with producer Bob Montgomery, and in 1979 **Raw Silk**, a compact showcase produced by Stephen Goldman and highlighted by a spine-tingling interpretation of Jerry Butler's(▶) **I Stand Accused.** The album also gave Randy her first writer credit for **I Got Myself A Happy Song.**

So far Randy's albums had only been released in the States, but Warners were prompted to release **Raw Silk** in Britain and Europe (and later **Everything Must Change** and **Miss Randy Crawford**) because of her success with the Crusaders. They were on the look-out for a guest singer for one of their rare vocal tracks and because of Sample's personal recol-

monds(▶) and the Heptones(▶) in 1977 with their most celebrated single to date, **Two Sevens Clash**, a stark foreboding prophecy of civilisation in chaos. In every way this single and the subsequent album encapsulated the spiritual definition of the word culture—a word fundamental to Rastafarians who seek to discover their cultural roots in Africa.

Central to the single that topped reggae charts in Jamaica and Britain, garnering favour in New York too, are the songwriting and voice of group protagonist Joseph Hill. This tall gangly boss-eyed man fuses the voice of Burning Spear(▶), the songwriting ability of Bob Marley(▶) and the philosophy of black militant Marcus Garvey. This winning formula quickly established Culture in the first division of Caribbean music and they were snapped up by the UK's reggae-hungry Front Line subsidiary of Richard Branson's Virgin Records.

Hill began his recording career as a solo artist in 1972 cutting a single, **Behold The Land**, at Jamaica's Studio One(▶). It was released by producer Clement Coxsone Dodd when Culture became popular. Although they have slipped in grace from the days of their chart domination, the group will be remembered for the extremely prolific and artistically gratifying period between **Two Sevens Clash** and 1979, when five first-rate albums slotted into the charts.

At the turn of the decade—about the time Virgin pulled the plug on reggae—Hill and his producer Sonia Pottinger came to a creative impasse, and although Culture's infrequent live performances continued to sell out, their languid recordings failed to please.

A single with the British Kingdom label showed that Hill had not lost all of his creative genius. **Disobedient Children** sold well enough for Culture to return to the studio to cut an album, the first new material in over two years.

Recordings:
Two Sevens Clash (—/Lightning)
Cumbole (—/Front Line)
Innocent Blood (Joe Gibbs/—)

Miles Davis

Miles Davis's own music has been majestic, his influence on others—not least the dozens of superb musicians who have played in his various bands—immeasurable. He is not only one of the all-time greats of the jazz world, his impact has been felt in the worlds of funk, soul and rock as well.

Born in Illinois in 1926, Miles Dewey Davis began his career playing alongside Charlie Parker and a host of other modern-jazz greats in the seminal Billy Eckstine(▶) Band. When Parker left to form his own quintet, Davis went with him and they worked together until 1948. Davis then teamed with arranger Gil Evans and formed his own band.

Though a commercial failure and only lasting a few months, this band did cut the classic **Birth Of The Cool** album, for Capitol, which featured the imaginative arrangements of a young white jazz musician, Gerry Mulligan.

In the early '50s, Davis's trumpet led several groups featuring many of the great musicians of the day, including Sonny Rollins, J. J. Johnson and Art Blakey. In 1955, he

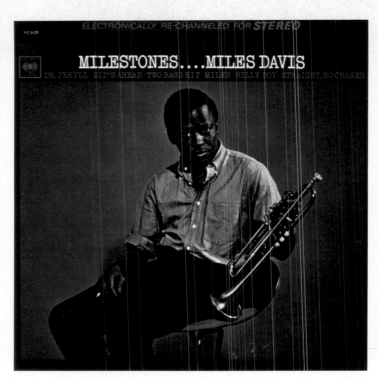

Milestones. Courtesy Columbia Records.

formed his legendary Miles Davis Quintet with the late John Coltrane, Red Garland, Paul Chambers and Philly Joe Jones, cutting the memorable **Working** and **Steaming** albums for Prestige.

In 1959 Davis made **Kind Of Blue** (Columbia) with Cannonball Adderley(▶) and Bill Evans—an album regarded by many as his finest. In an orchestral setting, with Gil Evans' arrangements, he cut the brilliant **Miles Ahead, Porgy And Bess** and **Sketches Of Spain** sets, also for Columbia. At that period, his group included Herbie Hancock(▶), George Coleman, Ron Carter and Tony Williams, an aggregation which cut **Four And More.**

When tenor saxophonist Wayne Shorter joined Davis in the mid-'60s, the style of the band was changing direction, leaning heavily on the progressive rock music of the West Coast, with an emphasis on electric bass and electric piano. At one time, Davis was featuring three electric keyboards (played by Herbie Hancock, Chick Corea(▶) and Joe Zawinul(▶)) plus British electric guitarist John McLaughlin.

Heard to good effect on **In A Silent Way, Bitches Brew**, and other Columbia albums, this electric band was the most commercially successful Miles Davis ever led and won him accolades as a hero of the rock movement, starring at the major rock venues and concerts (captured on **Live At The Fillmore**). Davis continued in this direction right through till 1977. He then went into a retirement which lasted till 1981, when he re-emerged to record **The Man With The Horn** for Columbia but, sadly, this set lacked his earlier magic and was not very well received.

Recordings:
Birth Of The Cool (Capitol)
Kind Of Blue (Columbia/CBS)
Milestones (Columbia/CBS)
Sketches Of Spain (Columbia/CBS)
Nefertiti (Columbia/CBS)
Bitches Brew (Columbia/CBS)
In A Silent Way (Columbia/CBS)

Right: Miles Davis. A dynamic influence.

Defunkt

Totally dominated by trombonist/leader Joe Bowie, Defunkt are a New York-based six-piece with a uniquely iconoclastic approach to what more orthodox even-tempered soul bands would call funk.

From a base of pure jazz (he's the brother of jazz trumpeter Lester), Bowie presides over a sizzling cauldron of all the toughest elements of contemporary East Coast black music. But even amid the seemingly haphazard bilious crossfire of such tunes as **The Razor's Edge**, the individual solos, particularly from guitarist Kelvyn Bell, are tight, meticulous and virtuously short.

At the age of 15, Bowie was backing various blues artists, including Little Milton(▶) and Albert King(▶), in his hometown of St Louis. He subsequently co-led such jazz aggregations as the St Louis Creative Ensemble and Human Arts Ensemble. Seeking greater exposure, Bowie moved to New York where with the assistance of his jazz-trained confederates, he began assimilating and interpreting the air of steely urban danger which now pervades Defunkt's music.

Recordings:
Defunkt (Hannibal)

William DeVaughn

An ex-government draft technician from Washington DC, DeVaughn graduated from local Washington outfits to have his biggest solo success with his first release, the self-penned and funded **Be Thankful For What You've Got**, in 1974. A devout Jehova's Witness, DeVaughn unashamedly bases his smooth melodic style on that of his premier influence, Curtis Mayfield(▶).

Recordings:
Be Thankful For What You've Got (Omega/Chelsea)

The Mighty Diamonds

Currently one of the most popular reggae vocal groups recording, the Diamonds (as they were originally known) surfaced in the Trenchtown ghetto of Kingston, Jamaica, in the latter half of the '60s. Donald 'Tabby' Shaw, lead vocals, and Fitzroy 'Bunny' Simpson and Lloyd 'Judge' Ferguson, harmonies, spread their reputation for soft, soulful closely-knit vocal arrangements at talent shows, prior to entering a recording studio in 1969 with producer Rupei Edwards to make **Girl You Are Too Young**. Bunny had previously sung alongside Jah Lloyd in the Mediators.

By the turn of the decade Lloyd was entering record production and he invited the trio to work with

him. Other producers interested in the Diamonds were Stranger Cole, Derrick Harriot(▶) and hitmaker Bunny Lee with whom they made their UK chart breakthrough, **Jah Jah Bless The Dreadlocks**. In 1975 they made a move that not only showered them with international acclaim, but put a new producer and his studio on the reggae map. Jo Jo Hookim and his brother Ernest, the engineer at the Channel One studio, had assembled an in-house band, the Revolutionaries(▶), revolving around the distinctive rim-shot drumming of Sly Dunbar(▶).

The Diamonds sang two Stylistics(▶) songs, **Country Living** and **Hey Girl**, prior to recording the song that gave them national prominence, **Right Time**. Written by the group and extolling the prophecies of Marcus Garvey over a rock-steady rhythm, its effect was shattering. Suddenly everyone wanted Channel One and Diamonds records. Singles **Jailhouse, Have Mercy, Why Me Black Brother Why** and **Them Never Love Poor Marcus** were snapped up and the following year Britain's Virgin Records released the **Right Time** album.

In November of that year, the group went to New Orleans to work with R&B producers Allen Toussaint (▶) and Marshall Seahorn. An album **Ice On Fire** contained some group compositions and their renditions of Toussaint's **Sneakin' Sally Through The Alley** and **Get Out Of My Life Woman**. Despite its obvious commerciality it alienated their fans and flopped.

Reuniting with the Hookim brothers in 1978, the Mighty Diamonds recorded one of their favourite songs, **Tell Me What's Wrong,** which utilised the rhythm of Dennis Brown's(▶) Studio One(▶) hit **No Man Is An Island**.

After a two-year sabbatical the group returned to chart prominence in 1981 with the exquisite **Pass The Kouchie** and the album from whence it came, **Changes,**

Reggae Street. Courtesy Shanachie Records.

co-produced and co-ordinated by Gussie Clarke. Their songwriting was better than ever and their harmonies loaded with emotion.

Recordings:
Right Time (—/Virgin)
Planet Mars Dub (—/Virgin)
Changes (Music Works/Rough Trade)
Reggae Street (Shanachie/—)

Manu Dibango

Born in Douala, Cameroon, in 1934, Dibango was introduced to music, like so many of his American counterparts, through attending church as a child. His parents were both choristers and young Manu followed suit. At the age of 15, he

Below: Manu Dibango grooves to his Afro rhythms.

came to Europe where he took up the piano and began seriously studying music theory and harmony.

His acquaintance with the soprano saxophone came about in the early '50s when, after spending the summer as a counsellor at a children's camp for young Africans, he was presented with a saxophone as a gift from one of his young charges.

Feeling that he had at last found his true instrument, he signed his first recording contract in Brussels, in 1952. He subsisted on a broadly jazz-based output until, in 1960, almost 10 years after leaving Africa, he encountered a group of Congolese musicians and decided to return to African music. He subsequently returned to Africa itself, where he fully rediscovered the roots of his developing Afro style. Based in Zaire, he soon found fame throughout the entire African continent.

Back in Europe, Dibango released, and had moderate success with, a string of single releases, such as **Salt Pop Corn** and **Soukouss,** and early Afro-jazz dance albums like **O Boso**.

Titling his music Afro-Quelque Chose (Afro-Something), he tapped the mainstream of the developing disco scene throughout the '70s with tracks like **Soul Makossa, Big Blow** and **Sun Explosion**. The unbridled exuberance of such early recordings was suffused when Dibango signed to Island Records, where his albums **Gone Clear** and **Ambassador** maintained a clever but low-key linkage between Afro rhythms and jazz rock instrumentals, and also brought in a mellow jazzy reggae style with tracks like **Kumbale Style** and **Night Jet**.

Recordings:
Manu Dibango (Decca/—)
Afrovision (Decca/Island)
Gone Clear (Island/—)

Dillinger

Lloyd Bullock (aka Dillinger) surfaced on the Jamaican sound-system(▶) circuit in early '70s

with a unique style of toasting, using the microphone to expound complete stories, his subject matter running the gamut of youth culture.

Another DJ, Dennis Al Capone, spotted young Bullock's talent and invited him to perform an occasional slot with El Paso Sound. This led to a tentative recording for Prince Tony's High School International, which issued his first single, **Fat Beef Skank**.

Working with producers Yabby U, at Channel One, and Coxsone Dodd(▶), at Studio One(▶), widespread notoriety ensued with Bullock's definitive singles **CB200** (an ode to his own Japanese motorbike), **Plantation Heights** and **Cocaine In My Brain**. After the release of **Cocaine** . . . (1976) he discovered a new and previously

Above: Dillinger . . . Dreadlocks image and witty toasting.

untapped audience with the emergent punk scene in Britain.

He signed to A&M Records (1981) who, with an eye on the expanding reggae market in America, put him in a studio with producer Larry Sevitt to record **Melting Pot**, a leaden collection of songs that lacked the wit and

Bionic Dread. Courtesy Island Records.

drama of earlier works. Still trading upon his own legend he recently became the model for Anthony Waldren (aka Lone Ranger), the only other Jamaican DJ to successfully imitate his wonderfully deranged style.

Recordings:
Ready Natty Dread (Winro/—)
Badder Than Them (A&M)
Top Ranking Dillinger (—/Third World)

The Dramatics

One of the greatest vocal groups of all time, the Dramatics have amazingly never had a hit outside of

Above: Always tremendous live performers, the Dramatics are working hard to recapture former glories.

America. Formed in 1964 in Detroit and featuring Ron Banks, Lenny Demps, Larry Reed, Rod Davis, Elbert Wilkins and Robert Ellington, they originally signed to Motown(▶) in 1964 but were never recorded and soon joined the smaller Golden World label which during 1965 was giving Berry Gordy some cause for concern. They released several singles, including the (UK) Northern soul(▶) favourite **Inky Dinky Wang Dang Doo**, before Gordy bought the entire company and closed it down.

In 1966 The Dramatics signed with Sport Records and had their first minor hit in 1967 with **All Because Of You**. In 1968 they met Detroit-producer Don Davis, who signed them to Memphis-based Stax(▶) label, but success eluded them and the group was dropped when the label was sold to Paramount Films in 1969.

After much line-up changing and near disbandment the group was introduced to writer Tony Hester. With the departure of Ellington, Reed and Davis and the arrival of William Howard, the new Dramatics—under the guidance of Hester and Don Davis—re-signed to the once again independent Stax and hit paydirt in 1971 with the joyfully uplifting **Watcha See Is Watcha Get**, a No. 3 soul and No. 9 pop hit. The follow-up **Get On Up And Get Down** was also a smash and their third Stax outing was the classic **In The Rain**, a No. 5 pop and No. 1 soul hit in April 1972. Other pop and soul hits followed in 1973, **Toast To The Fool**, **Hey You Get Off My Mountain** and **Fell For You**. Like fellow Detroiters the Temptations(▶), the Dramatics mixed their sweet soul titles with message songs, often with an anti-drugs flavour, viz **Beware Of The Man With The Candy In His Hand** and **The Devil Is Dope**.

By 1974 the Stax empire was crumbling and rather than renew their contract the group joined forces with another Davis-produced outfit, the Dells(▶), for a one-off outing **The Dells Vs The Dramatics** on the Chess(▶) subsidiary Cadet, a classic album of the '70s which gave them one more hit with **Door To Your Heart**.

In 1973 L. J. Reynolds and Lenny Mayes had joined to replace Wilkins, giving the group two writers and producers of immense talent in Reynolds and Banks. During the Cadet period they recorded enough tracks with Davis to make another album and signed to ABC. **Dramatic Jackpot, Drama V,** and **Joy Ride** were all smash albums. When ABC was sold to MCA in the late '70s the group remained, although their excursions into disco were mainly facile. By 1980 their albums were losing sales and although their soul chart status was still great, pop crossover eluded them. In the same year Ron Banks began outside production with the Five Special and L. J. Reynolds went solo on Capitol Records.

10½ and **The Dramatic Way** were the last MCA albums and although a splendid return to form, neither sold enough to tempt them to stay. The group signed with Capitol Records in 1982 and were set to make a full return to hit status. Consistency has always been their byword.

Recordings:
Dramatic Experience (Stax)
Best Of The Dramatics (Stax)
Whatcha See Is Watcha Get (Stax)
Drama V (ABC)
The Dells Vs The Dramatics (Cadet/—)
Dramatic Jackpot (ABC)
10½ (MCA)
The Dramatic Way (MCA/—)
New Dimension (Capitol/—)

Mikey Dread

Born Michael Campbell in Port Antonio, Jamaica, in 1954, Dread joined the Jamaican Broadcasting Corporation as an engineer, but quickly graduated to presenting his own reggae show, and subsequently cut his first single, **Love The Dread,** for his own Dread At The Controls label (1977).

He made his name as a DJ/toaster (1981) with the now infamous **Jumping Master** rhythm cut with Roots Radics. He has subsequently re-recorded many versions of the same rhythm, most of them contained on **Master Showcase** (1981). Currently he is experimenting with sing/jay—a combination of singing and toasting.

Recordings:
Dread At The Controls
  (Evolutionary Rockers/Trojan)
World War Three (—/DATC)

George Duke

Californian George Duke (born 1946) has encompassed the full spectrum of music in his career, from his heady days as a youngster with Jean-Luc Ponty, to his current work with Stanley Clarke(▶). Duke's early influence was jazz, and he was prompted in his enthusiasm by a Duke Ellington concert. 'After the performance, I was screaming at mother to get me a piano', recollects Duke.

At high school, he worked with a variety of groups, before starting his own jazz trio, which worked at a local club in San Francisco. His education was furthered at the San Francisco Conservatory where he majored in trombone and composition, and minored in piano.

Duke's trio continued to work local nightspots, and frequently backed visiting jazz musicians and singers, including Bobby Hutcherson and Sam Rivers. The first of Duke's excursions into full-time music was with the Don Ellis Big Band, and then, after persistent communication with Jean-Luc Ponty's producer, he was hired to record in Los Angeles with Ponty, who also took him on his American tour.

Ponty and Duke played a variety of dates, including some rock venues. The lack of an acoustic piano forced Duke onto an electric keyboard at one such gig. He liked the club's sound, and decided to record there shortly afterwards. At this session he was seen by Frank Zappa, who invited him to join the Mothers Of Invention. The band's mixture of doo-wop, rock and jazz puzzled Duke: 'One day, we'd be working with a symphony orchestra, the next, hammering out rock 'n' roll', he says.

After a year with Zappa, Duke replaced Joe Zawinul in Cannonball Adderley's(▶) band, but he rejoined the Mothers in 1972, adding synthesisers and vocals to his repertoire. Jean-Luc Ponty was also with the band at this time. When the by then primarily jazz-influenced Mothers disbanded, Duke joined forces with Billy Cobham(▶) in a short-lived project. He then began developing his own group, which resulted in the 1977 album **From Me To You**. Duke has half-a-dozen solo albums to his credit but although his solo career has progressed satisfactorily, (notably the **A Brazilian Love Affair** hit single) the chance to work with other musicians still appeals to him.

His latest collaboration is with Stanley Clarke, as the Clarke/Duke Project. They had previously worked together on Duke's debut album in 1977, and the follow-up, **Reach For It,** a year later. Duke has also ventured successfully into production work, including Dee Dee Bridgewater's(▶) **Bad For Me** album.

Recordings:
From Me To You (Epic)
Reach For It (Epic)
Don't Let Go (Epic)
Follow The Rainbow (Epic)
Master Of The Game (Epic)
A Brazilian Love Affair (Epic)
Clarke/Duke Project (Epic)

Below: George Duke. No longer screaming.

Sly Dunbar & Robbie Shakespeare

In a genre dominated by producers, and where musicians are invariably relegated to the second division as a consequence of the kudos given to singers, drummer Sly (Noel Charles) Dunbar and his bass-guitarist partner Robbie (Robert) Shakespeare have done much to redress the balance. Furthermore, they can be heard on more modern reggae records than any other musicians and in developing new styles and techniques discovered a hit sound identifiably their own.

Born on May 10, 1952, Dunbar— he obtained the nickname Sly because of his taste for Sly Stone's(▶) music—joined his first band at the age of 15 on leaving school. The Yardbrooms led to RHT Invincibles, the Volcanoes and Skin, Flesh and Bones (subsequently called the Revolutionaries(▶)), with whom he stayed for four years during a residency at Jamaica's 'Tit For Tat' Club.

Dunbar's first recording was the international hit **Double Barrel** with Dave and Ansel Collins. Other important session contributions included Joy White's **The First Cut Is The Deepest**, the Upsetters'(▶) **Night Doctor** and a reggae interpretation of James and Bobby Purify's(▶) **I'm Your Puppet,** with Jimmy London.

Employed by producer Jo Jo Hookim at the Channel One studio, the Revolutionaries, featuring Dunbar's bold double-time rimshot drumming, revamping Studio One(▶) rhythms, quickly became the toast of Jamaica. Later Dunbar was joined by Shakespeare who had also been apprenticed in many styles of music from a residency at another nightclub. Their friendship cemented during a spell with the Aggrovators. As the most in-demand drum and bass team in reggae they have never been unemployed since. Establishing themselves as musicians and arranger/producers on the Mighty Dia-monds'(▶) **The Right Time** album, the duo have worked with scores of other artists including Gregory Isaacs(▶), Bunny Wailer(▶), Johnny Clarke(▶), Dennis Brown(▶) and Wailing Souls(▶).

Sly 'n Robbie, as they were now known, began working on their own projects, developing the mechanical rhythms utilised by premier band Black Uhuru(▶) and the reggae/funk backdrop of Grace Jones'(▶) androgynous dance music. These projects, and their relaunching of the Taxi label, have made them the most potent production team in reggae.

Recent recordings with Island Records' house band Compass Point All Stars and Gwen Guthrie suggest imminent crossover into general pop music.

Recordings:
Sensimilla (Black Uhuru) (Island)
Nightclubbing (Grace Jones) (Island)
Sly And Robbie Present Taxi (Taxi)
Sly Wicked And Slick (Virgin)

Errol Dunkley

Born in Jamaica in 1950, Dunkley began singing at the age of nine as a regular competitor in weekly talent shows held at the Queens Club, West Kingston, and was singing professionally at 11.

Initially signed to Prince Buster's(▶) label and singing with Junior English in the School Boys vocal group, he stimulated local interest when he cut a version of Gloria Lynn's **You're Gonna Need Me** and later, **You're Lying Girl,** both for producer Joe Gibbs and issued on the Amalgamated label.

During the mid-'60s he teamed up with producer Rupie Edwards and Gregory Isaacs to create the African Museum co-operative label. He subsequently scored with the singles **Movie Star** and **Three In One,** a medley of his hits with Gibbs.

By 1973 Dunkley was becoming recognised as both a singer with a seductive timbre to his voice and as a songwriter with flair. Turning down an invitation to tour Canada, he travelled to the UK at the request of producer and sound-system operator Count Shelley.

He became a household name in 1979 with the release of his own composition **O.K. Fred** which reached the UK pop top 20. That year he could do no wrong, scoring on the reggae charts with singles **School Days, Come Natural** and **Rush No Badness.**

Launching his own Natty Congo label at the turn of the decade, he struck again in 1981 with the infectious **Happiness Forgets** and **Little Green Apples.**

Recordings:
Profile (—/Third World)
Darling Ooh (—/Trojan)

Cornell Dupree

The combination of Cornell Dupree's distinctive guitar style, Chuck Rainey's bass, Richard Tee's electric piano and Bernard Purdie's(▶) drumming made up the classic New York session team for Atlantic(▶) in the late '60s to early '70s, working with King Curtis(▶), Aretha Franklin and many others.

Born, like King Curtis, in Fort Worth, Texas, Dupree was discovered by the sax great on one of Curtis's trips home in 1961. 'I was 19 or so at the time and Curtis sent me the air fare to join him in New York where we backed people like Aretha Franklin and Esther Phillips(▶) and I started getting on recording dates.'

Dupree's recording credits include sessions with B.B. King(▶), Lena Horne, Harry Belafonte(▶), Freddie King(▶), Wilson Pickett(▶), Donny Hathaway(▶), Grover Washington(▶), Dusty Springfield, Hank Crawford(▶), Sam and Dave(▶) and Oscar Brown Jr(▶). Among his classic solos are those on Brook Benton's(▶) **Rainy Night In Georgia** and Aretha's **Rock Steady.**

Still an extremely active session player, he is part of the working band Stuff(▶).

Recordings:
Teasin' (Atlantic)

Dynasty

Dick Griffey, head of Solar Records, has two trios on his roster, Shalamar (▶), a two-boy-one-girl vocal outfit, and Dynasty, who are two girls and one boy, and although both groups employ the Solar session mafia, Dynasty's material has always been a little harder-hitting.

Solar house producer Leon Sylvers, once a member of Capitol Records' 10-piece band the Sylvers(▶), auditioned bass player Kevin Spencer who became part of the Sylvers and got to meet Griffey. Detroit-born, Los Angeles-raised Nidra Beard and New Orleans-raised Linda Carriere used to be part of a song and dance troupe known as DeBlanc. The two had met in Los Angeles, joined the troupe, and when it broke up in 1975, went on to a group called Starfire.

Simultaneously, Nidra was performing with the Sylvers on live dates, because several female members of the recording group were minors. Leon Sylvers introduced Nidra and Linda to Dick Griffey, and Griffey formulated his new concept, bringing Nidra, Linda and Kevin into a cohesive unit as Dynasty.

Their first album release, **Your Piece Of The Rock,** in 1979, spawned a massive club hit, **I Don't Want To Be A Freak.** The following year's release gave birth to three hit singles: **I've Just Begun To Love You, Something To Remember** and **Do Me Right.** Retaining the same mixture of aggressive funk and smooth vocals, Dynasty scored again (1981) with the single, **Love In The Fast Lane** from the album **The Second Adventure.**

Recordings:
Your Piece Of The Rock (Solar)
Adventures In The Land Of Music (Solar)
The Second Adventure (Solar)

Below: It's cheaper than a 747, Maurice! Earth, Wind & Fire take flight.

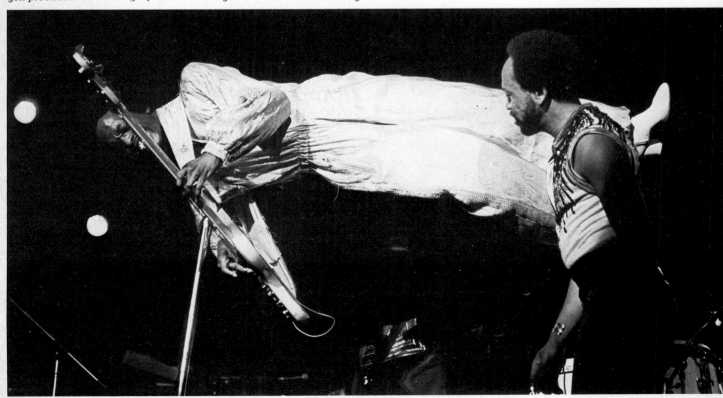

Earth, Wind & Fire

Allied to their fascination with the moribund quasi-science of Egyptology, Earth, Wind & Fire's emphasis on stage spectacle and all things metaphysical imparts an aloof mystique which is light years removed from the earthy street wisdom and soulful intimacy of previous black music giants.

The group image and musical mastery which have made them the most acclaimed soul dance band in the world are largely the responsibility of one man—Maurice White, formerly a session drummer with the legendary Chicago jazz and blues label Chess(▶).

The son of a doctor, White was born in Memphis, Tennessee, but lived in Chicago from the age of 16. Against his father's wish that he should enter the medical profession, White decided to attend the city's Conservatory of Music. From there he joined Chess and worked with, among others, John Coltrane, Muddy Waters(▶), Howlin' Wolf(▶) and jazz pianist Ramsey Lewis(▶), who subsequently invited White to join his trio.

During a four-year tenure with Lewis, from 1966 to 1970, White appeared on 10 of Lewis's albums and made several trips to the Middle East where he became increasingly fascinated with Egyptology, astrology and several other branches of mystic science. He began studying under mystic masters and cites this as a turning-point in his life. His newly elevated consciousness allowed him to envisage the sort of group which would appeal directly to his own generation, but also attract a multi-cultural audience. Accordingly, he split with Lewis and went to Los Angeles to pursue the project.

The first Earth, Wind & Fire aggregation released two albums on Warner Brothers which were slightly out of step with the current sound and sold only moderately. The group's continuity of style and success really began when they switched to Columbia and released **Last Days And Time** in the early part of 1973, and its follow-up **Head To The Sky** later in the year. With scant media attention, but a great deal of brassy uplifting momentum, both albums went gold.

On **Last Days And Time** White introduced the kalimba, an electrified modification of an ancient African percussion instrument. The kalimba has become an integral feature of the band's sound and was duly adopted as the name and logo of Maurice White's production company.

In 1974, with the release of their third Columbia album, **Open Our Eyes**, all the elements of E,W&F's world-dominating combustible dance music were being marshalled. The album had been recorded in the halcyon seclusion of James Guercio's ranch in Caribou, Colorado.

In the early part of 1975, a third White brother, drummer Fred White, joined Maurice and bass player Verdine in the band. The line-up was complete. Earth, Wind & Fire returned to Caribou, where Maurice later set up home in a house made of glass. They recorded **That's The Way Of The World**, which contained their first international breakthrough, the single **Shining Star**, a song which earned them their first Grammy for Best Performance By A Vocal Group in 1975.

White described the album as a 'musical score', and it was used as the soundtrack to a rather mediocre music-biz insight type film, in which Earth, Wind & Fire more or less portrayed themselves as a rock and soul band. (In fact their first LP on Warners, **Sweet Back,** had already been used as the score to Melvin van Peebles' 1971 'ghetto gang' movie, *Sweet, Sweetback's Baadasses Song.)*

In addition to **Shining Star**, the album highlighted falsetto lead singer Philip Bailey, whose heroic vocal on the track **Reasons** was a promise of more to come. That promise was redeemed with a staggering vocal performance on the track **Imagination**, from E,W&F's 1976 offering, **Spirit**. Indeed, the entire album was a breathtaking showcase of consistency, quality and sheer excitement, from the polyrhythmic attack of cuts like

Raise! Courtesy CBS Records.

All 'N' All. Courtesy CBS Records.

Getaway and **On Your Face** to the ethereal beauty of the brief title-track.

In the wake of such a landmark, their next LP, **All 'N' All**, containing the star track **Serpentine Fire**, went platinum almost before its release. It ultimately achieved double platinum sales and the band followed up, at the end of 1978, with a very timely **Best Of** collection.

Apart from containing the best tracks from previous albums, the **Best Of Earth, Wind & Fire, Volume 1** documented the band's show-stealing performance in Robert Stigwood's film *Sgt Pepper's Lonely Hearts Club Band,* with the inclusion of their version of **Got To Get You Into My Life.** Most film critics agreed that, amid a cast including the Bee Gees and Peter Frampton, only E,W&F emerged with any credit at all. The song earned them one of their total of three Grammy Awards in 1979.

In the same year, the group embarked on a mammoth worldwide tour, compounding their musical impact with one of the most ambitious, spectacular and expensive stage shows ever presented. Designed by master illusionist Doug Henning, the show featured levitation, vanishing acts and a dazzling display of lasers and crash-bang pyrotechnics. The show is

Above: The majestic Maurice White of EW & F.

reputed to have cost £130,000 to put together, and an additional £5,000 a night to perform. The specially constructed stage had to travel overseas by ship, since it was too bulky to be transported by air.

Following top-heavy critical acclaim for their stage effects, E,W&F have since maintained a wary balance between stunning theatrics and considerable musical potency as a live act. For the last five years or more, full-time sax player Andrew Woolfolk's efforts have been supplemented by the group's binding relationship with the Phenix Horns, a powerhouse brass section, comprising saxophonist/arranger Don Myrick, trombonist Lois Satterfield and trumpeters Rahmlee Michael Davis and Michael Harris. These four, plus Woolfolk, provide an empathetic abundance of Wind, to match the Earth and Fire of White's rhythm arrangements. As the very spinal column of E,W&F's most bombastic dancers, the Phoenix Horns provide White with yet another instantly recognisable trademark.

I Am, in late 1979, yielded the group's highest hits-per-album ratio yet, with perhaps their most interestingly varied collection: **Star** was their brass-driven stock in trade, but they also had chart-topping outings with **Boogie Wonderland,** featuring vocals by the Emotions(▶), only a moderately successful trio of sisters until White began to write for and produce them, and **After The Love Has Gone,** the group's first real down-tempo soft-focus single success.

After the tried and tested hit-bound formula of **I Am,** White became rather more experimental for E,W&F's 1980 release, **Faces.** It was the band's first studio double album, and aside from providing elbow room for one or two instrumental solos (notably Al McKay's screeching axe-heroics on **Back On The Road**) it lacked the textural variation to make optimum use of the space available.

The most radically experimental component of the album, and perhaps the major justification for the two-record format, was the 7-minute-40-second title track—a racy, free-form instrumental with elements of hard rock and jazz over an insistent Latinate percussion. It was ambiguously, if tolerantly, received by critics and fans alike, although if it was with this record that White hoped to 'create the sound of the '80s', as he put it at the time, a measure of its success was that the group cheerfully returned to the single-album hit package with their next LP **Raise,** in 1982. They scored with familiarly à la mode hits **Let's Groove** and **I've Had Enough,** and with customary panache, the stage effects for their accompanying world tour featured Maurice and a full size Darth Vader substitute exchanging thunderbolts in a pantomime duel to the death.

Independently of the almost self-perpetuating hit machine which is Earth, Wind & Fire, Maurice's Kalimba Productions services, among others, the Emotions and Deniece Williams(▶); singer Philip Bailey has made several outside guest appearances; keyboard player Larry Dunn has been closely involved with jazz and funk sax player Ronnie Laws(▶) ever since Laws was a member of the early E, W&F line-up, while the Phenix Horns are now probably the most sought-after freelance brass section in the world.

Recordings:
Head To The Sky (Columbia/CBS)
Open Our Eyes (Columbia/CBS)
That's The Way Of The World (Columbia/CBS)
Gratitude (Columbia/CBS)
Spirit (Columbia/CBS)
All 'N' All (Columbia/CBS)
The Best Of Earth, Wind & Fire Vol. 1 (Columbia/CBS)
I Am (Columbia/CBS)
Faces (Columbia/CBS)
Raise (Columbia/CBS)

Clint Eastwood and General Saint

Operating out of London this pair of DJ toasters have taken the art of reggae rhythm track voice-overs to previously unassailed commercial and inventive heights. Their forté is humour, which they apply in thick doses, utilising their Jamaican patois to relate stories varying in content from sexual shenanigans to nuclear holocaust.

Eastwood began his career as a guest DJ in his native Jamaica, working with Ray Symbolic, Echotime, Virgo, Gemini and Stereograph sound systems, later making a reputation on vinyl for wacky fast talk. Between 1978 and '80 his most popular singles included **Angel Face** and **Follow Fashion** and albums **Death In The Arena, Jah Lights Shining** and **Sex Education.**

Also from Jamaica, Saint moved to Britain around the same time as Eastwood, in the early '70s, and built up a staunch following, appearing with one of the country's brightest sounds, Frontline International.

The pair joined forces to record a tribute to sound-system operator General Echo, who was killed in a gun battle with the Jamaican police (1980). Taking their cue from Studio One leading lights Papa Michigan and General Smiley, they cut **Tribute To General Echo,** which topped the UK reggae charts. The follow-up, **Another One Bites The Dust,** issued in spring 1981, showed them to be astute humorists and topped the reggae - charts for more than two months, even nudging into the bottom of the national pop charts —a rare achievement.

With the release of their **Two Bad DJs** album the same year, a sensational nationwide tour and an appearance on national television, the duo is set for a lively and intriguing future.

Recordings:
Two Bad DJs (—/Greensleeves)

Rupie Edwards

Born Robert Edwards in St Andrews, Jamaica, in March 1942, Rupie comes from a musical background, his father was a piano tuner and his mother sang in the church choir. He has had two solo singles in the British pop-charts and in two decades of Caribbean music, from ska to rockers, he has assisted in the careers of numerous other singers.

He started recording when 24 for Clement Coxsone Dodd. By 1966 he had built his own studio and launched Success Records with singles **Exclusively Yours, Burning Love** and **Don't Let My Teardrops Fall,** each a prime cut of his distinctive romantic crooning.

By the early '70s he had bought his own record shop and was fast becoming an in-demand producer. Among those to have benefited from his help are Gregory Isaacs(▶), the Heptones(▶), the Mighty Diamonds(▶) and Errol Dunkley(▶). His international status was elevated with the UK hit **Irie Feelings (Skanga)** in 1974, and **Leggo Skanga** the following year, both issued by Creole's Cactus division.

Recordings:
Dub Basket (—/Cactus)
Dub Basket Chapter 2 (—/Cactus)
Rupie's Gems (—/Cactus)

Hortense Ellis

Born in Trenchtown, Kingston, Jamaica, in 1949, the sister of famed singer/songwriter/producer Alton Ellis(▶), Hortense's influences were Ella Fitzgerald(▶) and Aretha Franklin(▶). She began recording in the mid-'60s with producer Ken Lack. Among her earliest Jamaican hits were **I Shall Sing, Brown Girl In A Ring** and **Hell And Sorrow.**

Hortense has concentrated on live performances in Jamaica and Britain in between raising a family. In 1978 she enjoyed chart success with **Unexpected Places.** She re-

Reflections. Courtesy Ballistic Records.

recorded it two years later for the reactivated Burning Rockers label in the UK, who failed to cross it over from reggae to the pop charts.

Recordings:
Jamaica's First Lady Of Song
(—Third World)
Reflections (—/Ballistic)

The Emotions

Hailing from Chicago, Jeanette, Wanda and Sheila Hutchinson, who now make up the Emotions, began as a child gospel act, the Heavenly Sunbeams, under the staunch direcion of father Joe Sr, in the mid-'50s. Touring local churches, and picking up the breadth of experience which was to stand them in such prosperous stead, the girls evolved a repertoire of some 150 songs—mostly sacred, some secular, with even the odd operatic area included.

The group's name changed to the Hutchinson Sunbeams, but they maintained the same diet of mostly spiritual music until 1968, when they inherited their present name from a local all-male group who it seems 'weren't seriously intending to build a career in the music business'.

They came to the attention of Pervis Staples, himself of an equally renowned Chicago gospel family, who placed them with local label Twin Stacks. The girls turned out a couple of regional hits before Twin Stacks folded and they were pacted to Stax(▶), in 1969.

There they benefited from the prodigious talents of the writing/production team of Isaac Hayes(▶)/David Porter(▶) on songs like **The Best Part Of A Love Affair, Stealing Love** and **When Tomorrow Comes,** although it was with sister Sheila's own **So I Can Love You** that they made their debut on Stax subsidiary Volt and scored their first national chart entry.

Sister Jeanette made the first of two departures in 1970, to be temporarily replaced by the girls' cousin Theresa Davis, veteran of another Chicago trio, Our Ladies of Soul.

The group continued to impinge on the R&B charts and on the lower reaches of the pop charts, notably with **Show Me How** in 1971, a cover of Luther Ingram's(▶) **My Honey And Me** in 1972, and **From Toys To Boys** in 1973, but thereafter their hits became fewer.

With the demise of Stax, they took a year off to develop their

Left: The Emotions—petite soul from the Windy City. The girls are now under the guiding hand of Earth, Wind & Fire's Maurice White.

songwriting, before being rediscovered by Earth, Wind & Fire's(▶) main-man Maurice White, who signed them to his Kalimba Productions company. Under White's direction, the Emotions have enjoyed renewed fame and fortune since their debut Kalimba/Columbia album, **Flowers,** in 1977. **Rejoice,** later the same year, **Sunbeam,** recalling their childhood gospel stardom in 1978, and **Come Into Our World** in 1981, all sold well.

The sisters have toured internationally with the Commodores(▶) and had their biggest single success ever with a song from the **Rejoice** album, **Best Of My Love,** written by White and Earth, Wind & Fire guitarist Al McKay. They also provided the stentorian vocal on one of E,W&F's biggest singles, **Boogie Wonderland.**

During their early tenure with Kalimba/Columbia, sister Jeanette was again temporarily replaced, this time by the girls' younger sister Pamela.

Recordings:
Sunshine (Stax)
Heart Association (Stax)
Flowers (Columbia/CBS)
Rejoice (Columbia/CBS)
Sunbeam (Columbia/CBS)
Come Into Our World
(Columbia/CBS)

The Ethiopians

Starting as a vocal duo comprising Leonard Dillon and Stephen Taylor, the Ethiopians cut several small hits for Studio One(▶) in 1966, including **Owe Me No Pay Me, Gonna Take Over Now** and **What To Do,** before enjoying their biggest hit with **Train To Skaville** in 1967. They followed this with two more 'train' theme songs, **Train To Glory** and **Engine 54,** with an album featuring the latter tune being released in 1968 on the WIRL label.

A brief sojourn with Sonia Pottinger produced **I Need You** and **Cool It Amigo,** among others. They then enjoyed their most fruitful collaboration, with producer (Sir) J.J. Johnson. In this period, 1969-1971, they had many big hits with tunes like **Woman Capture Man, Hong Kong Flu, Well Red, Everything Crash, Wreck It Up, What A Fire** and **The Selah.**

From 1971 to 1975 the Ethiopians recorded for a variety of producers, including Derrick Harriott(▶) (**Lot Wife**), Winston Riley (**Promises**), Prince Buster(▶) (**Monkey Money**), Alvin 'GG' Ranglin (**Israel Want To Be Free**), Rupie Edwards(▶) (**Solid As The Rock, Splish Splash, Hail Rasta Brother Hail**), Geoffrey Chung (**Conference Blues, Another Moses**), Joe Gibbs (**Jump-up Action**).

In 1975, Taylor was killed in a car accident. Dillon, the real guiding force of the group, carried on alone, using a variety of back-up singers. In 1978, he released an album **Slave Call** produced by Winston 'Niney' Holness and came full circle in 1981 when he returned to Studio One to record an album containing a re-cut **Everything Crash,** replete with syndrum, for Clement Dodd.

The Ethiopians come from the Jamaican vocal-group tradition established by the Maytals(▶), although Dillon's style is more meditative than gospel-based like Toots'. There are two main themes

in the Ethiopians' music; one is commercial with standard love themes, and the other is a deeper, more spiritual Rasta-influenced strain. A sorely neglected talent, Leonard 'Sparrow' Dillon has made a distinctive and important contribution to Jamaican music which deserves to be more widely heard.

Recordings:
Engine 54 (WIRL)
Reggae Power ((—/Trojan)
Slave Call (-/Third World)

Yvonne Fair

Born in Virginia, raised in New York, Yvonne Fair was a member of the Chantells(▶) before joining James Brown(▶). After five years with J.B., she was introduced

The Bitch Is Black. Courtesy Motown Records.

to Motown producer, Norman Whitfield, by Chuck Jackson(▶). At Motown, she recorded several tracks, and the company released four singles before Whitfield found time for her, three years later, but eventually he produced her first album. She has also appeared in the feature film, *Lady Sings The Blues.*

Recordings:
The Bitch Is Black (Motown)

The Fantastics

The New York-based soul vocal group the Velours arrived in London for their first UK tour in the late '60s to find themselves being billed as 'The Tempting Temptations'—and being asked to imitate that group's act. They liked Britain, however and, renaming themselves the Fantastics, became regular visitors and enjoyed a minor hit with the Tony Macauley/Roger Greenaway penned **Something Old, Something New.**

John Cheatdom, Richard Pitts, Jerome Ramos and Donald Haywoode always put on a good stage show and their reputation as a successful live act, though not translating into massive record sales, has enabled them to continue working the circuits right into the '80s.

Recordings:
The Fantastics (Bell)

Joe Farrell

Born in Chicago in 1937, tenor-sax player Joe Farrell studied flute at the University of Illinois and still frequently records using that instrument, as on his **Flute Talk** set on Xanadu.

After a period jamming in New

York, Farrell joined the Maynard Ferguson Big Band in 1959, making his recording debut with that outfit. In 1965 he became a member of the Jaki Byard Quartet and of the Thad Jones/Mel Lewis Orchestra (appearing on the latter band's **Live At Village Vanguard** set).

In 1972 he was a founder member of the Return To Forever outfit put together by Chick Corea (▶). Now firmly entrenched in the jazz-funk groove, Farrell has turned out a consistent stream of albums for C.T.I.(▶), Warner Bros., and most recently Xanadu, as well as recording with Santana, Billy Cobham(▶), James Brown(▶), Aretha Franklin(▶), and the Band amongst others.

Recordings:
Moon Germs (CTI)
Outback (CTI)
Night Dancing (Warner Bros/—)

The Fatback Band

The Fatback Band started their career on member Bill Curtis's own Fatback label in the early '70s with a line-up based around Curtis, drums; Johnny King, guitar, and Johnny Flippin, bass. **Street Dance, Let's Do It Again, Street Walk** and **To Be With You** gave them an opening run of American R&B chart successes with infectious street-funk items, the rhythm section being rounded out with the fat horn sound of Earl Shelton, saxophone; George Williams, trumpet, and George Adam, flute.

Signing to the major Polydor label in the mid-'70s, the Fatback Band became enormously popular among black music audiences on both sides of the Atlantic but, with their music rooted in dance-orientated highly rhythmic instrumentals with vocal chants, the lack of any strong melodic quality prevented them making the important crossover into the pop market.

From their first two Polydor albums, **Keep On Steppin'** and

Yum Yum, released in 1975, came a stream of disco monsters: **Keep On Steppin', Wicki Wacki, Yum Yum (Gimme Some)** and **(Are You Ready) Do The Bus Stop.** When George Adam left, Saunders McCrae, keyboards, and Richard Cromwell, trombone, were added. In 1976, two more albums, **Raising Hell** and **Night Fever,** featured the hit singles **(Do The) Spanish Hustle, Party Time** and **Night Fever.**

After the departure of Johnny King, the line-up consisted of: Bill Curtis, drums; Kenny Ballard, guitar / vocals; Johnny Flippin, bass / vocals; Calvin Dukes, keyboards/vocals; Tom Copola, synthesiser; Richard Cromwell, trombone; George Williams, trumpet/ vocals, and Earl Shelton, saxophone.

Following their sixth album, **NYCNYUSA,** in 1977, the group's role as producers of disco staples seemed to wane, their earthy brand of funk being eclipsed by the technical wizardry of the new generation of bands which were moving black music into the '80s.

Still recording albums regularly, the group lives on but no longer as major chart contenders, though the 14 albums they had cut up to 1982 (the first for Perception, the next six for Polydor, the rest for Polydor's associated Spring label) have provided countless hours of dancing pleasure.

Recordings:
People Music (Perception/—)
Keep On Steppin' (Polydor)
The Best Of (Polydor)
Brite Lights, Big City (Spring)
14 Karat (Spring)
Tasty Jam (Spring)
Gogolo (Spring)

Fat Larry's Band

This band is an informal collection of musicians masterminded by five-foot-three-inch, 230-pound Larry James. Philadelphia-born James was originally the drummer for the Delfonics(▶) back in 1972,

Above: The prolific Fatback Band keep giving us people music.

but joined Blue Magic(▶) when they lost their backing group.

In 1976, Larry and his pals cut an album for the Philly label WMOT that was distributed by Atlantic(▶), but as the album was being released, negotiations with Atlantic broke down, and the album got somewhat lost. WMOT then signed a deal with Fantasy, who put Fat Larry's Band on the revived Stax(▶) label. Meanwhile, in Britain, Fat Larry's Band were having a hit single with **Boogie Town,** and the first UK album release was a concoction of the two US releases, plus other tracks, including **Centre City** and **Fascination.**

Off The Wall. Courtesy Fantasy Records.

The world was picking up on Larry James in 1979, and he even found time to put together other projects—Slick and Philly Cream, who had one-off club hits, **Space Bass** and **Sexy Cream,** respectively. Later in 1979, a third US album release for Fat Larry's Band produced the worldwide hit, **Lookin' For Love Tonight.** After a slight lull and further changes in distribution deals, FLB resurfaced in 1982 with a worldwide hit single, **Act Like You Know.**

Recordings:
Feel It (WMOT)

Off The Wall (Stax/Fantasy)
Lookin' For Love Tonight
(WMOT)
Act Like You Know (WMOT)

Fela Kuti

Fela Ransome Kuti was born in 1938 in Abeokuta, the oil-rich province of Ogun, Nigeria. At the end of the '50s he received a grant to study medicine in London, England. He abandoned this project, however, and turned to Trinity College of Music, spending five years studying jazz, and forming his own band, Koola Lobitos. His music was a mixture of highlife rhythms and jazz melodies, often with romantic lyrics. Back home in Nigeria in 1963 he scored his first hit single **Onifere.**

At that time Jim Lawson was the undisputed King of Highlife, but Kuti was convinced he was better and, knowing the mechanics of the media, he led a party of journalists to Lawson's home. After 10 minutes of insulting Lawson, Kuti and the press departed. The following day Kuti's destiny was sealed with the newspaper headline: 'Fela Ransome Kuti: The Idol's Biggest Rival! The Public Must Decide Between Them!'

Kuti's Lagos club, The Afro Spot, quickly became a thorn in the side of the Nigerian authorities, its walls covered with posters of leading black nationalists and radicals. Kuti dropped his middle name Ransome (meaning son of slave) and replaced it with Anikulapo (which means traditional hunter protected by charms). Naming his club and house Kalakuta (meaning rascal) Republic and surrounding it with electrified fences was his reaction to continuing police harassment. In January 1977 he boycotted Festac, the second Pan-African cultural festival held that year in Lagos. To the humiliation of the authorities, who had tried in vain to have him arrested for possession of drugs, the press and musicians spent all their free time with Kuti at Kalakuta.

A week after Festac, the army raided Kalakuta committing many atrocities and killing Kuti's mother; Kuti has won all the subsequent court cases pertaining to that day.

In November 1978 he played the Berlin Jazz stage with his massive Africa '70 band, including roadies, musicians, dancers and singers—his go-go girls, all 27 of whom he married! At the end of the German tour he disbanded the group (but kept the wives!).

With the advent of a civilian government in Nigeria, Kuti has created his own political party, Movement Of The People, which will contest the next general election in 1983. Meanwhile he continues to cut ambitious multi-ethnic albums, despite continuous harassment by the authorities.

Recordings:
Why Blackmen Dey Suffer
(—/African Song)
Black President (—/Arista)

Roberta Flack

Born in Black Mountain, North Carolina in 1940, Roberta moved at a very early age to Arlington, Virginia, where she and an extended family, including grandmother, aunt and uncle, shared a small, basement apartment. Though her family were affiliated to the local AME Zion

Above: Roberta Flack—full of emotion and style.

Church, Roberta opted for the musical faith-with-fervour of the nearby Baptist church where she became accustomed to hearing artists like Sam Cooke(▶) and Mahalia Jackson. She began to cultivate her own musical potential with piano lessons at the age of nine developing a taste for jazz, blues and R&B.

Four years later, Roberta had turned her attention to the classics, and her piano playing was of sufficient proficiency to win second prize in a national, black talent contest, with a rendition of a Scarlatti sonata. Following a distinguished academic path, Roberta continued to develop her musical acumen and was enrolled on a full music scholarship at the Howard University at the age of 15. There she began to train her exquisite voice and took every opportunity to become involved in the school's many and varied music activities, conducting her sorority's vocal quartet and accompanying singers of a variety of styles. For extra cash, Roberta gave private piano lessons and succeeded her mother as local church organist.

The sudden and unexpected death of her father interrupted Roberta's musical development as she was forced to take a succession of teaching jobs to support herself. She eventually became a piano accompanist to opera singers at Washington DC's Tivoli club and she secured her own five-nights-a-week residency playing blues and R&B at another club. Roberta extended her live engagements and eventually came to the attention of a passing Atlantic Records producer. He is said to have been 'stunned' by the experience and hurriedly set up an audition, for which Roberta turned up with 600 songs and actually played 42 of them in three hours. Invited to do a demo session, she gave a further demonstration of her professionalism, recording 39 songs in a total of nine hours' studio time.

The next year, 1969, saw the release of Roberta's debut album **First Take,** which included Ewan MacColl's ethereal folk ballad **The First Time Ever I Saw Your Face.** Prompted by the song's inclusion in the soundtrack of the Clint Eastwood film *Play Misty For Me,* Atlantic released it as a single two-and-a-half years later when it became Roberta's first US No.1 and a name-making international hit.

In the meantime, Roberta had released another album and collaborated for the first time with Donny Hathaway(▶) for a couple of singles, **You've Got A Friend** and **You've Lost That Lovin' Feelin'.** This heralded the release of the album **Roberta Flack & Donny Hathaway** and the beginning of their sadly short-lived, but perfectly complementary partnership.

Roberta's reputation continued to grow, and her achievements were recognised of the municipal governors of Washington DC where she was feted and presented with the keys of the city; April 22 was declared Roberta Flack Day. Her crowning glory came perhaps in 1973 when she was presented with a Record of the Year Grammy award for **The First Time Ever . . .** and her current single **Killing Me Softly With His Song** (reputed to have been dedicated to writers Norman Gimble and Charles Fox, to singer/songwriter Don MacLean) was simultaneously at No.1 in the charts.

Not yet satisfied with her multifarious musical interests, Roberta bowed as self-producer on the 1975 set **Feel Like Makin' Love,** from which the title track was an international hit. She consolidated her reputatation as an artist/producer with the stately set **Blue Lights In The Basement,** in 1977, yielding another Hathaway duet, **The Closer I Get To You.**

Following Hathaway's death in January 1979, Roberta spent the rest of the year putting together an album which included a legacy of two Hathaway collaborations (including the poetically apposite **Back Together Again**) for which she attracted the assistance of Stevie Wonder(▶), who wrote and contributed a guest 'rap' on the single **Don't Make Me Wait Too Long.** The album, released in 1980, was called **Roberta Flack Featuring Donny Hathaway.**

Recordings:
First Take (Atlantic)
Chapter Two (Atlantic)
Quiet Fire (Atlantic)
Roberta Flack & Donny Hathaway (Atlantic)
Killing Me Softly (Atlantic)
Feel Like Makin' Love (Atlantic)
Blue Lights In The Basement (Atlantic)
Roberta Flack (Atlantic)
Roberta Flack Featuring Donny Hathaway (Atlantic)

The Floaters

Under the avuncular guidance of James Mitchell and Marvin Willis of the Detroit Emeralds(▶), the Floaters, a five-piece vocal group also from Detroit, hit the world charts like a freak tornado in 1977. The song, from their eponymous debut album on ABC, was **Float On,** a stunningly simple and ethe-

Below: Far from floating on, the Floaters sank without trace.

Floaters. Courtesy ABC Records.

real two-chord ballad in which the individual members introduced themselves, star-sign by star-sign, and then proceeded to describe their ideal women.

Lavished with awards by the top trade magazine *Billboard*, the group followed with the singularly unsuccessful **Magic** album and then, so far as the charts were concerned, disappeared as rapidly as they'd arrived.

Recordings:
The Floaters (ABC/Anchor)
Magic (ABC/Anchor)

King Floyd

Wardel Quezergue, noted Jackson, Mississippi-based keyboard man, came up with an attractively simple jerk rhythm for King Floyd's **Groove Me** (1970) and introduced the world to 'the Malaco Sound' with a two-million-seller. Two albums for Chimneyville, licensed nationally to Atlantic(▶), revealed Floyd as a classy singer in the traditional Southern soul mode, but his career soon foundered.

Recordings:
Groove Me (Cotillion/Atlantic)
Think About It (Atco/Atlantic)

Sonny Fortune

Alto-saxophonist / flautist Sonny Fortune was born in Philadelphia in May 1939, studying at Granhoff School Of Music in the late '60s before moving to New York where he played with Elvin Jones, Buddy Rich and McCoy Tyner.

He joined Miles Davis's(▶) group in the early '70s and stayed until 1975, forming his own quintet the following year with trumpeter Charles Sullivan and cutting the **Waves Of A Dream** and **Awakening** albums for A&M Horizon.

In 1977 he signed to Atlantic(▶), moving into the jazz-funk fusion idiom with the albums **Infinity Is** and **Serengeti Minstrel**, and also recording with trumpeter Tom Browne(▶).

Recordings:
Waves Of A Dream (A&M)
Infinity Is (Atlantic)
Serengeti Minstrel (Atlantic)

Rodney Franklin

Born on September 16, 1958, in Berkeley, California, Franklin attended Washington Elementary School, whose administrator was Dr Herb Wong, a noted jazz journalist and DJ who ran a jazz education programme for the very young. At the age of six, Franklin was playing alto sax and organ in the school's jazz workshop.

Inspired by Herbie Hancock(▶), Chick Corea(▶) and Oscar Peterson, Franklin began to concentrate on keyboards, playing in the workshops and bands of his educational institutions.

In 1977, he left school to go on the road with percussionist Bill Summers, and then signed as a solo artist with Columbia Records. After recording his debut album **In The Center**, a series of jazz-fusion instrumentals, he was fortunate enough to be employed for three different artists' tours, Freddie Hubbard(▶), Marlena Shaw(▶) and John Handy(▶).

From 1980's maturing second album came a single, **The Groove,** a lively piano instrumental, which contained gaps of silence, generating a dance known as 'The Freeze' in which dancers would stand still for those few silent seconds. It was a worldwide crossover hit.

Endless Flight. Courtesy Columbia Records.

Although his third album, **Rodney Franklin,** did not contain a single smash, it was a fine mixture of vocal and instrumental jazz/funk/pop fusions, featuring guest vocalists.

Mike Post's theme for the highly popular television show, 'Hill Street Blues', provided Franklin with his second big single, taken from his fourth album **Endless Flight.**

Recordings:
In The Center (Columbia)
You'll Never Know (Columbia/CBS)
Rodney Franklin (Columbia/CBS)
Endless Flight (Columbia/CBS)

Funkadelic

See P. Funk.

Eric Gale

Possibly the most highly regarded of all the studio guitar players, Eric Gale has enhanced the records of a host of major artists from Aretha Franklin(▶) to Grover Washington Jr.(▶). As a leader in his own right, he has been responsible for some of the more worthwhile recorded examples of the jazz/funk/MOR genre, his playing always a model of taste and economy.

Brooklyn-born of Barbadian parents, Gale started playing guitar in his early teens and was still at school when he began working the R&B circuit with artists like Maxine Brown(▶), Jackie Wilson(▶) and the Flamingos. Nevertheless, it was not until after he left university that he decided to become a full-time musician. After some years on the road he broke into the charmed circle of New York session musicians.

Early studio experience included sessions with King Curtis(▶) and Jimmy Smith(▶), and over the next few years he contributed to the recorded work of dozens of top names in jazz, rock and soul. These included, among others, Marvin Gaye(▶), the O'Jays(▶), Frank Sinatra, Diana Ross(▶), Ashford and Simpson(▶), Gato Barbieri, Steely Dan, Billy Joel, Paul Simon and Phoebe Snow. He also played in Aretha Franklin's(▶) stage band.

In 1973 Gale became house guitarist for CTI(▶), and produced his first album as a leader, **Forecast**, also moving temporarily to

Above: Eric Gale, the guitarist as session superstar.

Multiplication. Courtesy Columbia Records.

Jamaica. Switching to CBS in 1976, he initiated a series of albums which, while not musically revolutionary, combined creative playing and commercial viability. A must for guitar players, his albums are rarely less than interesting though sometimes bland.

For the last few years he has combined his session and solo work with playing with the hot session man's band Stuff(▶), and has recently been seen in Paul Simon's movie *One Trick Pony* with his beloved Gibson guitar by his side.

Recordings:
Forecast (CTI)
Ginseng Woman (Columbia/CBS)
Multiplication (Columbia/CBS)
Part Of You (Columbia/CBS)
Touch Of Silk (Columbia/CBS)

The Gap Band

Three brothers from Tulsa, Oklahoma, Ronnie, Charles and Robert Wilson evolved their multi-instrumental and vocal talents during their heavily gospel-influenced youth. Their father was a minister and their mother led the family in the church choir. Their road to Los Angeles and the music industry big time was strewn with minor musical adventures, including brushes with Leon Russell, Ike Turner(▶), Billy Preston(▶) and D.J. Rogers(▶), till in 1979 they debuted with the Lonnie Simmons-produced **Gap Band I,** on Mercury.

Playing an array of instruments between the three of them—various keyboards, bass, percussion and brass—they are almost self-contained musically. Their self-penned material is impressively varied and ranges from the cool class of ballads like **You Can Count On Me,** through the exquisitely melodic (if tongue-in-cheek) pop of **The Boys Are Back In Town,** to the disco raunch of **Baby Baba Boogie, Burn Rubber On Me** and **Oops Upside Your Head** (their biggest hit to date and a song which sparked off a whole new dance craze).

Recordings:
The Gap Band I (Mercury)
The Gap Band II (Mercury)
The Gap Band III (Mercury)

Lee Garrett

An accumulation of personal problems and a lack of musical direction appear to have prevented Lee Garrett from fulfilling his obvious potential. Blind since birth, Mississippi-born Garrett had a brief songwriting partnership with fellow sufferer Stevie Wonder(▶), during which he collaborated on much of the material for Wonder's album **Where I'm Coming From,** and co-wrote the Spinners'(▶) hit **It's A Shame.**

Restively alternating between such direct musical involvement and a career as a disc jockey, Garrett is still able to conjure up a golden touch as a songwriter, even if such songs as his recent hit, **You're My Everything,** bear the influences of his former partner.

Recordings:
Heat For The Feets (Chrysalis)

Gloria Gaynor

Former American 'Queen of Disco' (as opposed to Donna Summer(▶), who despite her American origins and success there was really 'Queen of European Disco'), Gloria Gaynor remained something of a one-trick pony until she and disco music tumbled out of fashion together. Her career, however, was rallied to a pitch of even greater significance by her original interpretation, in 1979, of the superbly defiant womens' anthem, **I Will Survive.**

Gloria was born and raised, in the company of five sisters and a brother, in Newark, New Jersey. She evolved her style of shimmering, high-voltage vocal delivery through the influence of successive popular male singers of her childhood, beginning with Frankie Lymon and the Teenagers(▶), who were at the height of their popularity when Gloria was eight.

Against the background of a strong family interest in music (she claims her brother 'could harmonise with the water pipes'), Gloria strove towards a music career throughout her teens, picking up her first professional engagement when she was 18. Thereafter, she worked infrequently in New Jersey clubs and toured for a short time with a local band called the Soul Satisfiers, before being discovered by the man who would become her manager, Jay Ellis,

Below: Sweet-voiced disco Queen Gloria Gaynor.

while singing at The Wagon Wheel in New York. Within three months, Ellis had secured her a recording contract with Columbia, for whom she cut her debut single, **Honey Bee.**

When MGM took over her contract shortly afterwards, they also gained control of **Honey Bee** which they promoted to minor hit status on both the East and West Coasts. It was with her second single, an extended locomotive version of the Jackson 5's(▶) hit **Never Can Say Goodbye,** that Gloria established herself in the international pop charts.

Side one of Gloria's debut album linked **Honey Bee, Never Can Say Goodbye,** and an *à la mode* version of another old Motown(▶) hit, the Four Tops'(▶) **Reach Out,** in an early example of the 'segue' technique, allowing the 'Disco Queen' to command attention on the club floor for the entire side of an album.

Following the release of **Reach Out** on single, only a discofied **How High The Moon** made any particular impact from the second album, **Experience Gloria Gaynor.** From a chart point of view, it would be safe to say that Gloria's fortunes dwindled. The proliferation of new names and faces which made up the 'Eurodisco' boom of the mid-to-late-'70s did nothing to advance her cause.

However, she was brought sharply back to public notice in 1979, when her gale-force rendition of the Perren/Fekaris song **I Will Survive** became the most eloquent and expressive jolt to the cosy world of male chauvinism ever to achieve mass acceptance: an oft-recorded banner song, it was a true landmark in popular music. To add authenticity, Gloria was able to claim that the words of the song closely mirrored her own experiences.

Recordings:
Never Can Say Goodbye (MGM)

The Best Of Gloria Gaynor (Polydor)
Love Tracks (Polydor)

The Gibson Brothers

The Gibson Brothers—Chris, percussion, guitars; Patrick, drums, vocals; Alex, piano, vocals—were born in Martinique, in the French West Indies, although they spent most of their lives in Paris, where they started their mixture of Latin and Caribbean disco. Signed to Zagora Records, their fourth single, **Cuba,** caught the attention of Island Records' Chris Blackwell, who released the single and signed the band.

In 1980, they moved to Epic Records for the **Quartier Latin** set.

Recordings:
Cuba (Island)
On The Riviera (Island)
Quartier Latin (Epic)

Jim Gilstrap

Los Angeles-based session singer, veteran of hundreds of great soul records, Jim Gilstrap leapt to prominence in 1975 with the lilting mid-tempo **Swing Your Daddy,** written and produced by Kenny Nolan, and arranged by Gene Page. A year later, **Love Talk** was a minor hit, but Gilstrap then went back to singing on other people's records.

Recordings:
Swing Your Daddy (Roxbury/ Chelsea)
Love Talk (Chelsea)

The Gladiators

The story begins in the mid-60s when Griffiths, Fearon and Sutherland worked together as mason contractors. During meal breaks they would arrange harmonies and augment their sweet soulful singing with acoustic guitars. First group release for Wirl Records (1967) was **Train Coming Back,** although Griffiths had previously sung **You Are The Girl** with the Ethiopians(▶) on the flip of their enormous hit, **Train To Skaville.**

In 1968 they made the trek to Studio One(▶) to record a number of tracks, of which only **Hello Carol** was ever released, positioning itself at the top of the Jamaican charts for seven weeks. As proficient instrumentally as they were as singers, they made a name arranging rhythms for Burning Spear(▶) and Yabby U among others, and by 1972 had set up their own music school in Olympic Way, Kingston.

Returning to the recording limelight in 1974 the Gladiators scored with some of their best-loved songs: **Bongo Red** (versioned by Tommy McCook as **Bongo I),** **Roots Natty, Jah Jah Go Before Us, Serious Thing** and **Beautiful Locks,** issued in Britain by Fab and credited to Francis. Leaving Coxsone Dodd, they pacted with producer Prince Tony Robinson, who softened their rootsy sound for a debut album, **Trenchtown Mix Up** (1976), on Virgin. Lighter in content, it included a selection of new Griffiths' songs and covers of earlier classics, and a brace of Wailers(▶) tunes, **Soul Rebel** and **Rude Boy Ska.** The **Proverbial Reggae** album

(1978) brought them back to the trenchant rhythms and glistening harmonies of their first recordings, and the popularity of that album instigated their first UK tour that year.

Griffiths and Fearon had lost none of their songwriting flair in **Naturality** (1979), and by the following year were confident and capable of self-producing **Sweet So Till,** employing some of the very best JA session players. But with declining popularity they teamed up with Eddy Grant(▶) in London for **Gladiators,** an uneven work by their standards, the trio having a crack at a number of musical styles with limited success.

Recordings:
Trenchtown Mix Up (Front Line)
Proverbial Reggae (Front Line)
Naturality (Front Line)
Sweet So Till (Front Line)
Gladiators (Virgin)

G.Q.

At the age of 11, G.Q. guitarist, Rahiem LeBlanc, sat on the porch of his home, situated on the fringes of South Bronx, New York. He began playing Sly Stone's(▶) **Sing A Simple Song.** G.Q. bass player, Keith 'Sabu' Crier, also of similar age, walked by, was intrigued, and stopped to listen. LeBlanc and Crier then worked their way through their teenage years, playing in a variety of bands: Sabu and the Survivors, Sons Of Darkness, the Third Chance and Rhythm Makers.

They signed a six-year contract with a small, independent label but after discovering that the label was incapable of helping their careers, the extended period of their contractual obligation was a frustrating time. Meanwhile they recruited Herb Lane—for keyboards—and Paul Service, who had been at high school with Rahiem, as a drummer. The quartet found themselves a manager, Tony Lopez, who changed their name to G.Q. (Good Quality).

The six-year contract, however, taught the quartet much about studios, live work, and the need for patient diligence. They took one of their tapes to producer Beau Ray Fleming and played it to him on his car stereo. Fleming invited Larkin Arnold (Arista Senior Vice President) and Vernon Gibbs to come to a South Bronx basement to hear

Face To Face. Courtesy Arista Records.

the group. The group's first number was **Disco Nights (Rock Freak),** which the executives made them play several times.

Two weeks later G.Q. were in the studio. In 1979, Arista released the first album, **Disco Nights.** The title track plus **Make My Dream A**

Above: The original G.Q line-up, with recently departed drummer Paul Service.

Reality went on to become two of the biggest disco records of the year. 1980 yielded **G.Q. Two**, from which came the hit single **Standing Ovation**. In 1981, Paul Service left the group, and G.Q. used session drummers to record their third album **Face To Face**.

Recordings:
Disco Nights (Arista)
G.Q. Two (Arista)
Face To Face (Arista)

Graham Central Station

Graham Central Station was formed from a collaboration between former Sly & the Family Stone(▶) bass player Larry Graham(▶) and an American band called Hot Chocolate. Graham had been recruited to produce an album for the band (no relation to the British group of the same name) at the time when he was contemplating his departure from the Family Stone.

Release Yourself. Courtesy Warner Bros Records.

The initial line-up of Graham Central Station was Hershall Kennedy, keyboards; guitarist David Vega; Willie Sparks, drums; Patrice Banks, percussion; and Robert Sam, keyboards. Sam had previously been with Billy Preston(▶), while Kennedy and Sparks had backed Little Sister, former vocalists with Sly & the Family Stone.

Their brand of orchestral funk, led by vocal gymnast Graham, was continually successful from the mid-1970s, and they were much in demand as a concert attraction. The band's solid but predictable product earned them a stream of hit singles, including **Can You Handle It** (1974), **Feel The Need** (1974) and **Your Love** (1975), and their third album **Ain't No Bout-A-Doubt It** (1975) went gold within three months of release.

Although GCS had been one of the first soul-dance bands out of the gate, they had made little musical progress compared to the adventurous developments within such contemporary units as Earth Wind & Fire(▶) and Funkadelic. Graham experimented with a synthesised voice through his bass guitar for the aggregation's fifth album **Now Do U Wanna Dance** (1977), which featured new drummer Gaylord Birch (ex-Pointer Sisters(▶)) and guitarist Gail Muldrow (replacing Sparks and Banks). But the formula had run its course, and a further album indicated a likely demise for the band. Graham himself instigated the end for GCS

Below: Larry Graham. No longer the station master, now on solo tracks.

when he began a solo career with the excellent **One In A Million You** (1980) leaving behind a decade of lusty R&B music.

Recordings:
Ain't No Bout-A-Doubt It (Warner Bros)
Graham Central Station (Warner Bros)
Mirror (Warner Bros)
Now Do U Wanna Dance (Warner Bros)
Release Yourself (Warner Bros)
My Radio Sure Sounds Good To Me (Warner Bros)

Larry Graham

Larry Graham's startling change in direction, from out-and-out funk to ballads, has proved what many felt about this fine artist, for tempering of style, considered production, and astute choice of song, have given Graham new authority.

This powerful singer/multi-instrumentalist started his career in his mother's trio. Dell Graham had encouraged her son to play a variety of instruments, and by the time he was eight years old Larry was proficient on keyboards, guitar, drums and saxophone. He played guitar with the trio, which featured Dell on piano and vocals, but was soon experimenting with bass guitar.

Word spread quickly in the tightly knit Bay Area community that Larry Graham was a talent for the future and he was recruited by local DJ Sylvester Stewart into the nucleus of a new band known as Sly & the Family Stone(▶). Graham's mellow, elastic vocals were a perfect foil for the aggressive tenor of the re-named Sly Stone, and they worked together for more than six years, producing a collection of national hits.

When Graham left the Family Stone in 1972, his immediate plans were in production, and his first project was with a band called Hot Chocolate (not to be confused with the British band of the same name). Graham soon decided on a more permanent relationship with this band from his adopted home in Oakland, California—he was born in Beaumont, Texas—and, with an adjustment in personnel, re-named them Graham Central Station. This successful outfit was nominated for a Grammy as Best New Group and went on to record eight albums for Warner Bros, including the standouts **Release Yourself** and **Ain't No Doubt-A-Bout It**.

In 1980, and with over 10 years' success behind him, Larry Graham entered a new phase of his career, as a solo artist. His first album, **One In A Million You**, saw Graham utilise his instrumental talents—as bass player, drummer, guitarist, percussionist and keyboard player. The title track, a Sam Dees song, was a hit on both sides of the Atlantic, and Graham seemed completely at ease in his new role.

A new album, **Just Be My Lady**, again featured Graham's measured vocals on a fine selection of ballads. Having taken advantage of his wide vocal range, Graham himself seems certain where his future lies: 'When I was performing with Graham Central Station, I noticed the biggest response was for ballads. It was obvious audiences wanted more.'

Recordings:
One In A Million You (Warner Bros)
Just Be My Lady (Warner Bros)

Eddy Grant

Edmond Montague Grant was born in Plaisance, Guyana. In 1960 he followed his parents to London where in 1967, at the height of the British flower-power movement, he and four other London-based musicians formed the R&B/pop band the Equals, consisting of Grant (guitars), brothers Lincoln Gordon (guitar) and Derv Gordon (vocals), and white musicians Pat Lloyd (bass and rhythm guitar) and John Hall (drums).

Their catchy dance songs set to rhythms of jangling electric guitars and their outrageous bleached Afro hairstyles appealed to the record-buying public and between 1968 and '71 they notched up eight top-20 singles. The most popular were **Baby Come Back** (which made No.1), **Viva Bobby Joe** and **Blackskin Blue-Eyed Boys**, all released on President Records.

In 1972 Grant quit the Equals to concentrate on producing other artists. He formed Marco Music Productions and began working with the Pioneers(▶), 96 Degrees Inclusive and the Equals for Phonogram Records. This was just the first step towards his ultimate goal —a totally black-owned independent record company and distribution network.

Grant has always been a shrewd businessman and he had shrewdly invested his Equals' royalties in property. Thus, by the middle of the '70s, phase two began with the formation in Guyana of Ice Records, paid for with the proceeds from his property deals. His Caribbean base was used exclusively to issue his own records and those by his brother Rudi (aka The Mexicano).

In 1977, Ice Records was established in Britain, Nigeria and Canada. After numerous splits the Equals finally gave up the ghost and Grant issued his debut solo album, **Message Man**. The album had been recorded at his Coach

House Recording Studio in North London, with Grant playing practically every instrument.

It was an uneven affair, yet included one marvellous track, **Jamaican Child,** which found him moving further away from his pop past and towards a mid-Atlantic reggae sound where the bass and drums were firmly Jamaican but the rest of the rhythm section and the overall production distinctly Anglo-American. The album caused a sensation in Nigeria where it earned a gold disc.

His search for a new sound found the right chemistry the following year with his magnum opus, **Walking On Sunshine,** again recorded almost single-handed in his studio. The first side is devoted to a three-part **Frontline Symphony** saying all there is to say about the bass drum and synthesisers. Public reaction to the album was slow. In 1979, London DJs began playing a remixed version of part of the symphony, **Living On The Frontline,** and within weeks he was back in the UK top 10 for the first time since his days with the Equals.

Some of the proceeds from this success were used to buy the former British Homophone record pressing plant from his former manager Eddie Kasner, owner of the President label. This was the next step in Grant's Ice Dream, producing and pressing his own records. The following year he enjoyed a successful tour of Europe where his reputation for eclectic dance music was spreading fast. He found time to record a third solo album, although the finished work, **Love In Exile,** was merely a poor attempt to retread ideas from his previous recordings.

Since then he has encountered problems finding the hit formula that was once so easy for him. Of his most recent recordings the double set, **Live At Notting Hill,** recorded on-stage during the 1981 Caribbean Carnival in West London, is the best showcase for his exuberant personality, deep gutteral voice and imaginative use of multi-layered percussion.

In 1982, after years of complaint about the UK climate, he shipped his London studio lock, stock and barrel to Barbados where he now resides, working exclusively on his own material. Ice Records continues to function in the UK under the guidance of his brother Alpine.

Recordings:
Walking On Sunshine (Epic/Ice)
Can't Get Enough (—/Ice)
Live At Notting Hill (—/Ice)

Al Green

Perhaps it's a question of management, perhaps it's personal philosophy, perhaps it's being in the right place at the right time—fate, in a word—that decides which performers transcend national barriers and go on to tread the boards of the world's greatest musical auditoriums. Major black acts like Diana Ross(▶), Gladys Knight & the Pips(▶) and B.B. King(▶) have risen from the ranks of R&B to become international personalities, arguably at the expense of aesthetic qualities. Al Green was taking similar giant strides up the ladder of repute until a bowl of boiling grits came his way.

Al was born in Forrest City, Arkansas, on April 13, 1946, and his musical grounding came from singing in the family gospel group,

the Greene Brothers, from the age of nine. The family moved north to Grand Rapids, Michigan, in 1959 and it was there that Al made his initial foray into secular musical styles, joining a local group, the Creations, and recording some sides for the Zodiac label.

Progress was slow, however, until early in 1967 when two group members, Palmer Jones and Curtis Rodgers, persuaded Al to sing one of their compositions so that they could produce a disc for the quaintly named Hot Line Music

Have A Good Time. Courtesy London Records.

Journal label. Thus emerged **Back Up Train,** a gently haunting love-song credited to Al Greene (still with the extra 'e') & the Soul Mates, which climbed into the R&B top 10 early in 1968, crossing over to the top 50 in the Hot 100. Two subsequent 45s in similar style, **Don't Hurt Me No More** and **Lover's Hideaway,** sold well enough locally but failed to break nationally and with discontent festering in the group at their failure to maintain initial impact, the Soul Mates split, leaving Greene high and dry.

Picking up the pieces, he continued as a solo performer, soon to be spotted at a Texas gig by Willie Mitchell(▶), the renowned R&B musician/writer/producer, scouting for Hi Records(▶) in Memphis, to which Al was promptly signed. At first the result was a variety of styles, including the impassioned deep soul balladry of **One Woman,** the crisply funky **You Say It** and the thumping power of **Right Now Right Now.** Bluesy undertones were also prevalent (he cut a superb version of Roosevelt Sykes' vintage **Driving Wheel)** and it was an interesting combination of blues and funk which yielded the first major hit on Hi for Al Green (now minus the third 'e'), a powerful, ponderous treatment of **I Can't Get Next To You,** reviving the Temptations'(▶) 1969 chart-topper.

Six months later, in the summer of 1971, Green was back in the upper reaches of the charts with yet another change of musical direction. **Tired Of Being Alone,** an easy-tempo beat-ballad, clutched tightly at Green's gospel roots. The mood is set with gentle, mellow rhythm topped by staccato horn punctuation, while Green's delivery, in partly restrained, almost tearful tenor, draws on soaring emotional falsetto and crooning soulful melisma, supported by harmonic precision from the trio Rhodes, Chalmers & Rhodes, a sound lifted bodily from the Baptist choir heritage. Top 10 R&B, top 20 pop was the result, and a formula had emerged which was to generate a lengthy succession of smash hits over the next half-dozen years.

Follow-up **Let's Stay Together** topped the charts, both R&B and

Above: Al Green's Southern Soul was a prime feature of the '70s. He now finds solace in gospel music.

pop, in February 1972, and **Look What You Done For Me, I'm Still In Love With You** and **You Ought To Be With Me** all climbed to just short of the summit, sounding not dissimilar—and there lay the drawback with Green's amazing run of success. The material—mostly written by Green himself or in partnership with Willie Mitchell or trumpeter Wayne Jackson—was at least adequate, but the music was usually from the same nucleus of Memphis studio musicians, and the inventiveness of producer Willie Mitchell began to wane. Even album-cuts by other writers tended to slip into the predictable groove, the main relief coming with the occasional burst of down-home gospel like the title-track of the 1976 LP **Have A Good Time.** Generally there was little variety, though it may sound harsh to be too critical of a winning formula, and even Al's vocals began to suffer from overkill in wistful introversion, almost a parody of himself.

On-stage, Green purveyed an image of an eternal Romeo, playing heavily to the female element in his audience—his UK debut at London's Rainbow Theatre in the mid-1970s had him performing love-songs at somewhat regimented tempo, and casting plastic roses into the front-stalls. The roses were still in the act on his return to London in 1980, but by then his repertoire had phased into a succession of his own golden oldies.

The love-man image was to be his 'Waterloo', however, when a jealous female fan broke into Al's apartment while he was taking a bath and tipped a basin of boiling hot grits down his back. Green suffered severe skin burns, and was unable to record or peform for some time. During this lay-off, he 'found' religion again, thanking God for saving his life, and took to preaching occasionally around Memphis.

He was back in the studio in 1977 to cut the highly-rated **Belle Album,** from which **Belle** was a fair hit, an intense soulful ballad with a return to a more vocal passion, then 1978 brought a fresh approach with an LP **Truth 'n' Time.** A pleasing version of **To Sir With Love** had some chart action in hypnotic beat-ballad style, while the funky flip **Wait Here** filled disco floors its crisp punchy beat, Green producing himself with more energy than ever Willie Mitchell had generated!

By 1980 Al Green had forsaken the R&B world, leaving Hi Records to sign with the religious organisation Word, whereon his 'born-again' gospel LPs have enjoyed good sales, gaining gospel chart placings and Grammy nominations.

Recordings:
Back Up Train (HLMJ/Action)
Gets Next To You (—/London)
Have A Good Time (Hi/London)
Belle Album (Hi/London)

Marcia Griffiths

See I Threes

Herbie Hancock

Herbert Jeffrey Hancock, born on the South Side of Chicago on April 12, 1940, took up keyboards at the age of seven because a friend of his had just acquired a piano. His classical studies were interrupted when he heard a fellow student play jazz. Realising that he did not have the capacity to improvise, he locked himself away with George Shearing and Oscar Peterson records, methodically dissecting their styles by notating their every solo.

After enrolling on an engineering course at Iowa's Grinnel College in 1956, Hancock formed a 17-piece concert band. He began arranging and composing, and changed his major to music composition. He returned to Chicago after he'd completed his course and began sitting in at clubs around town. In the winter of 1960, Donald Byrd's(▶) pianist got stranded in the snow and couldn't make it to Chicago. Byrd asked around town to find the best replacement, and most people recommended Hancock. Aged 20, Hancock became a permanent member of the band.

Byrd was recording for Blue Note Records and convinced them that, because Hancock was soon to be drafted, they should quickly record him. Hancock missed the draft, but in 1963 **Takin' Off** was released, featuring Freddie Hubbard and Dexter Gordon. This album contained **Watermelon Man**, with which Mongo Santamaria had a big hit single. Such was the success of **Takin' Off** that Blue Note drew up a long-term contract, and Hancock formed his own music publishing company.

From 1963 to 1968, Hancock was a permanent member of Miles Davis(▶) groups. As one of a quintet that also included Wayne Shorter, Ron Carter and Tony Williams, Hancock can be heard on **Nefertiti, Sorcerer, Miles In The Sky, Frilles De Kilimanjaro** and **In A Silent Way**. For the last three LP's, Hancock had begun to use an electric piano. During his years with Davis, Hancock still recorded albums of his own with Blue Note, such as **Maiden Voyage, Inventions And Dimensions, Empyrean Isles, Speak Like A Child** and **The Prisoner**.

Hancock's fame spread when Italian film director Michelangelo Antonioni commissioned him to write the soundtrack for his film *Blow Up*, and American actor, Bill Cosby, asked Hancock to write the music for a television special—that music was released as **Fat Albert**

Rotunda in 1969.

In 1968, Hancock left the Miles Davis Quintet, and in 1971, having formed his own sextet, he released **Mwandishi**, an album with more deeply developed electronic sounds and improvisation. (**Mwandishi** is Swahili for 'composer'.) Following his 1972 album **Sextant** —which was profoundly influenced by his friend and fellow musician Charles Buster Williams—Hancock took up Nichiren Shoshu Buddhism. In 1973, he migrated to Los Angeles, and released a jazz-funk album called **Headhunters**, which instantly exceeded the combined sales of all his previous albums. **Headhunters** was followed by the equally successful **Thrust, Death Wish, Man-Child**, and **Secrets**, an album that actually produced a Grammy award-winning soul/R&B hit single, **Doin' It**.

Hancock's reaction to his unexpected commercial status was to go right back to classical jazz. He reunited the Miles Davis Quintet, with Freddie Hubbard on trumpet instead of Davis. The first concert by the V.S.O.P., as they became known, was at the Newport Jazz Festival of 1976. The enthusiastic reaction they met with prompted them to do an American tour in 1977. In 1978, Herbie Hancock and Chick Corea undertook a worldwide dual acoustic-piano tour.

That same year, Hancock began to use the Vocoder, a vocal synthesiser that allowed him to sing, using his keyboard as a voice. His **Sunlight** album (1978) even yielded a pop hit single, **I Thought It Was You**, utilising the Vocoder

Headhunters. Courtesy Columbia Records.

gimmick to good effect. In 1979, he reached out to disco audiences with **Feets Don't Fail Me Now.** CBS drew together a **The Best Of** compilation later in that year. For his 1980 album, **Monster**, Hancock contracted out most of the song-writing and singing, and the record yielded several pop hits.

A collaboration in 1982 with Rod Temperton produced the **Lite Me Up** set, which encouraged further chart action.

Selected Recordings:
Takin' Off (Blue Note)
Maiden Voyage (Blue Note)
Fat Albert Rotunda (Warner Brothers)
Headhunters (Columbia/CBS)
Thrust (Columbia/CBS)
Feets Don't Fail Me Now (Columbia/CBS)
The Best Of Herbie Hancock (Columbia/CBS)
Monster (Columbia/CBS)

Below: Hancock plus Vocoder equals hit after hit.

Magic Windows (Columbia/CBS)
Lite Me Up (Columbia/CBS)

John Handy

Dallas, Texas-born (in 1933), alto-sax player John Handy first came to attention through his work with Charlie Mingus on such albums as **Blues And Roots** (Atlantic) and **Mingus Ah-Um** (Columbia). Unlike most post-Charlie Parker sax players, Handy managed to create a sound which was all his own and in the mid-'60s formed a quintet with violinist Michael White which became a major draw on the jazz festival circuit, cutting a notable album **Jazz At Monterey** (Columbia).

Handy developed a strong affinity with Indian music and cut an album, **Karuna Supreme**, with Ali Akbar Khan for MPS. In the mid-'70s he signed to Impulse and moved into the jazz-funk idiom, scoring a chart hit with **Hard Work** which was a disco smash. Since switching to Warner Brothers he has been unable to repeat this commercial success despite solid output.

Recordings:
Jazz At Monterey (Columbia/CBS)
Karuna Supreme (MPS/—)
Hard Work (Impulse)
Carnival (Warner Bros)

Derrick Harriot

Harriot surfaced on the Jamaican Ska(▶) scene during the '50s with his school vocal duo Sam and Harriot, having begun singing in church. In 1957 he was entering talent shows at Kingston's Palace Theatre, which brought his act to the attention of sound-system and label operators Duke Reid and Clement Coxsone Dodd(▶), who secured regular employment for his duo.

The following year Harriot assembled doo-wop/ska group The Jiving Juniors, cutting the single **Lollipop Girl** for Reid, and two sides, **Over The River** and **Sugar Dandy** (subsequently covered by Millie), for Dodd. In 1962, as a solo singer with his own labels, Musical Chariot and Crystal, Harriot scored on the Jamaican charts with his own composition **I Care** and a cover of Donnie Elbert's(▶) **What Can I Do**, his biggest selling single to date.

He assembled the Crystalites in 1967 with Jackie Jackson, bass; Hux Brown and Lyn Tait, guitars; Joe Isaacs, drums, and Bobby Ellis, keyboards, to back and produce other artists. His successes included **John Jones** (Rudy Mills), **Stop That Train** (Keith and Tex) and **Sinner Man** and **Sufferer** (The Kingstonians).

During the '70s, the bulk of his output was aimed at the older, MOR audience. Yet he did score on the reggae singles charts with a version of Pete Wingfield's **Eighteen With A Bullet**, and **Skank In The Bed** and **Born To Love You.**

Harriot shaped the chirpy rock-steady sound of the '60s and is spoken of with reverence by many Jamaican artists.

Recordings:
Life Of Contradiction (Joe Higgs/—)
Reggae Chartbusters Seventies Style (Crystal/—)

Donny Hathaway

Making his early mark in the music business as a session musician, songwriter, arranger and producer, Donny Hathaway eventually made it as an artist in his own right, but his extremely promising career was tragically cut short by his suicide in 1979.

Born in Chicago on October 1, 1945, Hathaway was raised in St Louis by his grandmother Martha Cromwell, a noted gospel-music performer, and attended Howard University in Washington DC where he majored in musical theory.

While in the capital city, he played local clubs with a jazz outfit, the Ric Powell Trio, and met Curtis Mayfield(▶) who invited him to join his new Curtom label in Chicago as a staff producer.

While with Curtom, Hathaway recorded duets with June Conquest as June and Donnie, then moved on to a staff job at Chess(▶) before going freelance and working with Uni, Kapp and Stax(▶), and such artists as Jerry Butler(▶), Woody Herman, Carla Thomas(▶) and the Staple Singers(▶).

Above: Donny Hathaway. An all-time soul giant.

It was at a music-trade convention that he met King Curtis(▶) (who supplied the spine-tingling solo on **Giving Up**, a feature of his superb **Donny Hathaway** set). Curtis also introduced him to Atlantic Records(▶), who recognised his innate talent and signed him as a singer, songwriter and producer.

Hathaway's perceptive **The Ghetto** was a big 1970 hit; **I Love You More Than You'll Ever Know** scored in 1972 and when Atlantic teamed him up with Roberta Flack(▶) the same year (Roberta was an acquaintance from Washington days with whom he had already been working as a producer and arranger) they were rewarded with a top-five US hit in **Where Is The Love.** Their later hits were the compelling **The Closer I Get To You** (1978) and **Back Together Again** (1980). Every effort should be made to obtain **Donny Hathaway** and **Donny Hathaway Live,** the definitive recordings by this giant talent.

Recordings:
Donny Hathaway (Atlantic)
Everything Is Everything (Atco)
Extension Of A Man (Atco)
Roberta Flack And Donny Hathaway (Atlantic)
Donny Hathaway Live (Atlantic)

Richie Havens

Richie Havens' single-minded approach to music does not comply with standard black musical forms like jazz, R&B, soul and funk, and has left him high and dry after two decades of solid grafting. New York-raised Havens (born 1941) took early inspiration from his piano-playing father, but with money a rare commodity in the Havens' household, he was unable to pursue his initial ambitions. His first serious step as a musician was at the age of 14 when he joined the McCrae Gospel Singers.

Havens began playing guitar professionally in the early '60s, having moved to Greenwich Village during the folk boom. He attracted sufficient attention to cut a couple of albums, **The Richie Havens Record** and **Electric Havens**, before signing to Verve and starting the most productive period of his career.

Mixed Bag, his debut for Verve, pointed the way to his future, containing as it did a mixture of Havens' own compositions and pop standards, although he is best represented by the 1969 album **Somethin' Else Again.** This powerful collection contained all the Havens' classics — **No Opportunity Necessary, No Experience Needed, Inside Of Him, Run Shaker Life** and his impassioned tirade about the Klu Klux Klan, **The Klan.**

Havens moved from cult status to brief pop stardom after his appearance at the Woodstock Festival, where his percussive guitar playing (using an open E tuning), aggressive vocals and swirling stage movements provided a unique balance to the giant rock bands of the day.

Sadly, this was to prove the musical highlight of his career, despite a brief flirtation with the singles chart (both in the UK and US) with **Here Comes The Sun** in 1971. His more recent albums are lacklustre, although every effort should be made to acquire the Verve recordings, including the double LP set **Richard P. Havens, 1983,** and the work for his own production company Stormy Forest.

Recordings:
Somethin' Else Again (Verve)
Mixed Bag (Verve)
Richard P. Havens, 1983 (MGM)
Stonehenge (Stormy Forest/ Polydor)
Alarm Clock (Stormy Forest/ Polydor)
Great Blind Degree (Stormy Forest/Polydor)
Compilation:
A State Of Mind (Verve)

Isaac Hayes

12 years on from **Hot Buttered Soul,** it's easy to forget just what an effect Isaac Hayes had on the course of black music and pop music in general. The elements he pioneered or popularised — the extended song workout, the 'soul rap', the symphonic treatment, the wah-wah guitar — have all been worked by others to the point of parody, while his own recent output has been at best mundane. At the same time, Hayes' contribution to the development of Stax(▶) Records, his session work and songwriting abilities, have been relegated to the level of a historical footnote. It is perhaps time for re-appraisal.

Born in Covington, Tennessee, in 1943, Isaac Hayes was raised by his grandparents in conditions of considerable poverty. The family moved to nearby Memphis when he was in his teens, and Hayes played saxophone in his high school band and then in various night clubs. Hayes was also proficient on piano, and was eventually accepted by the elite of musicians who comprised the Stax(▶) studio session men. He played on some of the seminal Stax sessions of the early '60s, adding classy piano to many Otis Redding(▶) and Sam and Dave(▶) sides.

Furthermore, with David Porter(▶), Hayes wrote many of Sam and Dave's classic '60s songs, including **You Don't Know Like I Know, Hold On, I'm Comin', Soul Man** and the beautiful ballad **When Something Is Wrong With My Baby.** Along with Stax boss Jim Stewart they produced most of Sam and Dave's material as well, and wrote for other artists in the Stax stable.

Hayes put his production expertise on his own work for the first time in 1967 with the album **Presenting Isaac Hayes** (later re-titled **Blue Hayes.**) A relatively straightforward bluesy offering, the album made little impact, perhaps because it had never originally been intended for release, being the result of a boozy jam session during which the engineers had left the tapes running. It was not until 1969 and the advent of **Hot Buttered Soul** that recognition came; but how spectacular it was.

Hot Buttered Soul. Courtesy Stax.

Hot Buttered Soul was originally one of a massive Stax two-week recording binge of some 27 albums featuring virtually every artist on the label and was recorded to make-up the number required by Gulf Western subsidiary Paramount who had just bought Stax from its founders Jim Stewart and Estelle Axton. But within three months the album had outsold every album the company had on release, taking the No. 1 position on the soul and jazz charts and reaching the upper echelons of the pop listings. By the end of 1970 the album went platinum.

Looking back, it is not hard to see why the LP had such an impact. It was certainly different; no other artist outside jazz had stretched a number (**By The Time I Get To Phoenix**) to 18 minutes plus. Spoken introductions, while by no means new, had never been so heavily emphasised. Again,

Below: All that glitters was certainly gold for Isaac Hayes in the late '60s and early '70s.

while others had used large orchestras before, Hayes used layers of strings almost symphonically, especially on his treatment of **Walk On By**. The combination of factors made it all sound very new and revolutionary; but it seems likely that the major reason for **Hot Buttered Soul's** huge success lay not in its musical novelty but in the fact that it was intensely romantic sexy music that appealed to a wide cross-section of people, and not just to committed soul fans. Hayes' voice was never really a soul voice; it was a deep, dark brown crooner's voice perfectly suited to the kind of material he specialised in—ballads. He never sounded completely comfortable on up-tempo songs.

Whatever the reason for its appeal, Hayes had certainly hit on a lucrative formula. He repeated the format on **To Be Continued** and **The Isaac Hayes Movement** (Jerry Butler's(▶) **I Stand Accused** received the soul-rap treatment on the latter), and expanded it for the film soundtrack album **Shaft** released in late 1971. Written to accompany one of the first black 'tec movies, the **Shaft** music varies from fairly mundane mood music to the exciting title track whose use of guitar effects set a style for action soundtracks for the next decade. **Shaft** was also an international hit single, making No. 4 in the British charts.

1971 also saw the release of the double album **Black Moses,** on the cover of which Hayes appears as a robed Messiah, and can probably be regarded as the year Hayes peaked. By this time he had a massive stage show on the road, featuring a 40-piece orchestra with girl singers and strings; Hayes himself appeared stripped to the waist and hung about with thick gold chains. A live double album, **Isaac Hayes Live At The Sahara Tahoe,** was released in 1973, and it captures well the combination of talent, originality, schmaltz and camp that Hayes was presenting at this time.

By 1974 Hayes' career was beginning to wane. He released two film soundtrack albums that year, **Tough Guys** and **Truck Turner** (he also starred in the latter movie), but they were only moderately successful. In 1975 he moved to ABC Records and recorded the first of a series of disco-orientated albums of varying quality both artistically and commercially. In 1976 he

scored a hit in Britain with **Disco Connection,** and the following year released a double album made with Dionne Warwick(▶), another major artist having difficulty staying in the limelight.

The Best Of... Courtesy Stax.

Almost unbelievably, considering the millions of dollars he must have made, he was declared a bankrupt at this time. The last few years have seen him continuing to record, without major success and sometimes in a style that seems almost self-parodying. He has also resumed his acting career, appearing in TV series like 'Starsky and Hutch' and taking a major part in the futuristic thriller movie *Escape From New York*. Hayes is without doubt a highly talented man who has carved a certain niche for himself in the history of black music, and it is not beyond the bounds of possibility that he could make a major impact again.

Hints of such a possibility came when he cut an album of duets with Millie Jackson(▶) in 1979.

Recordings:
His Greatest Hits (Stax)
Chronicle (Stax)
Hot Buttered Soul (Stax)
To Be Continued (Stax)
Lifetime Thing (Polydor)
Royal Rappin's (with Millie Jackson) (Polydor)
Best Of Shaft (Stax)
Golden Hour Presents Isaac Hayes (—/Golden Hour)

Leon Haywood

Born in Houston, Texas, Leon Haywood started his career in local clubs before moving to Los Angeles and becoming a pianist, first with

the Big Jay McNeely Band and then with Sam Cooke(▶).

His 1967 Fat Fish album **Soul Cargo** highlighted his jazz-tinged organ work, but by the mid-'70s he was establishing himself as a soul vocalist with a penchant for disco-slanted up-tempo items like **Come And Get Yourself Some, Double My Pleasure** and **Don't Push It, Don't Force it,** which brought him hits on both sides of the Atlantic.

Recordings.
Soul Cargo (Fat Fish/Vocalion)
Come And Get Yourself Some (20th Century)
Double My Pleasure (MCA)
Intimate (Columbia/CBS)
Leon Haywood Naturally (20th Century)

Heatwave

Formed in Europe, based in its early years in England, and with a multi-national line-up, Heatwave is, nevertheless, essentially an American soul outfit, built around Dayton, Ohio-born brothers Johnnie and Keith Wilder.

After serving with the US Army and being based in Germany, the Wilders decided to stay in Europe and form a band when their tour of duty ended. Their first recruit was keyboard player and songwriter Rod Temperton (born Hull, England). Temperton had been writing songs and playing in a German band but, disillusioned, he was about to return home when he noticed an advert in a music paper. The advert had been placed by the Wilder brothers and was also noticed by Los Angeles-born guitarist Eric Johns.

Spanish bass-player Mario Mantese met Johnnie Wilder in Switzerland, as did drummer Ernest 'Bilbo' Berger. Czechoslovakian-born Berger had fled from his native land to West Germany. Now stateless, he has passport problems which have sometimes interfered with Heatwave's touring plans. Completing the original line-up was second guitarist Jessie Whitten, from Chicago.

This septet—Johnnie and Keith Wilder, Temperton, Berger, Johns, Mantese and Whitten—found initial success on the British ballroom/disco/air-base circuit playing a mix

Below: The multi-national Heatwave.

of cover versions of then current soul and pop hits along with Rod Temperton originals.

Their debut album, produced by one-time British pop star Barry Blue, was released in 1976 and contained three major hit singles, **Too Hot To Handle, Always And Forever** and **Boogie Nights,** which latter sold in excess of two million copies worldwide and established the band's reputation in America.

Soon after the album had been recorded, Whitten was stabbed to death while on a visit home in Chicago. His place in the band was taken by British-born Roy Carter, formerly a member of the Foundations(▶). Using the same producer and with Temperton writing the up-tempo numbers, while Johnnie Wilder contributed the ballads, Heatwave's second album, **Central Heating,** was released in 1977 and yielded another two hit singles, **The Groove Line** and **Mind Blowing Decisions.**

Mind Blowing Decisions had been covered from the album by reggae artist Tyrone David. Johnnie Wilder was so impressed with this version that he released a 12-inch single of Heatwave's original with a reggae extension dubbed on at the end and this proved a winner in discotheques around the world.

Following a serious car accident, Mantese developed an extreme form of paralysis, caused by a blood clot on the brain, which left him with an inability to control his finger movements. His place in Heatwave was taken by British-born Keith Bramble while Eric Johns also left the band and was replaced by the Wilders' cousin Billy Jones.

In 1978, the Wilders took their international septet—three Britons (Temperton, Carter and Bramble), three Americans (the two Wilders and Jones) and a Czech (Berger)—back to America for a wildly successful tour. One bill, in Rhode Island, featured Rufus(▶), Kool and the Gang(▶) and Chic(▶) as well as Heatwave. The third Heatwave album, produced by Phil Ramone, was also a 1978 event though, apart from the minor hit **Razzle Dazzle,** its material lacked the earlier flair.

Temperton quit the band in late 1978, and his role on keyboards was divided between ex-Fatback Band (▶) member Calvin Duke and Keith Harrison. As a freelance songwriter, Temperton went on to compose highly successful material for Patti Austin(▶), Michael Jackson (▶), Quincy Jones(▶), George Benson(▶), Rufus(▶), the Brothers Johnson (▶), Bob James (▶), Aretha Franklin(▶) and Herbie Hancock(▶).

In February 1979, Johnnie Wilder was involved in a car crash which left him totally paralysed from the neck down. Showing incredible bravery, he fought back from seemingly helpless disability and now moves around in a stylish wheel-chair which possesses a wide range of facilities operated by lip and chin movements. Utilising laser controls, Wilder can, with a mere facial movement, manoeuvre his four-speed chair and operate various electrical appliances, including a tape deck and phone. The chair can even be plugged into a studio mixing console.

Johnnie Wilder still produces his band and sings on studio dates and, parked in the theatre wings, at concerts too but his on-stage role has been assumed by British-born J. D. Nicholas.

Shortly before Wilder's accident, there was another line-up change

when Roy Carter left to pursue a career in record production.

For Heatwave's fourth album, **Candles,** co-produced by Johnnie Wilder and the band's long-time engineer James Guthrie, the vocals were shared by Keith and Johnnie Wilder and J. D. Nicholas. Rod Temperton wrote five songs for this set which gained more commercial success than its immediate predecessor with hits like **Gangsters Of Love** and **Jitterbuggin'.**

Recordings:
Too Hot To Handle (Epic/GTO)
Central Heating (Epic/GTO)
Hot Property (Epic/GTO)
Candles (Epic/GTO)

Eddie Henderson

Dr Henderson nearly became an athlete, but decided to pursue music instead, alongside his career in medicine and psychiatry. A member of Herbie Hancock's(▶) group for several years, Henderson then signed to Capricorn as a solo artist, making two albums for them, before moving on to cut two albums for Blue Note.

In 1977, this multi-talented trumpet and flugelhorn player (born New York, 1940) became a Capitol Records artist, recording an initial album, **Comin' Through,** that produced a world-wide pop hit with **Prance On.**

His next album, **Mahal,** released in 1978, was written for and played on by the kind of friends he's been collaborating with all his career: James Mtume, Bernie Maupin, Paul Jackson and Hubert Laws(▶).

Recordings:
Realization (Capricorn)
Inside Out (Capricorn)
Comin' Through (Capitol)
Mahal (Capitol)

Michael Henderson

Born in Yazoo City, Mississippi, in 1951, Henderson has led a charmed existence, playing many styles with the great musicians. Moving to Detroit, he got his first professional bass-playing job aged 14, sessioning for Billy Preston(▶), The Jackson 5(▶) and Martha Reeves(▶). Stevie Wonder(▶) then employed him for a three-year touring stint, directly after which Aretha Franklin(▶) hired him for her band, where he stayed for another three years. Spotted by Miles Davis(▶), he was invited to tour and record.

After meeting Norman Connors (▶), Henderson recorded his first single, singing **Valentine Love,** and wrote two tracks for Connors' **You Are My Starship** album, the title track and **We Both Need Each Other,** a duet that introduced Phyllis Hyman(▶) to the world.

After signing to Buddah in 1976, Henderson began to develop his singing, cutting a series of satisfying soul albums, and another track with Phyllis Hyman, the hit single **Can't We Fall In Love Again.**

Recordings:
Solid (Buddah)
Goin' Places (Buddah)
In the Night Time (Buddah)
Wide Receiver (Buddah/Arista)
Reach Out For Me (Buddah/Arista)
Slingshot (Buddah/Arista)

Nona Hendryx

Born in Trenton, New Jersey, Nona was heard singing in her local church by Sarah Dash. Sarah suggested they form a duo and the pair scored with local R&B hits, before becoming members of Patti LaBelle & the Bluebelles(▶), along with Cindy Birdsong, who later joined the Supremes(▶). When Cindy left, the trio shed the uniform femininity of conventional female vocal groups, changed their name to Labelle(▶), and donned space-age/sensual costumes, sometimes more spectacular than their material.

From 1971 to 1976, Patti, Nona and Sarah made some impact with their rock/R&B fusion. In 1977, Nona cut an eponymous debut, and has since continued her career in a solo capacity.

Recordings:
Nona Hendryx (Epic)

The Heptones

In their heyday during the mid'70s the Heptones reggae vocal trio was poised to equal Bob Marley and the Wailers(▶), both artistically and in popularity, thanks especially to the singing and writing of Leroy Sibbles. It is unlikely that they will ever regain that status, yet on the strength of recordings made during that period they will go down in history as one of the finest exponents of their genre ever to emerge from the Caribbean.

The original personnel—consisting of Sibbles (born 1949), Barry Llewellyn (born 1947) and Earl Morgan (born 1945)—were all born and raised in the Trenchtown ghetto of Kingston, Jamaica, and met at Kingston Senior High School. A prototype Heptones formed by Morgan had disbanded before it really began, the other singers going on to form the Cables. Sibbles (an arc welder), Llewellyn and Morgan (a mechanic) quit their jobs in 1965 and made initial unsuccessful recordings with producer Ken Lack.

Above: Night Food. Courtesy Island Records.

Switching to Clement Coxsone Dodd, at his Studio One(▶), in 1966, they enjoyed instant success with a single penned by Sibbles, **Fatty Fatty.** Set to a strident beat it topped the Jamaican charts despite a total radio ban owing to the overt sexuality of its lyrics.

Jamaican music was then changing from the energetic ska(▶) to the slower, more sensual rock-steady beat. The Heptones adapted easily, recording a string of hits with Coxsone, including **Soul Power, Equal Rights, Freedom Line, Suspicious Minds** and **How Can I**

Leave, then scoring with Joe Gibbs' productions on **Cry Baby, I Miss You, Hypocrite** and **Freedom To The People,** the last song playing a vital role in the election of Jamaica's People's National Party in 1972.

Having left Studio One in 1971 they joined forces with producer Danny Holloway, at Harry J's Studio, to record the epic **Book Of Rules,** co-written by Llewellyn and Harry Johnson (aka Harry J), which was to become a highlight of their first Island Records album, **Night Food.** The album signalled the re-emergence of the group from the trough they had gone through in the early '70s when rock-steady gave way to the tougher, more militant reggae rhythms. It included a re-recording of **Fatty Fatty** and an interpretation of Holland/Dozier/Holland's(▶) **Baby I Need Your Loving.**

With their songwriting and harmonies attaining unparalleled heights, the Heptones switched their base of operations briefly to Canada in 1973 and the same year appeared at New York's Madison Square Gardens. In 1976 they toured the UK with Toots and the Maytals(▶) and on returning to Jamaica found their single **Country Boy** topping the charts.

That same year, with both the UK and USA gripped by Heptones mania, Island Records issued their seminal **Party Time** album. It had been recorded at Jamaica's Black Ark Studio, the home of eccentric producer Lee Perry(▶) who they had met at Studio One. The set features a sterling version of Bob Dylan's **I Shall Be Released** and climaxes with Perry's opus magnum of racial oppression, **Sufferers Time.** The songs of romance and ghetto-ology are glued to Perry's distinctive elastic, hi-hat rhythms and no reggae collection is complete without a copy.

Soon after its release, Sibbles quit to embark upon what has been an erratic solo career. Meanwhile, the Heptones had always supplemented their income with studio session work and Llewellyn and Morgan filled in with that for a year until they recruited Naggo Morris and cut an album, **Good Life,** with

producer Jo Jo Hookim at Channel One.

The following year they refuted all accusations of creative redundancy with the splendid **Better Days** collection that dominated the top of the UK reggae charts for three months and led to a headlining slot at a 1979 awards show staged by the British music paper *Black Echoes.*

Recordings have been sporadic and uneven of late. However, in their salad days nothing could match the beauty of their harmonies on vinyl or stage. Much of their craft has become the blueprint for a new generation of Jamaican singers.

Recordings:
Sweet Sixteen (Studio One/—)
On Top (Studio One/—)
Freedom Line (Studio One/—)
Heptones & Friends (Joe Gibbs/Trojan)
Cool Rasta (—/Trojan)
Night Food (Island)
Party Time (Island)
Good Life (—/Greensleeves)
Better Days (—/Third World)

Joe Higgs

Joseph Higgs (born May 1940 in Kingston, Jamaica) is one of the great unsung heroes of West Indian music. His songwriting and deft harmonies were the blueprint for many international bands, yet he has achieved little more than a cult following despite two active decades in the music industry.

Along with many Jamaican music innovators he graduated from the Alpha School, Kingston, and soon gained recognition writing material for what were to become top flight acts: Toots and The Wailers(▶), Jimmy Cliff(▶) and Delroy Wilson(▶). He divided his time between his own playing and teaching music at the Central Music School. Among those to benefit from his singing and guitar tuition were Bob Marley(▶) and members of the em-

Below: Eddie Holman evoking memories with Hey There Lonely Girl.

bryonic Wailing Souls(▶).

By the late '50s he had formed a singing duo with his close friend Delroy Wilson. Higgs and Wilson's music was firmly rooted in American R&B, during the pre-ska and rock-steady era. This was clearly illustrated by their singles, **Pretty Baby, I Long For The Day, The Rob** and **Come On Home.**

Wilson left for America in the mid-'60s and Higgs responded by embarking on a solo career that after almost two decades has enjoyed only limited success. He recorded many fine singles for a variety of producers, including **I Am The Song, You Hurt My Soul** and **Burning Fire.** He was recognised first and foremost as a songwriter and refused many offers from producers Coxsone Dodd and Duke Reid to write exclusively for them.

In 1976 he recorded his first album, **Life Of Contradiction,** issued outside Jamaica on the now defunct Vulcan label. For the next three years he hovered around the limelight, cutting notable singles such as **Sons Of Garvey** and **Sound Of The City** for Jimmy Cliff's Sunflower label. Since then he has remained inactive, with the exception of a handful of projects for Bunny Wailer(▶) and Jack Ruby. Wailer's Solomonic company planned the release of another sought-after Higgs album in 1982.

Recordings:
Life Of Contradiction (—/Vulcan)

High Inergy

Initially a quartet comprising Linda Howard, Michelle Rumph and sisters Vernessa and Barbara Mitchell, High Inergy were signed to Motown(▶) in 1976, and groomed as a female Jackson 5(▶), singing very commercial soul.

Never quite achieving what the company had hoped, the group have had sporadic unspectacular chart success with singles such as **You Can't Turn Me Off, We Are The Future, Shoulda Gone Dancin', Make Me Yours, I Just Wanna Dance With You, Goin' Through The Motions.** Loosing Vernessa in 1978, the girls have now recorded six albums in total.

Recordings:
Turning On (Motown)
Shoulda Gone Dancin' (Motown)
Hold On (Gordy/Motown)
High Inergy (Gordy/Motown)

Marcia Hines

Although born in Boston, Massachusetts, Marcia Hines has become established as the most successful female performer and recording artist in the history of the Australian music industry. At 16, she answered an ad seeking black cast-members for an Australian production of *Hair*, and after three years in that musical she played Mary Magdalene in the Australian run of *Jesus Christ Superstar.*

In 1975, Marcia signed to Wizard/Miracle Records and her first five albums sold in excess of 600,000 units in Australia alone—**Marcia —Live Across Australia** selling more than 100,000 double album sets. Her mixture of R&B and pop material, plus her aggressive and commanding presence and delivery brought back concert memories—the result of her exhaustive touring.

Take It From The Boys. Courtesy Logo Records.

In 1979, Marcia was licensed to British label Logo, who began repackaging her material for the European market. In 1981, she signed a worldwide deal (excluding Australia and New Zealand) with Logo and later that year, released her first British-recorded album.

Recordings:
Take It From The Boys (Logo)

Hi Tension

See British Funk.

Loleatta Holloway

If the disco boom of the late '70s had one favourable effect, it was that it imparted new action into the careers of several established artists, and launched some lesser-known but equally talented singers to a plateau of fame hardly dreamed of. The latter is the case with vivacious southern belle Loleatta Holloway.

Loleatta trod the familiar path from church choir activities to gospel groups, and the mid-'60s saw her established as a recording and

Queen Of The Night. Courtesy Salsoul Records.

touring member of the Caravans, a renowned female gospel quartet led by Albertina Walker, and including sometime members Shirley Caesar and Dorothy Norwood. She recorded albums on Savoy subsidiary Gospel, and on Scepter's Hob outlet with the group before switching to a secular persuasion, and a contract with Atlanta-based Aware Records.

An eponymous 1973 album, produced by her husband Floyd Smith, included the works of songsmiths like Ashford & Simpson, Sam Dees and Charles Jackson & Marvin Yancy, and early 1975 brought chart status with **Cry To Me,** a superb soulful, lyrical ballad penned by Dees. Aware folded soon afterwards, owner Michael Thevis being indicted on pornography

Above: Loleatta Holloway: Worn out disco heart?

charges, and Ms Holloway was signed to Salsoul-distributed Gold Mind, continuing the Dees' connection with R&B hit **Worn Out Broken Heart.** But it was the beaty sound of **Hit And Run,** produced in Philadelphia by Norman Harris, that spurred Loleatta's career to gain disco acceptance, including a memorable promotional tour of the UK. A successsion of albums have followed, each blending some danceable material with more aesthetically-satisfying soulful balladry.

Recordings:
Cry To Me (Aware/—)
Queen Of The Night (Salsoul)
Loleatta (Gold Mind/Salsoul)
Help Is On The Way (with the Caravans) (Gospel/—)

Eddie Holman

There can be few soul fans who are not familiar with the impassioned falsetto strains of Eddie Holman's greatest hit, **Hey There Lonely Girl,** which first charted on ABC in 1969, then went on to enjoy revitalised British popularity in 1974.

Eddie was born in Norfolk, Virginia, in 1946, and was steered towards an entertainment career very early in life, being trained at the Victoria School of Music and Art in New York City, then moving to Cheyney State College in Philadelphia. It was in Philadelphia that his recording career began, and **This Can't Be True** charted on Parkway late in 1965. By 1969 Holman had joined ABC, **I Love You** opening his chart account. The successful **Lonely Girl** and **Don't Stop Now** followed, and pleasing versions of Tommy Edwards' **It's All In The Game** and the Skyliners' **Since I Don't Have You,** were delivered in that ear-catching melodic falsetto.

With a pedigree also including a disc on Ascot, Eddie maintained the Philly connection with **My Mind Keeps Telling Me** on GSF, penned by Ron Baker, then a couple of outings on Silver Blue, **You're My Lady** produced by

Bobby Martin, and **I Believe In Miracles,** reverting to the Peter DeAngelis production which had yielded the ABC hits. With the onset of the disco era, 1977 saw Holman signed to Salsoul, where **A Night To Remember** used the Baker-Harris-Young talents well for a strong album, but this seems to have been Holman's swansong.

Recordings:
I Love You (ABC/—)
A Night To Remember (Salsoul)

Honey Cone

Carolyn Willis, a veteran of hit record sessions with Lou Rawls(▶), Johnny Mathis(▶) and O. C. Smith (▶), joined Shellie Clark (a onetime member of Ike and Tina Turner's(▶) Ikettes and back-up singer for Little Richard(▶)) and Edna Wright (an ex-member of Ray Charles'(▶) Raelets and background singer for the Righteous Brothers(▶) and with Johnny Rivers) to form Honey Cone.

Based in Los Angeles, the trio went to Detroit to sign with Holland/Dozier/Holland's(▶) then infant Hot Wax label and cracked it with their first record, **While You're Out Looking For Sugar** (1969).

Even bigger successes came with **One Monkey Don't Stop No Show** and **Want Ads** but, despite their cutting edge (which made the Supremes(▶) sound positively MOR) and undoubted talents, their stint as hit-makers was relatively short lived and by the mid-'70s they had passed into black music history.

Records:
Honey Cone (Hot Wax)
Sweet Replies (Hot Wax)
Soulful Tapestry (Hot Wax)

Hot Chocolate

Although never great album sellers, Hot Chocolate — Errol Brown vocals, Harvey Hinsley, guitar; Larry Ferguson, keyboards; Patrick Olive, bass; Tony Connor, drums—have been among the most consistent producers of hit singles of the last decade, scoring heavily in both the

US and the UK charts. Their success is largely due to lead singer Errol Brown, whose unusual voice and distinctive compositions combine to give the group an instantly recognisable sound.

The multi-racial group was put together by Brown in 1970 after he and some friends had a near-hit with a reggae version of John Lennon's **Give Peace A Chance** on Apple. Brown and original bass player Tony Wilson then took some songs to Rak boss Mickie Most, who immediately signed them and recorded one of the songs, **Love Is Life**, as a single. The record made No.6 in the British charts and started a string of hits that has remained unabated.

Brother Louie, an unusual song about mixed marriage, was covered in the US by Stories and made No.1 in 1973. It was a precursor to success in the US market for Chocolate themselves—**Emma**, released in 1974, was the first of many singles that hit big on both sides of the Atlantic. 1974 also saw the release of the band's first album, **Cicero Park.**

In 1975 Tony Wilson left to concentrate on a solo career and production, Patrick Olive switched from congas to bass and the present line-up was crystallised. Since then big hit followed big hit—**A Child's Prayer, You Sexy Thing, Don't Stop It Now, So You Win Again, Every 1's A Winner** and the uncharacteristic ballad **I'll Put You Together Again** being among the most notable.

A surprisingly powerful live act, Hot Chocolate tour regularly, and their recording output continues undiminished.

Recordings:
Every 1's A Winner (Infinity/Rak)
Going Through The Motions (Infinity/Rak)
Hot Chocolate's Greatest Hits (Big Tree/Rak)
Class (Infinity/Rak)

Cissy Houston

Cissy Houston first appeared on record (with RCA) in 1958 as youngest member of the Drinkard

Singers gospel group. By the age of 16 she was directing her own choir, which led to the formation of a unique team of recording-session back-up singers that included her nieces Dee Dee and Dionne Warwick(▶) and Judy Clay. Their first session was with rock 'n' roller Ronnie Hawkins and his musicians, the Hawks (who later became the Band).

After working with Aretha Franklin(▶), Neil Diamond, Maxine Brown(▶), Dusty Springfield, and countless others, the group (now with a changed line-up, Cissy Houston being the constant factor) was launched on a career of its own as the Sweet Inspirations (on Atlantic). Besides notching their own hits (notably **Sweet Inspiration** and **Why Am I Treated So Bad?**) the Sweet Inspirations became regular backing singers (on record and on stage) first for Aretha Franklin and then for Elvis Presley.

The group broke up in 1970 and Cissy toured with Darlene Love and Dee Dee Warwick backing Dionne Warwick, and began a solo recording career recording for such labels as Commonwealth United, Atlantic(▶) (as part of Herbie Mann's Surprise), Janus and Private Stock. She could also be heard on radio and TV ads for Texaco on both sides of the Atlantic!

Recordings:
Presenting Cissy Houston (Commonwealth United/ Major Minor)
The Long And Winding Road (Janus/Pye International)

Thelma Houston

Jimmy Webb once described Thelma Houston's talents as 'Everything great about the female black voice'. It was Webb who gave the Leland, Mississippi-born, California-raised, singer her first breakthrough with the critically acclaimed **Sunshower** album, which included a distinctive version of the Rolling Stones' classic **Jumpin' Jack Flash.**

Managed by Fifth Dimension mentor Marc Gordon, Thelma built the right contacts and in 1972 split from Gordon to sign with Motown.

Her great moment came in 1977 with the disco monster **Don't Leave Me This Way.**

Besides singing, Thelma has acted in numerous movies, including *Norman . . . Is That You?, Death Scream* and *The Seventh Dwarf,* as well as on stage.

Recordings:
Sunshower (Dunhill/Stateside)
Thelma Houston (Mowest)
Don't Leave Me This Way (Motown)
Never Gonna Be Another One (RCA)

Freddie Hubbard

Trumpeter Frederick Dewayne Hubbard (born Indianapolis, April 7, 1938) studied French horn in high school and won a scholarship to a music conservatory where his fellow students included the late guitarist Wes Montgomery.

Moving to New York at the age of 20, he became a regular at Count Basie's club from 1958, worked as a sideman with Sonny Rollins(▶) and Quincy Jones(▶) and in 1961 joined Art Blakey's famed Jazz Messengers. He then worked in Max Roach's group, signing in his own right for Blue Note, for which label he cut numerous albums both as a leader and as a sideman.

On switching to Creed Taylor's CTI(▶) label in the early '70s, he recorded in a more formally arranged large group setting to broaden his commercial appeal, gradually evolving a disco-orientated funk-jazz style, especially on his later albums for Columbia.

He has not neglected his jazz roots, however, and still sometimes records with a small combo, as on his 1980 Freddie Hubbard Quintet set **Live At The North Sea Jazz Festival.**

Recordings:
First Light (CTI)
Red Clay (CTI)
Keep Your Soul Together (CTI)
The Love Connection (Columbia/ CBS)

Keith Hudson

Multi-instrumentalist Hudson (who was born Trenchtown, Kingston, Jamaica, March 18, 1949) embarked upon a career in music at the age of 15, carrying Don Drummonds'(▶) trombone. By 1968 he was writing and producing for Ken Boothe(▶) and John Holt(▶). He played a crucial role in the development of '70s DJ music, producing classic discs with Dennis Al Capone (**Spanish Omega**) and Big Youth(▶) (**S-90 Skank**). He also brought to prominence Skin, Flesh And Bones, an early incarnation of the Agrovators and the Revolutionaires(▶).

Recordings:
Flesh Off My Bones (—/Atra)
Rasta Communication (Joint International/Greensleeves)

Hues Corporation

June 1974 saw the Los Angeles-based trio of St Clair Lee, Fleming Williams and ladyfriend H. Ann Kelley skate to the top of the American pop chart with their rousing disco opus **Rock The Boat,** one of the records which set off the whole disco boom in the US.

The record was also a British hit,

making No. six. **Rockin' Soul,** from their second album, gave Hues Corporation another major American hit but they failed to maintain the momentum.

Recordings:
Freedom For The Stallion (RCA)
Rockin' Soul (RCA)

Willie Hutch

Willie McKinley Hutchinson was born in Los Angeles in 1946, but spent his formative years in Dallas where he sang with the Ambas-

The Mark Of The Beast.
Courtesy Tamla Records.

sadors. On returning to LA, Hutch worked for Johnny Rivers' Soul City Records, and then briefly for Venture, before moving to Motown (▶) and creating a career for himself as a writer/producer/performer. He co-wrote the Jackson 5's **I'll Be There** (1970), arranged the vocals on their **Got To Be There** and **Never Can Say Goodbye** singles, and produced and wrote **Mr. Fix It Man** for Sisters Love in 1972. Hutch also co-produced Smokey Robinson's(▶) debut solo album, after Robinson's split with the Miracles(▶).

Above: Always in tune—versatile Willie Hutch.

Hutch's first album as a performer was **The Mack,** a film soundtrack, released in 1973, which spawned two successful singles, **Brother's Gonna Work It Out** and **Slick.** The next 18 months saw a number of Hutch releases, including his best album to date **The Mark Of The Beast.** The 1976 release **Concert In Blues** featured the disco hit **Party Down,** and Hutch has since recorded several solid and satisfying albums, with **In Tune** (1979), his first for Whitfield Records, a stand-out.

Recordings:
The Mack (Tamla)
The Mark Of The Beast (Tamla)
Concert In Blues (Tamla)
Havin' A House Party (Motown)
In Tune (Whitfield)

Think It Over. Courtesy Private Stock Records.

Phyllis Hyman

Phyllis Hyman, the oldest of seven children, was born in Philadelphia and grew up in Pittsburgh. She sang in Pittsburgh's All-City Choir, and received the first music scholarship given by a business college. In 1971, she became a professional singer, forming a group called the New Direction for a six-month American tour. When the tour ended the group disbanded, and Phyllis went to Miami, to sing in clubs. She began a residency at Rust Brown's Club on West 96th Street, New York City, in 1975, attracting many celebrities. As a result, Jon Lucien asked her to appear on his **Premonitions** album, and she also guested on Norman Connors'(▶) **You Are My Starship.**

Soon after touring with Connors, Phyllis was signed to Buddah Records, and her first album, **Phyllis Hyman,** was released in **1977.** She then signed to Arista Records and recorded **Somewhere In My Lifetime** (1979) and **You Sure Look Good To Me** (1980).

You Know How To Love Me. Courtesy Arista Records.

Phyllis is a six-foot exquisite fashion model, her face and body being used to promote many beauty products. As an actress she made her Broadway debut in the 1981 musical production *Sophisticated Ladies.* Her performance was nominated for a Tony Award, and she received the Theatre World Award for the most promising new talent. Also in '81, Arista released her **Can't We Fall In Love Again?** set.

Recordings:
Phyllis Hyman (Buddah)
Somewhere In My Lifetime (Arista)
You Sure Look Good To Me (Arista)
Can't We Fall In Love Again? (Arista)

Ijahman

Born Trevor Sutherland in Jamaica in 1945, he followed his family to London, in 1961, living there for 13 years. After a three-year stint in a UK jail for a minor offence, he returned to Jamaica and in 1974 recorded his first single, **Jah Heavy Load.** A reggae chart hit, it was later included on the first of two albums for Island Records, **Haile I Hymn (Chapter 1),** a collection of lengthy, deeply spiritual songs set to a light semi-acoustic backing, and **Are We A Warrior.**

His third album, **Tell It To The Children** (1982), is a radical departure, displaying the influence of American R&B.

Recordings:
Haile I Hymn (—/Island)
Are We A Warrior (—/Island)

Tell It To The Children (—/Tree Roots)

The Independents

The Independents (Chuck Jackson, the unrelated Maurice Jackson, Helen Curry and, from the second album on, Eric Thomas) burst onto the soul scene in 1973 and had a quick flurry of enormous hit singles, including **Leaving Me, It's All Over, The First Time We Met, Just As Long As You Need Me** and **I Just Want To Be There.**

The group was a vehicle for the writing and production talents of member Chuck Jackson (born Greenville, South Carolina, March 22, 1945) and Marvin Yancey (born Chicago, May 31, 1950), and broke up when the pair decided to concentrate on their writing and production work for other acts, notably Natalie Cole(▶).

The Independents recorded for Scepter, but Jackson should not be confused with Scepter's other Chuck Jackson(▶), the '60s solo star.

Recordings:
The First Time We Met (Scepter/Pye International)
Discs Of Gold (Scepter/Pye International)

Luther Ingram

Born in Jackson, Tennessee, Luther Thomas Ingram was raised in the Mid-West, gaining early experience singing in Baptist Church choirs. Moving to New York, he met up with veteran producers Jerry Leiber and Mike Stoller(▶) (who had previously worked with the Coasters(▶), Drifters(▶) and Elvis Presley among others), who got him a deal with Smash. But his version of **I Spy (For The FBI)** dipped out, Jamo Thomas getting the hit. Ingram was then signed by producer Johnny Baylor to the tiny KoKo label, which had a national distribution deal via Stax(▶).

My Honey And Me (issued on Stax in the UK) did well in the discos, and then, from his second LP, came his masterpiece—the moving ballad **If Loving You Is Wrong (I Don't Want To Be Right),** subsequently covered by Millie Jackson(▶), Rod Stewart and others.

A major Stateside hit, the record was never released officially in Britain because of wrangles over the advance monies demanded, but it did sell more than 50,000 copies on import.

Recordings:
I've Been Here All The Time (KoKo/—)
If Loving You Is Wrong (I Don't Want To Be Right) (KoKo/—)

Inner Circle

Formed in Jamaica in 1968 by brothers Roger 'Fat Man' Lewis (lead guitar) and Ian 'Munty' Lewis (bass) upon leaving school, and including other musicians from comfortable middle-class areas of the island, Inner Circle played a residency at Kingston's Tunnel Club until it was destroyed by fire. The group split, some members leaving to form Third World(▶), while the brothers accepted session work at Dynamic Sound Studio.

Re-assembled with Calvin McKensie, drums; Bernard 'Touter'

Harvey and Charles Farquharson, keyboards, they won the 'Best Band' contest on Jamaica's influential Johnny Golding Show (1972) and during subsequent two years recorded hit single **I See You** and albums **Dread Reggae Hits** and **Heavy Reggae** for Top Ranking label.

Early in 1974, ebullient vocalist Jacob Miller, whose previous solo hits included **Tenement Yard** and **Forward Jah Jah Children,** complimented the equally rotund Lewis brothers by accepting the job of lead singer. His warm scat singing and flair for songwriting, and his appeal as a sex symbol, quickly established him as the nucleus of the band, their sound varying from reggae to disco. Inner Circle's first hit together was **All Night 'Till Daylight** and in 1975 they played an energetic and widely praised set at New York's first reggae festival at Madison Square Gardens.

Capitol Records signed the band and in 1977 they unleashed the album **Reggae Thing** and in 1978 **Ready For The World.** Both sets captured the excitement of their live performances, the latter veering more towards jazz, although neither sold in quantity. Nevertheless, their popularity placed them third after Bob Marley(▶) and Peter Tosh(▶) on the bill of the 1978 One Love Peace Concert, in Jamaica. Later that same year they signed to Island Records.

Their first album under this deal was **Everything Is Great** and it received all the promotional drive Island could afford, including a heavily publicised 1979 UK tour with the Average White Band(▶). Critical acclaim for the album and shows failed to ignite anything more than curiosity from reggae fans, who were bemused by the spectacle of three huge men with dreadlocks performing music often better suited to chic funk discotheques.

Other albums followed, consolidating their popularity in the States, but in 1980, tragedy struck when Miller was killed in a car crash in Jamaica. Without Miller, they slipped out of the public eye.

Responding to invitations to tour the US again, the group enlisted Twinkle Brothers'(▶) protagonist, Norman Grant, as a replacement. The tour was a success and A&M Records were reputed to have offered the group a sizeable advance on a recording contract if Grant remained.

He declined the invitation, A&M withdrew the offer, and in 1982 Inner Circle returned to Top Ranking with **B.M.W.,** a much rootsier album recorded in Miami with vocalist Trevor Brown.

Recordings:
Everything Is Great (Island)
New Age Music (Island)
B.M.W. (Top Ranking/—)

The Intruders

The million-selling teen anthem **Cowboys To Girls** was the most important record cut by Philadelphia-based Samuel 'Little Sonny' Brown, Phil Terry, Eugene 'Bird'

Cowboys To Girls. Courtesy Gamble Records.

Dautrey and Robert 'Big Sonny' Edwards. Signed to Kenny Gamble and Leon Huff, the Intruders had several minor hits including **Win, Place Or Lose (She's A Winner)** and **I'll Always Love My Mama** and built a following via Phillybased TV shows put together by DJ/promoter Georgie Woods and his partner Jimmy Bishop in the early '70s.

Below: The late Jacob Miller, IC's early inspiration!

However, they were later eclipsed by such heavyweights as the Spinners(▶), the O'Jays(▶), Harold Melvin and the Blue Notes(▶) and the Stylistics(▶).

Recordings:
Cowboys To Girls (Neptune/—)
Together Again (Gamble/—)
Energy Of Love (Philadelphia International)

I-Roy

Roy Reid (aka I-Roy) was one of the most popular Jamaican DJ toasters to emerge on the island's sound-system(▶) circuit in the '60s. Inspired by King Stitt and U-Roy(▶) he established and operated the Turbo Sonic Sound and Soul Bunny, a weekly reggae discotheque at Victoria Pier in St Catherine's, where he still resides.

Building a reputation for witty, politically incisive lyrics, he made his first recordings with Spanish Town producer Harry Mudie, **Musical Pleasure** and **Drifter,** circa 1971. His popularity increased when he took the reins of King Tubby's Hi Fi that same year and cut his first album, **Presenting I-Roy,** produced by Gussie Clarke and issued in Britain by Trojan Records. Soon he was producing his own material and during the early '70s made the island's charts with singles **Buck And The Preacher** and **Dread In The West,** and albums **Hell And Sorrow** and **Truth And Rights.**

A long creative spell with Britain's Virgin Records culminated (1980) with the Dennis Bovell(▶)-produced **Whap'n Bap'n** album. A radical departure from his earlier recordings, it was a successful fusion of Jamaican toasting and American rapping, intended to broaden his audience appeal.

Recordings:
The Best Of I-Roy (—/G.G.)
Cancer (—/Front Line)
The General (—/Front Line)

Gregory Isaacs

Isaacs has been a reggae superstar for a decade. His strength is in his totally unique voice of sandpaper and glue, coupled with a broad songwriting base. His R&B equiva-

*The Best Of Gregory Isaacs.
Courtesy CG Records*

lent is Marvin Gaye(▶), another artist who has made a career out of combining sensuality and ghetto-ology.

Born in July 1951, Isaacs attended schools in Jamaica's Fletcher's Land and Denham Town districts prior to joining his first vocal group, the Concordes. As a youth he followed the obligatory path for aspiring reggae singers and enter-

Above: I-Roy, straight to a toaster's head.

ed himself for the Vere Johns Opportunity Talent Contest. Shortly after, he cut his first studio teeth with producer Rupie Edwards(▶), who issued Isaacs' self-composed **Another Heartbreak** on the Success label. The relationship with Edwards spawned the **Each Day, Too Late** and **Black And White** singles, while, for Prince Buster(▶), he recorded **Dancing Floor.**

Isaacs quickly comprehended the pitfalls of becoming over-dependent on producers who too often issue unfinished material. He wanted total control, and by 1973 he and Errol Dunkley(▶) had established their African Museum label that would allow them to flex their production muscles on their own recordings and on those of other artists. In fact, the pair went on to collaborate on one track, the ever popular **Movie Star**—later versioned by Big Youth(▶).

Isaacs' UK chart breakthrough came in 1974, though he had toured the country three years earlier. The song that did it was **Love Is Overdue** on Trojan's Attack subsidiary. The same label later issued the singer's first album, **In Person,** a collection of some of his most popular songs of that time.

The mid-'70s was his most prolific period. Singles produced by himself and by others flooded the ethnic charts in Jamaica and Britain: With Winston Niney Holiness, **Bad Da,** for Lloyd Campbell **Promises,** and for Prince Tony **Fly Little Silver Bird.** His own productions included such notable tracks as Bob Marley's(▶) **Bend Down Low, Sinner Man, Help Us Get Over** and **Gimme Mi Gun,** which was later reactivated as a toast by Doctor Alimantado.

By 1976 Isaacs had provided African Museum with a distribution outlet, Cash & Carry. He had taken a firm grip of his own destiny

and the public responded by making that year his best to date. African Museum released material that was stunning in its quality and provided further evidence that Isaacs was a major songwriting force. There simply wasn't anything to match **Black A Kill Black** or **Extra Classic** (the latter was used as the title of a UK compilation album).

Virgin Records' Front Line reggae outlet was keen to share some of the Gregory Isaacs' action and, between 1978 and '79, issued two first-rate albums, **Soon Forward** and **Cool Ruler,** which did so well that Isaacs was henceforth known by the moniker 'Cool Ruler'. He is now also known as 'Lonely Lover', the title of another album.

Another UK label, Charisma, previously associated with the rock band Genesis, had launched its Pre label and was quick to sign Isaacs up when his Virgin deal expired. Albums **The Lonely Lover** and **More Gregory,** each supported by sell-out British and European tours, didn't move in the quantities that both parties had hoped for—Isaacs has since claimed that their poor showing was due to lack of promotion. He and Pre split in 1981 and the singer is presently in possession of a batch of new material but without a major company to back it.

A concrete move was to employ the services of Don Taylor who had previously managed both Bob Marley(▶) and Marvin Gaye(▶). Thus Isaacs is a completely autonomous music-making machine of the highest calibre and it can't be long now before he achieves the crossover acceptance that he so rightly deserves.

Recordings:
In Person (Treasure Isle/Trojan)
Cool Ruler (—/Front Line)
The Best Of Gregory Isaacs (—/GG)
The Best Of Gregory Isaacs Vol. 2 (—/GG)

Israel Vibration

Cecil 'Skeleton' Spence, Albert 'Apple' Craig and Lascelle 'Whiss' Bulgin were victims of the polio epidemic that swept across Jamaica in the late '50s. Severely crippled, they met and built up a common bond in music in 1976 at the Mona Heights Rehabilitation Centre.

Since the day they decided to form a reggae vocal group they have fought against prejudice from both the medical profession, for growing dreadlocks and for their abiding belief in Rastafari, and ironically also from other Rastas who refused to work with them because of a misguided belief that Jah (God) is punishing them.

Producer Tommy Cowan spotted them at one of the many Kingston talent shows they entered and with his assistance they issued their first single, **Why Worry,** in the summer of 1978. Cowan's confidence in their songwriting and vocal prowess paid off the same year with an album, **Same Song,** and an increasing number of live engagements. Audiences were stunned at the sight of three handicapped singers delivering their protest songs on crutches.

The trio reacted to the spread of political gang warfare on the island in 1979 with the hit single **Crisis** and a second album. By the turn of the decade they shifted axis and released what amounted to a love song, **Love Can Conquer,** on their own label.

Recordings:
Same Song (Israel Vibes/EMI)
Unconquered People (Israel Vibes/—)

I-Threes

Following the departure of Peter Tosh(▶) and Bunny Wailer(▶) from the Wailers(▶), Bob Marley(▶) was anxious to replace his principal backing vocalists, and recruited three young ladies — Marcia Griffiths, Judy Mowatt and Rita Marley—to complement the burgeoning Marley sound.

Known as the I-Three, the girls had pursued solo ambitions with various degrees of success until their collaboration and, since Marley's untimely death, have returned to solo careers. They did not record as a group outside of their appearances with Marley.

Judy Mowatt was originally a member of the Gaylettes, working with the group until 1973, and they enjoyed chart action with **Way Over Yonder** and **I Shall Sing.** She quit to launch a solo career, but within a year had joined Marcia and Rita (Bob Marley's long-time companion) as the I-Threes. She combined her work with Marley by raising a family, and continuing a solo recording career. Her most recent work is **Mr D.J.** (1982).

Marcia Griffiths (b. 1954) had attained a considerable amount of success as a singer before her participation with the I-Threes, having recorded with Clement Coxsone Dodd(▶) by the time she was 10, and scoring a huge international hit in 1972 with Bob Andy(▶) and **Young Gifted & Black.** The follow-up **Pied-Piper** also charted. Marcia has recorded four solo albums, the most notable being those produced by Sonia Pottinger in the late '70s, **Naturally and Steppin'.**

Rita Marley also worked with

Clement Coxsone Dodd as a solo artist, and had Jamaican hits in the late '60s, early '70s, with **Pied Piper** and the Beatles' **Yesterday**. She had previously been a member of the Soulettes. Since joining the I-Threes, Rita has scored with **Many Are Called, Play Play** and her only solo album **Who Feels It Knows It**, much of it recorded while Bob Marley was dying of cancer.

Recordings:
Judy Mowatt:
Mellow Mood (Tuff Gong/—)
Black Woman (Asgama/Grove Music)
Mr. D.J. (Ashama/—)
Marcia Griffiths:
Naturally (Sky Note)
Steppin' (High Note/Sky Note)
Rita Marley:
Who Feels It Knows It (Shanachie/Trident)

Jermaine Jackson

When the Jackson 5(▶) switched labels from Motown(▶) to Columbia, it was no surprise that Jermaine Jackson decided to remain behind—after all, he had married the boss's daughter!

Born Gary, Indiana, December 11, 1954, Jermaine LaJaune Jackson recorded his first solo album, **Jermaine**, n 1973 at a time when Motown were using the phenomenal success of the J5 as a launching pad for the brothers to enjoy parallel solo careers.

While Michael Jackson(▶) immediately made it big in his own right however, Jermaine Jackson's career was slower in taking off and, following a second 1973 album **Come Into My Life**, there was a delay until the end of 1976 before his third set was released.

In between, he had married Hazel Joy Gordy, daughter of Berry Gordy, on December 15, 1974, and become involved as songwriter and producer for aspiring new

Below: The X-rated Millie Jackson.

I Like Your Style. Courtesy Motown Records.

Motown act Switch who had given him a cassette of their material when they met in a lift at Motown.

Utilising Motown's house staff of writers, arrangers, producers and musicians, **My Name Is Jermaine**, which appeared shortly before Jermaine and Hazel's first child was born, was no more successful than the two previous albums.

Feel The Fire appeared in 1977 and a fifth album, **Frontiers**, in 1978 but there was still no exciting sales response to his mix of soul and pop.

As a member of the Jackson family he was still in the public eye and the media liked his good looks but the comparative lack of commercial success might have bruised the ego of someone less persistent.

Things finally took off in 1980 when Stevie Wonder(▶)—someone who could be expected to bring zest to anyone's ailing recording career—co-wrote, co-produced and played on much of **Let's Get Serious** which included the worldwide hit singles **Let's Get Serious** and **Burnin' Hot**.

His seventh album, **Jermaine** (which re-used the title of his second set!), was released later in 1980 and featured the hit single **You Like Me, Don't You** while his

eighth LP, **I Like Your Style**, with Wonder still casting a parental eye over him, was vocally his most assured to date.

Recordings:
Jermaine (Motown)
Let's Get Serious (Motown)
I Like Your Style (Motown)

Michael Jackson

Lead singer of the Jacksons(▶) since their discovery in 1969, Michael, the youngest performing Jackson till Randy joined, has also led a successful solo career since 1971. Beginning with **Got To Be There** in 1971, he scored half a dozen massive hits for Motown(▶), including revivals of **Rockin' Robin** and the movie theme **Ben**, before the entire Jackson clan left the company for Epic in 1977.

In 1978 Jackson co-starred with Diana Ross(▶) in the ill-fated movie version of *The Wiz*, but did not supply any solo recordings to Epic until 1979 when the Quincy Jones (▶)-produced **Off The Wall** album was released. Including new songs by Jackson, Paul McCartney and Heatwave's(▶) Rod Temperton and featuring top Los Angeles session musicians as well as the Brothers Johnson(▶), the album quickly achieved No.1 status in America and around the world, and is now reputed to be the biggest ever selling album by a black performer.

Virtually every track from the album has now been released on 45, and, at least in America, it achieved top-10 status. In 1981, demand for new material by Jackson was so great that Motown were able to reissue an old track, **One Day In Your Life**, and see it sail effortlessly to No.1 on the British charts.

Michael's solo success helped the Jackson's career to come to the top in the early '80s, but by mid-1982 there was still no sign of a follow-up to **Off The Wall**.

Recordings:
The Best of Michael Jackson (Motown)
Off The Wall (Epic)
The Wiz (MCA)

Millie Jackson

If the Board Of Film Censors had their jurisdiction extended to the world of records then Millie Jackson would be rated 'X'. Hers is most definitely adult entertainment—with no holds barred.

Songs berating two-timing men, and replete with four-letter expletives, are her forté. Her famous raps pull no punches—she tells it exactly the way it is, all of which goes a long way to explain her enormous impact. Add to her material one of the best female soul voices ever heard—yes, she does rate in the Aretha Franklin(▶), Nina Simone(▶) and Randy Crawford(▶) league—and you have the secret behind a stream of hit singles and albums and standing-room-only concerts.

Her career all started as a bet. She was out at a New York club with some friends one night in 1964 and they dared her to get up on stage and sing with the band, which included some other friends. She did it, and she's been singing ever since.

Millie was born in the small town of Thompson, Georgia, in 1944, and, with her father away in New

Jersey looking for work, was raised by her grandparents. Her grandfather was a preacher and that meant church six days a week, and the Tennessee Ernie Ford Show once a week was her allowed dose of TV—and that only because he ended each show with a hymn!

Rebelling, she ran away at age 14 and was eventually allowed to join her father in Newark, New Jersey. Starting work as a model she moved to New York but, with the advent of 'Black is beautiful', the market became flooded with aspiring black beauties and she quit.

Discovered by songwriter Billy Nichols, she was taken to MGM by Don French. After a flop with her one single **A Little Bit Of Something** she switched to Spring, who were having some success with Joe Simon(▶). Raeford Gerard produced her first Spring album **Millie Jackson**, which included the **A Child Of God, My Man Is A Sweet Man** and **Ask Me What You Want** hit singles, all of which earned her nomination as 1972's Most Promising Female Vocalist.

It Hurts So Good, title cut of her second album, featured in the *Cleopatra Jones* movie, and by her fourth album **Caught Up** she had developed her own brand of concept package, exploring the emotions of a love triangle, taking a stage further the format developed by her contemporary Laura Lee(▶).

The album was a monster, her first gold set, and the idea was developed further with **Still Caught Up** by which time she had perfected the soul-rap intro, which was further exploited in subsequent albums such as **Lovingly Yours** and **Free And In Love** and on her celebrated stage shows where she really did get lowdown-and-dirty, at one moment insulting, the next seducing, the male members of her audience (captured on disc on **Live And Outrageous**).

Mother of two daughters, she has herself probably been through many of the traumas she describes on vinyl, though she now describes herself as being 'happily divorced'!

Recordings:
It Hurts So Good (Spring/Polydor)
Caught Up (Spring/Polydor)
Still Caught Up (Spring/Polydor)
Best Of Millie Jackson (Spring)
Feelin' Bitchy (Spring)
Live And Uncensored (Spring/Polydor)
Royal Rappin's (with Isaac Hayes) (Polydor)

Bob James

White American Bob James (born 1939) has been contributing keyboards to jazz, and jazz-fusion albums for more than a decade.

Worked with Sarah Vaughan as accompanist/musical director from 1966-68, and on sessions for Quincy Jones(▶), Dionne Warwick(▶), and Roberta Flack(▶) between 1968-72.

Signed as exclusive producer for Creed Taylor's CTI/Kudu(▶) labels in 1973 for whom he recorded four solo albums as well as working with Eric Gale(▶), Groves Washington(▶) and Stanley Turrentine(▶). He formed Tappan Zee, a label distributed by CBS, to promote other jazz-fusion artists such as Richard Tee, Wilbert Longmire(▶) and Mongo Santamaria.

Recordings:
Heads (Tappan Zee/CBS)
Touchdown (Tappan Zee/CBS)

Lucky Seven (Tappan Zee/CBS)
H (Tappan Zee/CBS)
One On One (with Earl Klugh)
(Columbia/CBS)
All Around The Town—Live
(Tappan Zee/CBS)
Sign Of The Times (Tappan
Zee/CBS)

Rick James

Rick James has long braided hair, wears supertight leather pants and knee-high boots, smokes a lot of dope, makes love to innumerable women, and lives life in the fast lane. He was born James Johnson and raised in Buffalo, New York, in the mid-1950s. His mother, Betty Gladden, had separated from her husband when James was three, and involved her two sons, James and Roy, in a numbers racket; it was the only way she could support them.

At 15, James joined the US Naval Reserve, but regretting the hastiness of his decision he went Absent Without Leave. He fled across the border to Canada, where he shared an apartment with a then unknown folk singer named Neil Young. They formed a band called the Mynah Birds, went to Detroit, and got signed to Motown, but nothing was ever released. While in Canada, James called himself Ricky James Matthews. At that time, he was into the occult, and a Canadian witch told him that he should change his name to Rick James, and that he would make it in eight years. She was right.

After the Mynah Birds, James

Street Songs. Courtesy Motown Records.

kicked around Canada, South America, and then came to London, where he formed a blues band called Main Line, playing guitar and harmonica as well as singing.

Finally he returned to Buffalo. It was around the time that George Clinton's(▶) many bands were establishing themselves. Rick felt he couid produce something funkier, punkier and hornier. He went into Cross Eyed Bear Studios in nearby Clarence, and emerged with some tapes, going back to Motown to show them what he was doing, with a view to obtaining some kind of employment, or advice. Motown bought the tapes, and in 1978 released them under the title **Come Get It!** The album spawned the big hit **You And I.**

His second album, **Bustin' Out Of L Seven**, was followed by his first American tour. By then, Rick had a backing group, the Stone City Band; some backing vocalists, the coloured Girls; and a horn section, the Punk Funk Chorus. The tour enhanced his image of flamboyance and eroticism, and generated great interest in the product to come.

Severe hepatitis endangered his life for a while but in December 1979 **Fire It Up** arrived, and instantly outsold his previous albums. During that year, Rick produced the debut album by a new Motown artist, Teena Marie(▶); the album, **Wild And Peaceful**, contained a big hit, **I'm Just A Sucker For Your Love.** James and Marie have continued to contribute to each other's albums ever since, and is invariably backed on her albums by many of James's musical entourage.

In 1980, Rick produced the debut album for the Stone City Band entitled **In 'n' Out**. Also in that year, Rick took a vacation in Barbados, where he composed his comparatively relaxed fourth album, **Garden Of Love**, but the public did not respond to the idea of their urban hero lying on a tropical beach.

In 1981, as well as producing the Stone City Band's follow-up **The Boys Are Back**, Rick returned to the city with his fifth album, **Street Songs. Street Songs** went double platinum in America, and songs like **Give It To Me Baby** and **Super Freak** made the British population yearn for a Rick James tour. A package containing James, Teena Marie, Cameo(▶) and the Sugar Hill Gang travelled round America in 1981, playing to capacity crowds.

Recordings:
Come Get It! (Motown)
Bustin' Out Of L Seven
  (Motown)
Fire It Up (Motown)
Garden Of Love (Motown)
Street Songs (Motown)

Al Jarreau

Born in Milwaukee, Wisconsin, Al Jarreau received a BS at Rpon College and an MS in psychology at the University of Iowa. Maybe his understanding of the mind explains the sensitivity with which this singer approaches songs. Basing himself around jazz material, Jarreau has now sung his and others' songs on six albums.

As a young man, Jarreau sang at private parties, dances and local jazz festivals, taking his major influences from Nat 'King' Cole(▶), Billy

Above: Rick James has become an '80s superstar.

Eckstine(▶), Sarah Vaughn and Ella Fitzgerald. At the age of 25 he became a 'rehabilitation counsellor', but a friend of his opened a club in San Francisco and Jarreau got a job singing there. From working at the Half-Note Club with George Duke(▶), he moved on to Los Angeles. At the Troubador in Hollywood he was spotted by talent scouts and signed to Warner Brothers.

1975 saw the release of **We Got By,** although it was European audiences that first picked up on the versatile and gymnastic voice of Jarreau. A double live set, **Look At The Rainbow,** recorded in Europe, was released in 1978. His native land eventually began to acknowledge him with the release of **All Fly Home** (1978).

Breakin' Away. Courtesy Warner Bros Records.

In 1981, Al Jarreau had a series of pop hit singles. The album that precipitated this was his sixth release **Breakin' Away**, with **We're In This Love Together** and the title track further widening his audience.

Recordings:
We Got By (Warner Brothers)
Glow (Warner Brothers)
Look At The Rainbow (Warner
  Brothers)
All Fly Home (Warner Brothers)
This Time (Warner Brothers)
Breakin' Away (Warner Brothers)

Garland Jeffries

Born and raised in Sheepshead Bay, Brooklyn, Jeffries worked with Lou Reed, John Cale and Eric Burdon in the mid-60s, cultivating his rock leanings. These were manifest on his debut album with the band Grinder's Switch for Vanguard. After abortive pacting to Arista, Jeffries enjoyed a lengthy and memorable relationship with A&M, the rock/reggae fusion of **Ghostwriter** being an impressive work of classical proportions. It did well in Europe, and Jeffries followed this success with consistent output for CBS.

Recordings:
Ghostwriter (A&M)
American Boy And Girl (A&M)

The Brothers Johnson

The Brothers Johnson, George and Louis, were born in Los Angeles on May 17, 1953, and April 13, 1955, respectively. Their parents and elder brother Tommy had moved there from Mississippi some years previously.

With Louis just seven years old and playing bass, George, Tommy, and cousin Alex Weir, formed themselves into the Johnson Three Plus One, playing school dances, parties, and opening shows for major artists at local concerts. Later, when Louis was 12 and George 13, they found themselves supporting acts such as Bobby Womack(▶), David Ruffin(▶) and the Supremes(▶).

In 1971, soon after graduating from high school, George accepted an offer from Billy Preston(▶) to go on the road. Louis couldn't go because he hadn't finished his studies, although he joined a year later. The brothers toured Europe and the States, and contributed songs to Preston's **Music Is My Life** and **The Kids And Me** albums before leaving in 1973.

Quincy Jones(▶) produced their first four albums, their association with him beginning in 1975, while Jones was recording his **Mellow Madness** album. Introduced to Jones by mutual friend Joe Greene, the brothers ended up contributing four songs to his album: **Is It Love That We're Missin', Listen (What It Is), Tryin' To Find Out About You** and **Just A Little Taste Of Me.**

So impressed was Jones that he took the brothers on his spring tour of the States and Japan, securing them a deal with A&M Records in 1976. In 1977, the first Brothers Johnson album, **Look Out For No. 1,** was released. George and Louis who had, by now, been playing their instruments for 17 and 15 years respectively, were accomplished musicians, to say the least. Tall, thin, cool George became known as 'Lightnin' Licks' because of his calculated and decisive fills. Louis, aggressive, stocky and frantic, was called 'Thunder Thumbs' because of his fast and dynamic lines, and the harsh treatment he dished out to his strings.

Although categorised as a funk act because of their choice of single releases, the Brothers Johnson's albums mix fine ballads with the funk, with pop and jazz influences spliced between the R&B. Their first-ever single was the mellow funk of **I'll Be Good To**

Look Out For No. 1. Courtesy A & M Records.

You, a platinum debut single, while the album 'merely' went gold.

The following year, using a Shuggie Otis song, the brothers earned a worldwide hit single, **Strawberry Letter 23**, taken from their second album. Tours were undertaken, and live audiences marvelled at the power of the two guitarists.

After a less spectacular third album release in 1979 (an LP suffering from a lack of memorable material), their fourth album, which arrived in 1980, was written with the help of Quincy Jones' new friend, Rod Temperton, British ex-keyboard player for—but still principal songwriter of—Heatwave(▶).

Having just revitalised the careers of Rufus(▶) and Michael Jackson(▶) with the **Masterjam** and **Off The Wall** albums, respectively, Temperton and Jones created a wonderfully commercial album, **Light Up The Night**, complete with a worldwide smash, **Stomp.**

The brothers had been privileged to work with a master producer for four years and observe closely the workings of his craft. For their fifth album, **Winners** released in 1981, they undertook production responsibilities themselves, obtaining a hit single under their own steam, **The Real Thing.**

Recordings:
Look Out For No. 1 (A&M)
Right On Time (A&M)
Blam (A&M)
Light Up The Night (A&M)
Winners (A&M)

Linton Kwesi Johnson

Poets are unfashionable and a black poet, by that rule, ought to be starving! In fact that couldn't be further from the truth for Linton Kwesi Johnson. Reflecting the frustrations, aspirations and poverty of an oppressed black urban society, Johnson has found himself at the nucleus of a British black militant movement. This he has achieved with his poetry, spoken in Jamaican 'patois' accompanied by reggae music, and

with his contributions to a variety of radical publications, most notably **Race Today,** a black-orientated magazine based in Brixton, in South London, the scene of several violent street clashes between black youths and the police.

Johnson was born in the rural Clarendon County of Jamaica in 1952, moving to Britain in 1963 with his mother, and settling in Brixton where he has lived ever since. He attended Tulse Hill School and subsequently achieved an honours degree in sociology at the University of London, having studied at night school to meet the entrance requirements.

His first job was with a tailor's firm; later he moved to the civil service. Yet if his days were boring, his nights were spent in the company of the British Black Panthers who taught him disciplined political action by directing his own growing political awareness. He reacted to the writings of American black activists Eldridge Cleaver and Malcolm X in 1974 with his first volume of verse, **Voice Of The Living And The Dead.** The following year he published **Dread Beat And Blood.** Both are stark, witty, yet often disturbing, accounts of black culture in a white urban environment, mostly taken from Johnson's own experiences.

In November 1977, Virgin Records issued a 12-inch four-track discomix that featured two poems from **Dread Beat and Blood.** It was credited to Johnson's alias of that period, Poet and the Roots. The following August, the company issued an album **Deat Beat and Blood.** Produced by Dennis Bovell(▶), it is a landmark in British reggae, incorporating eight poems, the street violence inherent in each played out in the drama of the music.

Between then and 1980, Johnson went on to record three more albums, all issued in the UK by Island Records, namely **Forces Of Victory**, including the moving **Sonny's Lettah (Anti-Sus poem)**; **Bass Culture**, musically more adventurous, illustrating his fondness for jazz; and the third an instrumental dub compilation. He has formed his own LKJ label and

presently divides his time between writing, recording, touring and encouraging other black writers and poets.

Recordings:
Forces Of Victory (—/Virgin)
Bass Culture (—/Island)

The Jones Girls

Detroit-born Shirley, Brenda and Valorie Jones signed their first recording contract with GM Records, in the late-'60s. More than 10 years later, they're at last being handled by a company with the will and resources to properly exploit their talent. As a vocal trio, they have recorded for Holland/Dozier/Holland's(▶) Music Merchant label and Curtis Mayfield's(▶) Curtom company, although neither produced hit singles.

Their close gospel-founded harmonies have provided backing

The Jones Girls. Courtesy Philadelphia International Records.

vocals for the likes of Aretha Franklin(▶), Lou Rawls(▶), Norman Connors(▶) and Teddy Pendergrass(▶). From 1975 to 1978 the Jones Girls toured the world, having acquired the job as backing singers for Diana Ross'(▶) live shows. Diana gave them their own 15-minute set and they were spotted by Leon Huff and Kenny Gamble, and signed to Philadelphia International Records.

You're Gonna Make Me Love Somebody Else, a track from their debut LP of the same title, was released in 1978 and entered the American and British charts. Their follow-up the next year was bolstered by live appearances and outsold its predecessor. Their most recent album, **Get As Much Love As You Can** released in 1982, finally did justice to their unique mellifluous soulful vocals and included the worldwide hit **Nights Over Egypt.**

Recordings:
The Jones Girls (Philadelphia International)
At Peace With Woman (Philadelphia International)
Get As Much Love As You Can (Philadelphia International)

Grace Jones

Grace Jones believes that there was some genetic mix-up between her twin brother and herself. He played with the dolls. They were born in Jamaica, moved to Syracuse, New York, then Grace began a career modelling in Paris. Turning to singing, she began to develop a bisexual delivery, combining high fashion with theatrical and sensual disco.

Her two most recent albums,

Nightclubbing. Courtesy Island Records.

Warm Leatherette and **Nightclubbing**, were recorded with the legendary Sly Dunbar(▶) and Robbie Shakespeare(▶).

Recordings:
Portfolio (Island)
Fame (Island)
Muse (Island)
Warm Leatherette (Island)
Nightclubbing (Island)

Quincy Jones

The remarkable career of Quincy Jones spans 30 years and virtually every conceivable kind of job in the music industry, from musician, arranger, writer, A&R man and executive to president of his own record company. Although today known the world over for his production chores for Michael Jackson(▶), the Brothers Johnson(▶), Rugus(▶) and for his own recordings, Jones by no means confines his career to black music.

Quincy Jones was born in Chicago in 1934, and raised in Seattle where, in 1948, he met the then 16-year-old Ray Charles (▶) who was about to embark on a career that would eventually

I Heard That... Courtesy A&M Records.

change the shape of black music. Charles inspired Jones' initial interest in music, although at this time Charles was a pretty blatant copyist of the Nat King Cole(▶)/Charles Brown school of mellow piano and guitar-led blues balladeering. Soon Charles was to hit the road which, by 1952, led him to a contract with Atlantic Records(▶).

Rather than accompany Ray Charles into the netherworld of the chitlin' circuit, Jones chose instead to enrol in the Berkley School of Music. Here he maintained a rigorous regime of up to 10 classes a day. He paid his way through college by gigging in local Boston strip joints and nightclubs. Regular trips to New York fired his enthusiasm for jazz

Before graduation, he got his first professional job as a member of the trumpet section of the Lionel Hampton Big Band; he had met Hampton during his trips to New York. As a member of the orchestra Jones was able to tour many parts of the world and on one trip to France he was inspired to go back to musical study in order to develop his real love—writing and arranging. He studied for many years under the famous teacher Nadia Boulanger, who could also count among her pupils the classical composer Stravinsky.

Living in Paris for about six years led Jones into a job with one of France's top record labels, Eddie Barclay's Disque Barclay. In addition to his studies and the job, Jones also undertook outside work and quickly built up a reputation as one of Europe's leading composer/arranger/conductors and won for himself numerous European awards.

By 1961, though, after an attempt to keep afloat an 18-piece band, he was bankrupt and forced to return to New York. Luckily his European reputation had preceded him and Irving Green, then President of Mercury records, offered him a position as musical director for the company. Within a year he was promoted to Vice President of A&R, the first black man ever to hold such a position in a white corporation. In May 1963 he produced his first No. 1 pop single, Lesley Gore's **It's My Party**, and her follow-up **Judy's Turn To Cry**. At roughly the same time came his first charted album under his own name as a leader, **Big Band Bossa Nova**.

He recorded several albums for Mercury as well as producing many acts, including Billy Eckstine(▶) and Sarah Vaughan. He was also in demand as an arranger and it says much for Green's faith in him that Jones was allowed to do freelance work for artists like Frank Sinatra, Tony Bennett, Johnny Mathis(▶) and old friend Ray Charles while still employed by Mercury Records.

Smackwater Jack. Courtesy A&M Records.

One aspect of music that Jones wished to handle at this time was movie scoring. As a student he had spent many hours in cinemas listening to the classic works of film composers like Bernard Herrmann and Miklos Rosza. His opportunity came in 1965 when director Sidney Lumet asked him to score his new film *The Pawnbroker*. Jones' work for this movie was so well received that it led an almost unbroken run of movie soundtracks for seven years. Among the notable films to enjoy his music were: *In Cold Blood, Bob And Carole And Ted And Alice, The Anderson Tapes, Cactus Flower, In The Heat Of The Night* (working again with Ray Charles). *They Call*

Quincy Jones. His prodigious output as producer, performer, arranger and composer is pretty much all things to all men.

Me Mr. Tibbs, Mirage, Walk Don't Run, Dollars and *The New Centurions*. He also scored two television series, 'Ironside' and 'I Spy'.

In 1969 Jones signed with A&M records and began to record a new series of albums under his own name which brought the best musicians in jazz together under his aegis. These were undoubtedly the first signs of the emerging sounds of jazz/funk. **Walking In Space** became Jones' first charted album since 1962 and included the hit single **Killer Joe**, his first R&B chart entry, in 1970. **Walking In Space** won a Grammy for Best Jazz Performance By A Large Group. Among the soloists were Freddie Hubbard(▶), Ray Brown, Rahsaan Roland Kirk and Eric Gale(▶). 1970's album **Gula Matari** was also nominated in several categories, as was 1971's **Smackwater Jack**. He won a Grammy again in 1972 with the theme from his last major movie score, *The Anderson Tapes*. In 1973 **Summer In The City** won a Grammy for Best Instrumental Arrangement.

By 1973 he had tired of movie scoring and, well entrenched in his own career as a performer, turned his mind again to producing other acts. In 1973 he was responsible for the brilliant but very poorly received Aretha Franklin album, **Hey Now Hey, The Other Side Of The Sky**, and from 1974 onwards he concentrated on his own career and the development of his own discovered talent. That year he enjoyed the hit **If I Ever Lose This Heaven**, featuring Minnie Riperton(▶) from the album **Body Heat**; and the LP constituted another first for Jones, winning a gold record award. 1975 brought **Mellow Madness**, which introduced the Brothers Johnson to a waiting public. In 1976 he produced the Brothers' debut album for A&M as well as his own **I Heard That!!**

For the next six years Jones enjoyed an unbroken string of smash albums for himself and others; **Sounds And Stuff Like That, Master Jam** (for Rufus), **Off The Wall** (for Michael Jackson—reputed to be the most commercially successful black music

LP ever), **Light Up The Night** (for the Brothers Johnson). Among the singers and writers he nurtured to vast success in this period were Rod Temperton (writer for Heatwave), James Ingram, Patti Austin(▶), Leon Ware(▶), Jim Gilstrap(▶) and Al Jarreau(▶).

In 1980, after the phenomenal success of **Off The Wall**, he formed his own label, Qwest Records, with Warner Brothers. The debut release was by George Benson(▶)—an artist who would be temporarily on the logo—and it proved to be Benson's greatest success, spawning such hits as **Give Me The Night** and **Love X Love**. With his own success, **The Dude**, Jones entered the '80s at a commercial peak in his career. The second Qwest release was Patti Austin's **Every Home Should Have One**, again a large scale chart success.

Quincy Jones has been nominated for Grammys and Oscars more than 30 times and has won on more than a dozen occasions, an achievement culminating in his near clean sweep of the board in the 1982 Grammys for his 1981 hit album **The Dude**.

Although briefly returning to scoring for the immensely successful TV series *Roots* in 1977, Jones seems to have settled down to a multi-faceted career as producer, arranger and talent discoverer, and shows little sign of returning to his own roots in pure jazz.

Recordings:
Smackwater Jack (A&M)
I Heard That!! (A&M)
Sounds And Stuff Like That (A&M)
The Dude (A&M)
The Best Of Quincy Jones (—/A&M)

Margie Joseph

Born in Pascagoula, Mississippi, in 1950, Margie Joseph cut **Why Does A Man Have To Lie** (OKeh) at Muscle Shoals(▶) in 1967 and joined Stax(▶) two years later with the Bobby Womack(▶)-penned **What You Gonna Do**, produced in New Orleans by Willie Lee Turbinton.

After two classy Stax albums,

which revealed her as a great interpreter of soulful lyrics, she switched to Atlantic(▶).

Recordings:
Margie Joseph Makes A New Impression (Volt/Stax)
Phase Two With Love (Volt/—)
Margie Joseph (Atlantic)
Margie (Atlantic/—)

Judge Dread

The giant bearded figure of Alex Hughes, aka Judge Dread, had a chequered early career in debt-collecting, wrestling, male modelling and as a bouncer at the Flamingo Club, home-base for soul and reggae music in London at the time.

Following the lead of the Jamaican 'sound system', Dread put his own mobile discotheque show together and, again following Jamaican trends, began toasting: that is, half talking, half singing over recorded backing tracks.

Building a mass following among white skinhead cult youngsters (who had adopted reggae as their own in the late '60s), Dread and his manager Ted Lemon wrote the lewd **Big Six** (Big Shot 1972), based on Prince Buster's(▶) **Big Five**—and recorded in 10 minutes at a cost of six pounds. He followed through in the same vein with **Big Seven** (which made the top 10 in Britain) and **Big Eight**, which all earned massive sales despite being banned by radio stations, as was his 1975 version of the earlier Jane Birkin/Serge Gainsbourg sex hit **Je T'Aime**.

Recordings:
Dreadmania (Big Shot)

Janet Kay

Born in London, England, on January 17, 1958, Janet Kay Bogle first came to the attention of the reggae-buying public in summer 1977 when, after a chance encounter with members of Aswad(▶), she cut her debut single—a version of Minnie Riperton's **Loving You**—for Alton Ellis(▶). It topped the reggae charts, but her major breakthrough came two years later with her national hit **Silly Games**. An active member of Black Theatre Co-operative she divides her time between singing and acting.

Recordings:
Capricorn (—/Solid Groove)

K.C. & the Sunshine Band

The nucleus of this band comprises two Florida-born white musicians: Harry Casey and Richard Finch. Both began as backroom boys in the Florida recording world. Having completed high school, Casey worked in a record shop, making frequent visits to distribution and record companies. At Tone Distributors, he met producer/singer Clarence Reid and Steve Alaimo(▶), co-owner and head producer of Tone's associated record company TK(▶). Casey then began to hang around TK's offices, trying to gain employment, without success.

Finch was already working at TK. He'd been playing bass with a local group, and had also got to know Clarence Reid. Finch worked in the Tone warehouse and was subsequently hired as a part-time studio-maintenance engineer at TK.

In January 1973, Clarence Reid got married, and the reception was held in Betty Wright's(▶) house. The music at the reception was played by a junkanoo band whose sound excited Casey no end. Having become personal assistant to Betty and Timmy Thomas(▶), Casey was now on a better footing with their record company, TK Records.

Casey was joined by Betty's brother, Philip, on guitar, and Rick Finch on bass to form the Sunshine Band and they wrote, arranged, produced and performed on **Blow Your Whistle**, released on TK in 1973 a massive international club hit.

Adding drummer Robert Johnson and guitarist Jerome Smith, their follow-up single was **Sound Your Funky Horn**, which made a worldwide sales impression in pop terms. Now in-demand writers and producers for TK, it was Casey and Finch who put together the backing track and guide vocal for George McCrae(▶) to record his worldwide pop-soul hit, **Rock Your Baby**.

Basically, a singles band, 'the Miami sound' produced by K.C. and the Sunshine Band was highly commercial R&B. Throughout the '70s the group followed up with pop hits such as **Queen Of Clubs, Get Down Tonight, That's The Way I Like It, Shake Your Booty**, and a song used in the soundtrack of the film *Saturday Night Fever*, **Boogie Shoes**. After a late '70s lull, the group were back with their biggest hit ever, the ballad **Please Don't Go**, in 1981.

Recordings:
The Sound Of Sunshine (TK/Jay Boy)
Who Do Ya Love (TK)
Do It Good (TK)
Greatest Hits (TK)

Below: What Cha' Gonna Do For Me. *Chaka Khan can't be serious!*

Eddie Kendricks

Eddie Kendricks (born December 17, 1940) made the long trip from his home in Alabama to Michigan, and worked with the Cavaliers, the Primes, and another Motown group, the Elgins, before establishing himself as one of the dual lead vocalists with the Temptations(▶). His dynamic falsetto was a feature of many of the Temptations' singles during their all-conquering '60s period, including **The Way You Do The Things You Do, You're My Everything**, and **Just My Imagination**.

Kendricks left the group in 1971 and scored his first major hit as a solo artists with **Keep On Truckin'** (1973). This was followed by **Boogie Down** (1974), from the album of the same name, which featured the Crusaders' Wilton Felder(▶) and the successful solo/session guitar player Dennis Coffey. In 1975, Kendricks hit with the poignant but vigorous **Shoeshine Boy**, and maintained the momentum with **Happy** (1975) and **He's A Friend** (1976). Until the mid-'70s, Kendricks managed to escape the image-builders at Motown, who liked to see their performers as sophisticated 'men about town'. He did record some pop standards, including David Gates' **If** and Jim Croce's **Time In A Bottle**, but retained a hard edge, and all of his substantial reputation. Motown, however, were going through a transitional period, with their roster being seriously depleted and established artists suffering a decline in sales.

Kendricks felt the need for a change, claiming lack of record company support, and duly signed with Arista Records in 1977. His one and only album for the label, **Vintage '78**, was a mediocre offering, although **Ain't No Smoke Without Fire**, with its staccato guitar passage outshining Kendricks, was a minor hit. In 1980, he joined Atlantic Records and debuted with **Love Keys** in the

spring of 1981, recorded in his home state of Alabama. Producers Randy Richards and Johnny Sandlin eased Kendricks back nicely into a soul groove, with songs from the Holland brothers and Lamont Dozier and David Pomeranz, coupled with the driving Muscle Shoals' Horns.

Thankfully, Eddie Kendricks has avoided the 'whatever happened to . . ?' syndrome, but his most meritorious work was with the Temptations, which is a disappointing reflection on a solo career spanning 11 years and 13 albums.

Recordings:
All By Myself (Motown)
Boogie Down (Motown)
Eddie Kendricks (Motown)
At His Best (Motown)
The Hit Man (Motown)
Love Keys (Atlantic)

Chaka Khan

Chicago-born Chaka Khan quit school at 16 and started singing a wide spectrum of music in a variety of local clubs, eventually fronting a group which purveyed a mixture of soul, rock and pop. The band later adopted the title Rufus(▶), and won a major record deal and a mass

Rufus. Courtesy Warner Bros. Records.

following both for their records and for their colourful stage presentation.

Wearing a spectacular choice of alluring costumes, her rampant head of hair fashioned into numerous dazzling styles, the petite and curvacious Chaka fronted Rufus from 1972 to 1977, belting out such hits as **Tell Me Something Good, Once You Get Started, Dance With Me** and **Hollywood**.

Her raucous yet honeyed larynx was the group's prime focal point and it was obviously just a matter of time before she branched out as a solo. In 1978 she signed to Warner Brothers and her debut album yielded the worldwide smash **I'm Every Woman**, written by Ashford and Simpson(▶). Produced by Arif Mardin, **Chaka** also featured a smash-hit duet with George Benson(▶) on **We Got The Love**.

On the cover of Chaka's second solo album, **Naughty** (1980), is a picture of the child she had been carrying at the time of recording Rufus's **Rags To Riches** album back in 1974. The little girl is shown putting on make-up in front of a mirror, the image of her mother. Unfortunately, though, the music lacked such winsome appeal and the album made but a ripple. More successful was **What Cha' Gonna Do For Me**, the title cut from her third album, still using producer Mardin and the East Coast Warner Brothers' session mafia.

To emphasise her versatility, Chaka took part in a 1982 project organised by Lenny White(▶). **Echoes Of An Era** was an album in which eminent jazz musicians recreated the jazz music of the '50s, Chaka exquisitely rendering the classics of the idiom with consummate ease.

Recordings:
Chaka (Warner Bros)
Naughty (Warner Bros)
What Cha' Gonna Do For Me (Warner Bros)

Evelyn King

One day while in Kenny Gamble and Leon Huff's Sigma Sound Studios in Philadelphia with Bunny Sigler(▶), playing guitar on a Lou Rawls(▶) song, Theodore Life stepped out of the door to get a soda, and heard this fantastic voice singing its heart out. He looked up, and all he could see was a 16-year-old girl cleaning up the corridor. Evelyn and her mother Mrs King were the regular cleaners at the studio and Life proceeded to make this particular clean-up woman an international star.

Born in the Bronx, New York, on June 29, 1960, Evelyn moved to Philadelphia with her family when she was 10. From her debut album **Smooth Talk** (1977) came the single release that was one of the biggest pop hits of the year, **Shame**. Nicknamed 'Champagne', because of her charming and vivacious personality, Evelyn 'Champagne' King made two more albums with Life, but neither the LPs nor the 45s could make a similar impression to her opener.

Evelyn was still very young when her second and third albums refused to take off, but she bounced back in 1981 with a worldwide hit album and single, **I'm In Love**. The single (written by Kashif Saleem, ex-keyboard player with B.T. Express(▶), and the other tracks on the album, were a radical and successful change in sound. Half the album was produced by Saleem, Morris Brown and Lawrence Jones; the other half by Rodney Brown and Willie Lester, integral members of Prelude Records, the company that introduced Sharon Reid, Bobby Thurston(▶) and Gayle Adams.

Recordings:
Smooth Talk (RCA)
Music Box (RCA)
Call On Me (RCA)
I'm In Love (RCA)

Bo Kirkland and Ruth Davis

Two individually fine singers, Bo Kirkland and Ruth Davis came together from different backgrounds and locations while they were independently signed to Frank Slay's label, Claridge. Ruth originates in Arkansas, and arrived at her first recording contract via a victory in a Los Angeles radio station talent contest, following which she functioned as a backing singer for such as Ray Charles(▶). Billy Preston(▶) and Tina Turner(▶).

Bo, from Yazoo, Mississippi, graduated from a high school band, Mike and the Sensations, before being signed by Slay.

The Bo and Ruth alliance produced an album of the same name, which included one notable self-penned international hit, **You're Gonna Get Next To Me**, in 1977.

Recordings:
Bo & Ruth (Claridge/EMI)

Kleer

In 1971, Woody Cunningham (drums) Norman Durham (bass) and Richard Lee (guitar) acted as backing group for a Baltimore-based vocal group, the Choice Four. The following year, the three of them moved to New York, and became Pipeline, playing local clubs. In 1973, Paul Crutchfield joined on vocals and percussion. Pipeline met Monte Rock, and became the Jam Band in Rock's Disco Tex show. In 1977, they took the name Universal Robot Band, recorded an album, and played support on various American tours.

Taste The Music. Courtesy Atlantic Records.

As Kleer they were heard by Dennis King, a producer and engineer at Atlantic Studios, who took their demo tape to the label. A debut album **I Love To Dance** was released in may 1979, produced by King and the band, which immediately provided single success with **Keep Your Body Working**. The band have since released three more LP's.

Kleer augment their sound with vocalists Isabelle Coles, Melanie Moore and Yvette Flowers, plus keyboard players Terry Dolphin and Eric Rohrbaugh.

Recordings:
I Love To Dance (Atlantic)
Winners (Atlantic)
License To Dream (Atlantic)
Taste The Music (Atlantic)

Earl Klugh

Detroit-based Klugh is that rarity, an acoustic guitarist playing contemporary jazz. His choice of material and instrumentation actually classifies him as a crossover/MOR artist, but his strong melodic sense and excellent technique mean that most of his records warrant more than cursory attention.

A former compadré of George Benson(▶), Klugh uses top session men like Steve Gadd and Ralph MacDonald(▶) to ensure continuing listenability. He has recorded prolifically since 1977, first on Blue Note and then on United Artists, and more recently with Bob James (▶) on the Columbia label.

Recordings:
Dreams Come True (United Artists)
Late Night Guitar (United Artists)
Crazy For You (Liberty)
One On One (with Bob James) (Columbia/CBS)

Jerry Knight

See Raydio

Kool and the Gang

In 1964, Robert 'Kool' Bell formed the Jazziacs with brother Ronald, and friends Dennis Thomas and Robert Mickens. These school boys from Jersey City, New Jersey, had been listening to the leading jazz artists of that time and they fused that music with their own concept of dance styles.

The same year, the 14-year-old Kool took his gang as far as New York City, playing support sets for the likes of McCoy Tyner and Pharoah Saunders, but their days were mostly spent in their own neighbourhood playing local clubs and functions.

During the next five years, they expanded to incorporate four more musicians, and then signed to De-Lite Records in 1969 under the name Kool And The Gang. The line-up now consisted of: Ronald Bell, tenor sax; Claydes Smith, guitar; George Brown, drums; Robert Bell, bass; Dennis Thomas, alto sax; Rick West, keyboards; and Robert Mickens, trumpet.

Dispensing with the expense of a vocalist, the music's emphasis

remained on rhythm and instrumental improvisation, a fusion of funky R&B/jazz and afro styles. Their popularity had been confined to the United States, but in 1973 three singles from their **Wild And Peaceful** album reached out to world markets: **Funky Stuff**, **Jungle Boogie** and **Hollywood Swinging**.

Their **Open Sesame** single, taken from their 1976 **Love and Understanding** album, was part of the soundtrack of the film *Saturday Night Fever*. Around that time, another Gang favourite, **Summer Madness**, a long, rambling, jazz-structured, gentle-funk song was used for the film *Rocky*. Sylvester Stallone being seen working out to the Gang's horny jam.

Kool And The Gang. Courtesy De-Lite Records.

De-Lite changed distribution deals from Polydor to Phonogram, and the Gang's sound was soon to change as well. They brought in producer Eumir Deodato, who had previously been arranging and producing albums of heavily orchestrated and very classy instrumental jazz fusion. His main claim to fame had been in 1973, when he'd released a hit single called **Also Sprach Zarathustra (2001)**, which was a jazzy version of the theme from Stanley Kubrick's film *2001 (A Space Odyssey)*.

The combination of Deodato's engineering expertise and the group's decade's worth of experience produced a commercial blockbuster of an album in 1979. **Ladies Night** was brimming over with hit singles, the eventual winner being

Below: Kool And The Gang, shifting to harmonies.

the title track.

Hot on the heels of that was another set, **Celebrate**, from whence came the hit single **Celebration**. With worldwide interest in the group escalating, their album release of 1981, **Something Special**, rapidly turned platinum, and was fertile enough to spawn three massive hits: **Steppin' Out**, **Get Down On It** and **Take My Heart**.

The Kool and the Gang sound has changed immeasurably over 10 years, the main emphasis shifting from instrumentals to vocals, the Gang's harmonic arrangements being now one of their strongest features. Deodato has sharpened their sound to make them more suitable for dance-hall sound systems instead of smoky live venues.

The current line-up is: James 'JT' Taylor, lead vocals; Robert 'Kool' Bell, bass; George Brown, drums; Ronald Bell, tenor saxophone; Amir Bayyan, keyboards; Charles Smith, lead guitar; Dennis Thomas, alto saxophone; Robert Mickens, trumpet; Clifford Adams, trombone; Michael Ray, trumpet, flugelhorn.

Recordings:
Kool And The Gang (De-Lite)
Live At The Sex Machine (De-Lite)
Music Is The Message (De-Lite)
Wild And Peaceful (De-Lite/ Polydor)
The Best Of . . . (De-Lite)
Love And Understanding (De-Lite/Polydor)
Ladies Night (De-Lite)
Celebrate (De-Lite)
Something Special (De-Lite)

Patti LaBelle

Patti LaBelle and the Bluebelles are an interesting example of a group who managed to effect a smooth and successful transition from initial 1950s-type doo-wop styling into 1960s gospel-influenced soul, and even underwent another metamorphosis to emerge as a market-force in 70s funk and rock.

Patricia Holt (Patti LaBelle) was born on October 4, 1944, in Philadelphia, growing up with Cindy Birdsong with whom she joined a local group, the Ordettes. Their friends Sara Dash and Nona Hendryx(▶) were members of the Del Capris. In late 1961 the four girls got together to form the Bluebelles, making their disc debut with **I Sold My Heart To The Junkman**, shrill and eager and a top 20 hit on Newtown in early 1962. Four releases later, with Patti now taking label-credit, the passionate **Down The Aisle** reached the top 40, followed in early 1964 by the spare but soulful intensity of **You'll Never Walk Alone**, picked up from the re-named Nicetown by Parkway, whereon a similarly distinctive treatment of **Danny Boy** also scored.

A move to Atlantic(▶) brought a change to more contemporary soul styling, and songs like **All Or Nothing**, **Over The Rainbow**, **Groovy Kind Of Love** and **Take Me For A Little While** maintained the group's chart status, though by the late 1960s sales were declining. Cindy Birdsong split to join the Supremes(▶), and the remaining trio underwent a change of image.

Guided by British manager Vicki Wickham (of *Ready, Steady Go* TV show fame), the group became Labelle and steered towards a harder musical image with rock overtones, joining Warner Bros (1972) then RCA before landing at Epic in 1974 with the **Nightbirds** LP, produced by New Orleans' genius Allen Toussaint(▶). **Lady Marmalade,** aspiring to heady chart placings, combined ear-catching lyrics, arrangement and performance with disco impact. Hits continued for the group on Epic, but the image began to wear thin and the girls went their separate ways, Patti still on Epic, Sara on Kirshner, and Nona becoming a background voice for disco groups.

Recordings:
Over The Rainbow (Atlantic)
Pressure Cookin' (RCA)
C'Est La Vie (—/DJM)
Nightbirds (Epic)

Lakeside

A vital part of Dick Griffey's Solar Records' machinery is a self-contained nine-piece band, combining pop, funk, rock and R&B. Lakeside originate from Dayton, Ohio, and first came together in 1969. The band's line-up, as it has always been, is: Fred Alexander, drums; Norman Beavers, keyboards; Marvin Craig, bass; Fred Lewis, percussion; Tiemeyer McCain, vocals; Thomas Oliver Shelby, vocals; Steve Shockley, guitars; Otis Stokes, vocals; Mark Wood, vocals.

Employing cinematic themes for each album—cowboys, pirates, Arabian knights—the band has had occasional single success, their biggest being 1978's **All The Way Live** and 1981's version of the Beatles' classic, **I Want To Hold Your Hand.** The members of the group also write for, and play on, their fellow Solarites' recordings.

Recordings:
Shot Of Love (Solar)
Rough Riders (Solar)
Fantastic Voyage (Solar)
Keep On Movin' Straight Ahead (Solar)
Your Wish Is My Command (Solar)

Denise LaSalle

Denise LaSalle is one of those gritty Southern soul singers whose popular recognition is rather spasmodic, despite a string of records combining artistic merit and commercial potential. A large-framed lady with a cuddly figure, Denise delivers her often raunchy lyrics in a manner perhaps too black for general media acceptance, and most of her records have failed to gain British release.

Born Denise Craig in Greenwood, Mississippi, she moved to Chicago and took her name from a main highway in that city. She recorded first for Chess(▶) (1967) then for Parka (1970) without success before launching Crajon Productions with husband Bill Jones. Through this company, material recorded in Memphis was placed with Westbound, whereon the gently insistent brassy lilt of **Trapped By A Thing Called Love** rose to top 20 hit status in summer 1971. **Now Run And Tell That** and **Man-Sized Job** were smaller hits, both written by Denise, whose creative composing talent is evident throughout many of her albums.

The Crajon-Westbound Memphis connection continued through to 1976 with a succession of R&B

Fantastic Voyage. Courtesy Solar Records.

hits, both chunky beaters and searing balladry, then, following a summer hit with **Married But Not To Each Other,** Denise moved to ABC Records, handling much of her own production and continuing to write strong lyrical songs. The contract has yielded a creditable series of albums, including **Second Breath, The Bitch Is Bad** and **Under The Influence,** then ABC metamorphosed into MCA for **Unwrapped, I'm So Hot** (paradoxically a rather weak 'disco' set) and **Satisfaction Guaranteed,** each yielding R&B hit singles of varying note.

Recordings:
Doin' It Right (Westbound)
Trapped By A Thing Called Love (—/Janus)
The Bitch Is Bad (ABC/—)
Under The Influence (ABC/—)
Second Breath (ABC/—)
Unwrapped (MCA/—)
Satisfaction Guaranteed (MCA/—)

Yusef Lateef

Born William Evans in Chattanooga, Tennessee, in 1921, Yusef Lateef has recorded over 30 al-

The Many Faces Of Yusef Lateef. Courtesy Milestone.

bums with Savoy, Prestige, ABC, Impulse, Atlantic(▶) and CTI(▶). In the '50s he became interested in the Ahamdayyan movement of Islam and adopted his new name.

A 'Multi-reedman' his instruments include tenor and soprano saxophone, flute, oboe, shahnai, argole, bassoon, rabat, and various bamboo flutes. He played with Dizzy Gillespie and Cannonball Adderley(▶) before forming the Yusef Lateef Quartet in 1963, which moved into the jazz fusion market of the '70s.

Recordings:
Autophysiopsychic (CTI)
Gong (Savoy)

Latimore

Miami-based singer/keyboard player Benny Latimore brought a strong blues' flavour to contemporary soul music, with his deep smooth vocals, almost in the Billy Eckstine/Brook Benton(▶) mould.

Born in Charleston, Tennessee, on September 7, 1939, Latimore spent the '60s as arranger, conductor, pianist, singer and opening act for Steve Alaimo(▶), working the Las Vegas-Lake Tahoe-Miami cabaret circuit. It was Alaimo who became his producer and took him to TK Records(▶) in Miami (where Alaimo became vice-president).

Stormy Monday, If You Were My Woman and the **Latimore** album established an early reputation cemented by the success of his 1974 No.1 **Let's Straighten It Out** and the touching ballad **Jolie,** written by rock star Al Kooper, who co-produced with Alaimo and played piano on the session.

Recordings:
Latimore (Glades/President)
More More More Latimore (Glades/—)
Latimore III (Glades/—)
Let's Straighten It Out (Glades/—)
Dig A Little Deeper (Glades/—)

Below: The blues influenced singer-keyboard player Latimore.

Hubert Laws

Born in Houston, Texas, in 1939, this senior member of the famous Laws family plays flute. Below Hubert are Ronnie(▶), Eloise(▶) and Debra(▶). In 1954, Laws played in an early line-up of the Crusaders(▶), then known as the Swingsters, whilst also studying classical flute at Texas Southern University.

Moving to Los Angeles in 1958, Laws became a member of Mongo Santamaria's band. Recording albums for Blue Note, then for CTI (▶) between 1975 and 1977, Laws has since signed with Columbia. The excellent live CTI album, **The San Francisco Concerts**, featured Bob James(▶) on keyboards and Harvey Mason(▶) on drums.

Recordings:
The Chicago Theme (CTI)
Afro Classic (CTI)
The San Francisco Concerts (CTI)
Say It With Silence (Columbia/CBS)
Land Of Passion (Columbia/CBS)
Family (Columbia/CBS)

Ronnie Laws

Born (1950) and raised in Houston, Texas, saxophonist/flautist Ronnie is part of a famous musical family. His brother Hubert(▶) is a flautist, and his two sisters, Eloise(▶) and Debra(▶), are both singers. Living near the Laws family were some guys who later went on to become the Crusaders(▶), and it was ex-Crusaders' trumpet player Wayne Henderson who introduced Laws to their then record label, Blue Note, in 1976.

At high school, Laws had a group called the Lightmen and, resisting the temptation to take his muscular, six-foot frame into baseball, he enrolled at the Stephen F. Austin College in East Texas. Having graduated at 21, he moved to Los Angeles. His first professional break was in an early line-up of Earth, Wind & Fire(▶). Joining the group in 1972, he played with them for 18 months, and can be heard on their **Last Days In Time** set.

After playing with Hugh Mase-

Every Generation. Courtesy Blue Note Records.

kela(▶) for a short while, he became a solo artist and, soon after signing with the jazz label Blue Note, Wayne Henderson produced his debut album **Pressure Sensitive**. Blue Note signed Laws as a jazz artist, but when his fusion debut became the biggest album the label had ever released, they didn't bother to question his judgement.

As a saxophonist and flautist, Laws has always been highly respected in the jazz world, and now

in the '80s he has begun to create enormous excitement among funk fans, fusing the two musics, though declining to make out-and-out dance music.

He has subsequently established himself as a fine tenor vocalist, which perfectly complements his fluid alto styling.

Recordings:
Pressure Sensitive (Blue Note)
Fever (Blue Note)
Friends And Strangers (Blue Note)
Flame (United Artists)
Every Generation (Blue Note)
Solid Ground (EMI Liberty)

Barrington Levy

Born in Kingston, Jamaica, in 1963, Levy's distinctive whining voice and ghetto patois phrasing has placed him in the vanguard of a new generation of young singers who have a firm grip on the reggae market with songs that range from romance to politics.

Coming under the wing of producer Henry 'Juno' Lawes, whose shrewd business acumen made him quick to spot the potential of a ghetto youth who wrote his own material, the singer gained prominence with the single **Looking My Love** on the Bust label. Re-titled **It's Not Easy**, it appeared on his debut album, **Live And Learn**.

Levy's Jamaican and UK chart breakthrough came in autumn 1979 when the single **Shine Eye Gal** on Jah Guidance struck. He followed with the singles **Revelation, Moonlight Lover, Hunting Man** (re-titled **Bounty Hunter** as the title track from his second and arguably most accomplished album) and **Lose Respect**. He has since worked with Linval Thompson(▶) (**Poor Man Style** album for Trojan in 1982), yet seems most comfortable with Lawes and the Roots Radics band.

Recordings:
Shine Eye Gal (—/Burning Sounds)
Englishman (—/Greensleeves)

Linda Lewis

Sweet and raunchy, Linda applies a rangy thrust to a gamut of quality material, whether self-written, purpose writen, or thoughtfully treated cover-version.

Born in the docklands of London's East End, Linda attended both stage school and convent school. As a child actress she appeared in a number of films, including *Taste Of Honey*, and the Beatles' *Hard Days Night*. She sang with various London bands before releasing her first solo album, **Say No More**, on the Bell label in 1971, which was voted Best Album of the Year by a Newcomer, in an English poll.

She did two more albums for Bell, **Lark**, in 1972 and **Fathoms Deep**, in early 1974, building up a live reputation and scoring her first hit single with **Rock-A-Doodle-Doo**, in 1973.

Switching to Arista, in 1975, she has been produced and written for by Cat Stevens, Bert DeCoteaux, Allen Toussaint(▶) and her own husband Jim Cregan (Rod Stewart's guitarist), while to gratify her sense of restless musical adventure, she has hit with pure pop (**Rock—A-Doodle-Doo** and **Remember The Days Of The Old School Yard**), soul balladry (**This Time I'll Be

Above: Ronnie Laws, one of a very musical family.

Sweeter**), gutsy R&B (a version of Betty Everett's storming **It's In His Kiss**) and even Gilbert & Sullivan (**The Moon And I**).

Recordings:
Not A Little Girl Anymore (Arista)
Woman Overboard (Arista)

Light Of The World

Disenchantment with life in general and the lack of touring American soul stars led to the spawning of black music groups in British cities. From North London came one of the most significant, Light Of The World, who became forerunners of British Funk(▶).

The band came together in late 1978 and consisted of Everton McCalla, drums; Jean Paul 'Bluey' Maunick, guitar; Canute 'Kenny' Wellington, horns; Neville 'Breeze' McKreith, guitar; Chris Etienne, percussion; David 'Baps' Baptiste, horns; Peter Hinds, keyboards, and Paul 'Tubbs' Williams, bass. These eight, with the help of Nigel Martinez on drums, recorded **Light Of The World** (1979).

Soon after its release, Chris Etienne was tragically killed while on tour. Bluey chose to leave the group after this incident and Nathaniel 'Nat' Augustin and Ganiyu 'Gee' Bello were recruited as replacements.

Two singles were released from the first album, **Swingin'** and Mid-

Round Trip: Courtesy Ensign Records.

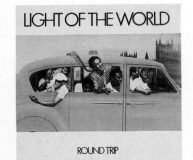

night Groovin'. The third single, recorded with the new line-up, was **The Boys In Blue**.

The second album **Round Trip** was released in 1980, with Mel Gaynor replacing McCalla. **London Town, I Shot The Sheriff** and **Time** were all successful singles from this set. In 1981, having developed a passionate British cult-following, the members broke up into three bands. Tubbs and Peter Hinds joined up with Bluey to become Incognito(▶), Kenny, Baps and Breeze became Beggar & Co(▶), Nat and Gee retained the Light Of The World name.

A 1981 album entitled **Remixed** contained new edits of old material. Also in 1981, Nat and Gee released their first product, a single, **Ride The Love Train**. In 1982, Tubbs rejoined, and with Nigel Martinez producing, **Famous Faces** brought British funk up alongside its American counterpart in terms of production and arrangement.

Recordings:
Light Of The World (Ensign)
Round Trip (Ensign)
Remixed (Mercury)
Famous Faces (EMI)

Limmie And Family Cooking

Limmie Snell, Martha Stewart and Jimmy Thomas, a brother and two sisters from Canton, Ohio, went to No. 3 in the UK with their debut Avco release, the lilting **You Can Do Magic**.

Just to confuse things, Jimmy (a girl) usually sang lead and, on stage, swopped names with brother Limmie, and at one point they also considered changing Martha's name to Timmy . . . !

Jimmy and Martha started out in the Sugarcakes while Limmie (the man) had solo releases on Columbia, Mercury and Warner Bros and plays drums. As a group they scored with the re-make of the Essex(▶) hit **Walkin' Miracle**.

When the group broke up, Limmie settled in the US, working as a solo, then in the early '70s forming H20.

There have been no album releases.

Jimmy Lindsay

Born in Kingston, Jamaica, on January 26, 1950, Lindsay made his first record, **Prove My Love To You**, for Cue Records in the UK in the mid-'60s. An exile of the bands Pure Machine (rock) and the Nighthawks (soul), he switched to reggae in 1976 and the following year entered national charts with a version of the Commodores'(▶) **Easy**.

Pacted to the now defunct Gem label, Lindsay recorded two albums with his road band Rasuji. He is now completely independent with his own London-based Music Hive label.

Recordings:
Where Is Your Love (—/Gem)
Children Of Rastafari (—/Gem)

Dandy Livingstone

Born in St Andrews, Jamaica, in 1943 Dandy Livingstone cut his first record for Carnival Records, **What A Lie**, in 1967. With Tito Simon he sang in clubs and hotels as half of Sugar and Dandy. Solo recognition ensued with his album **Rock Steady With Dandy** which included his **Message To You Rudy**, reactivated to great effect in 1980 by the 2-Tone band the Specials.

He moved to London at the end of the '60s and took up a position in the A&R department of Trojan Records. There he cut two British pop chart hits, **Suzanne Beware Of The Devil** and **Big City** for the label's subsidiary outlet Horse.

What many consider to be his greatest achievements were captured on the excellent **South Africa Experience** album, released in 1977 in the UK only by Night Owl.

Recordings:
Conscious (—/B&C)
Doo Wop Style (—/Night Owl)
South Africa Experience (—/ Night Owl)

Wilbert Longmire

Young American guitarist Wilbert Longmire has followed the path so successfully trodden by George Benson(▶). His melodic sense and pleasant tone make as good a job of jazz/easy-listening as any other musician in this overcrowded field. Sidemen like Eric Gale(▶), Richard Tee and Idris Muhammad(▶) are another reason why most of his output is worth listening to.

Recordings:
Sunny Side Up (Columbia/CBS)
Champagne (Columbia/CBS)
With All My Love (Columbia/ CBS)

Lovers Rock

A uniquely black British phenomenon, the term lovers rock is used to describe an essentially romantic, feminine approach to pop/reggae. With the progression of ska(▶) and blue beat to rockers reggae in the '70s, the music became increasingly male-dominated and orientated. Lovers rock was designed to

(and does) bridge the gap.

In the mid-'70s, South London producer Dennis Harris acknowledged a demand for a softer, sweeter music and recruited musicians from a number of indigenous bands, notably Matumbi(▶), to launch the Lovers Rock label and the careers of singer T.T. Ross and vocal trio Brown Sugar.

In the autumn of 1975, the diminutive Louisa Mark sang **Caught You In A Lie** over a Jamaican rhythm track and stormed the reggae charts. The effect was shattering and it served as a catalyst for scores of young female reggae singers: 15,16,17, Paulette Miller, Jennifer Daye, Yvonne Curtis, Samantha Rose, Sister CC, Simplicity, Jackie Dale, Phillis Wilson and Cassandra included. Their music was often maligned for being light and insipid.(the artists often merely tools for shrewd record producers chasing a fast buck), yet there is no denying its popularity.

As with any genre, a handful of exponents strived for creative credibility. None better than Carrol Thompson(▶), Janet Kay(▶), Erica Gayle and Jean Adebambo who, by writing much of their own material and taking a central role in the production of their records, are all within striking distance of crossing over from a minority ethnic appeal to widespread national acceptance.

Love Unlimited

Diane Taylor and sisters Glodean and Linda James started out singing together in a church in San Pedro, California, before linking up with Barry White(▶), who married Glodean and turned Love Unlimited into major stars with their million-selling debut single **Walking In The Rain** (1972).

Working the same material as the Three Degrees(▶) with a mix of the soulful and the bland and a besequined high glamour image, Love Unlimited moved from Uni to 20th Century and had a run of successful albums, continuing meanwhile as Barry White's backup vocal group. The Love Unlimited Orchestra, a mass aggregation of strings and brass, which was

Champagne. Courtesy Columbia Records.

formed to play behind them and White, also scored in its own right with **Love's Theme**.

The lush orchestral sound, arranged by White and Gene Page(▶), was a perfect showcase for Love Unlimited's high-pitched three-part harmonies, but their star soon dimmed as they failed to come up consistently with the instantly memorable songs which their style demanded.

Recordings:
Love Unlimited (Uni/—)
Under The Influence Of (20th Century)
In Heat (20th Century)

L.T.D.

Jimmie Davis, keyboards; Jake Riley, trombone; Lorenzo Carnegie, saxes; Carle Vickers, trumpet, flugelhorn, flute; Abraham Miller, saxes—a quintet of friends from North Carolina—worked with Sam And Dave(▶) in the mid-'60s, but by 1968 were playing pop-music sessions to pay bills.

Love To The World. Courtesy A&M Records.

The band played with a rhythm section, and when their drummer failed to make it to a gig in Providence, Rhode Island, one night local lad Jeffrey Osbourne stepped in. The band preferred Osbourne to their regular.

Moving to California, the group became resident at a hostel known as Operation Breadbasket, a project set up by the Southern Christian Leadership Conference. At this

venue, A&M Records' Lou Adler spotted them, and asked them to back Merry Clayton(▶) at the Monterey Folk Festival in 1971.

Settling in Los Angeles, L.T.D. added bass player Henry Davis and keyboard player Billy Osbourne, and so became an eight-piece. A&M signed the group in 1973 and they were allowed to self-produce their first two albums, although a hit single was not in evidence. Adding guitarist John McGhee, the group used Larry and Fonce Mizell to produce their next album and, in 1977, they had a hit single with Skip Scarborough's **Love Ballad**.

Bobby Martin produced their fourth album **Something To Love** later that year, from which came a bigger selling hit, **Back In Love Again**. In 1978, with Martin still at the helm, the LP **Togetherness** yielded **Holding On** and **We Deserve Each Other**. Soon after then the band recruited drummer Alvino Bennett, so that Jeffrey Osbourne could come to the front as lead vocalist.

For 1979, L.T.D. provided a new album, **Devotion**; the singles from that Bobby Martin-produced set were **Dance'n' Sing'n'**, **Share My Love** and **Stranger**. As a 10-piece whose members had been playing with each other for more than a decade, the L.T.D. (Love, Togetherness and Devotion) sound has become tight, commercial, retaining its R&B roots, but aimed at singles' charts. As a self-contained outfit, their shows were slick and very professional, with Jeffrey Osbourne's outstanding lead vocals and personality providing a crucial focus.

Following the group's 1980 album release **Shine On** Billy Osbourne and Jeffrey Osbourne embarked on solo careers, and for the 1981 release of their eighth album, the group acquired two new members, vocalists Leslie Wilson and Andre Ray, and although their vocals didn't quite gell immediately, **Love Magic** produced a hit single, **Kickin' Back**.

Recordings:
Love, Togetherness And Devotion (A&M)
Gittin' Down (A&M)
Love To The World (A&M)
Something To Love (A&M)
Togetherness (A&M)
Devotion (A&M)
Shine On (A&M)
Love Magic (A&M)

Carrie Lucas

Carrie Lucas was Solar's first solo female singer (as well as being the lady of label boss Dick Griffey). Utilising the company's staff producers, arrangers and songwriters she makes vari-tempoed albums, with an emphasis on lush sensual arrangements and pop-orientated melodies. To date, she's released four LPs. From her second set came the disco smash, title track, **Street Corner Symphony**, resplendant with acappella harmonies. From her third came another disco hit, the punchy **Dance With You**. Her most recent LP **Portrait Of Carrie Lucas** (1980), produced the hit **Career Girl**.

This five-foot-nine-inch Californian native represents Solar's answer to Diana Ross(▶): beautiful glamorous, and highly commercial.

Recordings:
Simply Carrie (Solar)

Street Corner Symphony (Solar)
Carrie Lucas In Danceland (Solar)
Portrait Of Carrie Lucas (Solar)

Cheryl Lynn

Cheryl was born in Los Angeles, California, on March 11, 1957. She was once a competitor on the legendary TV programme, 'The Gong Show', where performers, at the mercy of an eliminating gong, can be curtailed after a few seconds, but Cheryl's singing lasted the maximum duration. A 90-second video of her appearance was played to CBS Records, who promptly signed her.

Her debut album came out in 1979, and her first single, **Got To Be Real**, was one of the biggest R&B records of the year. From her third album, **In The Night**, produced by Ray Parker Jr.(▶), came the 1981 hit, **Shake It Up Tonight**.

Recordings:
Cheryl Lynn (Columbia/CBS)
In Love (Columbia/CBS)
In The Night (Columbia/CBS)

Ralph MacDonald

A former Roberta Flack(▶) sideman, MacDonald became everybody's favourite session percussionist in the '70s. Unlike many of his profession, he has had some success with his efforts as a leader. Both his albums listed showcase superb studio bands, and while **Drum** features melodic material with recognisable structures, **The Path** demonstrates the tasteful use of synthesised drums. The latter's title track shows the evolution of rhythm from African roots to disco.

Recordings:
Sound Of A Drum (Marlin/TK)
The Path (Marlin/TK)

The Main Ingredient

New York-based, the Main Ingredient churned out a consistent crop of smooth-soul records for more than a decade. Formed in the late '50s as the Poets, the original line-up comprised Donald McPherson (born Indianapolis, July 9, 1941), Luther Simmons Jr (born New York, September 9, 1942) and Enrique Antonio 'Tony' Silvester (born Panama, October 7, 1941). They made their first records for Leiber and Stoller's(▶) Red Bird(▶) label before scoring R&B No. 2 in 1966 with **She Blew A Good Thing** (Symbol) and changing their name.

Linked up with producer Bert De Coteaux they scored with a lushly orchestrated sound influenced by what was coming out of Philadelphia at the time. **I'm So Proud, Spinnin' Around, Black Seeds Keep Growing** and others kept them on the charts through 1970-71 till McPherson died of leukemia on July 4, 1971.

Replacement lead singer Cuba Gooding (born April 27, 1944) brought them even greater success with the million-selling **Everybody Plays The Fool** (RCA) in 1972. The albums **Afrodisiac** (on which Stevie Wonder(▶) guested) and **Euphrates River** were also massive sellers, though later records became increasingly MOR in feel.

In 1974, Tony Silvester left the group to work as a producer (notably with the Imperials(▶)), while Gooding quit for a solo career with Motown(▶).

Recordings:
Tasteful Soul (RCA)
Bitter Sweet (RCA)
Afrodisiac (RCA)
Euphrates River (RCA)
Rolling Down a Mountainside (RCA)

Mandrill

Rock-orientated funk was the forté of Mandrill, a group of seven adept musicians who could play some 20 instruments between them. The group was built around the three Wilson brothers: Louis 'Sweet Lou' Wilson, trumpet, congas, vocals; Dr Ric Wilson, sax; and Carlos 'Mad Dog' Wilson, trombone, flute, guitar, vocals.

The brothers placed an advert in a New York newspaper and, after exhaustive auditioning, brought in Omar Mesa, guitar; Claude 'Coffee' Cave, keyboards, percussion/vibes and vocals; former stunt-man Charlie Padro, drums and percussion; and Fudgie Kae, bass.

Within six months of formation, the band landed a Polydor recording contract and their debut album went top 30 in the US chart. They drew 14,000 people to a concert in New York's Central Park and an amazing 150,000 to Philadelphia's Fairmount Park, while also successfully touring Spain, Morocco, Holland and Brazil.

By the time of their third album, **Consummate Truth,** in 1973, Mandrill were being hailed as potential superstars for their blend of Santana, Chicago, Crusaders(▶) and Sly Stone(▶) influences, working over a spectrum of material which took in rock, folk, soul, jazz and calypso elements, reflecting the group's mixed heritage (the Wilson brothers were of Panamanian descent, Coffee's mother was three parts Iroquois Indian and they'd all grown up street-wise in Brooklyn).

By the time they switched to United Artists in 1975, there had been some line-up changes, the Wilson brothers and Cave now getting their support from Tommy Trujillo, guitar, Brian Alsop, bass, and André 'Mouth Man' Locke, drums, with the band's home base having switched to Los Angeles. Unfortunately, the move West didn't work out and Mandrill quickly faded.

Recordings:
Mandrill Is (Polydor)
Consummate Truth (Polydor)
Solid (United Artists)

Chuck Mangione

Charles Frank Mangione was born in Rochester, New York, on November 29, 1940. Having moved to New York City in 1965, he began playing trumpet with the big-bands of Maynard Ferguson and Kai Winding, and was then offered a job with his boyhood idol, Art Blakey, playing with the Jazz Messengers for two-and-a-half years, in a band that included Chick Corea(▶), Keith Jarrett and his brother, keyboard player Gap(▶).

In 1975, Mangione signed to A&M Records. For the title track of his second album, **Bellavia,** he received a Grammy award for Best Instrumental Composition. His 1977 **Feels So Good** album, featuring his own quartet (Chris Vadala, saxophones, flutes; Charles Meeks, bass; Grant Geissman, guitars; James Bradley Jr., drums) has recently been certified double platinum.

Having worked with the Rochester and Hamilton Philharmonic Orchestras, conducted marching bands, and composed themes for films and television shows, Mangione's music, often using large arrangements, is a fusion of classical, military, popular, rock and jazz.

Recordings:
Bellavia (A&M)
Feels So Good (A&M)
Children Of Sanchez (A&M)
An Evening Of Magic (A&M)
Fun And Games (A&M)
Tarantella (A&M)

Gap Mangione

Gaspare Mangione was born in Rochester, New York, on 13, 1938. Gap and his younger brother Chuck(▶), the Jazz Brothers, landed a record deal with Riverside Records, releasing **The Jazz Brothers** in 1960, and **Hey Baby!** and **Spring Fever** the year after. Graduating from Syracuse University in 1965 with a BA in music and liberal arts, Gap Mangione released his first solo album on G.R.C. Records, **Diana In The Autumn Wind**, in 1968. This album was the first recording of brother Chuck's orchestrated pieces, and drummer Steve Gadd's debut session too. Then, before signing to A&M, there was the solo outing, **Sing-A-Long Junk**, for Mercury.

Jazz-fusion keyboard player Mangione's third A&M album **Suite Lady** has been his most successful, produced by ex-Crusaders'(▶) guitarist Larry Carlton, and containing the single **Mellow Out**.

Recordings:
She And I (A&M)
Gap Mangione! (A&M)
Suite Lady (A&M)

The Manhattans

The group's original five-piece line-up, consisting of Edward 'Sonny' Bivins Jr, Kenny Kelly, Winfred 'Blue' Lovett, George Smith and Richard Taylor, was formed in the '60s from the most enthusiastic individuals of rival street-corner doo-wop groups in New Jersey.

They arrived at their present four-strong aggregation through a combination of happenstance and tragedy: Alston, a North Carolinian, replaced previous lead singer George Smith, who died from brain damage in 1971 while, in 1978,. Taylor left to become a minister. But in one form or another, the Manhattans have been together for around 16 years and in the field of musical endeavour to which they are best suited—love balladry—they remain unrivalled.

Eager to identify with the bright lights and showbiz chic of nearby New York, the group had carefully chosen their name and were performing regularly in the big city by 1965. At one such early concert, at

Below: Chuck Mangione, former Jazz Messenger

the Apollo Theatre in Harlem, they were spotted by an executive from Carnival Records and promptly signed to the label.

Their debut single, the apposite **For The First Time,** became a local New York City hit. The Manhattans steadily built a name until they were nominated for The Most Promising Upcoming Group Award in 1968 for the single **I Want To Be Your Everything.** In 1970, they joined forces with manager Hermi Hamlin, who took them to King Records(▶) for whom they cut an LP, **One Life To Live,** scoring hits with **A Million To One** and the title track.

In 1973 the group signed with Columbia and released **There's No Me Without You.** But it was two years later, with the release of their self-titled album, that the world charts got their first taste of the kind of decorous balladry for which the Manhattans are renowned. **Kiss And Say Goodbye,** closely followed by a version of the old Timi Yuro hit **Hurt,** charted on both sides of the Atlantic.

Ever tasteful, the group has shown an ability to adapt various musical genres to its own impeccably muted deep-soul harmony. Their versions of the comparatively boisterous **Tomorrow,** from the Broadway musical *Annie,* and the country classic **Then You Can Tell Me Goodbye** both charted. They have done two movie soundtracks, *The Class of Mrs. Mac-Michael* and *Moving* and in 1977 they performed at The White House at President Carter's inaugural ball.

Recordings:
Manhattans (Columbia/CBS)
It Feels So Good (Columbia/CBS)
There's No Good In Goodbye
(Columbia/CBS)
Love Talk (Columbia/CBS)
After Midnight (Columbia/CBS)

Teena Marie

Mary Christine Brocker, who later changed her name to Teena Marie, is a blonde Californian singer. Berry Gordy, president of Motown(▶)

Records, chose Teena for a major role while auditioning actresses for a television show, and when the project got shelved, decided that he still wanted the lady on his label.

Teena had begun her career at 13, fronting a band that contained her brother and cousin. During high school, she formed another group which played concerts all over Los Angeles, allowing Teena to develop her guitar and keyboard playing as well as her attacking vocal style.

Her first album, produced by Rick James(▶), was released in 1979 and displayed the kind of R&B aggression synonymous with Motown vocalists, but not synonymous with petite young white ladies! The hit single from **Wild And Peaceful** was the James-style **I'm Just A Sucker For Your Love.**

Teena had co-written material for her first album, and by her second album, she was also co-producing. In 1980, you couldn't go into a disco without hearing a Teena Marie record. The albums **Lady T** and **Irons In The Fire,** released in that year, contained the worldwide hits **Behind The Groove** and **I Need Your Lovin'.** These LPs were produced by Richard Rudolph, husband and co-producer of the late Minnie Riperton(▶).

America was in for a shock when Teena began touring with her explosive friend Rick James in 1981; they had not expected to see someone so small, let alone someone white. Her fourth album contained the hits, **Square Biz,** the title track, **It Must Be Magic** and **Portuguese Love,** bringing Teena international recognition.

Much of her sound can be attributed to the backing tracks of the Stone City Band and Ozone, who have helped make this lady a major Motown artist. Ozone, a new Motown act, are now being produced by Teena.

Recordings:
Wild And Peaceful
(Tamla/Motown)
Lady T (Tamla/Motown)
Irons In The Fire (Tamla/Motown)
It Must Be Magic (Tamla/Motown)

Above: Bob Marley's influence on reggae, and black music in general, was immeasurable. He will be missed.

Bob Marley

Without Bob Marley, reggae music would still be largely confined to a handful of singers, bands and sound systems dotted around the Caribbean and among West Indian communities in the cities of Britain and North America. Through his devotion to the principles of Rastafari, Marley preached strength and social unity to oppressed peoples across the globe. His music crossed racial boundaries, providing black people with a new level of dignity. Since his death, there has been an uneasy vacuum within the music, as if it is marking time until another prophet, with the capacity to carry millions, takes up his role.

Robert Nesta Marley was born in St Anns, Jamaica, also the birthplace of his prophet, the black civil rights leader Marcus Garvey. His passport records his date of birth as February 6, 1945, although he later revealed that the actual date was nearer the middle of the month. His mother was Cedella Booker and his father Norman Marley, a captain in the British Army who had been stationed in Jamaica during the Second World War. Educated at Stepney School it was there he cemented close friendships with two youths who were to play important roles in shaping his career — Winston Hubert McIntosh (Peter Tosh(▶)) and Neville O'Reiley Livingstone (Bunny Wailer(▶).

Marley's passion for music was born from two sources. The first was his mother who sang gospel in the neighbourhood Apostolic Church. The other was his close fiend Joe Higgs(▶) whom he would visit to discuss religion and listen to discs by the Impressions(▶) and the Ink Spots(▶). Their falsetto harmonies were to become central to his own music in its formative days.

Lacking educational qualifications, Marley was shunted off by Cedella to find employment as an apprentice welder. He struck up friendships with Desmond Dekker(▶) and Jimmy Cliff(▶) and they and Higgs convinced Marley that he should develop his singing and learn to play the guitar.

At 16, he made his debut at Kingston's very first recording studio,

Federal, owned by producer Ken Khouri, a relation of the late Byron Lee of the Dragonaires(▶). Issued in 1961, the song entitled **Judge Not,** co-written by Marley and Higgs, was a plea for society not to hastily judge the principles of the ghetto rude boys for the way they dressed. He had set the scene for a message that was to make him famous. His next recording (often credited as his first) was **One Cup Of Coffee,** selected by Marley after seeing its author Brook Benton(▶) in concert with Dinah Washington(▶). Neither record made the slightest impression upon Jamaican record buyers and he was forced to return to the welder's yard.

Reunited with Wailer and Tosh, the two urged him to form a vocal group. This he did, enlisting singers Junior Braithwaite and Beverly Kelso, and calling the group the Wailin' Wailers. Jamaica was then being terrorised by rival gangs. Marley reacted to the street violence with **Simmer Down,** the first Wailin' Wailers release for Clement Coxsone Dodd's Studio One(▶). It was an instant success, selling in excess of 80,000 copies. Marley has since been reported as saying he received no royalties for the record, a resentment he carried with him for many years.

The Wailers' quintet, backed by the Skatalites(▶), recorded a string of hits with Coxsone under the banners of Wailin' Wailers and Wailin' Rudeboys. Their songs varied from the deviant rock-steady and ska of **Rude Boy, Rule The Rudie** and **Rude Boy Go To Jail** to the more soulful American-influenced ballads, **Lonesome Feeling, I Need You, Put It On** and **Wings Of Love.**

In 1966 the group underwent a traumatic change. Braithwaite quit to join his parents in America and Kelso and another occasional member, Cherry, also left. Marley, Tosh and Wailer continued to work with Coxsone, although they finally threw in the towel when the arguments over payment became too much to bear.

Cedella had moved to Delaware, USA, where Marley joined her, securing a job at the Chrysler car factory. His experiences on the assembly line were immortalised on a song, **Night Shift.** To his horror his promised quiet life was shattered when he received his military conscription papers. To avoid being drafted and shipped off to Vietnam, he returned to Jamaica.

Tosh and Wailer had failed at their respective solo ventures and with Marley back the threesome went to record with Chinese/Jamaican producer Leslie Kong, with whom Marley had cut **One Cup . . .** in 1962, and a man fast establishing himself as the island's top rock-steady producer. What was to have been a one-off affair was extended after the public's reaction to the seminal **Soul Shakedown Party** shook Jamaica by its roots. However, Kong suffered from asthma and cancer and his deteriorating health sadly brought this creative combination to an abrupt end.

Their next stop was the newly built Black Ark Studio belonging to Lee Perry(▶), the impish genius they had befriended at Studio One, where he had been employed as an arranger. This period is generally regarded as

African Herbsman.
Courtesy Trojan Records.

Natty Dread.
Courtesy Island Records.

the foundation of Marley's career. With Perry's idiosyncratic studio tuition the Wailers hit the public with songs that are part of the group's legend. **Duppy Conquerer,** their first international hit, **Small Axe, Trenchtown Rock, Soul Rebel, Don't Rock My Boat, Keep Your Love Light Burning, The Sun Is Shining, Lively Up Yourself** and Curtis Mayfield's(▶) **Keep On Moving** were their greatest achievements. Many of these songs will be familiar to second generation Wailers' fans as Marley re-recorded several of them for his Island Records albums.

Garvey's teachings on the subject of repatriation to Africa were beginning to filter through the group. Wailer rejected his previous lifestyle and became a devout Rastafarian. By 1967 both Marley and Tosh had absorbed the words of Garvey, possibly from discussions with their colleague. Fundamental to the ideology—many would say fundamental to reggae—is the consumption of vast quantities of ganga, i.e. Jamaican marijuana that grows in abundance on the island. Marley is reputed to have smoked his way through a pound of ganga a week. Possession is nonetheless illegal in Jamaica and in 1968 he was busted and served time in jail.

All the grievances that they had previously confronted Coxsone with were then applicable to Perry. Yet they couldn't deny him the skills he had taught them, in particular, the totally unique bass-and-drum rhythm section of Aston 'Familyman' Barrett and his brother Carlton. They were the toast of the island and to Perry's horror, when the Wailers quit the Black Ark they took the brothers with them.

Marley's admiration for Perry never faltered, however, and while contracted to Island he returned to his mentor to cut the singles **Jah Live** (1976) and **Punky Reggae Party.** Marley's drive led to the group creating its own label, a move almost unheard of in reggae at that time. Wailin' Soul existed for 18 months and enjoyed mixed successes. Marley wrote their major hit of the period, **Bend Down Low,** yet their inability to manage their own financial affairs led to its collapse. Another nail in the label's coffin was a ganga bust for Wailer, who served a year's prison term.

His career in disarray, Marley signed up to Johnny Nash's(▶) TAD label as a songwriter. Nash was concerned about his own flagging career, and, impressed by Marley, recruited his skill to inject new life into his recordings, taking him into a novel mix of soul and reggae. The relationship spawned some classic tunes, notably **Stir It Up,** which went to No. 1 on the UK pop charts, and **Guava Jelly,** both from the album **I Can See Clearly Now.**

With the payment he received, Marley returned to Tosh and Wailer with the blueprint for another label. It was Tuff Gong (Perry used to call himself The Gong), operating out of 127 King Street, Kingston. With re-recorded versions of **Trenchtown Rock, Screw Face, Hypocrite** and the melancholy **Satisfy My Soul** their destiny was assured.

Perry had helped the trio to learn their respective instruments: Marley acoustic guitar; Tosh keyboards and lead guitar; Wailer percussion, adding their musicianship to the Barrett brothers. It was a completely individual sound, a hybrid of rock-steady and reggae and they soon attracted the attention of Island Records' supremo Chris Blackwell.

Stories of why Blackwell signed the group vary. A fascination with Rastafari coupled to a strong belief that reggae could, if marketed correctly, become an international music force, seem the most likely reasons. In any case, Blackwell knew they would have to move cautiously. White European and American audiences couldn't be expected to change their tastes in music overnight and latch on to reggae immediately. Blackwell financed the sophisticated **Catch A Fire** album (1973), a strong collection of diverse songs, packaged in an imitation Zippo lighter sleeve, and it sold well enough for Blackwell to be as good as his word and take Bob Marley and the Wailers under the Island wing.

The group went to Britain later that year as the darlings of the rock chic. Blackwell's campaign had paid off, their album was nestling alongside those of the Eagles and the Rolling Stones, both in the charts and in high-street chain-store browser racks. They played four nights at London's Speakeasy and made an appearance on national television. On their departure(▶) they went to the US to join Sly and the Family Stone(▶) on tour.

On the face of it, the Wailers had cracked the nut. By the end of that year they had completed a second Island album, **Burnin',** and confirmed a second UK tour. The album paled in comparison to the previous one, yet it did contain the classic **I Shot The Sheriff** that rock guitarist Eric Clapton made into a hit single for himself. Suddenly the world was aware of the Rastaman.

But acrimony had set in within the group. Wailer refused to tour again and Tosh began to express an unease about the deal with Island. Neither was to perform as a Wailer again, although the termination of their artistic relationship couldn't extinguish a lasting mutual respect and friendship. To fill the vacancy in the harmony section, Marley's wife Rita, Judy Mowatt and Marcia Griffiths(▶) (all professional singers) were enlisted as The I-Threes. With American guitarist Al Anderson and Bernard 'Touter' Harvey, Marley went on to record the album that finally set the seal on his career.

Natty Dread (1975) was a landmark for Marley and the Wailers, combining the spiritualism of Rastafari with the humour and warmth of its creator's romantic moments. It contained compelling new versions of **Lively Up Yourself** and **Bend Down Low** and new compositions **Them Belly Full** and **No Woman No Cry.** Those songs were taken to London that summer and at a memorable night at London's Lyceum, still spoken of with reverence, the future of reggae was cast. A **Live** album of that show spawned the single **No Woman No Cry,** awarding Marley his first major UK pop chart hit.

Live, like no previous work of his, was a symbol of Marley's quest for justice among the world's peoples. It stretched back to the dignity of **Trenchtown Rock** and included a riveting **I Shot The Sheriff.** He couldn't have foreseen the riots of Miami, Bristol and Brixton, but he could express the explosion that he knew would result from oppression. By now the group was concentrating on tours of the USA and Britain where he was enjoying a strong and devotional cult following among black and whites, while in Jamaica every single was an automatic No. 1.

After the release of **Rastaman Vibrations** (1976) and the annual tours, Marley's position as an international musician and statesman made him a target for warring gunmen in Jamaica. In December of that year, at the height of pre-election political gang violence, seven armed men burst into his home at 56 Hope Road, Kingston. If his manager, Don Taylor, hadn't flung himself in front of the singer, Marley would have sustained more serious injury than four bullet wounds in an arm. Rita was also injured in the incident. The attack occurred on the eve of a concert he was due to appear at organised by the then ruling PNP party led by Michael Manley. Despite his injuries, Marley performed the concert although, immediately after he left Jamaica for the safety of an 18-month exile in Miami.

The magnificent **Exodus** album (1977) was recorded partly there and partly in London; the sheer political fury of that record played a vital role in drawing him back to Jamaica.

When he did return it was for one of the most moving spectacles ever witnessed on the island. In front of an estimated 20,000 people at Kingston's National Stadium he brought together in a handshake Manley and the opposition leader (now premier) Edward Seaga. The concert was the beginning of a temporary truce between the rival factions and a commemoration of a visit to Jamaica exactly 12 years before by Ethiopia's Emperor Haile Selassie, a man at the heart of Rastafarian philosophy of repatriation to Africa.

In all, Marley recorded 10 albums for Island, ranging in content, lyrically and musically, from the bald political sloganeering of **Exodus** (spawning hit singles **Exodus, Jammin'** and **Waiting In Vain**), **Survival** and the powerful **Uprising,** his last recorded album that included the epic **Redemption Song,** Marley's voice accompanied by just an acoustic guitar, to the mellower, reflective **Kaya** (1978).

It was almost inevitable that a man so identified with the struggles against class and racial oppression should be invited to perform at the

Bob Marley And The Wailers Live! Courtesy Island Records.

Above: Marley's impassioned beliefs fired his memorable live performances, where he was superbly supported by the Wailers and I-Threes.

celebrations of the birth of a new nation, Zimbabwe. The popular press couldn't get much mileage from something as mundane as an assassination attempt or the end of apartheid in a newly created African nation, but his affair with erstwhile Miss World, Cindy Breakspear, caused them all to sit up and take note.

Towards the close of an exhausting world tour (1980) Marley collapsed after a concert at New York's Madison Square Gardens and was taken to Sloane Kettering Hospital where cancer was diagnosed. Some months later it became known that he had a cancerous toe removed while in Miami three years before. The extent of his illness could be gauged by his decision to admit himself to the Josef Issels Clinic, on Lake Tegarn, Bavaria. Upon completion of the treatment he flew to Miami, to visit Cedella, en route for Jamaica. His discomfort must have been chronic and on May 8 he admitted himself to the Cedars Lebanon Hospital where he died three days later (May 11).

Since his death, countless tribute records have been released, none finer than Bunny Wailer's **Tribute** collection of Marley compositions. A film of his life is planned, incorporating vintage footage and there is a book *Bob Marley, Soul Rebel-Natural Rebel* by photographer Adrian Boot and journalist Vivien Goldman.

Recordings:
The Wailin' Wailers (Studio One/—)
The Best Of Bob Marley And The Wailers (Studio One/—)
Marley, Tosh, Livingstone & Associates (Studio One/—)
Bob Marley And The Wailers, Birth Of A Legend Parts 1 & 2 (Calla/CBS)
Soul Rebels (—/Trojan)
African Herbsman (—/Trojan)
Rasta Revolution (—/Trojan)
Present Soul Revolution Part Two (Upsetters/—)
Present Soul Revolution Part Three (Upsetters/—)
The Best Of The Wailers (Beverlys/—)
Catch A Fire (Island)
Burnin' ((Island)
Natty Dread (Island)
Rastaman Vibrations (Island)
Live (—/Island)
A Taste Of The Wailers (—/Island)
Exodus (Island)
Kaya (Island)
Babylon By Bus (Island)
Survival (Island)
Uprising (Island)
Black Out (Splash/—)
Chances Are (Warner Brothers)

Rita Marley

See I-Threes

Harvey Mason

Harvey Mason's contribution to black music has come as much through his work as a backing musician as it has from his own records. While still attending high school, drummer / percussionist, Mason (born Atlantic City, New Jersey, 1947) backed jazz musicians when they came to the city's Winter Gardens, and after graduating he toured Europe with Errol Garner. Returning home in 1970, Mason's session career flourished as he contributed to countless records, film scores and commercials.

To date, Mason has appeared on hit albums by George Benson(▶), Dee Dee Bridgewater(▶), Grover Washington Jr(▶), Ron Carter(▶), Deodato, Carole King, Bobby Lyle, Phil Upchurch(▶) and the Brecker Brothers. He became a member of Herbie Hancock's(▶) Headhunters, which helped him move towards the jazz-funk fusion later heard on his own records. He signed with Arista in 1975 and his albums are populated with artists returning the compliment for his work, including Hubert Laws(▶), Herbie Hancock, Merrie Clayton(▶), Ray Parker Jr(▶), Stanley Clarke(▶), Verdine White of Earth, Wind & Fire(▶) and Ralph McDonald(▶).

Mason's **Groovin' You** album of 1979 brought him title-track single success, and from his **M.V.P.** album of 1981 **How Does It Feel** was the hit. Mason has also found time to produce albums by Esther Phillips(▶), Lee Ritenour(▶) and Shirley Brown(▶).

Recordings:
Marching In The Street (Arista)
Earthmover (Arista)
Funk In A Mason Jar (Arista)
Groovin' You (Arista)
M.V.P. (Arista)

Mass Production

A 10-piece band, who originally came from Richmond, Virginia, and made their debut album in 1976, Mass Production play a commercial fusion of jazz and funk. Club reaction to their dance material has kept them together.

They now consist of Agnes Kelly, vocals; Larry Marshall, vocals; Ricardo Williams, vocals; James Drumgole, horns; Gregory McCoy, saxes; Emanuel Redding, percussion; Kevin Douglas, bass; Leroy Bryant, guitars; Samuel Williams, drums; Tyrone Williams, keyboards.

Recordings:
Masterpiece (Cotillion)
In A City Groove (Cotillion)

Matumbi

Presently inactive owing to a profusion of solo activities, this premier-division reggae ensemble was formed in South London in 1972 by vocalist Tex Dixon. Other members included Uton Jones, drums; Dennis Bovell(▶), guitar; Errol Pottinger, guitar; and Bevin and Glaister Fagan and Nicholas Bailey, vocals.

Under a name that in Africa means rebirth, they served their musical apprenticeship backing a number of visiting Jamaican reggae singers. This led to a five-year contract with Trojan Records and their first recordings, **Brother Louis** and **Wipe Them Out.** Commercial success came in 1976 with **After Tonight**, written by Bovell and Pottinger, and later with a version of Bob Dylan's **Man And Me.** The former dominated the British reggae charts for weeks and was the biggest selling reggae single of the year.

Despite this, Trojan was unhappy with the group's choice of material. Members were already taking on individual projects to satisfy their creative appetites. When the label learnt that its band was backing Louisa Mark on another big record that year, **Caught You In A Lie,** it reacted with an injunction. Jah Bunny had been drafted to replace drummer Jones and in 1978 Bailey and Dixon quit to pursue solo careers, the former as Nick Straker (notching hit singles in pop idiom).

EMI was one of several major record companies seeking a way-in on the expanding reggae market. With the resources of an international corporation at their disposal, the band recorded its first studio album, **Seven Seas.** It was backed by a big publicity campaign and a British tour supporting Ian Dury.

In 1979 they released one of the

Point Of View. Courtesy EMI Records.

most sophisticated British reggae albums ever, **Point Of View**, complete with stylish, eye-catching packaging. Produced by Jamaican Errol Thompson, the doo-wop pastiche title track was extracted for single release. It reached No. 33 on the national charts and then, like the album, bombed out. The group never quite recovered from this. Two other albums followed, yet they lacked the spark of earlier recordings.

While the group sat out its contract with EMI, Bunny quit to join the Cimarons(▶), Bovell built his own studio, where he produces rock and reggae artists in addition to his own material, and Glaister Fagan and Blake have enjoyed consistent UK chart action as the Squad.

Recordings:
The Best Of Matumbi (—/Trojan)
Point Of View (—/EMI)
Dub Planet (—/Extinguish Records)

Maze

In 1971, Frankie Beverley, now lead vocalist and keyboard player of Maze, formed a band called Raw Soul, a group that was part of an emerging Philadelphia soul scene.

Having recorded two singles, Beverley thought it might be best to change location altogether to establish an individual identity away from the Philly International(▶) sound. So percussionists Roame Lowry and McKinley Williams, along with keyboard player Sam Porter and Beverley all piled into a bus, and headed out to San Francisco.

In California they began producing music that had the sound of a TSOP (The Sound Of Philadelphia) record, but with laid-back West Coast rock arrangements. Adding Robin Duhe, bass; Wayne Thomas, lead guitar, and Joe Provost, drums, Maze were signed to Capitol Records in 1976. From their debut album, **Maze Featuring Frankie Beverley**, came two R&B hit singles, **While I'm Alone** and **Look At California**, and a disco hit, **Happy Feelin's**; the album eventually turned gold.

For most of the second LP, **Golden Time Of Day**, Ahaguna G. Sun replaced Provost on drums. This gold album, released in 1978, featured the R&B hit, **Travellin' Man**. The special Maze mixture of R&B and soul, written and sung by the bluesy Beverley, generated a passionate cult-following. Their third gold album, **Inspiration**, produced a pop hit single, **Feel That You're Feelin'**.

The fourth set, released in 1980, was really a turning-point in terms of world sales. Billy 'Shoes' Johnson replaced Sun on drums, and Ron Smith replaced Thomas on guitar. The title track of the album, **Joy And Pain**, contained a chorus that so encompassed the warm spirit of the band and their music that at their live appearances the audience always ended up singing along on that song. Other hit singles from **Joy And Pain** included **Southern Girl** and **Look In Your Eyes**.

It was, though, Maze's concerts that were spreading their gospel most effectively. To see the band's faces and hear them talk conveyed even more of the emotion and amicability of their music. So, in November 1980, a concert recorded at the Saenger Theatre, New Orleans, became Maze's fifth release, **Live In New Orleans**.

Issued in 1981, this double set soon went gold. Three of its sides were the concert, featuring all of their hits, and a fourth side comprised four studio tracks, one of which, **Running Away**, became a hit single; all four new tracks were soon incorporated into the stage show. Just before the fifth album was recorded, Philip Woo was added as an extra keyboard player, to allow Beverley freedom to sing and aid the audience during the momentous **Joy And Pain**.

Recordings:
Maze Featuring Frankie Beverley (Capitol)
Golden Time Of Day (Capitol)
Inspiration (Capitol)
Joy And Pain (Capitol)
Live In New Orleans (Capitol)

Van McCoy

Born in Washington DC in 1940, Van McCoy was a member of the Starlighters with brother Norman. Friends Shep and the Limelights (of **Daddy's Home** fame) took them to George Goldner's End label in New York where they had three singles before splitting up in 1961.

McCoy became staff producer

Above: George McCrae, who rocked us in the mid-'70s.

and writer at Scepter/Wand, working under Luther Dixon and with the Shirelles(▶), Chuck Jackson(▶) and others. He then landed a staff job with Leiber and Stoller(▶) and became writer with Columbia's Blackwood Music.

He wrote for Bobby Vinton, Gladys Knight and the Pips(▶), Barbara Lewis, Aretha Franklin(▶), Ruby and the Romantics(▶) **(When You're Young And In Love**, later a hit for the Marvelettes(▶)). He formed his own publishing company in 1967 and penned **I Get The Sweetest Feeling** for Jackie Wilson(▶). He also had hits with Brenda and the Tabulations, and discovered Faith, Hope and Charity who became his long-time protégés.

When Thom Bell(▶) stopped working with the Stylistics(▶), legendary A&R men (and bosses of Avco Embassy label), Hugo and Luigi, called McCoy in and despite criticism for the super-lush nature of his productions and arrangements, he gave them massive hits.

Hugo and Luigi then invited McCoy to record an instrumental album of Stylistics' songs in near symphonic style. It sold moderately, but follow-up album **Disco Baby** (1975) was timed just right for the disco explosion and yielded **The Hustle**, an international hit. This success led to a string of similar albums featuring McCoy's keyboard work and a full orchestra of big name soul session men.

Recordings:
Disco Baby (Avco Embassy)
The Disco Kid (Avco Embassy)
The Real McCoy (Avco Embassy)
Lonely Dancer (Avco Embassy)

George McCrae

If your first hit is as massive a success as **Rock Your Baby** proved to be for George McCrae, anything that follows is bound to be an anti-climax. The song, which did much to launch the mid-'70s disco craze and sold many millions of copies, was written by H.W. Casey and Rick Finch (of K.C. and the Sunshine Band(▶)) with George's wife Gwen(▶) in mind, but she turned it down and George cut it

instead—as only his second record—with dramatic consequences.

Whereas Gwen had originally been the star of the family, with George happy to be her road manager, suddenly the situation was reversed. George was projected into the limelight and though they toured and recorded together the change in roles eventually led to the break-up of their decade-long marriage which had produced two daughters. Born on October 19, 1944, in West Palm Beach, Florida, George McCrae was a somewhat tipsy sailor out on the town when he first met Gwen in a Pensacola restaurant and was told to get lost. A week later he managed to get a date, a week after that they married!

McCrae had led his own group, the Jivin' Jets, before joining the Navy and after marrying Gwen and leaving the service, the couple began singing as a duet in West Palm Beach clubs, making their recording debut some years later with **Three Hearts In A Tangle** on Alston, part of Henry Stone's TK(▶) empire. TK then leased George's solo debut to United Artists and pacted Gwen with Columbia, while George took an increasingly background role on live dates.

Rock Your Baby hit No.1 around the world and follow-ups like **Let's Dance (People All Over The World)** had a certain charm, but his lightweight voice and somewhat lumbering stage movements were not the stuff of which soul superstars are made.

Recordings:
Rock Your Baby (TK/President)

Gwen McCrae

Born on December 21, 1943, in Pensacola, Florida, Gwen married George McCrae(▶), who enjoyed a multi-million seller with **Rock Your Baby**, a song which had been written for her to record.

With a gritty blues-slanted edge to her voice, Gwen has recorded a consistent run of aesthetically pleasing if only modestly commercially successful singles and albums for labels in Henry Stone's now defunct TK(▶) set-up. Particularly strong on story-style and rap records, as on **Let's Straighten It Out** (Cat 1978), she has the potential

to be another Millie Jackson(▶), given the right guidance.

Recordings:
Gwen McCrae (Cat/President)
Let's Straighten It Out (Cat/—
Melody Of Life (Cat/—)

McFadden And Whitehead

Philadelphia-born Gene McFadden and John Whitehead were signed to Philadelphia International Records(▶) in 1969, where they wrote songs for Teddy Pendergrass(▶), the O'Jays(▶), and Harold Melvin & the Bluenotes(▶). They did not release their first album until 1979, but their per-

McFadden & Whitehead. Courtesy Philadelphia International Records.

forming debut included **Ain't No Stoppin' Us Now**, which became a worldwide chart hit and club anthem. They are important figures in the formulation of the famous Philly sound which was behind many hits of the mid-'70s.

Recordings:
McFadden And Whitehead (P.I.R.)
I Heard It Through A Love Song (P.I.R.)

Freddie McGregor

Born in June 1956 in Clarendon, Jamaica, McGregor discovered music through his parents who were active in a church band and choir. Teaming up as a teenager with childhood friends Earnest Wilson and Peter Austin to form the Clarendonians, he left his rural home for Kingston and Clement Coxsone Dodd's Studio One(▶). Dividing his time between recording and schooling, McGregor and the group enjoyed local radio hits with **Rude Boys Gone Ah Jail, What A Bam Bam** and **Can't Leave Another.**

McGregor's young voice was fragile, almost feminine in texture (obvious early influences were the Impressions'(▶) records), and having established himself as a sought-after session vocalist he quit the trio in 1967 and went solo. Remaining with Dodd he scored with the singles **Just Once In My Life, Pledging My Love, Why Did You Do It** and **Do Good And Good Shall Follow You.**

In 1973 he was invited to become lead singer with the Soul Syndicate band who, despite limited recordings (notably **Love Ballad** and **Mark Of The Beast**), won a keen following on the strength of regular live appearances on the island. His increasing interest in the philosophy of Rastafari, manifest in his lyrics of that period, persuaded him to have a second crack at a solo career.

With producer Winston Niney 'The Observer', he released his debut solo album, **Mr. McGregor,** in 1977. Its melodic neo-folk songs and the singer's graceful phrasing took the reggae world by storm. it was enough to convince Dodd that he wanted him back and two years later they issued the immensely popular album of the hit single **Bobby Babylon.**

By then McGregor was a frequent companion of I-Three(▶) Judy Mowatt and an active member of the Rastafarian organisation, the Twelve Tribes. Later that year he hit again with another popular single, **Natural Collie.**

He remains an influential song-writer and a unique singer who, after almost two decades in reggae, still has much to offer. Most recently his records (**Roots Man Skanking**) have appeared on British label Greensleeves.

Recordings:
Bobby Babylon (Studio One/—)
Showcase (—/Third World)

Mel and Tim

Cousins Mel Hardin and Tim McPherson were born in Holly Springs, Mississippi. Gene Chandler(▶) signed them in 1969 for his own Bamboo label, and their second release, the self-penned **Blackfield In Motion,** eventually sold a million copies.

Further hits followed with Bamboo, until the company folded. In 1972 the duo signed with Stax, and hit again with **Starting All Over Again.** Although pleasant, the Mel and Tim sound was derivative of other duos like James and Bobby Purify(▶), and success was not sustained into the '70s.

Recordings:
Starting All Over Again (Stax)

Harold Melvin and the Blue Notes

Though the label credits read 'Harold Melvin and the Blue Notes,' it was the sensuously soulful Teddy Pendergrass(▶) who sang

lead on all the group's classic tracks, having previously been their drummer for six years.

As original lead singer when the group started out in 1954 (getting on record in 1956 via a hit on Josie with **If You Love Me**) and as the only founder member left, Melvin jealously guarded his star-billing, a stance bound to cause disgruntlement, and indeed it led to Pendergrass leaving for a career as a solo superstar in the mid-'70s.

After their initial hit, the 1960 Value release **My Hero,** taken from **The Chocolate Soldier,** gave them a second chart entry and they made noise with **This Time Will Be Different** on Uni in 1969. But it took Kenny Gamble, Leon Huff and their Philadelphia International(▶) operation to turn Harold Melvin and the Blue Notes into a major act; they were groomed to a slick stage presentation which enabled them to appeal to white cabaret audiences as well as their ethnic following.

The soulful **I Miss You** set things rolling, followed by the hauntingly poignant ballad **If You Don't Know Me By Now,** a monster in '72, then, in quick succes-

*Don't Leave Me This Way.
Courtesy Columbia Records.*

sion, **The Love I Lost, Where Are All My Friends, Wake Up Everybody, Satisfaction Guaranteed (Or Take Your Love Back),** and others, all featuring Pendergrass's stunning lead vocals showcased with a backdrop of smooth group harmonies from Melvin, Bernard Wilson, Lawrence Brown and Lloyd Parks (replaced by Jerry Cummings in 1974) and the impeccable 'The Sound Of Philadelphia' orchestrations.

With Pendergrass's departure, Harold Melvin and the Blue Notes switched to ABC in 1976 with a line-up consisting of Melvin, Jerry Cummings, Dwight Johnson, Bill Spratley and David Ebo, with guest appearances by Melvin's protégée Sharon Paige.

Recordings:
Harold Melvin And The Blue Notes (Philadelphia International)
Black And Blue (Philadelphia International)
Wake Up (Philadelphia International)
Greatest Hits (Philadelphia International)
Reaching For The World (ABC/Anchor)

MFSB

MFSB—Mother Father Sister Brother—had their biggest hit with **TSOP**—The Sound Of Philadelphia. That instrumental's title summed up what they were all about: a massive studio band which, besides recording in its own right,

provided the backings for a whole host of Philly hits like the O'Jays(▶), Harold Melvin and the Blue Notes(▶), Ronnie Dyson, the Intruders(▶), New York City(▶), the Three Degrees(▶) and Bunny Sigler(▶).

The core of the band were the musicians responsible for Cliff Nobles' million-selling instrumental **The Horse,** in 1968, then, in 1971,

Love Is The Message. Courtesy Philadelphia International.

as the Family, they recorded a version of Sly and the Family Stone's(▶) **Family Affair.** However, MFSB really broke through with **TSOP,** which was the theme for the popular 'Soul Train' TV show.

Producers Kenny Gamble and Leon Huff masterminded the aggregation with arranger/musical director Bobby Martin. Among the 28 regulars were Huff (on keyboards), Norman Harris, Roland Chambers, Bobby Eli and Ron Kersey (guitars), Lenny Pakula (organ), Zach Zachary (sax), Ronnie Baker (bass), Vince Montana (vibes), Larry Washington (percussion) and Earl Young (drums), and a string section put together by Don Renaldo.

Recordings:
MFSB (Philadelphia International)
Love Is The Message (Philadelphia International)
Philadelphia Freedom (Philadelphia International)
Universal Love (Philadelphia International)

Stephanie Mills

Stephanie Mills is a petite four-foot-nine-inch bundle of singer and actress. Born in Brooklyn, New York, in 1957, she auditioned for a part in a Broadway play at the age of seven and was accepted. The play, *Maggie Flynn,* ran for nine months. Stephanie then became a member of the off-Broadway troupe, the Negro Ensemble Company Workshop.

Aged 10, she won a talent contest at Harlem's Apollo Theatre and her prize was a four-week season there, followed by a week supporting the Isley Brothers(▶). In 1974, the first Stephanie Mills single, **I Knew It Was Love** on Paramount, was heard by Ken Harper, producer of *The Wiz,* the black musical based on *The Wizard Of Oz.* This Broadway smash, with Stephanie starring as Dorothy, ran for four years. (Stephanie appears on the original cast album.)

In 1979, she signed to 20th Century Fox Records, and her three albums to date, all successful in their own right, owe a debt of thanks to producers/writers/musicians James Mtume and Reggie Lucas. The title track of her first album, **Watcha Gonna Do With My Lovin',** and **Put Your Body In It,** were worldwide hits. The second album, released in 1981, included the pop chart hit, **Never Knew Love Like This Before.** On June 13, 1980, she married Jeffrey Daniel of Shalamar(▶) but they separated a little over a year later. Teddy Pendergrass(▶) invited Stephanie to duet with him on an album and a tour in 1981. Stephanie returned the compliment on her third album, and their **Two Hearts** single became her big hit later that year.

Recordings
Whatcha Gonna Do With My Lovin' (20th Century Fox)
Sweet Sensation (20th Century Fox)
Stephanie (20th Century Fox)

Below: The Sweet Sensation herself—Stephanie Mills.

Sugar Minott

In addition to recording some of the very best reggae music during the past five years, Sugar Minott made an important breakthrough by overcoming the purist school of prejudice which maintained that all good reggae must come out of Jamaica. His first major hit on arriving in Britain, **Lovers Rock**, not only revealed him as a singer/songwriter of enviable scope, but also established him as the focal point which British reggae so badly needed. A trail of first-class recordings have followed and the setting up of his Black Roots musical collective has been the first real push towards roping indigenous UK talent together.

Lincoln Minott was born in Maxfield Park, Kingston, Jamaica, on May 25, 1956. He attended Melrose Primary School and Kingston College Extension, finishing with full-time education when he was

Showcase. Courtesy Studio One Records.

19. He acquired his nickname 'Sugar' in his early teens because of his podgy frame: he was ribbed for having a belly full of sugar.

Minott entered his first talent competition at 14 and two years later was rehearsing with his lifelong friend and peer, Tony Tuff. Greatly influenced by Dennis Brown(▶), the pair joined the dis-

arrayed ranks of Derrick Howard's African Brothers. The group enjoyed limited success and in the early '70s Minott went solo and signed a one-year contract with Coxsone Dodd at Studio One(▶).

Working more or less as a studio apprentice, Minott sang everything from pop to gospel, and often sat in on percussion and guitar. From this period came such memorable cuts as **Wrong Doers, Is It True,** and later, with Prince Jammy producing, **Never Too Young** and an album **Bitter Sweet**, retitled **Save The Children** for the UK market.

Once in Britain, Minott's popularity spread at a meteoric rate and reached its first peak in the spring of 1980, when his version of **Good Thing Going** (previously covered by Michael Jackson(▶)) made the British national top 10. An astute business sense combined with an altruistic attitude towards his music and other young musicians have led him to maintain a diligent low profile despite many offers of recordings and concert tours.

Recordings:
Roots Lovers (—/Black Roots)
Black Roots (Mango/—)
Ghetto-ology Dubwise (—/Black Roots)
African Girl (—/Black Roots)

Misty-In-Roots

Formed in Southall, England (1974), this 11-piece reggae band backed Jamaican singer Nicky Thomas on his visit to Britain in 1975. By the mid-'70s Misty-In-Roots had secured a stoic cult-following by its muscular despatchment of rhythm and its alignment to the Rock Against Racism, Anti-Apartheid and Legalise Cannabis campaigns.

The group rejected recording offers from major companies and established the Peoples Unite label and a cross-cultural community centre. Appreciative audiences in Europe led to an impressive debut album being recorded in Belgium (1979), **Live At The Counter-**

Above: Misty-In-Roots. Although they won't ever achieve massive commercial success, they have a strong think-alike following.

Eurovision.

Recordings:
Wise And Foolish (—/Peoples Unite)

The Moments

Harry Ray from Long Branch, New Jersey, prolific songwriter/producer Al Goodman from Mississippi, and lead singer Billy Brown from Atlanta, Georgia, collectively known as the Moments, made a series of very successful smash pop/soul singles on All Platinum subsidiary Stang in the mid-'70s, including **Girls, Dolly My Love, Jack In The Box** and **Sexy Mama**.

As a slick sensual vocal trio, they attracted a large female audience. One live performance, at a women's prison, was recorded for a live album. In 1978, they changed their name to Ray, Goodman and Brown(▶) and moved labels to first Polydor then Mercury.

Recordings:
Those Sexy Moments (Stang/All Platinum)
The Moments' Greatest Hits (Stang/All Platinum)

Dorothy Moore

Jackson, Mississippi's Malaco company is a small localised operation, but though its output may be modest in volume, the quality has been very high and a distinctive 'Malaco Sound' has been evolved which has yielded the occasional massive hit (in both national and international terms), including King Floyd's(▶) **Groove Me** and Dorothy Moore's hauntingly attractive ballad **Misty Blue.**

Such artists' records have been leased to major companies to ensure proper promotion and distribution. Floyd was pacted to Atlantic, Dorothy Moore to Epic, though **Misty Blue** itself had been on Malaco (on Contempo in the UK).

A native of Jackson, Dorothy was born in 1947 and studied voice and piano while at Jackson State University, forming the Poppies with fellow students Petsey McCune and Rose Mary Taylor, and charting with **Cry Like A**

Below: Dorothy Moore's good formal education shows through in classy records and live performances.

Baby and **Lullaby Of Love** (Petsey went on to sing back-up with Helen Reddy, while Rose teaches French in Hawaii).

Leaving university, Dorothy pacted with Malaco and scored in 1976 with **Misty Blue**. The follow-ups **Funny How Time Slips Away** and **I Believe In You** also charted on both sides of the Atlantic.

Recordings:
Misty Blue (Malaco/Contempo)
Dorothy Moore (Epic)
Talk To Me (Epic)

Melba Moore

New York City-born Melba had her first success in the original Broadway production of *Hair*, and in 1971 she established herself as one of America's leading black actresses with her role in the black musical *Purlie*.

What A Woman Needs. Courtesy Capitol Records.

After a run of classy records with Buddah (arranged and produced by Van McCoy(▶)) and Epic during the '70s, she signed with Capitol Records in 1981, and with her first release for them began to utilise her singing and songwriting talents more fully. Having worked as a stage actress, she has a powerful delivery that touches all black musical forms.

Recordings:
Living To Give (Mercury/—)
This Is It (Buddah)
Melba (Epic)
What A Woman Needs (Capitol)

Morrissey Mullen

Self-taught musicians Jim Mullen, guitar (born Glasgow 1945), and Dick Morrissey, tenor sax (born Surrey 1940) first joined forces for the album **Up** (1975), produced by Average White Band's(▶) Molly Duncan.

Mullen (ex-Brian Auger, Kokomo) has strong jazz-rock roots, and is a perfect foil for Morrissey's fluid tenor styling, developed during a decade playing jazz clubs, and three years with British band, If, who cut seven excellent albums from 1969-72.

Forerunners of the British jazz-funk(▶) movement, Morrissey Mullen are well-respected concert and club performers, and have appeared at the Montreux Jazz Festival, where they were recorded for **The Atlantic Family** LP in 1978.

Recordings:
Up (Atlantic)
Cape Wrath (EMI)
Badness (Beggar's Banquet)
Life On The Wire (Beggar's Banquet)

Pablo Moses

Pablo Moses, real name Paul Henry, was born in Jamaica in August 1953, and, upon completing a graduate course in poetry, surfaced on the reggae charts with his own composition, **I Man A Grasshopper,** for the Jigsaw label in which he and many other local young emergent talents had personal stakes.

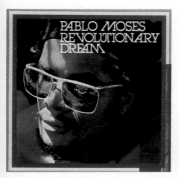

Revolutionary Dream. Courtesy Klik Records.

The song was about the meditative powers of ganga (marijuana) and was quickly followed by **Blood Dunza (Money).** This time Moses vividly portrayed the island's blacks who, come election time, turn on their brethren upon payment from unscrupulous politicians.

Two years later, both songs were included on an impressive debut album, **Revolutionary Dreams,** for Klik. It sold in excess of 6,000 copies and encouraged Moses to continue working under his deep-roots reggae banner. Producer Geoffrey Chung, an associate from Jigsaw, took him to Britain's Island Records.

A second album, **A Song** (1979), established Moses as an artist of strong intent. His music was increasingly militant and easily recognisable through his employment of synthesisers and keyboards. With his popularity on America's East Coast gaining ground, Island subsidiary Mango recently issued his seminal album, **Proverbs,** in the US.

Recordings:
A Song (—/Island)

Revolutionary Dream (Klik/ Different)
Proverbs (Mango/—)

Alphonse Mouzon

Today a highly-touted figure on the jazz-funk scene, Alphonse Mouzon started his professional career as drummer with 'King Of The Twist' Chubby Checker(▶) back in 1965 but soon switched to the musically more satisfying—if less well paying—jazz scene, working with Freddie Hubbard(▶) Roy Ayers(▶) (in 1970), Weather Report(▶) (in 1971), McCoy Tyner and Les McCann, as well as with Roberta Flack(▶) and Stevie Wonder(▶) on the soul side of things.

Signed to Blue Note, he started recording in his own right in 1971 and cut four highly rated albums for the label: **The Essence Of Mystery, Funky Snakefoot, Mind Transplant** and **Man Incognito.**

Following his first visit to Europe, he began recording his albums in Germany, cutting the **Virtue** and **Search Of A Dream** LP's for MPS Records and, in 1979, **Baby Come Back** for Metronome under the tag Mouzon Electric Band. That same year he wrote the worldwide disco hit **Poussez,** and in 1981 released the excellent **By All Means** and **Morning Sun** albums.

Best known as a drummer, Mouzon (born Charleston, South Carolina, November 21, 1948, and a New York resident since 1966) started out as a keyboard player and this helps account for his very distinctive style of drumming. On his own albums he handles vocals and much of the keyboard work, as well as his drum kit.

Recordings:
The Essence Of Mystery (Blue Note)
Funky Snakefoot (Blue Note)
By All Means (Decca/Excalibur)
Morning Sun (Decca/London)

Judy Mowatt

See I-Threes.

Junior Murvin

Born in Port Antonio, Jamaica, and originally known as Junior Soul, Murvin cut his first self-penned disc, **Miss Cushy,** with producer Sonia Pottinger. His multi-octave falsetto voice led him to join vocal groups with Max Romeo(▶) (The Hippy Boys) and Dennis .Brown(▶) (The Falcons).

International recognition followed the release of his Lee Perry(▶)-produced album, **Police And Thieves.** His own composition, it reached the UK pop charts twice, first in 1976 and again in 1980 when it was re-issued after being featured on the soundtrack of the reggae film, *Rockers.* It has since been versioned by DJ Jah Lion and is a popular stage number for the punk band The Clash. Murvin has scarcely recorded anything since.

Recordings:
Police And Thieves (Island)

Mystic Merlin

Clyde Bullard has a deep interest in illusionary magic, an interest which spread through his band who began to include magic in their stage shows. From their Brooklyn base Mystic Merlin—comprising Bullard, Jerry Anderson (guitar), Keith Gonzales (vocals), Sly Randolph (drums) and Barry Strutt (saxes and keyboards)—combine rock, jazz and R&B. Their debut album **Mystic Merlin** (1980) produced the hit **Just Can't Give You Up.**

Recordings:
Mystic Merlin (Capitol)
Sixty Thrills A Minute (Capitol)

Full Moon (Capitol)

Johnny Nash

Playing Johnny Nash's considerable recorded output from beginning to end is almost like taking a trip from one end of popular music to the other, for his career has seen him go from teen idol singing blatant pop, to MOR balladeer, into

I Can See Clearly Now. Courtesy CBS Records.

soul music and on into reggae. He has recorded with Paul Anka and country star George Hamilton IV, yet, on the other hand, he at one time used Bob Marley(▶) and the Wailers(▶) as his backing outfit!

Born in Houston, Texas, on August 19, 1940, Nash has led something of a nomadic existence, having at various times based himself in New York, Los Angeles, Jamaica, London and Sweden.

As a youngster Nash broke the colour bar on Texan TV when he starred in KPRC's 'Matinee' show, which earned him an ABC Paramount recording contract. A string of pop hits followed, **A Teenager Sings The Blues, A Very Special**

Below: Johnny Nash, former teen idol turned mid-'70s soul superstar.

Love, The Ten Commandments (with Anka and Hamilton) and **As Time Goes By** included, which with a seven-year residency on the Arthur Godfrey TV talent show, took him through the late '50s.

In the '60s, Nash was following the lead of Sam Cooke(▶) (who was a major influence on his style) by leavening soul material with MOR standards and show tunes, recording for Warner Brothers, Argo, MGM and other labels.

In 1965 he set up his own Jad and Joda labels in New York with business partner Danny Sims (producing the Sam and Bill US soul hit **For Your Love** that year) and started commuting regularly to Jamaica to record. He had fallen in love with the Caribbean while on location there at the age of 17 filming *Take A Giant Step,* in which he starred with Burt Lancaster (his other movies have included *Key Witness* with Denis Hopper, the Swedish sex film *Love Is Not A Game* and *I Want So Much To Believe*).

He charted in 1965 with **Let's Move And Groove Together,** then visited Byron Lee's(▶) studio in Kingston to record his own song **Hold Me Tight** (1968), which was a massive US hit and broke him into the UK top 10. He followed through in 1969 with **You Got Soul** and a re-make of Sam Cooke's **Cupid.** He also cut a 1969 album of duets with ex-Motowner Kim Weston(▶), produced by her husband Mickey Stevenson(▶).

By now his mix of silky American soul with a Jamaican reggae backing was nearing perfection

and on signing to CBS in London (Epic for U.S.) in 1971, he reached his zenith with the delicious Bob Marley composition **Stir It Up** and the self-penned American national chart-topper **I Can See Clearly Now. There Are More Questions Than Answers, Tears On My Pillow** and **Guava Jelly** were other superb offerings in the same mode.

Recordings:
Soul Folk (Jad/Major Minor)
You Got Soul So Hold Me Tight (Jad/Major Minor)
I Can See Clearly Now (Epic/CBS)
Tears On My Pillow (Epic/CBS)
Celebrate Life (Epic/CBS)

New York City

This four-piece Philly-inspired vocal soul group scored internationally with their attractive **I'm Doin' Fine Now** (1973), arranged and produced by Thom Bell(▶) and recorded at Sigma Sound.

John Brown was first tenor with the Five Satins and also sang back-up with the Cadillacs (his sister Estelle is a member of Sweet Inspirations(▶)); former basketball star Tim McQueen wrote much of the material and the group was completed by Edward Schell and Claude Johnson.

Despite a classy album based round the hit and a good follow-up set featuring a sleeve picture taken on THAT street crossing made famous by the Beatles' Abbey Road album, New York City soon faded.

Recordings:
I'm Doin' Fine Now (Chelsea)
Soulful Road (Chelsea)

New York Sky

See Skyy.

Dave 'Fathead' Newman

Dave Newman's raunchy sax playing and his punchy orchestrations (a big, round, brass sound doubling up on Charles' gospelly piano chords) played a major role in the rise to stardom of Ray Charles(▶) with whom he spent 12 years in the role of musical director. A native of Dallas, Texas, he also worked in the bands of T. Bone Walker and Lowell Fulsom(▶) (where he met Charles).

Newman's debut album was **Hard Times** (Atlantic) in 1968, and since then he has maintained a steady flow, bringing in the finest of jazz/R&B session men to play on his sessions and, like other jazz funkers, venturing into singing, with notable success on **Front Money** (1977).

Recordings:
House Of David (Atlantic/—)
The Weapon (Atlantic/—)
Mr Fathead (Warner Bros)
Front Money (Warner Bros/—)
Keep The Dream Alive (Prestige)

Billy Ocean

Trinidad-born but raised in Britain, Billy Ocean is one of the brightest talents to have come to the fore in the UK in the last few years. An excellent singer of his own melodic pop-soul material, he signed with GTO Records in 1975 and almost immediately hit No. 2 in the British charts with **Love Really Hurts Without You.** Three more big hit singles followed in quick succession—**Love On Delivery** in summer 1976, **Stop Me (If You've Heard It All Before)** in the autumn of the same year, and **Red Light Spells Danger** in spring 1977.

Then followed a low-profile period accompanied by the usual rumours of business problems. However, Ocean's second album, **City Limit,** was released in May 1980 and in autumn 1981 came his third LP, **Nights (Feel Like Getting Down).** The title track from this later album saw some action in the US and pointed to a promising future.

Recordings:
Billy Ocean (Epic/GTD)
City Limit (Epic/GTD)
Nights (Feel Like Getting Down) (Epic/GTD)

Odyssey

The exotic good looks which go with the Lopez sisters' Virgin Islands' heritage, combined with a conscientiously international and eclectic range of material, contribute greatly to Odyssey's broad appeal. They blend a very successful pot-pourri of style, among which they themselves cite Broadway tunes, R&B, Latin, jazz, pop and calypso. In addition, they have been known to try their hands at

Left: Billy Ocean—Life has its ups and downs.

reggae, and latterly, Swahili. In fact, almost any ethnic musical style seems to come within the ambit of this highly successful pop-oriented trio.

Connecticut-raised Lillian and Louise Lopez formed a trio with their sister Carmen and as 'The Lopez Sisters' made an auspicious start, headlining at 'The New Faces of 1968' festival at New York's Carnegie Hall. From there they toured Europe and Scandinavia for five months, returning to New York for session work.

Carmen dropped out of the group, whereupon Lillian and Louise recruited Manila-born Tony Reynolds, with whom they eventually recorded their first hit, **Native New Yorker.** Meanwhile, though, the group served a long apprenticeship in New York clubs, concerned more with their evolving stagecraft than with recording.

In 1976, the sisters were contracted to Chappell Music as writers and met writer/producer Sandy Linzer. The panoramic and melodic songwriting of Linzer perfectly matched the international flavour of Odyssey and the association culled hit after hit, over the space of three albums, beginning with the dreamy soft-focus disco of **Native New Yorker** (a gesture for which the city's municipal authorities have always been grateful and which was not at all spoiled by the fact that the group didn't contain a single native New Yorker!).

Before the group's second album, **Hollywood Party Tonight,** was recorded in 1979, Reynolds left, to be replaced by the lilting high tenor of Bill McEachern. A native of Fayetteville, North Carolina, McEachern had been singing since the age of eight and had most recently served seven years with the group We The People, before arriving on the New York session circuit.

In 1980 Odyssey's third and last album with Linzer produced a particularly high hit-ratio: the wildly percussive disco chant, **Use It Up**

Hollywood Party Tonight. Courtesy RCA Records.

And Wear It Out became a No. 1 pop hit in Britain, and was followed, in a dramatic change of style, by the stunning ballad **If You're Lookin' For A Way Out.** In the US, it went top 5, but there the chosen follow-up, **Don't Tell Me Tell Her,** was confined to the disco charts. The title track was also released on 45.

By the time of their 1981 album, **I've Got The Melody,** the partnership with Linzer was sundered by a mutual fear that it might grow stale. Steve Tyrell took over production, and with the loss of Linzer's writing abilities, the material for the album was drawn from a variety of sources. Amid conservative critical

Above: Odyssey's ability to blend ethnic musical styles to commercial pop has been consistently successful.

apprehension, the new partnership proved instantly and brazenly successful, particularly with the group's vocally dynamic version of Lamont Dozier's(▶) song **Back To My Roots**. In the context of the album, this had formed the middle section of an adventurous three-part suite, under the Swahili title **Baba Awa**.

Recordings:
Odyssey (RCA)
Hollywood Party Tonight (RCA)
Hang Together (RCA)
I've Got The Melody (RCA)

The Ohio Players

The Ohio Players started out as the Ohio Untouchables, supplying the instrumental backing behind Wilson Pickett's searing lead vocals on the Falcons' classic R&B hit **I Found A Love**, in 1962. That record appeared on the Lupine label, as did the Untouchables' own far less successful single **I'm Tired**.

The group had been formed in Dayton, Ohio, in 1959, by Robert Ward, Ralph 'Pee Wee' Middlebrook, Clarence 'Satch' Satchell and Marshall 'Rock' Jones. Having failed to find real success, original leader Ward broke up the band, but Satchell and Jones showed greater persistency and brought Andrew Noland, Greg Webster, Bobby Fears and Johnny Robinson in to form a new outfit under the name the Ohio Players.

They recorded some sides for TRC in 1967 and the following year were taken by producer Johnny Brantley to New York's Compass who released **It's A Crying Shame** and **Trespassin'** with no great impact.

A deal with Capitol in 1968 yielded the **Observations In Time** album, but it was not till they switched to Westbound that their ideas and the influence of people like Sly Stone (▶) and James Brown(▶) crystallised into something which was at the same time ultra-funky and eminently com-

mercial.

Adding Walter 'Junie' Morrison, the band went into a local studio in Dayton and cut an album which they leased to Westbound, who

Honey. Courtesy Mercury Records.

were based up in Detroit. Aggressive, heavy, horn-flavoured funk and sexually suggestive lyrical content made the Ohio Players' sound a winner and the breakthrough was helped by a succession of album-cover designs based on a consistent theme of sexual domination.

Pain was that first album and the gatefold sleeve featured a bald-headed whip-toting chick in a

Angel. Courtesy Mercury Records.

leather-studded bikini lording it over a submissive male. For **Pleasure** the same model was in chains, for **Ecstasy** both she and the man were chained; following a label change to Mercury in 1974, there was a different model, with long black tresses, who was featured suggestively fondling a fire hose for **Fire**, naked astride a coal-black horse for **Contradiction**, and dripping in **Honey** for the album of that name.

While very few Ohio Players' records crossed-over to the pop market, they were consistently heavy sellers among black audiences and, in the UK especially, with the disco crowd.

The Ohio Players were pioneers of 'street funk', basing their appeal largely on insistent hypnotic rhythms rather than melody, setting a style adapted and carried a stage further by the Fatback Band

Fire. Courtesy Mercury Records.

(▶), Kool and the Gang(▶) and, more recently, Rick James(▶).

Instant danceability was the keynote and the addition of the sparkling horn section and the innuendo of the vocals won them a massive — and fervent — following. They were outrageous, like Parliament/Funkadelic(▶), but without being anywhere near as bizarre—thus ensuring themselves a far wider audience.

By the end of the '70s, however, the freshness had gone and they seemed to be merely going through the motions, their record sales dwindling accordingly.

It's A Bitch. Courtesy Polydor Records.

In 1981 they pacted with Neil Bogart's Boardwalk Records and they now purvey a funk/pop fusion, including a measure of ballads, which is more melodic but far less horny than the output of their great days. The present line-up comprises: Ralph Middlebrook, saxophone; Leroy Bonner, vocals, guitar; Marshall Jones, bass; Marvin Pierce, horns; L. David Johnson, keyboards; Vincent Thomas, percussion; Jimmy Sampson, drums.

Recordings:
Pain (Westbound)
Pleasure (Westbound)
Ecstasy (Westbound)
Skin Tight (Mercury)
Honey (Mercury)
Contradiction (Mercury)

Olympic Runners

This British-based funk band recorded their US smash **Put The Music Where Your Mouth Is** in the unlikely setting of a converted schoolhouse in the sleepy Cotswold Hills' country town of Chipping Norton.

Blues-schooled white Chicago guitarist Joe Jammer, black American vocalist George Chandler, black bassist DeLisle Harper, black drummer Glen LeFleur (who later joined Gonzalez and was replaced by Glen Penniston), white British keyboard player Pete Wingfield (who scored a solo hit with the delicious and witty **Number One With A Bullet**, a falsetto-led/soul ballad on Island) were joined on stage and on record by their producer Mike Vernon, a white Englishman who learned his craft as a producer at Decca (working with a host of visiting American bluesmen and with Eric Clapton). With brother Richard, Vernon created Blue Horizon, a label dedicated to recording American blues, but which also launched Fleetwood Mac.

Setting up the Chipping Norton Studios, the Vernons recorded US soul band Bloodstone(▶) there with great success, while Mike Vernon also commuted to the US to produce American acts, logging a minor hit with Jimmy Witherspoon's re-make of the classic

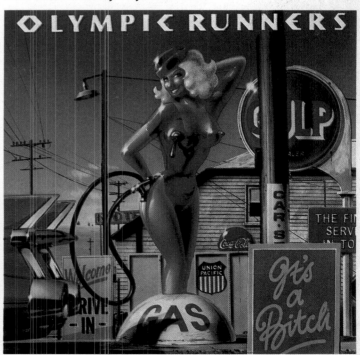

James Phelps' soul oldie **Love Is A Five Letter Word (Spelt M-O-N-E-Y)**.

Recordings:
Put The Music Where Your Mouth Is (London)
Out In Front (London)
Out Of The Ground (RCA)
Puttin' It On Ya (Polydor)

One Way

Detroit-born singer Al Hudson, a solo artist in the late '60s, met up with a group called the Soul Partners during his extensive travels. Making them his backing band, Al Hudson and the Soul Partners, later pruned down to just the Partners, began to make staple club recordings during the '70s, never really achieving crossover hit till the end of the decade, but touring successfully.

Singles such as **Spreading Love** and his 1979 worldwide hit **You Can Do It**, were the forerunners to the most recent hits, **Pull Fancy Dancer Pull** in 1981, and **Who's Foolin' Who** in 1982. Now called One Way, the band includes Dave Robertson, guitar; Kevin McCord, bass; Cortez Harris, guitar; Candyce Edwards, vocals; Gregory Green, drums; and Jonathan Meadows, drums. Recent hits have owed much to ex-vocalist Alicia Mayers, who left in 1980 to pursue a solo career.

Recordings:
Love Is ... One Way (MCA)
Fancy Dancer (MCA)

Johnny Osbourne

Jamaican-born Osbourne cut his first single, **All I Have Is Love,** for the Technique label in 1967 when 18. He subsequently joined Bobby Davis, Jackie Paris and Buster Riley, collectively the Sensations, applying his tender soprano voice to notable singles **Born To Love You, A Thing Called Soul** and **The Warrior**.

In 1969, having studied harmony with the original Wailers(▶), he joined his parents in Toronto,

Canada, where he surfaced shortly after as lead singer with the reggae band Ishan People. He recorded two albums with this ensemble, both produced by David Clayton Thomas, lead singer of Blood, Sweat & Tears.

Osbourne returned to Jamaica after 10 years, making an auspicious re-entry into the reggae charts with his single **Jealousy, Heartache And Pain,** cut with producer Clement Coxsone Dodd at Studio One(▶). That single triggered a phenomenal run of chart hits. His single **Fally Ranking** topped the UK reggae charts in the summer of 1980 and by Christmas such fine albums as **Truth And Rights, Fally Ranking** and **Fally Lover** had become best sellers.

The following year he made his UK stage debut topping the bill at music paper *Black Echoes'* annual awards show, walking away with the prize for best newcomer—ironical, considering the number of years he had been singing. His albums of that year, **In Nah Disco Style**, containing the immortal **Kiss Somebody** and **Warrior** (recorded three years earlier with Winston Niney), did brisk business.

Since then he has dropped back into seclusion with just sporadic single releases.

Recordings:
Truth And Rights (Studio One/—)
Fally Lover (—/Greensleeves)

Osibisa

In Britain in the early '70s it looked for a while as if Afro-rock might be the next big thing. Many Afro-rock bands were formed, several did well on the gig circuit, but the only one to achieve any lasting success was Osibisa. The band has now been together in one form or another for more than a decade, providing a stimulating blend of African and rock forms, both live and on record.

The band was originally formed around a nucleus of Teddy Osei (reeds, percussion), Sol Amarfio (drums), Mac Tontoh (bass, percussion) and Wendell Richardson (guitar). All, except Richardson, a

Mystic Energy. Courtesy Pye Records.

West Indian, were Ghanaians, and the group played a fresh and exciting music with the accent on African polyrhythms. They were an immediate success as a live act, and their first album, **Osibisa**, charted in the UK and made some progress in the US. Helped by the distinctive Roger Dean album-cover artwork, **Osibisa** put the band on the map and showed that there was a market for their atmospheric brand of music.

Osibisa and **Woyaya**, the follow-up, were probably the band's best albums, but over the course of the next few years they released a steady stream of records which were rarely less than interesting. Continual personnel changes—Richardson left, returned and eventually left again—nevertheless dampened the band's impact, and despite great popularity in Africa and the Far East, they never hit big in the US.

In 1976 Osibisa had two hit singles in the UK—**Sunshine Day** from the album **Welcome Home** and **Dance The Body Music** from **Ojah Awake**. Recent years have seen the band keeping a fairly low profile, their last release being **Mystic Energy** in late 1980.

Recordings:
Osibisa (MCA)
Woyaya (MCA)
Heads (MCA)
Welcome Home (Island/Bronze)
Ojah Awake (Island/Bronze)
Mystic Energy (Pye)

P. Funk

On reflection, we can see that P. Funk was not only a type of music, it was a philosophy. At the centre of the P. Funk organisation were George Clinton (born in Blainfield, Ohio) and, to a lesser extent, William 'Bootsy' Collins (born October 26, 1951, in Cincinnati, Ohio). Amongst the members of the P. Funk battalion, there were various different recording acts: Parliament, Funkadelic, Bootsy's Rubber Band, Parlet, the Brides Of Funkenstein, the Horny Horns, Eddie Hazell, Bernie Worrell and Fuzzy Haskins, recording for several different labels.

In the beginning there was a doo-wop group called the Parliaments comprising lead singer George Clinton, Raymond Davis, Calvin Simon, Clarence 'Fuzzy' Haskins, and Grady Thomas. Their backing band was made up of

Standing On The Verge Of Getting It On. Courtesy Westbound Records.

Eddie Hazell, lead guitar; Tawl Ross, rhythm guitar; Billy Nelson, bass; Mickey Atkins, organ; and Tiki Fulwood, drums.

Their first single **Poor Willie** was cut for ABC in 1956, and was followed by **Lonely Island** for New Records in 1958. Both were unsuccessful. The Parliaments then signed to Motown Records, but the recordings they did for Berry Gordy were not issued. In 1965, they recorded another single, **My Girl** for Golden World Records,

Never Stop Fighting. Courtesy Greensleeves Records.

Below: George Clinton, brain behind the P. Funk philosophy

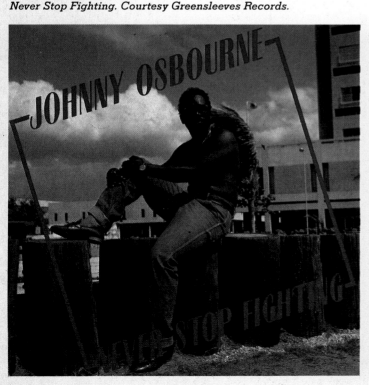

Above: William 'Bootsy' Collins, key member of P. Funk organisation.

Above: P. Funk's delightful 'Brides of Funkenstein'

Above left: Duane 'Blackbyrd' McKnight backs funky 'Bride' Dawn Silva (below).
Above right: Mike Hampton, a current P. Funker.

which also sunk without trace.

William 'Bootsy' Collins formed his first band the Pacesetters with his brother Phelps 'Catfish' Collins, Frankie 'Kash' Waddy and Phillipe Wynne(▶) in 1968. This quartet obtained employment at local record label, King Records, backing such artists as Arthur Prysock(▶) and Hank Ballard(▶).

When James Brown(▶), also signed to King Records, sacked his backing band, the Pacesetters became the new JBs.

Meanwhile, George Clinton's Parliaments were recording a single called **(I Wanna) Testify** for Revilot Records, which was their first hit. The year was 1967, when psychedelia was at its height, and George Clinton became profoundly affected by the movement, an influence on his life from which he never seemed to recover.

In the late '60s, Atlantic secured the rights to the Revilot back catalogue and released an album of old Parliaments material. Having lost the rights to his group's name, Clinton brought his backing band to the forefront, and called the collective Funkadelic, securing a contract on Westbound Records.

Clinton's music was a fusion of R&B and rock, the subject matter of the lyrics was centred around the appreciation of 'funk'—funk as the answer to the world's problems, funk as the elixir of life—Clinton's imagery portraying the black man where the white man rarely thinks of him, and his imagination going beyond the absurd into topical satire.

Stretchin' Out In. Courtesy Warner Bros Records.

Bootsy, Catfish, Kash and Wynne were JBs from 1969 to '71, then left James Brown, returning to Cincinnati to form the House Guests, a lively and garishly-dressed outfit. The Spinners(▶) approached the House Guests, wanting Wynne to become their lead singer, and the others to be their backing band, but only Wynne accepted, and the House Guests continued, looking and sounding very much like Clinton's Funkadelic. Mahalia Franklin, now a member of Parlet, knew of Funkadelic, and when she saw the House Guests, she sensed that a combination of the two bands would be dynamite. Meanwhile, Funkadelic had released three albums on Westbound: **Funkadelic, Free Your Mind . . .**

Above: Portraying the black man where white man least expects him, Santa Clinton shows off his badges.

Above: Bass guitarist 'Bootsy' Collins and his Rubber Band during 'Bootzilla' days. The chaos doesn't mask the musicianship.

And Your Ass Will Follow and **Maggot Brain.** Invictus Records, who still owned a piece of George Clinton, released an album of old Parliament material in 1970, entitled **Osmium.**

The collaboration of the House Guests and Clinton's outfit was on the Funkadelic album of 1972, **America Eats Its Young.** This was followed by **Cosmic Slop** and **Standing On The Verge Of Getting It On,** in 1973, Tawl Ross, Billy Nelson and Mickey Atkins having been replaced by Gary Shider, Cordell 'Boogie' Mosson and Bernie Worrell, respectively.

Because of disagreements with Westbound, Clinton shifted his music into Parliament, who had now got a deal with Casablanca Records. Westbound were still owed two albums, so when they changed distribution deals to 20th Century, Clinton was willing to complete his contractual requirements. And so the pattern developed. Using a massive pool of musicians and singers, Clinton and Bootsy fuelled their different projects with material.

P. Funk mania reached its peak in the mid-'70s, and a chaotic package entitled **Parliament Live —P.Funk Earth Tour** was released in 1977. Funkadelic's high point was with the release of their **One Nation Under A Groove** album in 1978 which spawned a worldwide pop hit of the same name.

As the '70s wore on, the public began to tire of the prolific output of this informal collective, and to lose track of the highly complex sub-plots going on within P.Funk material. Clinton had created a 'baddie', a character known as Sir Nose D'Voidoffunk, who tried to resist dance music, and because of this his nose had grown. Bootsy once stated, 'If you fake the funk, your nose will grow, when you hit the funk, you gotta dance, your

nose gotta shrink'. This was known as **The Pinocchio Theory,** which was also a hit single for Bootsy's Rubber Band in 1977. Bootsy himself had two alter egos: the original Bootsy was a rhinestone rock star, concerned with his public image, his ethics based on the principles of being 'cool'; 'Bootzilla' was Bootsy's aggressive side, a stack-heeled, bass guitar-thumping monster; 'Casper', a name taken from the cartoon character ghost, was Bootsy's friendly peace-loving side.

The P.Funk mob, resplendent in space-age/futuristic costumes and clown make-up, continued to churn out club record after disco hit, sometimes making an impact on the pop charts, but mainly feeding their own fanatical following.

At last count, the P.Funk troupe included: Parliament/Funkadelic: Bernie Worrell, Walter 'Junie' Morrison, Gary Shider, Mike Hampton, Rodney 'Skeet' Curtis, Cordell 'Boogie' Mosson, Tyrone Lampkin, Larry Frantangelo, Raymond Davis and Ron Ford; who are augmented by the Horny Horns: Fed Wesley, Maceo Parker, Rick Gardner, Richard 'Kush' Griffith; who also help out Bootsy's Rubber Band: William 'Bootsy' Collins, Phelps 'Catfish' Collins, Joel 'Razor Sharp' Johnson, Frank 'Kash' Waddy, Gary 'Mudbone' Cooper and Robert 'P-Nut' Johnson. These four groups are sometimes accompanied by the Brides Of Funkenstein: Lynn Mabry and Dawn Silva; plus the Bridesmaids: Sheila Horn, Babs Stewart, and Jeanette McGruder; and Parlet: Mahalia Franklin, Jeanette Washington, and Shirley Hayden. When the Brides and Bridesmaids play on their own, they're helped by Duane 'Blackbyrd' McKnight and Geoff 'Cherokee' Bunn. When Parlet play on their own, their band are: Ernestro 'Andrea' Wilson, Mannon Salsby,

Gordon Carlton, Jerome Ali, Donny Stirling, Kenny Colton and Janice Carlton.

Clinton plus 37 friends created the movement, and their '80s form is now known as the P.Funk All Stars, although they have yet to repeat past success.

Recordings:
Parliament: **Chocolate City** (Chocolate City/Casablanca)
Mothership Connection (Casablanca)
The Clones Of Dr Funkenstein (Casablanca)
Bootsy's Rubber Band: **Stretchin' Out** (Warner Brothers)
Parliament Live—P.Funk Earth Tour (Casablanca)
Bootsy's Rubber Band: **A-a-a-ah, The Name Is Bootsy, Baby** (Warner Brothers)
Funkentelechy Vs. The Placebo Syndrome (Casablanca)
Player Of The Year (Warner Brothers)
Funkadelic: **One Nation Under A Groove** (Warner Brothers)

Augustus Pablo

Born Horace Swaby in Kingston, Jamaica, in 1953, to a wealthy middle-class family with interests in horse racing, Pablo taught himself to play the piano whilst attending Kingston College. A close friend at the time was Tyrone Downie who later became keyboards player with the Wailers(▶).

Pablo was lent a melodica by a friend and became fascinated by the instrument. He switched over to it and immediately set about developing a highly individual reggae style that generates much of its instrumental beauty through the influence of Far-Eastern music. His first recordings were for producer Herman Chin-Loy (who coined the name Augustus Pablo)

between 1970 and '71: **Duck It Up** and **405.** Subsequent issues on his own Hot Stuff and Rockers labels included **Rockers Dub, Special** and **Jah Dread.**

A motorcycle accident laid him up between 1977 and '78. When he returned to the studio it was in fine style, to record the album **East Of River Nile,** setting the tone for his subsequent comand of this slightly bizarre aspect of reggae.

Augustus Pablo, Glen Brown, Joe White and Rue Lloyd are the melodica virtuosos featured on a recent retrospective collection issued in the UK on Trojan, **Melodica Melodies.**

Recordings:
This Is Augustus Pablo (Randys/Tropical)
Original Rockers (—/Greensleeves)
Africa Must Be Free Dub (Rockers/—)

Gene Page

Master arranger, noted for lush orchestrations, Gene Page grew up in Los Angeles and was taught his craft by his composer/pianist father. His brother, Billy Page, is a successful songwriter.

Page arranged the classic Phil Spector-produced **You've Lost That Lovin' Feelin'** by the Righteous Brothers(▶) and Dobie Gray's(▶) **The In Crowd,** then held staff jobs with first Reprise then Motown(▶), working with all latter's major artists in late '60s, before gaining recognition as regular arranger for Barry White(▶).

He continued working with Diana Ross(▶) (**Touch Me In The Morning,** 1973) and Marvin Gaye(▶), while also starring with his own Atlantic(▶)instrumental album **Hot City** (1974), produced by Barry White. The album was primarily a

Above: Gary Shider, complete with thing-length boots and nappy (!), is part of the current P. Funk troupe.

showcase for Page's orchestrations, though he also played keyboards on it.

Recordings:
Hot City (Atlantic)

Ray Parker & Raydio

When he broke his leg as a young boy, Ray Parker was confined to home and learnt to play guitar. At the age of 13 he formed his first group, the Stingrays, with two Detroit friends, Ollie Brown and Nathan Watts. His next band, which included Hamilton Bohannon(▶) and Michael Henderson(▶), was back-up group at the biggest club in town and supported such stars as Gladys Knight(▶), Stevie Wonder(▶) and the Temptations(▶).

In the early '70s Parker began recording, establishing himself as one of the most in-demand session guitarists in America, working for Motown(▶) and Invictus, then touring with Stevie Wonder in 1972. Having moved to Hollywood, where he bluffed his way into a Gene Page(▶) recording session, Parker was soon fully integrated into the Californian session scene. His songs began being recorded by Rufus(▶), Barry White(▶), Labelle(▶) and Bobby Womack(▶). One of them, **Keep On Doin' It,** recorded by Herbie Hancock(▶), was nominated for a Grammy.

In 1978, he assembled a band called Raydio, consisting of Arnell Carmichael, synthesiser; Jerry

Below: Ray Parker, great session guitarist; a successful songwriter.

Knight, bass; Vincent Bonham, piano. They recorded a namesake debut that included the hit **Jack And Jill.** For the second album, released in 1979, Knight and Bonham were replaced by Arnell's brother Darren and Larry Tolbert (drums) and Charles Fearing (guitar). Further hits ensued, including **You Can't Change That** and **More Than One Way To Love A Woman.**

Raydio maintained their high standards of commercial soul and funk with their third album, which contained the title track hit **Two Places At The Same Time** (1980). In 1981, retaining only Arnell Carmichael and Larry Tolbert, Parker recorded a fourth album, **A Woman Needs Love,** with the help of Jerry Knight(▶), Ollie Brown, Cheryl Lynn(▶) and J.D. Nicholas of Heatwave(▶).

Recordings:
Raydio (Arista)
Rock On (Arista)
Two Places At The Same Time (Arista)
A Woman Needs Love (Arista)

Billy Paul

Though very much a part of the famed 'Philly Sound', Billy Paul's jazz roots have always shown through. Born in Philadelphia on December 1, 1934, Paul had the distinction of singing with Charlie 'Yardbird' Parker in 1955, shortly before that genius of the jazz saxophone died.

Paul cut his first record, **Why Am I?,** for Jubilee when he was just 16 and another jazz great, Tadd Dameron, played piano on it. Besides his jazz leanings, Paul confessed a great admiration for Nat 'King' Cole(▶) (his manager, John Leavy, used to play bass for George Shearing who recorded **Let There Be Love** with Cole).

Despite being old school friends, it took Paul and Philadelphia International(▶) bosses Kenny Gamble and Leon Huff a long while before they got round to working together, Paul singing in jazz clubs while his friends were firmly entrenched in soul music. Eventually they cut him on a live jazz album then on two soul sets; **Ebony Woman** and **Going East,** which did reasonably well.

Below: Billy Paul, a man with strong jazz roots.

Brown Baby was intended as the single to be lifted from his next set, **360 Degrees Of Billy Paul,** but the sophisticated cheating—love song **Me And Mrs. Jones,** co-penned by Paul and Gamble, came out so well that it was released instead and promptly went gold, being a huge hit on both sides of the Atlantic in 1972.

Paul's subsequent records took him more into a standard Philly-soul groove and gave us such goodies as **The Whole Town's Talking, Thanks For Saving My Life** (both 1973) and **July, July, July, July** (1975).

Recordings:
360 Degrees Of Billy Paul (Philadelphia International)
War Of The Gods (Philadelphia International)
Got My Head On Straight (Philadelphia International)

Freda Payne

Born in Detroit, Michigan, Freda Payne left school to join the chorus of the Pearl Bailey Revue, and did some shows with Duke Ellington before being invited to front Quincy Jones'(▶) big band at the Apollo, then on tour.

Signed to ABC, her first album was on the Impulse jazz subsidiary and she toured the Far East and Europe (1965) with Bob Crosby's orchestra and had releases on MGM, but in 1969 swopped jazz for soul to score with **Unhooked Generation** on signing with Holland/Dozier/Holland's(▶) Invictus label.

She became an international star in 1970 with Invictus' biggest hit, the multi-million selling **Band Of Gold,** and had a million-seller with the anti-Vietnam War song **Bring The Boys Home.**

Freda has starred in Broadway plays, films and TV specials, but her recording career lost its impetus, though she had a succession of releases via ABC (from 1974) and Capitol (from 1976) making minor impact in discos with the latter label.

(Her sister Scherrie was a latter-day member of the Supremes(▶)).

Recordings:
Band Of Gold (Invictus)
Best Of (Invictus)
Payne And Pleasure (ABC/—)
Supernatural High (Capitol)

Scherrie Payne

See Supremes.

Peaches And Herb

In January 1965, Van McCoy(▶) walked into a Washington DC record store to promote his current product. Herb Fame, at that time a sales assistant, persuaded McCoy to audition him there and then in the stockroom. Fame convinced McCoy of his singing ability, and along with his partner Dave Kapralik, McCoy began setting a new trend. Male/female sweet soul duos were not in fashion, but McCoy felt the time was right, and found Herb a 'Peaches', Francine Barker. In 1965, the due had a string of soft, lilting, love-ballad hit singles, but when Francine decided to get married, the duo dissolved, and Herb joined the Washington police force.

McCoy, fresh from his 1975 single success, **The Hustle,** persuaded Herb to hang up his badge and try to find another Peaches. Herb found ex-Rondell, Linda Green. The resulting McCoy-produced album was not a success but, holding this partnership together, Herb was rewarded in 1978 when a Freddie Perren-produced album, **2 Hot,** yielded a massive club hit, **Shake Your Groove Thing,** and then a worldwide pop hit, **Reunited.** The duo have again surfaced, and we await fresh fruits.

Recordings:
2 Hot (Polydor)

Ann Peebles

Born in East St Louis on April 27, 1947, Ann Peebles was one of 11 children and started singing in her preacher father's Peebles Choir at the age of eight.

A solo gig at the Rosewood Club while holidaying in Memphis led to a contract with Willie Mitchell(▶)

I Can't Stand The Rain. Courtesy London Records.

at Hi(▶) and her magical 1970 debut album, **Part Time Love,** made her a cult figure overnight — critics and public warming to her gospel and blues slant on soul music.

Her re-working of older R&B hits like the title track, Bettye Swann's(▶) **Make Me Yours** and Jimmy Hughes'(▶) **Steal Away,** gave the album enormous strength but nothing was lost when Ann turned to a heavy leavening of more original material for her follow-up set **Straight From The Heart. 99 Pounds** (penned by her husband Don Bryant, also a Hi artist), **Slipped, Tripped And Fell In Love,** and a new version of Bobby Bland's(▶) **I Pity The Fool** all became hit singles.

One rainy night, Ann and her husband killed half-an-hour writing a new song. It was recorded the next day in just over an hour and and proved to be the record to establish her as an international star. **I Can't Stand The Rain** also provided the title for her third album and this time the Peebles/Bryant pairing contributed seven of the 10 songs, though the big hit from it, **I'm Gonna Tear Your Playhouse Down,** was not one of them.

Using the same Hi studio band as Al Green(▶), namely the Hodges brothers (Leroy, Charles and Teenie), drummer Howard Grimes plus the Memphis Horns (Wayne Jackson, Andrew Love etc.) and Willie Mitchell's production, Ann Peebles has been a very important component in the renowned 'Memphis Sound'.

Recordings:
Part Time Love (Hi/—)
Straight From The Heart (Hi/London)
I Can't Stand The Rain (Hi/London)
Tellin' It (Hi/London)
If This Is Heaven (Hi/—)

Below: Teddy Pendergrass turning the ladies on.

Teddy Pendergrass

In common with one other notable soul sex symbol, Marvin Gaye(▶), Pendergrass began his professional career, not as the gyrating woman-slaying front man, but as possibly the most remote member of any on-stage line-up, the drummer.

He was born in Philadelphia, in 1950, and raised in a deeply religious family. His regular church-going began at the age of two-and-a-half, but he was soon joining in the testifying and had a chance to witness the righteous singing and fire-and-brimstone 'stagecraft' with which gospel ministers are so adept at stirring up their congregations.

Regularly accompanying his mother to the nightclub where she worked, Pendergrass had his first access to a drumkit, and, with the assent of the management, plenty of time to practice. By the mid-'60s he was drumming in a local Philadelphian group, the Cadillacs, who were recruited, en bloc, as backing band for Harold Melvin and The Blue Notes(▶) in 1969.

The Blue Notes split up in acrimonious circumstances while on tour in the French West Indies, and when Melvin reformed the group, a year later, Pendergrass became the featured vocalist. This arrangement obviously appealed to producer/writers Kenny Gamble and Leon Huff who snapped up the group for their nascent Philadelphia International(▶) label.

Under the somewhat clumsy, but nevertheless just title, Harold Melvin and the Blue Notes featuring Theodore Pendergrass, the group joined labelmates the O'Jays(▶) and the Three Degrees(▶) to establish the sound of Philadelphia International and to become one of the hottest soul vocal acts in America. A string of hits through the mid-'70s included vibrant uptempo numbers like **Wake Up Everybody, Bad Luck** and **The Love I Lost,** and ballads **I Miss You** and the immensely powerful **If You Don't Know Me By Now.**

With the focus on the group's lead vocalist intensifying, 1976 saw the inevitable split. 'Theodore' became the more manageable diminutive 'Teddy' and Pendergrass struck out for solo stardom. After a short legal wrangle, he was able to re-sign with Philadelphia

International for whom his first solo offering was a very fine eight-track, self-titled album in 1977. Teddy's new persona was perhaps best characterised in the timbrous sensuality of **The Whole Town's Laughing At Me**, which was selected as the first single.

Pendergrass released one quality album per year until 1980, when the studio set, **TP**, was preceded by a live double, **Teddy Live! Coast To Coast**. He had been establishing a reputation as a charismatic stage performer whose appeal to the female members of the audience was so direct that his shows were often promoted with

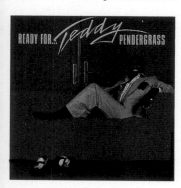

Ready For ... Teddy. Courtesy Philadelphia International Records.

strong hints that the ladies should leave their men at home and make it a girls' night out! Stories of underwear being thrown on stage and outbreaks of general hysteria were faithfully borne out by the ecstatic cacophany which pervaded this live double album.

A tour of the UK set for that year was postponed when Pendergrass became involved with the wife of Marvin Gaye who, as it happened, was touring for the same British promoter but, in April 1981, unheralded by any notable chart success in Britain, Pendergrass made his first speculative visit across the Atlantic, and although the re-release of **The Whole Town's Laughing At Me** received scant attention, reaction to his stage presence encouraged a return trip the following year, by which time British women were beginning to respond with a muted fervour.

Weeks after his return to the States, Pendergrass was involved in a horrific road accident. The crash occurred in the early hours of March 26, 1982, while the singer was returning home at the wheel of his Rolls Royce, after reportedly watching a basketball game. He was admitted to the spinal-chord department of the Thomas Jefferson University Hospital in Delaware, with injuries to his neck and vertebrae as well as internal injuries. Fears that Pendergrass may have become crippled for life were countered by encouraging reports from his record company that he was alert and cheerful in hospital and looked forward to resuming his career.

Recordings:
Teddy Pendergrass (Philadelphia International)
Life Is A Song Worth Singing (Philadelphia International)
Teddy (Philadelphia International)
Teddy Live! Coast To Coast (Philadelphia International)
TP (Philadelphia International)
Ready For Teddy (Philadelphia International)

It's Time For Love (Philadelphia International)

People's Choice

This second-division Philadelphia International(▶) act did well in the mid-'70s disco boom with the **Boogie Down USA, Do It Anyway You Wanna** and **We Got The Rhythm** dancers, led by keyboard player/songwriter Frankie Brunson's distinctive voice.

The rest of the line-up was: Guy Fiske, guitar; Roger Andrews, bass; and David Thompson, percussion.

Recordings:
Boogie Down USA (Philadelphia International)
We Got The Rhythm (Philadelphia International)

Philadelphia International

If Tamla Motown(▶) *was* the black record comany of the '60s, Philadelphia International Records (PIR) could lay claim to the '70s. At the centre of the organisation were Kenny Gamble and Leon Huff(▶), who first met up in 1964 when Huff played keyboards on a Candy and the Kisses' single, **The 81**, for which Gamble had written the song.

Huff, who had been working as a session musician in New York for Leiber and Stoller(▶), moved back to Philadelphia to replace Thom Bell(▶) in Gamble's group, the Romeos.

Besides freelance work in Philly for both Cameo-Parkway(▶) and the Jamie-Guyden group of labels, the duo supplemented their income from the Romeos by setting up their own Excel label in 1966, scoring a local smash with the Intruders(▶), changing the company name shortly afterwards to Gamble and hitting the national charts with further Intruders' recordings of Gamble/Huff compositions.

Greatest Hits. Courtesy Philadelphia Intl. Records.

Up until then the top Philadelphia label, Cameo (where Gamble had met his wife-to-be, soul singer Dee Dee Sharpe) folded in 1968, leaving a vacuum which the duo were intent on filling with the Neptune label, distributed by Chess. But the deal—and the label—foundered when Leonard Chess died and his brother Phil sold the company's assets to GRT.

Fortunately, Gamble and Huff had been piling up royalties from their outside production work, notably for Atlantic(▶) (with Archie Bell and the Drells(▶)) and Mercury (with Jerry Butler(▶)), and were thus

Phillybusters Vol. III. Courtesy Philadelphia International Records.

able to hold onto their own roster of artists while setting up Philadelphia International via a new distribution contract with the all-powerful Columbia company (CBS in the UK).

Working for Columbia at the time was Jimmy Bishop, an entrepreneur who was a former top radio DJ in Philadelphia and who, with partner George Woods (also a DJ), had become the city's leading concert promoter for both black and white acts (as well as having owned the promising Arctic label whose artists included the highly rated Barbara Mason). Bishop proved a worthy friend and eventually moved from the Columbia payroll to work directly for PIR and play a big role in establishing the label as a major force.

Just as Stax(▶) had done in Memphis and Fame had done in Muscle Shoals(▶), Gamble and Huff continued producing outside acts, at their Sigma Sound Studios base, including Joe Simon(▶) for Spring and Johnny Mathis(▶) for Columbia. as well as building their own ever-expanding artist roster.

An old friend who had been making quite a name as a cabaret jazz singer was brought in to the fold. Billy Paul(▶) gave PIR one of its earliest (and still biggest) hits with **Me And Mrs Jones** (1972) and followed through with further chart entries.

Utilising songwriters Victor Carstarphen, Carry Gilbert, Gene McFadden and John Whitehead (McFadden & Whitehead(▶)) with Gamble and Huff undertaking production duties and the famed MFSB(▶) team of session musicians playing, the 'Philly Sound' was created. Incorporating a large orchestra, the sound of Philadelphia was very full and rich, fixed in its R&B roots, and not self-consciously commercial. The public took to the sound because of its quality.

Early signings to the label included Harold Melvin and the Blue Notes(▶) (**The Love I Lost, If You Don't Know Me By Now, Wake Up Everybody**), the Intruders (**I Wanna Know Your Name, I'll Always Love My Mama**), the Three Degrees(▶) (**Dirty Ol' Man, When Will I See You Again**) and the O'Jays(▶) (**Put Your Hands Together, I Love Music, Use Ta Be My Girl**). Because Britain was

responding so enthusiastically to the Philly sound, Billy Paul, the O'Jays and the Intruders came over to Britain as a 'Philly' package tour in 1973.

As the '70s went on, Philly's roster altered. Harold Melvin and the Blue Notes went to ABC Records, leaving their lead singer, Teddy Pendergrass(▶) on PIR (Pendergrass maintained chart action with **The Whole Town's Laughing At Me, Close The Door, Only You**). New signings included Archie Bell & the Drells(▶) (**Dance Your Troubles Away, Glad You Could Make It, I've Been Missing You**), People's Choice(▶) (**Party Is A Groovy Thing, Cold Blooded And Down Right Funky, If You Gonna Do It**), Jean Carn(▶) (**Free Love, Don't Let It Go To Your Head**) and Lou Rawls(▶) (**See You When I Get There, Lady Love, Let Me Be Good To You**).

Previously employed as just a session keyboard player, Dexter Wansell(▶) worked his way right to

Ship Ahoy. Courtesy Philadelphia International Records.

the top of the PIR organisation, and apart from having a solo career, he writes and produces leading PIR artists, as well as being the present conductor of MFSB(▶), whose record, **TSOP** (The Sound Of Philadelphia), was a worldwide hit in 1975.

Singer/songwriter Jerry Butler(▶) signed to PIR and immediately had a hit single, **Cooling Out**. The Three Degrees went to Ariola/Arista in the late '70s, and their place was taken by the Jones Girls(▶), who instantly struck gold with **Your're Gonna Make Me Love Somebody Else.** Loyal song-writing partnership McFadden & Whitehead became PIR recording artists in 1979, releasing a single that became one of PIR's top-

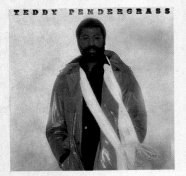

Teddy Pendergrass. Courtesy Philadelphia Intl. Records.

selling records, and one of the biggest club records of the year, **Ain't No Stoppin' Us Now.**

Since Gamble and Huff have delegated more responsibility to younger folk such as Wansell and McKinley Williams, and although the Philly sound is no longer in vogue, the quality of recordings remains high, with Teddy Pendergrass, the Jones Girls and the O'Jays taking PIR into the '80s.

Recordings:
Phillysound (Vol. 1 and onwards)
(Philadelphia International)

Players Association

The Players Association began as a studio band, masterminded by producer Danny Weiss, and multi-instrumentalist Chris Hills (drums, clarinet, guitar, synthesizer and vocals), featuring Joe Farrell(▶) on tenor sax and Jon Faddis (ex-Thad Jones/Mel Lewis, Charlie Mingus, Chuck Mangione) on trumpet and fluegelhorn.

Their brand of jazz/soul encompassed four fine albums, which included guest appearances by Michael Brecker(▶) (tenor sax) and David Sanbourne (alto sax and flute).

The band achieved single success with **Turn The Music Up** in 1979, before splitting a year later.

Recordings:
The Players Association
(Vanguard)
Born To Dance (Vanguard)
Turn The Music Up (Vanguard)
Ride The Groove (Vanguard)

Pluto

Born Leighton Shervington in Kingston, Jamaica, on August 13, 1950, Pluto began singing in the early '70s with local cabaret band Tomorrow's Children. His biggest commercial break came in 1976 with a solo performance with the patois/comedy disc **Dat,** which reached No. 6 on UK pop charts. Follow-up **Ram Goat Liver,** although similarly inspired, failed to create similar international amusement.

Living and recording in Miami, Pluto returned to chart in 1982 with the re-release of another tongue-in-cheek reggae cut from the **Dat** era, **Your Honour.**

Recordings:
Pluto (—/Opal)

Bonnie Pointer

In 1978, Bonnie left the Pointer Sisters(▶) and embarked on a solo career with Motown(▶), singing a more mainstream fusion of pop and soul. Motown president Berry Gordy decided to co-produce Bonnie's debut in 1978, from whence came **Free Me From My Freedom.**

With original co-producer Jeffrey Bowen now in total control, Bonnie continued carving a commercial niche with her follow-up LP in 1980.

Recordings:
Bonnie Pointer (Motown)
Bonnie Pointer 2 (Motown)

Noel Pointer

Violinist Noel Pointer was born in Brooklyn, New York, in 1957. Following extensive classical training and appearances with various orchestras, he began making a series of critically acclaimed but commercially unpalatable jazz-fusion albums, splicing rock and classical music into his violin-centred instrumentals.

His fifth album, **All My Reasons,** released in 1981, saw Pointer singing and making a concerted attempt to commercialise his refined and sophisticated sound.

Recordings:
Phantazia (Blue Note)
Hold On (Blue Note)
Feel It (Blue Note)
Calling (Blue Note)
All My Reasons (Blue Note)

The Pointer Sisters

Originally a four-piece when they emerged in the early '70s, the Pointer Sisters presented a slick and deliberately anachronistic jazz

and R&B based vocal act, with which they simultaneously created and cornered a market for close-harmony jazz nostalgia.

The sisters, Bonnie, Ruth, Anita and June, were raised by devoutly religious parents—both church ministers—and learned their trade singing in the choir of the West Oakland Church in their native California. In accordance with the religious tenets of their parents, the popular secular music of the day was not allowed in the house, and the sisters evolved a style of scat singing (a wordless form of vocal improvisation) from a rarified diet of local gospel and country music.

Their first recording contract was with Atlantic(▶) who steered them rigidly towards R&B, but after two failed singles, the formula was abandoned, as was the contract. The breakthrough came when they teamed up with San Franciscan producer Dave Rubinson, who engineered a new deal with ABC/Blue Thumb Records in 1973, and helped them to formulate a new musical policy.

For their first album on Blue Thumb, **The Pointer Sisters,** they appeared on the cover in period-style dress to complement the nostalgia-flavoured music within.

Steppin'. Courtesy ABC Records.

Above: From nostalgia and jazz to funk—the slick and glamorous Pointer Sisters.

They had an empathetic continuity of sound, almost exclusive to blood relations, as exemplified in the searing close-harmony jazz number **Jada's Coming Home.** They perpetuated the nostalgia image, both on stage and on record, throughout a handful of well-crafted albums on ABC/Blue Thumb, with some apposite original material, interlaced with individualistic renditions of such standards as **Salt Peanuts** and **That's A Plenty.**

The sisters' evolving skill as song-writers was acknowledged in 1975 with a Grammy award for **Fairy Tale,** by Anita and Bonnie, and their acceptance as country singers earned them the distinction of becoming the first black females to play the world mecca of country music, Nashville's Grand Ole Opry. But while expanding and diversifying their musical activities, they were becoming increasingly frustrated with the restrictions of their nostalgia image and in 1977 they released their last such album for ABC/Blue Thumb, **Having A Party.**

For a short while they disbanded. Bonnie, the most potentially glamorous of the four, had her image revamped accordingly and was signed to an ill-fated solo contract with Motown(▶). Ruth, Anita and June regrouped as a trio, with a brand new, hard-rocking image, and a record deal with Richard Perry, who produced the first of the new era Pointer Sisters' albums **Energy,** for his own newly formed Planet label in 1978. The combination met with instant success and no uncertain critical acclaim. Their radical stylistic departure had not been idly concocted and while drawing their material from such disparate sources as Bruce Springsteen, Allen Toussaint(▶), Becker & Fagan (Steely Dan), Sly Stone(▶) and Loggins & Messina, the new

Pointers' sound had all the confident expression and personality of their ABC/Blue Thumb recordings. Nor had they yielded any of the vivacity of their live performances in trimming down to a three-piece.

They retained this eclectic new-wave musical policy with their second Planet LP **Priority**, utilising material by Graham Parker, Bob Seger and Ian Hunter, and remaining, as they have done through two subsequent albums, under the production of Richard Perry.

Recordings:
The Pointer Sisters (ABC/Blue Thumb)
That's A Plenty (ABC/Blue Thumb)
Live At The Opera House (ABC/Blue Thumb)
Steppin' (ABC/Blue Thumb)
Energy (Planet)
Priority (Planet)
Special Things (Planet)
Black And White (Planet)

Prince

It usually takes many years to learn how to write, arrange and produce, but Prince still in his early 20s has made three albums, 99% of which he has written, sung, played on, arranged and produced. Born and raised in Minneapolis, Minnesota, Prince came from a musical background; his father is a band leader, and his mother is a singer. Minnesota's pop music is rock, so Prince's music has been affected by the contemporary giants of white music.

Controversy. Courtesy Warner Bros Records.

Aged 12, Prince fronted a band called Champagne that played hotel and high school dances. After five years, he split, and set about recording a demo. Several A&R men in New York offered Prince deals, but none would let him produce himself, so Prince refused them. A new demo of three songs resulted in Warner Brothers meeting his demands, and in 1980, his eponymous debut hit the streets. The following year, a follow-up album was released, and a single **I Wanna Be Your Lover** began to create chart rumblings and served as preparation for Prince's stage show.

While also being political, Prince's stage image, and much of his material is sex-orientated. On stage, his costumes are scanty, bordering on pornographic, and his visuals are sexually explicit.

Without a hit in Britain, Prince took the bold step of coming to Europe, knowing that his live sets would serve as the perfect form of promotion. In 1981, when his third album was released, the world was ready, and its title track, **Controversy**, received worldwide chart success. This topical extension of Prince's disregard for conservatism contained a recitation of The Lord's Prayer. The album covered both funk and rock, plus the highly-commercial fusion for which he has become famous. Although Prince's production cannot be commented on for its dynamism and clarity, he may have been right in his belief that he was the best qualified for the job.

Recordings:
Prince (Warner Brothers)
Dirty Mind (Warner Brothers)
Controversy (Warner Brothers)

Michael Prophet

Born Michael George Haynes in 1958 in Kingston, Jamaica, Prophet wrote his first song (inspired by the Bible), **Praise You Jah Jah**, at the age of 15. It was recorded five years later with producer Yabby U and is a highlight of Prophet's debut album **Serious Reasoning** (1980).

From one so young, the album is a stunning collection of mature, deeply spiritual songs that instantly established Prophet as a singer to watch. It was the subjet matter of his lyrics that caused Yabby U to award him his stage name.

Breaking with Yabby U, he nevertheless remained at Kingston's Channel One Studio with his new producer Henry 'Junjo' Lawes and the Roots Radics band, recording for the UK's Greensleeves label. Lawes was already enjoying some success with another young ghetto star, Barrington Levy(▶). Prophet and Lawes have since cut many marvellous sides, notably on the albums **Righteous Are The Conqueror** and **Michael Prophet** (both 1981), the latter spawning Prophet's hit single of that year, **Gunman**.

Prophet has played selected dates in the UK and proved himself a visually stunning performer, projecting a voice of immense timbre and emotion.

Recordings:
Serious Reasoning (—/Island)
Know The Right (Vivian Jackson/—)
Righteous Are The Conqueror (—/Greensleeves)

The Rass-es

Formerly known as the Royal Rass-es, the Rass-es is essentially a one-man band, showcasing the concepts, songwriting and voice of Prince Lincoln Thompson. By far the most important facet of Thompson and his work with the Rass-es is his concept of 'inter-reg', a broad-

Humanity. Courtesy United Artists Records.

ening of the rhythmic base of reggae, enabling the music to appeal to many differing and far-flung cultures. Throughout the mid-'70s Thompson and his group flourished with a steady stream of flawless gems.

Prince Lincoln Thompson, affectionately called 'Socks' ('Sax' in Jamaican patois), due to his fondness for red socks, joined his first band, the Tartans, when he was 19, and in 1970 tasted local notoriety with **Gonna Dance All Night** on Federal Records. As a showband the Tartans quickly went out of fashion and disbanded.

Thompson retreated from music and, having grown up in the Kingston ghetto, took his family to a smallholding in the secluded and less claustrophobic Hunts Bay area. There he cultivated the land by day and at night practised guitar and began writing songs. With greater confidence due to his improved musical proficiency he entered Studio One(▶) in 1974. Of those sessions with producer Coxsone Dodd, only four songs made it to vinyl, but two, **Live Up To Your Name** and **True Experience**, are still regarded as classics.

Although Thompson was quite capable of producing rich vocal harmonies in the studio by multi-tracking his distinctive falsetto voice, stage shows presented a

Left: Interesting and controversial, paying scant regard for conservatism—that's Prince's trademark.

Above: The gifted Prince Lincoln Thomson of the Rass-es.

problem and so in 1975 the Royal Rass-es were conceived, with Thompson augmented by backing vocalists Cedric Myton and Keith Peterkin. Harnessing a stronger vocal section and Channel One rhythms, the group was an instant success with such fine Thompson songs as **San Salvador** and **Humanity (Love The Way It Should Be)** which with Junior Murvin's(▶) **Police And Thieves**

Below: The Rass-es Thomson in London during his 1979 European tour to launch his Experience album.

were some of the most played reggae records of 1976.

On their own label, God Sent, the Royal Rass-es continued to expand 'inter-reg' with a number of singles, of which the most important was **Kingston 11** — a vocal tour of the ghetto area in which the trio were born and raised. This productive period for the Royal Rass-es is captured on their remarkable debut album **Humanity** that includes the definitive 'inter-reg' song **Unconventional People**.

By then, Cedric Myton had quit to join the Congos(▶) and Clinton 'Johnny Kool' Hall was recruited to replace him. In 1979, with their name shortened to the Rass-es, the fruits of their work at Harry J's studio were to be found upon a second album, **Experience**. This rhythmically innovative and adventurous collection of Thompson songs established them as an act to be reckoned with and impressive live shows on both sides of the Atlantic consolidated their position.

In 1980 Thompson embarked upon an experiment that was to have far-reaching effects for him and his group. His British label, Ballistic, and his manager/publisher John Telfer suggested that he should go to London to record part of a third album with singer/songwriter Joe Jackson, who had emerged during the new-wave boom of the late '70s and who confessed a strong interest in reggae.

Financial restrictions prevented Peterkin and Hall from accompanying Thompson to London. This marked their departure from the group and the Rass-es henceforth would consist only of Prince Lincoln Thompson. Critical acclaim for the Jackson collaboration **Natural Wild** did nothing to stimulate record sales and Thompson returned to Jamaica where he has remained silent, without a record deal, ever since. There were rumours of some recording activity in 1981, although there has been no vinyl evidence to support them. It appears for the time being at least that one of Jamaica's most gifted singers is for the second time in his career going through a period of reassessment.

Recordings:
Humanity (—/Ballistic—UA)
Experience (—/Ballistic—UA)
Natural Wild (—/Ballistic—UA)
Harder Na Rass — Dub Of Natural Wild (—/Ballistic—UA)

Ray, Goodman And Brown

Harry Ray, Al Goodman and Billy Brown, previously known as the Moments(▶), moved to Polydor Records in 1979, changed their name to Ray, Goodman And Brown, and moved into higher realms of romantic close-harmonied balladeering. From their debut album, **Ray, Goodman And Brown**, came widespread American successes such as **Special Lady** and **Inside Of You**. Their second album **RG&BII**, a year later, included **My Prayer** and **Happy Anniversary**.

Recordings:
Ray, Goodman And Brown
  (Mercury/Polydor)
Ray, Goodman And Brown II
  (Mercury/Polydor)
Stay (Mercury/—)

The Real Thing

Formed in the slums of Liverpool in 1970, the Real Thing comprised Chris Amoo, Ray Lake, Dave Smith, and original fourth vocalist Kenny Davis. They served a stultifying two years on the UK cabaret circuit, before their appearance on the TV talent show 'Opportunity Knocks' secured them their first recording contract with Bell Records, for whom they immediately debuted with the self-penned **Vicious Circle**.

Their second single, **Plastic Man**, became a turntable hit and a staple of their live performances, without selling in significant quantities (although the band were sufficiently fond of it to re-record it on a later album).

Three or four more singles failed to establish them, and the group

Can You Feel The Force. Courtesy Pye Records.

remained on the cabaret circuit (more or less compelled to cover other people's material) until Kenny Davis left. The remaining trio had their first exposure to a mass audience when they were selected to back rock singer David Essex on tour in the UK.

Emboldened by this wider exposure, the group made another strike for stardom, their first two hits, **You To Me Are Everything** and **Can't Get By Without You**, both in 1976, coming from the writing partnership of Ken Gold and Mickey Denne. At the same time, the group were brought back up to strength with the addition of Chris's brother Eddie, formerly of the much respected '60s vocal soul outfit, the Chants. It was this aggregation which released the Real Thing's eponymous debut album, on the Pye label, in October 1976.

Fronted by the heroic good looks and gravelly vocal thrust of lead singer Chris Amoo, the group had a succession of soulful mid-tempo hits through 1977 and 1978, including **You'll Never Know What You're Missing**, **Love's Such A Wonderful Thing**, **Whenever You Want My Love** and **Rainin' Through My Sunshine**, the pattern only being broken by their first full-tilt disco outing, **Let's Go Disco**, in the summer of 1978 (both the group and the song were featured in Joan Collins' disco-sex movie, *The Stud*).

By the end of the '70s, with the disco booom in full swing, the Real Thing grappled to keep up, notably with the John Luongo remix of **Can You Feel The Force**, a creditable addition to the spate of galactically themed post-'*Star Wars*' disco tunes.

Subsequently eclipsed by the full freneticism of the disco movement, the group laid low until, in March 1982, they appeared on the Calibre label with **Love Takes Tears**, a Johnny Bristol(▶) song, produced by Eddie Amoo, which successfully evoked the mellow and melodic class of their early successes with Gold and Denne.

Recordings:
Real Thing (−Pye)
Four From Eight (−/Pye)
Greatest Hits (−/K.Tel)

Revolutionaires

Revolutionaires were formed in 1974 as a session band at the famed Channel One Studio with producers Jo Jo and Ernest Hookim. Their reputation quickly spread and they cut classic rhythms for the Mighty Diamonds(▶), Dillinger(▶) and the Wailing Souls(▶) among others. The most consistent personnel were: Sly Dunbar and Barnabus (drums), Robbie Shakespeare(▶) and Lloyd Parks (bass), Ansell Collins and Tarzan (keyboards), Rad Bryan and Bo Peep (rhythm guitar), Earl Wire' Lindo (lead guitar), and Sticky and Skully (percussion). Prior to metamorphasising into the Aggrovators (mark II) Revolutionaires cut some splendid dub albums, including those listed below.

Recordings:
Revolutionaires Part 1 (Channel One/United Artists)
Revolutionaires Part 2 (Channel One/United Artists)

Rico

Rico Rodrgriguez, born on October 17, 1934, in Mark Lane, Kingston 2, Jamaica, was educated for 12 years at the Alpha Boys School, a Catholic institution that placed a heavy emphasis on musical tuition. The school was responsible for nurturing the first generation of great Jamaican musicians: from its classrooms came trombonist Don Drummond, trumpeter John 'Dizzy' Moore and saxophonists Lester Stirling and Roland Alphonso(▶), who together went on to form the horn section of the Skatalites(▶).

Initially attracted to the saxophone, Rico turned to the trombone in the early 1950s, sitting in with a number of Jamaican jazz players, including Eric Deans, and later joining Count Ossie and the Mystic Revelation Of Rastafari. He worked with a number of sound systems, notably those of Studio

One boss Coxsone Dodd(▶) and Duke Reid, and is featured on such classics as **Easy Snappin'**, **Judgement Day** and **Let George Do It**.

Arriving in London in 1961, he began playing with Georgie Fame & the Blue Flames and J.J. Jackson's(▶) 'The Greatest Little Show Band On Earth', with saxophonist Dick Morrissey in the line-up. Drifting into London's black music scene he cut two albums in 1969, **Rico In Reggae Land**, dedicated to Don Drummond who had just died, and **Come Blow Your Horn**. Neither these nor an improved third album, **Brixton Cat**, managed to properly capture his music.

Using the cream of Jamaican session musicians Rodriguez cut **Man From Wareika** in the early '70s, a limited edition dub version of which followed. This was the real Rico, fresh and inventive with dazzling virtuosity, even with an instrument as cumbersome as the trombone.

Hurled into the pop limelight by the Specials and by the Midlands Two-Tone ska revival movement in Britain at the beginning of the '80s, Rico is something of a celebrity, doing occasional solo shows and frequently popping up as a surprise guest.

Recordings:
Come Blow Your Horn (−/Trojan)
Rico In Reggae Land (−/Pama)
Man From Wareika (−/Island)
That Man Is Forward (−/Chrysalis)

Minnie Riperton

Minnie was born in Chicago on November 8, 1947, the youngest of eight children. She studied classical music and ballet as a child, developing a stunning five-octave range, and originally intended to make her career in opera. The impracticalities of this plan soon dawned and instead Minnie joined a local all-girl group, the Gems, whose recordings for foremost Chicago label Chess(▶) include the

Below: Minnie Riperton's talent is sadly missed.

The Best Of Minnie Riperton. Courtesy Capitol Records.

fondly remembered **That's What They Put Erasers On Pencils For**. In addition, Minnie began to sing on back-up sessions at Chess featuring Etta James(▶), Muddy Waters (▶), Ramsey Lewis(▶), Fontella Bass(▶) and the Dells(▶).

After the disbandment of the Gems, Minnie spent a year alternating between working as a secretary for the record company, and recording without success under the name Andrea Davis. When Chess put together a racially mixed group called Rotary Connection, Minnie joined the line-up. Although they were a successful live attraction, mostly as a support act on the rock circuit, their record sales were a little disappointing, largely because their music was too MOR for black audiences, their image too R&B for the pop market.

In the last days of Rotary Connection, Minnie recorded her first solo album, **Come To My Garden**, which was released on the Janus label, but did little business.

In a mood of some disenchantment, Minnie and husband/co-songwriter Dick Rudolph loaded their belongings into a mobile home and headed for the Florida town of Gainsville, where Minnie had made some friends while on a Rotary Connection tour. The two began writing in a warm, idyllic vein which reflected their happi-

ness in their new surroundings.

Meanwhile, an Epic Records' employee who had apparently been searching for Minnie since the break-up of Rotary Connection, eventually tracked her down and signed her to the label. Minnie moved to Los Angeles to record her debut album for the label, **Perfect Angel**. It was produced by Stevie Wonder(▶), and contained two Wonder songs (the rest being penned by Rudolph/Riperton).

Backed by Stevie's Wonderlove vocal group, Minnie evoked the summery raptures of her time in Florida on the Wonder-penned **Lovin' You**, her first international hit, in 1974.

Her second album on Epic, **Adventures In Paradise** (1975), contained 10 Rudolph/Riperton compositions, aided by co-writers Joe Sample (who also played on the set) and Leon Ware(▶). Without yielding a natural-born follow-up to **Lovin' You**, the album still went gold in the States.

At the age of 28, Minnie made the tragic discovery that she was suffering from a malignant breast cancer. She underwent a mastectomy operation and it was hoped that her condition would respond to subsequent chemotherapy treatment.

Naturally reluctant to talk about her condition at first, Minie was later increasingly forthright about it in public and became an active member of several cancer organisations. She became Chairman of the American Cancer Society in 1978, having received the society's Courage Award from President Carter the previous year.

Minnie turned out two more albums, even changing record label for the last one, before she eventually succumbed to her illness, at the Cedars Sinai Hospital, Los Angeles, on July 12, 1979.

Her consummate vocal artistry was lost to the world, save for one magnificent posthumous tribute: the album **Love Lives Forever** which was collated and produced by Minnie's husband from a batch of vocal tracks recorded just before her death.

With infinite patience, and much devoted care, Rudolph worked out arrangements, laid on rhythm tracks, and recruited the aid of a galaxy of Minnie's friends and admirers in the industry, to craft one of the singer's most attractive albums. Recorded contributions and sleevenote dedications came from, among others, Stevie Wonder, George Benson(▶), Peabo Bryson(▶), Michael Jackson(▶), Roberta Flack(▶) and Patrice Rushen(▶).

Recordings:
Perfect Angel (Epic)
Adventures In Paradise (Epic)
Stay In Love (Epic)
Minnie (Capitol)
Love Lives Forever (Capitol)

The Ritchie Family

One of the most successful 'manufactured' outfits of all time, the Ritchie Family was the creation of Jacques Morali, the writer and producer who went on to create the Village People(▶). The group's name was provided by producer Ritchie Rome, who cut a disco album, **Brazil**, in 1975, using the girls on backing vocals.

The original trio were Cheryl Mason Jacks, Cassandra Ann Wooten and Gwendolyn Oliver, but later the line-up was changed to Jacqueline Smith-Lee, Theodosia (Dodie) Draher, and Ednah Holt. At the height of the mid-'70s disco boom, the Ritchie Family scored their biggest success with the hit, **The Best Disco In Town** (1976). Basically their appeal lay in some hot rhythms; and they were also three gorgeous women. Because of their Morali connection, they were committed to film in the Village People feature, *Can't Stop The Music.*

Recordings:
Life Is Music (Polydor)
American Generation (Polydor)
The Ritchie Family (Polydor)

Lee Ritenour

As a session guitarist, Lee Ritenour (born Hollywood, 1952), has worked for Barbra Streisand, Steely Dan, Diana Ross(▶), Leo Sayer, Aretha Franklin(▶), Herbie Hancock(▶), the Brothers Johnson(▶), George Benson(▶), Norman Connors(▶), George Duke(▶), Stanley Clarke(▶) and Sergo Mendes (with whom he toured).

Ritenour's own music is a fusion of Latin, jazz and soul, and his albums, littered with the finest musicians in the business, have not had singles taken off them; pursuit of excellence and good music are his only aims.

Recordings:
First Course (Epic)
Captain Fingers (Epic)
The Captain's Journey (Elektra/Asylum)
Feel The Night (Elektra/Asylum)
Rit (Elektra/Asylum)
Rio (Elektra/Asylum)

Rockie Robbins

The rich and resonant voice of Minnesotan-native Rockie Robbins was eventually signed to A&M Records. After two albums of his romantic, slow and mid-tempo soul, producers Skip Scarborough and Jerry Peters finally made a third set count. The title track, **I Believe In Love**, scored high in the R&B singles chart of 1981.

Recordings:
Rockie Robbins (A&M)
You And Me (A&M)
I Believe In Love (A&M)

D.J. Rogers

A much-admired singer/keyboard player / composer / arranger / producer / session musician, Los Angeles-born D.J. Rogers worked with Rev. James Cleveland, was director of Watts Community Choir and cut five albums with the Los Angeles Community Choir while still in his teens.

He became a fixture on the LA studio scene, recording with Billy Preston(▶), Bobby Womack(▶), Helen Reddy and many others. In 1970 he met rock star Leon Russell and cut two albums for Russell's Shelter label (one of which has never been issued). He also wrote material for blues star Freddy King(▶) and worked on rock tours with Russell.

Signed to RCA in 1975, he recorded three albums for them— **It's Good To Be Alive, On The Road Again** and **Love, Music And Life**, having hit singles with **Say You Love Me, It's Alright Now** and **I Think I'll Make It Anyhow**—

Above: All rounder D.J. Rogers.

before signing with Kalimba Productions, run by Earth, Wind & Fire's(▶) Maurice White, and debuting with **Love Brought Me Back** (Columbia/CBS).

Recordings:
D.J. Rogers (Shelter/—)
It's Good To Be Alive (RCA)

Sonny Rollins

Though his own style owed much to the late Coleman Hawkins, Theodore Walter 'Sonny' Rollins himself was the most influential tenor sax player to emerge in the late '50s.

Born in New York on September 9, 1930, Rollins first recorded in 1948 and by the '50s was playing with the finest jazz musicians of the era. He was a member of the much-lauded Max Roach/Clifford Brown quintet from 1956-57, but in 1959 went into temporary retire-

Way Out West. Courtesy Contemporary Records.

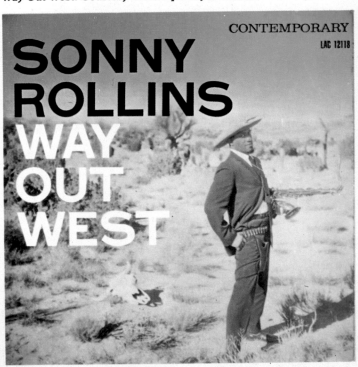

ment, forced on him by drink and drugs problems. He re-emerged in 1961 when he signed with RCA and cut the classic album **The Bridge** with white jazz guitarist Jim Hall.

In the '70s, Rollins began experimenting with electronically amplified sax and groups using other electronic instruments, which moved him out of the pure jazz field. His recent Milestone albums have all been in such vein.

Recordings:
The Bridge (RCA)
The Cutting Edge (Milestone)
Don't Stop The Carnival (Milestone)

Max Romeo

Romeo (born Kingston, Jamaica) first sang in church and at local talent shows, notably those promoted by Willy Francis. He cut his

first single, **Buy Me A Rainbow**, with producer Ken Lack in 1965. Four years later he stormed the reggae scene when his highly risqué single, **Wet Dreams**, climbed to No. 10 on the UK pop charts.

Subsequently embarrassed by the image that record projected of him, he surfaced in 1971 with a collection of sides, spiritual in focus, including **Pray For Me** and **The Coming Of Jah**. Since then he has maintained a strong cult following in Jamaica, America and the UK with singles like **The Power Fall On I, Mackabee Version, Three Blind Mice** and **Revelation Time**, the latter the title of a 1976 Lee Perry(▶)-produced album.

In March 1976 Island Records in the UK released the single, **War In A Babylon**, which topped the reggae charts

Recordings:
War In A Babylon (Mango/Island)
Holding Out My Love To You (Shanachie/—)

Diana Ross

One woman can be cited as the black female voice of the '70s and the limitless talents of Diana Ross look like making her a prime candidate for a similar accolade in the '80s.

Diana was born in Detroit on March 26, 1944, one of six children, to Fred and Ernestine Earle. At 14, she auditioned for a singing role in a high-school musical, but was turned down. Nevertheless, Florence Ballard and Mary Wilson decided to include Diana in their vocal group, upon the advice of Eddie Kendricks(▶), and, after recruiting Betty Anderson, the foursome called themselves the Primettes.

At the beginning of the '60s, they found themselves on local label, Lu-Pine Records. A dissillusioned Miss Anderson was replaced by Barbara Martin, and this line-up recorded two singles, **Tears Of Sorrow** and **Pretty Baby.** Through local sales, the group obtained local club bookings, and worked as sister group to Eddie Kendrick's the Primes, who later became the Temptations(▶).

Living locally was a guy called William 'Smokey' Robinson(▶), whose group the Miracles(▶) were signed to a new record company, Tamla Motown(▶). Diana, through Smokey, got an audition for the group with label boss Berry Gordy. Although Gordy didn't feel such a female group would be commercially viable, the girls obviously felt his mind could be changed. So, after school, they hung around the studio, and when session people didn't show up, they sang back-ups and hand-clapped.

That persistance finally paid off. In 1961, the Primettes were signed and their debut single was released on the subsidiary Tamla label. Soon after, the group changed their name to The Supremes(▶). They were moved to the company's main label, Motown, and their second single under this banner, **Let Me Go The Right Way,** was their first song to hit the American R&B charts.

From that day on, with singles such as **Where Did Our Love Go, Baby Love, Stop! In The Name Of Love, You Can't Hurry Love, You Keep Me Hanging On** and **The Happening,** the trio soon became R&B's premier black female vocal act.

In 1967, **Reflections** came out under the name Diana Ross & The Supremes, indicating a move towards a solo career for Diana. In June 1970, she released her first solo single, **Reach Out And Touch Somebody's Hand.** Still utilising the team of songwriters available from Motown, Diana found great success working with Nick Ashford and Valerie Simpson (Ashford And Simpson(▶).

Her first album was released in 1970, and working at a highly profitable speed, Diana had completed two more by the end of 1971, and four more by the end of 1973.

On January 21, 1971, Diana married businessman Robert Silberstein. Their marriage produced three girls, but on June 1, 1976, Diana filed divorce proceedings on the grounds of irreconcilable differences, gaining custody of their daughters.

Later in 1971, Diana began working on her first feature-film acting role, portraying Billie Holiday in the biographical *Lady Sings The Blues,* for which she was nominated for an Oscar.

Hit singles **Ain't No Mountain High Enough, Remember Me, I'm Still Waiting, Surrender, Doobedood'ndoobe, Touch Me In The Morning** and **All Of My Life** were followed by, towards the end of 1973, Diana teaming-up with Marvin Gaye(▶) to record an album, which included another hit, **You Are Everything.**

Still sounding very much part of the Motown sound, Diana's releases at this time were ballads, fully arranged, and delivered with an irresistible clarity and warmth that was taking her beyond the realms of mere immortality and into indispensability.

In 1974, Diana embarked on her second film, *Mahogany,* a fictional rags-to-riches tale of a young secretary's rise to become a top fashion designer. Diana designed her own outfits for the film, some 50 in total. Seemingly incapable of aging, she has always had a passion for clothing, and her beauty combined with her taste in cloths have much enhanced her appeal.

During 1974 and 1975, her singles' success rate lessened, but she re-emerged with **Theme From Mahogany (Do You Know Where You're Going To)** and **Love Hangover,** in 1976. The same year Motown obtained the film rights for *The Wiz,* a black musical version of *The Wizard Of Oz.* Diana asked Gordy if she could play the lead part of Dorothy, Gordy agreed. Co-starring with her in that film was Michael Jackson(▶), of The Jacksons(▶), a group she was instrumental in grooming when they'd first signed to Motown in 1969.

Although Diana's music became more up-tempo to meet the fashions of the late-'70s disco boom, 1977 and 1978 were lean years for her, singles-wise, until the release in mid-1978 of **The Boss,** her 15th album. Written and produced by Ashford and Simpson, hits tumbled off it, **The Boss, No One Gets The Prize** and **It's My House;** Diana became a floor-filler again.

In 1980, collaborating with Nile Rodgers and Bernard Edwards, the backbone behind Chic(▶), she recorded the **Diana** album, from which hit singles abounded—**Upside Down, My Old Piano** and **I'm Coming Out** winning massive sales. Her last album for Motown, having graciously honoured her entire contract, contained the hit **It's My Turn,** and with no interim, she signed a new deal with RCA for North America, and with Capitol for the rest of the world.

Diana Ross was Berry Gordy's finest piece of grooming, although the once intimate rapport with Gordy began to get violently stormy as she shied from re-signing with the label. Towards the end of her Motown days, her promotion budget had expanded greatly, and Gordy had invested millions in placing her face and figure on countless billboards and in every magazine.

Despite being offered a financially mind-blowing new contract, Diana wriggled free, and took her career one step further in 1981 by producing herself for the first time with an album from whence came a worldwide smash, a new version of the Frankie Lymon & The Teenagers(▶) **Why Do Fools Fall In Love.**

Charting simultaneously was the title song from the soundtrack of the film *Endless Love.* Written by Lionel Ritchie of The Commodores(▶), and sung by Diana and Ritchie, it was to be her swansong for the Tamla Motown label. A world wide hit, it reached No. 1 in many major markets, including a lengthy stay at the top of the US charts.

With video now a more widely-used media, Diana, naturally, is frequently visually recorded on cassette for promotional purposes, her ageless frame decorating innumerable posters with an even more sensual approach.

Below: Diana Ross has always moved with the times: In the 1980s she's as big box-office as she ever has been.

Recordings:
Diana Ross (Motown)
Everything Is Everything (Motown)
I'm Still Waiting (Motown)
Lady Sings The Blues (Motown)
Touch Me In The Morning (Motown)
Diana And Marvin (Motown)
Original Soundtrack Of 'Mahogany' (Motown)
Diana Ross (Motown)
Baby It's Me (Motown)
Ross (Motown)
The Boss (Motown)
Diana (Motown)
To Love Again (Motown)
Why Do Fools Fall In Love (RCA/Capitol)

Rose Royce

The members of the original Rose Royce octet grew up around the Los Angeles suburbs of Watts, Englewood, and West LA. Kenji Brown, guitar; Lequient 'Duke' Jobe, bass; Victor Nix, keyboards; Henry Garner, drums; Kenny Copeland, trumpet; Freddie Dunn, trumpet; Michael Moore, sax; Terral Santiel, congas; dropped out of college, intent on gaining musical experience, backing whoever came into town.

Eventually, they got an audition to back Edwin Starr(▶). He asked them to return the next day to be heard by his producer, Norman Whitfield(▶). The band's borrowed equipment soon had to be returned, and they realised that they weren't going to get many chances to impress a Motown producer.

They started backing Starr in 1973, under the group name of Total Concept Unlimited. Whitfield swapped them over to work with Yvonne Fair(▶), and changed their name to Magic Wand. Whitfield also used them for albums by the Temptations(▶) and Undisputed Truth(▶), for whom they soon became the regular backing band. All this time they had been creating for themselves, and planning a future, but they needed a vocalist.

*Rose Royce Strikes Again!
Courtesy WEA Records.*

Undisputed Truth played Miami, Florida, one night. The support band was called the Jewels, and their outstanding member was vocalist Gwen Dickey. The band told Whitfield about Gwen, and when she came to LA, she thought she was auditioning for Undisputed Truth. However, Magic Wand and Ms Dickey got on famously and, together they became Rose Royce.

Rose Royce's second album, **In Full Bloom**, was, strangely enough, recorded before their first. Michael Shultz, who was about to direct a film called *Car Wash*, asked Whitfield to write and produce the soundtrack. Whitfield thought that Rose Royce would make a bigger initial impression if he used the film as a vehicle for them. **Car Wash**, released in 1976, gave the band three hit singles in succession. The tapes from the first album were finally released in 1977. For this album, Victor Nix had been replaced by Michael Nash. **In Full Bloom** yielded several more hit singles.

Their biggest hit so far, **Love Don't Live Here Anymore,** came from their third album, **Rose Royce Strikes Again,** released in 1978. Following their fourth album, **Rainbow Connection,** Gwen Dickey and Kenji Brown left, to be replaced by Richee Benson and Walter McKinney, respectively. Following this, **Golden Touch** was released

Above: Gwen Dickey, Rose Royce's original exciting lead singer. See our front cover for another glimpse.

at the beginning of 1981, **Jump Street** arriving later on in that year.

Recordings:
Car Wash (MCA)
In Full Bloom (Whitfield/WEA)
Rose Royce Strikes Again (Whitfield/WEA)
Rainbow Connection (Whitfield/WEA)
Golden Touch (Whitfield/WEA)
Jump Street (Whitfield/WEA)

The Royals

The history of the Royals and of its central figure Roy Cousins has been dogged by disillusionment and frustration. But for all the setbacks and constant personnel changes the Royals have managed to carve a sizeable niche in the development of reggae. The story begins in the dusty backyards of Cockburn Pen, in Jamaica's infamous ghetto Kingston 11, in 1964, where Cousins and three long-since-parted friends, Eddie and Trevor on harmonies, and a certain Harry on guitar, dreamt of freeing themselves of the ghetto through music.

They made their first stab at recording in 1966, initially with the legendary Duke Reid and later over at Federal Records, with Ken Khouri. Another group, the Tartans, claimed that the track the Royals were cutting for Khouri had been stolen from them. We'll never know if the allegation was valid but the Tartans were popular at that time and to avoid a scandal Khouri dropped the Royals. The group was naturally upset, so much so that Trevor quit music altogether.

They returned in 1967 for Joe Gibbs, utilising a Studio One(▶) rhythm of Larry and Alvin's **Nanny Goat,** where they mocked the then No.1 group in Jamaica, the Pioneers, using the title **Never See Come See.** The Pioneers replied with the bitchy **Easy Come Easy Go,** which in fact was far from the case for **Never See Come See** was a hit on both sides of the Atlantic.

Cousins even collected the princely sum of 10 pounds (20 dollars) in royalties for it! Subsequent releases all flopped and after a disastrous relationship with Duke Reid's second-in-command Byron Smith, the Royals decided to call it a day.

Cousins still had his regular job with the Jamaican Post Office, which he had been wise enough to retain since leaving Tarrent School, and it was from his earnings there that he was able to re-enter the music business on his own terms — as artist and producer.

The Royals made their last record for an outside producer in 1973. It was the original Studio One versions of Cousins' marvellous **Pick Up The Pieces** and a million miles away from their music of the late '60s. The music had reached a new maturity with Cousins using his distinctive lisping vocal technique to its fullest. By 1974, with the formation of their own Wambesi label, the Royals were upon the threshold of Jamaica's premier music division. Politically and spiritually fired, Cousins' songs were emotive testimonies to an enslaved race: **Sufferer Of The Ghetto, Ghetto Man, Peace And Love, The Message** and **Blacker Black.** He was also branching out as a producer, cutting definitive sides with Gregory Isaacs(▶) and Lloyd Ruddock.

The very best of the Royals, songs recorded with determination after weeks of studio rehearsals, are to be found on the first and greatest of their albums, **Pick Up The Pieces,** released like all subsequent records in Britain by Ballistic—United Artists, and featuring the backing harmonies of Errol Davis and Carl Green. Four other albums, including a brace of dub collections, never quite reached the heights achieved by this first album.

Towards the close of the '70s Cousins was forced to break up the band and undergo intensive eye surgery to save his sight, threatened by severe cataracts. With the

medical treatment complete he re-emerged upon the scene in 1981 with a batch of new material for Kingston Records. All along he has made it clear that he *is* the Royals and that he can knock into shape just about any backing vocalist. He is a gifted man with a turbulent past; we can only wait to see if he can regain former heights.

Recordings:
Pick Up The Pieces (—/Ballistic-UA)
Ten Years After (—/Ballistic-UA)
Israel Be Wise (—/Ballistic-UA)
The Force Of Music—Liberated Dub (—/Ballistic-UA)
Freedom Fighters Dub (—/Ballistic-UA)

Rufus

Rufus are a stylish vocal/instrumental group, who have maintained a high standard of recorded work since the departure of Chaka Khan (▶); their final album together was **Camouflage** (1981), although Chaka and the band had recorded independently for two years before that.

Founded in 1970, Rufus was an offshoot of the American Breed, a lightweight pop outfit out of the Chicago area, who had scored in the late '60s with **Bend Me Shape Me.** After a couple of name changes (from Smoke to Ask Rufus and finally Rufus) and personnel, the band met again with Bob Monaco, who had been involved with the management of the American Breed. He cut a demo, took the group to Los Angeles, and fixed up a contract with ABC Records.

A satisfactory debut album, **Rufus,** attracted some attention, but it was on the release of their second LP, **Rags To Rufus,** that the band broke through, with two singles, **Tell Me Something Good** (a Stevie Wonder(▶) composition) and the thundering **You Got The Love,** hitting the US top 10. **Tell Me . . .** earned Rufus the 1974 Grammy Award for Best R&B Vocal Performance By A Group.

Further personnel changes ensued before the release of **Rufusized,** with the line-up consisting of Tony Maiden, guitar; Bobby Watson, bass; Nate Morgan, piano; Kevin Murphy, keyboards; Andre Fischer, drums; and Chaka Khan, vocals. Now an established recording unit, Rufus confirmed their status with concert performances alongside Stevie Wonder(▶), Santana, the Commodores(▶), the Beach Boys, Tavares and Elton John, with whom they appeared at the 100,000-seat Wembley Stadium in London.

After their sixth album, Chaka Khan launched her solo career, while Rufus cut **Numbers,** with John Robinson replacing Fischer on drums. Synthesist David Wolinski had joined on completion of the **Ask Rufus** album, replacing Nate Morgan. Although the band were obviously a different proposition without Chaka, **Numbers** was nevertheless an enterprising effort, featuring the excellent vocal work of Maiden and Wolinski.

The group reunited for **Masterjam,** their MCA debut produced by Quincy Jones(▶) which became their sixth gold album in seven years, then moved on to **Party 'Til You're Broke** (1981), which confirmed their solo identity.

Recordings:
Rufus (ABC)

Rags To Rufus (ABC)
Rufusized (ABC)
Rufus Featuring Chaka Khan
(ABC)
Ask Rufus (ABC)
Street Player (ABC)
Numbers (ABC)
Masterjam (MCA)
Party 'Til You're Broke (MCA)
Camouflage (MCA)

Patrice Rushen

Few artists began learning their craft at such an early age as Patrice Rushen, who was enrolled in a special music preparatory programme at the University of Southern California at the age of three. At the USC, they learnt about such things as 'eurhythmics'. 'Instead of talking about 8th notes and 16th notes, we talked about running

Straight From The Heart.
Courtesy Elektra Records.

notes and skipping notes, happy chords and sad chords,' she recalls.

Patrice was born on September 30, 1954, in Los Angeles. By the age of six she was giving classical recitals. At 12, having studied the piano for seven years, she got a littled bored and took up the flute, playing the instrument in the school orchestra. Patrice approached the jazz lab band, the Msingi Workshop, founded in her high school by a music teacher, Reggie Andrews. Andrews told her to enter her own combo in the Monterey Junior Jazz Festival competition, and she won. Andrews went on to co-produce her first five albums.

Patrice worked with Melba Liston's big band, with singer Abbey Lincoln, and then worked a summer with a black pop group, the Sylvers(▶). By the age of 20, Patrice had released two albums, **Prelusion** and **Before The Dawn**, mixtures of jazz and classical music, for the Prestige label. Her third and

last album for the label, **Shout It Out,** was her first venture into singing and funk. Having mastered her primary instrument, Ms Rushen was now composing, arranging, producing and playing her own bass and drums. **Shout It Out** was the beginning of her own vocalising and incorporated danceable rhythm tracks.

Her first session work was on Jean Luc-Ponty's **Upon The Wings Of Music.** From then on she began to be contracted for live and studio work. She has appeared on three albums· by Lee Ritenour(▶), with whom she worked at the Baked Potato Club. She recorded with Stanley Turrentine(▶), and that session included Ron Carter and Freddie Hubbard(▶). Her vocals and keyboard work augmented the last Minnie Riperton(▶) album, **Love Lives Forever.**

Patrice signed for Elektra Records in 1978 and in October released **Patrice,** turning down the offer of joining Herbie Hancock's(▶) touring band in order to pursue her own career. With the release of her fifth album, **Pizzazz,** she scored her first hit single, **Haven't You Heard,** and that achievement earned her major television appearances, and much publicity. With co-producer Charles Mims Jr, her sixth album, **Posh,** came out in November 1980.

Recordings:
Prelusion (Prestige)
Before The Dawn (Prestige)
Shout It Out (Prestige)
Patrice (Elektra)
Pizzazz (Elektra)
Posh (Elektra)

Brenda Russell

As Brenda Russell stood in a Toronto night club she was approached by the manager of a female vocal cabaret act called the Tiaras, who hired her without even hearing her sing.

Following a move to New York, Brenda landed a role in a travelling production of the musical *Hair.* This took her back to Toronto, where she met and married Brian Russell. Together they hosted a Canadian TV series, and Brenda had three Canadian hit singles, while also working as a DJ on a weekly Gospel radio show that required her to write a hymn every seven days.

Below: The sassy Chaka Khan
fronting multi-racial Chicago-
based band Rufus.

Above: Creative and influential, Gill Scott-Heron.

In 1973, they moved to Los Angeles, did TV and session work, and were signed to Rocket Records, with whom they made two albums, their songs being covered by Jermaine Jackson(▶), Rufus(▶), and Tata Vega(▶). When Brian and Brenda broke up, she and her producer Andre Fischer, a founder member of Rufus, approached A&M to see if they would sign her as a solo artist. In 1979, for Tommy LiPuma's A&M-distributed Horizon Records, Brenda released her first solo album.

Brenda's songs, keyboard work and voice, have appeared on the albums of Barbra Streisand, Bette Midler and Elton John.

Recordings:
Brenda Russell (Horizon/A&M)

Boz Scaggs

A member of the rock group the Steve Miller Band in the late '60s, Ohio-born Scaggs quit to pursue a solo career. His first effort, **Boz**

Slow Dancer. *Courtesy*
CBS Records.

Scaggs, was recorded for Atlantic at Muscle Shoals(▶) with local session men including Duane Allman(▶). It was an artistic but not a commercial success, and Scaggs signed with Columbia.

He moved more and more towards R&B-type styling, and the 1974 album **Slow Dancer,** produced by ex-Motown(▶) man Johnny Bristol(▶), consolidated his cult following. Massive acclaim came with his next album, **Silk Degrees,** released in 1977. Deeply influenced by soul and funk but much more than just a slavish imitation, the album spun off several hit

singles—**Lowdown, Lido Shuffle, What Can I Say, Harbour Lights**—and went double platinum. Subsequent albums were similarly styled and also successful.

Recordings:
Slow Dancer (Columbia/CBS)
Silk Degrees (Columbia/CBS)
Down Two Then Left
(Columbia/CBS)
Hits (Columbia/CBS)

Tom Scott

White reed player Scott (b. 1948) is a stalwart of the Los Angeles session scene who has made a raft of albums as frontman. An eclectic stylist who steps in and out of jazz, funk and rock modes, he was previously with Don Ellis and Oliver Nelson bands. Scored *'Uptown Saturday Nite'* and *'Conquest of the Planet of Apes'* movies.

Recordings:
Blow It Out (Epic)
Intimate Strangers
(Columbia/CBS)
The Best Of. . . (Columbia/CBS)

Gill Scott-Heron

Born in April 1949 in Chicago and raised by his grandmother in Jackson, Tennessee, Scott-Heron indulged his literary talents in his early teens by writing detective stories. His subject matter shifted to black politics after his guardian's death and he moved to New York. He attended Lincoln University, Pennsylvania, where he met his long-time musical associate and cultural collaborator, bass guitarist Brian Jackson. After Lincoln he went to Baltimore to take his masters degree in creative writing and, on completion, accepted a post at the University of Columbia.

At 19, Scott-Heron's first novel, *The Vulture,* was published. It was followed by a rap poem, entitled 'Small Talk At 125th And Lennox', and another novel, *The Nigger Factory.* The books sold well on the East Coast although it wasn't until Scott-Heron's poems were converted to songs—he took up keyboards and began recording with Jackson—that his reputation as a black radical with a jazz handle on funk started to spread.

The duo's first releases were for Bob Thiele's Flying Dutchman

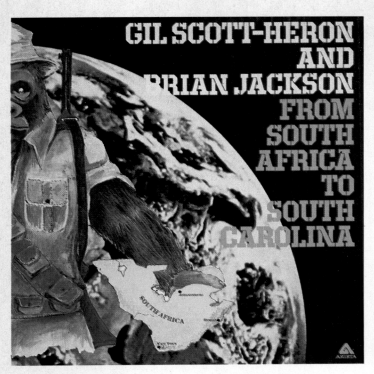

From South Africa to South Carolina. Courtesy Arista Records.

label: **Small Talk** . . . primarily an adaptation of Scott-Heron's book of poems, **Freewill, Pieces Of A Man** and a compilation of all three, **The Revolution Will Not Be Televised**, that later inspired Labelle's **Pressure Cookin'** album.

Another album, **Winter In America**, for Strata-East, spawned the single **The Bottle**, a telling observation of alcoholism that became a disco hit and was later established as a favourite with Britain's Northern-Soul clan. The single's popularity provided the partnership with enough ammunition to tour Europe in 1976.

Wide-scale recognition and popular acceptance came with his signing to Clive Davis's Arista label. He was the first act on the roster and his debut, **First Minutes Of A New Day**, backed by the Midnight Band brought him the international audience he sought.

In 1980, Jackson left for New Jersey where he began work on his own projects. Scott-Heron suffered the introverted **Real Eyes** album, a patchy transitional work, after the split. He bounced back a year later with the infinitely superior **Reflections**. The album contained his first major hit single for some time, **Storm Music**, set to a reggae rhythm, and **B Movie**, the sharpest indictment of the Reagan administration on record.

Recordings:
The Revolution Will Not Be Televised (Flying Dutchman/—)
From South Africa To South Carolina (Arista/—)
Bridges (Arista)
Secrets (Arista)
Reflections (Arista)

Robbie Shakespeare

See Sly Dunbar & Robbie Shakespeare

Shalamar

Jody Watley, born in Chicago, came to Los Angeles where she gained modelling experience in magazines and television. As well as being strikingly beautiful, she was an exceptional dancer. In LA she met Jeffrey Daniels, a native of the city. The two became dancing partners, and sneaked into recordings of 'Soul Train'. Very soon, the pair became darlings of the show, the cameras frequently turning to their superb syncopation.

Dick Griffey, bookings manager for 'Soul Train', decided to branch out into the recording world. With some LA session musicians and singers, he released a single called **Uptown Festival**, which was a disco medley of old Motown songs. The record was brought out under the name of Shalamar. The record became a success, and Griffey realised he would have to create an actual group. It was announced on 'Soul Train' that the show was forming its own group, and through public pressure Jody and Jeffrey were given voice tests, and became two-thirds of Shalamar. Howard Hewett became the third member. They began to sing on Shalamar records in 1978, and the second Shalamar album brought single success through **Take That To The Bank**.

Since Jody and Jeffrey had prin-

Friends. Courtesy Solar Records.

cipally been dancers, the choreography for their live shows was always way above run-of-the-mill R&B stepping. The trio, being good-looking as well, became heart-throbs of the Solar(▶) onslaught. In 1979, Solar had its first gold singles, one of them being **The Second Time Around**, taken from Shalamar's third album. Their pop and club chart success continued into the '80s, and on their fourth album, **Shot Of Love** their songwriting and instrumental skills began to be more prominently displayed.

Solar left RCA in 1981, and signed a new distribution deal with WEA. In order to honour their contractual obligations, Shalamar were forced to release their makeshift out-take of a fifth album, but stormed back in 1982 with their most polished album to date, **Friends**, their vocals and songs attaining a new sophistication. Undaunted by the fact that they were a 'fabricated' pop act, the three members have now gained musical status.

Recordings:
Uptown Festival (RCA)
Disco Gardens (RCA)
Big Fun (Solar)
Shot Of Love (Solar)
Go For It (Solar)
Friends (Solar)

Marlena Shaw

The title cut of Marlena Shaw's debut album **Out Of Different Bags** sums up a career which has shown her vocalising veering from jazz through easy-listening to soul music.

Born in New Rochelle, New York, and now the mother of five children, Marlena made her stage debut at the Apollo Theatre in Harlem when she was just 10.

Having married and started raising her family, she got a singing job in a New York lounge in 1963 and cut some demos which were sent to Columbia Records but rejected. Undeterred, she started working the East Coast club circuits and in 1966 landed a deal with Cadet which produced two albums, **Out Of Different Bags** and **Spice Of Life**, which latter contained her March 1967 R&B hit **Mercy, Mercy, Mercy**.

A five-year stint fronting the Count Basie Orchestra further developed the jazz/gospel fusion in her singing style and in 1972 she became the first female artist ever to sign for Blue Note, spending the next five years with the respected jazz label during which time she cut an album a year and enjoyed a 1976 R&B hit single with **It's**

Below: Marlena Shaw's music came out of different bags.

Better Than Walking Out.

Moving to Columbia Records in 1977 she was teamed with producer Bert De Coteaux for the biggest hit of her career with the Gerry Goffin/Carole King song **Go Away Little Boy** from the **Sweet Beginnings** album. But the LP was sadly mis-titled as, after two further sets, she was one of many artists ditched when Columbia savagely cut back their artist roster in the face of the recession and left without an outlet.

Recordings:
Out Of Different Bags (Cadet/Chess)
Sweet Beginnings (Columbia/CBS)
Take A Bite (Columbia/CBS)

Shirley & Co.

See Shirley & Lee

Joe Simon

A pioneer of the marriage between meaningful country songs and soulful interpretations, Joe Simon has, despite never quite being in the contemporary black music mainstream, always managed to make immensely satsifying records, while at the same time progressing his style into new fields, as shown by his classy disco records in the late '70s.

Born on September 2, 1943, in the sleepy Louisiana town of Simmesport, he was raised in the hurly-burly of Oakland, California, from the age of 15, but took his pleasures from listening to artists like Arthur Prysock and Ray Charles(▶) who were already using country material.

He sang with the Goldentones for a while and had releases on several labels, including Vee-Jay(▶) (where he cut enough tracks to fill an album), without much success till he took his talents to Nashville and signed for Sound Stage 7, a subsidiary which country label Monument had set up as an entrée into black music.

With producer John Richbourg, Simon gave the new label 16 hits in a glorious four-year spate of creativity, scoring first in 1964 with **Teenager's Prayer** and following through with the million-sellers **The Chokin' Kind** and **(You Keep**

Me) Hangin' On (not the Supremes' song of that name) as well as **No Sad Songs, Misty Blue, Message From Maria** and **My Special Prayer**. The Sound Stage 7 hits had a sound all of their own which was missing from his records when he switched to the Spring label in 1970, although it was replaced by something just as potent.

Initially, the company sent him to record in Philadelphia, with Gamble and Huff(▶) producing and Thom Bell(▶) arranging. The outstanding **Drowning In The Sea Of**

Above: Joe Simon the country soul singer.

Love proved the value of the experiment. Not wishing to get Simon stuck in a formula, Spring subsequently recorded him with a variety of producers at various locations (**Step By Step** with Raeford Gerald, an album with Brad Shapiro, others with his old partner John Richbourg).

Simon himself wrote, produced and sang the title track to the *Cleopatra Jones* 'blaxploitation' movie (recording for the first time with his own Mainstreeters backing band), and produced Millie Jackson's(▶) contribution to the soundtrack.

Whether emanating from Nashville, Muscle Shoals, the Chess studio in Chicago or New York, Simon's records have always had their own distinctive stamp and if his recent output has been somewhat disappointing it has been due more to a dearth of strong songs than any lack of conviction in his performance.

When Otis Redding died, many soul fans regarded Joe Simon as his natural successor, indeed the Redding family themselves chose Simon to sing Redding's favourite gospel song, **Jesus Keep Me Near The Cross**, at Big O's funeral. But over the ensuing decade Simon has proved that he is very much his own man with a style that has stood apart from his contemporaries, although never left behind or overshadowed by them.

Recordings:
No Sad Songs (Monument)
Greatest Hits (Sound Stage 7/ Monument)
Drowning In The Sea Of Love (Spring/Mojo)
Mood Heart And Soul (Spring/ Polydor)
Simon Country (Spring/Polydor)
Get Down (Spring/Polydor)

Sister Sledge

The Sledge Sisters, Kathy, Joni, Kim and Debbie, from Philadelphia, made their first single, **Weather Man**, with Thom Bell's(▶) brother Tony in 1973. Signed by Henry Allen to Cotillion Records in 1974, while still all under 20, they were given an image of innocence that was instantly successful. A single, **Mama Never Told Me**, was a worldwide pop smash.

It was some four years before Allen could find them a different image; this time he chose a 'sisterly love' approach. The girls' 1979 album, **We Are Family**, its material written, played by, and produced by Nile Rodgers and Bernard Edwards—the creators of Chic(▶) and in-demand music-makers at that time—yielded three worldwide hits, **He's The Greatest Dancer, We Are Family** and **Lost In Music**.

After that phenomenal success, the quartet went off the boil again. Throughout their career, they've maintained distinctive gospel-based harmonies, Allen finding different sounds to go beneath. Rodgers and Edwards produced the next album, but the Chic sound was going out of fashion. Narada Michael Walden(▶) produced the following LP **All American Girls** but that combination was not compatible.

Finally, with the girls starting to have babies, it was decided that they were old enough and wise enough to write and produce themselves. From their **The Sisters** album of 1981, they reworked Mary Wells'(▶) **My Guy** to successful effect.

Recordings:
We Are Family (Cotillion)
Love Somebody Today (Cotillion)
All American Girls (Cotillion)
The Sisters (Cotillion)

Skyy

This New York-based eight-piece who crossed over into the pop market with their fourth album, **Skyy Line**, consist of Solomon Roberts Jr, vocals/guitars; Gerald Le Bon, bass; Anibal Anthony

Skyy Line. Courtesy Salsoul Records.

Sierra, guitars; Tommy McConnell, drums; Larry Greenberg, keyboards, and the Dunning sisters (Denise, Delores and Bonnie), vocals.

The brainchild of Roberts and their producer, Randy Muller, leader and founder member of Brass Construction(▶), Skyy play a sophisticated mixture of dance tracks and ballads; their recent album **Skyy Line** contains the hit singles **Call Me** and **Let's Celebrate**.

Above: Sexy Sledge sisters still singing successfully.

Recordings:
Skyy (Salsoul)
Skyy Line (Salsoul/Epic)

Slave

Slave was born out of Dayton, Ohio, where four guys from that neck of the woods formed themselves into a band called the Young Mystics—it consisted of Floyd Miller, vocals, horns; Mark Adams, bass; Tom Lockett Jr, saxophones; and Steve Arrington, drums.

Trumpet player Steve Washington, from Newark, New Jersey, had come to Ohio to complete high school. As his uncle was Ralph 'Pee Wee' Middlebrook of the Ohio Players(▶) Washington went on tour with the group during vacations. In Ohio, he had a local band called Black Satin Soul that included Mark Hicks, guitar, and Tim Dozier, drums.

When the Young Mystics broke up, Arrington went to San Francisco. A few years later, on October 8, 1975, Washington formed the first line-up of Slave. It included Miller, Adams, Lockett, Dozier and Hicks. He also recruited Orion Wilhoite, saxophones; Charles Bradley, keyboards, and Danny Webster, vocals, guitars.

In 1977, Cotillion released Slave's first album, and they had their first hit single, **Slide. Hardness Of The World** issued later that year, seemed too-hurriedly put together and did little to increase their following. In 1978, **The Concept** gave them a hit single, **Stellar Funk**. Singing background vocals on that album were Steve Arrington and Starleana Young. In 1979, the title track of their **Just A Touch Of Love** album became a hit single. Singing background vocals were Starleana Young and Curt Jones. Steve Arrington sang lead on one of the album tracks, and later became the band's vocalist. After that LP, Washington and Lockett left Slave to put together Aurra, with Starleana and Curt Jones.

1980 brought **Stone Jam** and further hit singles, the title track and **Watching You**. With the hard-core nucleus of Adams, Webster, Miller and Arrington still present, Slave recruited Charles C. Carter, Delburt Taylor and Sam Carter, keyboards; Roger Parker, drums; and Kevin Johnson, guitar. Washington, Lockett, Jones and Starleana continue to contribute to Slave recordings, but Jimmy Douglass, engineer on early Slave albums, has now become co-producer.

Showtime was released in 1981, with Mark Adams' 'talking' lead bass guitar as prominent as ever. Many Slave songs have been created around Adams' phenomenal bass riffs. Where jazz bass sometimes 'walks', Adams' bass goes one step further and 'talks'. More hit singles arrived, including **Slap Shot** and **Wait For Me**.

Recordings:
Slave (Cotillion)
Hardness Of The World (Cotillion)
The Concept (Cotillion)
Just A Touch Of Love (Cotillion)
Stone Jam (Cotillion)
Showtime (Cotillion)

Lonnie Liston Smith

Lonnie Liston Smith was born in Richmond, Virginia in December 1940. His father was one of the original members of the Harmonizing Four, a gospel group that has existed for more than 50 years. At an early age, Smith directed his attentions towards the piano, tuba and trumpet, graduating from Morgan State College, Baltimore, with a BSc in music education.

His first professional job was at the State's Royal Theatre, as pianist in the resident backing band, providing accompaniment to everyone from the Supremes(▶) to Flip Wilson(▶). In 1964, he moved to New York, where he was fortunate enough to play with quite the most spectacular collection of musicians, spending months with one great, then moving on, absorbing different knowledge from each. In 1965, he was a member of Art Blakey's Jazz Messengers, which also included Chuck Mangione(▶). Replaced by Keith Jarrett, he then teamed with Rahsaan Roland Kirk, staying a year, before joining Pharoah Saunders' band. He subsequently

The Best of Lonnie Liston Smith. Courtesy CBS Records.

worked with Norman Connors(▶), Stanley Turrentine(▶) and Gato Barbieri.

In 1972, Smith began an 18-month gig with Miles Davis'(▶) band, recording on Davis' **On The Corner** and **Big Fun** albums. Following the experience, Smith felt he was ready to lead his own group and he formed the Cosmic Echoes which, initially, was made up of David Hubbard, saxophones/flute; Lawrence Killian, percussion; brother Donald Smith, flute/vocals; and Smith himself, keyboards.

His music has always been so fused, it would be impossible to categorise it. Following on from his lengthy apprenticeship, and then moving into the ever-changing commercial jazz market, the only constants in Smith's music have been that it is electronic, percussive and free. Unaffected by any desire to obtain a pop single, Smith has moved from company to company, making albums that sold well in jazz circles, and have frequently crossed-over into discerning disco-goer territory.

Recordings:
Renaissance (RCA)
Loveland (Columbia/(CBS)
Exotic Mysteries (Columbia/
  (CBS)
A Song For The Children
  (Columbia/(CBS)
Love Is The Answer (Columbia/
  (CBS)

Solar

Dick Griffey was born in Nashville in 1941. He attended Tennessee State University where, because he was a 230-pound natural, he played football for the university, but his problem was, in his words, that 'I never wanted to play on the team, I wanted to own it', so he dropped out and joined the Navy. He was stationed in Southern California, and after being discharged in 1961 he decided to settle in Los Angeles.

In 1966, along with an old school friend, Dick Barnett, he opened a 500-seat nightclub in LA called 'Guys And Dolls'. Barnett, then player-coach with the New York Knickerbockers basketball team, was hesitant at first because they didn't have money to finance the venture properly. Griffey, though, talked to three white lawyer friends —Sol Grayson, Melvin Belli and Sam Brody—and persuaded them to finance the opening. The nightclub, also a live venue, with Griffey as its entertainment manager, booked major acts such as the Impressions(▶), the Four Tops(▶) and the Temptations(▶); these concerts proved successful. Griffey turned his hand to large-venue promotions and soon became a

major promoter in LA, eventually graduating to Stevie Wonder's(▶) world tour of 1974.

'Soul Train', the American television music programme, was the financial responsibility of Don Cornelius, another black Los Angeles entrepreneur, who hired Griffey as his 'talent coordinator' in 1973, and Griffey booked acts for this syndicated show. In 1975, having taken the ratings of Cornelius's programme in an upwards direction, Griffey suggested they move into the record business. The two of them assembled the Soul Train Gang, Soul Train Records, and recorded a new theme for the show, **Soul Train '75.** The company signed the Whispers(▶), Shalamar(▶) and Carrie Lucas(▶), and on the strength of these moves, RCA Records agreed to begin distribution dealings with Griffey.

RCA had given Soul Train Records a $200,000 advance; by the summer of 1977 the company was $50,000 in the red. Early in 1978, Cornelius said he wanted out, so Griffey agreed to buy Cornelius's share off him gradually (Griffey has already completed that buying off). Later in 1978, RCA agreed to pay overhead and recording costs, and Griffey changed the the label's name to Solar (Sound Of Los Angeles Records).

In 1980, Griffey packaged a 70-city tour under the banner of 'The Solar Galaxy Of Stars', which encompassed the Whispers, Shalamar, Lakeside(▶), Dynasty(▶), and compere Vaughn West. Of the 60 people involved on the tour, 40 were musicians. It was a sophisticated and brilliantly budgeted version of the Motown Revue concept.

Griffey, as well as releasing a gospel album by his mother, Juanita G. Hines, has designed his roster so that none of his acts is similar. He has one female solo singer, Carrie Lucas; one male vocal quintet, the Whispers; one two-man/one-woman vocal trio, Shalamar; one two-woman/one man vocal trio, Dynasty; one eight-piece male vocal and instrumental group, Lakeside; one eight-piece female vocal and instrumental group, Klymaxx; one Rose Royce-style group, Midnight Star; one Chic-style group, the Sylvesters. Griffey's stage compere, Vaughn West, is also signed to the label; he is a

stand-up comedian in his own right.

Griffey has always maintained, 'Companies are built on hit acts, not hit records.' In order to develop his acts, he appointed a house producer, Leon Sylvers III, and keeps the label a minimal organisation, with his artistes playing and singing on each other's records. Sylvers was orginally a member of the Sylvers(▶) in their first incarnation as an eight-piece pop/soul outfit.

Since 1980, the year in which Shalamar's **The Second Time Around** and the Whispers' **And The Beat Goes On** became Solar's first million-selling singles, the company has doubled in size, and has achieved seven gold albums and one platinum. Griffey's attitude to the black music industry has remained constant throughout. He has said, 'Music is the greatest natural resource the black community has,' and was also quoted as saying, 'When I promote a concert, black kids put out my posters. If I have a party, blacks cater my party. I place tickets in the black stores and advertise their names on the radio. All black business people have a responsibility to help money circulate in black areas'.

In 1981, Solar moved to Elektra/Asylum for their distribution, Griffey's logic behind this being that Elektra/Asylum 'had no penetration in the black music market'; Solar would be the only soul music they would be representing; Solar would receive special · attention administered with a fresh approach.

As was Motown in the '60s, and Philadelphia International in the '70s, Solar is poised to become the hit-making factory of black music in the '80s. Griffey has said, 'If I sign a single artist, I expect him to sing like Donny Hathaway(▶), write like Stevie Wonder, dance like Fred Astaire, and look like Adonis.'

Stargard

Stargard were, initially, a three-piece vocal group consisting of Rochelle Runnells and Debra Anderson, from Los Angeles, and Janice Williams from Little Rock, Arkansas. Rochelle had gone to see Undisputed Truth(▶) at LA's Starwood nightclub, and there she

met their writer/producer Norman Whitfield(▶). At that same time, Rochelle had become one of Anthony Newley's backing singers. Newley's agent told Rochelle to find another girl, and she chose Debra. After touring the States, Debra left, and was replaced by Janice Williams. Soon after, Norman Whitfield rang the girls, and told them he wanted to form another group. The girls contacted Debra and Stargard was born.

Produced by Whitfield, the girls recorded the theme song for the Richard Pryor film, *Which Way Is Up?*, which became a big hit, and an album — **Starguard** — showcasing

What You Waitin' For. Courtesy MCA Records.

their talents was released in 1978. Fast on the heels of that came **What You Waitin' For.**

In 1979, they changed labels from MCA to Warner Brothers, and the trio appeared as the Diamonds (as in **Lucy In The Sky With . . .**) in the film of *Sgt. Pepper's Lonely Hearts Club Band*. In 1980, their third album, **Changing Of The Gard,** came out. Debra left the group soon after, but Rochelle and Janice recorded a fourth album, **Back 2 Back**, released in July 1981.

Recordings:
Stargard (MCA)
What You Waitin' For (MCA)
Changing Of The Gard (Warner
  Brothers)
Back 2 Back (Warner Brothers)

Candi Staton

One of the greatest exponents of the Southern 'deep soul' style of singing, Candi Staton was born in Hanceville, Alabama, and joined a girl gospel quartet at the age of five, graduating at 10 to the professional Jewel Gospel Trio and travelling throughout the Southern States.

In 1968, her brother took her along to '27-28a', a black club in Birmingham, Alabama, and got her to go up on stage. She sang the only secular song she knew, Aretha Franklin's(▶) **Do Right Woman,** and her performance brought her a booking for the following week. The headliner on that date happened to be the blind soul singer Clarence Carter(▶), who took her under his wing and eventually made her his wife.

Carter took his protégée to producer Rick Hall, boss of Fame Records, the original Muscle Shoals(▶) label, and she had an immediate US smash with her debut record **I'd Rather Be An Old Man's Sweetheart,** quickly following through with the superlative

Left: Stargard's stage show is superbly sensual.

I'm Just A Prisoner album.

When Fame's distribution deal with Capitol ended, Hall signed his label to the United Artists stable and though Elvis Presley had already enjoyed a massive hit with his version of the Mac Davis song **In The Ghetto** this did not stop Candi from notching a million-seller with her reading of it. From the same era, her definitive version of Tammy Wynette's **Stand By Your Man** showed just what a good Southern soul sister could make out of a class country song.

Her marriage to Clarence Carter at an end, Candi signed to Warner Bros and switched producers. Under Dave Crawford (renowned for his work with Wilson Pickett(▶)), her material became more urban in feel and tracks like her big hits **Young Hearts Run Free, Nights On Broadway** and **Victim** (the latter thanks to an extended 12-inch version remixed by Jimmy Simpson) became disco favourites. In 1982 she revisited the Presley songbook to hit with **Suspicious Minds**.

Recordings:
I'm Just A Prisoner (Capitol)
Young Hearts Run Free (Warner Bros)
House Of Love (Warner Bros)
Chance (Warner Bros)
Candi Staton (Warner Bros)

Above: Candi Staton has had single successes in the early '80s.

Steel Pulse

Handsworth Wood Secondary School, Birmingham, was the spawning ground for one of Britain's most imaginative and attractive reggae groups. Aligned to the punk movement of the late '70s, Steel Pulse fought hard to win greater stature and acceptance for UK reggae, which until then had been scorned as a diluted interpretation of Jamaican reggae.

Hinds, Gabbidom and McQueen were the original nucleus of Steel Pulse, advancing their craft in the local clubs and pubs of Birmingham. Determination and discipline resulted in the financing of their first single in 1976, **Kibudu, Mansetta And Abuku**, a song to link black youths of Western urban ghettos to their spiritual homeland, Africa. It was issued by a small independent label, Dip.

During the following 12 months other neighbourhood friends were brought in to bring the Steel Pulse

Above: Steel Pulse's Riley and Martin doing their Klan-bashing.

line-up to more or less what it is today: ex-funk band drummer Steve Nesbitt; Selwyn Brown, keyboards; Fonso Martin, vocals and percussion, and Michael Riley, vocals. Six strong, the group set about writing new material and designing stage costumes that were to present them in a uniquely visual manner, previously unheard of for reggae groups. They used convict uniforms, African robes, a pageboy suit and a preacher's gown and dog-collar!

Already the British rock press was showing interest in the group and later in 1977 they were invited to appear before a punk audience at London's Vortex Club. Their clipped rhythms and chanting harmonies, propelled by Hinds' angst, falsetto lead-vocals and songs that echoed the spirit of punk, quickly assured them of a sizeable white following. Frequent appearances at the Hope And Anchor, another punk venue of that time, were captured for posterity in 1978 with their inclusion on the Front Row Festival double album.

Anchor Records released their second single **Nyah Love** but it was in November 1977, while supporting Burning Spear(▶) on a nationwide tour, that the group was introduced to a mass reggae audience. Island Records, who had previously largely concentrated on Jamaican reggae, signed up the band and financed their debut album, **Handsworth Revolution**. This excellent set was the sum total of their then stage repertoire, with such fine songs as **Sound Check, Prodigal Son, Prediction, Macka Splaff** and **Ku Klux Klan,** for which Riley and Martin would don Klan costumes.

Riley's ignominious departure soon after the album's release, officially attributed to unreconcilable musical differences, found the group relying more upon Hinds and, in an attempt to draw a stronger black audience, carrying the banner of Rastafari. Increased African spiritual consciousness didn't stop Hinds from writing more songs of black political emancipation for a second album, **Tribute To The Martyrs.** A European tour with Bob Marley(▶) and the Wailers(▶), frequent benefits for Rock Against Racism and appear-

ances on UK television, which had clocked the reggae/punk alignment, kept them in favour and in work.

The release of a third album, **Caught You,** in 1980, and an only moderately successful tour with Jimmy Lindsay(▶) were the last to be heard from Steel Pulse. Undoubtedly ahead of their time, and caught between a roots reggae and rock audience, Steel Pulse returned to Handsworth to consider carefully their next move.

Recordings:
Handsworth Revolution (—/Island)
Tribute To The Martyrs (—/Island)
Caught You (—/Island)

Amii Stewart

Amii Stewart, a statuesque beauty from Washington DC, began acting at her local repertory company at the age of 16. As an actress, dancer and singer, she has appeared in feature films and stage musicals. Having come to London with the musical *Bubbling Brown Sugar*, Amii remained resident in the city, her career taking a slight change in direction, as she established herself as an international cabaret star.

Signing up with Hansa/Atlantic(▶) in 1978, she enjoyed worldwide disco hits with remakes of Eddie Floyd's(▶) **Knock On Wood** and the Doors' **Light My Fire.** Ironically, Floyd made more money as writer of the song than he had with his own version.

Recordings:
Amii Stewart (Hansa/Atlantic)
Paradise Bird (Hansa/Atlantic)

Stuff

Stuff—Gordon Edward, bass; Richard Tee, keyboards; Cornell Dupree, and Eric Gale, guitars; Christopher Parker and Steve Gadd, drums/percussion—is a permanent but part-time aggregation of New York's finest session musicians, whose music is a delight for anyone

Right: Stuff's Richard Tee, who's recorded solo, too.

who appreciates tasteful but funky musicianship. As session men, members of Stuff have individually played with just about every big name in rock, pop and soul, including Aretha Franklin(▶), Roberta Flack(▶), King Curtis(▶), Donny Hathaway(▶), Gladys Knight(▶), Paul Simon, John Lennon, Van McCoy(▶), James Brown(▶), Chick Corea(▶), George Harrison, Tom Scott(▶) and Quincy Jones(▶). As a group they have enhanced the efforts of artists like Al Jarreau(▶), Jimmy Witherspoon and Joe Cocker.

The seeds of Stuff were sown in the early '70s with Gordon Edwards' band Encyclopedia of Soul, and the current line-up has crystallised over the last few years. The band has been extremely successful as a New York club attraction and a festival favourite, and three members—Cornell Dupree, Eric Gale and Richard Tee—have recorded solo albums. Stuff's Warner Bros albums cover a wide range of material, but the playing is consistently inventive, cohesive and technically masterful. Unusually, the band tends to eschew massed electronics in favour of the natural sounds of their instruments.

Recordings:
Stuff (Warner Bros)
More Stuff (—/Warner Bros)
Stuff It (Warner Bros)

The Stylistics

From 1972 to 1977, the Stylistics recorded 17 hit singles which firmly established them as the No.1 vocal group of the decade, and although the last few years have been lean as far as chart success is concerned, their recent signing to Philadelphia International(▶) (and reunion with producer Thom Bell(▶)) augers well for the future.

Formed from a collaboration of two Philadelphia groups, the Percussions and the Monarchs, the Stylistics began recording for the Sebring label, before moving to Avco. Their first single under the Avco banner was **You're A Big Girl Now** (1970), which, despite its loose arrangement and archaic drum sound, was full of the smooth, powerful high tenor of Russell Tompkins Jr, a sound which immediately became the unit's trademark.

The introduction of Thom Bell to the producer's chair for **Stop Look & Listen** added the necessary artistry and sophistication to the Stylistics' vocal sound, although they had to wait for **You Are Everything** (1971) before achieving

top-10 status in the USA—the single was not a hit in the UK. **You Are Everything** was taken from **The Stylistics** album, which subsequently spawned **Betcha By Golly Wow**, breaking the group in Britain, and providing them with another top-10 45 in the US.

The Thom Bell/Stylistics partnership was maintained through until the summer of 1974—producing **I'm Stone In Love With You, Break Up To Make Up, Peek-A-Boo, Rockin' Roll Baby** and the majestic **You Make Me Feel Brand New**, a fitting finale to their work together.

Moving under the production aegis of Avco bosses Hugo and Luigi, already renowned for their work with Sam Cooke(▶), and with

Rockin' Roll Baby. Courtesy Avco Records.

arrangements by Van McCoy(▶), the Stylistics maintained their chart impetus, scoring immediately with **Let's Put It All Together** (1974) and keeping the association fruitful with **Star On A TV Show, Sing Baby Sing, Can't Give You Anything (But My Love)**, a UK No.1 in the summer of 1975, **Na Na Is The Saddest Word, Funky Weekend, Can't Help Falling In Love, 16 Bars, You'll Never Get To Heaven** and **7000 Dollars And You.**

Although much of the emphasis is focused towards Tompkins (born March 21, 1951), they are an all-round vocal outfit—witness their superior stage show—with talent in every department, particularly with the raw-edged tenor of Airrion

The Best Of The Stylistics. Courtesy of Avco Records.

Love (born October 8, 1949). Tompkins and Love went to school together, before joining the Monarchs in 1965. The other Philadelphia native was James Dunn (born February 4, 1950), who left in the late '70s. The line-up was completed by New Yorker James Smith (born June, 1950) and Herbie Murrell, from South Carolina (born April 27, 1949).

The Stylistics' recent album **Closer Than Close** is their second for the Philly International label, and with material again provided

by Bell (with Dexter Wansell), their star must surely soon be in ascendance once again.

Recordings:
The Stylistics (H&L/Avco)
Best Of The Stylistics (H&L/Avco)
Best Of The Stylistics Vol.II (H&L)
Rockin' Roll Baby (H&L/Avco)
Hurry Up This Way Again (Philadelphia International)
Closer Than Close (Philadelphia International)

Sugarhill

New Jersey-based Sylvia and Joe Robinson have been in the music business since the '50s (she had a million-seller with **Love Is Strange** as half of Mickey and Sylvia, with Mickey Baker(▶). They formed All Platinum Records and subsidiaries Turbo and Stang which released hit products from the Moments(▶), Linda Jones(▶), the Whatnauts, George Kerr, Rhetta Young, Chuck Jackson(▶), Brook Benton(▶), Shirley & Co (led by the Shirley of Shirley and Lee(▶) fame), Brother To Brother, and Donnie Elbert(▶). Sylvia herself had a new hit single in 1973 with **Pillow Talk,** an extremely sexual soul song, complete with cooing and groaning; a foretaste of the Donna Summer(▶) market that was soon to open up.

Dragged to a niece's birthday party at the Harlem World Disco,

Sylvia's imagination was set aflame by three young guys rapping down the microphone. Having created a new label, Sugarhill, she signed the boys up, gave them a rhythm and a name—the Sugarhill Gang—and created a new trend.

Sugarhill's initial and very substantial profits were made from that record, entitled **The Rapper's Delight**, a massive worldwide hit in 1979. The three young rappers were Wonder Mike, Master Gee and Big Bank Hank—real names Michael Wright, Guy O'Brien and Henry Jackson, respectively.

'Rapping' is the art of reciting rhyming couplets about topical subjects, using plenty of colloquialisms, over the top of strict 4/4 funk. Rapping began in American discotheques, with DJs talking through instrumentals or breaks. Fairly soon, popular rapping DJs were taken into studios and, using established or new rhythms, they'd cut records. **The Rapper's Delight** utilised Chic's(▶) **Good Times** rhythm, a superb backing track, and a major contributory factor to the success of the record.

Since that first release in late 1979, the Robinsons have signed other artists, both rapping and singing acts, with Grandmaster Flash and the Furious Five beginning to outshine their revolutionary brothers. One record in particular, **The Adventures Of Grandmaster Flash On The Wheels Of Steel** (1981), involved not only the con-

ventional rapping over a rhythm, but passages from Blondie's **Rapture** and Queen's **Another One Bites The Dust,** which Flash slotted into the mix. To make the single even more unique, and while still keeping to strict tempo, Flash stopped and started and repeated his mix, giving it an unnerving juddering effect.

Other signings to the label include Ferrari, Spoonie Gee, The West Street Mob, and Candi Staton(▶).

Donna Summer

Born in Boston, Massachusetts, in September 1950, Donna was one of six church-going children. She dropped out of high school, determined to be a singer, and left family comforts behind to tour with a white rock group called the Crow. Having played all round Boston, they got a gig at New York's Purple Onion club, but realised there was no future for them, and split up.

Melba Moore(▶), soon to leave the Broadway production of *Hair*, needed a replacement, and Donna auditioned. Although failing to get Melba's job, Donna was offered a part in the German production of the show. Following that, she appeared in *Godspell, The Me*

Below: Star-spangled Donna Summer . . . incurred the wrath of US moral societies.

Nobody Knows, and *Porgy And Bess.* After travelling round Europe, Donna settled in Mannheim, Germany.

In 1975, Oasis Records producers Giorgio Moroder and Pete Belotte were cutting an album with Donna, and she was repeating the phrase 'love to love you baby', a line from another song. Moroder and Belotte decided to lay tracks behind Donna singing that line, a backing track that transformed the song into a 16-minute 50-second epic, much of it singing, more of it moaning and groaning. This simulated orgasm, combined with the metronomic and electronic keyboard-centred disco rhythm, gave the song enormous notoriety.

Love To Love You Baby was banned from some radio stations, but having been picked up by Casablanca Records for American distribution, within weeks it sold 200,000 copies in New York City alone. Casablanca boss Russ Regan had been sent a copy of the record from Germany and forgot about it until someone dug it out from his collection during a party and it created a sensation, leading him to pick up the rights. Moral societies and feminist groups alike condemned the record, but it went straight to No.1 in many countries.

There then followed a series of sex-orientated albums, maintaining the sensual arrangements, but containing sparkling melodies that made Donna Summer the queen of the '70s disco boom. With little manipulation evident, Donna and her record company began exploiting her face and body and collectively created a brilliantly effective image of total innocence and charm running alongside blatant sexuality. Using what are widely believed to be the dreams of young girls, Donna ensured her audiences were not purely male, singing songs influenced by the romance of Cinderella and Sleeping Beauty.

On-stage, her highly feminine costumes and stunning choreography were beguiling. As her music matured, and robot-disco went out of fashion, Donna's computer tunes began to be interspersed with more traditionally arranged popular funk. In 1979, she attained two No.1 albums and two No.1 singles, as well as starring in the movie, *Thank God It's Friday* —from which a soundtrack album was released—a role that involved light acting and singing, and also featured the Commodores(▶).

Her singles, **I Feel Love, Down, Deep Inside, I Love You, The Last Dance, MacArthur Park** and **Heaven Knows,** were the prelude to her finest moment, a double-set called **Bad Girls.** Featuring some of America's best musicians, it included the hits **Hot Stuff, Bad Girls** and **Dim All The Lights,** and contained more of the human element associated with soul. Donna has never been acclaimed as a great singer, but the quality of her material and image have ensured that her records are constantly played in clubs and on radio stations.

In 1979, she duetted with Barbra Streisand on the one-off hit single, **Enough Is Enough.** In 1980, she signed to Geffen Records, recording **The Wanderer** on which her writing skills were given more exposure, with Moroder and Belotte still at the helm.

Recordings:
Love To Love You Baby
(Casablanca)

A Trilogy Of Love (Casablanca)
Four Seasons Of Love
(Casablanca)
I Remember Yesterday
(Casablanca)
Once Upon A Time (Casablanca)
Live And More (Casablanca)
Bad Girls (Casablanca)
On The Radio (Casablanca)
The Wanderer (Geffen)

The Sylvers

In the mid-'70s, many labels had a 'family' group, an act comprised of real-life brothers and/or sisters, playing commercial R&B, aimed at a very young 'teenybop' audience. In competition with the Jackson 5(▶), Cubie and the Stairsteps and the Osmonds, Capitol Records had the Sylvers, a nine-piece collection of brothers and sisters: Olympia-Ann, Leon Frank III, Charmaine, Jonathan, Edmund, Ricky, Angie, Pat and Foster. This group released several albums and had numerous lesser disco hits.

By 1981, the group had been pruned down to a five-piece, and were signed to Solar Records. Leon Frank III had become house producer, and Charmaine a house songwriter, so Foster, James, Pat, Ricky and Angie became the working act on Dick Griffey's roster developing a sophisticated style in the Chic(▶) mould. They released a magnificent album late in 1981, **Concept.** It was typical Solar with rich melodies, lively instrumentation, smooth vocals and sparkling production.

Recordings:
Concept (Solar)

Sylvester

Sylvester's brand of high-camp was just the ticket for mid-'70s disco, winning him notoriety and some very big hit records which crossed over from the gay scene to appeal to the mass discotheque audience.

Born in Los Angeles, Sylvester was a child gospel star before moving to San Fancisco at the height of 'flower-power'. 'Frisco was then the world centre of psychedelic culture and sexual freedom. Sylvester became a member of a highly camp nightclub group known as the Cockettes, a gig which enabled him to indulge his love of bizarre (and often transsexual) costumes (a role he later played well with a cameo appearance in the Bette Midler movie *The Rose*).

In 1973 he signed to Blue Thumb Records (a label which always had a penchant for the outrageous) but met little success on disc, though his extravagantly staged and highly

Mighty Real. Courtesy Fantasy Records.

flamboyant live appearances started winning a lot of attention. He switched to Fantasy in 1977, together with Grace Jones(▶), who can be credited along with Sylvester as having contributed most to the gay community's part in the '70s disco boom.

A debut album, titled simply **Sylvester,** was a mixture of fashionable disco rhythms and soulful ballads, Sylvester singing most of the time in a falsetto which ideally suited the unique blend of camp and gospel influences. Two of the very biggest songs of the disco era boom, **(You Make Me Feel) Mighty Real** and **Dance (Disco Heat),** were lifted from his second album, **Step Two,** released in 1978.

Sylvester's entourage included two female backing vocalists, Martha Wash and Izora Rhodes, who became known affectionately as Two Tons Of Fun (from their generous physique!) and recorded in their own right for Fantasy. Sylvester can also take credit for bringing another Fantasy star to public notice, Jeanie Tracy, who had also been part of Sylvester's troupe before recording her solo album.

With the waning of the disco boom, Sylvester's albums and singles have been less successful (he has moved on musically, away from a pure disco slant) and he has found greater reward in session singing, contributing to Herbie Hancock's(▶) **Magic Windows** album and Jeanie Tracy's **Me And You.**

Recordings:
Sylvester (Fantasy)
Step Two (Fantasy)
Mighty Real (Fantasy)
Living Proof (Fantasy)
Sell My Soul (Fantasy)

Above: From secretary to Motown star, Syreeta found the Wright track with a blend of soulfulness and sophistication.

Syreeta

Through persistent pursual of Brian Holland—of Holland/Dozier/Holland(▶)—Syreeta got signed to Motown(▶) Records. The label initially took her on as a secretary and back-up singer so that she could be orientated towards Motown's standards and styles. A song written by

The Best Of Syreeta. Courtesy Motown Records.

Ashford and Simpson(▶), originally meant for Diana Ross(▶), called **I Can't Give Back The Love I Feel For You,** was given to Syreeta and, under the name Rita Wright, her debut single was released in February 1968, but made little impression.

Two-and-a-half years later, she was still working at Motown, and feeling ignored, when Stevie Wonder(▶) walked into her office. He'd heard of her singing and songwriting abilities, and he had a song for her called **Win Your Love**. From that studio venture the relationship flourished. Stevie and Syreeta began to write together and by the time of her debut album in 1972 they had fallen in love and married. During the period between the first and second album, released in 1974, their marriage broke up, though they have remained firm friends.

It was another three years before Syreeta cut her third album, but from then on she began to work and grow at a more consistent rate. She re-married, had children, and her fourth album, released in 1977, featured G.C. Cameron(▶), and yielded hit singles.

Set My Love in Motion. Courtesy Motown Records.

Billy Preston(▶) signed to Motown in 1978. He and Syreeta had the same managers who united them for the soundtrack of the film *Fast Break*. The two had previously collaborated on Preston's 1975 **It's My Pleasure** album. Their first official duo album arrived in 1981, although they had seen singles success with **It Will Come In Time** and **With You I'm Born Again**.

Recordings:
Syreeta (Mowest/Motown)
Stevie Wonder Presents Syreeta (Motown)
One To One (Motown)
The Best Of Syreeta (Motown)
Set My Love In Motion (Motown)
Rich Love, Poor Love (featuring G.C. Cameron) (Motown)
Fast Break (with Billy Preston) (Motown)
Billy Preston & Syreeta (Motown)
Syreeta (Motown)

TK Records

This Miami-based group of labels, including TK, Glades, Cat and Alston, was established by white entrepreneur Henry Stone, who had been the most important distributor of black records in Florida and the Southeast USA.

Using K.C and the Sunshine Band(▶), the outfit led by prolific white songwriters H.W. Casey and Rick Finch (who have more than 500 published titles to their credit), supplemented by Latimore(▶), Little Beaver(▶) and other talents, TK churned out a whole flood of first-rate dance material in the early '70s, some leased to major companies like Columbia and Atlantic(▶), but most on the company's own labels.

Sadly, with the disco boom, TK turned its attention increasingly to an effete white-styled form of dance music which proved both an aesthetic and commercial disaster, leading eventually to the organisation's bankruptcy.

Amidst all the dross, though,

were some memorable recordings by Betty Wright(▶), Clarence Reid, Peter Brown(▶), Latimore(▶), Little Beaver(▶), Gwen McCrae(▶) and others.

A Taste Of Honey

At the centre of this group are two young ladies who could have equal success as high-fashion models. Janice Marie Johnson plays bass, and Hazel Payne plays guitar. With the help of Perry Kibble, keyboards, and Donald Johnson, drums, they recorded a debut album in 1978. Their first single, **Boogie Oogie Oogie**, was one of the most popular disco songs of that year.

The girls sing, compose, arrange and co-produce. Discarding the guys, they cut their third album **Twice As Sweet**, which was produced by George Duke(▶) and contained another smash, **Sukiyaki.**

Recordings:
A Taste Of Honey (Capitol)
Another Taste (Capitol)
Twice As Sweet (Capitol)

Tavares

Five natural brothers, Ralph Tavares, (first and second tenor), Arthur 'Pooch' Tavares, baritone; Antone 'Chubby' Tavares, tenor and falsetto; Feliciano 'Butch' Tavares first and second tenor and Perry Lee 'Tiny' Tavares, baritone; come from a large close-knit family.

The boys' father, a multi-instrumentalist, played clubs around the family's New Bedford, Massachussets, hometown and

raised them in a musical environment.

The Tavares are of black Portugese colonial extraction (from the Cape Verde Islands) and home in America was out in the country but the sound the group eventually evolved was to be of pure American city-slick sophistication.

It was elder brother John's idea to form a group. With Ralph, Pooch and Chubby joining him, they debuted in 1962 as the Del Rios. Then Pooch had to take time out for a minor operation and Tiny came in as his substitute. With Pooch back to health it was decided to keep

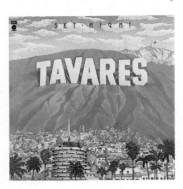

Sky High. Courtesy Capitol Records.

Tiny in the line-up and become a five piece under the name Chubby and the Turnpikes, soon abreviated to simply the Turnpikes.

By 1964 the group was fully professional, working clubs throughout New England, and five years later they got the chance to tour Italy as support act to Lola Falana. Believing foreigners would

have trouble with the name the Turnpikes, the boys decided to adopt their family name as the group's tag and became Tavares.

Returning from the tour they went back on the club circuit until being signed for management by Brian Panella who got them a recording deal with Capitol in 1973.

Johnny Bristol(▶) was brought in to produce their first album and it was a killer—the title track **Check It Out** giving them an immediate hit single.

Fresh from their successes with the Four Tops(▶) and others, the Lambert and Potter team was brought in to produce the **Hard Core Poetry** and **In The City** sets which yielded classic hit ballads in **Remember What I Told You To Forget**, and their first R&B chart-toppers—the mid-tempo **It Only Takes A Minute** and the potent **She's Gone.**

Switching to Freddie Perren's production, their fourth album, **Sky High**, included the hit singles **Don't Take Away The Music** and **Heaven Must Be Missing An Angel** (which quickly went gold, selling a total of more than three-million copies).

From **Love Storm**, the **Who-dunnit** (another R&B gold) and **Goodnight My Love** singles scored, while **Best Of Tavares** was a smash-hit album.

Tavares' seventh album, **Future Bound** (1978), contained their version of **More Than A Woman** which they had performed in the epic disco movie *'Saturday Night Fever'* (which also featured the Bee Gees' original rendition) while their eighth set **Madam Butterfly**, produced by Bobby Martin, featured

Below: Country boys Tavares have shown city slickness in a string of international hits.

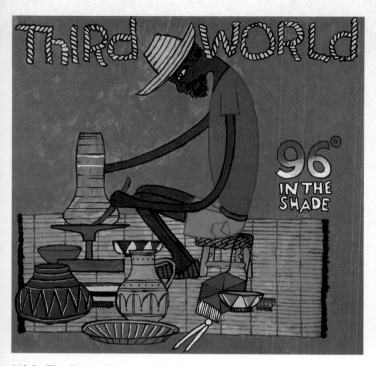

96° In The Shade. Courtesy Island Records.

Never Had A Love Like This Before.

By the close of the decade, Tavares could claim a string of 12 top-15 R&B singles, many of which were also pop hits internationally, and while the '80s opened rather quietly for them, they can be expected to bounce right back.

Unlike most vocal groups who have an elected lead singer (or maybe two sharing that role) with the rest just there to provide back-ups, Tavares share lead vocals among all five members, the choice of voice depending on the needs of the song.

Recordings:
Check It Out (Capitol)
Hard Core Poetry (Capitol)
In The City (Capitol)
Sky High (Capitol)
Love Storm (Capitol)
Best Of (Capitol)

Creed Taylor

See CTI Records.

T-Connection

Receiving most of their exposure in discotheques, T-Connection— now a four-piece group—who originate from Nassau, Bahamas, had their first single release in 1975. In 1977, having signed to TK Records(▶), they scored **Do What You Wanna Do**, which was one of the biggest club records of the year.

Now consisting of Theopilus Coakley, vocals, keyboards, guitars; Kirkwood Coakley, bass, drums; Anthony Flowers, drums; and David Mackey, guitars, they signed to Capitol in 1981.

Recordings:
Magic (TK)
On Fire (TK)
T-Connection (TK)
Totally Connected (TK)
Everything Is Cool (Capitol)
Pure And Natural (Capitol)

Richard Tee

See Stuff.

Third World

The supreme marriage of reggae and R&B took place in Jamaica in 1973 when an early manifestation of Inner Circle(▶) fragmented into those who wished to continue with orthodox reggae and those moving towards a fusion. Principal instigators of the move were Michael 'Ibo' Cooper, keyboards, and Stephen 'Cat' Coore, lead guitar. They were later joined by fellow Jamaicans Bunny 'Rugs' Clarke, lead vocals, Irvin 'Carrot' Jarrett, percussion, and British-born Willie Stewart, drums. Line-up was completed with the enrolment of Richard Daley, bass.

Third World travelled to England in 1975 and were signed up internationally to Island Records. They subsequently joined stable-mates Bob Marley(▶) and the Wailers(▶) on the now legendary British tour that summer, and in the autumn issued a tentative debut album **Third World**. The group spent the following year touring almost non-stop throughout the United States, taking their distinctive brand of uplifting universal reggae to audiences who had previously never seen dreadlocks or heard reggae beat.

With the release of the heralded **96 Degrees In The Shade** album, 1977 found the group concentrating on its home territory, touring the West Indies. The year climaxed with a series of critically acclaimed shows, *Explanations,* at Jamaica's Little Theatre, Kingston. Choreographed by Thomas Pinnock of the Jamaican National Dance Theatre, the show combined all aspects of theatre to illustrate many of the group's most spiritually important songs.

Their creative peak was third album **Journey To Addis**, containing the best-selling single (UK top 10) **Now That We've Found Love.** The record was a superior synthesis of reggae and disco forms. Its sheer exuberance made it appeal across-the-board to the otherwise segregated reggae, soul and pop buyers. Third World consolidated their position in the premier division with headlining European tours.

In 1981 they departed Island and signed a worldwide deal with the CBS organisation, which later issued the insubstantial **Rock The World** album, with mixed critical acclaim and poor sales, though it did spawn classy hit single **Dancing On The Floor** which was more disco than anything in form. However, the year wasn't lost. They played a memorable set at Jamaica's Reggae Sunsplash Festival, joined on stage by Stevie Wonder(▶).

Wonder invited the group to accompany him on a tour of the United States the following year and repaid them by producing their second album for the label, contributing two of his own songs, **Try Jah Love** and **You're Playing Us Too Close.**

Recordings:
Journey To Addis (Island)
You've Got The Power (Columbia/CBS)

Timmy Thomas

Why Can't We Live Together, which featured Timmy Thomas's voice backed by his own hypnotic organ work and nothing else, was surely the most distinctive sounding hit record of 1973. Two years later it was still topping charts in various far-flung territories, having sold more than a million copies.

Born in Evansville, Indiana, on November 13, 1944, Thomas studied music initially under Donald Byrd(▶) and Cannonball Adderley (▶) at the Stan Kenton Jazz Clinic and then reversed the usual black migration pattern by moving south to Memphis where he had a minor success with his debut record **Have Some Boogaloo.** Thomas became resident organist with the city's legendary Gold Wax(▶) label, backing soul hits by James Carr(▶), the Ovations, Spencer Wiggins and others.

After a spell teaching in Texas he moved to Florida where he became one of the first blacks to open a lounge bar in Miama Beach. A meeting with TK Records'(▶) boss Henry Stone led to the recording of **Why Can't We Live Together.** A somewhat smaller hit was **You're The Song (I've Always Wanted To Sing)**, but little has been heard of Thomas since the demise of TK in 1980.

Recordings:
Why Can't We Live Together (Glades/—)
You're The Song (I've Always Wanted To Sing) (—/Polydor)

Carroll Thompson

Born in Letchworth, Hertfordshire, England, Carroll developed her singing at an early age at her local church and devoted her spare time to songwriting. She originally planned to become a pharmacist, but at 16 she abandoned her studies and, following an advertisement in the UK music press, passed an audition with Hansa Records, who were recruiting personnel for Sugar Cane, a band that was being formed to exploit the label's phenomenally successful Euro/disco sound, represented by Boney M(▶) and Eruption(▶). Insubstantial material led to the project being temporarily shelved.

Carroll existed on session-work prior to being introduced to London record-shop owner and reggae producer, Leonard Chin. Their second single, **I'm So Sorry** (1978), her own composition, stormed the male-dominated reggae charts as did the subsequent **Simply In Love.** Dubbed 'The Queen Of Lovers Rock'(▶) she switched labels to S&G in 1980 and with her own production company, and with volumes of her own material, launched the careers of several impoverished East London reggae singers.

Below: Timmy Thomas, from backing keyboard man to solo hitmaker.

Recently, she has proven herself adept at covering a variety of musical styles, evident on her second single for another label, Excalibur, **Smiling In The Morning,** that utilised a hybrid of R&B and reggae rhythms. She is presently poised for well-deserved crossover from ethnic to international market.

Recordings:
Hopelessly In Love (—/S&G)

Linval Thompson

Born in Kingston, Jamaica, but spending much of his youth with his mother in Queens, New York, Thompson entered the music business in his hometown in 1975 with producer Phil Pratt. Much of those sessions remains on the shelf and it wasn't until he sang **Kung Fu Fighting** (not to be confused with the Carl Douglas song) with Lee Perry(▶) that anyone began to take an interest. Even then he had to persuade producer Bunny Lee, who was working in the newly built Channel One Studio, that he was as able as his long-time friend and Lee protégé Johnny Clarke(▶).

Eventually Thompson cut **Don't Cut Off Your Dreadlocks** and later that same year Striker Lee Productions, via Third World in the UK, issued a promising debut album of the same name. Pleased with the Channel One sound, Thompson employed Sly Dunbar(▶) drums, and Robbie Shakespeare, bass, among many noted session musicians, to record his excellent **I Love Marijuana** album in 1976.

Taking an active role in production, he set up the Thompson Sound label to work with other artists. His own music has a distinctly heavy quality and it was inevitable that he should choose to produce DJ/toasters Militant Barry, Ranking Dread and Tapper Zukie(▶). His solo recordings fared well too, the singles **There Must Be A way** coupled with a version of the Delfonics'(▶) **La La Means I Love You, Mister Boss Man** and **Look How Me Sexy** going high in the reggae listings.

He divides his time between his own militant-to-lovers singing and outside production. He is responsible for the epic Wailing Souls(▶) single, **Who No Waan Come** (1981) and Barrington Levy's(▶) **Poor Man's Story** album (1982).

Recordings:
I Love Marijuana (—/Trojan)
I Love Jah (—/Burning Sounds)
Look How Me Sexy (—/Greensleeves)

The Three Degrees

Favoured act of British royalty, the Three Degrees became one of the biggest black acts in the world by going upmarket and emerging as the undoubted queens of the world's cabaret circuit. They are especially popular in Britain and Europe with their glamorous be-sequined gowns, extravagant make-up and gushing show-biz persona.

They had started out, though, way back in 1965, as a pretty gutsy soul group on Swan Records in their native Philadelphia with **(Gee Baby) I'm Sorry,** at which time the line-up comprised Fayette Pickney, Linda Turner and Shirley Porter.

Take Good Care Of Yourself. Courtesy Philadelphia Intl. Records.

Under the guidance of their personal Svengali, Richard Barrett(▶), they were groomed for much bigger things. Taking a leaf from Motown's(▶) book, Barrett schooled them in fashion, posture and speech, as well as in song and dance, aiming them towards the supper-club type of audiences. Turner and Porter didn't stand the pace and were replaced by Sheila Ferguson and Valerie Thompson.

Following some rather less than successful records for Warner Bros, Metromedia and Neptune, the group hit top 30 in 1970 with the stunning **Maybe** on Roulette—a true deep-soul ballad performance of great intensity. More great soul records came on signing with Philadelphia International(▶), kicking off with the funky **Dirty Old Man** (1973) and following through with **Year Of Decision** (also 1973) and the haunting **When Will I See You Again** (1974).

Unfortunately, as Barrett's aspirations for his act's international superstardom came ever nearer to fruition, so the soulfulness of their material diminished, until they ended up singing what is best classified as easy-listening pop music. A switch of labels to Ariola in the late '70s produced a couple of good disco-dance items, but for the most part easy-listening dross filled their songbook.

A reported 1982 split with their long-term mentor Barrett is unlikely to bring any dramatic reversal of policy. After all, having found easy-street after such a long struggle, they can hardly be blamed for sticking with what their public wants, even at the expense of aesthetic considerations.

Recordings:
Three Degrees (—/Mojo)
The Three Degrees (Philadelphia International)
Take Good Care Of Yourself (Philadelphia International)
Gold (Epic)
New Dimensions (Ariola)
3D (Ariola)
Hits Hits Hits (—/Hallmark)

Bobby Thurston

An employee of the US State Department in Washington DC,

Bobby Thurston continued his clerical job even after his first international hit with **Check Out The Groove** in 1980, taking leave to visit the UK for a promotional tour.

His interest in music had started at high school where he was a member of the school band and choir. After graduation he formed his first band, Spectrum LTD, playing congas and singing backup vocals before taking over a lead vocal role when the line-up changed.

Discovered by producers Willie Lester and Rodney Brown, he signed with the disco-orientated Prelude Records, **Check Out The Groove** being culled from his debut album **You Got What It Takes.** Full of sizzling dance cuts, the follow-up album, **The Main Attraction,** received heavy club play on both sides of the Atlantic.

Recordings:
You Got What It Takes (Prelude)
The Main Attraction (Prelude)

Peter Tosh

Original member of the Wailers(▶), alongside Bob Marley(▶) and Bunny (Wailer) Livingstone(▶), Peter Tosh has since carved himself a solo career that expounds his fierce militant breed of Rastafarian rhetoric. Born Peter MacKintosh he was adept at playing the steel guitar, acoustic guitar and keyboards by the time he was 15. In his late teens he moved to the Kingston ghetto, Trenchtown, and met Marley and Livingstone to form the Wailers. From a background of poverty, repression and struggle the Wailers grew strong with their songs of social, political and religious attack. The trio shared equally the writing and arrangement of their music, with Tosh contributing such classic early Wailers' songs as **Get Up, Stand Up, One Foundation** and **400 Years.**

In 1974 the trio split and Tosh set about directing his revolutionary consciousness, which had been largely restrained while with the Wailers. Writing and producing records for the local Jamaican market, Tosh created increasingly

rebellious songs as he continued to exercise the revolutionary spirit inherent in black awareness reggae. Reflecting both personal events and a more universal notion of liberation from oppression, commitment to a cause charactererised the body of his work.

Early in 1975 he was beaten up at the hands of the Jamaican police. That experience prompted him to write and record **Mark Of The Beast,** which was instantly banned by both the major Jamaican radio stations. A long-time advocate for the abolition of marijuana laws, he followed through with **Legalise It.** Also banned by the radio stations, it became an instant hit in Jamaica and created a major cult following. Assisted by his one-time partner Bunny Livingstone, he began work on his first solo album **Legalise It,** early in 1976. This was a powerful testament from one who claimed to be constantly hounded by the authorities for his outspoken views, and his militancy was further emphasised in 1977 with the **Equal Rights** album.

Equal Rights was the most sharp-edged reggae production of its day, and included such memorable titles as **Apartheid, Jah Guide, Africa, Downpressor Man** and **Stepping Razor.** The title cut set the tone of the album: 'I don't want no peace, I want equal rights and justice'. He appealed to all blacks to recognise Africa as their common and true homeland; he warned of the dangerous results of oppression and racism and spoke of the spiritualism of Rastafari.

In 1978 Tosh was again savagely beaten up by the Jamaican police after being arrested on a 'possession of marijuana' charge. Bruised but undeterred, he parted with Virgin Records, who had released his previous work, and pacted with Rolling Stones Records. Jagger and Richard of the Stones were devout reggae fans and, as well as signing Tosh to their label, invited him to support them on an exacting North American tour. Bewildering musically and lyrically to American audiences, who only wanted to bang their heads to their favourite Stones chestnuts, the tour was notable for the teaming of Tosh's rhythm section Sly Dunbar(▶) and Robbie Shakespeare(▶) on drums and bass respectively.

This unit was to become the bedrock of subsequent Tosh recordings as well as developing into the most influential rhythm section to emerge from Jamaica in the '70s.

Tosh debuted for Rolling Stones Records with **Bush Doctor** (1978), a classic album from which was lifted for single release his version of Smokey Robinson's(▶) **(You Gotta Walk) Don't Look Back;** the definitive dub version of this, with Jagger and Richard on backing vocals, was pressed up as a limited edition and never officially released. Previous gems, the publicity from the beatings and a hot new album guaranteed the success of his Christmas UK tour of that year. The title of a track from the **Mystic Man** (1979) album **I Am The Toughest** (Tosh is a karate expert) became the catchphrase of the day and he was dubbed reggae's first lieutenant.

With his beloved monocycle by his side, Tosh came to London in 1981 to speak to the Press as a prelude to a third album for Rolling Stones Records, **Wanted—Dread And Alive,** and gave two shows at the capital's Rainbow Theatre prior to a major European jaunt. Tosh

Above: Controversial Rastafarian Peter Tosh, preaching equal rights and justice.

has softened with age and is prepared to talk less heatedly about the issues that dominate his work. In fact his desire to reach a wider audience instigated his version of the soul love-song **Nothing But Love**, which he duetted with Gwen Guthrie.

Tosh is a powerful, enigmatic figure in reggae who perhaps unwittingly courts controversy. At times capable of producing sublime music, he is a most charismatic artist who still has much to say.

Recordings:
Legalise It (Virgin)
Equal Rights (Virgin)
Bush Doctor (Rolling Stones)
Mystic Man (Rolling Stones)
Wanted—Dread And Alive (Rolling Stones)

Tower of Power

White groups like the Spiders, Loading Zone and the Generation (which became the excellent Cold Blood who cut a classy version of Sam and Dave's(▶) **You Got Me Hummin'**) dominated the Oakland, California, soul scene in the late '60s, while psychedelic bands held sway across the bay in San Francisco. When a new multi-racial 10-strong outfit got together in 1967, they called themselves the Motowns to make it clear where they were coming from, but a change of name two years later to Tower Of Power better reflected their pounding brass-laden style of music.

Tearing the place apart on an audition night at 'Frisco's legendary Fillmore Auditorium, they were encouraged by the venue's influential boss Bill Graham, and then introduced to hot producer David Rubinson, who signed them to his Atlantic(▶) distributed San Francisco label and released their debut set, **East Bay Grease**, in 1970 to critical acclaim but no great sales.

When the label folded the next

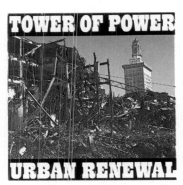

Urban Renewal. Courtesy Warner Bros Records.

year, the group signed to Warner Bros who brought in Steve Cropper of Booker T & the MGs(▶) to produce their **Bump City** LP in Memphis. The album charted nationally and the self-produced follow-up set contained a crop of 1973 hit singles, while their appearances at major rock concerts built a massive live following.

After the 1974 Warner Bros LP **Back To Oakland** they switched to Columbia in 1976. Their **Ain't Nothin' Stoppin' Us Now** and **We Came To Play** sets, the latter again produced by Steve Cropper and taking eight months in the making, brought their total album sales to more than four million units.

Regulars in a steadily evolving line-up were Steve 'The Funky Doctor' Kupka, baritone sax; Greg Adams, trumpet; Emilio 'Mimi' Castillo, tenor sax; Mic Gillette, trumpet/trombone; Francis 'Rocco' Prestia, bass; and, from the second album on, Lenny Pickett, tenor sax; Chester Thompson, keyboards.

Lead vocalists who served with the band included Rufus Miller, Lenny Williams(▶) and Edward MacGhee, while the horn section has recorded with several other artists, notably Elton John.

Recordings:
East Bay Grease (San Francisco/—)
Bump City (Warner Bros.)
Tower Of Power (Warner Bros)
Ain't Nothin' Stoppin' Us Now (Columbia/CBS)
Back To Oakland (Warner Bros)
Urban Renewal (Warner Bros)

The Trammps

The Trammps are a consistent aggregation of originally session singers and musicians from Philadelphia who, after working individually on hits for other artists, got together in the early '70s and for a decade have been established as a leading disco group, though their combined talent and style of delivery give them more lasting value as performers in the R&B idiom than such accolade might suggest.

Their first success came in 1972, when a brisk version of **Zing Went The Strings Of My Heart** made the R&B top 20 on Buddah, distinguished by a vocal arrangement contrasting lead tenor Jimmy Ellis with the bass voice of Earl Young, much in the style of the Coasters'(▶) version of 10 years earlier. **Hold Back The Night**, also on Buddah, met little success on release in the USA, but later became a British hit and a disco anthem of the mid-'70s.

From Buddah, the group moved in 1973 to Golden Fleece, a subsidiary of Philadelphia International, with Ellis and Young supported vocally by Stan Wade, Harold 'Doc' Wade, John Hart and Ron Kersey, while Ron Baker (bass), Norman Harris (guitar) and Earl Young's drumming formed a rhythm nucleus. Brisk numbers like **Love Epidemic**, **Trusting Heart** and **Where Do We Go From Here** produced a string of chart hits, while songs like **Down Three Dark Streets** proved the Trammps to be most able ballad performers.

In 1975 they moved to Atlantic(▶) whereon **Hooked For Life** and **That's Where The Happy People Go** maintained their chart status, and a consistent succession of dance-based LPs have followed, yielding occasional hit singles like **Disco Inferno** and **Don't Burn No**

Bridges. The Trammps now comprise a vocal unit of Jimmy Ellis (lead) Robert Upchurch (baritone) Earl Young (bass) Harold Wade (first tenor) and Stanley Wade (second tenor).

Recordings:
Legendary Zing Album (Buddah)
Disco Inferno (Atlantic)
Mixin' It Up (Atlantic)
Best of (Atlantic)

Tina Turner

From humble beginnings, Annie Mae Bullock, born in Brownsville, Tennessee, on November 26, 1938, rose to worldwide fame as Tina Turner. She aspired to combine sex and soul as a dynamic performer of R&B music, and was placed on a pedestal in the rock world when she starred as the Acid Queen in Ken Russell's acclaimed movie *Tommy*, based on the rock opera by the Who.

After recording and touring with husband Ike, and the Ike and Tina Turner(▶) Revue, Tina had her first solo venture in 1974 with a UA album, **Tina Turns The Country On**, musically enjoyable but a commercial flop. A year later she made the soul charts with **Whole Lotta Love**.

A hiatus followed before United Artists flexed their marketing muscles in 1978 to push Tina in a heavier image with an album tagged **Rough**. When that failed, they brought her to London in 1979 for disco eminence Alex Costandinos to try his hand at producing her in his idiom. The resultant LP, **Love Explosion**, also flopped, so Tina went home, signed an abortive deal with Roadshow, then was heard with Ike again on a Fantasy LP, **The Edge**, released in 1980 and featuring strong bluesy performances on some rock and soul hits.

Recordings:
Tina Turns The Country On (UA/—)
Rough (UA)

Twinkle Brothers

The Twinkle Brothers after a turbulent two-decade existence created renewed interest and increased their record sales in the early 1980s with a team of punchy hit records on their own label that recalled their heyday in the mid-'70s when their effervescent harmonies dominated the charts. The Twinkle Brothers are one Jamaican reggae group that has managed to exist outside of the Kingston music scene. Since 1962 when the group was formed by the three Grant brothers, led by principal songwriter Norman Grant, they have remained a close-knit unit based in Falmouth, Trelawny, on the island's north coast.

Triumphant annual winners of neighbourhood talent shows, in 1970 they embarked upon a fruitful two-year stint with key record producer Bunny Lee; **We Can Do It Too, Not Who You Know** and **Miss Laba Laba** charted, and the group also reaped the rewards of playing for tourists in expensive coastal hotels. In 1975 Twinkle Records Productions released the album **Rasta Pon Top** (they rerecorded the title track in 1981). It revealed them to be an exciting and versatile group with a strong gospel and soul influence within the songs that relied heavily upon

Rasta Pon Top. Courtesy Grounation Records.

the vocal harmony arrangements.

Hit after hit followed and Norman Grant even found time to record a selection of pop-orientated solo records. By 1976 with the release of the **Do Your Own Thing** album Norman Grant was finding greater expression in North American soul music. The album is notable for the doo-wop rendering of a song entitled **Too Late**. Signed to Virgin Records' now defunct reggae subsidiary Front Line, a wealth of new material sprang from Grant's pen. As a unit there were personality clashes which were manifest in the increasingly lacklustre playing. This was overcome for the fine last album for the label **Countryman**.

In 1981 Norman Grant joined Inner Circle(▶), who were robbed of a lead vocalist by the tragic death of Jacob Miller, on an American tour. Internal disputes within the Twinkle Brothers drove Grant to record the patchy **You Know Me** set without the band. Latest reports suggest that all differences have been settled and that new material and a major European tour are in the pipeline.

Recordings:
Rasta Pon Top (Grounation)
Do Your Own Thing (Carib Gems)
Love (Front Line)
Praise Jah (Front Line)
Countryman (Front Line)
Me Know You (Twinkle)

The UK Players

Out of Stevenage, Hertfordshire, come a young band, riding on the crest of the late '70s Brit-Funk wave. Their 1980 debut single, **Everybody Get Up**, was a massive British club hit, as was their follow-up in 1981 **Girl**. A transient line-up now stands at: Jim Ross, vocals/saxophones; Phil Bishop, guitar; Rusty Jones, drums; and Pat Seymour, keyboards. In 1982, they released their first album, the title track **No Way Out** also being issued as a single.

Recordings:
No Way Out (A&M)

The Undisputed Truth

Formed in 1970 as an outlet for Motown's(▶) top producer Norman Whitfield and his songs, the original line-up of the Undisputed Truth was Joe Harris, Billie Rae Calvin and Brenda Joyce Evans. Whitfield was facing criticism for using the same songs with all his notable assigned acts, Gladys Knight(▶), the Temptations(▶) and Marvin Gaye(▶).

Undisputed Truth's self-titled debut album did nothing to change this situation, containing as it did a version of **Smiling Faces Sometimes**, the major song on the Temptations' recently released **Sky's The Limit** album. The Temptations expected it to be their next single but Whitfield released the Undisputed Truth's version scoring a No.1 soul and a No.3 pop hit. The rift between Whitfield and the Temptations took a year to heal and was further aggravated by the release later in '71 of **Face To Face With Truth**, again including songs associated with the Temptations, along with new material like **What It Is**, which was later re-recorded with the Temptations.

The next Undisputed Truth album, **Law Of The Land** included what became their first single from the album, **Papa Was A Rolling Stone**, which peaked at No. 63 on the US pop charts in June 1972. Five months later it was No. 1 around the world for the Temptations. This caused a serious problem for the Truth and the two girls left, leaving Harris and Whitfield to take a little-known group, the Magictones, and turn them into the new Undisputed Truth.

Joe Harris, Tyrone Berkeley, Tyrone Douglas, Calvin Stevens and Virginia McDonald were the new line-up. No tracks featuring them actually appeared until 1974 (during 1973 **Law Of The Land** was a big hit single but 1973's album **Down To Earth** was a mishmash of old material), when the excellent

Help Yourself brought the Truth back to the top. 1974 was also the year of Whitfield's first full realisation of the group's potential with the album **Cosmic Truth**, which was influenced by heavy-rock developments and was in fact too rock-orientated for the US market. 1975's **Higher Than High** was closer to the emerging funk movement.

In 1976 Whitfield quit Motown to set up his own label via Warner Brothers, and took the Truth with him. The debut album on Whitfield Records, **Method To The Madness**, included the brilliant **You + Me Love** and another new line-up who wore wigs and make-up à la Parliament / Funkadelic(▶) and made the group more faceless than ever. After the success of Rose Royce, Whitfield lost interest in the undisputed Truth, who by the end of the decade were virtually forgotten. A sad end for what could have been one of black music's premier outfits.

Recordings:
Smiling Faces Sometimes (Gordy/Motown)
Cosmic Truth (Gordy/Motown)
Higher Than High (Gordy/Motown)
The Best Of The Undisputed Truth (—/Tamla Motown)
Method To The Madness (Whitfield/—)

Below: Tina Turner's solo career did not take off as expected.

Tata Vega

Born Carmen Rosa Vega, on October 7, 1951, in Queens, Long Island, New York, Carmen was nicknamed 'Tata' by her parents because it was the first word she uttered as an infant. Spotted by Berry Gordy, and signed to Motown(▶) Records, her debut album was released in 1976.

One of the few white artists on this label, Tata fuses many styles of music, but delivers with a distinctive and powerful R&B feel, producing commercial music, singing the songs of soul music's greatest writers. One such song, **Give It Up For Love,** taken from her 1979 album **Try My Love,** was a worldwide club hit.

Recordings:
Full Speed Ahead (Motown)
Totally Tata (Motown)
Try My Love (Motown)
Givin' All My Love (Motown)

Village People

An extremely successful offshoot of the late '70s disco boom, the Village People cleverly exploited the intimate connection that there has always been between disco and the gay scene. Each member of the group dressed in the style of a macho stereotype—cop, cowboy, construction worker—and their repertoire consisted of numbers like **Macho Man, In The Navy** and **I'm A Cruiser.**

Until his departure, the group's main asset was lead singer Victor Willis, a Levi Stubbs' sound-alike who helped them appeal to a wider audience, although their success rested solidly on the composing and production expertise of disco Svengali Jacques Morali.

The group's biggest hit was **Y.M.C.A.,** a paean to the hitherto unrecognised virtues of the Christian youth hostels, which charted internationally in 1978. But Village People have never quite recovered from their exposure in Allan Carr's disastrous movie musical *Can't Stop The Music.*

Recordings:
Cruisin' (Casablanca/Mercury)
Go West (Casablanca/Mercury)
Macho Man (Casablanca/Mercury)
Village People (Casablanca/Mercury)
Renaissance (Casablanca/Mercury)

Bunny Wailer

The most enigmatic of the original Wailers(▶), Bunny Wailer is just beginning to be recognised as a major songwriting and recording talent, almost a decade since departing from the group. Only his stubborn character, and his refusal to co-operate with any major recording company, stands between him and international acclaim. His music never falls short of excellence and it should only be a matter of time before he and his brand of reggae music take giant steps forward to widespread acceptance.

Born Neville O'Riley Livingstone in Trenchtown, Kingston, Jamaica, on April 10, 1947, and known locally as Jah B, he grew up under the same roof as Bob Marley(▶), after the latter had moved to the capital to pursue his career in music. Wailer would play percussion, and Marley guitar.

Above: Motown's Tata Vega broke through in 1979.

He quit the Wailers in 1974, after UK and American tours, just at the point when they were about to break internationally. Among his reasons were a dislike of touring (particularly travelling by aircraft) and a deep resentment and distrust of managers. His last recording with the group was the **Burnin'** album (1974) to which he contributed two songs, **Pass It On** (previously recorded as a solo single in 1963 with producer Ken Khouri) and **Hallelujah Time.**

Although still contracted to Island Records, Wailer formed his own Solomonic label and started work on his first solo album, **Blackheart Man** (1976). A deeply spiritual man and a devout Rastafarian, he

Blackheart Man. Courtesy Island Records.

took the title from a popular white term used to describe the 'evil' dreadlock-wearing Rastas, who live in the mountains of Jamaica. A monumental work, it failed to sell in any abundance, a result of his unwillingness to promote it, and a reluctance on the part of Island Records too perhaps, as they had their hands full with Bob Marley and the Wailers.

The set featured performances by Peter Tosh(▶), supported by the other Wailers, and contains two of Bunny W's finest songs, **Fighting Against Conviction,** written after his experiences in jail following a marijuana bust, and **Dreamland,** arguably the most poignant song of Rastafarian repatriation to Africa ever recorded.

With an increasing allegiance to the emancipation of blacks, Wailer returned to the recording studio for two more albums, **Protest** (1977) and **Struggle** (1978) which contained the hit singles **Bright Soul, Rock In Time** and **Power Struggle.** Island Records still had first option to release his material but they anticipated problems selling his spiritual and political philosophies to the rest of the world, thus the two latter sets and a fourth album, **In I Father's House** (1980) were released in the Caribbean only on Solomonic, now based in Retirement Road, Kingston. Wailer would commute there daily from his home in Portland, favouring Harry J's Studio for recording.

Still a close friend of the two other original Wailers, he often shared the same stage with them in Jamaica and in 1979 teamed up with Tosh for the single, **Anti-Apartheid.** Other significant single releases of this period were **Cool Runnings, Cease Fire, Gamblings** and **Tag A War.** These were only available on Solomonic, but sold well on import in both the UK and America.

By the turn of the decade, Wailer's music had undergone a drastic change. Perhaps due to his eagerness to establish Solomonic as the most influential label in the Caribbean, his music suddenly lost much of its introspection, becoming more accessible and ideal for radio programming.

Island took notice and issued the

Rock 'N Groove. Courtesy Solomonic Records.

album **Sings The Wailers** (1980) on both sides of the Atlantic. An invigorating retrospective collection, it found him delving into the Wailers' back catalogue to breath new life into Marley's **Hypocrite** and Tosh's **I'm The Toughest** (both originally circa 1967) and his own **Dancing Shoes** (circa 1966) among others.

An accomplished drummer and a skillful bas guitarist Robbie Shakespeare(▶) has said he learnt his most complex riffs from him), Wailer nonetheless enlists a variety of session musicians, which allows him to concentrate on production and the soulful falsetto voice that was once a cornerstone of the Wailers' sound.

Tribute. Courtesy Solomonic Records.

An early influence was the Impressions(▶) and he has since cut several Curtis Mayfield(▶) compositions. Mayfield's **Another Dance** was chosen for the **Rock 'N Groove** album (1981) which is a celebration of dance and says all there is to say about the thrill of reggae sound systems on the sublime **Dance Rock,** a cacophony of echo and reverb.

Despite inflammatory press reports surrounding his refusal to attend Marley's funeral in May 1981, Marley's death was a profound blow to him. The following year, after a plethora of insubstantial memorial releases, he issued his own **Tribute** album, interpreting many of his ex-colleague's finest moments.

With his music ever more commercial, without the slightest compromise either lyrically or emotionally, and with hints of an African tour, the '80s promise great things for Bunny Wailer.

Recordings:
Blackheart Man (Mango/Island)
Protest (Mango/Island)
Struggle (Solomonic/—)
In I Father's House (Solomonic/—)
Sings The Wailers (Mango/Island)
Rock 'N Groove (Solomonic/—)
Tribute (Solomonic/—)

Narada Michael Walden

Michael Walden was born in 1952 in Kalamazoo, Michigan. Having dropped out of university, he headed West with Deacon Williams and the Soul Revival rock troupe. When that broke up, Walden joined another rock group, the New McGuire Sisters, and moved to Miami.

Progressing out of rock, Walden became interested in the music of John McLaughlin's Mahavishnu Orchestra and the related teachings of McLaughlin's guru, Sri Chinmoy. At a Mahavishnu Orchestra concert in Connecticut, Walden told McLaughlin he'd like to meet his guru. Sri Chinmoy accepted Walden as a disciple, and named him Narada, which means 'Brings light, delight and compassion from heaven to earth and takes back to heaven from earth all of her sufferings'.

In December 1973, McLaughlin asked Walden to play in a new line-up of his band. They recorded **Apocalypse, Visions Of The Emerald Beyond,** which included a Walden composition and his clarinet playing, then, in 1975, **Inner Worlds,** which included four of his compositions. Walden then joined Jeff Beck's band, appearing on **Wired,** which principally featured Walden's songs. Late in 1975, Walden signed to Atlantic Records and, in summer 1976, his solo debut was released.

The **Dance Of Life,** his most recent and commercial set, contained several disco hits, including **Tonight I'm All Right,** and **I Should've Love Ya.** Having mastered the ability to produce a 'hit' sound, Walden became an in-demand producer, called upon by Sister Sledge(▶), Stacy Lattisaw(▶), and Angela Bofill(▶).

Recordings:
Garden Of Love Light (Atlantic)
I Cry, I Smile (Atlantic)
Awakening (Atlantic)
The Dance Of Life (Atlantic)

Dexter Wansell

Dexter Wansell joined Philadelphia International Records(▶) in 1972 as songwriter, arranger and producer for such artists as Billy Paul(▶), The Jones Girls(▶) and Jean Carn(▶). He has also performed similar duties for Archie Bell(▶), Carl Carlton and the Jacksons(▶). He became the conductor of MFSB(▶) in 1981, masterminding their **Mysteries Of The World** album.

In a solo capacity, Wansell's music veers towards a fusion of jazz and commercial R&B. From his third album **Voyager** (1978) came the R&B hits, **All Night Long** and **Disco Lights,** and his fourth album in 1979 gave us **It's Been Cool** and **Sweetest Pain.** Wansell is now predominantly an in-demand creator for other people.

Recordings:
Life On Mars (Philadelphia International)
What The World Is Coming To (Philadelphia International)
Voyager (Philadelphia International)
Time Is Slipping Away (Philadelphia International)

War

Self-proclaimed as 'The Music Band', War have celebrated 10 platinum or gold albums and as many smash hit singles since they were first launched on an unsuspecting world at the instigation of British rock singer Eric Burdon with his **Eric Burdon Declares War** album, on which they were heavily featured and got equal billing, the single **Spill The Wine** being lifted to go gold.

Emerging as an instrumental band on the West Coast in the '60s and recording under varied names, including the Creators, the Romeos, Señor Soul and the Night Shift, the group pruned its then very large membership and became War on meeting Eric Burdon. At that

Outlaw. Courtesy RCA Records.

time the line-up comprised: Lonnie Jordan (born November 21, 1948), keyboards; B.B. Dickerson (born August 3, 1949), bass; Charles Miller (born June 2, 1939), sax; Howard Scott (born March 15, 1946), guitar; Harold Brown (born March 17, 1946), drums; with Papa Dee Allen (born July 19, 1931), percussion, and white harmonica player Lee Oskar (born Denmark, March 24, 1948) being added in time for the two Burdon albums on which the group featured (**Black Man's Burdon** was the second).

Producer Jerry Goldstein, who also manages the band with Steve Gold, helped guide them towards a unique blending of jazz, funk, Afro-Latin, soul and roots R&B, at times highly melodic, at others relying on a hypnotically monotonous rhythm. It placed them firmly in the vanguard of progressive black acts.

Making a major impact on both black and white audiences, War had a memorable jam session in London with Jimi Hendrix(▶) in 1971, the video recording of which still awaits commercial release. It was Hendrix's last performance before his death.

Their first albums away from Burdon, **All Day Music** and **The World Is A Ghetto,** made them United Artists' hottest black act as the '70s got under way, and they kept the pressure up till 1974 when they had a year's lay off as a result of squabbles with management which, happily, were eventually resolved amicably. The title of their next hit single and album,

Below: War, evolving into one of the most progressive black acts.

Why Can't We Be Friends?, was therefore especially appropriate.

In 1975, the compulsive **Low Rider** scored in the US and saw them with a new label in the UK, Island, who gave them their first UK hit with the single the following year. Moving to MCA, the band continued to mine gold with the admirable **Galaxy** set (1977) and **The Music Band** (1979).

By 1980 War's line-up had evolved somewhat, Dickerson having been replaced by Luther Rabb a couple of years earlier, while girl singer Tweed Smith had been added on vocals, Pat Rizzo on horns, and Ron Hammond came in to give War a two-drummer sound. In 1981 the band switched to RCA.

Lonnie Jordan, Luther Rabb and Lee Oskar have all recorded in their own right while with the band, Oskar's **After The Rain** (MCA) set being worth seeking out.

Recordings:
All Day Music (United Artists)
The World Is A Ghetto (United Artists)
Why Can't We Be Friends? (United Artists)
Greatest Hits (United Artists)
Platinum Jazz (Bluenote)
Galaxy (MCA)
The Music Band (MCA)
Outlaw (RCA)

Anita Ward

At present one of the greatest one-hit wonders of all time, Anita Ward was born in Memphis, Tennessee, on December 20, 1957. Her initial singing was in the choir of Rust College, where she graduated with a major in psychology. Frederick Knight(▶) signed her to TK Records in 1978, and in 1979 they released her debut album. This ballad-orientated LP contained the disco song, **Ring My Bell,** which went gold within two-and-a-half weeks of its American release.

Recordings:
Songs Of Love (Juana/TK)

Leon Ware

Detroit-raised Ware has probably one of the best back-room reputa-

tions in contemporary soul, although major success as a solo artist has so far eluded him over the course of four very respectable albums.

As a songwriter, Ware has been responsible for hits by several top soul acts, a proud achievement which began in 1965 when he penned the gold-selling single **Got To Have You Back** for the Isley Brothers(▶). Since 1972, when he recorded his first solo set, **Leon Ware,** for United Artists, he has kept up the twin roles of freelance songwriter and sporadic solo artist, as well as diversifying into production, both for his own albums and those of other artists.

He wrote and produced Marvin Gaye's(▶) 1976 album **I Want You,** and also wrote for Syreeta(▶). Both projects were undertaken while Ware was contracted to Motown(▶) as a staff writer and producer in the mid-'60s to early '70s. Other writing credits include Michael Jackson's(▶) early solo hit, **I Wanna Be Where You Are,** and the Average White Band(▶) hit, **If I Ever Lose This Heaven,** which was originally recorded as a duet by Ware and Minnie Riperton(▶), during Ware's long collaboration with her and husband Dick Rudolph.

Recordings:
Inside Your Love (Fabulous/TK)
Rockin' You Eternally (Elektra-Asylum/WEA)

Delroy Washington

Born in Westmoreland, Jamaica, Washington moved to London in 1960 and at school became interested in music through his close friends Brinsley Forde (Aswad(▶)) and Locklsely Gichie (Cimarons(▶)).

In the early '70s, having been thwarted in his efforts to be a commercial artist, he met Bob Marley(▶) during the latter's debut UK tour and Marley convinced him that he should channel his energies into music. Washington subsequently joined a number of bands: the Mayfields, the Classics and Rebel Rebel.

Marley had introduced him to Island Records' Chris Blackwell who expressed an interest in releasing his fusion of reggae and

Mister Magic. Courtesy Kudu Records.

made **Reed Seed** in 1978, debuting, incidentally, as his own producer.

After dissatisfaction with conditions and promotion at Motown, Washington signed to Elektra, but without first extracting himself from his former deal. Contractual pressure from both labels have resulted in Grover alternating, album for album, between the two. He fulfilled his obligations to Motown with the **Skylarkin'** set in 1980, which ironically, was in fact a far more interesting enterprise than the comparatively flat **Paradise** he had presented to Elektra just a few months earlier.

Washington's biggest chart success came via a sturdy guest vocal performance from Bill Withers(▶) on the song **Just The Two Of Us** from the 1981 album **Winelight**.

Recordings:
Mr Magic (Kudu)
Soul Box (Kudu)
Reed Seed (Motown)
Paradise (Elektra)
Winelight (Elektra)

Sadao Watanabe

Watanabe is the most well-known of a new breed of Japanese crossover jazz artists. Because of the sheer quality of Japanese technology, some Western jazz musicians have chosen to record their albums in Japan, and because that country is so passionate about Western music, its own artists have begun to work with America's jazz greats.

Born in Utsunomiya in 1933, Watanabe began playing the clarinet at the age of 15. Through Japanese labels, and now via Columbia, there are some five Watanabe albums. His 1981 re-

lease, **Orange Express**, featured Dave Grusin(▶), Richard Tee, Eric Gale(▶) and George Benson(▶), while **How's Everything?**, a live set recorded in his home country, included the title disco hit.

Above: Sadao Watanabe puts an oriental slant to jazz-funk

Recordings:
Autumn Blow (Inner City)
California Shower (Inner City)
My Dear Life (Inner City)
How's Everything? (Columbia)
Orange Express (Columbia)

Weather Report

The two founding members and constant figures throughout Weather Report's story are Joe Zawinul and Wayne Shorter. Vienna-born Zawinul studied music at the Vienna Conservatory and then the Berkley School of Music before joining Maynard Ferguson's Band, where he met Shorter. Newark, New Jersey-born Shorter had played tenor and soprano saxophone with Horace

rock. Because of artistic differences, however, the deal fell through and Washington signed with Virgin instead. A sporadic recording and live performer, his last reggae chart hit in the UK was **Magic** in 1980.

Recordings:
Rasta (—/Virgin)

Grover Washington Jr

Born on December 12, 1943, in Buffalo, New York, Grover Washington was the son of a tenor-sax-playing father who introduced him to the instrument when he was 10 years old. Grover was raised and trained in a dedicated and disciplined musical environment, both at home and at the Wurlitzer School of Music where he took evening classes while still at high school. For two years he played baritone with the All City High School Band.

By the age of 14, and in his sophomore year at high school,

Inner City Blues. Courtesy Kudu Records

Washington was investigating the improvisational small-combo jazz of Thornel Schwartz, Larry Young and Don Gardner at a local Buffalo nightspot called the Pine Grill. At 16, he enlisted in a quartet of old school friends, calling themselves the Four Clefs, and with the full approval of his parents, left Buffalo

to take the band on the road. Four years later, they disbanded and Washington began to move around on his own, linking up for a while with organist Keith McAllister to play mostly society-type gigs.

In 1965 he was drafted, but wound up spending his entire two years' service playing in the band at his reporting point, Fort Dix, New Jersey, moonlighting whenever the opportunity presented itself by playing Philadelphia jazz clubs. In '67, Washington moved to Philadelphia and married. There followed a musically inactive period and bouts of depression.

His first break came when a guitarist friend, who was recording with Charles Earland, rang Grover because he needed a horn player to sit in on a recording session and Grover was subsequently invited to go on tour with him. Family responsibilities prevented this but the ball was now rolling and other opportunities cropped up, including recording and live session work with Joe Jones, Leon Spencer and Johnny 'Hammond' Smith. That latter association proved a very valuable springboard as Washington was soon to sit in on an album session with Hammond, under the production aegis of Creed Taylor. Taylor was suitably impressed and signed Washington to an exclusive recording contract with his CTI(▶) label.

It is widely rumoured that Washington got his big break when another of Taylor's stable, Hank Crawford(▶), failed to turn up in time for a recording session. His early albums like **Inner City Blues** won considerable attention thanks as much to superb arrangements as to Washington's solos. It was **Mr May** (1975), a sweet mixture of Washington's precise, even, but not too mannered playing style, a quartet of tightly structured jazz-funk tunes, and Taylor's famous uncanny ability to implant the essence of integritous jazz into a wholly commercial record, which took him to international prominence.

When Washington eventually left CTI he took up a contract with the Motown(▶) label, for whom he

Below: Wayne Shorter reeds the Weather Report!

Silver before joining Ferguson.

The pair went separate ways after leaving Ferguson, Shorter moving to Art Blakey's Jazz Messengers, Zawinul joining Cannonball Adderley's(▶) band (he wrote Adderley's classic **Mercy, Mercy, Mercy**). Shorter then became a member of Miles Davis'(▶) '60s quintet, along with Herbie Hancock(▶), Tony Williams and Ron Carter. In 1969, Davis asked Zawinul to write for his new album, thus Zawinul and Shorter were reunited, both appearing on Davis' **In A Silent Way.**

Weather Report are one of the most important and influential electric jazz outfits. Starting out in 1971 with Shorter, Zawinul, Miroslav Vitous and Billy Cobham(▶), the group has included, at one time or another, Alphonse Mouzon(▶), Airto Moreira, Don Um Romao, Eric Gravatt, Alphonso Johnson, Chester Thompson, Alyrio Lima, Alejandro Acuna and Manolo Badrena, and now consists of Zawinul; Shorter; Jaco Pastorious, bass; Peter Erskine, drums; and Robert Thomas Jr, percussion.

Their main claim to R&B fame is a one-off pop hit single, **Birdland**, taken from their 1978 **Heavy Weather** album. It is a song which has become one of the most radio-played instrumentals of all-time, the least you would expect from a combo that has contained such a breathtaking selection of musicians.

Recordings:
Weather Report (Columbia/CBS)
I Sing The Body Electric (Columbia/CBS)
Heavy Weather (Columbia/CBS)
Night Passage (Columbia/CBS)
Weather Report (Columbia/CBS)

Fred Wesley

See P. Funk.

The Whispers

When this five-piece vocal group were signed to Solar Records, they already had a decade's experience behind them. During the '70s they were one of many vocal groups vying with Motown(▶) acts like the Temptations(▶), the Four Tops(▶), Smokey Robinson(▶) and the Miracles(▶). Recording albums for various labels—Dore, Soul Clock and Chess-Janus(▶)—the group's passion for music and respect for each other held them together.

When Leaveil Degree replaced Gordy Hamilton in 1973, the group was signed to Dick Griffey's Soul Train Records, the forerunner of Solar(▶), and named after the influential 'Soul Train' networked TV show which Griffey co-produced. At present, the group consists of Nicholas Caldwell, Marcus Hutson, Wallace 'Scotty' Scott, Walter Scott and Leaveil Degree. In 1976 the act was switched to Solar, soon releasing a debut which included hit singles such as **Olivia** and **Headlight.**

Twin brothers, Wallace and Walter Scott, both tenors, were born on September 3, 1943, in Fort Worth, Texas. At the age of five they gave their first public performance, basing their style on the jazz vocal groups of the '50s. Growing up in Hawthorne, Nevada, and Los Angeles, the brothers worked as a duo, performing R&B standards.

Nicholas Caldwell was born on April 5, 1944, in Loma Linda, California. As the Whispers' principal songwriter, he decided not to join the Temptations, although he passed an audition for them in 1976. His first professional performance was for Sly Stone(▶), then a DJ in San Francisco.

Leaveil Degree was born on July 31, 1948, in New Orleans. Through singing in numerous street-corner harmony groups in LA, he met Scotty, who remembered him when Hamilton left. Marcus Hutson, born in St Louis, on January 8, 1943, was reared in Los Angeles.

In 1979, Solar had its first gold singles, one of them was the Whispers' **And The Beat Goes On**, taken from their second album **The Whispers.** 1980 was similarly productive, and from their third album came an equally successful single, **It's A Love Thing.** As part of the Solar machinery, the seasoned harmonies of these veterans were now gently laid across the sparkling and infectious rhythm tracks of Leon Sylvers' Solar session players.

As was to be expected, 1981's album release produced a hit, the title track **This Kind Of Lovin'. Love Is Where You Find It** (1982) contained the worldwide hit **In The Raw.** That album, the thirteenth in their career, and their sixth for Solar, was divided in two: side A was 'for dancin', side B was 'for romancin'. The quintet keep an even balance on their two styles, leaving the up-tempo writing to in-house Solar people, but arranging the ballads themselves, as they have been expertly doing for so long.

Recordings:
Headlights (Solar)
The Whispers (Solar)
Imagination (Solar)
This Kind Of Lovin' (Solar)
Love Is Where You Find It (Solar)

Barry White

Emerging from a lengthy career on the West Coast, notably producing with Fred Smith (and arranging) Bob and Earl's(▶) **Harlem Shuffle,** Jackie Lee's(▶) **The Duck** and Felice Taylor's Diana Ross soundalike **I Feel Love Coming On,** and on his own producing Love Unlimited(▶), Barry White established himself in the '70s as a soul superstar. Sadly, after some superb early records, he lapsed in to MOR theatrics, surrounding himself with orchestral overkill and bedecking his huge and ungainly frame with extrava-

Above: Key figure behind Weather Report, Joe Zawinul.

gant flowing clothes and lashings of diamond and gold, like a sort of black Liberace.

Born in Galveston, Texas, in 1944, White was raised in Los Angeles where he sang in the Upfronts. At 17, he entered the music business, arranging for Rampart Records and recording as Lee Barry before touring with Bob and Earl as their road manager.

Mustang/Bronco made him head of A&R in 1966 when he produced Felice Taylor. Upon the label's closure he met and masterminded Love Unlimited (one of whom, Glodean James, became his wife). **Walking In The Rain (With The One I Love)** was an inventively soulful record and gave the group a US No.1 hit on Uni, which led to a strong deal with 20th Century in 1972. Besides his own records and those of Love Unlimited, White also masterminded the massive Love Unlimited Orchestra, who scored with **Love's Theme.**

Astutely, White managed to include a contract for himself in the 20th Century deal and, showing a strong Isaac Hayes'(▶) influence, half-speaking, half-singing in rich warm tones, he scored with **Never, Never Gonna Give You Up, You're My First, My Last, My Everything, Can't Get Enough, Let The Music Play, Just The Way You Are** and other million-sellers, working with arranger Gene Page. This gave him a five-year run at the top during which his sales mounted while his soulfulness declined.

Recordings:
I've Got So Much To Give (20th Century/Pye International)
Rhapsody In White (20th Century/Pye International)
Let The Music Play (20th Century)

Lenny White

Lenny White was drummer for Return To Forever, the electric jazz quartet that included Stanley Clarke(▶), Chick Corea(▶) and Al Di Meola(▶). They released four albums, disbanding in 1976. White was born in New York City, on December 19, 1949. While attending the city's High School of Art and Design, he joined a local combo, the Jazz Samaritans (former members included Grover Washington (▶) and Billy Cobham(▶).

Below: The man they called the black Liberace, Barry White. Commercial success ran with artistic decline.

White was then drummer on Miles Davis' milestone fusion album, **Bitches Brew,** and recorded **Caravanserai** with Santana. His solo career began in 1976 with **Venusian Summer** (Nemperor). A further LP for this label **Big City** was followed by a move to Elektra for **Adventures Of The Astral Pirates.**

White formed Twennynine in 1979, comprising: Skip Anderson, keyboards, Barry Johnson, bass, Eddy Martinez, guitars, and Change(▶) vocalist Tanya Willoughby.

This aggregation have currently recorded three soul-styled albums, with some recent change in personnel including Jocelyn Smith and ex-Roy Ayers(▶) vocalist replacing Willoughby, and the addition of guitarist Steve Williams.

Recordings:
Adventures Of Astral Pirates
  (Elektra)
Streamline (Nemperor)
Best Of Friends (Elektra)
Twennynine (Elektra)
Just Like Dreamin' (Elektra)

Deniece Williams

Deniece grew up in Gary, Indiana, where, still attending high school, she worked in a record shop. The shop owner, after hearing her sing along to records, contacted Chicago talent scouts, who audited her and subsequently signed her to Toddlin' Town Records. Her first single, **Love Is Tears,** was a local hit.

Deniece, despite her minor success, was able to resist show business and enrolled in college, where she began working towards a nursing career. In 1969, Stevie Wonder(▶) heard one of Deniece's singles, and asked her to come on tour with him as a member of his backing group Wonderlove. Taking her young son on the road, Deniece (at the age of 20) toured for 18 months, before retiring to have a second child.

After rejoining the group, Deniece was still not totally sure that music was her profession, and again left, but returned soon after, participating in every Stevie Wonder album between 1972 and 1976, as well as contributing to albums by Roberta Flack(▶), Minnie Riperton(▶), D.J. Rogers(▶) and Weather Report(▶).

In 1975, however, she officially left Wonderlove to concentrate on a solo career in acting and writing. With the intention of selling some material to Earth, Wind & Fire(▶), Deniece sent some demo tapes to Maurice White, who was so impressed that he signed her to his own production company, Kalimba; she also signed a recording contract with CBS.

Her first album, **This Is Niecey,** released in 1977 and produced by White, contained a song, **Free,** born in a studio, and put together while with her Wonderlove compatriots—Susaye Green, Nathan Watts and Hank Redd—which became a worldwide No.1. It was the world's first exposure to Deniece's stunning vocal range. This startlingly mature beginning was a sensitive mixture of up-tempo and down-tempo pop and soul fused with jazz.

The follow-up single, **That's What Friends Are For,** was also a big worldwide hit. Deniece's songs, meanwhile, were being recorded

Above: Deniece Williams displays a stunning vocal range.

by Frankie Valli, the Soul Train Gang, Merry Clayton(▶), The Emotions(▶), Stanley Turrentine(▶), Nancy Wilson(▶) and Freda Payne(▶).

In 1978, as well as recording her second album, she toured internationally, supporting Earth, Wind & Fire(▶). During that tour, Deniece recorded a one-off duet with Johnny Mathis(▶), **Too Much, Too Little, Too Late,** which was another No.1, and prompted the duo to record an album, which was entitled **That's What Friends Are For.**

Having observed a master producer at work, Deniece was ready to co-produce her third album with David Foster and Ray Parker Jr(▶), from whence came the minor hit, **I've Got The Next Dance.** In 1981, leaving production duties to Thom Bell(▶), who radically altered her slick West Coast sound, she released a fourth album, **My Melody.**

Recordings:
This Is Niecey (Columbia/CBS)
Songbird (Columbia/CBS)
When Love Comes Calling
  (Columbia/CBS)
My Melody (Columbia/CBS)
That's What Friends Are For
  (With Johnny Mathis)
  (Columbia/CBS)

Lenny Williams

Lenny Williams was born in February 1945 in Little Rock, Arkansas. When he was 14 months old his family moved to Oakland, California. By the age of 19, he was married with two kids. Every Thursday night, a black radio station sponsored a talent contest at The Music Lounge. Week in and week out Williams went there and won the contest, earning 10 dollars at time to help support his family. One night in the early '60s, Fantasy boss Sol Zance saw him perform and signed him to his label, on which he cut a few singles.

In 1973, Williams became vocalist with the jazz/R&B/rock combo Tower Of Power(▶), staying with them for three years, cutting three albums. The next year he recorded **Lenny Williams** for Warner Brothers, produced by Eugene McDaniels(▶), and **Rise Sleeping Beauty,** produced by Chester Thompson for Motown(▶), neither made much chart impression.

Upon signing to ABC/MCA in 1977, hit albums and singles began to arrive. From his debut came **Shoo Do Fuh Fuh Oooh,** and he scored with **You Got Me Running** and **Midnight Girl** in 1978. Singing an R&B-based mixture of ballads and fast numbers, Williams developed the warm and refined tone which years of varying fortune had given him.

Love Current (1979) yielded **Doing The Loop De Loop** and **Love Hurt Me Love Healed Me;** **Let's Do It Today** a year later gave us **Ooh Child.**

Recordings:
Lenny Williams (Warner Brothers)

Rise Sleeping Beauty (Motown)
Choosing You (ABC)
Spark Of Love (ABC)
Love Current (MCA)
Let's Do It Today (MCA)

Viola Wills

Born and raised in the Watts district of Los Angeles, Viola Wills arrived at her first professional nightclub engagement in her late teens by way of a traditional, gospel church upbringing.

Breaking into recording, Viola was produced by Barry White(▶) on the LA-based Bronco label, in the mid-'60s, where she began to write and arrange her own material. Her international break came when she was personally selected by Joe Cocker to lead the Sanctified Sisters, an ad-hoc backing chorus who accompanied Cocker on his world tour of 1972.

Spurred by her success on the tour, Viola moved to Britain to resume her solo career. At Island Records' studio in the early '70s she cut and album for Goodyear, which was later released in the UK on the Charly label under the title **Without You.** The name was chosen to coincide with the singer's only significant solo success, an airy disco version of the 1957 Patience and Prudence hit, **Gonna Get Along Without You Now,** which made the British charts on the Ariola/Hansa label in 1979.

Recordings:
Without You (—/Charly)

Delroy Wilson

Born in Kingston, Jamaica, on October 5, 1948, Wilson first sang in church and later in local talent shows where he was spotted by Clement Coxsone Dodd who swiftly signed him up to a five-year recording contract at Studio One(▶). His first release was **Emy Lou** on Dodd's D. Darling subsidiary label. He followed with **I Shall Not Remove, Night People** and **Voodoo Man** among others.

By 1963 it was quite customary for ska producers and singers to slag each other off on vinyl, such was the competition, and Prince Buster(▶) was the target for Wilson and Dodd's vitriol on singles **Don't Believe Him, Remember Your Nest** and **Back Biter**. Wilson left Dodd in 1968 to join Bunny 'Striker' Lee's burgeoning hit stable. However, Lee was tied up with producing for the likes of Slim Smith(▶), Roy Shirley and the Uniques, and initially only found time to wax four sides, including a version of the Isley Brothers'(▶) **This Old Heart Of Mine**.

Since then Wilson has been a prolific, if slightly underrated, singer, constantly in the reggae charts, easily adapting from ska to rockers' reggae, and working with practically every Jamaican record producer of merit. A particularly fruitful spell was spent with Lloyd Charmers in 1976 with the issue of a cover of the Wailers'(▶) **I'm Still Waiting**.

More recent single successes include **Thank You For The Many Things, Sharing The Night Together** and **What's Going On**.

Recordings:
Cool Operator (ELS/—)
Twenty Golden Hits (—/Third World)
Sarge (Charmers/—)
Unedited (Hulk/—)
True Believer (—/Carib Gems)

Below: Bobby Womack grooves.

Just As I Am. Courtesy Sussex Records.

Bill Withers

Bill Withers is the epitome of the working man turned star. When picked up by Clarence Avant's Sussex label in 1971 he was still fitting toilets into airliners, and reputedly cut his first album, **Just As I Am**, between shifts. The cover of the album shows him in working jeans and T-shirt, carrying a lunchbox. Throughout his career he has remained unaffected and down to earth, more interested in perfecting his craft than in living the high life, more likely to engage in philosophical discussion than heavy nightclubbing.

As well as toilet fitting, Withers had done a spell in the Navy as a computer operator before hawking a batch of songs around the record companies. Avant signed him and put him into the studio with Booker T. Jones(▶) as producer. Jones co-opted fellow MGs Duck Dunn and Al Jackson and several other session luminaries, and the result was **Just As I Am**, one of the best debut albums of the '70s. Songs like **Harlem, Grandma's Hands** and **Better Off Dead** showed Withers to be a writer of great orginality, while **Ain't No Sunshine** was not only a hit but ended up being covered by everyone from Michael Jackson(▶) and the Temptations(▶) to Roland Kirk. Another distinctive factor was Withers' vocal styling, which combined soulful warmth with an almost folksy feel.

It was obvious that Withers (b. 1938) was far from being just another new soul singer, an impression confirmed by his next album, **Still Bill**. This teamed him with the ace rhythm section of Benocre Blackman on guitar, Melvin Dunlap on bass and James Gadson on drums, a team which became his regular touring band. All the songs were Withers' originals, two of which, the ironic **Use Me** and the gospelish **Lean On Me**, became top-10 hits. The latter song also broke him in Britain.

By now Withers was also playing live dates, displaying a likeably diffident persona and a generally low-key approach. Accompanying himself with workmanlike acoustic guitar, he projected an intimate feeling that was closer to the ethos of the folk-based singer-songwriter than that of the traditionally more aggressive black solo singer.

Further albums for Sussex followed, including a double live set in 1973, **Bill Withers Live At Carnegie Hall**. This repeated most of his famous songs and included a superb anti-war song, **I Can't Write Left-Handed**. In 1975 Withers split from Sussex to join Columbia, since which time his career has been peculiarly fitful. Several albums have yielded little more than pleasant moments, although he garnered considerable success with the single **Lovely Day** in 1978 The last few years have seen him more successful when guesting on other artists' records, such as The Crusaders'(▶) **Soul Shadows** and Grover Washington's(▶) **Just The Two Of Us** (which gained him a Grammy award). However, a man of Withers' undoubted talents can always be guaranteed to be keeping some in reserve, and we will almost certainly be hearing from him in the future.

Recordings:
Just As I Am (Sussex)
Still Bill (Sussex)
Live At Carnegie Hall (Sussex)
'Bout Music (Columbia/CBS)
Making Music (Columbia/CBS)
Menagerie (Columbia/CBS)
Naked And Warm (Columbia/CBS)
Greatest Hits (Columbia/CBS)

Bobby Womack

Bobby Womack (born in Cleveland, Ohio, on March 4, 1944) and his brothers Cecil (who later married Mary Wells(▶)), Curtis, Friendly and Harris sang gospel and got their recording break as the Womack Brothers on the Sar label run by Sam Cooke(▶) and his manager James Alexander. (They first met Cooke on a tour when he was singing gospel with the Soul Stirrers.)

Their first record was the Alexander song **Looking For Love** then, as the Valentinos, they switched to the associated R&B label and in 1962 cut **Looking For A Love** (later a hit for the J. Geils Band and re-recorded by Womack in 1972) and in 1964 sold 400,000 copies of the Bobby Womack-penned **It's All Over Now** (which was covered by the Rolling Stones).

Bobby Womack was working as Sam Cooke's regular guitarist (he plays left-handed), as well as playing on sessions for the Box Tops, Joe Tex(▶), Aretha Franklin(▶), Ray Charles(▶), the Sweet Inspirations, rock star Janis Joplin, jazzman Gabor Szabo and Jimmie and Vella (which session featured an incredibly short but brilliantly con-

Above: Betty Wright grabbed her lucky break with both hands.

ceived Womack guitar solo on **Heartbeat**, which he also produced). He wrote several hits for Wilson Pickett(▶), including **Midnight Mover**.

When the Valentinos folded after Cooke's death, Womack started to develop his own solo career, having little success with releases on Him, Checker, Atlantic(▶) and Keymen, but making an impact when he switched to Minit in 1967 with two albums in a strange mix of imaginative originals and re-worked MOR standards, having a hit with **Fly Me To The Moon**.

Moving to Minit's parent label United Artists in 1971, Womack gained confidence and increasingly concentrated on his own compositions (apart from a one-off venture with an album of country songs), recorded in a thoroughly contemporary way with extended instrumental passages and preaching-style raps.

The early to mid-'70s produced his best work, such as the **Communication** LP (1971), the **Understanding** LP (1972), which included **Harry The Hippie**, **I Can Understand It** (1972), **Check It Out** (1975) and the score for the black thriller movie *Across 110th Street*. His output became slightly stilted and cliché-ridden in the late '70s, but he showed a spurt of new vitality as black music moved into the '80s and, now recording for Columbia, regained lost ground and re-established his role as one of the most respected artists in black music.

Recordings:
Communication (United Artists)
Understanding (United Artists)
Original Score: Across 110th Street (United Artists)
A Portrait Of Bobby Womack (United Artists)
Facts Of Live (United Artists)
I Can Understand It (United Artists)

BW Goes C & W (United Artists)
I Don't Know What The World Is Coming To (United Artists)

Betty Wright

Betty Wright was just 11 years old when she turned up at a Miami record store to collect a copy of Billy Stewart's(▶) **Summertime** which she had just won in a radio station competition. Happily singing the song's tune, she was approached by two men who turned out to be singer Clarence Reid and his production partner Willie Clarke, who took her home to Mama and offered a recording deal!

Born in Miami on December 21, 1953, Betty had a musical background, working in the family spiritual group Echoes of Joy, with her four brothers and one sister, from the age of three. Sister Jeanette went on to become a member of Fire and sing back-up vocals for K.C. & the Sunshine Band(▶), while brother Phillip has played guitar with King Curtis(▶) and the Kingpins, Junior Walker(▶) and the All-Stars and in Betty's own band.

Travelin' In The Wright Circle. Courtesy Alston Records.

Signed to Reid and Clarke's Deep City label, Betty enjoyed a regional hit with **Paralyzed** when 13, and in 1970 was the only black performer, the only American performer, the youngest performer and the only performer to sing in both Spanish and English at the

Betty Wright. Courtesy Epic Records.

Spanish Fiesta in Caracas, Venezuela, earning herself spots on two major South American TV shows. She was presented with her first gold record on her 18th birthday.

Easing off to concentrate on her school studies, she was suddenly thrust back into prominence in 1978 when Clarence Reid cut her for his Alston label on the infectious **Clean Up Woman**, which became a massive hit. Signed to co-host a weekly TV talk and music show in Miami, she was five years into a show-business career before she had even graduated. Her precocious talent has continued through a run of superb albums and hit singles.

Recordings:
Explosion (Alston/RCA)
This Time For Real (Alston/—)
Live (Alston/—)
Travelin' In The Wright Circle (Alston/—)

Phillipe Wynne

Given the importance of this golden-voiced singer's contribution to the Detroit Spinners(▶) during a six-year tenure as lead vocalist, from 1971 to 1977, his attempted solo career has been markedly disappointing.

The joyously uplifting quality

and unusual phrasing of Wynne's voice characterised many of the Spinners' greatest hits, including **Could It Be I'm Falling In Love**, **Games People Play**, **One Of A Kind (Love Affair)** and the famous duet with Dionne Warwick(▶) on **Then Came You.**

Detroit-born Wynne cut an avuncular, rather than dashing, figure as a solo artist, and his first release on Cotillion Records in 1977, **Hats Off To Mama,** was accorded a tepid reception.

Recordings:
Starting All Over (Cotillion)

Tapper Zukie

Militant Jamaican reggae DJ Tapper Zukie made his vinyl debut shortly after his arrival in the UK in 1973 when, as operator/toaster of the Viego sound system, he was approached by Ethnic Fight label boss, Larry Lawrence. Fruit of those early sessions was the single **Jump And Twist.** Another London-based producer, Clen Bushay (aka The Bush Ranger), then worked with him on the splendid **Man Ah Warrior** album. They followed through with singles **Feeling High Version** and **A Message To Pork Eaters.**

Poor record sales led to his return to Jamaica, where he re-emerged in 1975 with promising sides for producers Lloydie Slim (**Judge I Oh Lord**) and the first of many for Bunny Lee (**Natty Dread Don't Cry**). He also launched his own Stars label, principally to promote a local youth combo, Junior Ross and the Spear.

1976 was unquestionably his most prolific and successful year. Apart from the album **MPLA**, his singles, **Ten Against One**, **Rockers** and **Pick Up The Rockers**, made him the biggest reggae singles act of the year and an inspiration to many fledgling DJs.

Signed to Virgin's Front Line subsidiary, a proliferation of recordings ensued between 1977 and '79, none better or more favoured than **She Want A Phensic.** Since then he has maintained an enigmatic silence.

Recordings:
Man Ah Warrior (Mer/Klik)
Peace In The Ghetto (Stars/Front Line)

Below: Phillipe Wynne hasn't done too well on his own.

The '80s

ALTHOUGH THE '80s have begun to display certain trends, the names of many of the players in the game are still the same; the institutions of soul music live on. A casual look at the charts of five years ago, 1977, will show that they feature artists who have since grown even bigger: Stevie Wonder, Diana Ross, Earth, Wind & Fire, the Jacksons, Kool and the Gang, the Commodores, Teddy Pendergrass, George Benson, Smokey Robinson, Marvin Gaye, Millie Jackson, Shalamar, Maze, Ashford & Simpson, the Brothers Johnson, Parliament/Bootsy's Rubber Band/Funkadelic, Ronnie Laws and Herbie Hancock. These are major league/first-division outfits, and although it's arguable that their music was better in the '70s, they continue to make music that is respected, as well as increasingly successful in commercial terms, and it seems unthinkable that they could ever grind to a halt.

Other acts that have been in existence for quite a while but have had sporadic bursts of chart success in the '80s are the Four Tops, Nina Simone, the Whispers, the Chi-Lites, War, the O'Jays, the Manhattans, Brass Construction, Bobby Womack, Roberta Flack, Gladys Knight and the Pips, Rose Royce, Natalie Cole and Billy Paul.

The acts that have more recently made instant and sizeable impacts follow no particular trend, and range from the '50s-style romantic crooning of Richard 'Dimples' Fields to the blatantly sexual pop-funk fusion of Prince. New bands making commercial R&B include Skyy, Lakeside, A Taste Of Honey, the Jones Girls, Sister Sledge, Cameo, Atlantic Starr, Aurra, and Kleer.

Among jazz favourites who have moved into more commercial music are George Duke, Dave Grusin, Grover Washington Jr, Quincy Jones, Ramsey Lewis, Donald Byrd, Eric Gale, Freddie Hubbard and Stanley Turrentine.

A new crop of balladeers has arrived with Deniece Williams, Randy Crawford, Patrice Rushen, Angela Bofill, Phyllis Hyman, Chaka Khan, Luther Vandross, Peabo Bryson and Patti Austin. Ballad lyrics have generally taken a lead from country music and often boast a lyrical content which reaches far beyond the confines of pure 'moon in June' romantic triteness.

Already a 'superstar' has emerged, someone whose first album arrived in 1978, and whose 1981 album was one of the biggest sellers of all times: Rick James. He combines the danceability of funk with the aggression of rock, and writes about two of the record-buying public's major preoccupations—sex and drugs—mixing in snatches of a rags-to-riches story, which appeals to everyone.

In a search for new music there has been a move to fuse

UB-40.

Rick James.

210

existing styles. Instrumental jazz musicians are introducing not only instrumental funk into their jazz, but sometimes vocal funk as well. Because of their musical environment, black artists from predominantly white states of America fuse pop, rock and rock 'n' roll into their funk. And because of the close proximity of the West Indies, other American artists are fusing reggae, calypso and soca. For sheer novelty value, some people have been splicing their songs with passages from classical music and/or utilising instruments more commonly associated with classical music.

While much of the earlier fire has gone out of black music, the overall standard of musicianship, and particularly of arranging, has improved immensely. Black session men, like their white counterparts, now tend to have had a formal musical education. Just as whites continue to play on black records, so black players are much in demand on recording dates for pop, rock and even country and western music.

Although British clubs are still playing predominantly American dance music, for the first time America is repaying the compliment, but not by playing what the British would strictly term 'dance music'. Some American discos have developed a great affinity for what the British have called 'blue-eyed funk', that is, black music interpreted by white pop acts—such as the Human League, Depeche Mode, Chas Jankel and Generation X. America is also beginning to pick up on 'Brit-Funk'—British black music acts—including Junior, Central Line and Imagination.

Following the pioneering work of Bob Marley and the Wailers, reggae is fast becoming generally accepted. Britain was the first nation to take to this Jamaican music, but America soon had its own reggae labels and shops, and reggae artists such as Black Uhuru, Third World, Gregory Issacs, the Mighty Diamonds, Dennis Brown and Burning Spear are now being widely recognised after many years of recording. Where once such music sold mainly to immigrant Jamaicans and a few hip young white fans, now (thanks to ever-increasing media exposure) it has attracted a following among the mass rock audience both in Britain and in America.

At long last black music in general has been accepted—not just by an international audience but by the record industry too—as an important art form. Today, labels lavish on their black artists the kind of attention and financial investment previously reserved for their white pop acts. No longer regarded merely as a source of a quick buck, the stars of black music are now taken seriously and treated with a fitting respect.

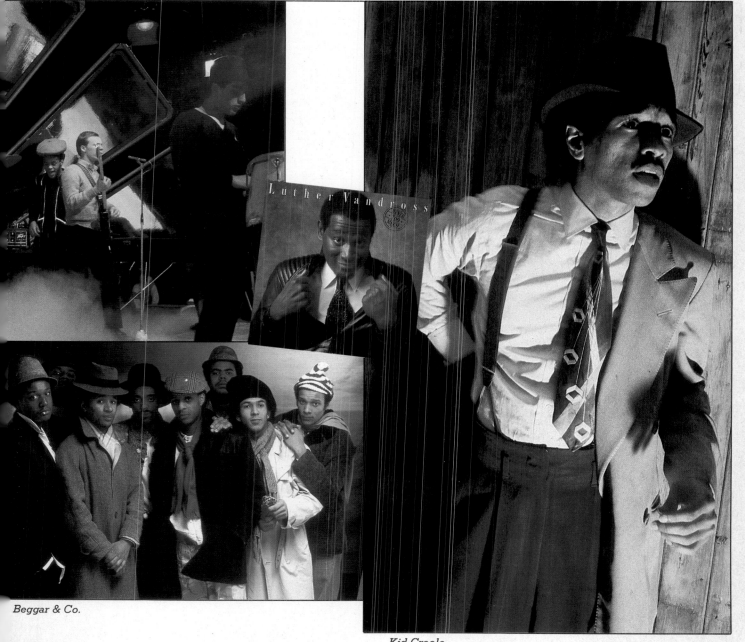

Beggar & Co.

Kid Creole.

Beggar & Co.

As Light Of The World(▶)—one of the '80s new breed of British jazz-funk groups—began to disband, three members broke away to make horn-flavoured funk. Beggar & Co., consisting of Neville 'Breeze' McKreith: guitars, vocals; Daid 'Baps' Baptiste: saxophone, flute, vocals; Canute 'Kenny' Wellington: trumpet, vocals, had immediate success with their first two

Monument. Courtesy RCA Records.

singles, uncompromisingly sounding as British as they chose. This was followed by an album, **Monument**, released in 1981, featuring former members of Light Of The World and Central Line(▶).

Recordings:
Monument (RCA)

Angela Bofill

Angela Bofill was born in West Bronx, New York City, and began composing songs when she was 12. While at New York's Hunter College High School, she formed a band called the Puerto Rican Supremes that played in church and at high school dances. She then attended the Manhattan School of Music.

While touring with Ricardo Morrero and the Group, she recorded a single **My Friend**, which got her nominated best Latin female vocalist in *New York Magazine*. At

Something About You. Courtesy Arista Records.

21, Angela left Morrero's band to go solo. She composed a multimedia jazz suite, **Under The Moon And Over The Sky,** which she performed in association with the Brooklyn Academy of Music. The suite is included on her first album.

Angela then became lead soloist with the Dance Theatre of Harlem Chorus, for whom she also arranged, composed and conducted. Dave Valentin, who had himself just signed to GRP Records, asked label bosses Dave Grusin and Larry

Rosen if they needed a girl vocalist. Angela's home-made demo won them over.

In November 1978, Arista/GRP Records released **Angie,** and followed this with **Angel Of The Night,** both produced by Grusin and Rosen. For her album **Something About You** Angela's producer was Narada Michael Walden(▶)

Recordings:
Angie (Arista/GRP)
Angel Of The Night (Arista/GRP)
Something About You (Arista)

The Breakfast Band

Trinidadians Winston Delandro, guitars; Annise Hadeed, percussion; Richard Bailey, drums; Englishmen Ken Eley, horns, and James Lascelles, keyboards; percussionist Tony Maronie from Dominique, and Japanese bass-player Kuma Harada, make up the multi-national, multi-racial line-up of the Breakfast Band. They had first met while session musicians for Johnny Nash(▶), Van Morrison, Kate Bush, Jeff Beck and others.

The band started as an informal outfit gigging at London's Dingwall's Club with the eventual line-up crystallising during summer 1980 and scoring with the disco smash **L.A. 14.**

Blending jazz with Latin and Caribbean influences (particularly the sound of Trinidad's steel bands), they co-operatively produced an acclaimed debut album **Dolphin Ride** on their own label in 1982.

Recordings:
Dolphin Ride (Breakfast Music)

British Funk

A rock world full of complacent, near middle-aged musicians, releasing records of deteriorating quality, their music surrounded by more hype than melody, was what sparked off the 'punk' revolution. British teenagers were tired of worshipping stars, most of whom seemed to be basking in American sunshine and to have no inclination to tour Britain. The kids' gesture of anger and frustration was an unmusical musical statement—a home-made cacophony that contained an exhilarating energy, and an exciting disrespect for the money-orientated music that was being fed them.

At the same time, British soul fans, realising that everything they loved was American, and knowing that personal appearances by their heroes were few and far between, decided that instead of just waiting for the next soul record or soul act to be imported, they were going to make their own music. Motown(▶),

Stax(▶), Atlantic(▶), Philadephia International(▶)—the soul artistes on these labels had dominated UK discotheques and charts. Black British-based artistes had charted occasionally since the '60s, but there was no concerted movement, and these performers could not live from their infrequent successes. P.P. Arnold, Zoot Money, Georgie Fame, Herbie Goins, the Equals, the Foundations, Jimmy James and the Vagabonds, Geno Washington, Johnny Johnson and the Bandwagon, Jimmy Helms—this had been British soul with many of the acts being expatriate black Americans or West Indians.

In the mid-'70s, pub bands, many of which consisted of white people made live British funk available to a wider audience. Bands such as Ace, the Average White Band(▶), Gonzalez(▶), Heatwave(▶), Kokomo, Moon, the Olympic Runners, Supercharge would also play on American air force bases and at ballrooms, polytechnics and discotheques around the country.

Places to dance increased in number. Certain venues began to be recognised as places where you could hear the best and newest records; DJs became celebrities among club followers; punters would form themselves into groups, known as

Below: Angela Bofill's home-made recipe works wonders.

'tribes'; tribes began to develop more sophisticated music tastes, and specialist record shops became fashionable, even hang-outs. Clubs, DJs and tribes all acknowledged each other, thus records could become club hits; the club and the record shop became the meeting-place of local and musically-aware people. It was a repeat of what had happened in the mod era of the mid-'60s, but this time on a bigger and more coherent scale. Some of these people formed themselves into bands.

By the end of the '70s, British funk outfits such as Hi Tension, the Real Thing,(▶) and Kandidate were having chart success at home, and sometimes abroad. Much of the excitement that spawned so many '80s bands was generated by two groups: Linx(▶) and Light Of The World(▶). Linx proved that the fairy tale could still happen in 20th-century life; it took one play of one record on one radio show for the industry to take out their cheque books. Light Of The World were an example of diligent professionalism, carrying their fast-developing sound around endless British venues.

A late-'70s American trend had been for established jazz artists to make more commercial even-tempoed music. This fusion they called jazz-funk. British funk, having added such bands as Beggar & Co.(▶), Central Line(▶), Imagination(▶) and the UK Players to its ranks, began to produce British jazz-funk groups such as Shakatak, Level 42(▶), Incognito(▶), Freeze, Morrissey-Mullen(▶) and the Breakfast Band(▶).

British funk of that period was a regurgitation of American styles and American giants such as Brass Construction(▶), the Ohio Players (▶), and War(▶), but as the young musicians moved into their twenties, their musical maturity helped them to catch up with the precise and crystal-clear production and engineering that Americans had earlier mastered. Other bands, Linx in particular, chose to sing in English accents and create a British funk sound.

Trends are beginning to emerge within British funk. Now that bands are an accepted form, female solo singers are also beginning to find their feet. Precious Wilson, Janice Hoyte, Gail Grier, Amii Stewart, Celena Duncan and Linda Taylor are gaining a following. Some of these singers are foreign expatriates, but they are finding Britain conducive to their music, and their music conducive to Britain.

British funk fusion has arrived—primarily white bands fusing pop and rock with what Brit-funkers have created. This has been termed 'blue-eyed' funk, played by bands such as Pigbag, Haircut One Hundred and Modern Romance. While bands such as Dexy's Midnight Runners and the Q Tips have also tried fusing '60s soul with '80s arrangements. A school of British funk producers is developing. Barry Blue, himself once a British pop star, produced the first Heatwave albums. Bob Carter has been instrumental in the creation of Linx's sound. Nigel Martinez, as well as writing songs for eminent American artistes, also produces at home. The number of funk and jazz-funk groups grows daily. Second Image, Funkapolitan,

Beggar & Co., comprising ex-Light Of The World members.

Above: Breakfast Band are riding high on a Dolphin.

Buzz, Savanna, Mirage, Cache, Cayenne and Touch are already having chart success.

On the West Coast of America, even the jaggedest funk has rounded edges. Those teeth are a little sharper on the East Coast. Across the ocean, Brit-funkers sometimes substitute sensual groanings with football crowd chanting, and exchange bumping for lurching; the songs refer to British landmarks; the characters, the humour and the personalities of the music-makers are unmistakably home-grown. Possibly because British funk is still a new music, its funk is even more earthy, more pure, more basic than its American counterpart.

Tom Browne

At the age of 11, Tom Browne took a year's piano lessons, but then changed to the trumpet, obtaining a place at New York City's High School of Music and Art. His early interest was classical music, and he played in brass choirs and orchestras, before a friend played him an Ornette Cole-

man album and turned him on to jazz.

Browne's first professional gig was with the Weldon Ervine group in 1975. He then joined Sonny Fortune's(▶) group, and is featured on Fortune's **Infinity Is** album. In 1976 he played on the Fatback Band's(▶) **Man With The Band** album. After leaving Fortune's group there was a four-month period in which he sat in at various clubs. One night, while sitting in with Lonnie Smith at Jimmy Boyd's Breezin' Lounge, Tom found himself on Smith's **Gotcha** album. Boyd is now Browne's manager.

George Benson(▶) took Earl Klugh(▶) to the Breezin' Lounge, and Earl told Dave Grusin(▶) and Larry Rosen, who had just formed GRP Records, about Browne. Browne's first release on GRP was **Browne Sugar** in 1979. The album featured two then-students at Tom's old school, 14-year-old Bernard Wright(▶) and 18-year-old Marcus Miller.

In 1980, Browne released **Love Approach,** which contained **Funkin' For Jamaica,** one of the biggest disco hits of the year. Since then he has recorded a run of jazz flavoured but highly commercial funk albums.

Yours Truly. Courtesy Arista Records.

Apart from Bernard Wright, Browne's musicians on his early albums included Patti Austin(▶), Lesette Wilson and Bobby Broom, all of whom have since embarked on solo careers.

Recordings:
Browne Sugar (Arista)
Love Approach (Arista)
Magic (Arista)
Yours Truly (Arista)

Central Line

Started in the East End of London, Central Line, consisting of Linton Eckles: vocals, Henry Defoe: guitars, Lipson Francis: keyboards, and Camelle Hinds: bass, are front runners of the British Funk(▶) movement, though their music encompasses many contemporary styles. After producing three singles, a fourth, **Walking Into Sunshine,** was a worldwide hit and heralded the release of their first album (1982), produced by ex-Heatwave(▶) member Roy Carter.

Recordings:
Breaking Point (Phonogram)

Champaign

Champaign are a seven-piece group from Champaign, Illinois, comprising Michael Day (guitar), (keyboards), Rena Jones (vocals), Dana Walden (keyboards), Howard Reeder (guitar), Michael Reed (bass), Paulie Carman (lead vocals), and Rocky Maffit (percussion). They released their debut album, produced by Leo Graham, in 1981. The album, a slick fusion of commercial R&B and pop, contained the crossover worldwide hit and title track **How 'Bout Us.**

Recordings:
How 'Bout Us (Columbia/CBS)

Change

Producers Jacques Fred Petrus and Mauro Malavasi met in Milan in 1975 and formed Goody Music to produce European acts. The most successful of these was Change who are led by guitarist Paolo Granolio and bass player David Romani. Their first album, **The Glow Of Love,** was recorded on the producers' own 24-track console in Bologna with lead vocals

added in New York by Luther Vandross(▶) and Jocelyn Shaw.

A year later, the second album, **Miracles,** further established their well-arranged and highly-structured disco sound and produced the hit single **Searching.**

Recordings:
The Glow Of Love (Warner Brothers)
Miracles (Warner Brothers)

Coffee

In 1980, Coffee, the US vocal trio comprising Lenora Dee Bryant, Glenda Hester and Elaine Sims, recorded **Slippin And Dippin,** produced by Leo Graham. This set included their disco classic **Casanova.** The girls, singing a mixture of slow and fast dance music, returned in 1982 with

Slippin' And Dippin'. Courtesy Phonogram Records.

Recordings:
Slippin' And Dippin' (Delite/ Phonogram)
Second Cup (Delite/Phonogram)

Gene Dunlap

Detroit-born Dunlap pursued his musical talent from the age of four, when he obtained his first drum kit. His part-time job at a musical instrument store while at high school brought him in contact with fellow employee Earl Klugh(▶), and the two quickly formed a band, which split before they had an

Party In Me. Courtesy Capitol Records.

opportunity to record.

Dunlap's first recorded composition was on Grant Green's final album, **Easy.** He then played drums with Roy Ayers(▶) appearing on three albums, before re-uniting

Second Cup, and an established formula.

Above: London's Central Line are travelling fast.

with Klugh in 1977 to tour the world and record on three of the guitarists' LPs.

Signed to Capitol Records in 1980, Dunlap cut his debut album (with vocals provided by the Ridgeways—Gloria, Esther, Gracie and Tommy), which contained a mixture of jazz-soul fusion club tracks and ballads, including the crossover hit single **It's Just The Way I Feel. Party In Me** released in 1981, featured him singing, and was altogether less impressive.

Recordings:
It's Just The Way I Feel (Capitol)
Party In Me (Capitol)

Richard 'Dimples' Fields

Having bought The Cold Duck Music Lounge in San Francisco, Fields put himself on in cabaret. His largely female audience gave him his nickname 'Dimples' be-

Dimples. Courtesy Boardwalk Records.

cause of his broad grin. Influenced by the 'crooners' of the '50s and '60s, Fields perfected his romantic vocal delivery over many years.

Following unsuccessful recordings on small labels, Fields signed to Boardwalk Records in 1981, where his first album **Dimples** yielded three American hit singles: **I Like Your Lovin', She's Got Papers On Me** and the persistent funk of **I've Got To Learn To Say No!**

Below: Richard Fields shows how he got his nickname.

Recordings:
Dimples (Boardwalk/Epic)
Mr Look So Good (Boardwalk/
Epic)

Freeze

See British Funk

Imagination

From within a number of mid-'70s London-based black groups emerged a trio—Lee John, Ashley Ingram and Errol Kennedy—whose music and image produced immediate worldwide funk and pop chart success. Their persona, like that of Linx(▶), defied the laws of black stereotypes. In collaboration with their writers and producers Tony Swain and Steve Jolley, Imagination developed an ideal, uncategorisable vocal style and music. Various tracks from their debut album, released in 1981, scored in numerous countries.

Recordings:
Body Talk (R&B/MCA)

Incognito

Former members of Light Of The World(▶), one of the forerunners of the late '70s black British scene, began to get involved in separate musical projects in 1980, the most prominent involving bass player Paul 'Tubbs' Williams and keyboard player Peter Hinds. They started Incognito with original Light Of

Incognito. Courtesy Ensign Records.

The World guitarist Jean Paul Maunick and drummer Jeff Dunn. Their debut album, **Incognito**, re-

Above: Imagination in the flesh.

leased in 1981, contained jazzier British funk than that played by LOW.

Recordings:
Incognito (Ensign)

Junior

Junior Giscombe hurtled to prominence in 1982 with the Stevie Wonder(▶) soundalike **Mama Used To Say** which, besides scoring in his native UK, reached No. 2 on the American soul charts.

Managed by Stevie Wonder's former personal assistant Keith Harris, Junior Giscombe was the first black British artist to appear on the *'Soul Train'* TV series.

Recordings:
JI (Mercury)

Kandidate

See British Funk

Kid Creole & The Coconuts

The most internationally successful act signed to Michael Zilkha's modernist/disco and jazz label Ze, Kid Creole & the Coconuts revolves around Kid Creole, the flamboyant cavalier alter-ego of songwriter and producer August Darnell. Born Darnell August

Browder in Haiti in 1951, he later moved with his family to New York, obtaining his street credentials in the Bronx. Graduating in English he spent some time teaching before securing a job writing songs for Chapell Music. The company didn't take to his propensity for Latin songs and they mutually agreed to part company.

Jobless, he and his brother Stony joined forces to construct the now legendary Dr Buzzard's Original Savannah Band, which in the mid-70s cut two albums for RCA, and a third for Elektra entitled **James Munroe HS Presents Dr Buzzard's Original Savannah Band And Goes To Washington**. It was never released outside the US.

Because they had recorded for two labels, the brothers were subsequently involved in litigation. Stony kept the original band together while Darnell, with Andy Hernandez (the Coati Mundi of **Me No Popeye** fame), started the Coconuts, with his wife Addy among the backing vocalists.

The group debuted for Ze in 1980 with **Off The Coast Of Me**, which delivered the minor hit **Maladie D'Amour**. It met enthusiastic media reaction but this euphoria wasn't matched by album sales. A second album, **Fresh Fruit In Foreign Places**, an agreeable salsa concept cruise, affirmed the group's status with its beau monde following on both sides of the Atlantic. Darnell's production

reputation spread to Britain where he produced Funkapolitan's first UK hit, **As Time Goes By**, and their debut album. In the autumn of 1981 he started work on a solo album. A sampler of those sessions, **Christmas On Riverside Drive**, became the standout track on a Ze compilation, **A Christmas Record**.

Recordings:
Off The Coast Of Me (Ze)
**Fresh Fruit In Foreign
Places** (Ze)

Fern Kinney

Fern Kinney was born in Jackson, Mississippi, and it was there that she sang in her first group, the Poppies, who also included Dorothy Moore(▶). Through a series of deep-soul singles, including records on the Atlantic(▶) label, Fern developed a cult following.

In 1977, she signed to Malaco Records, who released her first album in 1979. One track, **Together We Are Beautiful**, became hit No.1 in the British national charts.

Recordings:
Groove Me (Malaco/WEA)
Fern (Malaco/WEA)

Stacy Lattisaw

Born and raised in Washington, DC, diminutive Stacy has already recorded three albums for Henry Allen's Cotillion label, and she's not yet reached 20. At the age of 11, supporting Ramsey Lewis(▶), Stacy performed a five-song set in front of 30,000 people. Allen, who had signed four young girls—Sister Sledge(▶)—some years earlier, knew young talent when he heard it and promptly signed Stacy.

Stacy's Van McCoy(▶)-produced debut in 1979 had a fraction of the effect of her follow-up **Let Me Be Your Angel**, produced by Narada Michael Walden in 1980. From that album came the worldwide smash **Jump To The Beat**.

Recordings:
Young And In Love (Cotillion)
Let Me Be Your Angel (Cotillion)
With You (Cotillion)

Debra Laws

Debra Laws is a member of the famous Laws musical family. An ex-student of the New York School of Performing Arts, she left the Houston, Texas, family home in 1970 and moved to Los Angeles, where she provided vocals for the albums and concerts of her famous brothers, Hubert(▶) and Ronnie(▶). They produced a debut album for her in February 1981.

Recordings:
Very Special (Elektra)

Eloise Laws

Born Houston, Texas, 1949, Eloise Laws is the middle of the famous Laws' children, sandwiched between flautist Hubert(▶) and saxophonist Ronnie(▶).

Unlike her brothers, Eloise has preferred to work in the soul mainstream rather than the funk idiom and finally began breaking

Left: Kid Creole; his flamboyancy gives the ladies a lift.

2

afterwards. From that album came the fifth single, **Starchild**.

Recordings:
Level 42 (—/Polydor)

Linx

David Grant was born and raised in Hackney, East London. Peter Martin, more commonly known as Sketch, originates from Plaistow, East London. Sketch worked as an assistant in a central London hi-fi store. One day Grant walked in, the two talked and decided to write together.

Sketch had listened to Jimi Hendrix(▶) in his youth, while Grant had been influenced by Motown(▶). Some months after their meeting, they wrote a song, and took a tape of it to record companies, who universally rejected it.

Still songwriting, and still working to finance themselves, they came up with a new idea. With the help of keyboard player Bob Carter and drummer Andy Duncan, they recorded another of their songs called **You're Lying**, produced by Grant, Sketch and Carter. They pressed 1,000 copies of this, and gave it to various DJs. City Sounds, a record shop in Central London, agreed to sell it.

Radio London DJ Robbie Vincent played the record on his show one Saturday, and over the following week, City Sounds sold out of the single. It became an enormous club success, and the industry that had rejected Linx a few months previous, now chased them with open chequebooks.

Linx signed with Chrysalis Records, a company who did not have a black music act on their roster at the time and who had not heard the original tape. To Chrysalis' credit, they allowed Grant and Sketch a mostly free rein on their image and publicity. Because of this and the rock element in their music, the Linx cause was taken up by the white musical and national daily press.

After **You're Lying**, released by Chrysalis in mid-1980, came **Rise And Shine**. The first album, released on March 20, 1981, in-

Above: Self-help brought success to London's Linx.

through via Liberty in 1980 after a decade of hard graft and unsatisfactory recording deals.

Her first recordings, in 1969, were for CBS who tried to steer her in an MOR direction. Then, three years later, Holland/Dozier/Holland(▶) saw her as a possible replacement for Freda Payne(▶) who had just left the company, signing Eloise to their Music Merchant subsidiary.

The Phil Spector(▶) 'wall of sound'-influenced production on **Love Factory** made no chart impact but the record did become an in-demand item among British 'Northern Soul' freaks three years later.

A short stint as an anonymous member of the Fifth Dimension(▶) followed before Eloise returned to H/D/H to cut her **Ain't It Good Feeling Good** album.

Far Out Productions' boss Jerry Goldstein (who also manages and produces War(▶)) signed her then to ABC for the 1978 LP **Eloise** but the contract ended when ABC sold their operation to MCA and for two years she contented herself with singing back-up for brother Ronnie before landing a new deal with Liberty. They paired her with the creative production/arranging team of Linda Creed and Thom Bell(▶) for the **Eloise Laws** album which featured some critically acclaimed ballads leavened with up-tempo items.

Recordings:
Ain't It Good Feeling Good
(Invictus/—)
Eloise (ABC/—)
Eloise Laws (Liberty)

Level 42

British funk band Level 42 was born, very quietly, on the Isle of Wight, UK, in the autumn of 1972.

It was to be eight years before their first record was released. To begin with the band was a loose collection of young boys that included present members, brothers Phil and Boon Gould, Mike Lindup and Mark King. Phil met Mike Lindup at the Guildhall School of Music and Drama. Mike had just been at Chethams Music School in Manchester while Phil was about to embark on a scholarship at the Royal Academy of Music.

In the autumn of 1979, Mark, Phil and Mike got together, and were joined by Boon at the outset of 1980. Andy Sojka, the head of a London independent label, Elite, signed them, and produced their first two singles. **Love Meeting Love** came out on Elite in the summer of 1980, but a larger record company offered Level 42 a long-term contract, and **(Flying On The) Wings Of Love**, although produced by Sojka, came out on Polydor Records later in 1980.

For their third single, **Love Games**, released in March 1981, Level 42 chose veteran British musician and producer Mike Vernon to produce them. **Turn It On** followed in July 1981, and the first album **Level 42**, arrived a month

Below: Formal musical training is allied to street funk by Level 42.

Above: Hitmakers UB40, no longer unemployed.

Never Too Much. Courtesy Epic Records.

cluded the first two singles, and two further singles made impressions on the pop chart, the title track **Intuition** and **Throw Away The Key.**

Within the space of 18 months, Linx could claim four British hit singles, were generating enormous curiosity in America, and had created one of the most exciting fusions heard for a decade. They udertook their first tour after the release of their second album, **Go Ahead,** towards the end of 1981.

Recordings:
Intuition (Chrysalis)
Go Ahead (Chrysalis)

Midnight Express

See British Funk

Mirage

See British Funk

T.S. Monk

T. S. Monk, son of Thelonious Monk, is the leader of a New York-based vocal trio of that name consisting of sister Boo Boo Monk and Yvonne Fletcher.

In 1981, Sandy Linzer—the producer behind Odyssey(▶)—co-wrote and produced an album of bumpers and smoochers, repeating the process with the trio in **More Of The Good Life** in 1982.

Recordings:
House Of Music (Mirage/WEA)
More Of The Good Life
   (Mirage/WEA)

Ojah

See British Funk

The Reddings

The two sons of the late Otis Redding, Otis III and Dexter, and their cousin Mark Locket, constitute the Reddings. With Dexter: bass, vocals; Otis III: guitar; and Mark: keyboards, drums, vocals, they recorded **The Awakening,** an album of soul, funk and jazz for Russell Timmons' Washington-based Believe In A Dream Records (BID), released in 1981.

The band, all from Macon, Georgia, are managed by Otis's widow, Zelma.

Recordings:
The Awakening (BID)

UB40

UB40 is the official name of the British unemployment benefit form and it accurately illustrates the stark urban landscape that spawned this multi-racial Midlands reggae band. When the group assembled during 1977, few of the members owned their own instruments and even fewer could play anything. Yet within three years the group had become one of the most innovative and commercially viable acts in the country, with a string of top-10 hits under its belt.

Original membership consisted of Ali Campbell, vocals, rhythm guitar; Earl Falconer, bass guitar; Jim Brown, drums; Brian Travers, saxophone; Norman Hassan, percussion; Robin Campbell, lead guitar; Jimmy Lynn, keyboards, and Timi Tupe 'Yomi' Abayomi Babayemi, percussion. Lynn left in 1979 and was replaced by Mickey Virtue. Later that year, after only a handful of gigs, Yomi returned to his native Nigeria. Shortly before the group entered a recording studio for the first time they were joined on stage by Astro who nominated himself as resident toaster.

Demo tapes cut with local producer Bob Lamb were enough to interest several influential radio DJs and, with increasing exposure, the group was signed to the Graduate label. Their relaxed mellifluous reggae was captured on their second single, **King,** which took them straight into the UK national pop charts.

Invited to join rock group the Pretenders on a major British tour in 1980, the group became an overnight sensation. Their subsequent album, **Signing Off** (also produced by Lamb), became one of the few reggae albums to reach national pop 30. By the end of that year the group had genuinely outgrown its amateurish beginnings. They parted company with Lamb and Graduate (leaving the latter because of the label's decision to exclude the anti-apartheid **Burden Of Shame** from their debut album in South Africa), and formed their own Dep International label for all subsequent releases.

Since then they have produced their own material, contained on two albums. Popular and influential, their material retains their view of the harsh realities of what they see as living in a Western economic wasteland founded upon colonialism.

Recordings:
Signing Off (—/Graduate)
Present Arms
   (—/Dep International)

Luther Vandross

Before embarking on a solo career with Epic Records, Vandross was one of the most in-demand session vocalists in the world, backing superstars such as David Bowie, Bette Midler and Carly Simon, as well as contributing to Quincy Jones'(▶) projects. Vandross was also an informal member of the Italian disco outfit, Change(▶), and has contributed songs to the sound-

tracks of films such as *The Wiz* and *Bustin' Loose.*

New York-born Vandross eventually got the chance to commit his seasoned and rich tones to vinyl in his own right on his 1981 **Never Too Much** album. Both the title track and **Sugar And Spice** were successful singles.

Recordings:
Never Too Much (Epic)

Bernard Wright

Having started on piano at the age of four, Wright played in his first band four years later. At 13, he toured with Lenny White(▶). Tom Browne(▶), a neighbour in Queens, New York, told Dave Grusin and Larry Rosen about Wright, and they signed him up. Wright contributed keyboards and a composition to Browne's debut.

Wright's first LP, **'Nard,** recorded when he was 16 and released in 1981, featured danceable funk and an acoustic version of Miles Davis' **Solar,** with Grusin and Rosen producing.

Recordings:
'Nard (GRP/Arista)

Yarbrough And Peoples

Cavin Yarbrough and Alisa Peoples sang in the same Dallas church choir. Cavin was a member of a local band that contained the Wilson Brothers, soon to become The Gap Band(▶). Having been recommended to Gap Band manager/producer, Lonnie Simmons, Cavin and Alisa went to Los Angeles, where Simmons and Jonah Ellis produced **The Two Of Us,** which contained the worldwide hit, **Don't Stop The Music.**

Recordings:
The Two Of Us (Mercury)

Young & Company

In 1971, William, Mike and Kenny Young were part of a band called the Young Movement, touring around their home state of New Jersey. William used to record with Slave(▶) and Aurra, where he met drummer Dave Reyes. Another ex-member of Aurra was bassist Buddy Hank. The three brothers recruited Reyes, Hank, and vocalist Jackie Thomas, to form a commercial funk outfit.

In 1980, Young & Company gained worldwide success with a single, **I Like What You're Doing To Me,** although there is no album release to date.

Appendix

Sheer pressure of space prevents us giving a full entry to the following acts but we would like to record our appreciation of the contribution they have made to black music.

Act One: had disco rave **Tom The Peeper.**

Faye Adams: had R&B number-ones with **Shake A Hand** (1953), **I'll Be True** and **Hurts Me To My Heart** on Herald.

Johnny Adams: classy New Orleans-based soul singer who joined Nashville's SSS label in 1969 for classic **Release Me, Reconsider Me** and **I Can't Be All Bad** hits.

Marie Adams: 19-stone Texan lady who scored British number-one as member of Johnny Otis Show's Three Tons Of Joy with **Ma He's Making Eyes At Me** in 1957 as well as having solo hits on Peacock.

African People: Italy-based black group who had **Stop Pushing** album on Polydor (1971).

Afrique: featuring David T. Walker on guitar and Chuck Rainey on bass cut **Soul Makossa** for Mainstream in 1973.

Jewel Akens: had 1965 million-seller with **The Birds And The Bees.**

Lee Allen: the sax soloist on dozens of New Orleans R&B hits, including those of Fats Domino, he scored with his own instrumental **Walking With Mr Lee** in 1958.

Lee Andrews and the Hearts: had late '50s doo-wop classics on Philly-based Swan label.

Sil Austin: worked in Tiny Bradshaw's band before cutting string of saxophone-led instrumental hits in late '50s.

B

Baby Ray: recorded great Imperial soul/R&B album including **Sadie The Avon Lady, The House On Soul Hill** and **Wild Side Of Life.**

Bessie Banks: fondly remembered for her original of **Go Now.**

Len Barry: 1966 blue-eyed soul smashed out of Philadelphia with **Like A Baby** and **1-2-3.**

Harold Battiste: worked for Specialty in New Orleans, with Little Richard and Lloyd Price in his charge. Later discovered Irma Thomas, Ernie K. Doe, Chris Kenner, Barbara George and others and masterminded white rock artist Mack Rebennack's R&B-influenced new guise as 'Dr John The Night Tripper'.

Beginning Of The End: had 1971 Alston disco smash **Funky Nassau.**

The Artistics: Chicago uptown-soul vocal quartet who scored on Brunswick in late '60s with **I'm Gonna Miss You** and others.

Richard Berry: born New Orleans, moved to Los Angeles where he co-wrote prolifically

Otis Clay.

with Jesse Belvin. Wrote and, with his band the Pharoahs, recorded original of **Louie, Louie** (later pop hit for Kingsmen) making No.2 in US R&B chart.

Big Blues: African and blues roots mixed for some great '70s albums on Uni.

Billy Bland: had 1960 Old Town classic **Let The Little Girl Dance.**

The Blues Busters: formed 1962, comprising Phillip James and Lloyd Campbell. Their soulful harmonies owe a debt to Sam Cooke with whom they toured in Jamaica in early '60s; recorded seminal **Tribute To Sam Cooke** album. Hit singles include **Thinking Of You** and **Priviliged.** Presently in vogue in Canada with '**Hits**' album — melodies of contemporary pop hits set to reggae rhythm.

The Bobettes: New York 12 to 14 yr olds who hit in 1957 with **Mr Lee**; the girlie quintet had even bigger success three years later with **I Shot Mr Lee.**

James Booker: New Orleans organist prominent on many sessions in the Crescent City as well as scoring in own right with jaunty 1960 instrumental **Gonzo.** Later worked with rock stars Dr John and Doobie Brothers.

Earl Bostic: swinging alto sax player who sold a million copies of **Flamingo** for King in 1951.

The Box Tops: Memphis-based blue-eyed soul outfit featuring lead voice of Alex Chilton, though the superb songwriting/arranging/ production of Chips Moman, Dan Penn and Spooner Oldham were the real key to the success of **The Letter, Choo Choo Train, Cry Like A Baby, Soul Deep** and a mighty version of B.B. King's **Rock Me Baby,** all of which successfully married pop and soul.

Jan Bradley: recorded **Mama Didn't Lie.**

Al 'T.N.T.' Braggs: explosive stage act; had lots of records via Duke/Peacock.

Brenda And The Tabulations: Philadelphia mainstays who had string of '60s soul hits, notably **Dry Your Eyes** (Dionn).

Brick: displayed funky sounds of Atlanta, Georgia, with **Brick/Good High** LPs (1976).

Brighter Side Of Darkness: catchy **Love Jones** charter for 20th Century put the vocal quartet on the map briefly in 1973.

Tina Britt: Florida-born, Philadelphia-raised, Tina Britt cut a super bluesy album, **Blue All The Way,** for Minit in late '60s.

Buster Brown: blues/R&B singer/harmonica-man who had great **Fannie Mae** on Fire in 1960.

Clarence 'Gatemouth' Brown: Texas R&B guitarist maestro/vocalist, who cut mass of worthwhile sides for Don Robey at Peacock and of late has recorded with country star Roy Clark.

Roy Brown: New Orleans star, who was major influence on Bobby Bland, Little Richard, James Brown and Jackie Wilson, and remem-

bered also for **Good Rockin' Tonight** (1948) and **Hard Luck Blues** (1950).

Milt Buckner: veteran and much recorded R&B organist.

Billy Butler: talented brother of superstar Jerry. Remembered for OKeh '60s hit **Right Track.**

Bobby Byrd: James Brown's longtime right-hand man and an original Famous Flame; great dancer, organist — and songwriter.

C

Linda Carr & the Love Squad.

C.J. & Co. gave a Detroit slant to disco soul for Westbound with Mike Theodore/Dennis Coffey-arranged-and-produced **Deadeye Dick.**

Terry Callier: cut smooth soul albums for Elektra in late '70s.

Choker Campbell: Motown bandleader and session musician.

Capitols: '60s Atlantic soul group; **Cool Jerk** was their classic.

Linda Carr and the Love Squad: her dulcet tones scored in 1975 with **Cherry Pie Guy** for Wes Farrell's Chelsea label, produced by Kenny Nolan.

Mel Carter: signed by Sam Cooke to Derby then had run of hits for Imperial in mid-'60s.

George Chandler: British-based American soul singer; vocalist with the Olympic Runners and Gonzalez.

Checkmates Unlimited: had what was reputedly the most expensive-to-produce single ever made when Phil Spector used a mass orchestra for their version of **Proud Mary.**

The Chords: had one gem, **Sh-Boom** (1954), and later recorded as the Chordcats without success.

Tony Clarke: classic records at Chess — **The Entertainer, Coming Back Strong, Ain't Love Good, Ain't Love Proud.**

Judy Clay: session singer on hits for Wilson Pickett, Don Covay and others, she enjoyed duet hits with Billy Vera (**Storybook Children**) and William Bell (**Private Number** and **My Baby Specialises**).

Otis Clay: had Chicago R&B hits with One-der-ful and Memphis success via Hi.

The Cleftones: Big Apple doo-woppers, who recorded **Little Girl Of Mine, Heart And Soul** and **Lover Come Back To Me.**

Dennis Coffey: white Detroit session guitarist. Novel mass-guitars sound on funk instrumentals. Released albums on Sussex and Atlantic.

Cold Blood: white rock band heavily influenced by soul scene. Cut classic version of Sam and Dave's **You Got Me Hummin'** for Atlantic-distributed San Francisco label.

Lyn Collins: went from back-up singer with James Brown to solo stardom with **Think (About It), Rock Me Again And Again And Again And Again And Again And Again** in mid-'70s.

The Cookies: Beatles covered their infectiously lilting hit **Chains.**

Bill Cosby: comedian of 'I Spy' fame, cut funky send-ups of soul biggies, backed by Watts 103rd Street Rhythm Band.

Lou Courtney: scored with **Skate Now, Shing-A-Ling,** produced by Jerry Ragovoy.

Clydie King: one-time Ikette, one-time leader of Brown Sugar, session singer extraordinaire.

Creative Source: vocal group vehicle for talents of arranger Paul Riser. Cut classic version of Bill Withers' **Who Is He And What Is He To You?** and fine albums on Sussex.

The Crests: multi-racial East Coast close-harmony outfit remembered for **Sixteen Candles** and **The Angels Listened In.**

Cymande: British-based West Indian funkers, they recorded in London and Chicago and had heavy album sales in US but won little recognition at home.

D

The Darnells: scored for Tamla Motown with their '64 debut **Too Hurt To Cry, Too Much In Love To Say Goodbye** then sank straight back into obscurity.

Betty Davis: ex-model, ex-Mrs Miles Davis; mixed sex and soul; remembered as the **Nasty Gal.**

Ronnie Davies: mid-'60s member of vocal trio the Tennors who scored with singles **Ride Your Donkey** and **Girl I've Got To Get You Off My Mind.** Subsequent work with producer Bunny Lee maintained interest.

The Daylighters: had **Oh Ma, Teach Me How To Uncle Willie** of which there was a great UK cover version by Zoot Money too.

Delaney and Bonnie: Bonnie was the only white girl ever to be a member of Ike and Tina Turner's Ikettes. With husband Delaney she cut some great soul duets on Atlantic.

Del-Vikings: integrated Pittsburgh-based vocal group who scored big in '50s with **Come Go With Me** and **Whispering Bells.** Chuck Jackson was later a member before going on to big solo career on Wand.

Deodato: talented arranger/instrumentalist who had massive hit with exciting jazz-funk version of **Theme From 2001, Also Spracht Zarathustra.**

The Dixie Cups: their Red Bird hits **Chapel Of Love, People Say** and the Creole chant **Iko Iko** assured the New Orleans girlie trio of a place in pop history.

Willie Dixon: staff writer/producer/bass player/A&R man at Chess who enjoyed hits with Howlin' Wolf, Muddy Waters, Sonny Boy Williamson, Buddy Guy and others, and in his own right.

Bill Doggett: Philadelphia-born R&B organist, hit big in 1956 with chunky **Honky Tonk** on King. Prolifically recorded.

Jack De Johnette: fine jazz drummer who has played with Chick Corea, Freddie Hubbard, Stanley Turrentine, Miles Davis and countless others.

The Dominoes: led by Billy Ward, the first group for both Clyde McPhatter and Jackie Wilson. Bill Brown sang lead on their 1951 classic **Sixty Minute Man.**

Don and Bob: Chicago-based vocal duo who hit for Chess with freewheeling version of **Good Morning Little Schoolgirl.**

Don and Dewey: Don 'Sugarcane' Harris and Dewey Terry cut originals of **Big Boy Pete, I'm Leaving It Up To You** and **Justine.** Harris later played R&B violin with Johnny Otis, Frank Zappa and John Mayall.

Eric Donaldson: three times winner of Jamaica's annual song festival. Climax of this kudos was single **Cherry Oh Baby** in '71, selling over 400,000 copies. Hits kept rolling with **Sweet Jamaica** ('77) and **Land Of My Birth** ('78).

Carol Douglas: New Yorker who enjoyed short stint as 'Queen Of Disco' in 1976 thanks to **Doctor's Orders.**

The Dovells: Philadelphian quintet led by Len Barry (of subsequent **1-2-3** renown) notched eight dance-craze charters for Cameo Parkway between 1961-64, including the memorable **Bristol Stomp** which made number-two in U.S. A white group with a black sound: 'Sometimes we were great, sometimes we stank,' Barry recalled later.

Tom Dowd: Atlantic staff engineer. Worked on hits for Joe Turner, Ray Charles, Coasters, Drifters and also artists at Stax before becoming producer for Young Rascals, Aretha Franklin, Eric Clapton and others.

Big Al Downing: had rock 'n' roll, R&B and soul hits from 1956 with variety of labels then had renewed success with **I'll Be Holding On** in mid-'70s disco boom, while his brother Dan Downing scored in same era with **Lonely Days And Lonely Nights.**

Gene Dozier and the Brotherhood: heavy funk instrumentals. Great **Blues Power** album on Minit in late '60s.

Dr. Strut: Five-piece commercial, instrumental jazz outfit who recorded albums for Motown during '70s.

Eddie Drennon and BBS Unlimited: cut '76 disco dazzler **Do The Latin Hustle.**

Patti Drew: had great albums on Capitol and a singles smash with **Tell Him.**

Duprees: White American vocal unit, who recorded a minor masterpiece in 1970 with **Check Yourself.**

Dyke and the Blazers: had the original hit **Funky Broadway** (later covered by Wilson Pickett).

Ronnie Dyson: starred in 'Hair' then had hit with **When You Get Right Down To It** with Columbia before recording much-applauded **One Man Band** album with writer/arranger/ producer Thom Bell in Philadelphia.

Ecstasy, Passion and Pain: signed to Roulette, produced at Sigma Sound in Philadelphia, they were a four-guy/two-girl soul-harmony act.

Tommy Edwards: **It's All In The Game** was written by former US vice-president in 1912. Edwards' warm tones took it to number-one in 1958 (it was hit again later for Four Tops).

Bobby Emmons: white Memphis session keyboard player who cut R&B instrumental album **Blues With A Beat On An Organ** for Hi.

The Escorts: group of convicts who recorded their 1973 Alithia album **All We Need Is Another Chance** live at Rahway State Prison.

Esquerita: Capitol Records' answer to Little Richard, but he flopped till he recorded organ/instrumental **Green Door** for Minit in 1962 under real name of Eskew Reeder.

Executive Suite: had Philly-sound winner in '74 with **When The Fuel Runs Out.**

Faith, Hope and Charity: vocal outfit master-minded by Van McCoy.

Fantastic Johnny C: a Phil LA Of Soul hit with Jesse James-written and -produced **Boogaloo Down Broadway** gave Johnny Corley a brief taste of the limelight in 1968.

First Choice: Philly filly trio masterminded by Stan Watson and Norman Harris, who scored with **Smarty Pants** and **Armed And Extremely Dangerous** in 1973 on Philly-Groove.

The Five Satins: their classic R&B ballad **In The Still Of The Night**, an American hit in 1956 and again in 1960, was cut in basement of New Haven church.

Five Stairsteps: Curtis Mayfield-produced Chicago family group led by pre-teen Cubie.

Flaming Ember: Holland/Dozier/Holland's blue-eyed soul quartet. The Dunbar and Wayne partnership co-penned their 1970 golden goodie **Westbound No.9** on Hot Wax.

The Flares: originally worked with Leiber/ Stoller as the Flairs, and scored in '61 with the joyous dancer **Foot Stompin'.**

The Flirtations: after minor success on East Coast, Viola Billups, and sisters Earnestine and Shirley Pearce moved to UK and scored with **Someone Out There** and **Nothing But A Heartache** to become an institution on the late '60s-early '70s cabaret circuit.

Phil Flowers: Cut **Our Man In Washington** album on Dot.

Foxy: multi-racial Miami funk band who released **Get Off.**

Friends Of Distinction: two girls/two guys harmony group in the mould of Fifth Dimension had 1972 million-seller on RCA with **Grazing In The Grass.**

Harvey Fuqua: leader of the Moonglows, long serving Motown writer/producer; man behind the Nitelighters, New Birth and Sylvester.

The Futures: classy mid-to-late '70s Detroit vocal quintet; owed not a little stylistic debt to the Four Tops. Their best was haunting disco ballad **You Got It (The Love That I Need)** on Philadelphia International in '78.

The Fuzz: group member Sheila Young wrote much of the femme trio's material. Cut enjoyable 1971 album for Roulette.

Rex Garvin and the Mighty Cravers: Cut 1966 R&B/disco classic **Sock It To 'Em J.B.** which eulogised James Bond.

Barbara George: New Orleans songthrush who scored in '61 with **I Know** on AFO.

The Goodies: Stax vocal group (not to be confused with the British comedy team of same name!).

Earl Grant: string of MOR/R&B organ-instrumental and vocal records culminating in '61 million-seller **Ebb Tide.** Died 1970, Mexico, in car smash.

Garland Green: had success on Uni with **Jealous Kind Of Fella.**

Grey and Hanks: Len Ron Hanks and Zane Grey self-produced class disco albums on RCA and scored with **You Fooled Me** in 1978.

Jackie Hairston: Otis Redding protégé organist was great on mood-laden **Hi-Jack** (penned by Redding).

Thurston Harris and the Sharps: went top-10 in '57 with cover of Bobby Day's **Little Bitty Pretty One.**

Roy Head: white Texan R&B star very popular with black audiences, with a penchant for hard-rocking items like his 1964 number-two **Treat Her Right** (Backbeat).

Bobby Hebb: at age of 12, Bobby Hebb became first black artist to appear at the legendary Grand Ol' Opry home of country music in Nashville. Hebb's 1966 Jerry Ross-produced **Sunny** was one of the first true crossover records, figuring in soul, country and pop charts.

Donald Height: remembered for **Talk Of The Grapevine.**

Willie Henderson: remembered as Chicago's **Dance Master.**

Donna Hightower: Carruthersville, Missouri-born, Chicago-raised, Donna made name with jazz greats Ben Webster, Quincy Jones, Oscar Peterson, then moved to Belgium and cut twist and soul sides for Barclay.

Rosetta Hightower: American soul singer (one time member of the Orlons), married to British jazzer Ian Green. Settled in London and cut classy CBS album (1970).

Jessie Hill: had 1963 New Orleans classic **Ooh Poo Pah Doo** for Minit.

Ernie Hines: singer guitarist who recorded with Bar-Kays and MGs for his **Electrified** album on We Produce in 1972.

Below: James Brown's backing band, the J.B.'s.

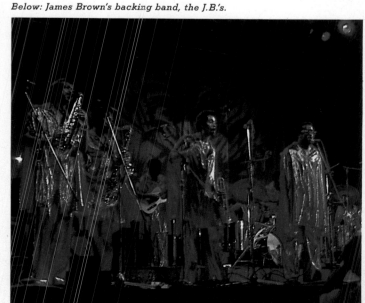

Sheila Hylton.

Joe Hinton: from The Spirit Of Memphis gospel group to pop chart success with the soulful classic **Funny (How Time Slips Away).**

Jimmy Holliday: wrote songs for Ray Charles then earned success in own right with **The Turnin' Point, Spread Your Love** and duets with Clydie King.

Honey Boy: aka Keith Williams, Honey Boy was on bottom rungs of the UK pop charts ('72) with own song **Sweet Cherry.** An actor and cabaret artist, he continues to cut well-balanced soulful reggae records, with **Dark End Of The Street** (Empire '72) one of his most consistent and popular albums.

Linda Hopkins: released memorable album of gospel-fervour duets with Jackie Wilson, with **Shake A Hand** the stand-out cut.

Jimmy Bo Horne: Miami dance master, scored for TK's Sunshine Sound in late '70s with disco smashes like **Dance Across The Floor** and **Spank.**

Rhetta Hughes: had nifty re-make of **Light My Fire** on short-lived Tetragrammaton label.

Hugo and Luigi: New York Italians Hugo Peretti and Luigi Creatore bought Roulette Records from George Goldner in '57, sold out to Morris Levy and Henry Glover in '59 and then produced the Isley Brothers and Sam Cooke for RCA. In 1973 they headed the new Avco label and wrote and produced for the Stylistics.

Paul Humphries and the Cool Aid Chemists: ace West Coast session drummer with his own band; hit with **America Wake Up.**

100% Proof Aged In Soul: recorded **Somebody's Been Sleeping In My Bed** on Hot Wax 1970.

Ivory Joe Hunter: had string of '40s R&B ballad classics and a 1950 million-seller with **I Almost Lost My Mind.** His compositions

gave hits to Nat Cole, Pat Boone, the Five Keys, Elvis Presley and others. Died Memphis, 1974, aged 60.

Sheila Hylton: Jamaican air hostess turned singer. Recorded Lloyd Bennett's **Breakfast In Bed**, and also **Don't Ask My Neighbour** in '79. Best known for rendition of **The Bed's Too Big Without You**, written by Sting of Police.

The Incredible Bongo Band: had scorchingly rhythmic disco stormer with **Bongo Rock '73.**

Jackie Ivory: Arkansas-born organist, released classic 1966 instrumental album **Soul Discovery** on Atlantic which included version of **High Heel Sneakers.**

Deon Jackson: Detroiter, scored for Calla/Atco in 1966 with **Love Makes The World Go Round.**

Debbie Jacobs: displayed LA sophistication on 1979 disco smash **Undercover Lover** (MCA) written by Paul Sabu.

Hank Jacobs: had '60s R&B organ classics on Sue with **So Far Away** and **Monkey Hips And Rice.**

Jay and the Techniques: five white musicians fronted by two black singers, from Philly. Jerry Ross produced their 1967 soul classic **Apples, Peaches And Pumpkin Pie.**

The J.B's: James Brown's superfunky backing band featuring Maceo Parker and Fred Wesley. Listen to **Pass The Peas.**

Jeannie And The Darlings: regular singers on Stax sessions, their own Volt single **Standing In The Need Of Your Love** (1969) was a delectable slab of Memphis soul.

Johnny Jenkins: Otis Redding was driver for Jenkins' R&B combo the Pinetoppers. In 1970, Jenkins signed to the Capricorn label (run by Redding's manager Phil Walden) and issued bizarre R&B/swamp rock album **Ton-Ton Macoute** to critical acclaim and mass public indifference.

The Jive Five: hit with **My True Story** for Beltone in '61 then in '70s changed name to Jyve Fyve and had a comeback with some good soul sides for Avco.

Mable John: Little Willie John's sister, flopped at Motown but cut soul classics like **Your Good Thing** (1966) at Stax.

Lou Johnson: had **Message To Martha** smash and later cut an album for Stax.

Plas Johnson: performed soaring sax solos on discs by B.B.King, Thurston Harris, Johnny Otis, Larry Williams, Bobby Day, Screamin' Jay Hawkins, Marvin Gaye and many others.

Joe Jones: New Orleans bandleader who scored gold in 1969 with R&B novelty disc **You Talk Too Much** and went on to manage the Dixie Cups and Alvin Robinson.

Lonnie Jordan: War mainman who also cut solo albums: his 1978 **Junkie To My Music** was a gem.

Louis Jordan: enormously influential jump-blues singer/sax man remembered fondly for **Let The Good Times Roll, Caldonia** and **Saturday Night Fish Fry.** Died 1975.

K

Kaygees: spin-off from Kool and the Gang.

Chris Kenner: 1961 million-seller **I Like It Like That** and another big hit, **Land Of 1,000 Dances,** both of which he co-write, made Kenner one of New Orleans' big soul stars.

Theola Kilgore: had **The Love Of My Man.**

Anna King: Philadelphia-born member of the James Brown Revue, scored in own right with series of soulful records for Philips in '60s, including **Make Up Your Mind** and **I Don't Want To Cry.**

Earl King: Solomon 'Earl King' Johnson, important New Orleans singer/guitarist who sang with backings by Huey 'Piano' Smith and the Clowns and was a major influence on Little Richard, Lloyd Price and Larry Williams. He turned to more of a mainstream blues style in '70s.

The Kingsmen: white 'garage punk' group whose version of Richard Berry's **Louie Louie,** featuring a garbled vocal, was an accidental R&B masterpiece.

Curtis Knight: of black/Red Indian extraction, he is best remembered for his work with Jimi Hendrix.

Robert Knight: brought Nashville flavour to soul with 1968 Rising Sons/Monument hit **Everlasting Love** and scored again in 1968 with **Love On A Mountain Top.**

L

Claudia Lennear: sultry lady on Warner Bros who had good versions of **From A Whisper To A Scream** and **Everything I Do Gonna Be Funky** in '73, recording one half of her album in New Orleans with help from Allen Toussaint.

Barbara Lewis: displayed smooth soul with **Baby I'm Yours** on Atlantic.

Bobby Lewis: his original of **Tossin' And Turnin'** (Beltone) topped US chart in 1961.

Dave Lewis: R&B/soul organist, scored with **Givin' Gas** in 1963. Based in Seattle, Washington.

Hopeton Lewis: won the annual Jamaican Song Festival (1967). His single **Boom Shakalaka,** cut with producer Duke Reid, stormed the island's charts. International recognition came in 1973 when Trojan released **Grooving Out Of Life** which nudged into bottom of UK pop charts. Following year **The Dynamic Hopeton Lewis** was released in Jamaica and UK on Dynamic and Dragon respectively. Has since made living playing tourist clubs and hotels on north coast of island.

Smiley Lewis: New Orleans R&B artist who scored big in 1955 with **I Hear You Knocking** (years later a UK hit for Dave Edmunds).

Little Mac and the Boss Sounds: had great organ-led instrumental version of Wilson Pickett's **In The Midnight Hour.**

Little Willie Littlefield: hit with the original of Leiber and Stoller's famed **Kansas City** (then called **K.C. Lovin)** on Federal in 1952.

Lowrell: remembered for **Mellow Mellow Right On** (AVI, 1979).

Barbara Lynn: New Orleans-based song-thrush, scored at age 18 in 1962 with Huey Meaux-produced **You'll Lose A Good Thing** and enjoyed seven top 100 hits for Jamie before stint on Atlantic.

Tami Lynn: scored for Atlantic with Bert Berns -penned/Wardell Quezergue-produced **I'm Gonna Run Away From You,** a hit all over again when re-released in 1971, thanks to UK's Northern Soul scene.

Gloria Lynne: New Yorker, toured with Ella Fitzgerald, Count Basie, cut run of jazz-flavoured smooth soul albums in '60s.

M

Willie Mabon: his lewd **I Just Got Some** was a big favourite in UK mod discos in early '60s. He had several US R&B hits on Chess.

Herbie Mann: white jazz flautist whose albums always had a strong R&B/soul content and were memorable more for contributions of such class sidemen as drummer Billy Cobham and vibist Roy Ayers than for his own musicianship. He ripped off the tune of Willie Mitchell's **Mercy** for his extended **Memphis Underground** (Atlantic) but result was an undeniable masterpiece.

Bobby Marchan: the **Get Down With It** man, whose hit was covered by Little Richard and Slade.

Maxine Nightingale.

Arif Mardin: Atlantic staff arranger who worked with most of company's black acts. Cut own well-received instrumental album **Glass Onion** for the label in late '60s.

Louisa Marks: spotted at London talent contest by sound system operator and label owner Lloyd 'Coxsone' Blackman. He subsequently recorded her and single **Caught You In A Lie** stormed reggae charts and became bedrock for lovers rock, (predominantly female pop reggae). Other hits were **Keep It Like It Is,** Michael Jackson's **Even Though You're Gone** and Jones Girls' **Six Six Street.**

Barbara Mason: had top-10 hit in 1965 with her self-penned **Yes I'm Ready** on Artic label out of her native Philadelphia. Cut a succession of smooth Motown-flavoured ballads and mid-tempo items.

Percy Mayfield: 1950 R&B chart-topper with **Please Send Me Someone To Love.** Had '63 classic **River's Invitation.** Wrote **Hit The Road Jack** for Ray Charles.

Al Mathews: American soul singer who settled in Britain, had pop hits then hosted BBC radio soul show as DJ.

Milt Mathews: remembered for 1971 **For The People** album.

Toussaint McCall: released delicious organ-backed slow soul ballad **Nothing Takes The Place Of You** in 1967.

Bobby McClure: had duets with Fontella Bass, and good solo records too.

Jack McDuff: organist veteran of some 30 jazz/funk albums.

Michael McGloiry: Californian session guitarist who turned solo artist in early '80s, vocalising on minor commercial funk hits.

Big Jay McNeely: West Coast bandleader/sax player with brash, punchy slant on R&B and athletic stage act (he was first to play sax while lying on his back!). His 1959 R&B hit **There Is Something On Your Mind** also charted for New Orleans singer Bobby Marchan the following year.

Huey P. Meaux: Cajun songwriter/producer who has worked with Archie Bell and the Drells, Chuck Jackson, T-Bone Walker and many other black artists.

Miami: recorded **Party Freaks** funker for TK's Drive label, featuring lead singer Robert Moore.

Ras Michael and the Sons Of Negus: principal exponents of fundi drum, nyah bingy chant music, their sound owes more to African rhythms than to the cosmopolitan rhythms of Jamaica. They in turn were inspired by Count Ossie and the Mystic Revelations. Their cult following far exceeds their record sales.

Midnight Movers: Wilson Pickett's super talented '60s back-up band who also had records of their own via Elephant V, Buddah **(Follow The Wind)** and other labels.

Mighty Sam: had **Papa True Love** on Amy.

The Mirettes: Los Angeles-based femme trio, scored in '68 with cover of Wilson Pickett's **In The Midnight Hour.**

McKinley 'Soul' Mitchell: had 1967 Chicago soul-ballad classic **The Town I Live In** on One-Der-Ful.

Phillip Mitchell: talented Southern songwriter and recording artist.

The Monotones: their **Book Of Love** was R&B classic on Argo in 1958.

Bobby Moore and the Rhythm Aces: had classic 1966 Muscle Shoals recording **Searching For My Love.**

The Morwells: currently comprising Blacka Morwell Wellington, Bingy Bunny and Flabba Holt, this seminal band of top session musicians has lasted almost two decades and their many hits include **Swing And Dine** and **In God We Put Our Trust.** Some of their best work is captured on album **Best Of The Morwells** released 1981 by American Nighthawk label.

Musique: Eurodisco-influenced New York team, their somewhat lewd Prelude hit **In The Bush** (1978) was a dancefloor success.

N

New York Port Authority: six-piece who cut classy **Three Thousand Miles From Home** album for Invictus in 1967.

Maxine Nightingale: British-born soul vocalist who had massive hit single in 1975 with **Right Back Where We Started From.**

Noble Knights: King Curtis' backing band in the 1950s and early '60s.

Cliff Nobles: had early instrumental Philly hit **The Horse.**

Freddie North: of the rich, smooth voice. Jerry Williams Jnr (aka Swamp Dogg) cut some great deep-soul sides on him for Nashboro, circa 1975.

The Nutmegs: New York vocal group, notched hit with debut Herald release **Story Untold** in 1955. Lead singer Leroy Griffin died in 1969 smelting-furnace accident, being replaced by his nephew Harold Jaynes who led group on a revival of **Story Untold.**

O

Odetta: gospel/folk lady with strong R&B crossover following in '50s and '60s. Had early influence on Bob Dylan.

Spooner Oldham And Dan Penn: a session keyboard player at Rick Hall's Fame Studios in Muscle Shoals, Oldham and his partner Dan Penn (both of them white) wrote host of soul classics for Percy Sledge, James Carr, James and Bobby Purify, Clarence Carter and other black artists.

The Olympics: West Coast vocal trio remembered for the '60s classics **Western Movies** and **Hully Gully.**

P

Sharon Paige: showcased with Harold Melvin and the Blue Notes.

Earl Palmer: drummer in Dave Bartholomew's band backing Fats Domino, Shirley and Lee, Little Richard and others in '50s. Settled in Los Angeles in 1957 to become in-demand session man working with all top black artists recorded in the city and many white stars too.

Bobby Parker: remembered for 1961 R&B masterpiece **Watch Your Step** (V-Tone) and its flip, **Steal Your Heart Away,** revived later by the Moody Blues.

Little Junior Parker: had a string of superb blues/R&B records from **Mystery Train** in 1953 (covered by Elvis) through till his death while undergoing surgery in 1971. Zenith came with the Bill Harvey/Joe Scott Band accompanying him on **Next Time You See Me** and **Barefoot Rock** for Duke in '60s.

Patterson Singers: gospel group who cut some great soul sides and worked with ace producers Dave Crawford and Brad Shapiro.

John Patton: Blue Note organist remembered for **Along Came John** and **Silver Meter** which also featured Grant Green's superb guitar.

Pockets: eight-piece, American funk outfit, signed to Earth, Wind & Fire's Kalimba Productions, produced by E.W.F. bass player Verdine White. Existed during late '70s.

The Politicians: Hot Wax act fronted by staff writer/producer McKinley Jackson circa 1972.

Presidents: Van McCoy arranged and produced the vocal trio's delicious 1971 Sussex smash **5-10-15-20 (25-30 Years Of Love).**

Arthur Prysock: warm-voiced vocalist in the Billy Eckstine/Brook Benton mould. Had many fine records on Verve, Bethlehem, King and Old Town in a long lasting career.

Red Prysock: singer Arthur Prysock's tenor-saxophone playing brother was in bands led by Tiny Grimes and Tiny Bradshaw before,in '50s and '60s, recording his own honking R&B/rock 'n' roll instrumentals for Red Robin, King and Mercury.

R

Luther Rabb: member of War and had good solo recordings too, like **Get On The One And Dance.**

Teddy Randazzo: Italian American who sang in black R&B style before moving into song-writing and production, notably for Little Anthony and the Imperials.

Rare Earth: white Detroiters, given own Rare Earth label by Motown. Cut run of strong funk-laced blue-eyed soul albums which appealed to black-music and rock fans alike.

Rasputin's Stash: much-vaunted funk outfit signed, and richly fêted, by Atlantic Records; quickly disappeared, despite fine opening single **Your Love Is Certified.**

James Ray: his originals of **If You Gotta Make A Fool Of Somebody** and **Itty Bitty Pieces** in 1961-62 gave this New Yorker a brief residency in the R&B charts.

Redbone: soul-laced Red Indian Band who hit big with **Witch Queen Of New Orleans.**

Jimmy Reed: master of the R&B end of Chicago blues with his hypnotic if monotonous classics for Vee-Jay, inlcuding **Baby What You Want Me To Do, Big Boss Man** and **Shame Shame Shame,** a minor UK hit in 1964.

Della Reese: sang gospel with Mahalia Jackson and with Clara Ward Singers then became one of first black pop stars — pop chart number-two with **Don't You Know** (1959).

Ras Michael & the Sons of Negus — "How could a black man name Mr. Brown?".

Clarence Reid: Miami-based singer/song-writer/producer and boss of Alston label.

Sir Mack Rice: member of Detroit's Falcons with Wilson Pickett and Eddie Floyd. Later recorded classy solos for Stax.

Rimshots: All Platinum instrumentalists.

John Roberts: cut '60s dance mover, **Sockin' One Two Three.**

Alvin Robinson: New Orleans' guitarist (with Joe Jones' band) turned singer; Coasters and Rolling Stones covered his **Down Home Girl** '60s classic.

Freddy Robinson: subtle blend of blues/jazz/soul guitar wizardry on others' recordings and had his own albums for World Pacific and Stax.

Vickie Sue Robinson: New Yorker who appeared in 'Hair' and 'Jesus Christ Superstar' then caught the disco wave with mid-'70s hits for RCA.

The Romeos: Philadelphia group which featured Kenny Gamble, Leon Huff and Thom Bell.

The Royalettes: Teddy Randazzo produced the lush sound of the girlie foursome's '60s biggie **It's Gonna Take A Miracle.**

S

Oliver Sain: important St. Louis bandleader and record producer; worked with Fontella Bass and scored in own right with **Bus Stop** disco smash.

Salsoul Orchestra: studio band for Salsoul Records, who had hits of their own with highly orchestrated Philadelphia slant on the disco-sound.

San Remo Strings: instrumental Motown combo, big favourites in Northern Soul circles with 1971-cut **Festival Time.**

Evie Sands: white femme singer, started with Cameo Parkway, later enjoyed soul hits via Red Bird group of labels.

Mongo Santamaria: Puerto Rican bongo player. Big hits with **Watermelon Man** and **El Watusi** in '60s then prominent as a jazz-funk session man in '70s.

Calvin Scott: signed to Stax but recorded in LA, blind singer musician who recorded classy **I'm Not Blind, I Just Can't See** album.

Freddy Scott: from Providence, capital of America's smallest state, Rhode Island, he moved to New York, signed to Bert Berns' Shout label and hit with deep-soul masterpieces **Are You Lonely for Me?** and **Cry To Me** in mid-'60s.

Peggy Scott and Jo Jo Benson: cut beaty gospel-tinged hits for SSS International circa '68, notably **Lover's Holiday** and **Picking Wild Mountain Berries.**

The Sensations: they cut new ground in mid-'50s, being one of first black male groups to feature a girl lead singer, scoring an early hit with **Yes Sir That's My Baby** then enjoying a further chart run in early '60s with **Music Music Music, Let Me In** and **That's My Desire.**

Dee Dee Sharp: wife of Philadelphia International co-founder Kenny Gamble. Recorded solo — selling a million with **Mashed Potato Time** — and in duet with Chubby Checker.

The Sharpees: **I'm So Tired Of Being Lonely** — one hit, one masterpiece.

Bim Sherman: started singing in Jamaica with embryonic Morwells. Biggest solo successes were **Golden Locks** and **Evergreen.** Currently producing futuristic reggae with UK based On-U Sound label.

The Showmen: led by General Norman Johnson, they cut landmark **It Will Stand** for Minit with producer Allen Toussaint in 1961. Johnson later led the hit Invictus group Chairman Of The Board.

The Showstoppers: Solomon Burke's two younger brothers and two young friends cut one classic record in Philadelphia: **Ain't Nothin' But A Houseparty,** moved to UK, then faded.

The Silhouettes: Philadelphian doo-woopers, the 'Sha-na-na-na' chant from their 1958 million-seller **Get A Job** inspired the white rock 'n' roll revival band Sha Na Na.

Danny Small: remembered for his gospel sytled soul standard **Without Love (There Is Nothing),** recorded by countless performers, but none better than Clyde McPhatter in 1958.

Huey 'Piano' Smith: New Orleans session pianist for Guitar Slim, Earl King, Smiley Lewis, Lloyd Price and Little Richard. Later formed the Clowns vocal band to score with **Rockin' Pneumonia And The Boogie Woogie Flu** (1957) and other novelty classics.

Slim Smith: Jamaican remembered for rare soulful voice, combining best of Curtis Mayfield and Sam Cooke. Teamed up with Lloyd Charmers and Jimmy Riley between '66 and '69 in the Uniques and later joined other seminal JA combo the Techniques prior to launching solo career with producer Bunny Lee. Jamaican hits included **My Conversation** and **Time Has Come.** Committed suicide 1973.

The Solitaires: their beaty **Walking Along** scored in 1958. Cecil Holmes emerged from this Harlem vocal group to become a major record executive with Buddah.

Soul Brothers Six: released **Some Kind Of Wonderful** on Atlantic.

Soul Clan: Atlantic put their soul superstars Burke, Joe Tex, Don Covay and Wilson Pickett together to work as the Soul Clan.

Jimmy Soul: his calypso-influenced **If You Wanna Be Happy** sold a million and made US number-one in 1962.

Soul Survivors: went top-five pop and had R&B hit with 1966 debut **Expressway To Your Heart,** but black radio stations stopped playing their records when they learned the New York-based group was white.

Sound systems: the reggae radio network, Jamaican answer to American discotheques in the early '50s, playing imported US R&B to people starved of musical entertainment. Among the greatest were King Edward, Lord Comic, Coxsone Downbeat (later of Studio One fame) and King Everald. With the arrival of the Duke Vin system in the UK during the mid-'50s rock steady had made it to Europe. Count Suckle, Fanso, Count Shelly, Coxsone Outernational (run by Lloyd 'Coxsone' Blackman) were other important UK systems. Sound systems for many provide the only opportunity to hear new imported and indigenous reggae music. Of most influential sound systems operating in UK, Fat Man Hi Fi, Jah Shaka and Frontline International are most respected.

Joe South: Southern white session-guitarist who played on Aretha Franklin's Muscle Shoals' cuts, wrote songs for the Tams and others and in 1968 went top-10 with his own singing on the soulful **Games People Play** for Capitol.

Raul de Souza: Brazilian slide and valve trombonist with three jazz/latin/funk fusion albums on Capitol.

Bob B. Soxx and the Blue Jeans: had classic Phil Spector-produced million-seller in 1962 with **Zip-A-De-Doo-Dah.**

The Spaniels: cut seven years of doo-wop ballads and jumping R&B items for Vee-Jay from 1953 on.

Jesse Stone: black arranger who brought King Curtis into the session scene and, often under his real name of Charles Calhoun, wrote hits for the Drifters **(Money Honey),** Joe Turner **(Shake, Rattle And Roll),** Roy Hamilton **(Don't Let Go),** and others.

Bill Summers: hit the discos in 1978 with latin and jazz-tinged chapter **Straight To The Bank** on Prestige.

Sweet Charles: James Brown protégé of '70s.

Herbie Mann.

T

Bobby Taylor And The Vancouvers: Canadian-based Motowners who scored with **Does Your Mama Know About Me,** co-written by then-member Tommy Chong of subsequent Cheech and Chong comedy team fame.

Felice Taylor: Supremes' soundalike; Barry White produced her 1966 success **I Feel Love Coming On.**

Koko Taylor: Chess's **Wang Dang Doodle** lady.

Richard Tee: ace session keyboard man and veteran of a thousand Atlantic studio gigs.

Teen Queens: sisters of the Cadets' Aaron Collins, Betty and Rosie scored big with **Eddie My Love.**

Temprees: three Memphis guys who cut trio of delicious smooth-soul harmony albums on We Produce between 1972 and 1975.

Jamo Thomas: had **I Spy For The F.B.I.,** a great '60s disco smash.

Jimmy Thomas: one-time member of the Ike and Tina Turner Revue, settled in Britain in late '60s to work solo and in various groups.

Nicky Thomas: climaxed five years of singing in native Jamaica when self-penned **Love Of The Common People** reached number 9 in UK pop charts. Thomas and his label Trojan struck again with their breezy reggae sound with another single, **Images Of You.**

Gary Thoms Empire: had **7-6-5-4-3-2-1 Blow Your Whistle.**

Willie Mae 'Big Mama' Thornton: her original of **Hound Dog** topped the R&B charts in 1953. She toured with the late Johnny Ace and later became a fixture on blues' revival tours.

George Torrence: remembered for **Licking Stick.**

Ed Townsend: ace producer who wrote **Let's Get It On** for Marvin Gaye, **Finally Got Myself Together** for the Impressions, **If You Want It** for the Main Ingredient, **The Love Of My Man** for Theola Kilgore, and **Foolish Fool** for Dee Dee Warwick, plus material for the Treniers, the Shirelles, Jimmy Holiday, Brook Benton, Maxine Brown, Gloria Lynn and Chuck Jackson as well as having own **Now** album on Curtom in 1976.

Nat Townsley Jnr: recorded **I Fell In Love With God** (ABC).

The Toys: three girls who took a Bach melody, turned it into the sweet, soft soul of **Lovers Concerto** and sold a million on Dyno-Voice in 1968.

Trussel: eight-piece band out of Virginia. Signed to Elektra in late '70s and had worldwide soul hit with **Love Injection.**

Sammy Turner: turned the nursery song **Lavender Blue** into a soul classic — with help from Leiber and Stoller.

Spyder Turner: his cover of Ben E. King's **Stand By Me** featured clever impressions of the soul stars of the day. Made minor comeback during mid-'70s disco boom.

Titus Turner: prolifically recorded in a range of styles from jump blues, rock 'n' roll, R&B ballad, soul, right through to funky disco, he is best known as writer of **All Around The World** and other standards.

T.V. and the Tribesmen: masterminded by Huey P. Meaux, they made waves with cover version of Robert Parker's **Barefootin'.**

U

The Unifics: displayed New York uptown soul with **Standing In The Court Of Love** on Kapp.

V

The Van Dykes: three Texans who got it on with **Tellin' It Like It Is** (Bell).

The Vibrations: had two hits in 1961, **The Watusi,** in their own right, and **Peanut Butter,** as the Marathons. Also scored in '64 with **My Girl Sloopy** and '68 with **Love In Them There Hills.**

Voices Of East Harlem: 17-strong choir which cut much-acclaimed **Right On Be Free** album for Elektra in 1970 with Cornell Dupree, Chuck Rainey, Jerry Jemmott, Richard Tee and Ralph McDonald among the sessioneers.

W

Baby Washington: gifted singer/songwriter, Jeanette 'Baby' Washington scored for Sue with classic **That's How Heartaches Are Made** in 1965.

Ella Washington: cut soulful Nashville-recorded ballad **He Called Me Baby** (Sound Stage 7) a minor hit in 1968.

Jerry Washington: South Carolina raised, he worked out of New York and scored with **Right Here Is Where You Belong** in '75.

Tony Wilson.

Waters: three girls and a guy, they were Blue Note's venture into the vocal soul market with their eponymous album of 1975.

Wah Wah Watson: seminal session guitarist with one of the most distinctive styles in the business.

Tony Joe White: white swamp-rock exponent from Louisiana who scored 1969 funk-soul hit with **Polk Salad Annie.** His further Monument records, including ballad **Roosevelt And Ira Lee** (with lyrics centred on problems of integration), the dancer **Soul Francisco** and his original of **Rainy Night In Georgia** had strong soul flavour.

Spencer Wiggins: recorded great '60s deep-soul records out of the Fame Studios in Muscle Shoals.

Wild Cherry: white six-piece funk band who cut superb **Play That Funky Music** stormer on Epic in 1976.

Maurice Williams and the Zodiacs: much covered **Stay** was — at 1 min 57 sec — one of shortest hits ever.

Otis Williams and the Charms: had million-seller in 1955 with **Hearts Of Stone** and another the following year with **Ivory Tower,** both on King.

Al Wilson: West Coast soul man, remembered for **Do What You Gotta Do, The Snake** and '74 million-seller **Show And Tell.**

Reuben Wilson: organist who cut a string of funky R&B/jazz albums for Blue Note and Lester Record Corporation from late '60s through into mid-'70s.

Tony Wilson: ex-Hot Chocolate, cut delicious **I Like Your Style** sole album and single on Bearsville in 1976.

Pete Wingfield: white British session keyboard-player with a penchant for black music. Has recorded with Freddie King, Bloodstone, Jimmy Witherspoon and other black acts as well as being member of the Olympic Runners and scoring solo hit in 1975 with his falsetto soul-ballad **Eighteen With A Bullet** (Island).

The Winstons: remembered for **Colour Me Father.**

Brenton Wood: Los Angeles-based, had hit in '67 with novelty ballad **Oogum Boogum Song,** followed through with **Gimme Little Sign,** then slipped into obscurity.

Michael Wycoff: Californian session keyboard player and background vocalist, signed to RCA as solo artist in early '80s. Has already had minor soul hit singles.

Y

Lonnie Youngblood: tenor-sax wielding veteran of All Platinum/Stang/Turbo sessions; also recorded in own right.

Young Hearts: LA threesome, who had good sweet-soul albums on Minit and 20th Century in early '70s.

Young Holt Unlimited: bassist Eldee Young and drummer Redd Holt split from Ramsey Lewis Trio in 1966 and scored with Canadian pianist Ken Cragen as Young Holt Unlimited, **Soulful Strut** going gold in 1968.

Timi Yuro: better known for her country records, white singer Timi Yuro had incredibly soulful voice in Esther Phillips' mould and cut some brilliant R&B/soul-flavoured records — her two differently tempoed soul versions of Hank Snow's **I'm Movin' On** being sheer genius.

Index

This index does not set out to be comprehensive, but concentrates on those personalities whose names recur throughout. It also provides an alphabetical guide to any acts and artists of stature not given their own entry in the book, and supplements the cross-reference system (denoted by ▶) used throughout. References to main entries are indicated here by **bold** type.

Picture Credits

The publishers would like to thank all the record companies who have supplied record sleeves (credited in captions) and photographs of their artists to make this such a dynamically and colourfully illustrated volume. We also thank *Black Echoes* magazine, London, for opening their considerable and valuable archives so that we could select many interesting and often rare photographs of performers. In addition, many individual photographers have supplied excellent photographs shot under less-than-ideal conditions; we appreciate their efforts, which appear as follows:

Front cover: Phil Gorton. **Front endpapers:** Background, Keith Bernstein; colour photos bottom left and top right, Keith Bernstein. **Page 1:** Bottom left, Keith Bernstein. **2-3:** Colour photographs, Keith Bernstein. **4-5:** Background and colour photos left and centre, Keith Bernstein. **6-7:** Background, Keith Bernstein; centre and right, London Features International (hereafter referred to as LFI). **9:** Top left, Phil Gorton. **10:** Top left, Keith Bernstein; bottom right, Phil Gorton. **11:** Left and right, Phil Gorton. **16:** Phil Gorton. **20:** Top, Phil Gorton. **24-25:** Phil Gorton. **41:** Bottom, Neil Kenlock. **45:** Top Left: Keith Bernstein. **49:** Top, Phil Gorton. **55:** Top, Barry Plummer. **60:** Top left, LFI. **62:** David Redfern. **75:** Top right, LFI. **79:** Top, Barry Plummer. **81:** Bottom, Barry Plummer. **91:** Barry Plummer. **100:** Top, Barry Plummer. **101:** Keith Bernstein. **104:** Top, Barry Plummer. **121:** Top, Barry Plummer. **122:** Keith Bernstein. **123:** Top, David Redfern. **134:** Bottom, Barry Plummer. **136:** Top, Keith Bernstein. **137:** Top, Phil Gorton. **141:** Top, Keith Bernstein. **159:** Bottom, Barry Plummer. **168:** Barry Plummer. **169:** Barry Plummer. **171:** Top, Barry Plummer. **178:** Bottom right, Phil Gorton. **179:** Top left, Keith Bernstein; top right, centre and bottom, Phil Gorton. **180:** Phil Gorton. **181:** Top and bottom left: Phil Gorton. **185:** Bottom, LFI. **186:** Top and bottom, Phil Gorton. **189:** Barry Plummer. **190:** Top, Phil Gorton. **194:** Bottom, Keith Bernstein. **195:** Top, Barry Plummer. **202:** Bottom, Barry Plummer. **205:** Bottom, Phil Gorton. **206:** Top, Phil Gorton. **207:** Dennis Morris. **208:** Bottom, Barry Plummer. **213:** Bottom, LFI. **214:** Bottom, Terry Lott. **216:** Bottom, LFI. **217:** Top left, LFI. **Back endpapers:** Keith Bernstein.

PRINTED IN BELGIUM BY proost INTERNATIONAL BOOK PRODUCTION

AUG 3 0 1983